The Penguin Book of

Rock & Roll Writing

EDITED BY CLINTON HEYLIN

Illustrated by Ray Lowry

VIKING

VIKING

Published by the Penguin Group
Penguin Books Ltd, 27 Wrights Lane, London W8 5TZ, England
Penguin Books USA Inc., 375 Hudson Street, New York, New York 10014, USA
Penguin Books Australia Ltd, Ringwood, Victoria, Australia
Penguin Books Canada Ltd, 10 Alcorn Avenue, Toronto, Ontario, Canada M4V 3B2
Penguin Books (NZ) Ltd, 182–190 Wairau Road, Auckland 10, New Zealand

Penguin Books Ltd, Registered Offices: Harmondsworth, Middlesex, England

First published 1992
1 3 5 7 9 10 8 6 4 2
First Edition

Typeset by DatIX International Limited, Bungay, Suffolk
Set in 11¾/14½pt Lasercomp Sabon
Printed in England by Clays Ltd, St Ives plc

A CIP catalogue record for this book is available from the British Library

ISBN 0-670-845590

Contents

Contents

3. YOU SAY YOU WANNA REVOLUTION?

This section deals with the decade (1967–77) when rock music was regularly rent asunder by abrupt shifts in the music.

4. I HAVE SEEN THE FUTURE . . .

A selection of articles which demand the recognition of new talents or simply attempt to convey the sheer impact of seeing/hearing the likes of the Stones, the Doors or the Pistols for the first time.

Contents

5. ON THE ROAD AGAIN

This section details a quintessential rock & roll experience – going on
the road – from the viewpoints of both musicians and writers.

6. VOICES FROM THE OTHER SIDE

This section allows the musicians to have their own say, whether it be

Contents

commenting on their own work, their influences or satirizing aspects of rock journalism.

7. SATIRES AND SHORT STORIES

This is the fiction section, featuring a series of spoof albums and examples of fan worship going badly wrong.

8. THE BIZ

This section deals with the often discordant relationship between the music and the machine.

Contents

9. THE PROMISE IS BROKEN

This section deals at length with a favourite theme in writings about rock music: the fall from grace.

Contents

10. AND IN THE END

Finally, the casualties. A relentless catalogue of those who have lived fast, died young.

Introduction

'Oh my God! Where's Zaphod Zebedee, my all-time favourite rock critic? What about that magnificent piece he wrote on Missouri's premier mud-flat metal merchants, the Slugs, in the second issue of *Who Took the Bomb*!? Call yourself an anthologist.'

What was it you wanted? It ain't here. Anthologies of poets who died at twenty-one are considerably easier than collections drawn from mounds and mounds of mass media mutterings in magazines where quality (indeed literacy) controls are often absent. So encased within the *Penguin Book of Rock & Roll Writing* you will find some eighty needles in a haystack.

It is thirty-five years since Elvis emerged from the Memphis melting-pot, twenty-five years since a young student by the name of Paul Williams began publishing the first mimeographed rockzine, *Crawdaddy* – the true genesis of rock criticism. In that time rock & roll has grown conceited. It has also had its share of great writers, both lyricists and commentators.

This hefty tome is designed to let the commentators have their say. The basic idea for this anthology seemed pretty simple – a book which would collect together the best of the last twenty-five years of rock writing. Part history, part literature, part reference source, part hyperbole, part disillusionment, part parting gesture, the *Penguin Book of Rock & Roll Writing* would be all things to all rockers. An oracle-cum-bible in just 200,000 words and eighty testaments.

A scant glance at the list of contributors will hint at the casualties of my self-imposed constraints. No Robert Hilburn, no Mikal Gilmore, no Peter Guralnick – all of whom I would ideally have liked to induct into my Knights of Rockprose (don't look for adjective-merchants like Dave Marsh, Andy Gill or Adam Sweeting either). Yet I would like to think that there are more fine exponents of the form within than without and that there will be features *and* writers new to you, no matter how well versed in rock's writers you may be.

I trust that most of the major English and American magazines who through-the-years have devoted column inches to rock music have been judiciously represented. The sheer diversity is certainly striking. *The New York Herald Tribune, Jazz & Pop, Crawdaddy, New Musical Express, Village Voice, East Village Eye, Melody Maker, New York Rocker, Creem, New York, The Real Paper, Sounds, Rolling Stone, Punk, Forced Exposure, Spin, International Times, Let it Rock,* the *Cleveland Edition, Ramparts, The New York Times, Cheetah, The Face* and the *New York Post* are all represented within.

I should note (before someone else does) that none of the recent wave of English monthly music mags – *Q, Vox* and *Select* – is represented. This is more a comment on contemporary editorial wisdom than on the quality of contemporary writers. The current editors seem to prefer concentrating almost exclusively on verbatim interviews and pages and pages of Chicken McNugget-size reviews of recent 'product'. Rather than providing an opportunity to discourse on one of the half a dozen notable releases each month (can there really be more?), reviewers are asked to assess the results of two years in a rock artist's life in two hundred words. And for those whose lives are too full to even read such bite-sized reviews, we have the star-rating system. If it gets a box it's got to be four stars – *capisce*!

This is not an entirely English malaise. The two major American music magazines – *Spin* and *Rolling Stone* – now devote precious little space to any but the album of the month. Though *Spin* and assorted American fanzines have kept the rock feature alive, *Rolling Stone*, like its English copyists, has seemingly forsaken The Feature. A scan of all the issues of *Q* to date and an entire eighties wad of *Rolling Stones* yielded exactly no usable features, surely a considerable waste of literary resources?

And what, pray tell, have I got against (say) Van Morrison, Neil Young or Deep Purple, all of whom might warrant inclusion but are absent from these pages? My intent in putting the *Penguin Book of Rock & Roll Writing* together was to provide the reader with an overview of the major shifts in rock music while at the same time representing the best writers who have worked in the field. To paraphrase George Bush, there will always be casualties.

Further juggling was required to ensure that the best of both English and American rock presses was judiciously represented. Ironically, there has been considerably more newsprint expended by the English music press, which has always had at least three weekly music magazines along with a variable number of monthlies, from the heyday of *Zigzag* and *Let it Rock* in the early seventies to the Q-clone industry of the present day. The best of American rock writing has often been confined to the 'quality dailies', cultural weeklies and up-market fanzines.

The final and most troublesome quandry when selecting material was framed by the question: Yes, but is it rock (& roll)? I was never entirely sure what it was that all these scribes were writing about. The *Penguin Book of Rock & Roll Writing* it says. But in delving into the professed subject matter — that rock & roll music — I needed to ponder: Is it 'only rock & roll'? Is rock & roll 'here to stay'? Did God give rock & roll to you? We all recognize rock & roll when we hear it. It's just everyone else who fails to appreciate the sledgehammer sludge of the Slugs.

Since I've cobbled together this 'book about rock & roll', perhaps I should call on the experts — my contributors. The scribes of the form. They should know what rock & roll is. Charlie Gillett, in paragraph one of his definitive history of its origins, *Sound of the City*, seems pretty sure what it means:

In tracing the history of rock & roll, it is useful to distinguish rock'n'roll — the particular kind of music to which the term was first applied — both from rock & roll — the music that has been classified as such since rock'n'roll petered out around 1958 – and from rock, which describes post-1964 derivations of rock'n'roll.

All clear? Anyone want to try and run by me again the difference between rock'n'roll and rock & roll? Still, Gillett has established one important distinction, rock'n'roll from rock. But then there is rock and there is Rock, *n'est-ce pas*? At least Jon Landau says there is:

In 1963 the Beatles shattered the dreariness of the music business. And with them came rock, the music of the sixties, and a music quite different from rock & roll.

Of the two, rock is a music of far greater surface seriousness and lyric complexity. It is the product of a more self-aware and self-conscious group of musicians ... And while it borrowed extensively from rock & roll styles, it was a fundamentally different kind of music.

That seems to settle it. Rock & roll is a fifties phenomenon after which it was quietly laid to rest by Fabian's phantoms. But perhaps Landau's perspective reveals more about the context from which it was offered than the one it sought to assess? After all, the man's no clairvoyant, 'I have seen the future ...' claims notwithstanding. The dead giveaway here is 'rock, the music of the sixties'. I can see the sepia tints of nostalgia misting up Landau's contact lenses even now.

Naturally, the godfather of punk journalism, Lester Bangs, chose not only to disagree with Landau and Gillett but to dispute their view of 'rock [& roll] history' altogether, this time from the other side of the chasm created by punk. In his rather charmingly entitled essay – 'In Which Yet Another Pompous Blowhard Purports to Possess the True Meaning of Punk Rock' – Bangs is refreshingly unconcerned about the terminology:

For performing rock & roll, or punk rock, or call it any damn thing you please, there's only one thing you need: NERVE. Rock & roll is an attitude, and if you've got the attitude you can do it, no matter what anybody says. Believing that is one of the things punk rock is about. Rock is for everybody, it should be so implicitly anti-élitist that the question of whether somebody's qualified to perform it should never arise.

But it did. In the sixties, of course . . . in the sixties rock & roll began to think of itself as an 'art-form'. Rock & roll is not an 'art-form'; rock & roll is a raw wail from the bottom of the guts.

Thus Bangs placed rock with rock'n'roll, part of rock & roll's past, and asserted a simple truth: punk rock = rock & roll. As was Cochran. As was the Stones. As was T. Rex. Huh? There is a line but you don't know it's there until you trip over it. If it's all rock & roll then we can all go home and write our very own 'My Favourite – and therefore q.e.d. the Best – 10,007 Singles of Rockpopsoul'.

Discerning rock & roll from rock, Rock, rock'n'roll and Rolling Rock is only half the fun. Since Presley started selling records, rock & roll has been entangled in an at-times-unnervingly-symbiotic relationship with pop music. Rather than accepting the guilt and strangling its bastard-twin at birth, Pop has preferred to treat rock & roll as its errant son.

Soon enough we arrive at the point where pop and rock are used interchangeably. Which perhaps justifies the degree of bile Joe Carducci heaped on those who choose to preserve this incestuous relationship in his recent polemical work *Rock and the Pop Narcotic*. Carducci provides a damning indictment of those scribes of the form who have accepted the pop/rock symbiosis for their own, primarily sociological, ends:

The more I thought about it the more crucial an examination of the relationship between rock music and pop music seemed . . . These two musics are generally thought to overlap far more than they in fact do. Indeed, the pop success of rock bands in the 1960s seems to have convinced many – even among music professionals such as players and critics – that the two are one and the same. This idea has been poison to the discourse on rock music because it has led to pressure to forsake the rock approach for that of pop/Tin Pan Alley. In this way rock criticism (born in the 1960s) attempts to subvert rock music in order to enforce the notion that rock and pop are – or should be – one.

Carducci is one of the few modern commentators prepared to deal with the thorny issue of rock vs. soul a.k.a. Did the honkies steal the blues? Carducci gets his say on the subject in section nine (as does Charles Shaar Murray, who advocates that the debt can never be underestimated). I consider it self-evident that rock is 'a white boy's club'. Why is another question.

When rock'n'roll went Rock, the white man appropriated, purloined and generally took out an extended loan on the tenure of rock. The debt to its black roots is touched on in section one but once the reader passes beyond prehistory and into the realms of rock criticism, rock (& roll) becomes an essentially guitar-based, white man's means of letting rip.

So that's it. I trust that the sheer quality of much of the writing will inspire you to dust off some of those old black platters (or, if you insist, small silver discs).

Have fun.

Clinton Heylin
March 1992

1. Prehistory

"Believe me, this kid would have been bloody enormous if he hadn't been born to a family of illiterate grape-treaders in a remote Sicilian village."

Despite the fact that this section deals with the birth of rock & roll, all but two of the selected features postdate the advent of rock criticism, and only one is contemporary. Article 1, from the rear-cover of Presley's second R C A album, is drawn from the one medium that, in the years before rockcritdom – pre-BritBeat, pre-Crawdaddy – lent itself to musical critique, the album sleeve-note.

The sleeve-note was already well-established by the time rock & roll roared into town and was able to take in the full range from gushing hyperbole to insightful overview. Most early prose on rock & roll was black or white, the whitewash of the teenzine or the blackboard jungle of paranoia. Us or Them.

Features 2–5, postdating the introduction of Rockspeak, recall this period of innocence. The articles representing this prehistoric period advance from the unashamedly utopian – Nik Cohn's golden age valediction 'Classic Rock' – via a detailed disposition of its roots by Charlie Gillett (an excerpt from his seminal The Sound of the City), *to Lenny Kaye's 'Best of Acappella', which matches the historic detail of Gillett with a Cohn-like wistfulness.*

The arrival of the Beatles in the US signalled the end of rock'n'roll's first era, giving a renewed impetus to 'that rock & roll music'. Tom Wolfe's profile of one of rock & roll's great eccentrics, Phil Spector, reflecting its post-BritBeat perspective in dealing with one of the giants of the First Era, represents a halfway house between serious sociology and the burgeoning 'rock' aesthetic.

Elvis

ANON.

Though album sleeve-notes would give way in the mid sixties to the garish psychedelic montage, they deemed to serve in the pre-teen days of rock & roll as an index to the contents within. The 1956 Elvis album remains a supreme example of the form. If rock & roll predates 'rock criticism' by a good ten years, here is a valiant attempt to come to terms with the Presley phenomenon – and it's both contemporaneous and contextual.

It was a cold, rainy night on Broadway. The time, January 1956, a TV theatre studio between 53rd and 54th Streets. The occasion, the first network telecast of a country singer unknown to the pop world, a youngster of unusual talents with some uncertainty about displaying them before a national audience.

Although Elvis Presley's debut was gained through spectacular local fame and following, its publicity had not attracted the world at large. An artist who had set numerous Southern centres on their ear, Presley was facing a majority of viewers as cold and unprepared as the citizens of Siberia.

In New York very few had braved the storm. The theatre was sparsely filling with shivering servicemen and Saturday-nighters, mostly eager for the refuge from the weather. Outside, groups of teenagers rushed past the marquee to a roller-skating rink nearby. Just before show time, a weary promoter returned to the box-office with dozens of tickets, unable even to give them away on the streets of Times Square.

What happened that night, and during the days following, is now history. The national gaze was pivoted to Presley *en masse*, the rain above was quickly transformed into a deluge of acclaim all over the country. In the South, people understood and were delighted by the success of their 21-year-old prodigy. Elsewhere this enthusiasm was carried first by amazement, later by a sizzling controversy.

At its source was the 'Why?' of Elvis Presley's wildfire popularity. Many have confused the issue with social problems, real in themselves but meaningless when the terms are begged, borrowed and stolen for musical criticism. As a result, most of the analytical sour grapes soon turned into useless vinegar, or else were sweetened by the critics' 'discovery' of Presley's talents in time.

The answer to this 'Why?' lies somewhere in the welter of feelings and trends which have become focused through Presley's powerful style. A way to find it is to add them together, then try to equate the sum with his incredible following over the world.

Of commercial folk music Presley is perhaps the most original singer since Jimmie Rodgers. His rhythmic style derives from exactly the same source of Deep South blues and jazz as that which inspired the late Blue Yodeller. Nor is it any coincidence that their birthplaces in Mississippi are less than a hundred miles apart.

Some say it is a reaction to present-day confusion that has caused rhythm and blues writers to simplify their songs with repeated tones and a heavy after-beat – in other words, to create rock & roll. If so, Presley was the first to extend to it the Rodgers interpretation, followed with his own. However, his folk characterization is still most natural and forthright.

Presley's belting delivery accounts for a truly sensational reaction among teenagers. Important to this is his enthusiasm for music by the Blackwood Brothers, the Statesmen and other quartets in the South. There has never been a great difference between rhythm and gospel songs except, of course, for the lyrical content; in fact, the latter are far more rhythmic where staging is concerned. It is essentially the fervour, the animation and boundless spirit of gospel singing that Presley admires, and which has been absorbed into his own dynamic performances.

We can better understand this if we consider how often 'revival' numbers have hit in the popular field. Here Presley favours beat and ballad singers alike, in such different personalities as Billy Daniels and Bill Kenny – which leads to this possible answer for the 'Why?' of his unprecedented appeal: Elvis Presley, by combining the four fields (country, gospel, rhythm and pop) into perfect unity, is unique in music annals and experience.

Five Styles of Rock & Roll

CHARLIE GILLETT

If it took ten years for rock & roll to acquire its first critical coterie, it was a further five before it could claim its first serious historian. Charlie Gillett's The Sound of the City, *first published in 1971, remains the best account of the origins of the sound and the fury, exemplified by this distillation of rock & roll into its five prototypical forms.*

In the years 1954 to 1956, there were five distinctive styles, developed almost completely independently of one another, that collectively became known as rock'n'roll: northern band rock'n'roll, whose most popular exemplar was Bill Haley; the New Orleans dance blues; Memphis country rock (also known as rockabilly); Chicago rhythm and blues; and vocal group rock'n'roll. All five styles, and the variants associated with each of them, depended for their dance beat on contemporary Negro dance rhythms.

The styles gave expression to moods of their audience that hitherto had not been represented in popular music. Each style was developed in particular regions or locales and expressed personal responses to certain experiences in a way that would make sense to people with comparable experiences. This grass-roots character gave styles of rock'n'roll their collective identity, putting it in sharp contrast with established modes of popular music, which were conceived in terms of general ideas formulated in ways that made the finished product available for millions of people to accept.

I

Northern band rock'n'roll, exemplified by Bill Haley And His Comets, was concerned mainly with expressing high-spirited feelings of togetherness. Haley had little of the romantic appeal familiar to the fans of Frankie Laine or Eddie Fisher. More quaint than good-looking, Haley rested his appeal on his music, which he had been developing for ten years before the general audience discovered him in 1953. Haley's earliest records were in conventional country and western style; by 1947 he had begun experimenting with it. As he recalled in an interview much later, '. . . the style we played way back in 1947, 1948 and 1949 was a combination of country and western, Dixieland, and the old style rhythm and blues.'

The 'old style rhythm and blues' he referred to was probably the roaring, riff-laden music of bands like Lionel Hampton's, itself a simplified descendant of the Kansas City jazz, committed to creating as much excitement as possible, with musicians playing solos on one or two notes, lying on their backs or climbing on pianos or basses, or playing their instruments above their heads in search of thrilling visual effects. Contrasting the enjoyment of the audience at this kind of dance with the staid reaction of audiences where white dance bands played, Haley saw the chance for change.

'We decided to try for a new style, mostly using stringed instruments but somehow managing to get the same effect as brass and reeds . . . Around the early fifties the musical world was starved for something new . . . the days of the solo vocalist and the big bands had gone. About the only thing in fact that was making any noise was progressive jazz, but this was just above the heads of the average listener . . . I felt then that if I could take, say, a Dixieland tune and drop the first and third beats, and accentuate the second and fourth, and add a beat the listeners could clap to as well as dance, this would be what they were after. From that the rest was easy . . . take everyday sayings like "Crazy Man Crazy", "See You Later, Alligator", "Shake, Rattle And Roll", and apply what I have just said.'

It wasn't quite as easy as Haley suggested. Another group, Freddie Bell and the Bellboys, tried the same formula with 'Giddy-Up A Ding Dong' (Mercury) but had much less success, despite being featured with Haley, the Platters, and Alan Freed in the film *Rock Around the Clock*. And in 1955 Haley's own Comets left him to form the Jodimars, who sang 'Let's All Rock Together' (Capitol) in the prescribed fashion without impressing the customers. (Boyd Bennett's 'Seventeen' did confirm, however, that in 1955 a record with little musical quality and banal lyrics could satisfy the popular audience; a singer called Big Moe chanted the words tonelessly, while the band played a rough beat. Bennett, a protégé of the Louisiana honky-tonk singer Moon Mullican, had no other hits.)

II

One of the first of Haley's successors in covering rhythm and blues material for white audiences was Pat Boone, whose first big hit 'Ain't That A Shame' (Dot) remained in the Top 10 for fourteen weeks through the summer of 1955. Whereas Haley had developed his style of rock'n'roll himself, Boone had been surprised and rather shocked when he had been asked to record the up-tempo 'Two Hearts, Two Kisses' as his first release for Dot, a southern independent company based in Gallatin, Tennessee. He had been accustomed to slow ballads, of the kind well established in the popular and country and western markets. With the rest of middle-class America, Boone regarded rhythm and blues material as being rather crude, musically and lyrically. None the less, he went on to record 'Ain't That A Shame', 'Tutti Frutti', and a succession of cover versions of other rhythm and blues hits.

In contrast to Bill Haley, Boone was young and good-looking and had a more expressive voice. But unlike Haley, he did not seem to be involved with the spirit of the musicians behind him, and he was important to rock'n'roll only in the role he played bringing a little conservative respectability to the music's image. Although his early success delayed the mass public's awareness of real rock'n'roll/rhythm and blues singers, it may also have indirectly generated interest in them. A few disc jockeys, for example, played the original versions of the Boone hits 'Tutti Frutti' and 'Ain't That A Shame', and when the original singers became better known, Boone retreated to the ballads he seemed from the start to have preferred to record.

'Ain't That A Shame' and 'Tutti Frutti' were both originally recorded in the New Orleans dance blues style, by Fats Domino and Little Richard respectively, and Boone's cover versions used instrumentation closely based on the New Orleans arrangements. In these records the rhythms were looser, less mechanical than in the northern band rock'n'roll records, and the singers were more prominent. There was rarely any singing by the band, and the musicians accepted a supportive role.

Fats Domino, working with Dave Bartholomew, a local big-band leader and trumpeter, as his recording supervisor, co-writer and session bandleader, helped to evolve the New Orleans dance blues through a remarkable series of records which began with 'The Fat Man' (for Imperial), a big hit in the rhythm and blues market in 1949–50. At that time Domino sang in a high, exuberant tenor, and played piano with a distinctive boogie-influenced style that featured chords with both hands. The effervescent good humour of his fast records was eventually discovered by the popular music audience, which in 1956, after he had achieved many hits in the black market, raised 'I'm In Love Again' into *Billboard*'s Top 10. Domino's follow-up to 'I'm In Love Again' was a slow version of the standard 'Blueberry Hill', sung with impressive control and apparently no effort at all. Domino's curious 'creole' accent immediately identified his records, and he maintained a long string of hits, including both infectiously happy songs and plaintive appeals.

A feature of virtually all Domino's records was a tenor sax solo, taken usually about two-thirds of the way through, often by either Lee Allen or Herb Hardesty. These solos were probably shortened versions of the solos that would have been played at dances, and they matched the relaxed control of Domino's voice. Like his singing, the sax tone was melodic, economical, warm and slightly rough.

Although Little Richard came from Georgia and did not record for the same company as Domino, he often played with the same musicians. But in contrast to Domino's cool style, Little Richard was intensely involved in everything he sang, exhilarating his audiences with a frantic, sometimes hysterical performance which was distinguished by pure-voiced swoops and whoops out of a raucous shouting style.

With Little Richard, the rock'n'roll audience got the aggressive extrovert to enact their wilder fantasies, and his stage performance set precedents for anyone who followed him. Dressed in shimmering suits with long drape jackets and baggy pants, his hair grown long and slicked straight, white teeth and gold rings flashing in the spotlights, he stood up at, and sometimes on, the piano, hammering boogie chords as he screamed messages of celebration and self-centred pleasure.

Both 'Long Tall Sally' and 'Rip It Up' became standards in the repertoire of almost every rock'n'roll singer, for the spirit of Little Richard affected and influenced most singers who followed him. Compared to Domino, Little Richard, musically and stylistically speaking, was coarse, uncultured and uncontrolled, in every way harder for the music establishment to take. Among the white rock'n'roll singers, Elvis Presley was similarly outrageous as compared with his predecessors Bill Haley and Pat Boone.

III

Presley was the most commercially successful of a number of Memphis singers who evolved what they themselves called 'country rock' and what others, record collectors and people in the industry, have called 'rockabilly'. Country rock was basically a southern white version of 12-bar boogie blues, shouted with a minimum of subtlety by ex-hillbilly singers over an accompaniment featuring electric guitar, stand-up bass, and – from 1956 – drums, still taboo in Nashville. The style evolved partly from the imaginative guidance of a Memphis radio station engineer, Sam Phillips, who entered the recording business by supervising sessions with local blues singers and leasing the masters to a number of independent companies (Chess in Chicago, owned by the Chess brothers, or Modern/RPM in Los Angeles, owned by the Bihari brothers). The success of some of these singers, notably B. B. King and Howlin' Wolf, encouraged Phillips to form his own label, Sun, and two of the singers he recorded for his own label, Little Junior Parker and Rufus Thomas, had hit records in the Negro market.

The Memphis blues singers used small bands which featured piano, guitar and saxophone. No particular dominant style linked them all, but common to many of their records was a kind of intimate atmosphere created by the simple and cheap, but unorthodox, 'tape delay echo' recording technique of Phillips. The singers invariably made their personal presence felt on the records, menacingly in Howlin' Wolf's case, impatiently in Junior Parker's. These recordings, and other more traditional blues, and rhythm and blues records issued by Sun, were known to a substantial number of white youths through the South, and presented a source of song material and stylistic inspiration that was in many ways more satisfactory than the orthodox country and western culture.

Jimmie Rodgers sang the 'white blues' in the twenties but Elvis Presley was the first to make it work as pop music. According to the legend of his recording debut, his discovery by Sam Phillips was casual and lucky. Presley is said to have attracted the attention of Phillips when he used Sun's studios to cut a record for his mother's birthday present; Phillips encouraged him to make a record with proper accompaniment, and the two men were rewarded with a local hit from one of the sides, 'That's All Right'.

The story of Presley's discovery has the elements of romance, coincidence and fate that legends need, and in fact seems to be true, but it is likely that if Phillips and Presley had not met, two other such people would soon have done what they did – merge rhythm and blues with country and western styles and material, and come up with a new style. In the panhandle of west Texas, in Arkansas, in north Louisiana and in Memphis, there were other singers whose cultural and musical experience were comparable to Presley's; indeed, some of them followed him into the Sun studios, while others tried studios in Nashville and Clovis, New Mexico.

It is difficult to assess how great a part Sam Phillips played in influencing his singers – among other things, by introducing them to blues records – and how much they already knew. Presley told one interviewer:

'I'd play [guitar] along with the radio or phonograph, and taught myself the chord positions. We were a religious family, going round together to sing at camp meetings and revivals, and I'd take my guitar with us when I could. I also dug the real low-down Mississippi singers, mostly Big Bill Broonzy and Big Boy Crudup, although they would scold me at home for listening to them. Sinful music, the townsfolk in Memphis said it was. Which never bothered me, I guess.'

In the same interview, Presley stressed the importance of Phillips:

'Mr Phillips said he'd coach me if I'd come over to the studio as often as I could. It must have been a year and a half before he gave me an actual session. At last he let me try a western song – and it sounded terrible. But the second idea he had was the one that jelled. "You want to make some blues?" he suggested over the phone, knowing I'd always been a sucker for that kind of jive. He mentioned Big Boy Crudup's name and maybe others too. I don't remember. All I know is, I hung up and ran fifteen blocks to Mr Phillips's office before he'd gotten off the line – or so he tells me. We talked about the Crudup records I knew – "Cool Disposition", "Rock Me, Mama", "Hey Mama", "Everything's All Right", and others, but settled for "That's All Right", one of my top favourites . . .'

What Presley achieved was certainly not 'the same thing' as the men he copied. On 'That's All Right' and 'Mystery Train' (written and first recorded by Junior Parker for Sun), he evolved a personal version of this style, singing high and clear, breathless and impatient, varying his rhythmic emphasis with a confidence and inventiveness that were exceptional for a white singer. The sound suggested a young white man celebrating freedom, ready to do anything, go anywhere, pausing long enough for apologies and even regrets and recriminations, but then hustling on towards the new. He was best on fast songs, when his impatient singing matched the urgent rhythm from bass (Bill Black) and guitar (Scotty Moore). Each of his five Sun singles backed a blues song with a country and western song, most of them already familiar to the respective audiences; each sold better than its predecessor, and increasing numbers of people discovered Presley either through radio broadcasts or through his stage appearances.

But Presley did not reach the mass popular music audience with his Sun records, which sold mainly to audiences in the South and to the minority country and western audience elsewhere. Only after Presley's contract was bought by RCA–Victor did his records make the national Top 10, and the songs on these records were not in a country rock style. At Victor, under the supervision of Chet Atkins, Presley's records featured vocal groups, heavily electrified guitars, and drums, all of which were considered alien by both country and western audiences and by the audience for country rock music. Responding to these unfamiliar intrusions in his accompaniment, Presley's voice became much more theatrical and self-conscious as he sought to contrive excitement and emotion which he had seemed to achieve on his Sun records without any evident forethought.

Presley's success for Sun, and later for RCA–Victor, encouraged Phillips to try other singers with comparable styles and material, and attracted to his studios young southeners with similar interests. Carl Perkins and Warren Smith from the Memphis area, Roy Orbison from west Texas, Johnny Cash, Conway Twitty and Charlie Rich from Arkansas, and Jerry Lee Lewis from northern Louisiana, brought songs, demonstration tapes and their ambitions to Phillips, who switched almost completely from black singers to white singers once the latter became commercially successful.

Not all of the singers were as obviously influenced by blues styles as Presley was. Carl Perkins and Johnny Cash, for example, both sang in a much more predominantly country and western style. But, as with Bill Haley, the music and particularly the rhythms of all of them had the emphatic dance beat of rhythm and blues. 'Rockabilly' effectively describes this style, which differed from the northern band rock'n'roll of the Comets. Rockabilly has much looser rhythms, no saxophones, nor any chorus singing. Like the New Orleans dance blues singers, the rockabilly singers were much more personal – confiding, confessing – than Haley could ever be, and their performances seemed less calculated and less prepared. But unlike the lyrical, warm instrumentalists in the dance blues, the instrumentalists in rockabilly responded more violently to unpredictable inflections in the singer's voice, shifting into double-time for a few bars to blend with a sudden acceleration in the singer's tempo. Presley's 'You're A Heartbreaker' (his third single for Sun) typifies the style, as does Carl Perkins's 'Blue Suede Shoes'. The latter was the first million-selling record in the rockabilly style, and brought a new dimension to popular music in its defiant pride for the individual's cultural choice.

Later, in 1956, Johnny Cash made *Billboard*'s Top 20 with another Sun record, 'I Walk The Line', much closer to conventional country and western music in both style and material, and in 1957 the Louisiana pianist–singer Jerry Lee Lewis, heavily influenced by Little Richard, had the first of several big hits with his boogie-based 'Whole Lotta Shakin' Goin' On' (also for Sun). Rockabilly became a major part of American popular music, as much in its continuing inspiration for singers from outside the South as in the occasional commercial successes enjoyed by the rockabilly singers other than Presley.

IV

The nearest equivalent to rockabilly among black styles was the 'Chicago rhythm and blues' style of Chuck Berry, perhaps the major figure of rock'n'roll, and Bo Diddley. Many of the black singers who had recorded around Memphis before Presley (among them Howlin' Wolf, Elmore James and James Cotton) moved to Chicago during the early fifties, where they helped Muddy Waters and others develop the Chicago bar blues style – loud, heavily amplified, shouted to a socking beat.

Chicago became the hotbed for any black musician trying to make a living from the blues, many of whom hoped to work for Muddy Waters or Howlin' Wolf and to record for Chess or its subsidiary Checker. Muddy's harmonica player Little Walter gave Checker two of its biggest rhythm and blues hits in the early fifties with 'My Babe' (1952) and 'Juke' (1955), and the Chess label's big rhythm and blues hits of the period were by the soft-voiced club pianist, Willie Mabon: 'I Don't Know' (1953) and 'I'm Mad' (1954). In 1955 the company became one of the first rhythm and blues indies to break into the pop market with Chuck Berry and Bo Diddley, two guitar-playing singers who recorded with blues musicians but aimed their lyrics and dance rhythms at a younger audience.

'Maybellene' was a 'formula' song, carefully constructed to meet the apparent taste of the recently emerged mass audience for rock'n'roll. The song lived out the fast-car fantasy:

> As I was motorvatin' over the hill,
> I saw Maybellene in a Coupe-de-ville
> Cadillac rollin' on the open road
> Tryin' to outrun my V-8 Ford

Berry has since said that he conceived 'Maybellene' as a country and western song which he originally called 'Ida May'. But disc jockeys Alan Freed and Russ Fratto were 'motivated' to play the record regularly – by being credited as part-authors – and the result was instant rock'n'roll. The beat was much cruder than any Berry ever used again, echoing Bill Haley more than anyone else, and the shouted-back chorus lines were also derived from the Comets' style. Berry's clear enunciation probably enabled his record to 'pass for white' on the radio stations that generally kept such stuff off the air.

The stations could not have made the same mistake with 'Bo Diddley'. Even worse, the rhythm was a bump-and-grind shuffle, which could not be rendered any the more innocent by such lines as: 'Bo Diddley bought-a-baby a diamond ring . . .' The record hardly had the impact on radio stations that 'Maybellene' had, but it ensured demand for 'Bo Diddley' at high school dances.

Both singers had immeasurable influence on other rock'n'roll singers and styles. Berry particularly as a songwriter and guitarist, Diddley as the interpreter of one of the most distinctive rhythms of rock and roll.

V

'Vocal group rock'n'roll' was the loosest of the five types of rock'n'roll, bracketing the groups who sang mainly fast novelty songs together with those which specialized in slow ballads. Where the other four styles developed in reaction to the evolution of electrically amplified guitars and to the emphatic back-beat from drummers, the vocal group style was almost a throw-back to earlier eras; almost, but not quite.

Most of the black vocal groups who emerged in this period were young, inexperienced and amateur singers whose rehearsals were in improvised settings without the benefit of musicians to help with the arrangements. To compensate, each of the back-up singers had to evolve a part which was more concerned with rhythmic and percussive impact than with harmonic sophistication, and it was often the ingenious chants that attracted attention to their records.

But although the rehearsals may have been a cappella (without

17

instruments), most of the records were made with hastily convened back-up bands, often the bare minimum of guitar, bass and drums, with sometimes a saxophone player in the solo break. The paradox for the supervising A&R man was that the less he interfered with a group's own arrangement, the better, although a few companies did find sympathetic arrangers who learned to tidy up the groups' ideas without making them merely conventional. In New York, Atlantic benefited from Jesse Stone's coaching efforts with the Chords, whose 'Sh-Boom' made the pop charts in 1954, while Al Silver of Herald Records sent both the Turbans ('When You Dance') and the Nutmegs ('Story Untold') to Leroy Kirkland for help with their arrangements. The most productive team in this period was George Goldner and Richard Barrett, who were respectively the supervisor and arranger at the session which produced 'Why Do Fools Fall In Love?' by the Teenagers featuring Frankie Lymon, issued on Goldner's Gee label at the end of 1955.

'Why Do Fools Fall In Love?' was in many ways the definitive fast novelty vocal group record of the period, combining an unforgettable web of back-up noises with a classic teenage-lament lyric. Bass singer Sherman Garnes kicked the song off: 'Ay, dum-da di-dum dah dum . . .' and in came Frankie, wailing high in his little boy's cry: 'Ooh-wah, oo-ooh wah-ah'. And then, with the rest of the group weaving in and out, the saxman Jimmy Wright honking along with them, came the song itself, as simple as a nursery rhyme, and as effective, but sung with such heartfelt conviction that it sounded – like the group's name – teenage, not kindergarten.

The record made the Top 10 in the States, and then took off around the world, topping the charts in Britain where none of the previous black vocal group records had made any impact. But although the Teenagers had a couple more hits (which was better than most novelty-oriented vocal groups managed), they soon faded into the swamps of obscurity, and Frankie Lymon's life wasted away to an inevitable death from a drug overdose in 1968.

Of the other novelty groups who made their mark early, the Crows had no more success after their first hit, 'Gee', made the pop charts on George Goldner's Rama label in 1954; that record was hardly more than a repetition of the title, chanted over a simple dance beat, and mainly served to prove that the teenage audience was starved of records with an emphatic off-beat. The Chords were next up, with 'Sh-Boom', and down they went too, followed by the Charms from Cincinnati, who lasted long enough to chalk up two hits, 'Hearts Of Stone' and 'Ling Ting Tong', and then one more in 1956, 'Ivory Tower', billed as Otis Williams and his Charms, all for DeLuxe Records. In 1955, the El-Dorados ('At My Front Door', Vee Jay), the Cadillacs ('Speedoo', Josie) and the Turbans took their turn on the wheel of fortune, and in 1956 another of George Goldner's groups, the Cleftones, made it with 'Little Girl Of Mine'. Each record implanted itself in the minds of listeners, and several attracted cover versions at the time and revival versions since; but for most of the singers involved, it was back to day jobs at best, or hustling on the streets at worst. The term 'novelty group' seemed to be a euphemism for one-hit wonder. The one notable exception was the Coasters, who made their mark in 1957 with the Leiber–Stoller productions of 'Young Blood' and 'Searchin'', and sustained a career of hits until 1964.

For slow groups, career prospects were potentially much better, because they could hope to move into the supper-club and cabaret world where Las Vegas was the ultimate target. The paradox was, could a group meet the needs of that world and yet satisfy the criteria for play on the teen-oriented rock'n'roll radio shows? Buck Ram, manager of the Platters and writer of several of their hits, proved that it could be done.

Although there were slow groups making the rhythm and blues charts from all areas of the States, the three which made most impact on the pop charts in rock'n'roll's breakthrough period were all based in Los Angeles: the Penguins, the Teen Queens, and the Platters. Both the Penguins and the Teen Queens turned out to be one-hit wonders, but their records were typical of an on-going West Coast style which had previously surfaced on the rhythm and blues charts via 'Dream Girl' by Jesse and Marvin (Specialty, 1953), and 'Cherry Pie' by Marvin and Johnny (Modern, 1954). In both cases, the singers slurred and dragged their phrases to ludicrous extents in order to declare their heartfelt devotion, and this was the sound that the Penguins brought to the nation in 'Earth Angel'.

For the professionals in the industry, 'Earth Angel' was seen as undeniable proof that the youth of the day had lost their marbles. Was the singer male or female? (Male: Cleveland Duncan.) Where was the song? 'Earth Angel [thud, from the drummer], earth angel [thud] [pause] will you be mine? [thud].' To compound the felony, the record featured the bane of all professional musicians, triplets, where the pianist just held a chord and hammered it three times on every beat; so simple, no self-respecting musician could bear to do it. But it made for hypnotic dancing, and was what worked. Dootone Records had its one and only hit, and encountered some of the attendant problems when Buck Ram moved in as manager of the group and took them off to Mercury Records along with his other protégés the Platters.

The Platters had been just one of the countless black vocal groups in Los Angeles, recording for Federal in all the current styles without ever establishing a distinct identity, but after their move to Mercury all the focus was put on to the voice of lead tenor Tony Williams. The first recording for the new label was of a song (written by Ram) which the group had already recorded for Federal with no success, 'Only You'. This time around, the record went unnoticed again for three months before it began to get play, yet it came to represent a milestone in the era's music.

The back-up singers in the Platters never sounded as interesting as most of the other groups of the day, and in many ways the group's records could have been billed as by Tony Williams. He had a genuinely good voice, obviously influenced by gospel, and he threw in a kind of hiccup on the high notes which became his trademark. Swooping up to stratospheric heights, he declared the now familiar undying devotion in 'Only You', and followed through with a better song (again written by Buck Ram), 'The Great Pretender'. Tailor-made to showcase the high-flying voice of Williams, this topped the American pop chart, and set the group up for a long career, achieving Ram's declared ambition to launch 'the new Ink Spots'. Later records veered away from the triplet, teen-ballad idiom of the first two hits, but that idiom became part of the basic rock'n'roll heritage for better or (quite often) for worse.

These five styles of rock'n'roll covered most of the records which broke through to the pop charts from 1954 through 1956, and basically set up the 'ingredients' which were mixed together in slightly varying combinations for the next thirty years by musicians, producers and singers aiming at the 'youth market'. Bill Haley's brand of northern band rock'n'roll was probably the least influential, being the end, rather than a beginning, of a tradition; sometimes derided for his old-fashioned image, Haley was in fact an astute bandleader who outlasted most of his contemporaries by accommodating the back-beat rhythm that was required of the new dance music.

The piano-and-saxophone orientation of New Orleans rock'n'roll gradually lost favour during the sixties, when the majority of groups featured guitars as both lead and rhythm instruments, inspired equally by Memphis-style rockabilly and Chicago-style rhythm and blues. The gospel attack of Little Richard had incalculable influence, both directly and through the other gospel-styled singers who found more favour after he had crashed into public view. And many of the performers who synthesized these influences worked as groups, incorporating vocal harmonies which took off from the Teenagers and the other vocal groups. Between them, these styles provided the basis for all the major artists and producers of the sixties – obviously the Four Seasons, the Beach Boys and the Motown groups in the States, and the Beatles and Rolling Stones in Britain, and less obviously but just as certainly, Bob Dylan and Sly Stone. In most cases, the second generation were able to make more from their records than the innovators had, in terms of money, fame and prestige, as they reclaimed the music from the businessmen who tried to reproduce the effects of rock'n'roll without risking the personal elements that had been fundamental in the first place.

The Best of Acappella

LENNY KAYE

The sheer diversity of rock's roots ensured a widescreen sound from which it could distill and then disperse. Lenny Kaye's 'The Best of Acappella' deals with one obscure strand, culled from the era when rock & roll was eternally 45. Reflecting on Acappella at a time when rock had dropped its roll (1970), Kaye was seeking to remind both himself and his readers that rock & roll is/was/will always be a simple music.

It used to be that you could only find it in little, out of the way places. There was a cut on the first Captain Beefheart album, an Anglicized version by Them on their first effort, another on the Amboy Dukes' *Migration*. Or you might hear it in the midst of a jam session somewhere, flowing out amid laughter and shouts of hey-I-remember-that, a little I-IV-V progression and then into

'Teen Angel'. Frank Zappa once devoted an entire album to it (*Ruben and the Jets*), but fell prey to the too-easy temptation to parody.

But now the rock'n'roll revival is fully upon us. The music of the First Phase is all around; Chuck Berry is at the Fillmore, Fats Domino just recently had an almost-hit record, the Coasters are again recording and appearing. On another level, there was a Pachucho record hop at the Family Dog a while ago, Cat Mother is singing about Good Old Rock & Roll, and a group named Sha-Na-Na played oldies-but-goodies at the Scene to screaming crowds and rave reviews. We're almost back in 1958 again, with people starting to dig out their old 45s, immersing themselves in such as Dion and the Belmonts, the Big Bopper, the Earls and the Fascinations, doing the ol' hully-gully as they walk down the street.

It's nice to see rock nostalgia happening; more than that, it's nice to see something past nostalgia happening. The old values seem to be on their way back; as the decency rallies proliferate, we are slowly entering a new phase of the old outlaw days of rock'n'roll. The cycles are turning, my friend, around and around once more, and we're coming home at last. Goodbye, Fillmore East; hello, Brooklyn Fox.

But I don't really want to write a thing on late fifties/early sixties rock'n'roll: that topic deserves a book and (sadly) will probably get one in the near future. Rather, this is about a stream within a stream within a stream; a little thing that happened once a long time ago, something that began, went round in its own little circle, died after a time. Call it a movement if you will – art historians would like that term. Call it a subculture, or maybe a microcosm of a much larger rock society – sociologists would like that. Call it an 'experiment with the polyphonic possibilities of the human voice within a set and limited structural framework' – musicologists would like that. Or call it a genre, or a style, or a fad. Anything your little heart desires.

But I call it Acappella music, which is what it was known as then, though all of us had to have the word explained at one time or another. 'Hitting notes', in the language of the street, and this is probably the most fitting title, since it was born on the street, on the corners of the small cities and large metropolises. Somebody tried to make it a Star once; they almost succeeded, but it ultimately toppled over from its own weight, coming back, in the end, to the very place where it was born, the place where it probably still remains today.

This, as they used to say in the movies, is its story.

The formula was very simple. You would be at a dance (or a party or just sitting around on somebody's front stoop), and things were draggy so you would go in the bathroom (or hallway or stay on the same old stoop) with four (or six or twenty) other guys and sing (and sing and sing). The songs were standards; there was 'Gloria' (of course), and the lead singer's voice always cracked when he reached for the falsetto part. There was 'Diamonds And Pearls', a must from the Paragons, then 'Valerie' for the crying and melodrama, 'What's Your Name' 'cause it had a boss bass part, finally into 'Stormy Weather', that perennial old classic:

> Don't know why
> (a-don't know why)
> There's no sun up in the sky
> It's Stormy Weather
> (Stormy wea-ther, wah-doo) . . .

Acappella, not to be confused with the classical a cappella, means 'without music'. We were told that on the first all-Acappella album ever released, called *The Best of Acappella*, Vol. 1. They weren't quite right, as it turned out – there was very definitely music involved. What they really meant to say was that there was no musical accompaniment, no background instrumentation. Acappella groups had to rely solely on their voices (helped a bit at times by an echo chamber), using them to provide all the different parts of a song. This tended to put a greater emphasis on the role of the back-up part of the group, pushing the lead singer into a slightly less prestigious position. There was none of this limp Supremes background humming that is so prevalent today – Acappella groups really had to work, nearly scat-singing their way through the highs and lows of a song.

The movement began sometime in late 1962 or '63 with a group called the Zircons. The original Zircons (for there was a second, less creative group later) were probably together for about five days, at least long enough to cut a record which ultimately became the first big Acappella single. It was called 'Lonely Way', and sold somewhere above three thousand records. In these days of the Big Huge, three thousand really doesn't sound like much, but for an Acappella record, appealing to a limited audience in a limited area, the number was quite substantial. There had been a few other groups who preceded the Zircons (notably the Nutmegs who had made a lot of practice tapes in the style), but it was they who broke the initial ice, receiving some airplay on AM stations and promptly breaking up over it.

'Lonely Way' was, and still remains, one of the finest Acappella songs produced throughout the entire history of the style. Many of the later productions had a tendency to be hollow; there were holes in the arrangements and you really missed the presence of the back-up music. Not so with 'Lonely Way' – the harmonies were full and vibrant, the arrangement tight and tasteful, everything working together toward a melodious whole. I had the record for two weeks before I even realized they were singing alone.

After the Zircons, the Acappella movement went into full swing. In what surely must be a famous first, the style was not fostered by radio airplay, by record companies, or even through personal appearances by the groups themselves. Instead, the driving forces behind Acappella, those who promoted, financed and ultimately pushed it, were by and large record stores. And to fully understand this, we must do up a little background history.

Rock in the fifties, though it followed somewhat national trends, was basically regional in nature. Southern California birthed a peculiar brand of pachucho-rock; Tex-Mex had the Buddys – Holly and Knox; Philadelphia gave the world dances, *American Bandstand* and Fabian, and New York had the groups. The groups, together for a day or a year, often recording under a variety of names, sprang up at record hops or teen variety shows, here today and gone tomorrow. As a conservative estimate, I would say that close to ten thousand records by fly-by-night groups on similar fly-by-night labels were released in the late fifties and early sixties. And slowly, again mostly around New York, there grew up a little fandom around these groups, calling itself by various names – 'oldies fans', 'R&B lovers', etc. – who became really involved with the kind of music these groups were producing. In time, as the Top 40 began to play fewer and fewer of these combinations, the movement was pushed underground; groups like the Ravens, the Moonglows, the Five Satins, the Paragons, slowly became the chief proponents of the older music. At a time when most radio stations were slowly sinking into the morass of Bobby Vee and Tony Orlando, groups like the Cadillacs and the Diablos were busily keeping the faith alive.

This fascination with groups has carried over to present day rock and I've always been at a loss to figure out why. Even today, a group stands a better chance of being listened to than does a single artist; there is more glamour, more ... well, something about a group that calls forth stronger loyalties. Whatever, this rock and roll underground, though it had no connection with the radical movements of the day and indeed was probably very hostile toward all *outré* forms of behaviour, resembled very much the early days of progressive rock. There was the same sense of boosting involved, the same constant grumblings that the radio played shit and if only they would program some good groups . . . And if you can remember turning people on to the Airplane (or even grass) for the first time, you might be able to imagine what it was to turn someone on to Acappella records. ('Now here's this fine group', arm around shoulder, slowly leading toward the record-player, a weird glint in the eye . . .) You were simply doing missionary work – taking care of God's business here on earth – and you just knew that He looked down and that He saw it was good.

In the true spirit of supply and demand, this group-oriented underground spawned record shops designed to meet their needs. Even at the height of their popularity, there were still only a few, maybe one or two per city, sparsely spread in a ragged line from New York to Philadelphia. In New York there was Times Square Records, later followed by the House of Oldies and Village Oldies on Bleecker Street. In Hackensack, New Jersey (soon to be a major centre of Acappella – no foolin'), was the Relic Rack. Newark boasted Park Records, which gave away free coupons so that you stood to gain one record for every ten, and Plainfield had Brooks Records, a store which had the dubious honour of having the dumbest salesgirls in existence. There were also a few in South Jersey, mostly around Trenton, one in Philadelphia whose name I can't remember, and maybe two or three others. The Acappella underground was not exactly a mass movement.

Times Square Records, located in the 42nd Street subway arcade, was the biggest and best. It was run by Slim, a tall, gangling man who knew everything there was to know about rock and roll, assisted by Harold, who knew nearly as much. Slim was a strange character, looking for all the world like a Midwestern con man, always ready to show you this or that little goodie which he had just gotten in. He used to write for some of the little hectographed magazines that sprang up around the movement, little rambling columns that talked about the health value of Benson & Hedges, his ex-wife, all the new records Times Square was going to find and sell at outrageous prices. In a sample column, from *Rhythm and Blues Train*, he covered tapes that you could have made from the Times Square files, the fact that no one bought in 'Saki-Laki-Waki' by the Viscounts on Vega label so that the cash price they would pay was now two hundred dollars, a few upcoming inventions of his (including air-conditioned streets), and finally finished with a joke about the best thief in the world, who stole a tyre off one of the wheels of his car when he was doing fifty.

Slim really came into his own when he had an FM radio show which appeared in odd corners of the dial on occasional Sunday afternoons. He used to play some fine music, new Acappella releases, also rarer records from the Times Square stock. 'And now,' he would say, 'here's "Sunday Kind Of Love" by them Medievals, worth ten dollars at Times Square Records', and then, 'pop', there it would be, probably the first time it had ever been on a radio station, rescued from some dusty old file of DJ records.

But if Slim was a world in himself, his store was a veritable universe. Records lined the walls, sparkling in all manner of colours. One of the sneakier ways to make a record rare in those days was to release a limited number in a red (or green, or yellow) plastic edition. Times Square had them all, Drifters 45s in purple, a copy of the long sought-after 'Stormy Weather' by the Five Sharks in a full five-colour deluxe edition, others in varying hues and shades. Alongside the rows of hanging records were huge lists, detailing the prices Times Square would pay for rare records. Elvis Presley efforts on the Sun label went for ten dollars; 'Darling I'm Sorry' by the Ambassadors would bring the bearer a princely two hundred dollars. The rarest record of all, which Slim never actually succeeded in obtaining, was the old 78 version of 'Stormy Weather' by the Five Sharps, complete with sound effects of thunderstorms and rain. (In the end, he was forced to gather together a collection of drunks and name them the Five Sharks in order to re-cut and re-release the record.) If you have the Five Sharps version, you could have made yourself an easy five hundred dollars.

The nicest thing about Times Square Records, or any of the shops for that matter, was that they never minded if you just hung around the store, listening to records, rapping, trading and buying on your own. The clerks loved to talk, loved to show you obscure oldies, loved to find out if you could teach them anything in return. After a while, the stores became regular meeting halls, places where the groups hung out, where the kids brought their demos, where you could hear any number of versions of 'Gloria' or 'Pennies From Heaven', or 'Ten Commandments Of Love'. It was a big club, and you could join if you had ever even remotely heard of Sonny Till and the Orioles.

But though Times Square was the headquarters, the Relic Rack actually started the whole thing off. Hackensack, New Jersey, is an unlikely spot for anything resembling a music centre. It's dumpy, stodgily middle class, right on the outskirts of the pleasant pastoral spots of Secaucus and Jersey City. Yet its one asset was that it had a fine record shop, one where you could find nearly anything you were looking for and one which had the same set of vibes as Times Square Records.

The Rack, in the person of Eddie Gries, had experimented for a time with bringing out re-releases of some of their rare oldies on their own label, Relic. They had some success and so, nearly simultaneously, Times Square followed suit. After a time, there was an assortment of things out on these private labels, some Acappella and some not, all managing to do moderately well. The important thing here, though, was not so much in the labels themselves, but in the fact that when the Zircons proved Acappella could actually sell, at least in a limited circle, the labels were already in existence to push and provide a vehicle for the music. Which brings us, finally, to the Star itself.

Acappella music grew out of the fifties rock underground, which coalesced around an assortment of loosely termed R&B groups all held together by this series of specialty record shops. The music itself was primarily more a style than anything else, using basically interchangeable words and phrases. Like blues, the thing was not in what you did, but rather how you did it. To generalize, we can divide the output into two main types, the Fast song and the Slow song. The Fast song was up-tempo, lots of sharp vocal work in the background, heavy emphasis on the bass, lead singer on top merely filling up the rest of the balance. In the context of Acappella music, it had more of a tendency to fall apart since even the most spirited singing could not usually make up for the loss of rhythm instruments. In these fast songs, all the holes could never really be filled adequately and the result, except in selected instances, was usually choppy, sounding weak and thin. Its good feature, however, was that it usually provided the most freaky vocal effects then present on record. In their push to clean up the loose ends, back-up vocalists were really hard pressed to find suitable accompaniment. Some of the results are like the Del-Stars' 'Zoop Bop', a song which was easily five years ahead of its time. Consisting of little more than a collection of indecipherable syllables, rhythmic effects and skilful use of the echo chamber, the record comes off as one of the first psychedelic golden oldies.

The Acappella form truly found itself, however, in the Slow song. Essentially a ballad, it was soft, the background singers filling out the lead vocal, coming in over, under and through it at various times. When successful, the effect could be haunting in its starkness and purity. The Vi-Tones once made a record called 'The Storm' which is nothing less than unearthly, minor in mood, creating feelings I know I could never put down on paper. Acappella was really a true return to essentials, finding the emotions that could be represented by simple harmonies, using only the human voice as its instrument. When it was done well (something that often eluded the dozens of groups who relied on showy vocal pyrotechnics), it could be incredibly gripping and powerful.

We could get really hung up in drawing analogies to present-day rock here, but it's much too tempting to find any number of parallels in the rise and fall of Acappella and compare them with what has been happening over a like period of time in rock. Acappella began with a handful of groups, all highly polished in a crude sort of way, proud of their craft and creating a superior collection of recordings and performances. Then, as the movement's sense of self increased (much as in the curse of Marcuse's *One-Dimensional Man*), the quality began regressing. It began to be self-conscious of what had formerly been unconscious and contrived results were hardly listenable. Pale imitations sprang up, filled with sloppy singing and off-key harmonies. Strangely, all this happened at a time when Acappella was actually increasing in popularity; the amount of good stuff simply decreased in a kind of inverse ratio. And Acappella, not having the numerical power nor the resiliency of rock, could not afford to have its strength so diluted – it had to keep being produced at a high level in order to survive. But once the downfall started, there was no stopping it. When Acappella finally died, there were few left around to mourn it.

But all that is much nearer the end of the story. Acappella's Great Groups come well at the beginning, and most managed to retain their high positions until the whole thing began to fade out of sight. We've already spoken about the Zircons; the newer group that sprang up to take their name was not nearly as good, producing one fine song ('Silver Bells'), and then concentrating on shlock versions of 'Stormy Weather' and the like. This newer group actually got around to producing an album (on Cat-Time label), but it was significant only in the negative.

But the other large groups of Acappella managed to stay together, and several of them kept on producing more and better stuff. The Young Ones, who became popular almost at the same time as the Zircons, were probably almost as well known, maintaining a high quality in their records (with resultant rise in reputation). The group was from Brooklyn, ranged in ages from eighteen to twenty and managed to coalesce one of the truly unique sounds in Acappella, thanks to a lead singer who had the capacity to sound nearly castrato at certain times. Their first record, on the Yuusels label, was called 'Marie', a near-standard stereotypical Slow song:

> He made the mountains
> He made the tree
> And He made a girl
> When He made Marie

But for whatever reason, the Young Ones took this song and really did a Job on it, creating out of it one of the most moving records of the whole period. Though 'Marie' contained some musical background, the Young Ones soon moved over to Slim and the Times Square label and began producing Acappella records.

While there, they came up with several passable songs and two truly Great ones. The first of these was easily the finest version of 'Gloria' yet available, a tremendous reading of a song which had been done over and over and over, sometimes nearly to death, by some huge number of groups. But even better than that was their Acappella version of 'Sweeter Than', a remake of the Passions' oldie of 'This Is My Love'. From the opening note to the final, bell-like harmonic rise at the end, the song had Classic written all over it.

If the Young Ones represented some of the best that Acappella had to offer, the Camelots certainly showed the versatility of the style. For one, they produced the best up-tempo song, 'Don't Leave Me Baby', a record that featured a bottom line any present-day bass guitarist would be happy to make his own. The Camelots' success was mainly due to their incredibly rich harmony, a sound which brooked no faltering or loose moments; they were on top of their material at all times. Of all the groups, they made the best effort to go commercial, recording for both Laurie and Ember records, but, like the others, they have long since disappeared.

Underneath this top layer of groups were three or four secondary combinations, all of which had varying moments of excitement from them. I have a warm spot in my heart for the Savoys, hailing from Newark, who came out with some fine material on the Catamount label. They and a group called the Five Fashions were the stars of the best Acappella album ever put out, *I Dig Acappella*, featuring a cover photo of a plump girl in a bathing-suit overseeing gravestones with the names of the groups on them (*I Dig* . . . get it?), containing some twenty cuts of sheer Acappella proficiency. There were the inevitable bummers, of course ('She Cried' by the Rueteens, the Zircons' 'Unchained Melody'), but on the whole, it was the finest statement that the Acappella movement had yet made. It still is, by the way, and I can think of no better way to introduce anybody to music 'without music' than to play them any one of half a dozen cuts from the album.

It would be nice to report that the other albums that came out were as consistent as *I Dig Acappella*. 'The Best of Acappella' series on Relic only lived up to its name with the first volume and continued downward from there. Except for selected groups (the

Citadels, a revival of the old Quotations, a few others), the series degenerated into a collection of poor imitations, flat harmonies and gimmick groups. They would feature Joey and the Majestics – 'A twelve-year-old lead singer!' – songs done in barber shop harmony, the first Acappella song done in a foreign language, any number of other superficial hypes. My personal favourite from all of these winners was a group called Ginger and the Adorables, who appeared on the cover of Vol. IV, five chicks who really looked as if they could roll your back until it began to break. Unfortunately, they couldn't sing worth a damn. In the liner notes, we were told that:

> Ginger and the Adorables (also known as the Lynettes) are from West Orange, New Jersey. They were discovered by Wayne Stierle while singing outside a local candy store. Lead singer is Ginger Scalione, 16; first tenor is Jill Tordell, 16; second tenor is Gail Haberman, 14 . . .

The period of decadence was about to set in.

Withal, you could feel Acappella slowly fading away. It was losing steam, fighting a weighted battle against a nearly overwhelming onslaught of crap. But in November of 1965, as the whole thing was entering its twilight, Acappella had its finest moment. The occasion was the first Acappella show, sponsored by the Relic Rack, featuring all the groups that we had heard but never seen, people like the Savoys, the Five Sharks, the (new) Zircons. It was to be quite an Event; except within a small hometown radius, Acappella groups almost never appeared anywhere. They were simply much too esoteric and obscure. As the night drew closer, it seemed as if a huge party was about to take place; good feelings were spread all around.

As it would happen, the night was fated: the entire East Coast was struck by the Great Blackout. But Hackensack, for some unknown reason, was one of the few remaining pockets of light. And it was exciting to be at the theatre; a kind of community existed between the people who came, a spiritual bond which said that there is one thing that binds us all together – one thing that we have that the Others outside don't even know about. There was a sense of belonging, of participation in a small convention of your own personal friends. We were all together.

Now I suppose that it would be logical to describe a pseudo-mystical experience at this point, complete with stars and flashing red lights. It would bring things to a dramatic finale, tie together all the differing streams of narrative we've started up and left hanging, round everything off in a nice warm ball. But I can't do that, simply because it just didn't happen. The groups came out; I remember seeing the Five Sharks, a new group called the Meadowbrooks who did a few nice things, maybe a couple of others, but the air was never charged with the feeling that something Wonderful was taking place. The music was good, we all liked it and applauded like mad, but the Magic simply wasn't there.

The reason that nothing like that could happen was because the people on the stage were essentially no different than us. There was no charismatic distance between us down here and them up there, no feeling of the performer and his relation to the audience. These people weren't professionals; they were only doing the same things that we had been doing all along, leaning up against the wall, laughing a lot, trying to sing. They might have done it a little better than we could, but that was irrelevant.

It was fun. Like a sing-along, or a hootenanny. Like being in one of those 1890s ragtime places where people get drunk and sing the old songs. Like being home. And so, when it was over, we left and said it was fine, 'cause it was, especially when that big bass hit that riff, *damn* he had a low voice (trying it) *bah-doo bah-doo* and what about the falsetto from the Sharks *oo-whee-ee-oo-oo* yeah but remember . . .

*

There was another concert somewhere along the line, a lot more records, more groups, more everything. But toward the end, no one really cared very much. Acappella died because the confines of its own small world could not contain it when it became too large; it simply could not keep up enough quality per record. Toward its final days, when people like Stierle were producing Acappella's brand of bubble-gum music, when groups like the Autumns recorded limp versions of 'Exodus', when it became nearly impossible to separate the good from the bad, many of the old fans began drifting away. And I was one of them, picking up on the Beatles, the Stones, on newer things with the vitality that Acappella once had, but somehow lost.

But because I still remembered, I went down to Times Square Records the other day, just to check it out, to have some sides played, to find out what had happened in the years I had been away.

There was a sign on the door, saying the store was to be closed soon. It had moved from the old large location to a smaller, very cramped hole in the wall. Slim was gone, of course, and skinny little Harold was gone also. All that remained was a pale junkie behind the cash register who would doze off each time I would ask for a record. I wandered around inside, feeling fairly lost, remembering how things once were and irrationally wishing they might return again.

I asked the guy at the store what had happened. 'Nobody likes the old music any more,' he told me. I said that was sad. He shrugged and dozed off again.

I left a little while after that. He was right, of course. Even the rock'n'roll revival will probably pass right over Acappella music, over the Five Satins, over the Orioles, even over the rainbow. Which is really too bad. In passing over all of them, it'll miss the heart of the whole thing, avoiding the meat and picking up some of the filler, bypassing a lot that might be nice to have in these days of giant festivals and supergroups.

Acappella was not the stuff of which you could make mountains. It was simple music, perhaps the simplest, easy to understand, easier to relate to, and so maybe it's not so bad that Acappella will be passed over after all. It would be lost at the Fillmore or the huge stadiums, swamped by the electrical energy that is so much a part of the contemporary scene. Acappella is meant to be personal, music for street corners and bathrooms, for happy memories and good times.

A stream within a stream within a stream. Folk music of a very special kind.

Classic Rock

NIK COHN

Though Nik Cohn's Awopbopaloobop *purported to be a straightforward résumé of the first decade of rock & roll, there was always a polemical bent to Cohn's prose. Originally published in 1969, under the title* Pop From the Beginning, *it sought to contrast the Classic Rock of Cochran, Berry and Penniman with the shallow sophistry of what came in its wake.*

Rock'n'roll was very simple music. All that mattered was the noise it made, its drive, its aggression, its newness. All that was taboo was boredom.

The lyrics were mostly non-existent, simple slogans one step away from gibberish. This wasn't just stupidity, simple inability to write anything better. It was the kind of teen code, almost a sign language, that would make rock entirely incomprehensible to adults.

In other words, if you weren't sure about rock, you couldn't cling to its lyrics. You either had to accept its noise at face value or you had to drop out completely.

Under these rules, rock turned up a sudden flood of maniacs, wild men with pianos and guitars who would have been laughing stocks in any earlier generation but who were just right for the fifties. They were energetic, basic, outrageous. They were huge personalities and they used music like a battering ram. Above all, they were loud.

It was a great time – every month would produce someone new, someone wilder than anything that had gone before. Pop was barren territory and everything was simple, every tiny gimmick was some kind of progression. Around 1960, things evened out and much of the excitement died out. Pop had become more sophisticated, more creative, more everything. But the fifties were the time when pop was just pop, when it was really something to switch on the radio and hear what was new right that minute. Things could never be so good and simple again.

For instance, the first record I ever bought was by Little Richard and, at one throw, it taught me everything I ever need to know about pop. The message went: 'Tutti frutti all rootie, tutti frutti all tootie, tutti frutti all rootie, awopbopaloobop alopbamboom!' As a summing up of what rock'n'roll was really about, this was nothing but masterly.

Very likely these early years are the best that pop has yet been through. Anarchy moved in. For thirty years you couldn't possibly make it unless you were white, sleek, nicely spoken and phoney to your toenails – suddenly now you could be black, purple, moronic, delinquent, diseased or almost anything on earth and you could still clean up. Just so long as you were new, just so long as you carried excitement.

*

Most of the best early rockers came out of the South: Elvis from Mississippi, Little Richard from Georgia, Buddy Holly from Texas, Jerry Lee Lewis from Louisiana, Gene Vincent from Virginia. These were the states where the living had always been meanest, where teenagers had been least catered to, and where, therefore, the rock kickback was now most frantic.

Anyhow, the South was by far the most music-conscious section in America, it always had been. It had huge traditions in R&B, country, trad. and gospel, and its music was in every way more direct, less pretentious than that up north. Mostly, it had a sledgehammer beat and pulled no punches. Down here, rock was an obvious natural.

The only innovation was that the rockers made use of all the sources around them. Up to this time, whites had used country, Negroes had used R&B, and the two had never remotely overlapped. Now everyone incorporated anything they could lay their hands on, and it was this mix-up of black and white musics that gave southern rock its flavour.

Of all the great southern rockers, just about the most splendid was the aforementioned Little Richard Penniman out of Macon, Georgia.

He was born on Christmas Day 1935, one of thirteen children, and had a predictably harsh childhood. At fourteen, he was singing solos with the local gospel choir. At fifteen, he was blues-shouting, dancing and selling herb tonic in a medicine show. From there, he got into a variety of groups, made a sequence of nothing records, and finally in 1955, when he was twenty, sold a million copies of 'Tutti Frutti'.

He looked beautiful. He wore a baggy suit with elephant trousers, twenty-six inches at the bottoms, and he had his hair back-combed in a monstrous plume-like fountain. Then he had a little toothbrush moustache and a round, totally ecstatic face.

He played piano, and he'd stand knock-kneed at the keyboard, hammering away with two hands as if he wanted to bust the thing apart. At climactic moments, he'd lift one leg and rest it on the keys, banging away with his heel, and his trouser rims would billow like kites.

He'd scream and scream and scream. He had a freak voice, tireless, hysterical, completely indestructible, and he never in his life sang at anything lower than an enraged bull-like roar. On every phrase, he'd embroider with squeals, rasps, siren whoops. His stamina, his drive, were limitless and his songs were mostly total non-songs, nothing but bedrock 12-bars with playroom lyrics, but still he'd put them across as if every last syllable was liquid gold. He sang with desperate belief, real religious fervour: 'Good golly, Miss Molly, you sure like a ball – when you're rockin' and rollin', I can't hear your momma call.'

As a person he was brash, fast, bombastic, a sort of prototype Mohammed Ali ('I'm just the same as ever – loud, electrifying and full of personal magnetism'), and right through the middle fifties he was second only to Elvis. Most of his records sold a million each: 'Long Tall Sally', 'Lucille', 'The Girl Can't Help It', 'Keep A Knockin', 'Baby Face'. They all sounded roughly the same: tuneless, lyricless, pre-Neanderthal. There was a tenor sax solo in the middle somewhere and a constant smashed-up piano and Little Richard himself screaming his head off. Individually, the records didn't mean much. They were small episodes in one unending scream and only made sense when you put them all together.

But in 1957 he suddenly upped and quit. No warning – he just stopped touring, stopped making records, and went off to play piano in a Seventh Day Adventist Church off Times Square.

Apparently, he'd been in a plane and a fire had broken out. Richard got down on his knees and promised that if he was spared, he'd give up the devil's music for ever and devote himself to the gospel instead. 'And God answered my prayers and stopped the fire.'

So he announced that he was giving up, but his entourage thought he was crazy and laughed at him. Then Richard, in a typically flash performance, took his many rings from his fingers and flung them into the sea. Almost $20,000 worth: 'I wish I'd seen the face of the man that caught those fish. A king's ransom, all courtesy of Little Richard.' And he quit on the spot. At least, that's the story he tells, and it might be true. Some of his stories are.

Five years he kept it up, made no records, gave no interviews. But in the early sixties he began to cut gospel records, and from there it was inevitable that he'd go back to rock again. He didn't get any further hits, but he was still a name. Several times he toured Britain, and each time he went down a storm.

The first time I saw him was in 1963, sharing a bill with the Rolling Stones, Bo Diddley and the Everly Brothers, and he cut them all to shreds. He didn't look sane. He screamed and his eyes bulged; the veins jutted in his skull. He came down front and stripped – his jacket, tie, cuff-links, his golden shirt, his huge diamond watch – right down to flesh. Then he hid inside a silk dressing-gown, and all the time he roared and everyone jumped about in the aisles like it was the beginning of rock all over again.

Objectively, he didn't even do much. Anyone else that has a great stage act always has an obvious selling point: James Brown has speed, Johnnie Ray has pain, Elvis has sex. Little Richard had none of that. All he had was energy.

He howled and hammered endlessly. On 'Hound Dog', he dropped down on his knees and grovelled, and still he howled. It was all gospel – 'that healing music, makes the blind see, the lame to walk, the dead rise up.' He kept it up so long, so loud, it made your head whirl. Good hard rock; he murdered it and murdered us. When he was through, he smiled sweetly. 'That Little Richard,' he said, 'such a nice boy.'

*

Fats Domino came from further back. In fact, he was almost pre-pop. As early as 1948, he cut a big hit called 'Fat Man', and he'd already tucked about ten smashes under his belt by the time that Bill Haley came along.

At this period, he sold mostly around his home town of New Orleans and worked for a strictly Negro market. The music he peddled was a nicely relaxed line in R&B, backed by tightly knit small bands, and everything he did was casual. Fats himself wrote the songs, played piano and sang.

When rock came in and R&B was acceptable, the fat man very quickly cashed in. He had whole strings of American hits and by 1960 he'd sold upwards of fifty million records. Fifty million is a lot of records. Officially, he's also credited with twenty-two individual million sellers, which puts him ahead of everyone outside of Elvis and the Beatles.

Mind you, it has to be said that these figures make him sound a lot bigger than he ever was. Most of his alleged million sellers were only regional hits and he never made much sustained impression on British charts. All the same, he was a figure. More important, he made good records.

The way he was so lazy and good-humoured, he was a bit like an updated Fats Waller. Most of his best songs – 'Blue Monday', 'I'm Walking', 'Blueberry Hill' – were dead simple, straight ahead, and Fats sang them as if he was having himself a time. When he was at his best, he conjured up small-time coloured dance halls on Saturday night – he played a bit, sang a bit and everyone got lushed. Good-time music, that's all it was and it hit the spot just right.

In 1967 he did a Sunday night show at the Saville in London and the audience was made up of rockers from way back – all greased hair, drainpipes and three-quarter coats. Fats weighed in at sixteen stone and smiled all the time. He ran through his hits and diamonds glittered on his fingers and he wore bright orange socks.

When he came to his finale, he went into an endless and very corny workout on 'When The Saints Go Marching In'. It went on and on and on. Fats glistened and gleamed all over, his band cavorted like circus clowns and it was all a bit embarrassing. At the end, Fats got up and started to push his piano across the stage with hard thumps of his thigh. He was past forty and not fit and it was a very wide stage. By the time he was halfway across, he was flagging. The music rambled on and Fats was bent almost double with effort. It was a very ludicrous situation – the rockers stormed forwards at the stage, willing him on, and he kept heaving, he wouldn't give up. And it took him maybe five minutes but finally he did make it and everyone cheered like mad.

Two of the rockers jumped up on stage and lifted his hands, holding them aloft like he was a winning fighter. They were big kids and Fats, for all his weight, is quite squat. He stood shaking between them and he looked vulnerable, almost old. Everyone was rioting. Fats streamed sweat and kept smiling but he also looked a bit confused. Very likely, no one had gone quite that wild for him in ten years.

Another noble rocker was Screamin' Jay Hawkins, who had been around ever since the middle forties. He wore a zebra-striped tailcoat, a turban, polka dot shoes. He began his act by emerging flaming from a coffin, and he carried a smoking skull called Henry; he shot flame from his fingertips; he screamed and bloodcurdled. At the end, he flooded the stage with thick white smoke, and when it cleared, he was gone.

'I used to lose half my audience at the start, when I came up screaming out of my coffin,' he said. 'They used to run screaming down the aisles and half kill themselves scrambling out of the exits. I couldn't stop them. In the end I had to hire some boys to sit up in the gallery with a supply of shrivelled-up elastic bands, and when the audience started running, my boys would drop the elastic bands on to their heads and whisper "Worms".'

Jay's biggest hit was the original version of 'I Put A Spell On You', and he had other triumphs with things like 'The Whammy' and 'Feast Of The Mau Mau'. Actually, he had quite a pleasant baritone, but on stage, he'd only screamed and ghouled. 'I just torment a song,' he said. 'Frighten it half to death.'

Then there were the Coasters, who had the most sly-sounding lead singer in the whole of the business, not to mention the most lugubrious bass. The lead, Carl Gardner, played the school bad boy. He sang like he had some bubble gum permanently stashed away inside his cheek, and everything he did was sneaky, pretty hip. Then he was a loudmouth, a natural-born hustler, and all the time the bass groaned and grumbled below him, the voice of his conscience speaking. The lead took no blind notice.

Mind you, they could hardly miss. For a kick-off, they had the most prolific songwriters in rock going for them: Jerry Lieber and Mike Stoller, a partnership that hustled upward of thirty million records in five years. Lieber and Stoller also wrote some of the best early Elvis hits, notably 'Hound Dog' and 'Jailhouse Rock', but they were natural humorists, and Presley was just a bit straight for them. The Coasters were ideal.

Lieber and Stoller churned out stuff that was inventive, wry, and sometimes very shrewd – a running commentary on the manifold miseries of being teenage – and the delinquent talents of Carl Gardner did the rest with no sweat. Between them, they came up with some very funny records.

The format was simple: they got a fast shuffle going, reeled off the assembled lyrics, and then stuck a frantic yakety sax chorus into the middle. It was a comforting scheme of things. You always knew what was coming and could relax. So the lead snickered, the bass moaned, and everyone was happy.

Probably their most classic effort was 'Yakety Yak', a knockdown and drag-out row between a bullied teenager and his monstrous parents. The teenager, of course, is seen as martyr. He spends his whole time tidying his room, doing homework, washing, generally flogging himself.

From there they went on to further explorations of teenage hell, 'Charlie Brown' ('Why's everybody always picking on me?'), 'Poison Ivy' and 'Bad Blood'. Each one was perfect in its own way, but the whole style was completely geared to rock attitudes, and when times changed, they were among the first to slip.

They're still around, though, and occasionally a new single filters through. Nothing vital is changed. The lead still sounds maybe fifteen years old and carries himself as if he's just seen his geometry coach slip on a shrewdly planted banana skin. The bass still groans. They live in a cut-off private world and everyone is sweet sixteen for ever.

Chuck Berry was a bard; classic rock's definitive chronicler, interpreter and wise-guy voyeur. He wrote endless Teen Romance lyrics but sang them with vicious, sly cynicism and this is the clash that makes him so funny, so attractive.

His most perfect song was 'You Never Can Tell', an effort that gets a lot of its flavour from the knowledge that it was made soon after Chuck had served a hefty jail sentence for transporting a minor across a state boundary without her parents' consent:

> It was a teenage wedding and the old folks wished 'em
> well,
> You could see that Pierre did truly love the mademoiselle,
> And now the young monsieur and madame have rung the
> chapel bell –
> C'est la vie, say the old folks, it goes to show you never can
> tell.

A jangle piano rambled away legato in the background and there were great swirling sax riffs and Chuck himself more intoned than sang, sly and smooth as always, the eternal 16-year-old hustler. That was it – the Teendream myth that's right at the heart of all pop and 'You Never Can Tell' expressed it more exactly, more evocatively than any of the other fifty thousand attempts at the same theme.

Of course, this is all very naïve and undeveloped by comparison with what has come since, but then Bogart proved thirty years ago that, in mass media, you don't need to be a monster intellectual to be great. In fact, it's a definite disadvantage if you are. What you do need is style, command, specific image and these are the exact things that Chuck Berry has always been overflowing with.

Basically, what it boils down to is detail. Most pop writers would have written 'You Never Can Tell' as a series of generalities and it would have been nothing. But Chuck was obsessive, he was hooked on cars, rock, ginger ale and he had to drag them all in. That's what makes it – the little touches like the cherry-red Jidney '53 or the coolerator.

Chuck was born in California in 1931, grew up in St Louis and, when he was older, got to be a hairdresser. By nature, he was an operator and he was always going to be successful. The only question was how. So he tried singing, he wrote, he made progress. In 1955, he had his first national smash with 'Maybelline' and from then on he was a natural Mister Big.

As a writer, he was something like poet laureate to the whole rock movement. He charted its habits, hobbies, hang-ups or celebrated its triumphs or mourned its limitations and he missed nothing out. 'School Days' pinned down exactly that school-kid sense of spending one's whole life listening for bells and 'Johnny B. Goode', guitar-slinger, created a genuine new folk hero and 'Roll Over Beethoven' should have been adopted as the universal slogan of rock. But almost best of all was 'Sweet Little Sixteen'. Nothing summed up better the twinned excitement and frustration of the time:

Sweet little sixteen, she's got the grown-up blues
Tight dresses and lipstick, she's sportin' high-heeled shoes
Oh but tomorrow morning she'll have to change her trend
And be sweet sixteen and back in class again.

Beyond his writing, he played a very fair blues guitar, Chicago-style, and sang in a voice as waved and oily as his hair. On stage, his speciality was the duck walk, which involved bounding across the stage on his heels, knees bent, body jackknifed and guitar clamped firmly to his gut. Then he would peep coyly over his shoulders and look like sweet little sixteen herself, all big eyes and fluttering lids. He had a pencil moustache and had the smoothness, the cool of a steamboat gambler. A brown-eyed handsome man, in fact.

Just when things were going so well for him, he made his mistake with the minor and was put away. By the time he got out again, in 1963, rock was finished but the British R&B boom was just getting underway and he was made blues hero number one by the Rolling Stones, who started out playing almost nothing but Chuck Berry songs. Almost as a matter of course, he'd landed on his feet.

He was brought over and made much of but turned out to be hard to deal with. He was arrogant, rude. When he liked to turn it on, he could be most charming but often he couldn't be bothered. First and last, he was amazingly mean.

There's an authenticated story about him that, on his first British tour, he used to study the evening paper nightly and check to see if there had been any fluctuation in rates of exchange. If there was any deviation in his favour, no matter how small, he'd demand payment in cash before he went on. On one night, this supplement came to 2s. 3d.

By and large, white rockers were a lot less impressive than their coloured counterparts. After the wildness of Little Richard, the lyricism of Chuck Berry, they sounded samey and half-hearted. As personalities too, they were less colourful, less articulate. Mostly, they were plain boring.

The major exception was Jerry Lee Lewis, a pianist and shouter from Louisiana. He used R&B and country in about equal doses and attacked the keys in very much the same style as Little Richard, bopping them with fists, feet, elbows and anything else that was handy. Towards the end of his act, he'd climb on top of the piano, hold the mike like a lance and stay up there until the audience got hot enough to dash forward and drag him down.

His great gift was that, no matter how frantic he got, his voice remained controlled and drawling country. He seemed to have a lot of time to spare, an unshakeable ease, and this gave him class.

He had long yellow crinkly hair that fell forward over his eyes when he worked and a thin, slightly furtive face. He always reminded me of a weasel. And when he got steamed up, he'd sweat like mad and his face would collapse into nothing but a formless mass of heaving, contorting flesh. Still, his voice would be strong, easy. As stage acts go, it was hardly pretty but, definitely, it was compelling.

After he'd rampaged through his earliest hits (the apocalyptic 'Whole Lotta Shakin' Goin' On' and 'Great Balls Of Fire') he did a 1958 tour of Britain and immediately plunged neck-deep into trouble. He had brought his young wife with him. His very young wife, as it turned out. Her name was Myra and Jerry Lee said she was fifteen. Later, he admitted that she was only thirteen. He also said that, at twenty-two, this was his second marriage. His first had been at fourteen ('Hell, I was too young').

The British press duly disgraced itself. It howled blue murder, screamed baby-snatcher, and finally got the tour cancelled. Jerry Lee flew out in disgrace. 'Hell, I'm only country,' he pleaded, but no one took any notice.

Before the cancellation, he'd had time to do two concerts and, doomed by so much bad publicity, they were disasters. In the first, Jerry Lee dashed out in a pillar-box red suit and smashed straight through two numbers without let-up. He was brilliant, by far the best rocker Britain had then witnessed, and he half won his audience round. Then, before going into the third, he took out a golden comb and very delicately swept his hair back out of his eyes. It was a fatal move. Someone yelled 'Cissy!' at him and from there on it was solid murder. Finally, Jerry Lee just upped and walked off stage. The curtain came down. Pandemonium.

All of which goes to show how superficial the rock revolt had really been. On paper, Jerry Lee's marital junketings were exactly calculated to improve his prestige, make him into an even better symbol of rebellion. In practice, it only took a fast burst of pomposity in the papers and the kids were just as appalled as their parents. And when Jerry Lee left his hotel, he was hissed and insulted and spat upon.

Jerry Lee wasn't downcast. Arriving back in New York, he announced that his concerts had been 'Great, just great' and that, as he'd left 'three thousand stood and cheered'. There are people around who'll tell you that he's the greatest pop figure ever. I wouldn't agree, but he certainly rates. I also like his attitude. 'You are either hot or cold,' he says. 'If you are lukewarm, the Lord will spew you out of his mouth.'

Buddy Holly was really called Charles Hardin Holley and first came out of Lubbock, Texas, with broken teeth, wire glasses and halitosis, plus every last possible kind of country southerness. He wasn't appetizing. In fact, he was an obvious loser.

On the other hand, he had a voice, he wrote natural hit songs, and what's more, he was by no means prepared to sit tight in the background and churn out smashes for other artists. He said he wanted to sit in his front room and watch his face singing to him out of the television screen. He was very firm about this. So a man called Lloyd Greenfield, a tough, no-nonsense agent, took him up and changed him into another person. Buddy had his teeth capped, his breath cleaned, his hair styled, his wire glasses exchanged for big impressive black ones, his voice toned. Then he was put into high school sweaters and taught how to smile. Suddenly, he was all-America.

The whole saga was straight out of Stan Freberg – Holly sang lead with a group called the Crickets and promptly cut a succession of monster hits with them: 'That'll Be The Day', 'Oh Boy', 'Maybe Baby'. By 1958, growing big-time, he had dumped the Crickets and gone solo, clocking up a further sequence of million sellers on his own: 'Peggy Sue', 'Rave On', 'It Doesn't Matter Any More'. He was smooth, he was clean. He had a smile straight off a toothpaste ad, and his new black glasses were major trend-setters. In every detail his career was perfect, and in February of 1959, just to round it off, he got killed in an air crash at Fargo, North Dakota. He was then twenty-two years old.

Long-time rock fans have always been bitterly divided about him. He wasn't a hard-core rocker, being too gentle and melodic, and this eccentricity can be construed either as backsliding or as progression. Even ten years after his death, it isn't an academic question; I have seen rock preservation meetings reduced to brawling knuckle-dusted anarchy about it. On the wall of a pub lavatory in Gateshead, there is a scrawled legend: 'Buddy Holly lives and rocks in Tijuana, Mexico.'

He was all adenoids – twanged them like a catapult, propelled each phrase up and out on a whole tidal wave of hiccoughs and burps. As sound it was ugly, but at least it was new. It was also much copied; Adam Faith, for one, built his early career largely around his variations on it. For that matter, so did Bobby Vee.

Holly's breakthrough, in fact, was that he opened up alternatives to all-out hysteria. Not many white kids had the lungs or sheer hunger to copy Little Richard, but Holly was easy. All you needed was adenoids. The beat was lukewarm, the range minimal

– no acrobatics or rage or effort required. You just stood up straight and mumbled. Even the obvious beaters, things like 'Rave On' or 'Oh Boy', were Neapolitan flowerpots after 'Tutti Frutti'.

In this way Buddy Holly was the patron saint of all the thousands of no-talent kids who ever tried to make a million dollars. He was founder of a noble tradition.

Killed in the same air crash that took care of Holly were Ritchie Valens and the Big Bopper. Valens, at seventeen, had already made some of the direst records in pop. The Bopper, on the other hand, had made one of the all-time best: 'Chantilly Lace'.

His real name was J. P. Richardson; he was a Texan disc jockey, and 'Chantilly Lace' was his only hit. A fat man in his late twenties, he wore vast baggy striped suits, and jackets halfway down to his knees and the trouser seats big enough to hide an army in, and he owned a grin of purest lip-smacking lechery, a monster. 'Chantilly Lace' is his testament.

He's in a phone booth, ringing some girl, and he's having to hassle like mad to get a date out of her. He sweats, he giggles, he groans. He drools, overflows himself.

You can feel him wriggling his fat shoulders in delirium, his joke suit around him like a tent, his eyes bugging and his bottom lip hanging slack: Chantilly lace and a pretty face, giggling talk, wiggling walk, pony-tail hanging down, Lord, makes the world go round round round, makes him feel real loose like a long-necked goose. And all this time he's melting.

He's getting nowhere, of course, but he doesn't give up; he campaign shouts like a southern Democrat. The result doesn't matter anyhow; it's the performance that counts. 'Ooh, baby,' he howls. 'You know what I like. You KNOW.' And when he says that, he bursts, he just disintegrates.

*

Eddie Cochran was pure Rock.

Other people were other kinds of rock, country or high school, hard, soft, good or bad or indifferent. Eddie Cochran was just Rock. Nothing else. That's it and that's all.

There's not much fact on him: he was born in Oklahoma City, October 1938, youngest out of five children. His family moved to Minnesota, then to California. He grew up to be one sweet little rock'n'roller, a nice looker, and he made records and had hits. He played good guitar and worked on sessions in Los Angeles. He wrote songs, got to be quite big. He even toured England. And on 17 April 1960, he was killed in a car crash on the A1. He was then twenty-one years old.

As a person, there's even less on him. He looked like another sub-Elvis, smooth flesh and duck-ass hair and a fast tricksy grin, the full uniform. He was quiet, a bit inarticulate, a bit aggressive, and he cared mostly about his music. He was polite to journalists, helpful even, but had nothing much to tell them. I was once told that he had a deep interest in toads but I have no evidence on it. He was nothing special. He just came and went.

What made him such pure Rock? In a way, it was his very facelessness, his lack of any detailed identity. With so little for anyone to go on, he seemed less a specific person than an identikit of the essential rocker, a generalized fifties' blur, a bit pretty and a bit surly and a bit talented. Composite of a generation.

But he was something more than that, his songs were perfect reflections of everything that rock ever meant. They were good songs, hard and meaty, but that wasn't it. In every detail, they were so right. So finally rocker.

'Summertime Blues', 'My Way', 'C'mon Everybody', a few more – there were only maybe half a dozen things that did him full justice but, between them, they added up to something more than somewhat.

There is almost a continuous storyline running through them. Eddie is still at school and hates it. Lives at home and hates it.

Works in his holidays and hates that worst of all. Still, he's a pretty ready kid, can handle himself. And he runs in some kind of gang, he's leader of the pack. Eddie Cochran, no punk or palooka of '59.

When he gets very lucky, his father gives him the car for the night and then things are wild. Of course, after he gets back home, four in the morning, bushed and busted, he is kept in for a fortnight but that's the name of the game: he can't win. The world rides him. When he works, he's paid chicken-feed. When he enjoys himself, he is automatically punished. Tough.

Still, when he walks down the street so nice and slow, his thumbs hooked into the belt-loops of his blue jeans, his hair all plumed and whirled, the girls look up from their chewy mags, sip Coke through a straw and they think he's cute, real cute. Sure good-looking, he's something else.

And that's about where it ends; that was rock, those were the great rockers.

Looking back through what I've written, I'm struck hardest by two things – just how good the best of rock really was, and just how sadly most of its practitioners have ended up.

I suppose the trouble was only that rock was such committed music, such a very specific attitude, so tied to its time, it wasn't possible for real rockers to ever move on. Of course this is a stock problem in any field – revolution so quickly becomes boring – but the thing about pop is that its generation cycles last five years at the very most.

Never mind: the best rock records stand up still as the most complete music that pop has yet produced. Everything about it was so defined – all you had to do was mix in the right ingredients, stir well, and you had a little rock masterwork on your hands. It was that simple, that straightforward, and finally, that satisfying.

Of course, classic rock wasn't ever anything like as complex, as creative, as the music is now. Does that matter? It was Superpop. On its own terms, it was quite perfect.

America After the Beatles

NIK COHN

Cohn recalls that brief period when the British Beat combos seemed intent on sweeping American pop music into the garbage can of history, in the interim before Dylan mustered some folk-rockin' angels for a counter-attack.

If the Beatles meant a lot in Britain, they meant very much more in America.

They changed everything. They happened at a time when American pop was bossed by trash, by dance crazes and slop ballads, and they let all of that bad air out. They were foreign, they talked strange. They played harsh, unsickly, and they weren't phoney. Just as they'd done in England, they brought back reality.

Beyond that, they happened at a time when the whole of American teenage life was bogged down, when there was an urgent need for new leaders and, along with Bob Dylan, that's just what they became.

Because they weren't fake or computerized themselves, they brought it home exactly how conformist America had really become, they woke people up, they crystallized all kinds of vague discontents. They didn't sermonize, they didn't have to. Just by existing, they played a major part in turning dissent from an intellectual left-wing indulgence into something that involved maybe thirty per cent of all American teens.

Still, that's roughly what they'd done in England, too, so how come they meant much more in America? Mostly, it was a question of scale.

In England, after all, teenage rebellion had always been something quite amiable and formalized. It starts fashions, sells records, makes fun for the people, but it doesn't change much, it causes no revolutions. Over the years, it moves things very gently along, but, come right down to it, England simply isn't ugly enough to make white kids feel passionate.

But in America, in the sixties, teen dissent has become something more than fashionable. On the whole, it's about real diseases, real social insanities, and it may end up making changes. And, because they're influential in all this, the Beatles have become more than they'll ever be here, they've gone beyond entertainment and they've turned into serious social influences, they matter.

At a less exalted level, when they first broke through, they stirred a hysterical cult for all things British, a fad that's only just dying down now.

This was simple: one look at the Beatles, long hair and Scouse accents, big mouths and all, and America decided that something strange must be going on here, that London must be some kind of continuous space-age fun-fair, one endless parade of boutiques and discotheques and hip trattorias, Carnaby Streets and King's Roads.

Immediately, England became the epitome of everything elegant, enlightened, deeply switched-on, and its exports became automatic triumphs.

English pop had it fat in there and most everyone cleaned up – the Rolling Stones, the Animals, the Yardbirds, the Kinks, Manfred Mann, Donovan, Dusty Springfield. And not only pop but actors, designers, hairstylists, models – Julie Christie, Mary Quant, Vidal Sassoon, Michael Caine and, climactically, Twiggy.

Two groups, in particular, made it much bigger in the States than they'd ever done at home – the Dave Clark Five and Herman's Hermits.

Dave Clark had been a film extra and he was handsome, he had smooth skin and white teeth and a dazzling smile, he was clean-cut as hell. He played a bit of drums and he formed his own semi-professional group around Tottenham.

After a time, they made records, very crude and chaotic but quite danceable, and soon they had a number one hit, 'Glad All Over'. They had no pretensions to musical class, they were only basic noise-machines and, predictably, after they'd lost their first impetus, they found the going erratic here.

When they got to America, though, Dave Clark smiled just once, flashed those perfect teeth of his, and they were made. For two years, they were hardly ever gone from the American charts and, every time they wavered, Clark only flashed his smile one time and they went right back on top again.

The odd thing was, he had no manager. He was advised by Harold Davidson, his agent, but nobody controlled him ever, nobody made his decisions for him. All on his own, he'd realized his potential and he'd pursued it, he'd grabbed everything possible. And it was really quite an impressive thing, any young boy being so sure of himself that he could set up as a million-dollar industry and not be conned, not stumble for a second. It was almost indecent.

Herman's Hermits were another strike for Mickie Most.

Herman himself was really called Peter Noone and he was a very young, very innocent-looking boy from Manchester. He had buck teeth and dimples, he looked about twelve years old, and he'd sometimes stick his finger in his mouth as he sang.

America being as matriarchal as it is, such little boy antics could hardly miss and they didn't. Mickie Most, who knows where the money is and has always concentrated on America more than anywhere, handed him one hit song after another and Herman came to be bigger even than Dave Clark.

Throughout this British invasion, the American scene stood stock-still. It grew its hair long, produced a few half-hearted imitations of the Beatles, and left it at that. For one year, the English ruled unchallenged.

The First Tycoon of Teen

TOM WOLFE

With religion or the Reaper claiming rockers at a disconcerting rate, the years between a sideburnless Presley's army discharge and the Beatles descending from Albion gave Tin Pan Alley cause to feel it could yet re-establish its domain. One shard of light was the Philly Sound, wrought from the hand of a true obsessive, Phil Spector. By the time Tom Wolfe's article on Spector appeared in the New York Herald Tribune – *in February 1965 – Spector's golden age (and hairline) was fast receding. Yet he remained one of rock & roll's most enigmatic (and influential) mavericks.*

Phil Spector is sitting in a little cream room in his office suite at 440 East 62nd Street with his back to a window that is practically on top of the East Side Drive. Twenty-four years old, he has a complex of corporations known as Phil Spector Productions. One of them is Mother Bertha Productions, named after his mother, Bertha. She works for his office in Los Angeles, but only because she wants to. The main organization is Philles Records. Spector has produced twenty-one 'single' Philles records since October 1962 and sold more than 13,000,000 copies. All rock & roll. His current hit, 'Walking In The Rain' by the Ronettes, has gone as high as number 20 on the 'Cashbox' chart and has sold more than 250,000 copies. His latest record 'You've Lost That Lovin' Feelin', by the Righteous Brothers, rose from the seventies to number 37 with a 'bullet' beside it, meaning 'going up fast'. He has produced seven albums. The first teenage tycoon! He is leaning back in the chair. He has on a suede jerkin, Italian pants, a pair of pointy British boots with Cuban heels. His hair hangs down to his shoulders in back. The beard is shaved off, however.

Danny Davis, his promotion man, is talking on the phone in the inner office. A fellow sits across from Spector with his legs crossed and a huge chocolate brown Borsalino hat over his bent knee, as if he were just trying it on. He says, 'Phil, why do you do –'

'I'm moving the whole thing to California,' says Phil Spector. 'I can't stand flying any more.'

'Why do you do these things?'

Spector – without his beard, Spector has a small chin, a small head; his face looks at first like all those little kids with bad hair and reedy voices from the Bronx, where he was born. But – an ordinary Phil Spector? Phil Spector has the only pure American voice. He was brought up not in the Bronx, but in California. His voice meanders, quietly, shaking, through his doldrum fury out to somewhere beyond cynical, beyond cool, beyond teenage world-weary. It is thin, broken and soft. He is only twenty-four years old, the first millionaire businessman to rise up out of the teenage netherworld, king of the rock & roll record producers.

Spector jumps out of the chair. 'Wait a minute,' he says, 'just a minute. They're making deals in here.'

Spector walks into the inner office gingerly, like a cowboy, because of the way the English boots lift him up off the floor. He is slight, five foot seven, 130 pounds. His hair shakes faintly behind. It is a big room, like a living-room, all beige except for eight gold-plated rock & roll records on the wall – some of Phil Spector's 'goldies', 1,000,000 sales each. 'He's A Rebel' by the Crystals. 'Zip-a-dee-doo-dah' by Bob B. Soxx and the Blue Jeans. 'Be My Baby' by the Ronettes. 'Da Do Ron Ron', 'Then He Kissed Me', 'Uptown', 'He's Sure The Boy I Love', all by the

Crystals. 'Wait Till My Baby Gets Home' by Darlene Love. And beige walls, beige telephones all over the place, a beige upright piano, beige paintings, beige tables, with Danny Davis crowding over a beige desk, talking on the telephone.

'Sure, Sal,' says Danny, 'I'll ask Phil. Maybe we can work something out on that.'

Spector starts motioning thumbs down.

'Just a minute, Sal.' Danny puts his hand over the mouthpiece and says, 'We need this guy, Phil. He's the biggest distributor out there. He wants the 1,000 guarantee.'

Phil's hands go up as if he were lifting a slaughtered lamb up on top of an icebox. 'I don't care. I'm not interested in the money, I've got millions, I don't care who needs this animal. I'm interested in selling records, O K? Why should I give him a guarantee? He orders the records, I guarantee I'll buy 1,000 back from him if he can't sell them; he sells them, then after the record dies he buys up five hundred cut-rate from somebody, sends them back and cries for his money. Why should we have to be eating his singles later?'

Danny takes his hand away and says into the mouthpiece, 'Look, Sal, there's one thing I forgot. Phil says this record he can't give the guarantee. But you don't have anything to worry about . . . I know what I said, but Phil says . . . Look, Sal, don't worry, "Walking in the Rain", this is a tremendous record – tremendous, a very big record . . . What? . . . I'm not reading off a paper, Sal . . . Wait a minute, Sal –'

'Who needs these animals?' Spector tells Danny.

'Look, Sal,' Danny says, 'this man never made a bad record in his life. You tell me one. Nothing but hits.'

'Tell him I'm not in,' says Spector.

'Sal –'

'Who needs these animals!' says Spector, so loud this time that Danny cups his hand around the receiver and puts his mouth down close.

'Nothing, Sal,' says Danny, 'that was somebody came in.'

'Joan,' says Phil, and a girl, Joan Berg, comes in out of another room. 'Will you turn the lights off?' he says.

She turns the lights off, and now in the middle of the day the offices of Philles Records and Mother Bertha Productions are all dark except for the light from Danny Davis's lamp. Danny crowds into the pool of light, hunched over the phone, talking to Sal.

Phil puts his fingers between his eyes and wraps his eyebrows around them.

'Phil, it's dark in here,' says the fellow with the large hat. 'Why do you do these things?'

'I'm paying a doctor six hundred dollars a week to find out,' says Phil, without looking up.

He sits there in the dark, his fingers buried between his eyes. Just over his head one can make out a painting. The painting is kind of came-with-the-frame surrealist. It shows a single musical note, a half note, suspended over what looks like the desert outside Las Vegas. Danny has to sit there huddled in his own pool of light talking to this 'animal' on the telephone.

'This is a primitive country,' says Phil Spector. 'I was at Shepheard's, the discotheque, and these guys start saying these things. It's unbelievable. These people are animals.'

'What kind of things, Phil?'

'I don't know. They look at, you know, my hair. My wife and I are dancing, and – I mean it's unbelievable – I feel somebody yanking on my hair in the back. I turn around, and here's this guy, a grown man, and he is saying these unbelievable things to me. So I tell him, like this, "I'm going to tell you this one time, that's all: don't ever try that again." And the guy it's unbelievable – he shoved me with the heel of his hand and I go sprawling back into a table –'

Spector pauses.

'I mean, I've studied karate for years. I could literally kill a guy like that. You know? Size means nothing. A couple of these' – he cocks his elbow in the gloom and brings up the flat of his forearm

– 'but what am I going to do, start a fight every time I go out? Why should I even have to listen to anything from these animals? I find this country very condemning. I don't have this kind of trouble in Europe. The people of America are just not born with culture.'

Not born with culture! If only David Susskind and William B. Williams could hear that. Susskind invited Phil Spector to the *Open End* television program one evening to talk about the record business. Suddenly Susskind and William B., station WNEW's old-nostalgia disc jockey, were condemning Spector as one kind of sharpie poisoning American Culture, rotting the minds of youth, and so forth. That was how it all hit Spector. It was as if he were some kind of old short-armed fatty in the Brill Building, the music centre on Broadway, with a spreadcollar shirt and a bald olive skull with strands of black hair pulled up over it from above one ear. There was something very ironic about that. Spector is the one record producer who wouldn't go near Broadway. His set-up is practically out in the East River, up by the Rockefeller Institute.

Susskind and Williams kept throwing Spector's songs at him – 'He's a Rebel', 'Da Do Ron Ron', 'Be My Baby', 'Fine Fine Boy', 'Breakin' Up' – as if he were astutely conning millions of the cretins out there with this stuff. Spector didn't know exactly what to tell them. He likes the music he produces. He writes it himself. He is something new: the first teenage millionaire, the first boy to become a millionaire within America's teenage netherworld. It was never a simple question of his taking a look at the rock & roll universe from the outside and exploiting it. He stayed within it himself. He liked the music.

Spector, while still in his teens, seemed to comprehend the prole vitality of rock & roll that has made it the kind of darling holy beast of intellectuals in the United States, England and France. Intellectuals, generally, no longer take jazz seriously. Monk, Mingus, Ferguson – it has all been left to little executive trainees with their first apartment and a mahogany African mask from the free-port shop in Haiti and a hi-fi. But rock & roll! Poor old arteriosclerotic lawyers with poky layers of fat over their ribs are out there right now twisting clumsily to rock & roll. Their wives wear stretch pants to the seafood shop. A style of life!

There have been teenagers who have made a million dollars before, but invariably they are entertainers; they are steered by older people, such as the good Colonel Tom Parker who steers Elvis Presley. But Phil Spector is the bona fide genius of teen. Every baroque period has a flowering genius who rises up as the most glorious expression of its style of life – in latterday Rome, the Emperor Commodus; in Renaissance Italy, Benvenuto Cellini; in late Augustan England, the Earl of Chesterfield; in the sad, volatile Victorian age, Dante Gabriel Rossetti; in late-fancy neo-Greek Federal America, Thomas Jefferson; and in teen America, Phil Spector.

In point of fact, he had turned twenty-one when he made his first million. But it was as a teenager, working within the teenage milieu, starting at the age of seventeen, that Phil Spector developed into a great American businessman, the greatest of the independent rock & roll record producers. Spector's mother, Bertha, took him from the Bronx to California when he was nine. California! Teen heaven! By the time he was sixteen he was playing jazz guitar with some group. Then he got interested in rock & roll, which he does not call rock & roll but 'pop blues'. That is because – well, that's a complicated subject. Anyway, Phil Spector likes this music. He genuinely likes it. He is not a short-armed fatty hustling nutball fads.

'I get a little angry when people say it's bad music,' Spector tells the man with the brown hat. 'This music has a spontaneity that doesn't exist in any other kind of music, and it's what is here now. It's unfair to classify it as rock & roll and condemn it. It has limited chord changes, and people are always saying the words are banal and why doesn't anybody write lyrics like Cole Porter any more, but we don't have any presidents like Lincoln any more, either. You know? Actually, it's more like the blues. It's pop blues. I feel it's very American. It's very today. It's what people respond to today. It's not just the kids. I hear cab-drivers, everybody, listening to it.'

And Susskind sits there on his show reading one of Spector's songs out loud – no music, just reading the words, from the Top 60 or whatever it is – 'Fine Fine Boy', to show how banal rock & roll is. The song just keeps repeating, 'He's a fine fine boy'. So Spector starts drumming on the big coffee-table there with the flat of his hands in time to Susskind's voice and says, 'What you're missing is the beat.' Blam blam.

Everybody is getting a little sore, with Susskind reading these simple lyrics and Spector blamming away on the coffee-table. Finally Spector starts asking Williams how many times he plays Verdi on his show? – Monteverdi? – D. Scarlatti? – A. Scarletti? 'That's good music, why don't you play that? You keep saying you play only good music. I don't hear you playing that.' Williams doesn't know what to say. Spector tells Susskind he didn't come on the show to listen to somebody tell him he was corrupting the youth of America – he could be home making money. Susskind: 'Well, ah, all right, Phil.' Everybody is testy.

Making money. Yes! At the age of seventeen Spector wrote a rock & roll song called 'To Know Him Is To Love Him'. He took the title off his father's tombstone. That was what his mother had had engraved on his father's tombstone out in Beth David Cemetery in Elmont, Long Island. He doesn't say much about his father, just that he was 'average lower-middle class'. Spector wrote the song, sang it, and played the guitar in the recording with a group called the Teddy Bears. He made $20,000 on that record, but somebody ran off with $17,000 of it and . . . well, no use going into that. Then he was going to UCLA, but he couldn't afford it and became a court reporter – one of the people who sit at the shorthand machine taking down testimony. He decided to come to New York and get a job as interpreter at the UN. His mother had taught him French. But he got to New York, and the night before the interview he fell in with some musicians and never got there. Instead he wrote another hit that year, 'Spanish Harlem'. And then – only nineteen – he became head of A&R, Artists and Repertoire, for Atlantic Records. By 1961 he was a freelance producer, producing records for the companies, working with Connie Francis, Elvis Presley, Ray Peterson, the Paris Sisters.

All this time, Spector would write a song and run all phases of making records, get the artists, direct the recording sessions – everything. Spector would work with these kids who make these records because he was a kid himself, in one sense. God knows what the music business biggies thought of Phil Spector – he already wore his hair like Salvador Dali did at that age, or like an old mezzotint of Mozart or something. And he was somehow one of them – the natives, the kids who sang and responded to this . . . music. Phil Spector could get in one of those studios with the heron microphones, a representative of the adult world that makes money from records, and it became all one thing: the kids comprehended him.

Spector had an ideal: Archie Bleyer. Bleyer was a bandleader who founded a record company. Cadence Records. Spector formed a partnership with two other people in 1961, then bought them out and went on his own as Philles Records in October of 1962. His first big hit was 'He's A Rebel' by the Crystals. Spector had a system. The big record companies put out records like buckshot – ten, maybe fifteen rock & roll records a month – and if one of them catches on, they can make money. Spector's system is to put them out one at a time and pour everything into each one. Spector does the whole thing. He writes the words and the music, scouts and signs up the talent. He takes them out to a recording studio in Los Angeles and runs the recording session himself. He puts them through hours and days of recording to get the two or three minutes he wants. Two or three minutes out of the whole struggle. He handles the control dials like an electronic maestro, tuning various instruments or sounds up, down, out, every which way, using things like two pianos, a harpsichord, and three guitars on one record; then re-recording the whole thing with esoteric dubbing and overdubbing effects – reinforcing instruments or voices – coming out with what is known through the industry as 'the Spector Sound'. The only thing he doesn't keep control of is the actual manufacture, the pressing of the records and the distribution.

The only people around to give him any trouble all this time are the distributors, cigar-chewing fatties, and . . . well, to be honest, there is a lot that gives Phil Spector trouble, and it's not so much any kind of or any group of people as much as his status. A teenage tycoon! He is betwixt and between. He identifies with the teenage netherworld, he defends it, but he is already too mature for it. As a millionaire, a business genius, living in a penthouse twenty-two stories up over the East River, with his wife, Annette, who is twenty, a student at Hunter College, and with a four-room suite downstairs on the ground floor as his office, and a limousine, and a chauffeur, and a bodyguard, and a staff – Danny and Joan Berg and everybody – and a doorman who directs people to Mr Spector's office . . . well, that makes Phil Spector one of them, the universe of arteriosclerotic, hypocritical, cigar-chewing, hopeless, larded adults, infracted vultures one meets in the music business. And so here in the dark is a 24-year-old man with a Shelley visage, a suede shirt, a kind of page-boy bob and winkle-picker boots – the symbol of the teen world – sitting in the dark in this great beige office – the symbol of the tycoon world – in the middle of the day, in the dark, tapping his frontal lobes with his fingers in the gloom.

One of the beige phones rings and Danny answers. Then he presses the 'hold' button and tells Phil Spector, 'It's the Rolling Stones. They just got in.'

Spector comes alive with that. He gets up on his ginger toes and goes to the telephone. He is lively, and he spins on the balls of his feet a little as he stands by the phone.

'Hello, Andrew,' he says. He is talking with Andrew Oldham, the manager of the Rolling Stones. And then he puts on a cockney accent, 'Are you all in?' he says.

The Rolling Stones – all right. The Rolling Stones, English group, and Andrew Oldham, are like him. They grew up in the teenage netherworld and made it, and they all want to have it all too, the kids' style of life and the adults' – money – and not cop-out on one side or the other, larded and arteriosclerotic. Phil Spector's British trip! That was where suddenly he had it all.

Phil Spector is here! The British had the ability to look at all sorts of rebel baddies and alienated thin young fellows and say coo and absorb them like a great soggy, lukewarm, mother's poultice. The Beatles, Beatlemania, rock & roll – suddenly it is all absorbed into the centre of things as if it could have been there all along if it only asked. Phil Spector arrives at London Airport and, Santa Barranza, there are photographers all over the place, for him, Phil Spector, and the next morning he is all over the centrefold of the London *Daily Mirror*, the biggest newspaper in the Western World, 5,000,000 circulation: 'The 23-year-old American rock & roll magnate.' He is in the magazines as the 'US Recording Tycoon'. Invitations go out to come to the receptions to meet 'America's outstanding hit-maker, Phil Spector'. And then he lands back at Idlewild and waiting are, yes, the same bunch of cheese-breath cabbies, and he takes a cab on back to 440 East 62nd Street and goes into his beige world – the phones are ringing and it is all the same, the same . . .

'Cigar-smoking sharpies,' says Phil Spector. He is in a livelier mood after the talk with Andrew Oldham. 'They're a bunch of cigar-smoking sharpies in record distribution. They've all been in the business for years, and they resent you if you're young. That's one reason so many kids go broke in this business. They're always starting new record companies – or they used to, the business is very soft right now. They start a company and pour all their money into a record, and it can be successful and they're still broke, because these characters don't even pay you until you've had three or four hit records in a row. They order the records and sell them and don't pay you. They don't pay you because they know they don't have to. You start yelling for the money and they tell you "What-ya mean, I have all these records coming back from the retailers, and what about my right to return records and blah-blah!" What are you going to do? Sue twenty guys in twenty different courts in the United States?

'They look at everything as a product. They don't care about the work and sweat you put into a record. They respect me now because I keep turning out hits, and after that they become sort of honest . . . in their own decayed way.'

Where does a man find friends, comrades, anything, in a world like that? They resent his youth. They resent his success. But it is no better with the kids. He is so much more mature and more . . . eminent . . . they all want to form 'the father thing' with him. Or else they want to fawn over him, cozen him, cajole, fall down before him, whistle, shout, stomp, bang him on the head – anything to get his attention and get 'the break', just one chance. Or one more chance. Spector can't go near the Brill Building, the centre of the music business, because the place is crawling with kids with winkle-picker shoes cracking in the folds who made one hit record five years ago and still can't realize that they are now, forever, in oblivion. They crawl all over the place, the way the small-time balding fatty promoters and managers used to in the days when A. J. Liebling wrote about the place as the Jollity Building.

Phil Spector steps on to an elevator in the Brill Building. The elevator is packed, and suddenly he feels this arm hooking through his in the most hideously cozy way and a mouth is closing in on his ear and saying 'Phil, baby, wait'll you hear this one: "Ooh-oom-bah-ay"', and Phil Spector is imprisoned there with the elevator inching up, '"vah ump nooby poon fan ooh-ooh ayub bay-ay" – you dig that, Phil? You dig that, don't you Phil? Phil, babes!' He walks down the hall and kids sneak up behind him and slip songs, music, lyrics into his coat pocket. He finds the stuff in there, all this ratty paper, when he gets home. Or he is leaving the Brill Building and he feels a great whack on the back of his head and wheels around, and there are four kids, in the singing stance, their heads angled in together, saying 'Just one bar, Phil: "Say wonna love boo-uh-ay-yay-bubby"' – while the guy on the end sings bass with his chin mashed into a pulpy squash down over his collarbone – '. . . "beh-unggh, beh-ungggh"'.

Status! What is his status? He produces rock & roll and therefore he is not a serious person and he won't join the Young Presidents or whatever kind of organization jaycee geniuses would join for their own good.

'Phil,' says the man with the hat, 'why don't you hire a press agent, a PR man?'

Phil is tapping his frontal lobes in the gloom. Danny Davis is hunched up in the little pool of light on his desk. Danny is doing his level best for Phil.

'Jack? Danny Davis . . . Yeah . . . No, I'm with Phil Spector now . . . Right! It's the best move I ever made. You know Phil . . . I'm in the best shape of my career . . . Jack, I just want to tell you we've got –'

'A press agent?' Phil says to the man in the hat. 'In the first place, I couldn't stand to hear what he'd say about me.'

'Got two tremendous records going, Jack, "Walking In The Rain", the Ronettes, and –'

'In the second place,' Phil says, 'there's no way my image can be bought.'

'And "You've Lost That Lovin' Feeling" by the Righteous Brothers,' says Danny. '. . . Right, Jack . . . I appreciate that, Jack . . .'

'The only thing I could do – you know what I'd like to do? I'd like to do a recording session in the office of *Life* or *Esquire* or *Time*, and then they could see it. That's the only chance I've got. Because I'm dealing in rock & roll, it's like I'm not a bona fide human being.'

'. . . Absolutely! . . . If there's anything we can do for you on this end, Jack, let us know. O K? Great, Jack . . .'

'And I even have trouble with people who should never say anything. I go over to Gristede's to get a quart of milk or something, and the woman at the cash register has to start in. So I tell her, "There's a war in Vietnam, they've fired Khrushchev, the Republican party is falling to pieces, the Ku Klux Klan is running around loose, and you're worrying about my hair!" '

America's first teenage tycoon – a business genius, a musical genius – and it is as if he were still on the corner of Hoffman Street in the Bronx when the big kids come by in hideous fraternity, the way these people act. What is he now? Who is he in this weird country? Danny talks in the phone in the little pool of light; Joan is typing up whatever it is; Phil is tapping his frontal lobes.

2. Rock & Roll Aesthetics

"Can you turn that racket down? I'm trying to write about coming trends in contemporary popular music and I can't hear myself think!"

Dylan is saddled with a quite horrible backing dominated by syrupy strings, amplified guitar and organ . . . The monotonous melody line and Dylan's expressionless intoning just cannot hold the interest for what seems like the six longest minutes since the invention of time.

This was the way 'Like A Rolling Stone' was described in the English music weekly Record Mirror *in the summer of 1965 – not the most obviously appropriate description of one of rock music's undisputed 24-carat classics. It was the ephemeral nature of this type of pop 'criticism' that prompted Paul Williams to begin publishing* Crawdaddy *in the early months of 1966.*

Pre-Crawdaddy, pop journalism was either seriously sociological (Why are these kids doing this?) or simply superficial (It's fab. Buy it). Rock & roll, with its many mutant forms, was already in its second decade. It was established as the dominant teen culture. And the Beatles, Byrds, Beach Boys and assorted beach nuts were applying brains to the beat. Rock had acquired a new reason.

Crawdaddy *began running features with titles like 'How Rock Communicates' and 'The Aesthetics of Rock'. Nik Cohn was right. A period of innocence was over. The first thing Adam did after he ate from the Tree of Knowledge was write a dissertation. Ah, but rock was so much older then, it's younger than yesterday now.*

Even if it all comes around again. After a decade of encroaching technical virtuosity and the ascendancy of the notion that a medium became art simply by writing about 'issues' – reinforced by the great

*divide into album and single acts – the 'punk' aesthetic finally kicked
in. Reactionary rather than revolutionary, punk's back-to-basics approach preferred noise to art (if this is Art, I don't wanna meet Paul),
and gleefully disparaged any sixties icon as it sought to return the
music to its Cohn-like state of innocence.*

*But punk was no spontaneous explosion. If Presley did not worry
why what he did worked, Patti Smith sure as hell did. The punk
brigade had its own retinue of defenders of the faith. Father-figure
Lester Bangs had been espousing a 'punk' aesthetic for years via tall
tales and telling tête-à-têtes in* Creem *magazine. His brief essay, 'In
Which Yet Another Pompous Blowhard Purports to Possess the True
Meaning of Punk Rock', concisely detailed this new aesthetic.*

*As punk's new order gave way to the new wave which duly became
the old order ('Meet the new boss/Same as the old boss'), the eighties
suffered its own sixties-style crises of conscience – only partially satiated by public gestures like Live Aid – both at the inability of punk to
change things and the increasing distance between* Pop *(-ular) and its
energetic kin,* Rock N. Roll. *My examples of eighties Rockspeak span
the various states of doubt voiced about the role of rock as it faces up
to an encroaching middle-age spread. Paul Williams, having returned
to espousing the creed, compares the eighties with the sixties in his
first book on rock in twenty years,* The Map – Rediscovering Rock &
Roll. *Barney Hoskyns prefers to belong to the Rockpopsoul/what's-in-
a-name world while Joe Carducci attempts to revive the iconoclastic
quality of punk in an increasingly disjointed music scene. His final
statement, 'Rock literature barely exists in reality', suggests the extent
of his disenchantment.*

How Rock Communicates

PAUL WILLIAMS

It is no coincidence that it was only after Dylan put a head on the rutting beast of rock & roll, youthful would-be academics abandoned their ivory towers for the uncharted domain of the rock critic. First volunteer and self-appointed editor of the first 'rock' magazine, Crawdaddy, *was 18-year-old Paul Williams. In the winter of 1965–6 Williams's mimeographed magazine was largely composed of his own ruminations, instantly addressing the need for a terminology.*

A great many considerations and puzzles that one meets sooner or later in all the arts find their clearest expression, and therefore their most tangible form, in connection with music.

> (Suzanne K. Langer, *Feeling and Form*)

I know you deceive me; now here's a surprise . . .

> (Pete Townshend, 'I Can See For Miles')

I have never consciously written a song through a personal experience or an inspiration. I never write about things that happen to me. A lot of writers will say they did a song because they were in a certain mood but that's never happened to me. I can write happy when I'm sad or sad when I'm happy. I just get an idea and work on it.

> (Smokey Robinson, interviewed in *Hit Parader*)

75

I got up this morning and listened to 'Heroes And Villains'. Awakening from deep sleep, unconsciousness spills hesitantly away, aspects of the real slowly mixing in with the rest of your mind. 'My children were raised you know they suddenly rise; it started slow long ago head to toe healthy, wealthy and wise . . .' Last week I was at Van Dyke Parks's home in the Hollywood Hills; the week before, chatting with Brian Wilson at the Kennedy International Airport. He hadn't heard Van's album yet. He'd been surprised to read about *Smiley Smile* in *Crawdaddy*. When *Smiley Smile* came out, I wondered why 'Heroes And Villains' didn't sound as good in stereo. Now I was listening to the single for the second time this morning. I stepped into the shower.

I don't know how I get these things on paper. Thoughts in my mind form words on a page through my fingers; concepts come together and generate ideas, and what can I point to to say, 'I intended that?' The reader himself has no certain idea what goes on as his eyes touch the paper. He receives. I have given. But how?

How do we get from one place to another? (Now I'm thinking out loud.) Space is conquered by movement. Freedom of movement is granted by lack of restraint. There are things I can move through – water, and air; there are things that detain me, like stone. I cannot walk through fire. How do we get from one place to another? We will ourselves to move through receptive media.

Then what are our vehicles for? They get us there safer, and faster, retarding our movement in time. We cover more space and less time. What is a vehicle for an image, a concept? Something that carried that concept, from here to there, in space and time. I hear music in New York that was recorded in Oklahoma; I hear it today and tomorrow; the musicians performed it last year. And the music itself is a vehicle, just like my words on the page. Pick up a concept, stick it in the music, send it on its way.

The medium. The medium. It's all pretty complicated. The medium carries the message, but that's not all there is to it. Some people relate to Bob Dylan's vision of the world. That doesn't have anything to do with the medium, that's something that's in his head. And now it's in your head. The music – the medium – delivered it intact.

But suppose you say you relate to the music itself. Now you're digging the package, right? But it's the music that communicates – the feeling you get from the melody, from the beat, from the sound of the words and all that interacting with the words themselves, the specific concepts. So maybe the package, the medium, is the message, since we can't quite separate Bob Dylan's vision from Bob Dylan's music. But . . . no, the music and the message aren't the same thing either. They aren't separable, but they aren't the same thing. You can't pry the painting from the canvas and the oils, but that doesn't mean the materials are the painting. Just a minute, Mr McLuhan.

Communication is transportation (uh, I'm just fooling around here; I wouldn't want to perpetrate new slogans). Time and space are things to pass through, art is the rearranging of the universe into patterns reflecting the artist's will. Message is a specific thing, a discernible thing. Will is not. Few artists deal with messages, few artists expect you to go at the physical body of their work with a scalpel and attempt to extract its essence. The artist's emotions and sense perceptions are transmitted by means of his work. He receives, and he sends so that you may receive. The medium is not important. The medium is inanimate, an object. What you receive – not a message, not a specific, but a sum of messages, an emotion, a vision, a perception – is a part of the artist. It's alive. It's reborn in you. Music. The notes are not important. Virtuosity means nothing. No one cares how well you rearrange the objects. You gotta have soul, baby, which just means it's gotta be you you're passing on, people receiving parts of people, living matter, animate stuff. The medium and the messages it contains are just so much nothing, trees falling in the forest with no one to hear, unless there is human life on both ends of the line, sending, receiving, transferring bits of human consciousness from one soul to another. Communication is the interaction between our personal worlds.

Stepping out of the shower, I put on the Byrds.

The Byrds go right at it. They are about as nice as you could be and still seem absolutely real, and few of us could think of groups we'd rather listen to. It's always what's there on the record that's stunning; not the quality or the cleverness of what's there, not the music or the intent of what's there, but the stuff itself – you hear it and you react, you feel good, you understand, you are entirely and personally involved. First you think: 'Wow, I really love the Byrds', and then you maybe stop to think about why you love them or what it is that you think is so good. Maybe you never even know, but the important thing is, they always get to you.

Anyway, they always get to me. And I have a lot of friends who for maybe a month after any given Byrds album comes out walk around muttering 'Wow' and saying that when they really think about it, the Byrds are their very favourite rock group. And then they forget for a while, until another Byrds record appears; and of course it's not thinking about the Byrds that impresses them but hearing the Byrds. And isn't this how it should be?

The Byrds more than anybody today have mastered communication. Part of it is that they're not afraid. Not on any of the important levels. They try, but they're not very conscious of what they're 'supposed to be' doing, and this is a saving grace. Such an ominous toy as the Moog becomes in their hands just a thing to make sound with at the beginning of 'Natural Harmony'. They aren't intimidated. They're in control, the music is completely theirs, there is no distance between man and machine because machine is appreciated as simply tool, extension of man, something to do things with. The same is true of the horns, strings, everything on *The Notorious Byrd Brothers*. The listener is absolutely not aware of strings on 'Going Back', not because he can't hear them – they're right there – but because he's hearing the song. In the best art you cannot see the artist's handiwork. You can only feel his presence, in what you're perceiving, you're overwhelmed by that and not concerned with examining it. You relate. Sex can be much closer, more direct, than we think the word 'close' means. So can looking at Picasso. So can listening to the Byrds.

Now that we are ready, now that they are ready, the Byrds do not ignore specifics. It is just the right time to sing about amphetamine, in the context of Memphis brass and waves of non-feeling; it is just the right time to follow that with further reflections on an overthought theme, going back, younger than yesterday, my back pages, underthought this time: a little bit of courage is all we lack, I'm going back. That means less and feels more. Vietnam is on this album. Vietnam is everywhere these days. Last year it would not have been proper; last year Vietnam and rock were not so close for us, we couldn't have made the bridge. This year some things are in all things, and the Byrds are us too, they feel that too, and what they feel is what's present on this album.

There is a natural progression, in my mind, from the Love album (*Forever Changes*) to the Dylan album (*John Wesley Harding*) to *The Notorious Byrd Brothers*. Self-awareness is the word I like to use, the artist aware of who he is and putting it right across, no distance, just presence. Horns, steel guitars, strings, rock stuff, harmonies, melodies, words ideas concepts phrasing are all part of it, all more and more natural and invisible as the person of the artist takes shape, takes form, becomes present in the living-room or wherever you listen, wherever you hear. Talking to a friend on the telephone, you get only voice, some words in straight-line order, inflection of voice, and a lot of memory, a lot of consciousness of who this person is from all you knew before. Listening to the Byrds, you have heard all those other albums, you know what you know, and you also have words in multi-leveled order, inflections, melodies and rhythms, every sort of rich communication directly to/with you.

On a Byrds album, how much distance is there between what the artist (several people, but singular on records) is trying to do and what he does? None at all, or not perceptible, or maybe we don't care what he was trying to do. He must have been trying to do this, he did this and it's incredible. No distance. Does this mean the medium's the message? No. Both these things are impersonal. This is all personal. The Byrds is the Byrds. The music and the group are the same concept, the same thing in our minds, the same thing on the record; the people are not the same as the music, but then the people in the Byrds are not the same as the Byrds, which is part of why they come and go so much. The Byrds is a true gestalt, successful in so far as six great albums and fifty-nine songs have been produced by that gestalt, successful in so far as that gestalt is known as a person to more people than most individuals are.

There is no distinction in time between Byrds' albums; more than any other group they are as good on their first album, as appropriate now on their first album, as they are now on this album, and I suspect this album would have sounded perfectly fine back then, three years ago. The Byrds are now, the Byrds have always been now. They don't just say those things, they feel them, they get in and around and through all those things they say and no one but the Byrds has more right to say 'Just like the day of birth our first awakening to this earth' and 'That which is not real does not exist.' 'Dance to the day when fear is gone.' The Byrds have abolished time, for themselves, and for us all if we listen enough.

The Aesthetics of Rock

RICHARD MELTZER

Fans of the latter-day 'Gulcher' Meltzer may find it hard to equate that writer with the young philosophy student whose term paper Paul Williams renamed 'The Aesthetics of Rock' and published in Crawdaddy, *subsequently burgeoning an entire tome of such beserk dia(rrhoea)tribes.*

Bob Dylan's greatest dive into the rock & roll domain, 'Like A Rolling Stone', represents an attempt to free man by rescuing him from meaning, rather than free man through meaning. John Lennon's two collections of writing, *In His Own Write* and *A Spaniard in the Works*, have shown his desire to denigrate all meaning and thus throw intentional ambiguity into all domains of meaning. And very definitely all meaning is similar, beginning with the most 'authentic' and continuing down the line. When told by Paul McCartney about a girl he encountered with the idea that God had advised her to marry Paul – 'I was trying to persuade her that she didn't in actual fact have a vision from God, that it was –' George Harrison interrupted with, 'It was probably somebody disguised as God.' Meaning by any other name, spells about the same.

Whereas James Joyce attempted to salvage meaning from semantic chaos, John would rather attain a cool semantic oblivion, and thus has written two books intentionally inferior to James Joyce's works.

One of Lennon and McCartney's maneuvers is to present

meaning in such a role that it becomes trite. Thus is the use of 'in spite of' in a positive sense reduced to triviality in 'Yes It Is':

> Please don't wear red tonight . . .
> For red is the colour that will make me blue
> In spite of you . . .

This very spirit of the song, with its assertively positive title, presents a frightening ambiguity between arrogance and possession of a unique vulnerability. 'When I Get Home' plays upon the mere appearance of a single word, 'trivialities':

> Come on, if you please
> I got no time for trivialities,
> I got a girl who is waiting home for me, tonight.

In the midst of apparent 'tragedy' in realizing a sudden revulsion at his semi-adulterous involvement with another girl, he can hesitate to give it the meaning of 'triviality'. But the five-syllable word is so strange in such a monosyllabic context that it is rendered incredibly inappropriate, and the need for meaning collapses.

Barry McGuire's 'Eve Of Destruction' presents a plethora of such words: 'Coagulatin'', 'Legislation', etc. The very appearance of such 'serious' subjects as war and segregation in a rock context is a denigration of their original significance. His absolute overstatement of theme renders disaster cool; his 'Don't you know we're on the eve of destruction' is so affirmative that one can feel comfortable with such knowledge. England's banning of this song is a really fine misunderstanding of how McGuire has rendered *Weltschmerz* trite.

In a world of such things as random values, metaphysical inconsistency, and the constant unavoidable interruption of pure aesthetic perception by random events from within and without, eclecticism is the only valid position; and other stances may be measured by virtue of their distance from the eclectic. Andy Warhol has devised one of the simplest of all schemes, the selection of a popular motif, from Troy Donahue, to floral prints, to Campbell's soup, followed by mechanical multiple reproduction of this motif, with the consistency and inconsistency being a function of the mechanism of creation. Rock & roll, however, cannot rely upon the selling power of random circumlocution of the originally acceptable motif, but turns toward the utter compression of popularly acceptable, yet eclectically arranged images. 'A Little Bit Better' by Herman's Hermits begins with the instrumental introduction from the Four Seasons Coca-Cola commercial, proceeds with the sinister spirit of the Rolling Stones' 'Play With Fire' (of course rendered innocent by Herman's contradiction), sung with the vocal style of the Zombies, to the tune of Chuck Berry's 'Memphis', and in possession of a title clearly reminiscent of the recent hit by Wayne Fontana and the Mindbenders, 'A Little Bit Too Late'. Wayne Fontana himself sounded like a clear version of the Kingsmen in his first hit, like the Searchers in his next. The Beatles have taken from visceral jazz saxophonist John Coltrane in 'Love Me Do', the gay Four Seasons in 'Tell Me Why', Larry Williams in 'I'm Down', and Bob Dylan and Scottish marching bands in 'You've Got To Hide Your Love Away'. They have used elderly African drum in 'Mr Moonlight', violins in 'Yesterday', timpani in 'What You're Doing' and 'Every Little Thing', packing case in 'Words Of Love', and unusual amplification maneuvers in 'I Feel Fine' and 'Yes It Is'. They have used double tracking on several records, sometimes so obviously that it can be easily noticed (John Lennon's harmonica line can be heard while he is singing lead vocal in 'I Should Have Known Better'. It does not matter if part of the Beatles' formula is visible; after all, even Lennon's bathing-suit is clearly visible in a bath-tub scene).

At the same time, rock has transcended any difficulties

encountered in the sociology of knowledge. Because it is so wantonly eclectic, any moment's linear connections can bear contradictory relationships to those of the next without difficulty. 'I Can't Stop Loving You' has succeeded 'I've Had It', 'Tequila' had led to 'Too Much Tequila', and 'Eve Of Destruction' and 'Dawn Of Correction' have appeared almost concurrently. William James has seen the impossibility of viewing philosophical constructs separate from the temperament which has led to them; rock has never for a second viewed the construct and temperament as anything but the same phenomenon, or noumenon for that matter. Quine has noted, 'The unit of empirical significance is the whole of science.' The unit of rock significance is the whole of rock & roll, and this is not merely the result of the failure of reduction.

The possibility of artistic evolution presupposes questions of evolving legitimacy and illegitimacy. Once a new approach has been legitimatized through acceptance it may be repeated; in the case of rock & roll the very process of legitimatization itself can pertain to rock & roll's total picture, and this repetition of course is driven into the ground, just as I have obliterated the concept of repetition by overuse so far in this very essay. But when the mere juxtaposition of a still extraneous element can lead to either friction within an art or between it and the audience (which to rock is equally internal), more than simple vulgarity and tastefulness are in question. Moreover, rock has dealt with legitimacy and illegitimacy in a manner which frequently annihilates the distinction. Often something is capable of being observed as both at home in a rock context and utterly alien. When Elvis Presley followed his early hardcore rock hits with a ballad, 'Love Me Tender', the music of which had been taken from Stephen Foster, several questions arose. Could Elvis now be considered a popular musician in the 'adult', Muzak-oriented sense? Was rock & roll, not even three years old as an identifiable movement, on the verge of fusion with this popular mainstream? Pat Boone built his entire early career on music ambiguously legitimate to both pop and rock, with titles like 'Love Letters In The Sand', 'Anastasia', 'There's A Gold Mine In The Sky', 'April Love', 'When The Swallows Come Back To Capistrano', and the Quaker 'Friendly Persuasion'. Perhaps he was interested mainly in attaining pop legitimacy for his own songs, imbued already with a pseudo-rock energy, without concentrating upon how that energy might enhance what he conservatively judged to be legitimate. The Platters, perhaps the biggest group during the early days of rock & roll, strained to sound so 'legitimate' that they have completely vanished. As rock developed, a significant change took place: ballads became illegitimate. That is, they were no longer ambiguous 'good' music but were now eligible for use by rock & rollers. Beauty could now re-enter rock & roll with full 'badness' to it; there was no longer a need to equate beauty with the sub-mundanely pretty, as Muzak necessitates: beauty was now free and ontologically energized.

'Soul' encountered a similar problem, resolved completely by Ray Charles. His early blues and gospel contained an intense, lyrical poignancy that seemed unbreachably removed from rock's trivial sentimentality. Charles's 'What'd I Say' and 'Swanee River Rock' alienated his work from its earlier more conservative legitimacy and introduced to rock a variety of soul far more 'righteous' than that of rhythm and blues. One of the first great ballads of this new era of rock was Conway Twitty's 'It's Only Make Believe', perhaps an indicator of the self-cognition necessary for such a transition beyond limitation by dubious distinction: 'People see us everywhere/They think you really care/But myself I can't deceive/I know it's only make believe.' The problem of delegitimatization has sometimes been reduced to a problem of trivialization. The Righteous Brothers' 'Unchained Melody' is a song recorded scores of times in a 'legitimate' context, but only they (actually only one Brother sings on the record, a dubious trivialization itself) could make it completely renderable through a rock context. The trick was to slur the phrase 'your love', in the final 'God speed your love to me', so that it is not clearly audible, even inaudible on a faulty transistor radio. Bob Dylan has brought his harsh folk songs of protest into rock & roll by following the latter's pleasure principle, recording for single releases (separate from his record albums) those songs which are the most aurally pleasing, as 'Like A Rolling Stone' and 'Positively Fourth Street'.

The Beatles have in their own work mirrored the entire development of rock & roll. They began with primitive emotional music ('Love Me Do'), went on to hardcore affirmative kineticism ('She Loves You') and triviality (Ringo's wail, 'Okay, George' during 'Boys'), progressed to highly sophisticated arrogance ('I Should Have Known Better') and straightforward profundity ('I'll Be Back'), pessimism ('Things We Said Today') and modern 'tragedy' ('No Reply'), while at all stages relating themselves to the roots with revivals ('Dizzy Miss Lizzie') and retrogressions to early noncognitiveness, written themselves ('I'm Down'). They have noted the evolution of multi-tracked recording, with 'Help!', a single-tracked recording, at its pinnacle. In this work, juxtaposed Greek-like lead and chorus seem separate in echoing each other, suggesting that the Beatles' self-restraint in limiting the song to a single track divided between George and Paul and John is a self-conscious comprehension of the effect of one being fully capable of echoing himself and yet refusing, a queer addendum to a movement continuously felt throughout rock & roll history. Representing the evolution of rock made conscious of itself (just as Chardin asserts man to be the crown of the natural evolution of the universe, made conscious of itself), the Beatles have made ontologically important the concept of anachronism. Just as the Parmenidean One 'at all times . . . both is and is becoming older and younger than itself', Beatlistic unity implies anachronism in its novelty, not just infinite extension of nostalgia.

Stylistically Conway Twitty resembles closely Elvis Presley, who is echoed by Terry Stafford, who sounds just like Del Shannon.

Marianne Faithfull can be thought of as an anemic Joan Baez; Adam Faith is essentially the same as Jimmy Soul both stylistically and nominally. By a convenient raunch epistemology, Dee Dee Sharp has resembled the Orlons, who in turn resemble the Marvelettes. The 'late great' Buddy Holly was posthumously heard in the singing of Tommy Roe and Bobby Vee, who has even used Buddy Holly's Crickets. The instrumental sounds of the Tornadoes and of Johnny and the Hurricanes display no distinct difference. Mel Carter is not readily distinguishable from the 'late great' Sam Cooke. Some vocals and harmonica solos by Dylan and Lennon have sounded so related that one rock & roll magazine said that they might be the same person in different disguises. Jay and the Americans sound like the Fortunes, who sound like the We Five, who sound like the Ivy League, who sound like the Beatles, who sound like the Zombies, who sound like the Searchers, who sound like the Everly Brothers, who sound like a multitude of white country blues singers, who sometimes sound like Negro country blues singers, who can sometimes sound like urban Negro blues singers, who sound like the Rolling Stones, who sound like the Nashville Teens, who do not even look like Jay and the Americans.

Germs

JULIE BURCHILL AND TONY PARSONS

Subverting each and every choice phrase, every enduring sentiment about rock & roll's unique synergy to the treadmill of Burchill's bile, Julie Burchill and Tony Parsons, in 1978's The Boy Looked at Johnny, deconstructed the history of rock & roll. But if Burchill's and Parsons's bangs'n'meltzered prose had its own verve, it failed to reflect its stylistic precursors spiritually.

Bob Dylan broke his neck – close, but no cigar.

Sealed integrity is reserved for the fêted self-immolated. Choking on their own idolized vomit allowed a fistful of White Youth Culture luminaires – Brian Jones, Jimi Hendrix, Janis Joplin, Jim Morrison – to escape the fate of life-sucking godhead, as did their fifties antecedents.

Fast-living, young-dying, good-looking icons like Eddie Cochran (killed in a car crash), Gene Vincent (fatally shell-shocked from Cochran's last ride), Buddy Holly, Ritchie Valens, Big Bopper (victims of the same plane crash), Jerry Lee Lewis, Chuck Berry (two primal paedophiles), Elvis Presley (drafted down the middle of the road), Little Richard (who – God forgive him – got religion) – all killed or castrated before their decade was dead.

But the sixties was a decade of iron-lung dinosaurs washing their hands of the blood of teen idealism – sated, sanitized and bloated after gorging on the carnal/chemical/mass-worship fruit of their assault on the heights.

Artistic pretension became self-parody as working-class heroes became cocaine-class tax-exiles. By January 1968, the Who were pure vaudeville – 'Smashing guitars used to be real anger; it isn't anymore. It's theatrical melodrama,' said the Mod who discovered Meher Baba and had a baby called *Tommy*.

The Fab Four got divorced, Eric Clapton gave up guitar-heroism for heroin and the Rolling Stones played tootsie with socialites and Satan. Hope I get rich before I get old.

Meanwhile, back in the States . . . garage bands erupted like coast-to-coast acne as a new generation of crew-cuts got to first base with the black R&B and soul that the all-pervasive Brit-Beat Invasion stole its licks from originally.

True to Asian and World War form, the Americans arrived

years late with an advanced state of technology. They may have been neophytes, but they could afford better equipment than anyone else.

Rock became the sole property of white dopes high on punk everywhere as bands like ? and the Mysterions, the Electric Prunes and the Magic Mushrooms came up out of nowhere and scored one hit before going straight back there. The lucky ones got jobs modelling Valderma.

This adolescent angst soundtrack was the first exposition of the trash aesthetic to get branded as 'punk rock'; a revolt into anti-style consisting of raw, basic, brazen flaunting of electric toys to pump out revenge anthems directed at the perennial Unholy Trinity of comfortable self-contained pain-inducers – real or imagined – in the affluent lifestyle of the average white American teenage boy circa mid sixties; their parents, their teachers and – most of all – their girlfriends.

But oblivion beckoned; the garage bands' enthusiastic celebration of solipsism was already dated, unfashionable and obsolete. Uncle Sam napalmed Vietnamese villages as His offspring burnt their draft cards. All across the nation, you could hear the hair grow as innocence discovered acid.

It took a Lenin to make Marx's philosophy recognizable; it took the Byrds, the Mamas and the Papas and Sonny and Cher to get Dylan on the AM playlist. Arthur Rimbaud and Woody Guthrie doing the Wall Street Shuffle hand in hand . . . they made his pop-psalms listenable and got across to an area where Dylan's influence was minimal – the singles chart.

But by this time the intelligentsia were concerned purely with albums, one eye on artistic merit and the other on bigger profits/prophets.

The Byrds never watered Dylan down but made him bearable . . . it's all right, ma, he's only whining. And Dylan learned from the pop groups; as well as being electric, his later work was mainly boy-meets-girl with the token protest thrown in whenever he remembered. Sonny and Cher believed in the songs they sang infinitely more than Dylan ever did; the crossover product, less nitpickingly political and more humane, is invariably more sincere than dogma – and therefore has more integrity, less pretension. When the Rolling Stones were on their very first tour of the USA, they slept on the floor of Sonny and Cher's mansion.

But in Haight-Ashbury there was an epidemic – here, dropping acid was more important than moving units. 'Raising of conscious-ness' was a luxury just the affluent could indulge in; Jimi Hendrix had black skin but was adopted by the hippies as their token Tom tab, the only black star on acid.

Hallucinogenic honkies like Jefferson Airplane, Grateful Dead, Moby Grape, Love and Captain Beefheart consumed LSD with the religious fervour of a penitent playing with rosary beads.

For the first time, rock was a vehicle for religious appetites. Even the Beach Boys had a Maharishi ('He's my Little Deuce Guri, you don't know what I got'), and everyone from the Rolling Stones to Frank Sinatra's third wife was going to Katmandu in their Kashmir sweater. Ringo may have returned from India complaining that it was 'just like Butlin's' but sanity was still a long way away and Brian Epstein was being buried.

Highbrow critics weaned on the classics swooned like bobby-soxers over Sergeant Pepper's Chemical Rebellion In A Cosmic Vacuum. Cannabis *sativa* nestled next to savoury canapés as Hampstead hors-d'oeuvres. Jimi Hendrix employed a stooge to sample every tab of acid for that pretentious little bouquet. The consumers of Alternative Product in their baubles, bangles and beads forsook surfboards and Liverpool accents for Hipperanto like 'high' and 'trip' ('tower block' and 'dole queue' were but a twinkle in the iris of enterprising entrepreneurs not yet out of business school). Rock had bartered its purity and vulgarity for raising of consciousness and respectability.

But even in the new aware rock & roll, the barricades were still built of papier mâché; be the first one on your block to have your boy come home in a headband! Elsewhere, the blood didn't taste of tomatoes. In Paris, left-wing students and trade unionists fought running battles with the *gendarmes* as the authorities desperately poured tons of cement over the instant artillery cobbled streets of the burning capital. The youth of Japan, Mexico, Greece and Germany would also have regarded the flashing of peace signs as high satire – but back in the USA, who needs unions when you've got the Mafia?

The blacks were burning Watts while the whites were burning joss-sticks, love being all you need when your idol's rich and your guru's smooth-talking. Any hint of a threat to the great American status quo was muzzled with a recording contract – it's a career man's life as a vinyl battery hen – and hitched to the corporation treadmill. Energies ostensibly committed to the annihilation of the establishment were enlisted in the lucrative perpetuation of nothing more subversive than the generation gap.

The prime example was the MC5, a Detroit band formed in 1967 by John Sinclair, 'Minister of Information of the White Panther Party'. Let's hear it for Mr Sinclair, as he tells you in his own words why they were formed!

The MC5 is totally committed to the revolution. With our music and our economic genius we plunder the unsuspecting straight world for money and the means to carry out our program, and revolutionize its children at the same time. And with our entrance into the straight media we have demonstrated to the honkies that anything they do to fuck with us will be exposed to their children. You don't need to get rid of all the honkies, you just rob them of their replacements and let their breed atrophy and die out, with its heirs cheering triumphantly around it. We don't have guns yet – not all of us anyway – because we have more powerful weapons – direct access to millions of teenagers is one of our most potent, and their belief in us is another. But we will use guns if we have to – we will do anything – if we have to. We have no illusions.

Neither had Judge Colombo when he awarded Sinclair a ten-year jail sentence for passing two free marijuana cigarettes to undercover narcotic agents with their sheriff's badges pinned inside their headbands. Scolded Colombo, 'He represents a person who has deliberately flaunted and scoffed at the law.' He waved a hand in dismissal, 'take him away.'

The MC5 themselves weren't exactly busting an alternative gut to bake good old John a hash cake with a file inside, to spring the dude and get back to the revolution. Far from it; they felt they'd paid their urbane guerrilla union dues to their sugar lump daddy Svengali with their first fab album waxing *Kick Out The Jams*. Recorded live, it was a fumbling mating of screeching, head-banging heavy metal and fashionable politico-platitudes delivered in best/worst Billy Graham Bible-banging self-righteous rhetoric.

No sooner was their conscience buried safely behind bars than the Angry Young Businessmen obsequiously got tight with rock critic Jon 'No H' Landau and smartly did an about-turn. With Landau handling production chores, the MC5 cut *Back In The USA*, pure pop pap sheep-dipped in transparent raiments of youth and rebellion. They came on like bitter Monkees, chortling tinny, three-minute, wishful-thinking hymns to teenage lust, sitting in the classroom at high school and fighting with cops.

But the album's title track had sounded infinitely more subversive when performed ten years previously by its cynical author Chuck Berry, a black man fresh from jail. He had handled the celebration of America with derisive humour; in the plump pink hands and mealy mouths of the MC5, 'Back In The USA' sounded as superficially sincere as a holiday jingle.

To Sinclair, the entire album must have sounded like a Dear John letter:

> Then one day I had a perfect plan
> I'd shake my ass and scream in a rock & roll band
> From now on there'll be no compromising
> Rock & roll music is the best advertising.

From inside, their ex-guiding light seethed, 'You guys wanted to be bigger than the Beatles and I wanted you to be bigger than Chairman Mao.' Despite their desperate attempt at mass acceptance, the album sold badly, not even recouping the advance Atlantic had paid them – thus gaining cult status and subsequently becoming one of the most vastly over-rated albums in the history of rock. When their third album *High Time* met the same indifferent fate, the band lost their recording contract and disappeared.

The band's lead vocalist Robin Tyner reappeared years later on a trip to England as an obese bespectacled journalist trading on past glories, who declined joints from strangers and who hefted his weighty torso on to a stage to guest with Eddie and the HotRods before a young audience who had never heard of him.

The demise of the MC5 was indicative of the fact that in the USA the youth didn't have to be contained; just corralled, like half a million radical sheep. Out of this grew the festival phenomenon, in which the kids got it together just enough to wallow in the mud.

Monterey in June 1967 (featuring the Who, Jimi Hendrix, Janis Joplin, Brian Jones and Otis Redding) was the dress rehearsal for Woodstock, August 1969 (three days of the Who, Janis Joplin, Joan Baez, Jefferson Airplane, Grateful Dead, Crosby, Stills, Nash and Young and many more). Love Nation show of unity; see the movie, buy the triple album! Those wonderful friends you'll remember forever!

The highway to Woodstock was clogged with an eight-mile traffic jam of car-owning hippies on their way to the fun, a freak summer thunderstorm turned the site to a quagmire of mud and – as the portable toilets overflowed – the police declared Woodstock a 'disaster area'.

The crowd of part-time bohemians at Woodstock was the size of a city, but the seemingly limitless supply of sex and drugs and rock & roll kept the contented kiddies too peaceful, placid and passive for any urban reality symptoms – hence the media myth of the festival as Birth Of A Nation social landmark. The gurgling inmates of Woodstock would have suffered severe spiritual starvation (it was a long walk back to Mom's apple pie) had not the local Women's Group of the Jewish Community Centre spoon-fed the Utopia frontiersmen 30,000 sandwiches, and had not Woodstock's 49-year-old dairy farmer owner Max Yasgur donated large quantities of milk and cheese. Even the outraged residents of Woodstock warmed to the helpless hippie nation when they too began to make a groovy profit out of the Aquarian Exposition.

Because the only 'supermarket' on the site was a chemical co-op selling hashish, marijuana, LSD, mescaline, psilocybin and opium. In the heat of the hedonistic goldrush to the Promised Swampland, it never occurred to the co-eds that their stomachs wouldn't be kept as full as the family freezer. For all their cunning counter-culture capitalism, the Big Daddies of Woodstock – 25-year-old Porsche-driving entrepreneur, Mike Lang, and 24-year-old investment concern boss, John Roberts – had forgotten that man cannot live on good vibes alone. There was no food in the land of plenty.

Which left the ravenous ravers at the mercy of charitable handouts, local daylight robbers and . . . now a word from our Sponsor (choke on it, suckers). Had the authorities felt at all threatened by the lumpenhippies, they would have let them eat love beads or sent in the National Guard with rubber bullets. As it was, they sent in the Air Force with 300 lbs of edible treats; despite the mounting protest against what this same army was dropping in Vietnam, the peanut-butter sure tasted swell. Manna from heaven, courtesy of President Nixon.

When the half a million campers went home after their three-day fling, the head of Monticello's constabulary was full of praise: 'Notwithstanding their personality, their dress and their ideas, they are the most courteous, considerate and well behaved group of kids I have ever been in contact with in my twenty-four years of police work.'

The smiling benevolence with which the police stalked the half-inherent Americana, half-drug-induced polite passivity of the Woodstock playpen was paralleled by the attitude of the Hell's Angels to the non-active mass of hippies, because the fundamental philosophy of both the hated cops and the revered Angels was founded upon the evolution of mindless machismo which Gore Vidal had nailed to the Stars and Stripes as *The M3 Line* – when Woodstock ended, Sharon Tate had been dead for seven days:

There has been from Henry Miller to Norman Mailer to Charles Manson a logical progression. The Miller–Mailer–Manson 'man' (or M3 for short) has been conditioned to think of women as, at best, breeders of sons, at worst, objects to be poked, humiliated, killed . . . M3 was born, emigrated to America, killed Indians, killed blacks, conned women . . . righteous murder stalks the land.'

Though the cops/Angels tolerated the hippies who opted out of the M3 brotherhood in favour of all-round euphoric apathy, both the boys in blue and the boys on bikes screamed in vehement panic at the activist minority of anti-war demonstrators, who had realized that no revolution was won by sitting stoned in a field.

Despite this, the reactionary rednecks on sparkling Harleys were elevated to folk-hero status by such counter-culture luminaries as acid-testing dilettante Ken 'Cuckoo Nest' Kesey and moronic marathon-rockers the Grateful Dead – all the hip guys love a bike-boy – whose leader Jerry Garcia provided references for the Angels when the Rolling Stones at the climax of a box-office smash-hit American tour decided to play a massive free festival to grab the top rock-hero rung, open to offers due to the Beatles being in the painful throes of divorce proceedings and Bob Dylan playing the part of hermit family-man.

For the Rolling Stones wanted no establishment 'pigs' at the Californian speedway of Altamont, just outside San Francisco – they would provide their own alternative police force.

It was fitting that the Stones, who with their myriad celebratory dabblings in Satanism, mindless violence, dirty hypodermic needles and other habits which were the direct antithesis of love, peace and tolerance, should choose to replace one crew of law-enforcers with another of even greater brutality. The doublethink was ripe for violent nemesis.

In the last month of the last year of the sixties, 300,000 people hooked down the depression cocktail of downers and cheap wine and set fire to mountains of garbage to fend off the freezing winter air as they huddled on the bleak hills around the Altamont speedway. The Hell's Angels had been paid $500-worth of beer for keeping the peace.

By the time Santana, the first act of the festival, were on-stage, the Angels were already brutalizing the audience. In front of the stage a young man was repeatedly kicked in the face and the set was interrupted by another Angel rushing across the stage to beat up someone else. When Jefferson Airplane played, guitarist Marty Balin was knocked senseless by a pool-cue wielding Angel for having the audacity to intervene in one of the many beatings being handed out by the Angels.

In complete control, the Angels drove their bikes straight through the packed crowd to park them by the side of the stage. At the end of Crosby, Stills, Nash and Young's set, a horde of stretchers were sent into the audience and came back carrying bloodied, unconscious bodies to the first-aid tent.

After a lengthy delay, the Stones themselves appeared and found themselves confined to a minute stage area surrounded by the jeering, openly contemptuous Angels who found a source of great mirth in Mick Jagger's dancing. As the Stones' third number

'Sympathy For The Devil' ground to a halt, a group of Hell's Angels some ten yards from the stage stabbed to death a young black man named Meredith Hunter, who had offended the Angels by attending the festival with his girlfriend who happened to be very pretty, very blonde and very white.

They made a movie of it, of course, in which Mick Jagger wept as he watched a video-tape slow-motion instant-replay of the murder and Keith Richard (whose cocaine bill after one 49-date US tour was a quarter of a million dollars) demonstrated considerably less compassion.

'People were just asking for it ... all those nude, fat people. They had victims' faces.'

'The kids are being hyped,' Lou Reed had said before Altamont, on peace and love versus his 'realism'. Reed and the Velvet Underground were exponents of twisted black East Coast pessimism in the face of flowery West Coast optimism, both loathed and feared by the hippies. Lou Reed had met John Cale in New York City, 1964, and the Velvet Underground were formed after making a big impression on Andy Warhol and his menagerie. The Velvets made their debut at the mixed media Exploding Plastic Inevitable show in 1966 and their first album appeared a year later, brimming with paeans to urban paranoia, smack glorification and sado-masochism. Failing to achieve chart placings, the nihilists pursued solo careers. From Detroit, also pretending to destroy themselves before anyone else could, came Iggy and the Stooges. James Jewel Osterberg aka lead singer Iggy Stooge achieved notoriety and a recording contract not so much by his warbling – he and his anonymous band were still hungover with sporadic attacks of doomy post-Doors mystical acid gloom which they dropped on their second album in favour of Iggy's patented routine of self-hate, self-abuse and self-degradation – as for urging the crowd to buy shares in his crucifixion.

Iggy's party-pieces included – dousing his body in burning wax! swan-diving on to broken glass! ripping his chest open with a broken bottle! smashing his teeth through his gums with the micro-phone and crooning 'The Shadow Of Your Smile'! covering his body in peanut butter!

'Basically I'm a nurd,' Iggy told the authors in late 1977. 'Look at my face, it's Alfred E. Neuman.'

Alfie gave the authors the shits, metaphorically. The authors gave Alfie the shits, literally. The day he minced into their office to ponce drugs, he was given a generous supply of laxatives. He gulped them greedily, causing the Mighty Poop (as we af-fectionately refer to him) to interrupt his gigs for the next forty-eight hours. Basically, he was a turd – and, as such, Born to Run.

He was racist and sexist, the hippie ideology seen through a microscope instead of rose-tinted shades. When the Stooges dissolved, Iggy turned whore and later committed himself to a sanatorium.

Really, both Iggy and Lou were just flamboyant closet-cases fronting amateur-hour wimp bands, the members of which would have been just as happy if they'd done acid-drops and 'believed' in love and peace. Though, significantly, Haight-Ashbury was eventu-ally destroyed by a soul-sucking plague of heroin – Alfred E. Iggy and Loopy Lou's own particular hype.

'Because it makes me feel like I'm a man/When I stick a spike into my vein' from the Velvet Underground's 'Heroin' summed up both Lou and Iggy most succinctly. This odd couple were to be the sixties legacy to the next generation, though wearing needles in one's arm was just as much an affectation as sporting flowers in one's coiffure . . . it just sounded more drastic on plastic.

The funky junkie duo would have languished in obscurity, growing evermore fat, flaccid and forgotten, had it not been for the cataclysmic David Bowie. *The Rise And Fall Of Ziggy Stardust And The Spiders From Mars* was Bowie's third album, released in the summer of 1972. Set five years before Doomsday, against a backdrop of Brave New World escapism, its naïve obsession with Space Age Science Fantasy – blatantly displayed in songs like 'Moonage Daydream', 'Starman', 'Lady Stardust', 'Star' and

'Ziggy Stardust' – reflected the resignation of a generation who had washed their hands of Earth after their failure to create a new world during their weekend picnic at Yasgur's farm.

Appealing to Bowie's own mid-twenties contemporaries who had converted to all things sci-fi after abandoning belief in mere mortals, and to a new generation of teenagers too young to know or care about the past glories of the leftover idols and restless for an icon of their own, *Ziggy Stardust* was a camp novelette starring ex-mime artist Bowie in the title role of rock star as leper messiah consumed by his ego.

Showing considerable integrity, a good business head and a dramatic sense of timing, Bowie revealed in an interview that he was bisexual, setting a precedent in a tight-lipped world of show business. Although bands such as Alice Cooper – standard heavy metal muzak fronted by the baby-doll-beheading fat ham Alice himself – T. Rex – androgynous imp singing purple prose jukebox classics – and Slade – platform-boot stomping would-be working-class heroes – had been around since the start of the decade, it took someone as intelligent and glamorous as Bowie to instigate the pop renaissance soon categorized as Glitter Rock, with exponents as diverse as Gary Glitter, Alvin Stardust and Sweet – chicken-in-a-basket brickie cabaret and hod-carriers in gold lamé hotpants – Elton John and Roy Wood – fat old Tin Pan Alley tunesmith tarts in more mascara than anyone since Dusty Springfield – Queen and Cockney Rebel – competent rock bands ordinaire fronted by portentous, preening, piss-pot bards – and Roxy Music, whose first and second albums contain the only truly timeless rock music ever recorded, and were infinitely more convincing in their themes of alienation than Bowie playing Captain Kirk to his lead guitarist's Mr Spock. Roxy Music, alas, ended not with a bang but with a simper when Bryan Ferry subsequently joined the aforementioned piss-pot parade.

By 1973, Bowie was influential enough to take his poor relations Iggy and Lou out of mothballs and serve them up for seventies consumption. He produced Reed's limp-wristed self-parody

Transformer and Iggy's vinyl tout *Raw Power* and was left at the altar on both occasions when Iggy and Lou flounced back across the Atlantic to resume their romance with heroin. Ungrateful bitches!

At least they were spared the soporific musical diet of Hip Easy Listening, Disco Fodder and Heavy Metal which had drenched young earbuds before Glitter Rock and regained its stranglehold by 1975. All three products matched the mood of economic crisis depression prevalent in a UK torn by one million plus unemployed and legions of school-leavers swelling their ranks every day, the three-day week, teeming assembly-line education and the Tory mis-rule culminating in miners' strike blackouts.

Coffee-table credibility Hip Easy Listening was an insipid aural palliative for and by jaundiced hippies of all ages and social standing, with the artiste as creator of product and his worth measured on the *Financial Times* index. Disco Fodder was mechanical, mindless, sanitized soul, in which Uncle Tom sported an Afro to provide the staple dancing ration of the nation's youth whose lives were similarly mass-produced; it was the perfect backdrop for a slipshod education running the line to the factory, office or dole. *Top of the Pops* played colonial host to a regular stream of nimble-toed melon chompers. Disco was the opiate of the prole – agent of social order, it featured no polemics beyond get down and boogie, party, party, and Dating Do's and Don'ts.

The epic Teutonic Anaesthetic Heavy Metal was brutally hamfisted renderings of blues-based white rock – a totally moronic and downered wipe-out which complimented the seventies' teen-age leisure activities of arson and alcoholism.

The emergence of Pub Rock in 1975 was a reaction against the giant stadiums at which the opulent rock aristocracy occasionally deigned to play, and against the slumming matrons who were getting backstage passes – Elizabeth Taylor and the Who and Princess Margaret with the Rolling Stones. The Pub Rock backlash was re-vamped R&B cranked out in small sweaty venues which had taken to serving live music along with the brown ale.

Mostly, the music itself was dire and derivative (a fact easily overlooked by a pub of pilchard-packed punters, pissed as newts) and, even with record company financial enthusiasm fired by trade press critical hyperbole, few Pub Rock bands transcended the rock 'n' bitter scene and moved on to greater things – the major problem being their inability to capture the live gig excitement on cold, hard, vinylized plastic.

But despite the demise of the Pub Rock ethos – which had always been strictly confined to the capital – the venues created by the aural movement remained and grass-roots rock combos had a ready made gig-circuit training ground in London for their lean years of apprenticeship. It was no longer uncool for a band to climb on stage without a P A system the size of Laskys' warehouse. In New York City, the club scene had been thriving for some time and had spawned a dead-on-arrival disaster-area outfit calling themselves the New York Dolls, who by 1975 had achieved the popularity of acne-blitzed transvestite lepers addicted to heroin. Formed in Babylon two years previously, the Dolls were the most blatant Rolling Stones rip-off of all time though paradoxically exuding ten times more nerve-bruising belligerent excitement than Mick and Keith's ritzy old tarts had ever mustered.

The New York Dolls starred tousled blond David JoHansen on lead vocals and audience-baiting, an ex-teenager pornlette who had graced such celluloid evergreens as *Studs on Main Street* and *Bike Boys Go Ape*. He danced like a white James Brown in chiffon and stilettoes flanked by rhythm guitarist Sylvain Sylvain, a manhandled Manhattan marionette with corkscrew curls, and lead guitarist Johnny Thunders, a back-combed brunette baseball jock turned junk rock starlet. As befitted a good Italian boy who loved his mother, Johnny would always execute a neat reverse duck walk for the sheltered privacy of the amplifiers whenever gripped with a new wave of nausea. Bassist Arthur Kane resembled a giant haystack turned hooker turned Bowery bum paralysed by paraffin while drummer Jerry 'Atric' Nolan looked like the sulky substitute he was, drafted in to the Dolls' rancid ranks after their original drummer Billy Murcia committed soap-skidding unintentional suicide after tarrying too long in the tub with a bottle of booze and a mountain of Mandrax.

Unrepentant poseurs, the Dolls wanted to be stars because there was nothing else left to be. Incompetent musicians, they owed more to Marilyn Monroe than to Elvis Presley, raking over the ashes of the living dead with their Famous Dopes On Opiates fashion-consciousness. On stage, JoHansen, Sylvain and Thunders raged around like crowd-conscious beauty queens with hostile possums housed down their G-strings (just to obtain that impressive bulge, one understands), frequently colliding and toppling off their rhine-stoned cowboy platforms, their three-minute masterpieces of solipsistic sleaze such as 'Pills', 'Trash' and 'Personality Crisis' very much the icing on the fairy cake.

Due to their self-imposed handicaps – Thunders and Nolan addicted to heroin and Arthur Kane a chronic alcoholic – and despite their recording contract with Mercury, their reputation as unreliable degenerates made it practically impossible for them to get a gig anywhere outside of Max's Kansas City. However, during a disastrous European tour they made such an impression on a tone-deaf East End tailor with a business in Chelsea that he followed the Dolls to Paris and later to New York and eventually became their manager. He tried to prevent the band coming apart at the seams, even working as a window-cleaner to supplement their income, relaunching them in threads of red leather before a huge hammer-and-sickle flag.

But neither the audience nor the Dolls took it seriously and the band began to disintegrate. During a residence in Florida, hard-won by the hustler acting as their manager, pin-cushion pair Thunders and Nolan escaped back to New York where they formed the Heartbreakers. Within two weeks the New York Dolls' erstwhile manager was back in his King's Road shop.

But the draper's potential had not bypassed the eagle eye of

Johnny Thunders: 'Malcolm McLaren is the greatest con-man that I ever met.'

In Which Yet Another Pompous Blowhard Purports to Possess the True Meaning of Punk Rock

LESTER BANGS

If Paul Williams was the founding father of rock journalism then Lester Bangs was the godfather of punk journalism. When 'punk' music was a strictly underground sub-genre, Bangs was espousing the creed in Detroit's very own Creem of the crop. On this occasion Bangs uses the unorthodox medium of a quickie pop-bio on the rise of Blondie to expound the origins of punk.

Punk rock was hardly invented by the Ramones in Queens, NY, in 1974–5, any more than it was by the Sex Pistols in London a year or so later. You have to go back to the New York Dolls.

The truth is that punk rock is a phrase that has been around at least since the beginning of the seventies, and what it at common means is rock & roll in its most basic, primitive form. In other words, punk rock has existed throughout the history of rock & roll, they just didn't call it that. In the fifties, when rock & roll was so new it scared the shit out of parents and racists everywhere, the media had a field day. This stuff was derided mercilessly, it was called 'unmusical', it was blamed for juvenile delinquency, sexual depravity (well . . .), if not the demise of Western civilization as a whole. It was said that the musicians could not play their instruments; in large part, by any conventional standards (what they used to call 'good' music), this was true. Does that matter now to the people who are still listening to those classic oldies twenty years later? It was said that the singers could not sing, by any previous 'legitimate' musical standard; this was also true. It was written off nearly everywhere as a load of garbage that would come and go within a year's time, a fad like the hula hoop.

Is any of this beginning to sound vaguely familiar?

The point is that rock & roll, as I see it, is the ultimate populist art form, democracy in action, because it's true: anybody can do it. Learn three chords on a guitar and you've got it. Don't worry whether you can 'sing' or not. Can Neil Young 'sing'? Lou Reed, Bob Dylan? A lot of people can't stand to listen to Van Morrison, one of the finest poets and singers in the history of popular music, because of the sound of his voice. But this is simply a matter of exposure. For performing rock & roll, or punk rock, or call it any damn thing you please, there's only one thing you need: NERVE. Rock & roll is an attitude, and if you've got the attitude you can do it, no matter what anybody says. Believing that is one of the things punk rock is about. Rock is for everybody, it should be so implicitly anti-élitist that the question of whether somebody's qualified to perform it should never even arise.

But it did. In the sixties, of course. And maybe this was one reason why the sixties may not have been so all-fired great as we gave them credit for. Because in the sixties rock & roll began to think of itself as an 'art-form'. Rock & roll is not an 'art-form'; rock & roll is a raw wail from the bottom of the guts. And like I said, whatever anybody ever called it, punk rock has been around from the beginning – it's just rock honed down to its rawest elements, simple playing with a lot of power and vocalists who may not have much range but have so much conviction and passion it makes up for it ten times over. Because PASSION IS WHAT IT'S ALL ABOUT – what all music is about.

In the early sixties there was punk rock: 'Louie, Louie' by the Kingsmen being probably the most prominent example. It was crude, it was rude, anybody could play it, but so what? It'll be around and people everywhere will still be playing it as long as there's rock & roll left at all. It's already lasted longer than *Sgt Pepper*! Who in the hell does any songs from that album anymore? Yet, a few years ago, some people were saying *Sgt Pepper* will endure a hundred years.

Seventies punk largely reflects a reaction against the cult of the guitar hero. Technical virtuosity was not a *sine qua non* of rock & roll in the first place and never should have become. Not that brilliant rock hasn't been made by musicians whose technical chops were and are the absolute highest. But see, that's JUST THE POINT. Just because something is simpler than something else does not make it worse. It's just the kind of hype a lot of people started buying in the late sixties with the rise of the superstar and superinstrumentalist concepts.

There was punk rock all through the sixties. The Seeds with 'Pushin' Too Hard'. Count Five 'Psychotic Reaction'. 'Talk Talk' by the Music Machine. And many others. It was simple, primitive, direct, honest music. Then, in 1969, Iggy and the Stooges put out their first album. Throughout the seventies, that and their subsequent two albums became cult items with small groups of people all over the world, who thought these records were some of the greatest stuff they had ever heard. They were also some of the simplest: two chords, a blaring fuzztone, Iggy singing lyrics as simple as 'Can ah cum ovah to-nat? Can ah cum ovah to-nat? Uh said uh we will have a real cool taam – to-naaat! We will hayuv – a reeal coool taam! To-naat!' Get it? It was, as Ed Ward wrote in *Rolling Stone* when it appeared, 'A reductio ad absurdum of rock & roll that might have been thought up by a mad DAR General in a wet dream.' Except where he was being sarcastic, I thought that was a compliment: the Stooges' music was brutal, mindless, primitive, vicious, base, savage, primal, hate-filled, grungy, violent, terrifying and above all REAL. They meant every note and word of it.

Enter the Dolls. They might have taken some cues from the Stooges, but who they really wanted to be was an American garage band Rolling Stones. And that's exactly what they were. Everything about them was pure outrage. And too live for the time – '72–3–4 mostly. They set New York on fire, but the rest of the country wasn't ready for it.

I was talking to a guitarist friend, and the subject of the Dolls came up.

'God,' she said, 'the first time they were on T V, we just couldn't believe it, that anybody that shitty would be allowed to do that! How did they get away with it?'

I felt like throwing her out of my house. They didn't 'get away' with anything. They did what they could and what they wanted to do and out of the chaos emerged something magnificent, something that was so literally explosive with energy and life and joy and madness that it could not be held down by all your RULES of how this is supposed to be done! Because none of 'em are valid! Rock & roll is about BREAKING the form, not 'working within it'. GIVE US SOME EQUAL TIME. Let the kid behind the wheel. Like Joe Strummer of the Clash says, 'It's not about playin' the chords right, for starters!'

The Meaning of Bile

BARNEY HOSKYNS

In a post-punk world the line between pop and rock may have become blurred. In his 1984 essay 'The Meaning of Bile', Barney Hoskyns, seeking to abandon the iconoclasm of punk journalism, attempts to find a niche for the 'rock critic' in this Rockpopsoul world.

Why do people read about pop?

What does it mean to write about pop, and what is the state of this writing?

These and more are just some of the thrilling questions that will be addressed over the next two or three thousand words.

But where do we start?

Well, where else but Steve Taylor? In last year's Virgin *Yearbook*, Steve contributed a piece entitled 'The Death of the Swiftian Function', its subject 'the changing face of rock journalism'. In it he argued, quite convincingly and quite eloquently, that *NME*'s sort of journalism was finished; that the runaway success of *Smash Hits* proved the only things pop's punters really wanted were the facts, presented glossily, reported efficiently.

Today's techno-teenagers were not, it transpired, interested in vast conceptual theses and long-winded spieling whose primary concern was autobiographical.

Dicing with heavily loaded terms, Taylor calmly lambasted *NME*'s pretensions to 'cultural arbitration' and 'market manipulation'.

'The journalist,' he stated, 'is no longer a folk figure on a par with the characters which he or she interviews.' Adding, 'It is telling that at the time of writing the *NME* does not have a single writer on its staff who is individually notorious or able to chivvy up circulation with controversy.'

When you start using terms like 'arbitration' and 'manipulation', you call into question the entire status and meaning of a music press. The trouble is, Taylor's answers are quite unsatisfactory – or else his vision of the link between music and 'media' is very naïve.

To start with, no pop writer could seriously claim to wield the power to arbitrate or manipulate taste. Of course s/he may adopt a supercilious, even despotic tone when urging the reader to listen (or not listen) to an act, but surely it is obvious to anyone that a single spin on daytime Radio One is worth three music paper covers in succession. Pop writers have no way of enforcing taste, and I cannot believe any of them wish to do so.

I think we are simply in the business of discussing what we take to be a subculture, constructed partly by – and partly for – young people of different sexes, classes, races. Apart from the fact that it's interesting to speculate on why Culture Club or Duran Duran sell so much vinyl, this has nothing to do with record sales. It's just interesting, it's part of what life is about.

Taylor's model of entertainment is built on that sturdiest of foundations: the notion of 'giving people what they want'. But what people want is a mixture of what is available and what is possible.

Simon Frith wrote an entire book to demonstrate (and argued the case superbly) that pop music is never just a commodity, something produced by record companies to be consumed by record purchasers. 'Consuming' implies a very straightforward economy – it suggests wastage and destruction in the very event of acquiring pop. And if that sounds like an accurate description of the rapid turnover in the teen idol trade, it scarcely accounts for the manifold uses people find for most pop music.

If leisure and recreation are the opposite of work, then they are surely the sphere in which people make meaning of their lives. Even when having fun, we use art to symbolize ourselves, for art is neither mirror nor hammer; it is the symbolic denotation of the complex of relations and contradictions that makes up the matter of our life.

The trap which Taylor so easily falls into is in setting up a hierarchy of 'importance', the gist of his reasoning being a wiser-than-hindsight fear that pop music isn't, after all, that important.

This would be fair if it meant that pop music had, after all, turned out to be unimportant for Steven Taylor; as a general statement it smacks of a stylistic tyranny. Nothing in this life is any more 'important' than anything else: Wittgenstein is no more 'important' than Paul Young, for the *Philosophical Investigations* do not change the basic facts of life any more than *No Parlez* does.

What culture is about is how we use the matter we are given, what choices we make, and how we relate people, ideas and feelings to each other; in other words, how we communicate, how we interpret.

A music paper is simply another way of opening up these choices and looking at them.

For Taylor, though, the new pop fan neither wants, nor indeed needs, any of this. All s/he needs is a consumer guide to the relevant desirables – a style kit.

We may think this an adequate provision for 13-year-olds, but that begs the whole issue of Teenage itself. Should we somehow grow out of pop music, face up to the more 'important' things in life? But what does that mean? Does it mean pop music is an immature way of living, that when you 'consume' pop you have no time or room for anything else? Surely not: surely pop music is simply a part of life.

The concept of 'importance' is just snobbish, and one that *The Face*, the magazine Taylor used to edit, continues to disseminate through the culture of youth: there is in *The Face* the constant sense that, somewhere out there, people are doing more stylish, more interesting, more 'important' things than you are. Suck on these sticks, hicks!

Taylor slyly develops the notion of what is 'important' by turning *NME*'s own legend against itself.

The fact that writers like Tony Parsons, Danny Baker and Paul Morley have 'moved on', become brighter stars in more powerful roles, is taken to mean that they have left behind the unimportance and triviality of pop writing, even though they are the very people who turned it into an art. So that Taylor's argument becomes at once that (a) the pop press no longer requires 'personality' writers, but that (b) pop press sales have fallen precisely because there are no more 'individually notorious' writers.

The implication is also of course that Taylor himself has moved on to something more important – i.e. been sucked into the vacuum of television. (Sorry, couldn't resist sticking the knife in somewhere.)

What I fail to see is why critics should have to choose between being individually notorious or blandly efficient. Scourge or toady: is there nothing in between?

Logically, then, Taylor's argument is that it is quite legitimate for a 13-year-old girl to masturbate to pictures of John Taylor (the capitalist economy of the orgasm being honest pop consumption) but quite pathetic, say, for a 22-year-old journalist to be reading cultural signs from the work of, say, the Birthday Party. Indeed, his final jab at us failed student intellectuals in Carnaby Street is the argument that we clutched at that heroic Aussie combo in a 'conceptual frenzy' of worship and rhetoric.

Now this is something I do personally own up to.

I do recall that, with a little help from Friedrich of the moustachioes and various other junkie polymaths, I did try to convey the impression that the broad future of the Western world roughly hinged on the music of this group. But that does not account for Taylor's reference to the 'embarrassing number of interviews' with the Birthday Party, that we are supposed to have run in the period '82–'83, nor the fatuous conclusion to his spleen, to wit: 'and still they never made *Top of the Pops*'.

Taylor is effectively proposing that if a band isn't in the Top 50, then it is pretentious to write about them. Thus it further becomes superfluous to exercise any discrimination in judging between, say, Culture Club and Duran Duran. They both sell masses, so let's just have the facts on both, presented, of course, anonymously and efficiently.

'The relevant details', 'serving a demand', 'responsible writing': Taylor's terms betray such an insidious conservatism.

'Relevant' – to what? What kind of 'service'? 'Responsible' – to whom?

In Taylor's universe, music papers become merely another adjunct or extension of promotion. If that really were the case, however, why would people read about music at all? Surely not just to discover what aftershave Simon Le Bon is wearing?

As far as good pop writers and readers are concerned, there are people working in music who are doing interesting things, making significant meaning of it. They are using and, if necessary questioning it: making a meta-music, a music about music. This is what Simon Frith called the 'punk vanguard', a line which could be stretched to include musics as different as the Gang of Four's, the Fall's, the Raincoats', and Einsturzende Neubauten's.

To those who write about this music, about 'difficult' groups, about jazz, music is quite as 'important' as it is important for Duran Duran to receive the royalties for *Rio*. Bohn's Germans and Cook's jazz avant-ists are people who simply are not competing in Taylor's universe of pure consumption. They are not writing 'hits'.

What is really insidious about the position of people like Taylor is its implicit anti-pluralism. Taylor himself has already polarized his one-dimensional universe between Wham! (presumably as honest market-force 'pop') and the Redskins (presumably as 'rock' becomes self-important again). And this is surely as narrow as the reverse view, which would, in Levi-Straussian terms, see the Redskins as 'raw', untreated, a voice of truth, and Wham! as 'cooked', synthetic, false. (Before one even begins to dissect these views, both 'Young Guns' and 'Lean On Me' were great records.)

The point is that *NME* no more needs to be seen backing a specific 'party' than *Smash Hits* does. It is a place for the discussion of the myriad details and intersections that comprise a state (always dynamic) of subculture. It is in turn 'telling' that Taylor quotes the bemusement of America's music press at the 'power' of our rags, when it was Jann Wenner, who at the inception of *Rolling Stone* in 1968 described it as 'sort of a magazine and sort of a newspaper' which would be 'not just about music, but also about the things and attitudes that the music embraces'.

It would be disingenuous of me to imply that we do not greatly depend on record companies for what we write about. Ideally, we wouldn't be bound to them, but if we weren't sent records or financed to join groups touring abroad, we'd have a lot less copy.

In principle, though, this system does not work to corrupt. My expense-paid put-downs of Prince and the Talking Heads in America may not have established me as WEA's all-time favourite journalist, but I can still go round there and scrounge free records and meals.

I hope what I've been saying serves in some way as a rejoinder to the position of Taylor. (I don't know what Jonathan Swift would have made of it. I feel that he would not have been very interested in Duran Duran.) What it does not and cannot fully answer is the question of what a pop writer is aware s/he is doing when s/he writes about pop music. Is good pop journalism necessarily something more than music criticism? Can we ask whether pop writing could be different, or better, if we are not even roughly sure what it is?

In a section on the rock press in *Sound Effects*, Simon Frith credits *NME* with a sociological outlook (which may or may not be received as a compliment: Frith originally wrote his book under the title *The Sociology of Rock*, a concept guaranteed to make any music fan run a mile). He claims we are more interested in pop's consumption that in its creative production.

In other words, we do not have sacred cow 'artists' whose development we trace through their *oeuvre*. We respond to pop's social use, its contexts, 'assuming that a youth culture still exists'. Whether or not he is right, the various aims of our pop criticism are still unclear.

As Frith puts it, 'criticism remains confused, as writers seek simultaneously to provide a consumer guide, to comment on a subculture, and to explore personal tastes.'

This confusion tends to result from a writer's self-preening – 'exploring personal tastes' sounds like a generous euphemism –

and juggling these three modes of criticism (guiding, observing, personalizing) requires a very clear head.

Naturally, even in *Smash Hits* there's no such thing as a pure consumer guide – and there are great writers still languishing on the pulp gloss rags – but bringing good music to a reader's attention is obviously a fundamental criterion.

As for 'commenting on a culture', often this is inadvertent, manifested in asides – as it were in parenthesis. Yet once you've slammed, say, five heavy metal albums in a row because you don't like the way they sound, you begin to ask yourself why they sound that way. Hence you confront the sub-subculture of heavy metal . . . in which area I shan't go into the matter of 'exploring personal tastes'.

When I review, though, what am I actually doing besides preening myself and earning a living? When I write about a soul album, for instance, what am I attempting to convey to the readership which – if our poll is anything to go by – is fundamentally uninterested in soul?

Well, given the comparative anonymity, i.e. visual and aural similarity, of many soul acts, I'm trying (a) to distinguish form, as in funk, blues, ballads, disco etc. . . . (b) to give a sense of the production style, i.e. whether it's rough or lush, simple or complex, how electronic it is, (c) to suggest whether the emotion of a song is located in the composition, the voice, the production, or all of these and (d) to see whether the music can be read within a wider frame of reference, such as black America.

These criteria are not levels or gradations (one more important than the next), but frames, contexts, widening outwards like Chinese boxes. By the time you reach the question of music's social function, even a moral frame becomes possible, in which context it is more usual to find writers attacking the hypocrisy or posturing of a white rather than black artist, since rock 'artists' are more prone to pretending to be something they aren't than soul ones. (Also there are a lot more white writers.)

There is, of course, the simple dilemma of musical pleasure, something again which Frith deals very well with.

For example, my favourite 'genre' of music is probably the soul ballad, and my absolute favourite song of the moment is 'After I Cry Tonight' by Memphis deep soulers Lanier & Co. The question is, how do I convey the utter perfection of this record without drifting into my usual hyperbole? Roland Barthes saw this problem the clearest when he asked 'Are we reduced to the dilemma of the predicable or the ineffable?'

In other words, when we try to describe a particular sound, say the voice or the guitar of the Lanier & Co record, do we root out the least vague adjective at our disposal, or do we just throw our hands in the air and exclaim 'God, this music is fab. Wow!' Or is there another way altogether?

Music is hard to describe very simply because it dissolves language. It resists our attempts to humanize or anthropomorphize it. We try to capture it in terms of visible or tactile sensation, yet we can never quite get our finger round it.

As Plato recognized quite a while ago (in Book III of *The Republic*), music is dangerous, not because it undermines law and order (although it can help to), but because it so directly involves loss of self, loss of the ability to put a word to a feeling.

Music is dangerous because it leaves you speechless. Even when a great singer is moving you with her account of a broken heart, it is not the verbal information she is providing that is 'moving', it is the way the language, in Barthes's words, is being 'worked at' by melody.

For Barthes, we predicate, we match an epithet to a sound – epithets like 'smooth', 'violent', 'luscious', 'abrasive' – to protect ourselves from loss of 'self'. Emotion being the break-point of language, of our construction of 'self' itself, we are unconsciously afraid of its annihilating us. Just as a pop critic finds herself being emptied by her emotions, she has quickly to summon a word to stop up the gap through which she is pouring out of herself.

Where is the thing in music that we are trying to describe? Is it, as George Steiner once asked, in melody, or in pitch, or is it in the dynamic relations between tone and interval? Even if pop writers were musicologists and could answer that question, could they explain, without resorting to adjectives, why one voice overwhelms them where another leaves them cold?

Barthes suggests it is possible. He speaks of a play between the rules and structure of a song – 'its tissue of cultural values' – and the volume, or 'grain', of a voice; the way it is forced or natural; the mood it makes out of words, the shape it gives to expression.

It thus becomes feasible to distinguish between Tyrone Davis and Paul Young without labelling the one subtle and the other crude, by observing what their voices do, their stress and delivery, the meaning they make out of received phrases; and this one does with verbs and nouns. So that a piece of music not is but does.

On another plane, what is the subcultural meaning of a Mutt Lange as opposed to a Steve Lillywhite rock production? What is it about these styles of sound that appeals to one person and not another? How does the sound itself overlap with the image its artist projects? And so on . . .

If music, in Frith's words, celebrates the inarticulate – emotion and style – then it is the pop writer's project to articulate that celebration. It is a way of looking and listening which must take its cue from the likes of Frith, and try to see how style breaks rules and how people use music.

Frith's most brilliant insight in *Sound Effects* is to see that problems of description – of labelling – are of precisely the same order as problems of market control. When a pop writer splits groups into codes of style, s/he is simply teaching the music business how to market and predict, how to divide.

In Steve Taylor's universe, pop music is no longer commenting on culture, it is substituting for it. It's a universe where youth sports an identifying badge and ticks off its idols, a universe where pop is dying of consumption.

Pop writing's greatest challenge is to jam the codes.

What the Sixties Had That the Eighties Don't Have

PAUL WILLIAMS

After a seventies sabbatical from the demands of rock criticism, Paul Williams's rediscovery of rock & roll in the eighties formed the basis of the best written 'rock' tome this side of Bangs, The Map. *In this excerpt, Williams contrasts the Third Decade of Rock with its formative days – the sixties.*

What the sixties had that the eighties don't have is an illusion of community. Despite the quality, the richness, the variety of rock & roll today, especially live rock & roll, this absence is sorely felt. There is something incomplete about even the best live shows. The prevalence of people wearing t-shirts with bands' names on them seems to me not so much a proclamation of identity as a plea for it. We hear ourselves in the music but when we look around we can't see ourselves in the crowd.

This loneliness is felt by the musicians as well. They can express their hearts and shout the truth so it bounces off the farthest walls, but what's missing is something bigger to be in service to. Some have found it for themselves, but only a very few – U2's Bono comes to mind – project a conviction that their audience is finding it too. I suppose Springsteen projected it and that's a big part of why he became so hugely popular. But the hunger he sensed and expressed has turned on him, I fear, so that regardless of his wishes in the matter he is now identified as the nourishment rather than the need. It's like you get out in front of the stampede and suddenly everyone thinks that maybe you are the mysterious IT we've all been running after. Express the hunger and we'll make you king; become king and we'll eat you alive and complain that there wasn't more meat on your bones.

For a few brief years in the sixties there was something like a collective illusion, a sense of working together in service to a real and imminent greater truth. We believed we were building something. That feeling was so satisfying that even today musicians and fans alike listen to the music that was made then and bemoan the loss of the intangible Something that made it all so special once. Why can't it be like that today?

The sad answer is, because the bubble burst, the magical sense of community came to naught and blew away, and it's hard to put an illusion back together again. The illusion of the sixties was one of social transformation, a birth of a new community from the ashes of the corrupt old order. The illusion was based on a very substantial (and, in hindsight, accurate) feeling of change taking place, old assumptions and old ways dying and new ways being born.

This did in fact occur, in many public and private realms of human perception and endeavour. But what failed to occur was the perpetuation of a sense of community and common purpose among those committed to ongoing transformation, revolution, personal and societal growth and change. The hippies, the peaceniks, the rock & rollers, the underground and the counterculture and their alternative media and lifestyles were all integrated back into the mainstream of society, and although the changes we spearheaded had a lasting impact, and touched more people than ever, the thrill of discovery, leadership and danger was gone. The sense of belonging to a tribe of great adventurers, caught up in the momentum of a historic time of change, disappeared; and here we are belonging to nothing but society as a whole with all its inertia and corruption and purposelessness again.

Rock & roll became an institution, big business, it even took on a sort of bread-and-circuses quality, a diversion to keep youthful, revolutionary energy inside the stadiums and off the streets. Rock & roll stars by their actions promoted the use of alcohol, cocaine, heroin and other spiritually debilitating drugs, and along with Richard Nixon and the other role models of the day promulgated a value system in which winning, staying on top, and amassing large sums of money were the only things that really mattered.

Punk came along in the mid–late seventies as a response to this, a revolution within the rock & roll ranks, and in many ways it was a successful revolution, the fruits of which are still very much with us today. Particularly musically, a kind of independence has been declared, and rock & roll's creative base has been significantly widened and revitalized.

The music is exciting again, there's a lot of different things happening and a plunge into the world of rock & roll in the mid–late eighties can be extremely stimulating and rewarding. But good music does not in and of itself create community – at least, not the very powerful expanded and expanding sense of community we had for a few years in the sixties.

The closest approximation of an illusion of community in the eighties music scene can be found at a Grateful Dead concert. Not only are the superficial trappings there, such as the common symbology of skulls, roses, lightning bolts, but there is an authentic commonality as well, in the thoughts and feelings expressed in each show and the understanding and response of the audience. I was at a Dead concert yesterday that subtly, indirectly, and very powerfully made reference to the wounding of the earth that occurred in the Ukrainian nuclear disaster, and went on to remind us of the earth's strength and resilience and also of our need to participate in its care. And I know that consciously and unconsciously the message was felt and received by everyone there – indeed, the 'message' comes not so much from conscious intention on the band's part as from the ability of their music to articulate the unconscious collective feelings of the people who are present.

At a good Dead performance everyone in the audience feels a sense of community, with each other and often with the human species as a whole, and in addition there is an actual community of Grateful Dead fans who live in different places but come together, barter, renew friendships, fall in love etc. at the shows. So there's real community, but there still isn't illusion of community in the particular sense I mean. For there to be illusion of community, as there was in the sixties, the scene would have to be more expansive, there'd have to be other bands around working with the same kind of energy and something approaching a similar level of popularity. There'd have to be a sense and an experience of all of us being part of some larger movement, some great rising tide of the times.

This illusion of community I'm talking about has to be inclusive, it has to carry with it a feeling that the great day is coming when the whole world will get on board and be part of this – it can't be restricted to appreciation for a single band, one group of musicians. That's a personality cult, not a movement. These comments are not meant as a reflection on the Grateful Dead, who have been social and musical innovators for twenty-one years, and who contribute at least as much to earth music today as they did to San Francisco music in the sixties, which is to say, a lot. They're a magnificent band. But even at a Dead concert it is possible to feel lonely, looking around and seeing all these people who don't even pretend to be committed to anything bigger than being at this show and maybe coming to the next one if they have the time and money. There is no real illusion generated that this beautiful day in the amphitheatre is part of a larger movement. It's just a Grateful Dead show, and it doesn't even hold out the promise of a world in which there are more Grateful Dead shows, since these boys are working about as hard as they possibly could be already.

Community may mean living together or liking the same band or going to the same church every Sunday. But 'illusion of community' is a movement, like the anti-slavery movement of the nineteenth century or the peace, love, rock & roll and expanded consciousness movement of the late sixties. Music takes on an extraordinary power during such moments of perceived common purpose and activity – it proclaims, amplifies, celebrates and unifies. The i ching says, in describing the great sacrificial feasts and sacred rites of ancient China, 'the sacred music and the splendor of the ceremonies aroused a strong tide of emotion that was shared by all hearts in unison, and that awakened a consciousness of the common origin of all creatures. In this way disunity was overcome and rigidity dissolved.' That stands as an excellent description of the 1969 Woodstock Music Festival.

The danger for people of my generation (I turn thirty-eight next week) and even for the generation that follows us is that we may be so attached to past glories – experienced first-hand or just heard tell of – that we miss the new and different glories of our present moment, as we stubbornly hold on to and hold out for the return of the-way-it-once-was. Ain't gonna return. Ain't gonna be another Beatles. Ain't gonna be another Woodstock. Might possibly be another all-encompassing illusion of community and common purpose, but if so it'll be different from the last one and anyway it's not the sort of phenomenon anyone can predict. What is for sure is that there's something even more important going on right now – by definition, because only what's happening now makes a difference.

What's happening now? Ten months into my journey, my rediscovery of rock & roll, what have I found? What message, if any, seems to be coming through the records I'm listening to and the shows I go to and the videos I watch?

The message I get is a personal one, but it has strong collective implications. It is that rock & roll is a resource, as much or more so today than it's ever been in the past. It is a healing music. It has a unique power to aid the individual listener in the process of locating himself or herself amidst the confusion and complexity of the modern world. In fact, the general purpose of rock & roll now is to allow people to discover and explore their own maps of personal and collective reality.

In a few months I'll be done writing this book about my own recent discoveries and explorations, but I can see already that my journey will continue, that in fact it's just beginning. The most satisfying thing I have learned about rock in these months is that it's not a shallow wilderness. The deeper I go into it the richer the scenery is, and the more paths there are to explore. 'In wildness lies the preservation of the world' – I grew up with a normal twentieth-century fear that there would be no wildness in my world or my children's world, no place for adventure, discovery, the unexpected, the unknown. When I got to college it felt like the end of the line, the end of youth, creativity and freedom. None of the tricks I'd used in the past seemed to work any more – dramatics, school newspaper, foreign languages – and the future looked stultifying. And then I got involved with the radio station, and started a rock & roll magazine . . .

And now, as my children become adolescents and I approach forty, the frontier has called me again, and the thing that amazes me is it's the same frontier I walked away from seventeen years ago because it was becoming too civilized. And I get out here and sure, there's dude ranches and shopping centres and whole bloody cities built on top of little settlements we established twenty years ago. But the territory as a whole has expanded so much that there's actually more wild country now than there was then, much more, and it seems like the more wonders I find the more there are left to discover. Rock & roll didn't grow up to fulfill the particular dreams I had for it; I guess I've been measuring it against those dreams in my mind all these years, and so I figured it hadn't grown up at all. But I was wrong . . .

> The well is there for all. No one is forbidden to take water from it. No matter how many come, all find what they need, for the well is dependable. It has a spring and never runs dry.
>
> (i ching)

Rock & roll exists outside of time, don't let my talk about the sixties and the eighties confuse you. The kids who listen to the Doors' first album or the Beach Boys' *Endless Summer* as though these records were made this year have got it exactly right. One of the disadvantages of the illusion of common purpose is that it naturally carried with it an illusion of progress. If rock & roll was part of this great collective effort towards some imminent and glorious new world, if the musicians and the audience were involved in an ongoing, evolving process of consciousness expansion, then we could and did expect each new record by the Beatles, the Stones, Bob Dylan et al. to be better than the previous one, a news report on how far we'd gotten and where we were heading to next. A positive aspect of this was the way it fostered a kind of creative ambition and competition, the Stones and the Beatles always trying to top themselves and each other. Of course it was ludicrous at times but it also did make them bolder, wilder, in a way it sustained that energy that we hear on a band's first record ('this will get their attention!') so that it kept going and kept building for six or seven years.

It was fun while it lasted, but it also left behind in me and probably a lot of other people a persistent illusion that this year's music is supposed to represent a moving forward from last year's music. To carry this kind of thinking to its logical conclusion, what's coming out now ought to be thirty or a hundred times better than 'Maybellene' or 'Milk Cow Blues', and if it isn't, rock & roll has failed to grow.

The flaw in the logic is this: progress isn't growth. When you're a kid there are these marks on the kitchen wall that show how much taller you are now than six months ago and six months before that; but if you go back to that kitchen at age thirty-something hoping to find out how much more you've grown since you got out of high school, you're in for a disappointment.

Putting aside definitions of growth for the moment, my idea of a timeless model of rock & roll as a whole would be an enormous jukebox with selections arranged in no particular order. Any time you look at it there's old stuff, new stuff, records you love and records you can't stand, current favourites and classics you've forgotten about, and lots and lots of things you've never heard before, some of which are sure to turn out to be wonderful, powerful, written and sung and recorded just for you.

Any time you want you can reach over to the jukebox and punch up 'Fun, Fun, Fun', by the Beach Boys and it'll sound like what rock & roll sounds like, and you can follow it with the Pretenders' 'Middle Of The Road' and Lisa-Lisa's 'I Wonder If I Take You Home' and Bob Dylan's 'Knocking On Heaven's Door' or any one of tens of thousands of other songs, album sides, videos, live performances (imaginary jukeboxes can play live performances, club, concert hall or arena, your choice), and it'll just be glorious rock & roll coming at ya. If you like you can check the footnotes for history, dates, all kinds of neat information (like baseball statistics), but that's strictly optional, the music keeps playing regardless of history, in an order determined only by serendipity and the whims of your head and heart.

And if someone tries to sell you a program that tells you which songs are worth listening to and what order to play 'em in, don't buy it. Only the map you draw for yourself can possibly bring you home.

The Thing of It and the King of Thing

JOE CARDUCCI

Carducci's Rock and the Pop Narcotic, *privately published in Chicago in November 1990, may well be the most important critique on rock music written in the last ten years. On occasions both aesthetically and historically dubious and blindingly myopic with regard to any info which might refute the absolute importance of American rock music, Carducci is also refreshing in his refusal to embrace Pop, preferring to leave by the back door with the family jewellery. His absolute distinction between rock and pop is the central tenet of a scathing but invigorating look at the increasing chasm between the rock aesthetic and the demands of the market-place.*

A band is a tough thing to be a part of. Every band is, in a sense, doomed to fail. Bands demand of their members relationships more akin to family than to co-worker. This means that ridicule and shame born of intimate awareness are always potential; however, the life-long experience at accommodation developed in family relationships is lacking. The work involved in writing, arranging, practising, recording and performing music is also more apt to bend egos than is more conventional work. Each individual musician's ego is on the line to some extent at every little artistic decision. It's more common for the music or the money to keep a band together than it is for camaraderie. For even when that is strong it tends to be quickly overwhelmed by the sheer quantity of time and tension involved, particularly in touring.

Greg Ginn (Black Flag, Gone) who spent upwards of a decade

in the rock band psych wards (let's hope he returns there soon) attributed the difficulty of keeping a band together to the fact that it must be a commune of sorts and most Americans aren't culturally prepared for this reality. Greg's legion of ex-bandmates might say they'd have gladly settled for a communal set-up, but then neither point quite accounts for the fact that Ginn as catalyst did make the whole thing go. It is interesting to speculate on the extent to which these tensions are desirable and necessary, though of course everyone has his breaking point. Certainly it is easy to trace the hatred that developed between Lennon and McCartney, but still neither, ex of the Beatles, did a damn thing worth listening to in rock terms (Lennon's Plastic Ono Band existed contiguous to the Beatles). As I said, 'Doomed'. When you think about it, those double insulated carpet-covered practice studios bands use look quite a bit like rubber rooms.

The variables in good rock bands' stylistic character may be innumerable, but invariably the art in rock music is found at that superheated nexus in performance where each musician, while playing his part in the material, hears and feels and anticipates with his imagination the greater whole as it is being reincarnated. This whole – a multidimensional simultaneity – is at once solid and evanescent: solid enough for a good band to swing with and improvise from, and evanescent enough for a lousy band to never reach. It is conjured up by three or four players like some phantom. It rises in their midst and people will pay to witness it. Any real musician chases that phantom in communion with other players until he dies or the market-place convinces him he's been a chump. This should not be confused with pseud musicians chasing psychological compensations and simple adrenalin rushes.

In other words: 'Rock & roll, the two kinds of syncopation arising from the fundamental rhythm, one discontinuous, the other continuous, merge in an eerie, oscillating stillness for which swing is a wonderfully accurate term' (Robert Cantwell – *Bluegrass Breakdown*).

In rock music, songwriting may be a significant aid in the conjuring, but it's still essentially a pretext for the art itself. Better songwriting and arrangement provide a more fertile base for performance. The tonal colouring of the music's chords and notes is frequently more telling than the tune itself. When the masters took the slaves' drums and left them with guitars, banjos and violins, what resulted was a rough physical approach to string instruments that was also a restless approach as the black players probed and bent the notes, searching for phantom African tonalities with the European scale. The southern white's interest in roughed up tonalities must have originated in the drivingly flat keening of Scottish/Irish marches and ballads.

But rock's use of song is similar to jazz's in that it is not the replication of a song that matters but what jam/spirit can be invoked in the musical use of the tune. A song that in its structure recalls previous rock experiences may better or more easily set up both the musicians and the audience for the performance, but as bands pursue their own musical paths the songwriting sometimes moves beyond such traditionally resonating dynamics. In such cases a band's audience may fall off to just those most intensively interested in music and its construction.

More common as a model for band evolution is the one in which the band begins with an extreme formalism that is both consciously aesthetic and rooted in limited musicianship. If there is real music in such a band a gradual reconciliation with mainstream dynamics is likely to follow improved musicianship and increased sense of security about making music.

A third model of musical development is, superficially at least, more static in that these bands continue to explore the same musical territory year to year, improving in ability but not straying from initial inspiration.

Recent examples of these three models might be Black Flag, the Butthole Surfers and the Tar Babies for the first, progressive model, and the Minutemen, Husker Du and Sonic Youth for the second or assimilative model, and Johnny Thunders, the Ramones and the Descendents for the third or affirmative model.

If there are lyrics to a rock performance their delivery by the vocalist may be a part of the process or apart from it. There is usually some amount of tension between a band's players and their singer. It's usually in part a product of envy but also rooted in musical issues. However, when the sex groupies and the mind groupies both line up after gigs in front of the singer it tends to turn off the players who may have written the music and in any case played it. When musicians let their pay-offs slip from musical ones to those supplied by the audience they are in trouble. These issues vary depending on whether the singer writes, plays an instrument, is the only vocalist, etc. Mike Watt of the Minutemen once mused that the band could never have survived with a vocalist that only sang given the high-strung nature of that trio's relationship. Meaning that in the politics of a band a singer without an instrument is essentially unarmed and out-numbered, and must turn his back to the players at the precise moment their resentments are made concrete by the live audiences.

Joy Division apparently had some kind of blood oath that if any of the four left the band the others would not continue. How new romantic! When the singer Ian Curtis left town for good the others cheated a bit and changed their name to New Order, and more tellingly made a dramatic switch from rock (art) to pop (craft). The name change, reference-wise, switched from victim identification to perpetrator identification. Never has this switch been made and executed by a band so clearly. On successive releases Joy Division had been pushing keyboards forward and guitars back in the mix – sweetening the sound – but they had still been playing a highly refined, yet Stooges influenced, rock music. But rock rhythm was traded for an electro disco one and New Order went down the sophistodance path emphasizing techno tricks and textures and eliminating guitars altogether. Curtis's lyrics had been straight and had emotional content; the remaining members could only substitute a canny, hip vacuousness in their place. The curious thing is that they made the same such musical substitute though no players changed. Joy Division's vocalist was certainly part of their rock nexus.

Instrumental rock helps make clear the essence of the rock process because the grip an instrumental performance can have on the listener is quite different and deeper. A vocalist invites the audience to focus on him and switch attention to the players only during their solos. A band without vocalist presents three or more equal foci of attention. In watching and listening to the players play without the literal distraction of words, and visual distraction of being addressed by a singer, the audience more properly become listeners. Bands where one of the key instrumentalists also sings, such as Eleventh Dream Day, and Lil' Ed and the Blues Imperials, effect an audience somewhere in between and likely temper any tension between singer and the others.

It seems that as the music audience (and Americans as a whole) have become less literate and more dependent on the electronic media, the involvement with music has also become more passive. Instrumental music, other than new age or Muzak, requires more involvement and a higher, more abstract involvement at that. A vocalist is perhaps most effective as the audience's vicarious stand-in for their own response to the music. His clear signs indicating how the music is to be taken aren't present in instrumental music. Thus the less literate or intelligent the listener the more likely he is to require that a singer determine his response to the music. (I'm of course exempting highly musical persons who may be entirely illiterate because they do not make up the bulk of the rock or pop audiences.) And again, a vocalist can indeed be a part of a band's musical process; it's just that too often he isn't.

Regarding exceptional singer/lyricists, this same tendency towards simplification for the literacy impaired can be observed today. Consider the prickly, multi-faceted pop and rock personae of earlier years: Frank Sinatra, Jerry Lee Lewis, Little Richard, Miles Davis, Bob Dylan, John Lennon, Jimi Hendrix, Neil Young. Think of how many records they sold. Now consider what passes for problematic pop personahood today: Prince or Madonna or Michael Stipe or Sting. It's enough to make you agree with all those sentimental sixties' burn-outs about the current state of music, except that their own tastes in contemporary personality worship are just as puerile and two dimensional as their children's. Bruce Springsteen, Bono, etc. Donovan was to Dylan as Prince is to Little Richard (or James Brown or Jimi Hendrix), as Springsteen is to Neil Young, as Bono is to Lennon. Marketing efficiency requires simplified personae just as it requires simplified melodies.

To find today's problematic musical personalities you have to look to the rock music scene (though it's probably filed under 'import' or 'punk' or 'hardcore'). There is where you will find Henry Rollins, H.R. Paul Hudson, Ian MacKaye, Jack Brewer, Glenn Danzig, Johnny Rotten, Curt Kirkwood and Jello Biafra. And think of how many records they have sold. Why, the feebs aren't hardly worth bootlegging! As rock music was removed from the pop world over the course of the seventies, tensions increased for bands seeking success in the market-place. In order to get or maintain golden sales figures, accommodations were made with the pop process that killed whatever rock potential such bands might have had. Thus were born such 'rock' half measures as Van Halen, Kiss, Def Leppard, Motley Crue, Quiet Riot, Twisted Sister, Bon Jovi and dozens of even lesser lights and lighter lessers. And as the younger, hipper males of the metal market opt for the full measures approach of Metallica and the rest, these light rock bands respond by pushing their pop into outright balladry and toward that market's females. This type of band does not persevere year after year working its collective ass off for small movements in record sales figures and concert grosses. They have no musical purpose to keep them too occupied. It is all or nothing (hits or quits) for them. If they fail to get signed or get dropped they break up and reassemble with others of their type to try again with slight modifications in look and sound. If it does click they ride it as long as it'll go, adapting to the pop sound trends as the years pass.

To what end all this activity? Either way these bands' records end up in the bargain bins.

For rock bands resigned to the dim commercial prospects of the day, the usual tensions are present but with some new twists. Without the cash prospects there tend to be no managers involved. In a band's early years one of its members typically is in charge of getting gigs and booking tours. The others put the pressure on him while putting up with his abuse over their freeloading. If this tension and the general poverty doesn't break up the band they may proceed to the point where they have saved or borrowed enough to record themselves. Demo cassettes go out to local clubs, local press, some fanzines, record labels like Homestead, SST and Sub-Pop. Nothing comes of this, and more general pissed-offness ensues. If the band doesn't break up at this point they may collect a small audience which spreads the word on them. In a couple of years they may become the toast of the local fanzine and get a good gig or two opening for touring independent label 'big shots'. They may get a small label to release their first record. It might chart all over the nation on college radio stations and still barely sell two thousand copies.

Despite criticism that he is spending too much band money on the telephone, the band 'leader' may manage to book a hodgepodge of tour dates that cover at least a few cities everybody's heard of. This first tour likely brings them to the point of breaking up within the first week. Hostile and incompetent sound men might botch the mix on cheap PA equipment which could get blown in which case the band would have to pay for it out of the door which was likely shit anyway so the promoter is probably stiffing them on the 'guarantee' to start with.

The pay to play reality sinks in after one week without a motel stop, without a change of clothes, without a shower, with three Dennys's meals a day, with a mad scramble for pot, heroin or cocaine in each new town, with girlfriends back home threatening to jump off bridges unless they leave the tour immediately. If the van breaks down at this point, or their equipment is stolen in New York, it's usually the end because the guy who's booked the tour has to take torrents of shit over all this for twenty hours a day and still keep on doing the job . . . No he doesn't.

If it had been this bad before, the sixties never would have happened. Back then the old Tin Pan Alley show biz infrastructure was still in place. Managers, distributors, promoters, disc jockeys, booking agents, record labels, all tended to deliver at a minimum level of competence (rip-off or no rip-off). This is no longer the case. Even the mob ain't what it used to be. Now new bands are signed to parodies of record labels that barely function above the level of fan clubs. The ambitious labels (SST, Twin/Tone, Touch & Go, Sub-Pop, Taang) capitalize themselves as they go and slow improvement in bands' situations may be possible here. Good bands must survive about four years of poverty trauma to get to where they are getting by rather than scraping by.

In an age of big conglomerates/big management/big media, touring the rock clubs of America in a van is the equivalent of fighting a ground war strategy in an age of strategic nuclear forces. Still, the body count does mount.

Along the road there are pit-stops of hospitality because there are so many bands in the same situation. And each time a band goes round it is easier because they have more friends among local bands and fans along the way. However, the dedication it takes to reach this minor pay-off point weeds out the part-timers and heavy drug users. This leaves the musicians, the ambitious, and the scenesters, those who use music as a framework within which to party nationwide.

Like the rock press and much of the audience, this rock scene doesn't often separate real music from hackwork. As often as in the overground market the underground accepts and defines itself in terms of surfaces: the look of the players, the attitude projected, the speed of the beat, the lyrics etc. This is the single most important failure of the rock underground. It encourages the real thing to aid and abet frauds and con artists in the name of assorted perceived solidarities: generational, cultural, political, social, class and rock. This only succeeds in camouflaging from the beginning whatever art exists within the form, and only serves the hacks (and those interested in disparaging rock music generally).

In rock's present situation as a largely non-pop form, the mainstream music industry (whether it be press, concert promoters, or media programmers) can only use such aesthetically bogus solidarity against rock music. Thus as contemporary rock seems more and more radical and hostile and difficult to the Industry, what little tokenism is offered is typically handed to the fraudulent parasites.

This is why NBC's *Saturday Night* producers turned down John Belushi's desire to have Black Flag on the program but agreed to have Fear on it. Fear were picturesque and conceptually pat. Thus there was nothing to Fear. This misplaced solidarity also contributes to the rock press's instinct to cover many second-hand and third-hand post-punk retreads while allowing the real stuff, musically speaking, to fight it out by word of mouth.

Not that many are really attempting to crash this party. This party requires too much work, too much attention – the full measure. It's the party next door, the pop party, where half-measure scams are rewarded, if the managers have sense enough to buy good songs, if the producer is hip enough to the current charts, if the engineer knows how to use the new technology, if the artist's look can tap into the audience's needs. It's that party where all the non-musical commotion is. The pop scam artist might just as well forget that his manager is ripping him off, his producer's got a tin ear (and nose), and his label's cutting corners on his latest release even as he rehearses stage moves for the tour. He should just go with the flow. Strut the walk. He should snort/ fuck/shoot/blow as much as possible before he's back on the street.

The pop scam is one big bowl of menudo, *comprende*?

There are serious pop artists but most of them are producers and songwriters. The ranks of serious pop vocalists haven't expanded much since Elvis led most subsequent such into the 'rock' music racket.

For the rock musicians today there can be plenty of oh so earthly rewards. Certainly, however, the eighties in total had less to offer than any previous decade. But this hasn't meant that there has been a correspondingly lower number of important rock bands. Art is after all at least a little bit outside of the laws of supply and demand.

Rock's musical reality is an active by-product of the playing of a band. Rock is not alchemy (adding black to white and getting gold), it is transubstantiation. It's not the notes, it's the jam between them. It is aggressive to the point of derailing from its rhythm and is unsafe at any speed. Its special value is that it is a folk form which exhibits a small band instrumental language, rather than mere accompaniment behind a vocalist. It's the place where rhythm and melody battle it out most intensively and in doing so create something more. Rock music is not identifiable by chart position, nor even by sound (say fuzzed-out old guitars), volume or speed.

If we accept that rock music is important as a music, then we must insist on a credible aesthetic definition no matter how insufficient words seem when considering music. Only then can our ability to discern the aesthetic reality of rock music in a pop world keep up with that pop world's rapacious material evolution toward an obliterating hegemony over market and mind.

It is easy to argue about which bands make it with this rock criterion but these arguments will be fruitless if they're simply fights over class/lexicon favourites. The musical criterion shakes out many who are quite ingenious and leaves many with nary a brain cell to spare; so be it. Not all of them that qualify are innovators either, least of all a consolidator such as Muddy Waters. He sensed an untapped potential of the musics of his day. But even in exploring the full musical possibilities of a narrow palette, a Robin Trower has been able to add significantly (whereas contemporaries of his such as Pat Travers or Mahogany Rush were merely milking a submarket). Whether anyone was listening to the offerings of a Saccharine Trust is a different question – not an aesthetic one. Another important point to emphasize is that not all artists who have influenced rock music are aesthetically speaking rock music artists themselves. The rhythmic engines behind Johnny Cash and the Tennessee Two, Captain Beefheart and the Magic Band, and the Velvet Underground, were generally running on non-rock fuels. This is no slight to them; as I've said, rock is not the only music worth listening to. And it's not giving any musics their due if it's decided that everything that is good must somehow be rock music. Yet, who could dispute the influence these three have had on many rock bands.

It is clear to me that there were just as many important rock bands in the eighties as there were in the much revered sixties, while in fact the much reviled seventies yielded more than either. The seventies' advantage was that it straddled both the resolutions of the sixties' progressions, and the punk inspired challenge to the aesthetic late in the decade.

The deceptive element in this exercise is the rockification of pop music that spread from the Chess, Sun and King studio-labels in the fifties to nearly all independent and major labels by the mid-sixties. This allows for much of the pop produced in the sixties to be appreciated in rock music terms. This is what allows for that period's reputation as a golden age of pop music. And it is what has led us to confusion over rock as a music ever since. Rock had been latent in some R&B, C&W, and even pop. Its birth was messily spread across the fifties and sixties and seemed to imply that rock was pop. In truth, these early rock hits were merely the exit wounds as rock left the body of pop.

By 1972, however, this rockification process had ended. Pop technology and process moved on again following its own imperatives which no longer overlapped rock's. For most of the seventies and all of the eighties rock music has existed outside of pop music. In the early seventies FM radio kept a viable rock music economy booming, but this radio also soon began to respond to its own evolving imperatives. These led to the tightened playlists of the AOR format. Quickly thereafter rock touring in the style then common became too expensive to be supported by the sales figures of records no longer getting significant airplay. Record label tour subsidies (contra royalties) near ceased, swinging the business relationship's power from the artist to the record label, and from the record label to the radio programmers. The new success equation required a band sell out to radio programmers in order to get tour support from their label.

Coming off the high times of the early seventies many bands refused to tour more economically in small halls and clubs. Perhaps they thought that would not fill the promotional purpose of touring; after all, they had played stadiums and festivals for audiences of 20,000 to 100,000 just a year or two earlier. Perhaps they didn't understand the musical damage done to themselves by not touring.

In any case, when pop pulled the media out from under rock, bands lost conviction and direction resulting in attempts to sell out, misconceived progress, or in simply more conservative approaches. Coupled with natural tendencies toward burn-out and self-indulgence, it was but a matter of a couple years before a qualitative void was opened up in rock music that could only be filled by regenerated rock forms such as punk and metal were to become.

Punk rock, for those who had cultivated an appreciation of rock music, seemed a long time coming and was quickly embraced and championed. The increasingly commercially designed rock of the mid seventies had left the most aggressively interested rock market bored. And pop music no longer allowed for rock hits such as 'Born To Be Wild', 'Purple Haze' or 'Hot Smoke And Sassafras'. Radio was dead to rock. Journey ruled the waves, and Pink Floyd even exploited the huge audiophile audience made up of fans of music reproduction technology. The modernists bought multiple copies of *Dark Side Of The Moon* in all formats (LP, cassette, 8-track, reel-to-reel, foreign pressings, etc).

The real rock music audience, aside from the white teen males who continued to line up for arena concerts, was part hipster, part record collector, part music fan, part groupie, part misfit. This rock intelligentsia, much of which hovered around the fringe of the music business, tended to overreact to punk rock in direct proportion to how starved it was for the straight stuff. And so assumptions about what punk meant or could accomplish were rampant.

With so many suddenly turned on to rock music again and picking up instruments for the first time, and harboring a commonly vindictive attitude toward the music industry's rock establishment, a heavy sanctimonious cool hardened around an easy contempt for musical skills and professionalism. Countercultural pretensions fed the egalitarian fantasies of the rad politically minded who, though despising society, required a subsociety of their own making to be their audience (read: mirror). Hence: 'Unite Against Society'.

Despite the general hostility to things hippie and sixties, these 'punks' in most instances were hoping to redo the social drama of that decade but in more realistic terms. But the fact that Reagan never precipitated a war seemed to send the rad corps into the realms of the fantastic. Claims like George Bush is a drug runner are after all not that far from Lyndon Larouche's claims that the

Queen of England is one. Bands with their feet on the ground concentrated on their music and, as far as lyrics went, with things internal.

A number of bands (Clash, Alternative TV, Dead Kennedys, Stiff Little Fingers, Sham 69, Minutemen) and fanzines (*Sniffin' Glue*, *Maximum Rock 'n' Roll*) encouraged everyone (the 'kids') to start up their own bands and fanzines. It sounded like a good idea at the time; everyone could sell each other their records, or better yet, put each other on their promo lists. What the hell, dads were paying for most of it. And so was born the youthtopia of One Thrash Nation Under Ron all playing at a style of 'music' necessarily reduced to noise in all aspects so that literally any four numbskulls (eight numbnuts) could bash it out. When pressed, the more serious of the politicos might actually offer that punks needed to be freed from the tyranny of musical considerations. With such a mindset what possible concern could it have been to them if their burrhead minions, in laying seige to the 'bourgeois' separation between artist and audience (at the sound of the bell) made it impossible for the band to actually play their music. Music itself seemed suspiciously 'bourgeois' to them; best just subvert it as well.

Much of the cool and sanctimony preferred by the new independent labels, distributors and bands was a quickly evolved, economically (and psychologically) compensatory marketing scheme. It happened that those involved actually believed they were hipper and morally superior to the Industry at large and thus made good salesmen, at least with the already converted. However, cool and sanctimony work well only in the launching phase; soon, in the maintenance and expansion stages for these distributorships, labels and bands, accommodation and reintegration skills were required. Few possessed them. The real bands limped along the marketplace, but the true believer/movement types either disappeared into the drug scene or segued into the newer boom markets (speed metal, death rock, hip hop), perhaps revealing as they did the negotiable nature of their 'ideology'.

Disillusion built in cycles as each new trend swept the underground scene and failed to resolve the rock/pop impasse either aesthetically or commercially. The Industry's equilibrium couldn't be destroyed or co-opted. Rock music or, more often in the underground, the mere 'musical' tantrums of the dispossessed could not be pushed through the Industry's media to reach the purported rock audience. Naturally that music, conceived in bitter repudiation of the mass taste, was not likely to subvert or redeem that taste. But some of the rock underground thought it could since rock had seemingly done so in the sixties. Unfortunately, much great rock music got painted with the same brush or even willingly fellow-travelled with such would-be bomb throwers.

In time the Industry did learn to take and sell the Talking Heads, Blondie, the Human League, the Blasters, the Cure, Adam and the Ants, Gary Numan, ABC, Depeche Mode and New Order without upsetting its own dominance, or jeopardizing dependable pre-punk sellers. MTV did not serve as the under-ground FM radio of the eighties as it initially promised, but it was able to balance the new Euro-hip with the standard industry rock cool: Depeche Mode and Bon Jovi rock 'n' rotation.

The older folks at *Bomp!* magazine and label (Greg Shaw also edited the *Mojo Navigator* from August 1966) might have known better what punk's significance was, but record collectors do tend to be out of touch with musical realities. *Bomp!* was the power pop standard bearer and featured think-piece after think-piece in the mid to late seventies about how punk rock was going to electrify the pop nation and lead directly to the rightful ascendence of neo moptop power pop to pop chart dominion, the so called Dwight Twilley Scenario. They also specialized in spectacular reaches of rationalization whereby they'd claim aesthetic value for the likes of Blue Ash, Milk and Cookies and the Paley Brothers.

But, of course, it was finally disco, not punk rock, that reshaped pop music in the eighties. Initially it was disco's rhythmic monotony as retooled by Kraftwerk and Blondie, but ultimately it was disco's technological approach as a studio music itself that rationalized the pop process for all time. Disco's modernist materialism easily accepted the pop imperative, whereas punk's ideal of gritty, physical artificeless performance did not. And so, where disco's influences were structural and procedural, punk's were mere spicing, encouraging more dramatic colourings and energies such as of the new metal scene, the hip hop, rap and go go scenes, and the college radio pop scene.

But as rock bands (even punk bands) broach the pop market-place today they are obliged to conform to the rationalized studio process devised and fueled by the disco producers of the seventies. The Replacements, REM and Camper Van Beethoven may each begin by recording their music played in real space and time, but finally they must submit to the digitally processed, computer-driven pop production process and its coterie of human retainers in order to attempt to make their major label distribution and promotion profitable.

Had Husker Du recorded a third album for Warner Brothers the plans were to program the percussion rather than to play the drums and record them. Only rock bands whose slop is a key element in their sound's attraction, such as Motorhead and Sonic Youth, can profitably exist on the fringe of major label distribution without such conformance. But mess today doesn't guarantee against machine-tooled die-cast pop tomorrow, witness the Replacements.

Even today's seemingly radical metal bands, those picking up on early seventies hard rock and early eighties hardcore, are submitting to these discoid processes in the recording of their music. But in their cases it isn't in hopes of gaining radio exposure because hard rock never has gotten that and never will. The high tech pop process is required in this metal scene in order to successfully tap into the young, upwardly mobile middle-class male consumer's sense of what is a quality product worthy of being purchased. His taste in cars calls for sleek lines and lots of chrome; in music it calls for a metallic male melodrama of an ice cold precision.

This revitalization of the metal scene followed the Industry's popularization of the new wave and the limp wave. What was called the New Wave of British Heavy Metal (begun by Judas Priest and Motorhead), yielded arena bands such as Priest and Iron Maiden and the pop metal radio sensation Def Leppard. The metal underground is far better connected to the metal mainstream because, like black and country forms, it is isolated by pop programmers, which tends to internally integrate the genre's scope. This has allowed Metallica, if not actually Motorhead, to fight it out with Ozzy Osbourne at the top of the charts (just as Run DMC and Dwight Yoakam compete at the top of their respective charts).

Still the disco legacy, enforced as it is by radio programmers, prevents a resolution of the pop/rock impasse. The new metal scene, even its underground part, is less conscious of rock music's aesthetic issue than the punk and hardcore scenes have been. This, despite metal's narrowly drawn musical aesthetic which we might have expected to be focused on rock essence. But here again it was largely look and sound style that determined success. Motley Crue and Twisted Sister strip-mined the fruited plain above while Metallica and its less effective alloys commenced deep-shaft mining below.

Hardcore bands like Corrosion of Conformity, Suicidal Tendencies and DRI made the switch to metal in a pitiful burlesque of a section of Black Flag's musical development. Ultimately Metallica, with its canny pastiche of ideas from Black Flag and Sabbath, tore open a platinum-sized market.

This new metal market was immediately glutted by invaders from a parallel universe of speed metal pseud bands playing out the same market-place ballet that the skinhead lemmings had choreographed five years before, right down to the arguments over who's a poseur and which band is more hardcore.

As this point (1990), the underground has largely been separated from its delusions of moral grandeur and is preoccupied with just 'staying alive'.

The punk and metal bands of the independent label underground developed their music without mass media involvement.
This has reinforced the characteristics which precluded mass
popularity and big bucks via the media, but it has also provided a
measure of freedom for those few bands musically inclined to take
aesthetic advantage of this otherwise bad situation.

Radio is hardly worth talking about with regard to
contemporary rock music. Even an exceptional rock station like
WXRT-FM in Chicago – frequently named station of the year in
radio trades for its unwavering refusal to be doctrinaire AOR or
CHR in format – nevertheless imply with their logo and advertising that their programming approach is akin to the 'fine arts' one
of crosstown classical music station WFMT. This correctly
implies as well an avoidance of contemporary rock music. The
leaden weight of past masters (Beatles, Stones, Kinks, Band, Little
Feat . . .) crushes the dirty stinking loud life out of the station's
anemic attempts at contemporary programming. The listener must
wade through yards of Dave Mason and Van Morrison in order
to hear an inch of even the goddamn Smithereens!

In other cities exceptions to AOR or CHR narrowcasting
reflect local colouring rather than any programming vision. So in
college-rich Boston the FM giants add the college radio Top 10 to
their playlists, and in Los Angeles (conspicuous consumption
capital of the world) KROQ milks suburban teens' delusions of
debauchery with élitist, limey fag wave conceit.

Radio has forfeited its programming decisions to the consultant
priesthood which has jumped into the pop cash trail, pockets
open. All of these consultants research the same trade publications,
the same trend stations, the same demographic slices, and they
come to the same conclusions: play the New Bohemians; don't
play the new Bitch Magnet. Since these priests know formats but
not rock music they can only be censors in the most general sense,
pop sentries stamping out the rock heresy. It is a simple task these
days. There is more pop on the market than the formats can

handle, so it is a programmer's market. Record labels must pay bribes via independent promoters to insure the proper attention is paid by the programmers at the crucial make or break point in an artist's major label career.

As the priests kill the faith, radio appears to be tying its wagon to MTV. The visual dimension humours novelty in the form of new faces and looks, and so MTV has been more likely to break new artists. Radio can let MTV live or die in its ratings game and just take from it what works, seasoning it for local palates. The rest of the game for radio is up to on-air personalities and cash giveaways. (While Morton Downey Jr did his talk-show on WMAQ-AM in Chicago the station's slogan was, 'Rock & roll without the records'.)

Under such cold war conditions rock music has survived and, aesthetically anyway, even thrived. Rewards are limited, and even then irrational. Metallica can jump to a major label and go platinum as their music improves, but even hacks like Anthrax sell half that, while Motorhead sells perhaps 90,000. Husker Du sold 100,000, but the World Party sell twice that. Angst sold 4,000 while Soul Asylum sells 40,000.

These figures mean nothing as far as aesthetics go, but it is important to understand the frustration experienced by great musicians in great bands as they watch shit climb even the 'alternative' charts while they are left to wipe their ass with yesterday's U2 reviews.

Inequities aside, a small amount of money can be made after a few years work by a band with its feet on the ground. This can provide said band with a life of sorts, and with promotion of its art to some degree.

No matter how loudly rock music speaks to its audience, it presently goes virtually unheard by the rock/pop culture at large. And much of what is heard by the rock audience itself shouldn't be. In the fifteen years since the Ramones picked up their instruments, the underground has humoured as much utter garbage as the mainstream has. The only abiding truth (value) in this ongoing cultural miasma necessarily has to be found in the specific music created by this or that individual band.

Some of these bands worked hard and intelligently and operated in rock forms more easily received by audiences and in doing so raised themselves somewhat from the market-place muck of imitation, fraud, genre-mining, image-mongering, trend-engineering and tomb-raiding. Others endured without prospering, and still more didn't last, or lasted only on a part-time or local basis.

This stark reality facing any contemporary rock band has fueled the desperate attempts at popification of rock. You hear these in the records of the Smithereens, Dream Syndicate, Georgia Satellites, X, Midnight Oil, I N X S, the Pursuit of Happiness, Concrete Blond and loads more. These are the rock half-measures of the eighties' punklings. Generally the most aesthetically successful such qualification of rock has been the roots rock approach. This approach is heard in the music of Joe Ely, the Blasters, Charlie Burton and Rock Therapy, Joe 'King' Carrasco, Steve Earle and the Dukes, Dwight Yoakam, the Cramps, the Kentucky Headhunters, N R B Q, the Paladins, Johnny Reno, Evan Johns, Flat Duo Jets, the Spanic Boys, Dash Riprock, the Tailgators etc. It is a testament to the fertility of rock's source materials that this could be so after nearly forty years.

The Industry succeeded in fastening its pop machinery to the rock boom of the sixties after stumbling through the fifties when rock & roll was first sparking off of its source musics. The nascent rock intelligentsia of the mid sixties (and the rock press that it became) tried to call the Industry on its blatant usurpations of rock as manifested in such pop careers as Pat Boone, Fabian and the Monkees. But, as the pop narcotic kicked in throughout the pop and rock cultures, the heavy-handed approach of squaresville managers and promoters was soon no longer necessary to the manufacture of pop confectionery. The musicians themselves were quickly pop-wise and quite eager to pull the pop scam on themselves (Paul Revere and the Raiders, Kiss, Journey, Van Halen, Devo, the Go Gos, Bruce Springsteen, ZZ Top etc). The difference that concerns us here between say, the Monkees and the Go Gos, was that the Go Gos were a band of musicians and made their own decisions, while the Monkees were actors who mimed playing 'their' music. The Monkees model still exists in some pop areas but it has basically been pushed aside because it is too much trouble. It is simpler and more efficient for the Industry to just find musicians who are mercenary enough to keep themselves in line. Whereas the Monkees chafed under their manager's rules (the actors actually could play their instruments) and eventually did win their freedom to function as a true band, the Go Gos purposefully surrendered theirs as best they could as they went.

When airplay tightens up, so do pop musicians. The Go Gos after all didn't start out with their lips sealed. Here then is the distinction that concerns us: the self-directed pop artist, even when more interesting than the outright Tin Pan Alley vocalist, nevertheless is not equivalent in aesthetic terms to the self-directed rock band. This given is determined by the disparity in musical potential between the rock process and the pop process. To the extent that the pop artist is able to cadge rock credibility while pulling the modern pop scam, he is a worse threat to rock music than the older more easily identified models of Industry pop hustle.

But our 'rock' intelligentsia doesn't recognize distinctions between the rock methodology and the pop methodology. The critics have become part of the pop Industry (Meltzer cited this development as his principle reason for exiting rockcritdom). Perhaps they are ombudsmen of some sort, but this has proven insufficient to defend and articulate rock music's aesthetic.

In any case, the rock press are members of the mass media and the mass media's true gift is obscurantism. We do not just witness reality via media; we do not just hear stories told via media; we witness the obliteration of reality's integrity (its meanings and contexts). Mass media corrodes faith and foundation. The rock press at this point simply expands (or contracts) its definition of rock to include (or exclude) that which it wishes (or doesn't wish) to write about. On Monday when the subject is Van Halen the rock definition shrinks. On Thursday when the subject is Tracy Chapman it expands. On Sunday when it's time for a revisionist appreciation of Frank Sinatra it is irrelevant. Doublethink? Triplethink? Most rock critics have been writing about pop and rock musics for twenty years now. They are confident in their ability to repeat and manipulate commonly accepted rationalizations. They know how they stand with their colleagues: safely.

They are tired of the involvement that rock music, as an essentially live, performance-based musical art, requires of them. They may be pushing forty or fifty and don't go out as often as they used to. If they do, they hang backstage at the comfortable clubs, not the joints.

And it is generally to see such New Wave of Retirement fare as Laurie Anderson, Philip Glass, Suzanne Vega, Julia Fordham, Sade, etc. They've latched on to the less strenuous (but nearly as interesting) pop world as if it were a life-saver. It is, in fact, a career-saver. Because what publication is going to pay them a living wage to cover all those no name eighties rock bands? Pop criticism requires nothing more than a radio and records. And if you get your records free by mail from the labels you need never leave your apartment (other than to check out that new restaurant that everyone says is so hot). With just a little sleight of mind, this pop circus gets presented as if it were the rock world. And soon enough, once hooked on the pop narcotic, the rock press is dead to rock music. It makes them nauseous.

Through this minefield of cross-purposed ideologies, sentiments, intuitions, deceptions and fashions, rock bands must be chasing that musical phantom gig after gig, tour after tour, practice after practice, sound-check after sound-check, recording session after recording session, in order to have a chance at maintaining the focus necessary to produce a music that rocks. Anything less than that and a band is on the slippery slopes of burn out, sell out, fade out, sham, miming and debasement. Unfortunately for the health of rock music, there are frequently large pots of gold and platinum at the bottom of those slopes.

The retreat into Tin Pan Alley (Broadway, bel canto, etc.) is inevitable when a musician rejects the band format, whether that musician is Linda Ronstadt or the dude from the Virgin Prunes.

These days the blues would have just had an abortion and the Industry would never have been disturbed. But then it could just as easily be said that country sired the bastard. We all know it takes two. However, reading the rock press on the subject you'd imagine some sort of asexual cloning had taken place in the fifties. And given the (sexual) nature of rock music, how could such a fiction be built up over so many years from so many sources?

Well, those sources are probably the most homogenous bunch of personality-type this side of mathematicians. There is no real dialogue within their ranks; there is rather group masturbation over this week's sexy issues.

Let's forget for the moment the political purposes for the press's misrepresentation. Whites in the early years of rock & roll noticed primarily the blackness of the music. Blacks noticed the whiteness of it. But blacks don't write the history of rock & roll. Some did throw out challenges to those writers after the fact, the gist of which were if blacks didn't get their share of success and money out of rock & roll in this racist society's pop market then they were at least due all the credit for having birthed it. (You have to prove ownership before you can prove theft.)

But this has never been proved, only asserted slyly by youthful rock critics of the sixties and seventies eager to please Little Richard and Huey Newton, thereby transcending the constipated world of their parents. The white rockers themselves were mostly pushing up daisies by the time rock criticism was born, and while they were rocking they would not have been likely to champion their country influences. They were hicks high on mobility (and other substances), and the perceived purity of country and western music was not then esteemed by them. (Jerry Lee Lewis for one would later find much esteem for it.) Furthermore, the white middle class of the urban and suburban areas up north and out west (whose interest was what made rock & roll a popular music) knew even less about country and western music than they did about rhythm and blues, and as the future titans of rock criticism were of this outsider/consumer rather than producer class, C&W constantly got, gets, and will get the shaft in discussions of rock's roots.

To deliver a realistic appraisal of where rock music is right now, politically correct falsehoods must be rooted out and destroyed. The only conceivable realpolitik justification for this one ended with the civil rights legislation of the sixties. Even then, lies of charity are of no real help to black Americans in their struggle to understand their culture. Too much damage is done down the line when this type of cultural condescension is taken at face value.

In terms of rock music today and the literature on it, this may seem a trivial matter. There are enormous problems facing any rock band attempting to get the music heard. But for the rock music establishment itself to be so thoroughly committed to lies that the very actors within the establishment (and even the underground!) have forgotten (or never even known) why they were first attracted to the music as music, continually contributes to choking the life out of important bands, thus further leaving the culture to pop confections.

Individual artists (say, painters) may never make a dime on their artistic production and still they can't be stopped from producing. They can and usually will find a way. A rock band, however, is a three to five person unit and its days are numbered to begin with. Make it futile for them economically and you accelerate their demise. Rock music today is vulnerable, not to attacks by the PMRC or other irrelevant bogeymen, but from attacks by the music business itself, the labels, the radio stations, the press, and the audiences they've created.

When the rock press succeeded in floating the premise that whites had stolen the music from blacks, they naturally moved on to suggest that white rock can only attain validity through homage to black forms (Rolling Stones, Gang of Four), or in liberal ('pro' black) consciousness-raising directed at the pop (white) audience (*à la* Beatles, U2, Springsteen).

The problem is that this has nothing to do with music, so in one fell swoop denies nearly all of rock music its due. And in any case, I would argue that it's the appropriation of black form by a Gang of Four and their attempt to 'salvage' that form via 'intelligent' (i.e. left-wing) lyrics that is racist in conception. More importantly, all this subversive conceptualizing leaves the body of rock music, from No Means No to UFO, uninspected and undocumented in the so-called rock music press.

Rock music has to be defined, but our definition will neither hold together nor aid us in reconsidering the music unless it focuses on the essence of what rock is as a music, and ignores the flashier conceptualized fictions. Again, rock music is not the lyrics, nor is it the notes or the distortion of the notes. It is not an attitude! (How typically New York, that one.)

The music is rock when it is guitar, bass and drums at the centre and they are played by musicians who know the language of the instruments enough to be expressive with them while playing hard. It is a musically risky proposition; mistakes will be made. It is difficult; practice is required. With the band's individual musicians each aggressively supplying their element, the sound made together can become more than the sum of its parts. This surplus value is the jam, and if it's there in the performing then a rock band is effecting a transubstantiation nearly as sublime as any priest's. Rock reaches the spiritual by way of the physical; it requires an aesthetic of fully integrated completion. And this takes the listener out of his critical mode, even out of his scamming on girls mode, when he comes upon it in a club. If this music had any less potential it never would have raised such a ruckus.

It wasn't Presley the man that was rock & roll, it was his band. As great a vocalist as he was, it is pure celebrity worship and sociological shorthand to harp on his importance to rock & roll and pop culture. He demonstrated quickly enough that whatever his talents he had little comprehension of what made rock & roll itself. His 1968 comeback concert seemed to indicate his compass was back on true north. But before you knew it he was doing a Tom Jones thing in Vegas.

Presley, of course, predated what came to be rock criticism. He had to make do with the old Tin Pan Alley business and artistic processes then in place. There was nothing else. The question before us now, though, is are we any better off for being thirty-five plus years from the beginning of the music, and twenty plus years from the start of serious analysis of the music? Is there the general awareness of what the definitions are, that you might expect for having had the benefit of so much wordage and tuneage over those years? Is there? Or has Tin Pan Alley, with its emphasis on song, voice, arrangement and production (which as a process is so much more comprehensible and desirable for the Industry) simply co-opted rock music from within while the writers jabbered on about grand concepts like Society, Myth, Hope, Faith, Compassion?

It is only when there has been a significant demographic shift towards youth in the prevailing market (mid fifties, late sixties) that the pop music audience has accepted a full-on rock approach. These periods allowed under-motivated bands, meaning musicians with little comprehension of or commitment to rock music, to produce quite exciting rock music. Their peers, dominating the market, indulged them. Blue Cheer in 1968 could naïvely believe that they might have a hit single (as they did). Pere Ubu in the late seventies could not, and were thereby compelled to find a more serious, durable motivation. (Blue Cheer later attempted a misconceived sell-out via the California hippie/folk scene, while Pere Ubu would leave rock in a reactionary élitist pique, break up, and then reform years later, chastened and shall we say listener-friendly.)

It may seem heartless to critique fifties artists for losing out artistically given the hostile business climate of that day, it certainly is easier and more fun to jump all over those sixties artists who sold out or nodded off, but it's an insult to those who did continue in the face of near silence (Muddy Waters, Charlie Feathers, Mac Curtis, Sleepy LaBeef, Carl Perkins, and for a while even Bill Haley, Jerry Lee Lewis and Chuck Berry) if the record is not kept straight.

If all we hear from the rock press is Elvis Presley and Buddy Holly, doesn't that diminish as well as overwhelm the odd paragraph tossed the way of the others? And doesn't it set the values for rock at the level of pop music, i.e. chart success, fame, sociology, product shipped, $? And once this value has been set, doesn't the occasional critical piece touting some new artist, whether they are real (Flipper), or hack work (the Unforgiven), then fall before aesthetically illiterate readers? Doesn't it read as mere travelogue to exotic subcultures? This is why the good won't sell any more and the bad won't sell any less even when the writer has it right. The press has so compromised itself that it cannot be said in all fairness that image and radio alone can sell records. A more clear-thinking rock press may have helped keep the media doors open to rock music. But nobody listens to people they can't trust.

Rock literature barely exists in reality.

3. You Say You Wanna Revolution?

" I'm glad to see that punk rock is at last losing it's rough edges and
is beginning to display a more considered, mature attitude."

Rock's prototypical aesthetes soon became self-conscious would-be revolutionaries. The emergence of its own Rockspeak helped spark the engine in the revolution-machine and the period 1967–77 marked a series of actions and reactions to rock's new-found conceits. Having come of age, it returned to adolescence and suffered its first fit of senile dementia, before coming around in mid menopause.

Beginning with the Summer of Love, centred on the San Francisco scene but paralleled by England's own folk'n'blues-in-rock-form boom, rock began its mutations in earnest. In the wake of Folk Rock came Country Rock, Jazz Rock, Prog Rock, Soft Rock, Hard Rock – indeed Anykindarock – before the inevitable reaction: Glam Rock and Punk Rock.

'You Say You Wanna Revolution?' deals with this decade of shifting sands, from Richard Goldstein writing about a nascent scene in San Francisco, praying that it will not allow temptation to dilute lofty ideals; through Jon Landau despairing at the impasse that rock music had seemingly reached by the early seventies; to Pete Fowler attempting to figure out where the divisions had begun by examining the stratas of English teen-culture.

Which brings us to the acolytes of punk: Caroline Coon, at the hub of English punk, and James Wolcott, witness to the early flowering of American punk at CBGB, write of a new generation ready to sweep rock's pretensions away, returning the music to some imaginary golden age. Paul Morley prefers to look forward to a new kind of rekindled rock & roll that will endure despite the continued presence of the going-thru-the-motions-merchants.

San Francisco Bray

RICHARD GOLDSTEIN

Richard Goldstein was the first rock critic to be given regular column inches in the hallowed portals of The New York Times *and the* Village Voice. *If, like many, he became disillusioned with the form when technical proficiency began to replace inspiration, his feature on the San Francisco bands came before the Bay Area's own media circus, the Summer of Love.*

The most fragile thing to maintain in our culture is an underground. No sooner does a new tribe of rebels skip out, flip out, trip out, and take its stand, than photographers from *Life-Look* are on the scene doing cover layout. No sooner is a low-rent, low-harassment quarter discovered than it appears in eight-colour spreads on America's breakfast table. The need for the farther-out permeates our artistic involvement. American culture is a store window which must be periodically spruced and redressed. The new bohemians needn't worry about opposition these days; just exploitation. The handwriting on the wall says: preserve your thing.

The new music from San Francisco, most of it unrecorded at this writing, is the most potentially vital in the pop world. It shoots a cleansing wave over the rigid studiousness of rock. It brings driving spontaneity to a music that is becoming increasingly conscious of form and influence rather than effort. It is a resurgence which could drown the castrati who make easy listening and devour all those one-shot wonders floating above stagnant water.

Talent scouts from a dozen major record companies are now grooving with the tribes at the Fillmore and the Avalon. Hip San Francisco is being carved into bits of business turf. The Jefferson Airplane belong to RCA. The Grateful Dead has signed with Warner Brothers in an extraordinary deal which gives them complete control over material and production. Moby Grape is tinkering with Columbia. And a fistful of local talent is being wined and dined like the last available *shikse* in the promised land.

All because San Francisco is the Liverpool of the West. Not many breadmen understand the electronic rumblings from beneath the Golden Gate. But youth power still makes the pop industry move, and record executives know a fad sometimes needs no justification for success except its presence in a void. There is the feeling now, as pop shepherds watch the stars over their grazing flock, that if the San Francisco sound isn't the next Messiah, it will at least give the profits a run for their money.

'The important thing about San Francisco rock & roll,' says Ralph Gleason, 'is that the bands here all sing and play live, and not for recordings. You get a different sound at a dance, it's harder and more direct.'

Gleason, jazz and pop music critic for the *San Francisco Chronicle*, writes with all the excitement of a participant. But he maintains the detachment of twenty years' experience. It is as though Bosley Crowther had set up headquarters at Warhol's Factory. Gleason's comprehension of the new sound is no small factor in its growth and acceptance by the hip establishment.

That Ralph Gleason writes from San Francisco is no coincidence. This city's rapport with the source of its ferment is unique. Travelling up the coast from the ruins of the Sunset Strip to the Haight is a Dantesque ascent. Those 400 miles mark the difference between a neon wasteland and the most important underground in the nation. San Francisco has the vanguard because it works hard to keep it. Native culture is cherished as though the city's consuming passion were to produce a statement that could not possibly be duplicated in New York. Chauvinism in Southern California runs to rhetoric about pulse and plastic, but up north it is have-you-seen-the-Mime-Troupe? and Haight-Street-makes-Greenwich-Village-look-like-a-city-dump.

Ten years ago, San Franciscans frowned on North Beach, but let it happen. Now, the city is prepared to support the rock underground by ignoring it. The theory of tacit neglect means a *de facto* tolerance of psychedelic drugs. San Francisco is far and away the most turned-on city in the Western world. 'The cops are aware of the number of heads here,' says Bill Graham who owns the Fillmore and manages the Jefferson Airplane. 'The law thinks it will fade out, like North Beach: What can they do? To see a cop in the Haight . . . it's like the English invading China. Once they own it, how are they going to police it?'

With safety in numbers, the drug and rock undergrounds swim up the same stream. The psychedelic ethic – still germinating and still unspoken – runs through the musical mainstream in a still current. When Bob Weir, rhythm guitarist with the Grateful Dead, says 'the whole scene is like a contact high', he is not talking metaphor. Musical ideas are passed from group to group like a joint. There is an almost visible cohesion about San Francisco rock. With a scene that is small enough to navigate and big enough to make waves, with an establishment that all but provides the electric current, no wonder San Francisco is Athens. This acropolis has been carefully, sturdily built, and it is not going to crumble because nobody wants to see ruins messing up the skyline.

Bob Weir of the Grateful Dead insists: 'We're not singing psychedelic drugs, we're singing music. We're musicians, not dope fiends.' He sits in the dining-room of the three-story house he shares with the group, their women, and their community. The house is one of those masterpieces of creaking, curving spaciousness the Haight is filled with. Partially because of limited funds, but mostly because of the common consciousness which almost every group here adapts as its ethos, the Grateful Dead live and work together. They are acknowledged as the best group in the Bay Area. Leader Jerry Garcia is a patron saint of the scene. Ken Kesey calls him 'Captain Trips'.

Together, the Grateful Dead sound like live thunder. There are no recordings of their music yet, which is probably just as well because no album could duplicate the feeling they generate in a dancehall. I have never seen them live, but I spent an evening at the Fillmore listening to tapes. The music hits hard and stays hard, like early Rolling Stones, but distilled and concentrated. When their new album comes out, I will whip it on to my record-player and if they have left that boulder sound at some palatial studio and come out with a polished pebble, I will know they don't live together in the Haight anymore.

But right now a group called the Grateful Dead is playing live and living for an audience of anybody's kids in San Francisco. Theirs is the Bay Area sound. Nothing convoluted in the lyrics, just rock lingua franca. Not a trace of preciousness in the music; just raunchy funky chords. The big surprise about the San Francisco sound has nothing to do with electronics or some zany new camp. Musicians in this city have knocked all the civility away. They revel in the dark, grainy sound of roots.

'San Francisco is live,' says Janis Joplin, of Big Brother and the Holding Company. 'Recording in a studio is a completely different trip. No one makes a record like they sound live. Hard rock is the real nitty-gritty.'

Ask an aspiring musician from New York who his idols are and he'll begin a long list with the Beatles or Bob Dylan, then branch off into a dozen variations in harmonics and composition.

Not so in San Francisco. Bob Dylan is like Christianity here; they worship but they don't touch. The sound of the Grateful Dead, or Moby Grape, or Country Joe and the Fish, is jug-band music scraping against jazz. This evolution excludes most of the names in modern pop music. A good band is a 'heavy' band, a 'hard' band.

Marty Balin, who writes for the Jefferson Airplane, declares: 'The Beatles are too complex to influence anyone around here. They're a studio sound.' Which is as close as a San Francisco musician comes to describing his thing. Their music, they insist, is a virgin forest, unchannelled and filled with wildlife. This refusal to add technological effect is close to the spirit of folk music before Dylan electrified it. 'A rock song still has to have drive and soul,' Balin maintains. 'Jazz started out as dance music, and ended up dead as something to listen to. If you can't get your effects live, the music's not alive.'

San Francisco musicians associate Los Angeles with the evils of studio music. This is probably because almost every group has made the trek south to record. And the music available on record so far is anything but hard rock (the Sopwith Camel, for instance, earned everyone's disfavour with a lilting good-timey rendition of 'Hello, Hello').

But resentment of Los Angeles goes much deeper than the recording studio. The rivalry between Northern and Southern California makes a cold war in pop inevitable. While musicians in Los Angeles deride the sound from up north as 'pretentious and self-conscious' and shudder at the way 'people live like animals up there', the northern attitude is best summed up by a member of the Quicksilver Messenger Service who quipped, 'LA hurts our eyes.'

Part of the Holding Company puts down the Byrds because: 'They had to learn to perform after they recorded. Here, the aim is to get the crowd moving.'

A member of the Jefferson Airplane says of the Beach Boys: 'What Brian Wilson is doing is fine but in person there's no balls. Everything is prefabricated like the rest of that town. Bring them to Fillmore, and it just wouldn't work.'

The technology involved in putting on a lightshow doesn't seem to bother San Franciscans, however, because what they're really uptight about is Southern California. There is a sneaking suspicion in this city that the south rules and The Bay is determined to keep at least its cultural supremacy untarnished. Even Ralph Gleason has little sympathy for Los Angeles music. 'The freaks are fostered and nurtured by LA music hype,' he says. 'The hippies are different. What's going on here is natural and real.'

The question of who is commercial and who is authentic is rhetorical. What really matters about San Francisco is what mattered about Liverpool three years ago. The underground occupies a pivotal place in the city's life. The Fillmore and the Avalon are jammed every weekend with beaded, painted faces and flowered shirts. The kids don't come from any mere bohemian quarter. Hip has passed the point where it signifies a commitment to rebellion. It has become the style of youth in the Bay Area, just as long hair and beat music were the Liverpool Look.

San Francisco is a lot like that grimy English seaport these days. In 1964, Liverpool rang with a sound that was authentically expressive and the city never tried to bury it. This is what is happening in San Francisco today. The establishment has achieved a much greater victory here than on the Strip: integration. The underground is open, unencumbered and radiating. The rest of the country will get the vibrations, and they will pay for them.

Which everyone thinks is groovy. The Grateful Dead are willing to sing their twenty-minute extravaganza, 'Midnight Hour', for anyone who will listen, and if people pay, so much the better. But Bob Weir insists: 'If the Industry is gonna want us, they're gonna take us the way we are. Then, if the money comes in, it'll be a stone gas.'

It will be interesting to visit the Bay Area when the breadmen have gutted every artery. It will be fascinating to watch the Fillmore become the Radio City Music Hall of pop music. It will be a stone gas to take a Greyhound sightseeing tour through the Haight.

But that's another story about another San Francisco. Right now, give or take a little corruption, it is new ideas, new faces and new music.

Which is what undergrounds are all about.

It's Too Late to Stop Now

JON LANDAU

Jon Landau's 'It's Too Late to Stop Now' reads primarily as an obituary of the sixties. Yet he uses the opportunity to review the changes wrought on rock & roll in the central years of the decade, when it seemed that 'Rock' could be a perpetually evolving form, before it began to devolve back into rock & roll.

Creative moments come at slow intervals and last a short time in any popular culture. Rock & roll was a distinct musical form for only a few years – according to Charlie Gillett, 1954–8. The years 1959 through 1963 were years of transition, in which the music manipulators became temporarily more important than the artists themselves and in which the artistry of the rock'n'roll years was formalized by unimaginative record companies and A&R men.

Only in the hands of a few independent-minded artists like Phil Spector and the Beach Boys, and companies like Atlantic and Motown, did the music continue to grow. In 1963 the Beatles shattered the dreariness of the music business. And with them came rock, the music of the sixties, and a music quite different from rock'n'roll.

Of the two, rock is a music of far greater surface seriousness and lyric complexity. It is the product of a more self-aware and self-conscious group of musicians. It is far more a middle-class music than the lower-class one that was its predecessor. And, while it borrowed extensively from rock'n'roll styles, it was a fundamentally different kind of music.

It was mainly played on guitars instead of pianos and horns, mainly by whites instead of blacks, mainly in groups of three, four or five musicians, instead of in nine- and ten-piece bands, mainly on FM radio (after 1967) instead of AM, and mainly in concert halls and specialized clubs, instead of in bars and state fairs. To replace record hops, liquor and transistor radios, there were lightshows, dope and headphones.

And yet both were essentially folk musics. The best music in both idioms came from men who recorded their own material, or worked very closely with a collaborator on it. While producers have been important in both fields, the music was essentially controlled by the performing artist – unlike the music from 1959–63. And in both situations there existed a strong bond between performer and audience, a natural kinship, a sense that the stars weren't being imposed from above but had sprung up from out of our own ranks. We could identify with them without hesitation.

As we move into a new decade and the Beatles recede into our musical past, one gets the sense that we are in the midst of a new, constructive period of transition – a prelude to some new approach to music in the seventies. It may well be that when someone writes a history of rock ten years from now, he will identify its creative period as 1964–8. Certainly the year 1970 will be viewed as one of the decline of one set of artists (groups) and the emergence of a new set (individuals, solo artists, acoustic artists).

Looking back at the last ten years, it seems obvious that the atmosphere of low expectation, common during the early sixties, contributed to the growth of many artists who became popular in the later sixties. It gave them time to learn their craft and an unhurried and unpressurized period. When fame finally summoned many of them in the wake of the Beatles, a surprising number were more than ready with their own musical statements.

In America, colleges, coffee houses and independent record companies like Elektra, Prestige and Vanguard became the havens of aspiring musicians seeking refuge from the poverty of commercial recording scenes during those years.

In England, the established music scene was dominated by people even stodgier than their American counterparts. With Cliff Richard's self-righteousness acting as a kind of norm of acceptability, few new groups were even given an opportunity to record. And yet, despite its inaccessibility through records, increasingly well-educated British young people turned away from pop and found a refuge in small clubs where groups like the Stones, Animals, and Mayall's various bands played blues and early American rock'n'roll.

As in the States, the commercial potential of this new thing was ignored by established companies which in turn gave musicians a chance to grow without being hustled into record contracts prematurely. The Beatles themselves were the classic example. It is therefore not surprising that when the Beatles proved the commercial viability of rock in 1964, there were so many groups prepared to follow through with their own distinctive music.

The Beatles established rock with the finality that Presley had established rock & roll. In their wake came two types of groups: the forerunners of mid sixties FM rock, who included the Yardbirds, Them, the Pretty Things, Manfred Mann, the Who, the Animals, and the Stones; and the rest – the pop establishment's attempt to update itself without accepting the cultural changes implied in the styles of the more adventurous and innovative groups. These children of Cliff Richard included Billy J. Kramer and the Dakotas, the Searchers, Freddie and the Dreamers, Herman's Hermits, and Gerry and the Pacemakers. Through the mid sixties these two different styles achieved high levels of popularity.

American groups were often natural but less interesting on stage. Mick Jagger's command of the stage may have been programmed, but it was perfect. Jim Morrison's more spontaneous, debauched style was merely vulgar. While English groups were comfortable with their pop-star identities, American groups would have been considered dressed up if they appeared in something other than jeans. These days American groups are more show conscious, while the English pop stars have taken to jeans.

Through the mid sixties, American rock was defining its own ambience and style. Through the flirtation with folk music in the early sixties many musicians found a unique source out of which to mold a new kind of rock, something distinct from what British bands were offering. Foremost among these were the Byrds, who transformed Dylan into rock more extensively than Dylan ever did himself. Their special talents allowed them to combine the prettiness of popular folk music with the drive and strength of rock rhythm. The results were usually among the best rock of the period.

The Buffalo Springfield had a similar talent and were more adventurous as songwriters, as well. Veering closer to the pop side of the music were the Mamas and the Papas and Simon and Garfunkel, both of whom became masters of the art of studio recording. While a bit too polished and successful to be called underground, the Lovin' Spoonful kept more of an informal image than any of their fellow groups. Somewhat less talented than the others, they were often the most spirited. And, like the others, they enjoyed huge A M successes in 1965 and 1966.

Most of these groups were concerned with attaining conventional success. In later years their music would appeal to the FM audience, but for the time being they committed themselves to the pop process. Other groups less concerned with (or less capable of) obtaining conventional success were creating a true underground: the Paul Butterfield Blues Band, the Blues Project and, eventually, the San Francisco groups. That city's musical development proved to be a fascinating story in its own right.

During the early and mid sixties San Francisco had the advantage of being shielded from the music business people of Los Angeles and New York. Because there were no firm practices already accepted on how to handle popular music, people there were free to invent their own. Ballrooms emerged as rock's first answer to folk clubs, discotheques and civic auditorium concerts with poor sound and lighting. The Fillmore eventually served as a model for every rock club in the country, and it is interesting (maybe even absurd) to recall that there was little regular presentation of rock in New York City until Bill Graham decided to open the Fillmore East.

In companionship to the Fillmore, K M P X started a new form of F M radio in San Francisco which quickly spread to other big cities. In two years' time F M became more significant than A M in affecting album sales and, more importantly, in successfully providing rock audiences with a style of radio and an outlet for music which suited their needs. The mass acceptance by rock audiences of F M, with its superior fidelity and variety, make it clear that the seventies will see the further demise of A M programming. In cities like Boston (W B C N) and Detroit (W A B X and W K N R) as well as on the West Coast, F M stations have already destroyed the primacy of A M radio for good. A new federal regulation requiring all 1973 cars carrying radios to have both A M and F M bands will hasten the process considerably.

In the mid sixties San Francisco was the only city to develop a consciousness about the importance of rock. That cultural awareness was the cushion for all other developments. Rock was not only viewed as a form of entertainment; part of the collective outlook held that music was the essential component of a 'new culture'. The almost religious fervour that surrounded rock in 1966 and 1967 was occasionally frightening. Like the infatuation with drugs, there was a sense of discovery going on that made it seem like nothing could ever be better and that nothing would ever change. Things were so good, who could ever get tired of them?

Moby Grape was the best performing band to come out of San Francisco, although few people in their native city recognized that. Perhaps there was a little too much Hollywood in the group for the new audiences and new performing style. Their first album for Columbia was by far the best first album from a San Francisco group. Regrettably, with so much talent in the group, they went the way of all hypes and spent three years trying to catch up with an unbelievably inflated press.

Janis Joplin, who came to national attention in the summer of 1967, was typical of a number of San Francisco musicians who had emigrated from Texas and the Midwest. The two most influential groups to come out of the city were the Jefferson Airplane and the Grateful Dead. Together, they defined an American style of improvised music that was quite different from the blues bands (Butterfield) that preceded them and the English groups (Cream) that would come after. The Airplane on record confined themselves to an elongated fabric of folk rock. Live, however, they jammed often and at length. Unlike British groups, their jams seldom centred around blues but instead displayed a more intellectual and complex approach that was loud but not hard. The Dead did involve themselves more with blues and, later on, country, but they too specialized in cerebral improvisation.

Both bands have grown considerably since they first became popular. *Volunteers* was an undeniably powerful statement about America after Chicago, while the Dead's *Casey Jones* shows them ready to adapt to anything. Both groups are something of a national institution and are the closest American bands to come to permanence.

In the wake of the success of San Francisco groups, American businessmen saw the potential in this new approach to popular music, dubbed it 'Underground Music', and started responding to what had already become a fact of life for hundreds of thousands of young people. In three years' time they would number in the millions.

During the late sixties, literacy, the first sign of civilization, struck rock hard, first in the form of *Crawdaddy* and Richard Goldstein's writing in the *Village Voice*, and then in the pages of *Rolling Stone*. Dissemination of news and publicity to the new audience became an amazingly efficient process, thereby accelerating the pace of change within the business itself.

All of these new conditions helped to make possible the second coming of the British rock groups, the British underground acts. In 1966, a harbinger of the future occurred. Having missed the boat in San Francisco, Atlantic records decided it had to expand from its R&B base and sign some of the English groups. This led to meetings with Robert Stigwood, the notorious English impresario. Stigwood offered Atlantic a package of two groups. One was put forward as the new Beatles; the latter was forced upon the company as part of the deal. The former was the Bee Gees; the latter was Cream.

Cream legitimized the whole new development with unimaginable force. In New York a new booking agency, Premier Talent Associates, evolved to specialize in British groups, and following the pattern of Cream's success helped establish the modern concept of a tour. It entailed extensive promotion of new releases on a regional basis. In each of the major markets of the country the group would appear at the local club, usually gaining FM airplay (where they would often turn up to do interviews), coverage in the local underground press, and word of mouth publicity from those who saw them.

This last was ultimately decisive. The tie-in between new releases, FM airplay, and appearances in selected markets was successfully used to build Jeff Beck, Jethro Tull, Joe Cocker and Led Zeppelin. It became a formula still rigidly adhered to today.

As in the late fifties and early sixties, towards the end of the decade the formula seemed to be taking precedence over creativity. A group of people emerged, sometimes producers, sometimes managers, sometimes engineers, who understood rock well enough from a technical point of view to manipulate it with above average success. Technological changes within the recording process itself helped to make this possible.

During the late sixties 8- and 16-track tape recorders became the standard of the industry. These machines not only improved the quality of recorded sound but made it easier to program. Producers and engineers, increasingly the equivalent of movie director and editor (or cameraman), have greatly increased their roles in the recording process. The negative consequence is a potential reduction in spontaneity and feeling. Over-dubbing as a recording technique has virtually eliminated the need for musicians to play together at all. Mixing, in turn, offers vast opportunities to affect the sound of the record after the actual recording has been done. Together they make it possible to formalize and standardize recorded sound to a higher degree than ever before.

Cream, more than any other group, established the importance of improvisation and instrumental facility as bases for new rock. They had no talent for and did not rely on singing or songwriting. The core of their live performance material was blues, although Cream was not merely a blues band – at their best they combined that musical form with rock in an expert and exciting way. At their worst, they indulged in a narcissistic display of technical virtuosity. Among other things they institutionalized rock 'jams' and long cuts, and they may well have pulled it off better than anyone who has tried since them.

Jimi Hendrix was the other major artist who helped elevate the importance of instrumental rock. While Cream maintained a detached image of themselves as craftsmen, Hendrix flaunted his decadence and outrageousness in an almost vaudevillian style. And even more than Clapton, he challenged people with his extensions of the guitar into all sorts of realms that had been overlooked, ignored or undiscovered.

The children of Cream and Hendrix – Jeff Beck, Ten Years After, Led Zeppelin, Grand Funk, and Mountain – were outgrowths of blues bands and used blues as the framework for developing individual styles. Beck was perhaps the first to take the more exhibitionistic elements of the approach and turn them into a virtual parody of improvised music. Ten Years After's Alvin Lee followed Beck with a primitive form of show-offishness that created brief moments of excitement and long hours of tedium.

Led Zeppelin has by now become the most popular of all the late sixties British bands. Like their predecessors, they build their style on doubling bass and guitar figures, thereby creating a distorted emphasis on the bottom sound range. It is a completely physical approach to sound that usually works better live than on records. Zeppelin's demeanour, like that of most of these groups, was loud, impersonal, exhibitionistic, violent and often insane. Watching them at a recent concert I saw little more than Robert Plant's imitations of sexuality and Jimmy Page's unwillingness to sustain a musical idea for more than a few measures.

I got a sense that the real mood of the band is ennui. I sat there thinking that rock could not go on like this. There are those who are prepared to buy it now, but there is no future in it, and that is why groups like Zeppelin take it all in now. They have no place to go, no place to grow into, no roots anywhere. And so there they were in front of 15,000 people, going through the motions – their 'act' – in order to pick up a paycheck. Fifteen thousand people sat through it all hoping that somehow their expectations would be fulfilled. They weren't, because, in the words of a fine Bob Dylan song, 'nothing was delivered'.

The changes of the late sixties were illustrated best at the three major festivals that took place between 1967 and 1969. The Monterey International Rock Festival signalled the decline of the then existing rock establishment and legitimized the underground. Out of Monterey came Jimi Hendrix, Janis Joplin and the Who, as well as increased mass acceptance of some San Francisco bands and Otis Redding. These relatively new names entirely over-shadowed the AM stars: the Association, Simon and Garfunkel, Scott McKenzie and even the Mamas and the Papas. One could witness the underground culture at a point of transformation into a mass culture.

The Woodstock Music and Art Fair, held only two summers later, signified the ultimate commercialization of that same culture. A fitting end to the sixties, it showed the country just how strong in numbers the rock audience had become, and just how limited its culture was. It was the last assembly, if not the only one, of virtually every name of any consequence to have emerged since Monterey, and it was held in front of the largest audience ever assembled. After it there was no place left to grow, no way for things to get any bigger, nothing that could be more exciting or gargantuan.

The energy and intensity of interest could only be imitated cheaply, then parodied; at Altamont, the anticlimax of it all, an audience once naïvely optimistic turned rancid with cynicism, a cynicism that was but a reflection of the stars whom they admired. The vibrations that emanated from the Stones' free concert showed at least a healthy sign that people had not forgotten how to be critical of both themselves and those whom they admire. And yet somehow one realized it couldn't be made up: Altamont showed everyone that something had been lost that could not be regained. This past summer saw exploiters and manipulators trying to pull off Woodstocks all over the country. The incompetence of Woodstock, an incompetence (and the resultant spontaneity) which was worshipped in the media, could not be institutionalized as a fixed part of the program by the new promoters.

The rock business has had a bad case of elephantiasis and everything that had been swept under the rug was now coming into the open: the greed, the hustle, hype and, above all, the lack of a long-range commitment to the music or the audience on the part of many groups, managers, agents and record companies.

More and more, it looked like people trying to take the money and run. And when decadence comes into the open, decline cannot be far behind. Presley was forced to look at his reflection in the face of Frankie Avalon. The Stones saw themselves parodied by the Doors. And Bob Dylan must have tired long ago of that sincerest form of flattery, imitation.

Skins Rule

PETE FOWLER

'Skins Rule' recognizes the central importance of the dictates of fashion in English pop music. Though more concerned with sociology than musical critique, Fowler's 1972 feature was one of the first to recognize a fundamental shift in rock music's audience base during the late sixties, even if he clearly does not subscribe to the view that the likes of Marc Bolan were simply returning the music to pre-teens, laying the foundation for punk.

> Of course, the whole thing is a game of seduction between me and the audience. My act is very sexual. I know it. I mean when you've got this guitar between your knees, putting out a lot of energy, strong or soulful music, it's going to be erotic whether you like it or not. I give them excitement, energy and my time. But it's not only an orgiastic exercise – I can be quiet and poetic too ... I've sort of become a rock & roll James Dean.
>
> (Marc Bolan talking to Donald Zec, *Daily Mirror*, 13 April 1972)

Strong stuff from the Metal Guru himself – Bolan is clearly

convinced that he'll be the one down in the annals of Rock History as far as the seventies are concerned. And, more important, everybody seems to believe him. It's not just in the pop press that we can find the interminable Bolan interviews and photographs of the golden boy in his latest lamé-suit – they're in the nationals too. Over the past couple of months, I've lost count of the number of features on T. Rex, and most of these features follow the same corny format – pictures of screaming teenyboppers, a long description of the effect of Bolan on his audience ('And of course at the end of it all a pair of pink panties thrown at the stage' – the *Daily Mirror* again), and an in-depth analysis of 'the unquestionable phenomenon in this year of Pop', usually written by Bolan himself.

This, really, is the starting point in the difference between Bolan-as-Idol and his predecessors. Bolan knows all the answers. There's no need for the Maureen Cleave type of journalist at all because all the reporter need do is listen to the words of The Man himself and get it down in writing. He really does write their features for them. Looking back to Presley and the Beatles, the change of direction is startling. No doubt about it, the Beatles were verbal, but on the question of their popularity, they were dumbfounded. Not once did they come up with anything approaching articulate. Elvis, of course, was even more reticent. He simply thanked God and his mother in the best American tradition.

Bolan's confidence in himself makes me more than a little suspicious, though this in itself doesn't add up to much of an indictment. Yet, other things do.

First, it must be obvious to all that the appeal of T. Rex isn't anywhere near as broad-based as that of the Beatles (or even the Stones) nearly a decade ago. There's just far too many kids who hate Bolan, and far too many who laugh him off. The Beatles were notable for the lack of teen-opposition (they cut right through the existing barriers in the 12–15 age bracket) and their only enemies were the old rock purists who couldn't stand to see some

171

bum English group getting a success out of old classics like 'Roll Over Beethoven' and 'Twist And Shout'. By eliminating an effective opposition, they helped to create a solid, united teen culture – which lasted in England from 1963 through to '66. The divisions that did 'exist' were fake divisions dreamed up by the press ('Dave Clark Five ousts Beatles' etc. or the 'Stones vs. Beatles dilemma'. No one would admit that most of the kids who bought the Beatles records also bought the Stones). There were no real schisms; the concerts given by the Stones in London in '63 and '64 at places like Ken Colyer's Studio 51 and the 100 Club were attended by students from London University, spivs from Soho, and the kids up for the day from the council estates in the suburbs. As the old sign used to read, 'Even GOD digs the Stones'.

Second, some awkward, damning facts. At the beginning of this year, BBC's Radio One presented a new kind of chart on the *Tony Blackburn Show*: the 100 best-selling number-one hits in Britain over the past decade.

For me, this chart is startling for one reason; the lack of T. Rex. Bolan, who claims his records are selling as well as the Beatles were at their height, only comes in this Top 100 at number 72 with 'Hot Love'. This means that 'Get It On' and 'Telegram Sam', the two other number ones T. Rex had in the period covered by the Top 100, have been outsold by several records from the same period; records such as 'Son Of My Father' by Chicory Tip (at 94) and ''Coz I Luv You' by Slade (at 93). Even 'Hot Love', their biggest seller, is nowhere near being the biggest record of the past eighteen months – above it are Rod Stewart's 'Maggie May' (65), Middle of the Road's 'Chirpy Chirpy Cheep Cheep' (42), Bennie Hill's 'Ernie' (36), George Harrison's 'My Sweet Lord' (25) and the New Seekers' 'I'd Like To Teach The World To Sing' (18). And T. Rex, remember, concentrates on selling 45s, not LPs.

The Beatles, incidentally, take positions 1, 2, 4 and 5.

*

That Marc Bolan is a self-made Fabian of his times rather than a Presley, I have no doubt. But evidence for his relative lack of success goes deeper than exposure of a few lies about record sales – it's something of a comment on the way teen culture has split itself up.

In short, it's got something to do with the skins who represent the biggest challenge to T. Rex and the other lesser 'orgiastic exercise' groups. For it's the skins who constitute, at the time of writing, by far the biggest single group among this country's teenagers. In the war for the kids' minds raging between Pupil Power, Bolan's hot-goblinism and Festival of Light, the skins have slithered in and won hands down. A walk through any provincial town will confirm this picture. It's the Crombies, it's the pocket handkerchiefs, it's the football badges that predominate. For every one little middle-class girl with sequins round her eyes, there must be two dozen in their two-tone mohair suits. It's a walk-over.

There are many similarities between the skinheads of the seventies and the mods of the sixties – they tend to come from the same sort of council-house background, they veer towards the same uniformity of dress (the girls drab two-tone suits of last winter echoing the mod girls and their below-the-knee-skirts of the winter of 1963–4), and even, in the spring of 1972, the scooter is making something of a comeback. But there are differences: the skinheads were, originally, a reaction against what many of the mods had become.

The mods were dominated by pop music and their lifestyle was dictated by it. They had their own groups: the Yardbirds, the Who, the Stones and the Small Faces. They had their own TV show in *Ready Steady Go*, compèred by their own representative in high places, Cathy MacGowan. They even had their own drugs, in Purple Hearts and other amphetamines. But all of it sprang from rock. Their idols, their trend-setters, were all from the pop world. 'Faces' was the word they used to describe them. Eric Clapton, for example: 'Eric [according to the first *Record Mirror* report on the group, 30 May 1964] is one of the most fashionable dressers in showbiz. In fact, the Yardbirds in general are regarded as the most fashionable group, but fashion-leader Eric is accosted by mod girls who blandly accuse him of being one of the top faces.'

As the old ad went: 'Everybody knows three feet make a yard, but every moddy knows that ten feet make the Yardbirds.'

If the mods idolized their Faces, the Rock stars in return loved the mods – it was this dialectic that was responsible for all the good things that happened in British rock in the mid sixties. Take the Who, or the High Numbers as they were originally known in the suburbs of London. The *Record Mirror* saw their first record (called, significantly 'I'm The Face') as 'the first authentic mod record', and noted that 'their clothes are the hallmark of the much criticized, typical mod. Cycling jackets, t-shirts, turned-up Levi jeans, long white jackets, boxing boots, black and white brogues.' All those early Who records were taken straight from the mod experience. The guy who sings 'My Generation', Pete Townshend said in November 1965, 'Well, he's supposed to be blocked . . . it's reminiscent in a way, because mods don't get blocked anymore . . . Pills was a phase.'

The mod movement was unstoppable – or so it seemed. The kids loved the groups, adored their Faces, and the groups loved the mod experience. It was all very close – and the result of this physical closeness (after all, you could see all the top groups except the Beatles at your local Big Beat Club) was the destruction of the 'star' mentality. Pete Townshend was no more a star than the kids who were dancing, blocked out of their heads, right in front of him, and the girl he eventually married was at one time in the audience at the Railway Hotel in Wealdstone, just one of the mod crowd.

Once the star syndrome got smashed, things happened. If Townshend or Jagger could make it, the feeling went, anybody could. This isn't meant to be a slur on their talent in any way –

it's much more a compliment. Groups simply sprang up relentlessly. Every week, it seemed, a new group was making it. One week it was the Stones breaking through – the result for us in London was that they left their Sunday afternoon residency at Studio 51 to tour the country. But not to worry. The 3–6 spot at the club was taken over by the Yardbirds. A few months later, they made it. Same thing happened – then it was the turn of Pretty Things. Groups just appeared out of thin air, and the reason for their emergence was the remarkable fluidity of an open scene. The mods were firmly rooted – and so were their stars. Theirs was a generation.

And yet, of course, it all ended. It's a sad irony that it was the mod experience that created the springboard for the first significant breakthrough made by English rockers in the States, for it was the incredible American successes of most of these groups that wrecked our own pop music. The mods were destroyed not by their 'growing up', as has sometimes been suggested, but rather by their very success.

If the focal point of rock in 1964 and 1965 was Richmond (or any of the London suburbs, for that's where it was all really happening), the focal point shifted in the later sixties towards the American West Coast. Rock was taken over by the students. San Francisco was primarily dope-centred, and the music became intellectual and hallucinogenic. Looking at individuals is the best way, perhaps, of getting the whole picture in perspective: one minute Eric Burdon was a good old Geordie rocker, the next he was a wet, weak-kneed stargazer ('When I think of all the good times that I've wasted having good times . . .'); Lennon shifted gear in 'Strawberry Fields Forever', a far cry from 'Eight Days A Week'. And Peter Townshend went from 'My Generation' to the idea of a Rock Opera, which eventually emerged in 1969. However much the Sunday papers might latch on to the 'significance' of *Tommy*, Townshend must know deep down that 'My Generation' had far, far more of an impact on the kids than anything he's done this side of 'Substitute'. Similarly, Stevie Winwood's maximum point of impact wasn't with Blind Faith or even Traffic – it was with 'Keep On Running' and 'Gimme Some Lovin'.

1967 was the great divide for rock. The mods lost their Faces to the new hippie movement. They were absorbed elsewhere. The golden age of 1967–8 was not so golden for everybody. Eddie is a 20-year-old apprentice in Birmingham – he remembers 1967 as being something quite different:

'I was 15 in '67, and all I remember is what a drag it all was. One minute we had the Spencer Davis Group playing here, and the Stones played here a lot, and the Yardbirds and the Animals. Then suddenly – nothing. Nothing at all. I hated fucking *Sgt Pepper* and that thing the Stones did with "She's A Rainbow" on it. Me and my mates spent most of the time in the pub after that. I mean, you could hardly dance to the Pink Floyd, could you?'

Nik Cohn is the only rock writer I've ever read who came close to the truth of that year. He was afraid of *Sgt Pepper* and rightly so. Rock became highly regarded by all the 'right' people. Rock columns suddenly appeared in the *Observer* and the posh weeklies. It became (dare I say it?) middle class by default. And, once this absorption took place, rock lost much of its strength and much of its popularity. The old Faces were much richer; they'd made it in the States after all. They had no need to tour round the dingy old clubs any more. Besides, who could afford them anyway? In effect, they became stars – or superstars, as they preferred to be called. They found their level, and it was a level divorced from those who had made their success possible in the first instance. Listen to this:

Both in the East and in the West music was separated into two forms. One was court music to entertain the aristocrats. The other was folk songs, sung by the people to express their emotions and their political feelings. But lately, the folk music of the age, Pop Song, is becoming intellectualized and is starting to lose its original meaning and function. Pop is supposed to stimulate people in the audience to think, 'Oh, it's so simple, even I could do that.' It should not alienate the audience with its professionalism but communicate to the audience the fact that they, the audience, can be just as creative as those on stage, and encourage them to make their own music with the performers rather than just sit back and applaud.

Sad, really, that that perfect summary of what I've been groping to say should have come from Yoko Ono (in *Rolling Stone*, 17 February 1972). For it was Lennon and the other Beatles who lost contact somewhere back in the late sixties: they became court musicians.

And, going back to good old Tony Blackburn's Top 100, it's all in writing. 'She Loves You' is at number 1, 'I Want To Hold Your Hand' is at number 2, and 'Can't Buy Me Love' is at number 4.

'All You Need Is Love', though, is at 53 and 'Eleanor Rigby' at 59. For all those who thought that the Beatles were the saviours of rock, there were at least twice as many who thought John Lennon was going round the twist.

In 1969, the backlash started. It had to happen sometime: once the star idea was reborn, once the gaps arose between artist and performer, once the focal point of the new culture became rooted in the States, the time was ripe for change. The skinheads came from the same areas that had witnessed the rise of the mods – the East End of London and the outer ring of suburbs. But whereas the mod had seen his 'enemy' as the rocker, and had rationalized his life style accordingly (Cleanliness vs. Grease; Scooter vs. Motor Bike; Pills vs. Booze), the new skinheads reacted against the hippies. Their hair was short to the point of absurdity, they were tough and went around in their 'bovver boots' for the express purpose of beating hell out of any deviants, and they wore braces. Braces! For God's sake, some sort of weird throwback to the thirties.

At Hyde Park in July 1969, they showed their strength. According to Geoffrey Cannon's report on the event, a free concert given by the Stones, it was 'A Nice Day in the Park'. It was things 'nice' that the skins objected to. John Peel and the other beautiful people saw everything as being 'really nice' – the skins wanted others to see them as really horrible.

The concert was odd. Here were the Rolling Stones, the old mod idols, being defended by the Hell's Angels, the descendants of the old rockers, and the whole scene was laughed at by the new skinheads, who were the true descendants of the old mods. After all, it seems likely that most of their elder brothers and sisters had spent their teens down Soho getting blocked on a Saturday night. The wheel had come full circle.

Since that concert, we've learnt to live with the skinheads. They have the same austerity of style as the early mods, and they hunt in packs like the mods tracked down the rockers on the beaches of Margate and Clacton.

Though their style has been determined to a large extent by their opposition to the hippies, other factors have played a crucial role and, in particular, the impact of the West Indian community. Many of the skin gangs have West Indians not only in the group but actually leading them, the short hairstyle having been, without doubt, lifted from the old Blue Beat days in the London clubs.

In Birmingham, a city with a large immigrant community, the pattern is especially evident. The skins will still profess to hate the niggers, but by 'niggers' they generally mean the Pakistanis. Their hatred of the Pakkis might appear crazily illogical in the light of their friendship with the West Indians, but there is a certain, cruel logic about it.

The logic of their hatred is this: the West Indian kids are mixing, and their influence is taking hold. They are beginning to

178

see this country as their home. The Indians and Pakistanis keep themselves to themselves and in Birmingham interaction between white working class and Asian is non-existent. To put it another way, the Indians and the Pakistanis are aspiring (if they are aspiring towards anything whilst they're living here) towards a middle-class set of values. They dress in carefully tailored suits, they are polite, they are nice. The West Indian kids on the other hand are more 'normal' in the skins' eyes. They get drunk, they like dancing, they like dressing up in skingear. They are willing to join forces.

There's nothing nice about the skins. And likewise there's nothing nice about their taste in music. They completely reject the music of the counter-culture. Nothing is more loathsome to them than the junk of progressive rock. Music is for dancing to. Music is for getting off with birds to. And the best music for that, they have decided, is reggae and Tamla Motown. Their love of this twin spearhead is, of course, a direct legacy of the impact of the West Indians in the late sixties. But their idolization of this music should not be mixed up with the mods' relationship to their Faces – it's something quite different. For the new relationship is essentially *impersonal*, whereas the mods related to a set of individual Faces, like Steve Marriott or Rod the Mod Stewart. The skins relate to *types* of music, like Motown. The Four Tops, to take an example, are not revered for being the Four Tops; they are simply one aspect of the Motown machine. If T. Rex has any appeal with this audience, it's on this same impersonal level, a brand name for formula-produced dance records.

Moreover, there's the question of distancing. A group like the Kinks could be seen 'live' every week somewhere round the country because the central factor of the mod-music scene was the live club appearance. The skins tend more towards discos, mainly because there are so few British groups they like.

The result of this has been important. Music is still important to the skins, but it's not of such overriding importance as it was for the mods. Music, it has been argued, was central to the mod experience. It dictated style. For the skinheads, music has become peripheral: style is in no way determined by it. If the skins do have Faces, they are elsewhere. They are out there playing on the football field.

'Only a few weeks ago, Charlie George scored an important goal at Derby, and then ruined the goal and dragged Arsenal's mighty name through the mud by facing the County crowd and jolting them with a double V-sign . . .' (Iain Mackenzie, the *Observer*, March 1972).

When the skins root for Charlie George at Highbury – they are rooting for themselves. For Charlie is simply one of them who's happened to make it out there on the stage. They hate the opposition, and so does Charlie. They adore him for his V-signs and his tantrums, just as they adore kicking in the teeth of an enemy fan.

Linking this with pop is interesting, for analogies suggest themselves with ease. Watching Charlie George at Highbury is, for the skins, much the same experience as watching the Who at the Railway Hotel in Wealdstone was for the mods. Or, to cross the Atlantic, the same experience as watching Johnny Cash at San Quentin was for the prison inmates. They are all watching their equals acting out their fantasies. And they can all hold on to these fantasies because those 'stars' on the stage are just the same as they are.

And this, for the skinheads, is the great difference between them and the mods. Their point of reference is different. The mods were inextricably tied up with pop. The skins are inextricably linked with soccer.

Before we ever heard of skinheads, we all knew about football hooligans – but it's only in the last three or four years that the problem has come through with any force. And this is simply because the area of 'play' for deviant teenyboppers has changed.

*

180

The skins have changed a lot since that first major public appearance at Hyde Park in 1969. The braces and the cropped hair gave way to the two-tone Trevira suits, and these in turn have given way to Crombies, and – for the girls – Oxford bags and check jackets. But their attitude to music hasn't changed that much, nor has their attitude to football. On most Crombie jackets, there is the obligatory football club badge, as central to the skins' uniform as a pocket handkerchief. But on none of their clothes is there any sign of pop worship.

This, really, is why Marc Bolan isn't as popular as he likes to make out. He's made no positive impression on the skins at all. Bolan is popular and it would be silly to completely write him off – after all, he has had four number ones on the trot – but the basis for his support is very narrowly confined. To be accurate, Marc Bolan is idolized by grammar school girls between the ages of eleven and fourteen (the skins, who might buy T. Rex records to dance to, don't idolize or identify with Bolan at all).

Other groups win support from this 'teenybopper' area and Slade are the best example. Slade, it might be remembered, were, at one time, a skinhead group, though if they ever were really skins I don't know. But it is a fact that they no longer enjoy much support from that area, if they ever did.

Meanwhile, although previous generation groups like the Stones and the Who can still fill a hall wherever they play, their support is not growing. It's a constant factor; those who have stayed with them through their changes over the past five years aren't giving them up, and they could still fill any of their old haunts if they so desired. But they're winning no new fans, and probably haven't for the last three or four years.

If this analysis is correct, then the rock perspective that exists is hopelessly out of balance, and has been for some time.

Together, these factors have helped perpetuate the skins' alienation from pop.

There have been signs, becoming increasingly evident these past few months, of a change of direction by some of the skinhead girls – two stars in particular have catapulted to superstar/idol status. At the moment of writing, Donny Osmond is at number 1 in the charts with 'Puppy Love', and David Cassidy at number 2 (with the Partridge Family) with 'Breaking Up Is Hard To Do'.

It's appropriate that both of these songs are old fifties' material and that the 'new' treatments given them are in essence no different than the original treatment given in the fifties by Paul Anka and Neil Sedaka: appropriate because the relationship between the fans with their idols is very close to that of parallel fifties' relationships. When some of the skinhead girls have finally latched on to pop idols, they have done it in such a way as to completely invalidate the British sixties experience – there is no greater proof of the ephemeral success of the Beatles era than the idolization of pretty boys like Cassidy and Osmond.

But the boys that these girls go around with – rather than the images they idolize – remain outside the pop experience, and it's this that strikes at the heart of rock. The bovver boys look like becoming the first major subcultural group not to produce any major rock stars! They, for rock, are the lost generation.

The survival of rock has depended on its position as the core of Male Teen Culture. But the bovver boys have rejected rock's traditional status. Which explains the lack of vitality in British rock in the early seventies.

A Conservative Impulse in the New Rock Underground

JAMES WOLCOTT

Despite happening within spitting distance of their own brownstone, New York's cultural weekly, Village Voice, *was surprisingly slow to write about the scene converging on CBGB, a seedy Bowery dive, home to the most exciting local scene in the seventies pre-punk milieu. CBGB's 1975 summer festival of unsigned bands finally convinced the* Voice *to send down a journalist.*

Arabian swelter, and with the air-conditioning broken, CBGB resembled some abbatoir of a kitchen in which a bucket of ice is placed in front of a fan to cool the room off. To no avail of course, and the heat had perspiration glissading down the curve of one's back, yeah, and the cruel heat also burned away any sense of glamour. After all, CBGB's Bowery and Bleeker location is not the garden spot of lower Manhattan, and the bar itself is an uneasy oasis. On the left, where the couples are, tables; on the right, where the stragglers, drinkers and love-seekers are, a long bar; between the two, a high double-backed ladder which, when the room is really crowded, offers the best view. If your bladder sends a distress signal, write home to your mother, for you must make a perilous journey down the aisle between seating area and bar, not knock over any mike stands as you slide by the tiny stage, squeeze through the piles of amplifiers, duck the elbow thrust of a pool player leaning over to make a shot . . . and then you end up in an illustrated bathroom which looks like a page that didn't make *The Faith of Graffiti*.

Now consider the assembly-line presentation of bands, with resonant names like Movies, Tuff Darts, Blondie, Stagger Lee, the Heartbreakers, Mink de Ville, Dancer, the Shirts, Bananas, Talking Heads, Johnny's Dance Band and Television; consider that some nights as many as six bands perform, and it isn't hard to comprehend someone declining to sit through a long evening. When the air gets thick with noise and smoke, even the most committed of us long to slake our thirst in front of a Johnny Carson monologue, the quintessential experience of bourgeois cool.

So those who stayed away are not to be chastised, except for a lack of adventurousness. And yet they missed perhaps the most important event in New York rock since the Velvet Underground played the Balloon Farm: CBGB's three-week festival of the best underground (i.e. unrecorded) bands. The very unpretentiousness of the bands' style of musical attack represented a counter-thrust to the prevailing baroque theatricality of rock. In opposition to that theatricality, this was a music which suggested a resurgence of communal faith.

So this was an event of importance but not of flash. Hardly any groupies or bopperettes showed up, nor did platoons of rock writers with their sensibilities tuned into Radio Free Zeitgeist brave the near satanic humidity. When the room was packed, as it often was, it was packed with musicians and their girlfriends, couples on dates, friends and relatives of band members, and CBGB regulars, all dressed in denims and loose-fitting shirts satorial-style courtesy of Canal Jeans. The scenemakers and chic-obsessed were elsewhere.

Understandable. Rock simply isn't the brightest light in the pleasure dome any longer (my guess is that dance is), and Don Kirschner's *Rock Awards* only verifies the obvious: rock is getting as arthritic, or at least as phlegmatic, as a rich old whore. It isn't only that the enthusiasm over the Stones tour seemed strained and synthetic, or that the Beach Boys can't seem able to release new material until Brian Wilson conquers his weight problem, or that the album of the year is a collection of basement tapes made in 1967. 'The real truth as I see it,' said the Who's Pete Townshend recently, 'is that rock music as it was is not really contemporary to these times. It's really the music of yesteryear.'

He's right and yet wrong. What's changed is the nature of the impulse to create rock. No longer is the impulse revolutionary – i.e. the transformation of oneself and society – but conservative: to carry on the rock tradition. To borrow from Eliot, a rocker now needs a historical sense; he performs 'not merely with his own generation in his bones' but with the knowledge that all of pop culture forms a 'simultaneous order'. The landscape is no longer virginal – markers and tracks have been left by, among others, Elvis, Buddy Holly, Chuck Berry and the Beatles – and it exists not to be transformed but cultivated.

No, I'm not saying that everyone down at CBGB is a farmer. Must you take me so literally? But there is original vision there, and what the place itself is doing is quite extraordinary: putting on bands as if the stage were a cable TV station. Public access rock. Of course, not every band which auditions gets to play, but the proprietor, Hilly, must have a wide latitude of taste since the variety and quality of talent ranges from the great to the God-condemned. As with cable TV, what you get is not high-gloss professionalism but talent still working at the basics; the excitement (which borders on comedy) is watching a band with a unique approach try to articulate its vision and still remember the chords.

Television was once such a band; the first time I saw them everything was wrong – the vocals were too raw, the guitar work was relentlessly bad, the drummer wouldn't leave his cymbals alone. They were lousy all right but their lousiness had a forceful dissonance reminiscent of the Stones' *Exile On Main Street*, and clearly Tom Verlaine was a presence to be reckoned with.

He has frequently been compared to Lou Reed in the Velvet days, but he most reminds me of Keith Richard. The blood-drained bone-weary Keith on stage at Madison Square Garden is the perfect symbol for Rock '75, not playing at his best, sometimes not even playing competently, but rocking, swaying back and forth as if the night might be his last and it's better to stand than fall. Though Jagger is dangerously close to becoming Maria Callas, Keith, with his lanky grace and obsidian-eyed menace, is the perpetual outsider. I don't know any rock lover who doesn't love Keith; he's the star who's always at the edge and yet occupies the centre.

Tom Verlaine occupies the same dreamy realm, like Keith he's pale and aloof. He seems lost in a forest of silence and he says about performing that 'if I'm thinking up there, I'm not having a good night'. Only recently has the band's technique been up to Verlaine's reveries and their set at the CBGB festival was the best I've ever seen; dramatic, tense, tender ('Hard On Love'), athletic ('Kingdom Come'), with Verlaine in solid voice and the band playing as a band and not as four individuals with instruments. Verlaine once told me that one of the best things about the Beatles was the way they could shout out harmonies and make them sound intimate, and that's what Television had that night: loud intimacy.

When Tom graduated from high school back in Delaware he was voted 'most unknown' by his senior class. As if in revenge, he chose the name Verlaine, much as Patti Smith often invokes the name Rimbaud. He came to New York, spent seven years writing fiction, formed a group called Neon Boys, then Television. The name suggests an aesthetic of accessibility and choice. It also suggests Tom's adapted initials: T. V.

'I left Delaware because no one wanted to form a band there,' he says. 'Then I came to New York and no one wanted to form a band here either.' Verlaine came to New York for the same reason every street-smart artist comes to New York – because it's the big league – even though he realizes 'New York is not a great rock & roll town.'

Still, they continue to arrive: Martina Weymouth, born in California; Chris Frantz, drummer, in Kentucky; David Byrne, singer and guitarist, Scotland. All attended the Rhode Island School of Design, and according to their bio, are 'now launching career in New York' – a sonorous announcement, yes?

These people call themselves Talking Heads. Seeing them for the first time is transfixing: Frantz is so far back on drums that it sounds as if he's playing in the next room; Weymouth, who could pass as Suzi Quatro's sorority sister, stands rooted to the floor, her head doing an oscillating-fan swivel; the object of her swivel is David Byrne, who has a little-boy-lost-at-the-zoo voice and the demeanour of someone who's spent the last half-hour whirling around in a spin-drier. When his eyes start ping-ponging in his head, he looks like a cartoon of a chipmunk from Mars. The song titles aren't tethered to conventionality either: 'Psycho Killer' (which goes, 'Psycho killer, qu'est-ce c'est? Fa-fa-fa-fa-fa-fa-fa'), 'The Girls Want To Be With The Girls', 'Love Is Like A Building On Fire', plus a cover version of that schlock classic by ? and the Mysterians, '96 Tears'.

Love at first sight it isn't.

But repeated viewings (precise word) reveal Talking Heads to be one of the most intriguingly off-the-wall bands in New York. Musically, they're minimalists: Byrne's guitar playing is like a charcoal pencil scratching a scene on a note pad. The songs are spined by Weymouth's bass playing which, in contrast to the glottal buzz of most rock bass work, is hard and articulate – the bass lines provide hook as well as bottom. Visually, the band is perfect for the cable-TV format at CBGB; they present a clean, flat image, devoid of fine shading and colour. They are consciously anti-mythic in stance. A line from their bio: 'The image we present along with our songs is what we are really like.'

Talking to them, it becomes apparent that though they deny antecedents – 'We would rather advance a "new" sound rather than be compared to bands of the past' – they are children of the communal rock ethic. They live together, melting the distinction between art and life, and went into rock because as art it is more 'accessible'. They have an astute sense of aesthetic consumerism, yet they're not entirely under the Warholian sway, for as one of them told me, 'We don't want to be famous for the sake of being famous.' Of all the groups I've seen at CBGB, Talking Heads is the closest to a neo-Velvet band, and they represent a distillation of that sensibility, what John Cale once called 'controlled distortion'. When the Velvets made their reputation at the Balloon Farm, they were navigating through a storm of multi-media effects; mirrors, blinking lights, strobes, projected film images. Talking Heads works without paraphernalia in a cavernous room projecting light like a television located at the end of a long dark hall. The difference between the Velvets and Talking Heads is the difference between phosphorescence and cold gray TV light. These people understand that an entire generation has grown up on the nourishment of television's accessible banality. What they're doing is presenting a banal façade under which run ripples of violence and squalls of frustration – the id of the vid.

David Byrne sings tonelessly but its effect is all the more ominous. This uneasy alliance between composure and breakdown – between outward acceptance and inward coming-apart – is what makes Talking Heads such a central seventies band.

A quote from ex-Velvet John Cale: 'What we try to get here [at the Balloon Farm] is a sense of total involvement.' 1966. But what bands like Television and Talking Heads are doing is ameliorating the post-sixties hangover by giving us a sense of detachment.

We've passed through the Dionysian storm and now it's time to nurse private wounds. Says Tina Weymouth, quite simply: 'Rock isn't a noble cause.'

The Ramones recently opened at a Johnny Winter concert and had to dodge flying bottles. During one of their CBGB sets, they had equipment screw-ups and Dee Dee Ramone stopped singing and gripped his head as if he were going to explode and Tommy Ramone smashed the cymbal shouting, 'What the FUCK'S wrong?' They went off-stage steaming, then came back and ripped into 'Judy Is A Punk'. A killer band.

'Playing with a band is the greatest way of feeling alive,' says Tom Verlaine. But the pressures in New York against such an effort – few places to play, media indifference, the compulsively upward pace of city life – are awesome. Moreover, the travails of a rock band are rooted in a deeper problem: the difficulty of collaborative art. Rock bands flourished in the sixties when there was a genuine faith in the efficacious beauty of communal activity, when the belief was that togetherness meant strength. It was more than a matter of 'belonging'; it meant that one could create art with friends. Playing with a band meant art with sacrifice, but without suffering. Romantic intensity without Romantic solitude.

What CBGB is trying to do is nothing less than to restore that spirit as a force in rock & roll. One is left speculating about success: will any of the bands who play there ever amount to anything more than a cheap evening of rock & roll? Is public access merely an attitude to be discarded once stardom seems possible, or will it sustain itself beyond the first recording contract? I don't know, and in the deepest sense, don't care. These bands don't have to be the vanguard in order to satisfy. In a cheering Velvets song, Lou Reed sings: 'A little wine in the morning, and some breakfast at night. Well, I'm beginning to see the light.' And that's what rock gives: small unconventional pleasures which lead to moments of perception.

Rebels Against the System

CAROLINE COON

Contrasting the fledgling English punk scene with its more established New York cousin, Coon details punks' rejection of rock's heritage, correctly outlining the potential for combustion that the likes of the Pistols and the Clash were not-so-quietly amassing.

Johnny Rotten looks bored. The emphasis is on the word 'looks' rather than, as Johnny would have you believe, the word 'bored'. His clothes, held together by safety pins, fall around his slack body in calculated disarray. His face is an undernourished grey. Not a muscle moves. His lips echo the downward slope of his wiry, coat-hanger shoulders. Only his eyes register the faintest trace of life.

Johnny works very hard at looking bored. Leaning against a bar; at a sound-check; after a gig; making an entrance to a party; on-stage; when he's with women. No actually, then he's inclined to look quite interested.

Why is Johnny bored? Well, that's the story.

This malevolent, third generation child of rock & roll is the Sex Pistols' lead singer. The band play exciting, hard, basic punk rock. But more than that, Johnny is the elected generalissimo of a new cultural movement scything through the grass-roots disenchantment with the present state of mainstream rock.

You need look no further than the letters pages of any *Melody Maker* to see that fans no longer silently accept the disdain with which their heroes, rock giants, treat them.

They feel deserted. Millionaire rock stars are no longer part of the brotherly rock fraternity which helped create them in the first place.

Rock was meant to be a joyous celebration; the inability to see the stars, or to play the music of those you can see, is making a whole generation of rock fans feel depressingly inadequate.

Enter Johnny Rotten. Not content to feel frustrated, bored and betrayed, he and the Sex Pistols, Glen Matlock (bass), Paul Cook (drums), and Steve Jones (guitar) have decided to ignore what they believe to be the élitist pretensions of their heroes who no longer play the music they want to hear. The Pistols are playing the music they want to hear. They are the tip of an iceberg.

Since January, when the Sex Pistols played their first gig, there has been a slow but steady increase in the number of musicians who feel the same way – bands like the Clash, the Jam, Buzzcocks, the Damned, the Subway Sect and Slaughter and the Dogs. The music they play is loud, raucous and beyond considerations of taste and finesse. As Mick Jones of the Clash says: 'It's wonderfully vital.'

These bands' punk music and stance is so outrageous that, like the Rolling Stones in the good old days, they have trouble getting gigs. But they play regularly at the 100 Club, which is rapidly becoming the venue at which these bands cut their teeth.

The musicians and their audience reflect each other's street-cheap, ripped-apart, pinned-together style of dress. Their attitude is classic punk; icy-cool with a permanent sneer. The kids are arrogant, aggressive, rebellious. The last thing any of these bands make their audience feel is inadequate.

Once again there is the feeling, the exhilarating buzz, that it's possible to be and play like the bands on stage.

We're back where we were in 1964. The Beatles, Stones, Kinks, Who, Them, Animals and the Yardbirds – in effect, a new wave – blasted out of the national charts the showbiz pop of Adam Faith, Bobby Vee, Cliff Richard and Paul Anka, which had replaced the initial vibrant explosion triggered by Bill Haley's 'Rock Around The Clock' and Elvis's 'Heartbreak Hotel' in 1956.

The last five years of rock can be compared to the early sixties when the rock stars of the fifties were wiped out. Buddy Holly's plane crashed. Elvis was drafted into the army, Chuck Berry was jailed. Car crashes killed Eddie Cochran and hospitalized Gene Vincent and Carl Perkins. The field was left open to the businessmen.

The parallels with today are uncanny.

What happened to the rock stars – the new wave – who revolutionized the scene from 1964–7? Jimi Hendrix, Jim Morrison, Brian Jones and Janis Joplin are dead. Clapton retired, and is only just returning, Dylan rested up for several years with a broken neck. Those who are left – the ex-Beatles, Stones, Who, Kinks, have become businessmen. OK, some are still playing rock & roll – but aren't they a little more motivated by making money than making music?

When these bands first shook the foundations of the established musical order they revelled in their image as *rebels*: misfits, outcasts. The Beatles played in Hamburg with toilet seats around their necks, the Who smashed expensive equipment they could ill afford every night, the Rolling Stones, with their long hair and tieless shirts, were chucked out of hotels and restaurants wherever they went.

These rock & rollers were the heroes of their generation because they rejected and broke through the restrictions which had kept teenagers bound to the outdated authority of their parents. Their music was loud, the clothes outrageous.

Most important of all, they were anti-élitist, voices from and of the people – or so we believed. They spoke our language. Every kid who sang along to 'My Generation', 'All Day And All Of The Night' and 'Let's Spend The Night Together' felt that he was as involved with the music as the musicians.

And the bands tried to keep it that way. When the Beatles felt they were becoming the acceptable face of rock with songs like 'Michelle', 'Norwegian Wood' and 'Yesterday', they zapped it back to the true believers with a mind-blowing concoction of backward tapes, multi-tracking and psychedelic weirdness that only youth could really understand.

The trouble is, in the last five years, the rock stars have become 'adults', they have forgotten that crucial to their appeal was their rebellious stance. Instead they are bending over backwards to become acceptable.

Mick Jagger, once the arch-deacon of iconoclasm, now couldn't be farther removed from his fans. It's no longer possible to imagine him as a man of the people, if he ever was – his yobbo accent doesn't wash any more. He's élitist, the aristocracy's court jester, royalty's toy. How long before his name appears on the Queen's honours list?

The Who are becoming Pete Townshend's private nightmare – trotting out their musical history, the seventies' Chuck Berry.

The Beach Boys and the Byrds, America's initial reply to the British eruption, haven't been a vital force in rock for eight years.

The Beatles are the fastest-expanding nostalgia industry yet conceived. On an individual level Paul McCartney and Wings is the only one to have maintained the tradition of an artist consistently performing for an audience, and he speaks mainly to the generation he grew up with.

To his credit, although Lennon is now a quiet family man, he, with Yoko, was the only rock giant to attempt to bring the rebellious protest of his generation to a political level which transcended the rhetoric of rock.

With few exceptions, the interim bands, the ones who sprang up while the old wild men were moving from cellar to penthouse, never transcended their music to become cultural heroes. The psychedelic bands like Jefferson Airplane, Grateful Dead, Soft Machine and Pink Floyd were musically important until they disintegrated with the underground, or disappeared into their own insularity.

Basically middle class, affluent or university academics, they set the stage for bands like Genesis, Jethro Tull, ELP, Yes, Rick Wakeman, Roxy Music and Queen, whose 'progressive rock' uses an increasing amount of technical apparatus, has become increasingly quasi-orchestral and quotes liberally from the classics.

All these bands have been acclaimed by the critics, sometimes justifiably. But the crucial element is missing. These musicians have always been gentlemen rockers and their music can only be played by people with similar academic temperaments. The music, although inspired, is far beyond what the average teenager, without expensive equipment, can reproduce in his own front room.

David Bowie is the one person the growing wave of third-generation rock fans seem to identify with. Although a musical stylist rather than an innovator, he's captured their imagination with a film and stage persona creating him as a mutant alien from another planet.

Thus he has brilliantly detached himself from the conventional jet set, rock star establishment. Unlike other stars whose private lives are totally disparate with their rock stance, Bowie's private life seems freaky enough, weird and secret enough to get him elected the first Punk Space Cadet.

There was a time when it looked as though Led Zeppelin and Bad Company might have carried the torch for raw, raunchy rock & roll but they became multi-national corporations, casualties of the business ethic.

The present state of rock came to a dramatic climax in May and June of this year, at the series of businessmen's conventions held at Wembley, Earls Court and Charlton.

The Who, the Stones, Elton John, David Essex, Steve Harley, David Bowie, Uriah Heep, all put on shows which, whatever they may have said and whatever attempts they may have made to overcome their self-imposed problems, had little to do with music and everthing to do with the kind of gestures these stars think is all that's needed to keep their fans happy.

194

The fans, wanting to give their heroes the benefit of the doubt, weren't as angry as they had the right to be. But a great many were heartsick, disillusioned and bored rotten.

Of course, thousands of people, especially those who grew up with Rock Giants, were still loyal fans, still buying the albums and having a good time. But this is simply not the atmosphere in which the new generation of rock musicians can thrive or have any desire to carry on from where the old guard has left off.

There is a growing, almost desperate, feeling that rock music should be stripped down to its bare bones again. It needs to be taken by the scruff of its bloated neck and given a good shaking, bringing it back to its sources and traditions.

The time is right for an aggressive infusion of life-blood into rock.

It's no coincidence that the week the Stones were at Earls Court, the Sex Pistols were playing to their ever-increasing following at London's 100 Club. The Pistols are the personification of the emerging British punk rock scene, a positive reaction to the complex equipment, technological sophistication and jaded alienation which has formed a barrier between fans and stars.

Punk rock sounds simple and callow. It's meant to.

The equipment is minimal, usually cheap. It's played faster than the speed of light. If the musicians play a ballad, it's the fastest ballad on earth. The chords are basic, numbers rarely last longer than three minutes, in keeping with the clipped, biting cynicism of the lyrics.

There are no solos. No indulgent improvisations.

It's a fallacy to believe that punk rockers like the Sex Pistols can't play dynamic music. They power through sets. They are never less than hard, tough and edgy. They are the quintessence of a raging, primal rock-scream.

The atmosphere among the punk bands on the circuit at the moment is positively cut-throat. Not only are they vying with each other but they all secretly aspire to take Johnny Rotten down a peg or two. They use him as a pivot against which they can assess their own credibility.

It's the BSP/ASP Syndrome. The Before Or After Sex Pistols debate which wrangles thus: 'We saw Johnny Rotten and he *changed* our attitude to music' (the Clash, Buzzcocks); or 'We played like this *ages* before the Sex Pistols' (Slaughter and the Dogs); or 'We are *miles* better than the Sex Pistols' (the Damned). They are very aware that they are part of a new movement and each one wants to feel that he played a part in starting it.

All doubt that the British punk scene is well under way was blitzed two weeks ago in Manchester, when the Sex Pistols headlined a triple, third-generation punk rock concert before an ecstatic capacity audience.

Participation is the operative word. The audiences are revelling in the idea that any one of them could get up on stage and do just as well, if not better, than the bands already up there. Which is, after all, what rock & roll is all about.

When, for months, you've been feeling that it would take ten years to play as well as Hendrix, Clapton, Richard (insert favourite rock star's name), there's nothing more gratifying than the thought: Jesus, I could get a band together and blow this lot off the stage!

The growing punk rock audiences are seething with angry young dreamers who want to put the boot in and play music, regardless. And the more people feel 'I can do that too', the more there is a rush on to that stage, the more cheap instruments are bought, fingered and played in front rooms, the more likely it is there will be the 'rock revival' we've all been crying out for.

There's every chance (although it's early days yet) that out of the gloriously raucous, uninhibited mêlée of British punk rock, which even at its worst is more vital than most of the music perfected by the Platinum Disc Brigade, will emerge the musicians to inspire a fourth generation of rockers.

The arrogant, aggressive, rebellious stance that characterizes the musicians who have played the most vital rock and roll has always been glamorized. In the fifties it was the rebel without a cause exemplified by Elvis and Gene Vincent, the Marlon Brando and James Dean of rock. In the sixties it was the Rock & Roll Gypsy Outlaw image of Mick Jagger, Keith Richard and Jimi Hendrix. In the seventies the word 'rebel' has been superseded by the word 'punk'. Although initially derogatory it now contains all the glamorous connotations once implied by the overused word – 'rebel'.

Punk rock was initially coined, about six years ago, to describe the American rock bands of 1965–8 who sprung up as a result of hearing the Yardbirds, Who, Them, Stones. Ability was not as important as mad enthusiasm, but the bands usually dissipated all their talent in one or two splendid singles which rarely transcended local hit status. Some of the songs, however, like 'Wooly Bully', '96 Tears', 'Psychotic Reaction', 'Pushin' Too Hard', have become rock classics.

In Britain, as 'punk rock' has been increasingly used to categorize the livid, exciting energy of bands like the Sex Pistols, there has been an attempt to redefine the term.

The new British bands emerging have only the most tenuous connections with the New York punk rock scene which has flourished for the last four years. Bands like the New York Dolls, the Ramones, Patti Smith, Television and the Heartbreakers are much closer, musically, to the Shadows of Knight, the Leaves and the other punk rock bands of the sixties.

And they dress almost exclusively in the classic punk uniform. Those not in Levis, sneakers, t-shirts and leather jackets are still pretending to be English rock stars circa 1965.

On the other hand, the British punk scene, far from glorifying, is disgusted by the past. Nostalgia is a dirty word. The music's only truck with yesterday's rock is an affection for one or two classics, 'Substitute', 'What'cha Gonna Do About It', 'Help', 'I Can't Control Myself', 'Stepping Stone': all vitriolic outbursts mirroring the spirit of the bands' own songs, which have titles like 'Pretty Vacant', 'No Feelings', 'Anarchy In The UK', 'You're Shit!' or 'I Love You, You Big Dummy'.

While New York cultivates avant-garde and intellectual punks like Patti Smith and Television, the British teenager, needing and being that much more alienated from rock than America ever was, has little time for such aesthetic refinements.

British punk rock is emerging as a fierce, aggressive, self-destructive onslaught.

There's an age difference too. New York punks are mostly in their mid twenties. The members of the new British punk bands squirm if they have to tell you they are over eighteen. Johnny Rotten's favourite sneer is: 'You're too old.' He's twenty.

British punk rock garb is developing independently too. It's an ingenious hodgepodge of jumble sale cast-offs, safety-pinned around one of the choice, risqué t-shirts especially made for the King's Road shop, Sex.

Selling an intriguing line of arcane fifties cruise-ware, fantasy glamour-ware, and the odd rubber suit, this unique boutique is owned by Malcolm McLaren, ex-manager of the New York Dolls, now the Sex Pistols' manager.

His shop has a mysterious atmosphere which made it the ideal meeting place for a loose crowd of truant, disaffected teenagers. Three of them were aspiring musicians who, last October, persuaded McLaren to take them on. They wanted to play rock & roll. They weren't to know what they were about to start and even now no one is sure where it will lead. All Steve, Glen and Paul needed then was a lead singer.

A few weeks later Johnny Rotten strayed into the same murky interior. He was first spotted leaning over the jukebox, looking bored.

New Pop UK

PAUL MORLEY

If the original punks attempted to lay to waste all those rock dinosaurs without the good grace simply to keel over from acquired mass. Their second-generation brethren sought to establish a new wave that could take over a vacuous mainstream. Paul Morley was one of the few critics to recognize that these bands were temporarily recreating the same sense of continuous affirmation previously achieved in the years between 'Please Please Me' and Pepper.

Predictably, the disdain flows freely following the punk move-ment's inevitable inability to complete wholesale changes in the structure and intent of the rock business. Two colleagues of mine, propelled by genuine bitter disillusionment at the voices and faces of the initial vanguard's failure to fulfill early fanciful ambitions and their apparent dive into complacent impotence and stylistic clichés, wrote an outraged reactionary overgrown pamphlet condemning the 'shambles'. The boringly controversial *The Boy Looked at Johnny* purported to conclude an era and all eras with wilful lack of optimism. It was a good laugh, but hard to take seriously. Many others, similarly motivated, smugly spit that everything is back where it started three years ago: a selfish, passive, isolated rock & roll dead end.

Anyone putting the last three years into sensible perspective, and taking into account the reasons British rock got into such a pitiful state at the beginning of the decade after the exciting endeavours of the late sixties groups, will immediately realize that the state of rock & roll is unprecedentedly healthy and full of fascinating potential. Punk has a valuable, volatile position, and the adapted and adopted relevance of the early basic need to inspire and sustain change, retain respect and relevance and maintain energy and humour has meant that punk has quickly evolved into a mature, multi-levelled, respectful and realistic movement with important impact and influence on the business. No overnight revolution, but a diversifying growth towards a sensitive, concerned rock & roll open end.

Some quotes from early important voices in the punk upsurge qualify the current activity. Howard Devoto reflects that the reason why rock music stagnated so shamefully in the seventies was 'primarily the musicians' fault'. And the Clash, when they boast 'What we're trying to do now is to be the greatest rock & roll band in the world and prove you can do it and still not be a junkie or an alcoholic or stuck up', put the whole thing into context. Where punk has arrived at, and where it's going to go, is molding a rock music that retains all the myths, imagination, romance and ambiguities of rock & roll whilst simultaneously insisting upon honesty, simplicity, adventure and relevance. Fun and accessibility without abuse, and often with a lot of poetry. Tom Robinson has said that he just got his band together 'because we wanted to play rock & roll, we all loved rock & roll', but after that – well, you just don't leave it at that. And that's a lot of the difference between rock & roll then and rock & roll now. Isolate all the music that is directly rooted in the '76 rebellion (and there's a hell of a lot of it, so that ain't hard) and it becomes apparent that punk has grown and is growing into a self-aware, active, alive movement that spreads literally week by week. Flawed and naïve, sure, but determined not to let slip this time. Musicians who care, however misguided.

Punk has considerably changed rock music, its shape and scope and motivations. It is just beginning. The systematic monopolizing of the business and the resultant threat of lack of choice is frightening, but such shadows are powerfully opposed by the alert, colour-ful forces of punk and its relations. The front prongs are already beginning to poke into the all but impregnable, obscenely bigoted American rock blanket and begin change there. Such activity can only be good for freedom of choice, thought and action.

Rock has never been so diverse and exciting. It's probably never wanted to before. The way that punk exploded into view, settled and developed, has been extraordinarily misunderstood, misinterpreted and poorly broadcast, even by those it should theoretically appeal to. As soon as it got over the accusations of contrived sensationalism, it had then apparently died out. But it was never a fad, so how could it die? It was a change, and the change continues – under any other name.

Look back to 1967, and the rich strain of precocious British rock musicians produced some extraordinary music over the next few months: Pink Floyd, Family, Traffic, Nice, Cream, Audience, Fairport Convention, Who etc. Achieving too much too soon, probably unprepared to accept and adapt to the pressure, the musicians of this beginning soon obliviously caused all the problems (and failed to react to them) that helped create the eventual smugness and complacency. Their adventure and neatly applied musical accomplishment ran into a brick wall; the musi-cians continued, caring little about their indulgence and isolation (America has its own parallels). The musicians' smugness about their early, often accidental successes erupted into intolerable narrow-mindedness about their newer music and its effects. The music became slicker, the morals slacker. 'Progressive rock' emerged out of the little, fascinating, psychedelic-oriented burst of the late sixties, a music of horrible hybrid and clinical, cynical technical superiority. Listeners lapped up its empty complexity: the dull doodlings of Yes, ELP, Genesis, Purple, Floyd, all of which could be traced back to the late sixties – the heavy rock army offered an awkward, equally deluded alternative. The music drifted further and further away from even the vaguest abstractions of what rock & roll is all about. It became, more and more, music to consume. Teenage fans growing up, intuitively repelled by the indulgence and irrelevance of this ironically regressive 'progressive' bastard, initially made do with glam rock and other pop perversions before most of that, too, got caught in the spiralling traps of fame, money and delusions, or just ran out of tricks.

Rock had effectively eased to a halt, even if economically you wouldn't have noticed. It needed one massive, exhilarating eruption to become a creative, authentic voice of the new generation, a reflection for the first time. It needed a total, unrelenting assault that was far greater than what the media could do with it, so its effects would resound way past its copy usefulness. All that happened and more.

A whole mass of young listeners frustratedly lashed out at the redundancy of 'rock', demanding an immediate, intimate youth music. They said it was 'punk', and it caused abrupt consternation and sensationalism; many feeling their secure positions threatened, ignored the emergence or absurdly dismissed it as a craze. The media exploited the dirtier parts of the movement, and that's what stuck in a lot of people's minds.

But the initial apparent quasi-nihilistic, mock-anarchistic fashion-hangers associated with punk and its intentions were stupid exaggerations of the small, ugly aspects of any kind of 'revolution' or petulant stamp for attention. The 'movement', avoiding misinterpretation with relish and thriving on the confusion and suspicion of the business and onlookers, was intent on sliding into, and profoundly shaking out of its petty and narrow perspectives, the rock culture. It was never necessarily anti-technique or wilfully, consciously crude, but simply about *change*.

The New Pop developed naturally out of the punk assault. The important thing about punk, musically and visually, was that it effectively engineered new forms of using rhythm and economy, and revealed awareness and sensitivity of how to perform and present. Visually and aurally, even when crudely stated, there were sharp and confident expansions upon rock's basic stale presentation. The undeniable *presence* of the initial punk groups was not only apparently alienating, but highly accessible and obviously fresh in its vigor and simplicity. And it's that, more than anything, that dragged punk groups into the charts and began opening doors. 1977, when controversy blotted natural progress, revealed at the time peculiar traces of the emergence of a new pop; 1978 solidly confirmed this new and colourful force; and 1979 already looks set to extend this trend with the early successes of Wire, the Members, the Pretenders, the Skids and Generation X.

Demands of the time have not only inspired angry alternatives, but placed bright new pop music into the best-seller lists, and thus our everyday lives, possessing distinct and definite looks, sound and sensitivity. Punk succumbed, if you like, but didn't sell out any pure original imperative. Not content with crouching in a corner, doodling and twitching, it stretched out to reach. Its effect is large. The New Pop has used the business as much as it's been used, if not more, and the advantages are more rich than money – individualism, entertainment, speculation – right there in the Top 30 and on our televisions.

1978's pop charts were visited by dozens of new pop groups whose inspirations and purposes can be traced back to 1976, or whom the open-mindedness introduced by '75 gave proper notice to: Buzzcocks, the Jam, Jilted John, Elvis Costello, Undertones, Lurkers, Dury, X-Ray Spex, Stranglers, Adverts, Ramones, Rezillos, Patti Smith, Tom Robinson Band, Sham 69, Blondie, Boomtown Rats . . . something for everyone; some derivative, some disturbing, some dumb. But loud, noisy, and even the more frivolous and fatuous giving off signs that they were *alive* and *thinking*. And in any year which can boast the presence in its charts of 'Hong Kong Garden', 'Public Image' and 'Shot By Both Sides' – something has happened. And is happening.

The New Pop is in effect just one level of where punk has
splintered. Its major benefit, almost as if it's a sacrifice, is supplying access and deflecting attention on to all corners of new rock
music. That's a positive function; a lot of barriers have been
broken down and kept down. Plus, there's such a rapid turnover
of new groups, and things happen so quickly, fade so easily, that
there's little chance of damaging isolation. And for considerable
change to have happened throughout the British rock structure, it
needed to begin with the best-seller lists. People must hear,
identify, continue; Buzzcocks, Jam, Blondie, vigorously and
creatively challenging the moping mighty monoliths like Floyd,
Bad Company, Led Zep; introducing aware, provocative mottos
on to the radio and the TV screens. So that preachers like Costello
can literally bite the hand that feeds and Lydon can lividly lecture
to the clumsy and crass media – and people listen. The point
about the New Pop and other punk splinters is that it will never
sit back. No dozing, but plenty of diversifying.

There's a continual avalanche of ambitious and invigorating
new acts that can't be ignored and who will replace or join
established acts, while the avenues New Pop opens and directs to
(showing that the unusual and unconventional can be attractive,
innovative and classic – and sell) should keep everything fresh and
regenerating. The next wave of New Pop continually surfaces: Joe
Jackson, Soft Boys, Members, Essential Logic, Vipers, Ludus, Stiff
Little Fingers, Bette Bright, UK Subs, Patrik Fitzgerald, Skids,
Rich Kids, 999, Wire, Pretenders, Penetration, John Cooper
Clarke, Secrets, Devo, Clash, Cure, Yachts, Only Ones will break
through this year. But of course, it's so unpredictable it could
even be the Human League, Mekons, Gang of Four or Doll by
Doll. The record labels are lumbering into a second forced but
noticeable period of accepting and marketing new acts, and
crucially the vast valiant range of active alternatives – other
splinters of punk, who've resisted slipping into the tangle but who
do need to communicate – receive full benefit of the reflected

glow. The diversity of contemporary rock (the New Pop, the 'distorted disco' music, the new breed of economic electronic exponents) that all developed from punk is vast and exciting – so how can punk have failed? If you expect to pay a quid for your albums or pay nothing to see musicians, then it probably has. In Britain, though, things have changed at all levels and will continue to do so. Rock – commercial, creative, critical; as entertainment, inspiration and education; inside the charts and outside – has never been stronger, and it's getting better. It's not only just woken up, it's alive and kicking, and you don't have to look that hard to see it.

It is, of course, the birth of rock & roll.

4. I Have Seen the Future . . .

" I've heard that he wasn't completely satisfied with it. For the next
one he wants the light shining out of *his* backside. "

Hyperbole: A figure of rhetoric whereby the speaker expresses more than the truth, in order to produce a vivid impression; hence, an exaggeration.

(Encyclopaedia Britannica, 1950).

The first time I heard Bob Dylan, I was in the car with my mother listening to WMCA and on came that snare shot that sounded like somebody'd kicked open the door to your mind: 'Like A Rolling Stone'.

(Bruce Springsteen, January 1988.)

We're back to 'Like A Rolling Stone' again. The road to Damascus approach to rock writing represents one of the greatest challenges to would-be exponents of Rockspeak. In the rock world, hyperbole rarely produces 'more than the truth'. So how exactly does one convey the impact of seeing the Velvet Underground live with the *EPI* (*Richard Goldstein*), *watching the Rolling Stones' American TV debut on the* Ed Sullivan Show (*Patti Smith*), *or hearing 'Pretty Vacant'* (*Roy Carr*), Marquee Moon (*Nick Kent*) *or* Horses (*Charles Shaar Murray*) *that first time?*

I have not confined the features in this section to concert and album reviews but included personal memoirs from Patti Smith and Danny Sugarman, as well as Byron Coley's welcome rediscovery of the art of the sleeve-note and even a major profile from Sounds *by John Ingham detailing his discovery of the Sex Pistols in a seedy Soho dive, affording them the opportunity to outline their manifesto for electrocuting the industry.*

The Rise of the Sacred Monsters

PATTI SMITH

Perhaps it took a poet to truly detail the impact of the Rolling Stones'
first appearance on American TV, an event as cataclysmic as the
Beatles' earlier Sullivan *debut. In the early seventies Patti Smith, part-*
time journalist and full-time poet, was wont to provide Detroit's Creem
with some of her more rock-oriented expositions. Notably . . .

Look back. it was 1965. Pa was shouting from the TV room.
'jesus christ! jesus christ!' flew up those stairs pumping in 3-D.
bad back widows . . . water moccasins . . . red snake long as a fire
hose. see our house was built on a long swamp. on easter a boy
died. he sank in the quick mud and the next morning he floated
up like ivory soap. Mama made me go to the wake. the afternoon
was hell hot. mosquitoes and steam were rising from the swamp.
the world series was on. the women sat around the casket. all the
men sat around the TV.

Which brings me back to pa. I ran in panting. I was scared silly.
there was pa glued to the TV screen cussing his brains out. a
rock'n'roll band was doing it right on the Ed Sullivan Show. Pa
was frothing like a dog. I never seen him so mad. but I lost
contact with him quick. that band was as relentless as murder. I
was trapped in a field of hot dots. the guitar player had pimples.
the blonde kneeling down had circles ringing his eyes. one had
greasy hair. the other didn't care. and the singer was showing his
second layer of skin and more than a little milk. I felt thru his
pants with optic x-ray. this was some hard meat. this was a bitch.

five white boys sexy as any spade. their nerves were wired and their third leg was rising. in six minutes five lusty images gave me my first glob of gooie in my virgin panties.

That was my introduction to the Rolling Stones. they did time is on my side. my brain froze. I was doing all my thinking between my legs. I got shook. light broke. they were gone and I cliff-hanging. like jerking off without coming.

Pa snapped off the TV. but he was too late. they put the touch on me. I was blushing jelly. this was no mamas boy music. it was alchemical. I couldn't fathom the recipe but I was ready. blind love for my father was the first thing I sacrificed to Mick Jagger.

Time passed. I offered up everything I didn't have. every little lamb. I can tie the Stones in with every sexual release of my late blooming adolescence. the Stones were sexually freeing confused american children. a girl could feel power. lady glory. a guy could reveal his feminine side without being called a fag. masculinity was no longer measured on the football field.

Ya never think of the Stones as fags. in full make-up and frills. they still get it across. they know just how to ram a woman. they made me real proud to be female. the other half of male. they aroused in me both a feline sense of power and a longing to be held under the thumb.

The *Aftermath* album was the real move. two faced woman. doncha bother me. the singer displays contempt for his lady. he's on top and that's what I like. then he raises her as queen. his obsession is her. 'goin' home'. What a song. so wild. so pump pumping. do it down in the basement. don't come 'til the last second. cockpit. cover you like an airplane. Stones music is screwing music.

They rechanneled hot rivers at 78 speed. they were a guide for every shifty white kid. who could get behind the sun-tanned soul of Jan and Dean? look back on the TAMI Show. Leslie Gore was Auntie Mama. the spastic moves of Gerry and the Pacemakers. god bless the marvellous majorette precision of Motown. the

TAMI show's saving grace was pure spade. until the last precious moments with the Rolling Stones. on that silver screen they were bigger than bed. my head spun. my pussy dripped. my pants were wet and the Rolling Stones redeemed the white man forever.

No wonder the Christian God banned the image. jealous bastard. he must have foreseen the black and white movie. who can reject the power of that image? real or 3-D the magic leaks thru. if you got it. and they had it.

I seen them live in 1966. in the heart of the february freeze. Frank Stefanko picked me up in a towtruck. we cruised thru every red light in South Phillie. it was my first white concert. now at the Roxy the spades danced on the ceiling. but this was different. these blonde screamers were after more than a party.

Mick ripped off his flowered shirt and did a fandango. satisfaction. tambourine on head he strutted like some stud. virgin fell off her folding chair and broke her leg. I sussed it all out. this was no TV this was real. I could enter the action. I got set to out stoneface Bill Wyman. the cornerstone of the Stones. relentless as Stonehenge. as a pyramid. any hard edged kid took to him. he was on stage right to catch some spit from Mick. then hell broke. handkerchiefs folded like flowers. a million girls busting my spleen. oh baudelaire. I grabbed Brian's ankle and held on like a drowning child. it seemed like hours. I was getting bored. I looked up. I yawned. Bill Wyman cracked up. Brian grinned. I got scared. I squeezed out and ran. like the altar boy who busts his nut to peek in the sacred chalice. once achieved what next? I left without my hat. I was soaking wet. sweat was freezing on my face.

The politics of speed. between the Buttons came out. that's when I zoomed in on Brian. I got obsessed with him. focused on him like some sick kodak Brian between the what? look at that cover. look at him. he's exposed. he's cold as ice. his powdery skin. his shadow eyes. a doomed albino raccoon. I seen them do 'Ruby Tuesday' on TV. Mick was on top he was the prince. decked in a mirrored shirt and shingled hair. he made his first public ballet bow. Brian was crouched down. he seemed covered with a translucent dust. Mr Amanda Jones.

By 1967 they all but eliminated the word guilt from our vocabulary. 'Let's Spend the Night Together' was the big hit. it's impossible to suffer guilt when you're moving to that song. the Flowers album was for loners and lovers only. it provided a tight backdrop for a lot of decadent fantasy. and by 67 fantasy had already got the best of me.

I never considered the Stones drug music. they were the drug itself. they took up where Martha and the Vandellas left off. real heatwave dancing music. thru demon genius they hit that chord. basic as Charlie's drum beat. as primitive as a western man could stand. find the beat and you dance all night. dive into Gimme Shelter full volume. it's always been easy to let it loose to the Stones. cause they're so cool. so worthy.

Plenty of body shot. they had their brain shot too. Remember 'We Love You?' the beat was hidden. it was far from western but when it needled ya you were shot up but good. madly intoxicating. erotic and extending. like the Satanic Majesty. real search party music. hang your lantern high. brain operation. then they backed it up with *Beggars Banquet*. pure hump hump. get that trojan.

Body and brain. they spell cocaine. the inner search light, speed and slow motion. perfect snow job. the results are alchemical. and if you can't afford it the Stones are it. *sticky Fingers. exile on Main street.* stick your nose in the speakers and get frostbite.

It was July 2. the doctor thought I was bats. he gave me morphine for the pain. he whispered sweet dreams.

That night stretched like a cloud. a hypnotic. I was aware of the droning of bees. in the garden the blonde woman was preparing a mixture of pollen and pure honey. Keith was twisting her arm. he had a leather erection. Mick was writhing. some dizzy ritual. the pollen made me wheeze. I laid in the grass and puked. the dew was cooling my hot leg. someone grabbed my ankle. bruising it. I was saved. I was suffocating in my own warm vomit. I gulped sweet oxygen and turned. Brian was still holding on. I wanted to speak to him but I got caught up in the lace border of his cuff. I traced the delicate embroidery until it stretched across my field of vision like Queen Anne's Lace.

It was morning. it was dazzling. it was July 3rd. by night fall the whole world knew that Brian Jones was dead.

I went home to America and threw up on my father's bed.

I was antique. he had returned to light and I was holding baby hair.

Brian was a length ahead. he was gonna dig up the great African root and pump it like gas in every Stones hit. but it wasn't time yet. unlucky horoscope. imagination and realization were ticking on separate time-pieces.

But Brian was in a hurry. running neck and neck with his vision was his demon. he would soon as stick his dick up the baby doll's ass. Shove pins in the heads of innocents. torn between evil energy and pure spirit. bad seed with a golden spleen. the Stones were moving toward a mortal mergence of the unspoken moment and that hot dance of life. but they were moving too late for Brian. so slow he split. in too.

Death by water. just a shot away from the heart of Ethiopia. rising to original heights. up and over Adams apple sauce. there are blonde hairs raveling in the Stones vital breath. ha ha. Brian got the last laugh.

And the sacrifices continue. moving toward the perfect moment. the miracle of Altamont. the death of the lime green spade. not shocking. necessary. the most graceful complete moment. compare his dance of death with Mick's frenzied movement. Mick's spastic magic. unlucky motor.

Give history a chance. St Meredith. his image in pure copper rising over the speedway. our jesus of Brazil.

Look back Altamont. our Rome. water babies. no flow. no one. gimme gimme. a private piece of the action. some footage. some tail. hold it to the ego like gold plate. no collective act.

And Mick was no flashing priest. a pretty sailor thrown in a cell of sissy athletes. all panting into anarchy. they pluck up Mick like the old fairy tale. split the goose that lays the slow golden eggs. shake the magic maker. extract that diamond tooth.

That's the western movement. that's the way of rock n roll. at my first school dance Jo-Jo Rose got stabbed. US Bonds was lip-synching 'Quarter to Three'. nobodies erecting monuments to Jo-Jo Rose. nobody's blaming US Bonds either.

Blame Mick Jagger? for what? for performing thru theory not grace. the alchemy was not there. the performer and the audience have got to be as intimate as the killer and his victim. like in *Performance*. takes two to make the radio. contact pill. if you can see it you can get it. Brian dreamed of it. Mick failed at it.

But you know he's redeemed. Mick did it. this is no stylistic trick. tuesday night July 25 1972 at Madison Square Garden. a sacred peep show. Pope don't bless my flashlight. I found my own way.

Born to be. born to be me. got my ticket for free. what would I wear? Keith Richards gear? bone in the ear? naaa. lay the flash aside. dress like *Don't Look Back*. just the right dark glasses. blow my last buck to be cool. grab that taxi. adjust my shades and light a Kool. pat my flask of Jack Daniel's. I get there. completely solitaire.

My seat juts out. overlook the ground floor. left handed stage view. nobody can get in my way. nothing but ramp and space. a box seat. tuesday was the off night. the double show day. rock stars make their own labor laws. inhuman work load. no party. no hip chicks. just fans. everyone a stranger. good. I could play at being a cool and perfect stranger myself. I sat there feeling incognito hot shit. then my stomach started feeling funny. detached jello. regulate my breath. be a breathing camera. the hungry eye.

Something snapped. I'm no screamer. I swear. when the roller coaster crashes. I hold my breath. I refuse to let loose. it's a matter of pride. but I cracked. my tear ducts burst. they were there in 4-D. fell on one knee. couldn't see. my brain cracked like an egg. the gold liquid spurted all over the stage. Mick bathed in it. Keith got his feet wet. then I calmed quick. it was like coming without jerking off. they hadn't even finished 'Brown Sugar' and I was cool as a snake. physically for me the concert was over. like hearing the punchline then sitting thru the long drawn out joke.

The rest was pure head motion. like viewing any ancient ceremony. pass the sacred wafer. transfixed my open laughter. My brain was open as a loft. no mere image. I was ashamed. they were just men. Charlie raised over like King Drum. Bill in red velvet. his bass way up. his classic dignity. Mick Taylor completing the triangle. the maypole.

Mick and Keith wove their magic round. Keith a drunken kid. he was moving so good. thin raunchy glitter. I don't care what anyone says. he's the real rolling stone. he got the silver. basic black guitar. like a convertible. like heartbreak hotel. his plexiglass one got stolen.

not without sacrifice. he was loosing his grip. he introduced the band. a long silence before Keith. death rattle. did he introduce Brian Jones? freeze that moment. I got no Maysley video to look back on. what was he saying? the silence was anything but golden. does the lion drown underwater? or does he swallow the golden fish? Brian swimming thru the crowd. I looked down. they were modulating. Jagger was apologizing. incoherent. drooling. the heat. the drink. I was in shock. my heart stopped thisshort. from stopping.

A Quiet Night at Balloon Farm

RICHARD GOLDSTEIN

Though there were few kind words expended on the Velvet Underground in their peak years, Richard Goldstein recognized the genesis of something new in their atonal thrust, witnessing one of their 1966 multi-media Exploding Plastic Inevitable shows.

The Velvet Underground is not a first-class car on the London transit system, but Andy's rock group. Sometimes they sing, sometimes they just stroke their instruments in a single, hour-long jam. Their sound is a savage series of atonal thrusts and electronic feedback. Their lyrics combine sado-masochistic frenzy with free-association imagery. The whole thing seems to be the product of a secret marriage between Bob Dylan and the Marquis de Sade. It takes a lot to laugh; it takes a train to cry.

Andy says he is through with phosphorescent flowers and cryptic soup cans. Now it's rock. He may finally conquer the world through its soft, teenage underbelly.

'It's ugly,' he admits. 'It's a very ugly effect when you put it all together. But it's beautiful. You know, you just look at the whole thing – the Velvets playing and Gerard dancing and all the film and light, and it's a beautiful thing. Very Vinyl. Beautiful.'

'Yeah, beautiful. There are beautiful sounds in rock. Very lazy, dreamlike noises. You can forget about the lyrics in most songs. Just dig the noise, and you've got our sound. We're putting everything together – lights and film and music – and we're reducing it to its lowest common denominator. We're musical primitives.'

That's John Cale, composer, guitarist and resident Welshman for the Velvet Underground. He plays a mean, slashing viola. And piano, when he has to. He and Lou Reed once shared a three-room flat on Ludlow Street and a group called the Primitives. Their place was cold (broken crates in a wood-burning fireplace looked very chic but also kept the blood circulating). The group was cold too, bassman Sterling Morrison recalls: 'Sometimes we'd do more jumping around in a night than the goddam waitresses. Before Andy saw us at the Café Bizarre (which isn't exactly the Copa of McDougal Street) we were busting our balls in work. Up to here. And you can't do anything creative when you're struggling to keep the basic stuff coming. Now it seems we have time to catch our breath. We have more direction – that's where Andy comes in. We eat better, we work less and we've found a new medium for our music. It's one thing to hustle around for odd jobs. But now we're not just another band; we're an act. See – when a band becomes an act, you get billing. You get days off. You don't just work nights – you're like, Engaged.'

Nightly at the Balloon Farm the Velvets demonstrate what distinguishes an act from a band. They are special. They even have a chanteuse – Nico, who is half goddess, half icicle. If you say bad things about her singing, she doesn't talk to you. If you say nice things, she doesn't talk to you either. If you say that she sounds like a bellowing moose, she might smile if she digs the sound of that in French. On-stage, she is somewhat less communicative. But she sings in perfect mellow ovals. It sounds something like a cello getting up in the morning. All traces of melody depart early in her solo. The music courses into staccato beats, then slows into syrupy feedback. All this goes on until everyone is satisfied that the point has gotten across.

Oh yeah; the point! John Cale sits dreamily, eyeing a Coke, pushes his hair back from his face to expose a bony nose, and observes: 'You can't pin it down.' (Granted.) 'It's a conglomeration of the senses. What we try to get here is a sense of total involvement.' (You mean acid, scoobie-doobie-doo?)

'Coming here on a trip is bound to make a tremendous difference. But we're here to stimulate a different kind of intoxication. The sounds, the visual stuff – all this bombarding of the senses – it can be very heady in itself, if you're geared to it.'

John Cale is a classicist. His first composition was 'written on a rather large piece of plywood'. He studied viola and piano at the London Conservatory of Music and came to the United States as a Leonard Bernstein fellow. His sponsor was Aaron Copland. 'We didn't get on very well,' John says. 'Copland said I couldn't play my work at Tanglewood. It was too destructive, he said. He didn't want his piano wrecked.'

Cale pursued his vision with John Cage. On the viola, he would play a single note for as long as two hours. Then he met Lou Reed, and the sound that John calls 'controlled distortion' was born.

The Velvets, with Nico and Andy and all that light, began to construct a scene around the title 'Exploding Plastic Inevitable'. They've done quite a bit of travelling since, and their reviews reflect the ambivalence a quiet evening at the Balloon Farm can produce. Said the *Chicago Daily News*: 'The flowers of evil are in full bloom.' *Los Angeles* magazine compared the sound to 'Berlin in the decadent thirties'. Even Cher (of Sonny and Cher) was heard to mutter: 'It will replace nothing except suicide.'

Dauntless, the troupe returned home. Now they are popping eardrums and brandishing horse-whips on a nightly basis. Their first album sounds a bit restrained (though a long, harrowing cut called 'Heroin' isn't exactly calculated to make the radio as a 'good guy sure-shot'). But it's still The Sound. And the group is brimming with innovation.

'We want to try an electronic drum,' says John. 'It would produce sub-sonic sounds, so you could feel it even when you couldn't hear it. We'd then be able to add it to a piece of music, and it would be like underlining the beat' (in cement).

On-stage, Gerard Malanga motions wildly. They have run out of records, and that means it's time for another set. John puts down his Coke and wraps a black corduroy jacket over his turtleneck. He slides his hair over his face, covering his nose again. Lou tucks his shirt in.

'Young people know where everything is at,' he says. 'Let 'em sing about going steady on the radio. Let 'em run their hootenannies. But it's in holes like this that the real stuff is being born. The university and the radio kill everything, but around here, it's alive. The kids know that.'

The girl in the bark stockings is leaning against the stage, watching them warm up. 'You can tell this is going to be a very atonal set,' she says. 'It's something about the way they handle their instruments when they first come on-stage.'

'Beautiful,' sighs her partner, rolling his larynx and his eyes. With a single humming chord, which seems to hang in the air, the Velvet Underground launches into another set. John squints against a purple spotlight. Lou shouts against a groaning amplifier. Gerard writhes languidly to one side. Sterling turns his head to sneeze. And Nico stands there, looking haunted. The noise, the lights, the flickering images – all happen. Everybody grooves.

From the balcony, Andy Warhol watches from behind his glasses. 'Beautiful,' he whispers. Sterling sneezes audibly but it seems to fit. 'Beautiful.' Gerard hands his partner a bull-whip and the girl in bark begins to sway. 'Just beautiful.'

It's My Life

DANNY SUGARMAN

Danny Sugarman, co-author and editor of a virtual bookshelf about the Doors, did not detail his first live encounter with Jim Morrison until he came to write his own tale of excess, Wonderland Avenue, *which here takes a slight detour down the road to Damascus.*

My mother was doing her hysterical concerned Jewish mother bit, galloping around the kitchen from phone to stove to refrigerator and back, the whole while bombarding me with questions I had very few answers for. She had to know who I was going with and everything about him. Who were we going to see? No one had heard of the Doors. Where were we going? Why was I going? Twelve-year-olds don't go to concerts . . . all her mothering fears were on red alert. She had to be certain Evan was a real, decent person taking me to a real concert, and not some child molester taking me to a drug orgy. She didn't trust him because he had a moustache, and what grown man invites a little kid to a rock concert? She didn't trust his motives. That he umpired Little League games only indicated he really liked little kids, and not necessarily in a healthy manner.

None of this mattered. I was going. 'I can take care of myself,' I reassured her, and to my surprise she believed me.

'OK,' she relented, 'but promise me, absolutely promise me you will be home no later than midnight.' Of course I promised, even though I had never been to a concert before and I had no idea how long they were. For this one, I had no idea the lead singer's idea of a fashionable entrance was to arrive on stage two hours after the scheduled start time.

After Evan and I arrived at Cal State Los Angeles, where the concert was being held in the gym, we unloaded the equipment he carried in his VW van. When most of it was set up on stage inside, I scrambled back inside the van to pull the microphone cables out from under the dashboard. Looking up I was shocked to see the dark outline of a figure through the windshield. I scurried back out of the van and the same dark figure blocked my exit.

'What the fuck do you thing you're doing?' he demanded.

'I'm helping Evan,' I stammered. 'This is his van.'

'Yeah? How do I know you're not stealing his stuff?'

I look around frantically for Evan. He was nowhere in sight.

'I'm not! I'm helping.'

'I should bring the cops.'

I was really spooked. I spilled the whole story out to this guy. 'I came here with Evan. He told me if I hit a home run he'd take me to see this band tonight and here I am.'

'Oh, so you're the kid who whacked Parker with the baseball bat?'

How did this guy know that? I was about to ask him when Evan appeared.

'I was just about to call the cops on this kid I caught stealing our equipment, Evan. What do you think we should do with him?'

'I think we should hang him by his ankles with these microphone cables and beat the shit out of him,' Evan said.

Now I didn't know whether to laugh or run.

'That's not a bad idea,' the guy said.

Evan winked, I breathed easier.

At that moment, a pretty red-haired girl came up and put her arm around the guy with the long hair. 'Hello, honey,' she said and kissed him on the cheek. He slipped his arm around her waist. 'Well, I guess I'll let you go this time, but watch it in the future.' Then they walked away.

'That was Jim Morrison,' Evan told me. 'You two oughta really get along fine; he's crazier than you are.'

A group called the Sunshine Company opened the show, followed by the Nitty Gritty Dirt Band. The audience was polite to the first band, but had become rude and impatient by the time the second was wrapping up their set. Then there was a long, long break.

The four members of the Doors were in the locker-room, which was serving as a dressing-room, underground and beneath the gym. They were completely unaware of the tension mounting upstairs back in the hall. The Dirt Band had left the stage early, about 10.45. The Doors were to go on at 11.15. It was already 11.30, the audience was growing increasingly intolerant, and it was becoming obvious I wasn't going to make it home by midnight. The stage was finally readied for the Doors at 11.45. Sixteen black Jordan amplifiers were erected into four individual towers looking like Greek columns – one stack of four on either side of the drum riser. In front of the stage, a lone, slightly bent, chrome microphone stand. Just to its immediate left, a red and black Vox organ with a silver, metal-flake bass keyboard by Fender riding piggyback on the organ's left shoulder.

222

At midnight the pre-recorded music from the PA was turned off and the audience tensed. But no Doors. I was standing between Evan and another man whom he introduced to me as the Doors' manager, Bill Siddons. 'Listen, how'd you like to do me a favour?' Bill asked.

'Sure.'

'Go downstairs and tell those guys it's show time.'

I dashed down the stairs and into the dressing-room, my enthusiasm barely contained, and repeated the message. I was met with darkness and silence. I had to peer into the room to make them out.

I heard a deep voice: 'Tell Bill we know.' I stood there and waited for more but when no more came, I decided I'd done the job I was asked to do and ran back upstairs. I relayed the message to Bill.

'Go and tell them I said now!'

'All right.'

More silence. No movement. I waited a while. What were they waiting for? Nobody talked. I left, ran back upstairs and told Bill they said 'all right'.

'Tell them the contract reads 11.15, and we're already over an hour late.' I didn't want to tell them that. Walking into the dressing-room was like entering the River Styx. But I didn't want to disobey. I went back downstairs, my legs getting tired by now, and told them what Bill said.

'Tell Bill we'll be right up,' the baritone answered. I climbed back upstairs.

'Tell them the audience is going ape-shit,' Bill asked me. I hobbled down the stairs and delivered the message.

'Let 'em, it's good for them.'

This time I tried to run back up the stairs with the reply, but I confess I walked two or three of them.

I told Bill. 'Why don't you go talk to them, I don't think they're listening to me,' I said.

'Don't take it personally,' he told me, 'those guys don't listen to anybody.' Thus fortified he gave me a new message. 'Tell them if we don't go on now, this second, we're gonna be in default, got that?' I nodded, afraid to speak for fear of forgetting the message. I trotted back downstairs and fed the information into the darkness. Silence.

'Tell him we don't give a fuck about the money.' I didn't want to tell anybody that.

'Tell him we're on our way,' another voice said. What were they doing in there anyway? I wondered. I was beginning to have real strange feelings about these guys.

Back upstairs, I gave Bill the latest news. 'Go watch for them at the top of the stairs and when you see them, come and tell me, OK?' The crowd was stomping and clapping and hollering for the Doors. I waited a good ten minutes at the top of the stairs. It was almost one o'clock. I had given up a long time ago getting home before two. Then I saw three musicians coming up the stairs. A tall, blond, well-dressed man who looked nice and wore rimless glasses; a frizzy-haired, slightly dazed-looking guy who looked like he was wearing a carpet over his shoulder and carried a burgundy Gibson guitar; and a colourful, almost pixie-looking guy with lousy skin. Where was the fourth guy, Morrison? Hadn't he heard me? Oh, shit. I'd assumed he was in the dressing-room.

I ran and told Bill they were coming. Three of them, at least. He said something into his headphone mike and the house lights dimmed. The audience hushed and inhaled. The place smelt of pot. I'd smelt it once or twice before, but not like this. A spotlight came on. 'Ladies and Gentlemen,' Bill Siddons' voice boomed throughout the gym, 'Please welcome the Doors!' Wild applause. The spotlight went out and you saw nothing but some buttons of red light beaming. The music started in total darkness. It sounded like a carnival was beginning. That was my first thought. Had the fourth guy made it? That was my next thought. Where was he? Was he coming? Had he heard me? Oh, shit. Was I in trouble with these guys already? I hoped not. I'd just met them!

Nothing in my life prepared me for the arrival of Jim Morrison.

I had gotten my seat, up front, up close in front of the front row, sitting cross-legged with dozens of other members of the audience, pressed tightly together. They sat alert, as if awaiting a lecture, not a concert. They knew something I didn't. I tried to be cool. I made some room for myself and tried to fit in.

Should I go back and get him? That was my last thought and I might as well have left it in another world. Then it happened.

I heard a scream, long, pained, thick and husky: loud enough and strong enough to wake me up. In his black leather, with long brown hair and angelic features, the singer was a phantom, staggering across the stage, about to fall but somehow keeping his balance, bellowing a long-winded series of screams and grunts. The rest of the band looked unconcerned. The keyboardist's eyes were closed, his head slowly winding from side to side in time with the music. The drummer was raising his hands and drumsticks in the air and bringing them down with an exaggerated motion. The guitarist stood stone still.

The lead singer was still yelling, but slower now, in time with the music, hard grunts.

He stopped, as if regaining awareness, and looked right in our faces, held our stare as the music began to build. He dropped back, and leapt forward, throwing his face at ours, his eyes agog, terrorized, tearing at the microphone. Hands a blur, on the verge of insanity, and he screamed again, the sound of a thousand curtains torn. The audience, who were already on the edge of their seats, were bolted and locked in the Doors' current. Jim crumpled on to the stage in a lifeless heap; the music pounding. I thought he was dead, electrocuted, maybe shot.

He rose from the ground slowly and did a beautiful leap straight up, as if jettisoned. He landed easily but staggered a bit as he approached the microphone. He touched it slowly, and blinked, opened his mouth to sing, but thought of something else and closed his mouth. (Has he forgotten the words?) The music continued, repeating itself, waiting for him to enter. The audience was frozen in expectation and attention. Morrison just rode it all, letting the music build and build, blind to stares. Then just when it felt like the room would blow its roof off, he slipped the words in, closing his eyes he sang:

> When the music's over
> When the music's over, yeah
> When the music's over, turn out the lights
> The music is your special friend,
> Dance on fire as it intends
> Music is your only friend . . . until the end . . . until the end

It was the end. It was the end of the world as I had known it. Nothing would ever again be the same for me.

It was 3.30 a.m. by the time we had finished, loading the equipment back in Evan's van. I felt different – lighter, freer. We were sitting on the kerb in the parking-lot talking about it, having a smoke, when a police car pulled up in front of us with its light shining in our faces. Evan and Bill got real nervous real fast. A cop got out of each door. One was a policeman, the other a campus security cop. The official cop said, 'Danny Sugarman?'

'Yes, officer?' My father had taught me to always be polite to cops.

'Your mother is looking for you,' the other one finished.

I Saw Rock & Roll Future and its Name is Bruce Springsteen

JON LANDAU

Jon Landau's review of a May '74 Cambridge, Massachusetts, concert by Bruce Springsteen and the E Street Band is surely the most legendary piece in this section. Landau's hyperbole generated an ad campaign from CBS that would be a source of intense embarrassment for Springsteen and Landau. From the original article, published in a local Boston freebie paper, CBS took the quotes required and left behind its skeletal context, which placed Springsteen at the crossroads of rock's past and present.

Tonight there is someone I can write of the way I used to write, without reservations of any kind. Last Thursday, at the Harvard Square Theatre, I saw my rock & roll past flash before my eyes. I saw something else: I saw rock & roll future and its name is Bruce Springsteen. And on a night when I needed to feel young, he made me feel like I was hearing music for the very first time.

When his two-hour set ended I could only think, can anyone really be this good, can anyone say this much to me, can rock & roll still speak with this kind of power and glory? And then I felt the sores on my thighs where I had been pounding my hands in time for the entire concert and knew that the answer was Yes.

Springsteen does it all. He is a rock & roll punk, a Latin street poet, a ballet dancer, an actor, a joker, bar band leader, hot rhythm guitar player, extraordinary singer, and a truly great rock

227

& roll composer. He leads a band like he has been doing it forever. I racked my brains but I simply can't think of a white artist who does so many things so superbly. There is no one I would rather watch on a stage today.

Bruce Springsteen is a wonder to look at. Skinny, dressed like a reject from Sha Na Na, he parades in front of his all-star rhythm band like a cross between Chuck Berry, early Bob Dylan and Marlon Brando. Every gesture, every syllable, adds something to his ultimate goal – to liberate our spirit while he liberates his by baring his soul through his music. Many try, few succeed, none more than he today.

It's five o'clock now – I write columns like this as fast as I can for fear I'll chicken out – and I'm listening to 'Kitty's Back'. I do feel old but the record and my memory of the concert has made me feel a little younger. I still feel the spirit and it still moves me.

I bought a new home this week and upstairs in the bedroom is a sleeping beauty who understands only too well what I try to do with my records and typewriter. About rock & roll, the Lovin' Spoonful once sang, 'I'll tell you about the magic that will free your soul/but it's like trying to tell a stranger about rock & roll.' Last Thursday I remembered that the magic still exists and that as long as I write about rock, my mission is to tell a stranger about it – just as long as I remember that I'm the stranger I'm writing for.

Weird Scenes Inside Gasoline Alley

CHARLES SHAAR MURRAY

By the time Patti Smith made her debut album, Horses, *in the summer of 1975, her performances with an ever-expanding band, endorsed by luminaries like Dylan and Springsteen, had been attracting enthusiastic*

*press for two years. She had also been writing her own brand of rock
& roll reviews for* Creem *since 1972. But Murray was writing for an
English audience largely unexposed to the New York hype and perhaps
unprepared for the unequivocal nature of Murray's endorsement.*

First albums this good are pretty damn few and far between.

It's better than the first Roxy album, better than the first Beatles
and Stones albums, better than Dylan's first album, as good as the
Doors and Who and Hendrix and Velvet Underground albums.

It's hard to think of any other rock artist of recent years who
arrived in the studios to make their first major recordings with
their work developed to such a depth and level of maturity.

Listen. Last April I saw Patti Smith play CBGB in New York,
and she knocked me flat on my ass, which was impressive since
my preconceptions weren't helping her any.

I mean, whenever an act is hyped to me – whether it's on a big
scale like Springsteen or even a few friends (either mine or the
act's) frothing at the mouth some – my first instinct is to come
right back at them with a big 'So what?' or 'Oh, yeah?'

What I mean is, like our American cousins say, I'm from Missouri. You gotta show me.

Believe me, Jim, she showed me.

OK, she's a lady poetess, which is generally not the stuff of
which rock heroism is made.

She also ain't too good-looking, if you're judging her by conventional gosh-what-a-cutie-nudge-nudge standards.

Plus she's from New York, which means that she isn't available
to be checked out at the grass roots by British audiences, which in
turn means that you're going to have to get hip to her through
media instead of discovering her for yourself – just the same way
that American audiences are going to have to learn about Dr
Feelgood via rock press rather than by those happy accidents that
we all know and love, etc.

Three strikes down. Foreign, female but not stereotypically attractive, and f'Chrissakes, a poetess.

Just the stuff to appeal to, let's say, a Mott fan from Bradford.

Thing is, it really doesn't work like that. If you add up what Patti Smith appears to be when viewed from a distance, and then go see her or (to get nearer to the point) listen to *Horses*, the result of a few weeks of madness and desperation in Electric Lady studios with famous Welsh person John Cale riding herd on the operation, the disparities become apparent.

Horses is some kind of definitive essay on the American night as a state of mind, an emergence from the dark undercurrent of American rock that spewed up Jim Morrison, Lou Reed and Dylan's best work.

Like Patti Smith herself, it's strange, askew and flat-out weird. It's neurotic and unhealthy and dank, a message in a bottle sent from some place that you and I have only been to in the worst moments of self-doubting defeated psychosis.

It's night-wailing, street corner blues, the midnight flight out of Gasoline Alley, to Desolation Row, a thrashing exorcism of public and private demons.

Horses is what happens when the fuses blow and the light goes out.

'Jesus died for somebody's sins, but not mine . . .' Smith's singing voice draws on her received black influences as well as the teenaged school of girl-group vocals.

The playing of her band (Lenny Kaye on guitar, Richard Sohl – known as 'DNV', an abbreviation of 'Death in Venice' – on piano, Ivan Kral on bass and latecomer Jay Dee Daugherty on drums) sounds kind of amateurish and off-the-wall at first, as does Smith's singing (she can't quite hit a low note straight on), until you realize that they simply lack the kind of standardized stylized mechanization that we've come to confuse with 'professionalism'.

In this and so many other ways, Patti Smith's album hips you to just what's wrong with a lot of other stuff you've been listening to, tips you off as to who's really doing it and who's just going through the motions.

The first dive into the maelstrom comes with 'Gloria', the old Van Morrison/Them rabbler-rouser beloved of garage bands since time immemorial.

It's done with grinding stickshift guitar played off against teeth-grinding methedrine piano, vaguely like the stuff Mike Garson was doing way down in the mix on *Aladdin Sane* and strategic areas of *Pin Ups*.

It's a stunning opener, achieving almost the same psychotic/sexual/dervish whirl as some of the Doors' longer, stranger rides.

In general, there's a Doors feel to the keyboards (particularly the organ) and a Velvets edge on the guitars, though this is purely coincidental, as no resemblance is intended to anybody living, dead or intermediate.

'Gloria' is followed up by the album's least impressive track, 'Redondo Beach', which is a New York impression of reggae (I detect the dread hand of Mr Cale in this track, though he doesn't actually perform on any instruments) and features Ms Smith doing a strange kind of JA Dylan vocal. Not the most immediate piece on the album, but kinda charming.

'Birdland', however, is the goods.

Building relentlessly over a slow, obsessive piano with a saw-toothed guitar whining someway in the distance, Smith wails like the proverbial lost soul – and here the shade of Mr Morrison looms inescapably over the proceedings right up until the final strands of shredded-wire feedback.

It's chilling as hell, so keep yer woollies on for this one, fear fans.

The first side rides out on a fair piece of decompression with 'Free Money' written for Smith's current old man, Allan Lanier of Blue Oyster Cult. It's got a kind of 'Johnny Remember Me' production on the voices and metallic Del Shannon-style rhythm guitar.

Choogling to orgasm, you might say.

When you get over to side two, you happen on to 'Kimberley', a song about Patti's sister of the same name and very Velvets about the bass and organ, though the latter instrument also has a fifties/Farfisa/Ray Mangarde vibe to it. It's based on an incident that occurred during a thunderstorm, and sounds it.

'Break It Up', co-written with Tom Verlaine of Television, follows.

Verlaine was Patti's last old man (anyway, he was when I saw the two bands together in April), and he plays guitar on the track, a kind of liquidly malevolent electronic burble.

It starts out as slow, almost blues, before the piano switches into that distant nursery echo type of riff that'd go down a treat as the soundtrack to a remake of *The Turn of the Screw*.

Next up is the album's unquestioned pièce de résistance, 'Land', the piece that completely skulled me out when I saw her do it at CBGB. It's the mélange of a mutated 'Land of a Thousand Dances' (Chris Kenner and Fats Domino would probably haveta undergo intensive care if they knew what she's done to their song, ma) and a scorching recitation about a kid getting beat up in a locker-room, blazing into a free-association sexual fight which utilizes the horse as a sexual metaphor in much the same way as Morrison used the snake.

Except that Jimbo was pretty much preoccupied with his own snake, and Smith's sexuality is far more outgoing as she rides the horse and the sea comes in and the sexual spiral of letting go/ breaking through inexorably begins again. Like Van Morrison said, it's too late to stop now.

Kaye balances vicious guitar razor-slashes against the relentless bass-heavy rhythm while it builds into a Velvety whirlpool.

The dissociation is dramatized by the over-dub juxtaposition of Patti singing the lyrics on one track and reciting/performing them on another.

It's a falling, possessed performance, fuelled by the kind of energy you run on when there's no energy left, a death-defying kamikaze leap into places you go when you want to either come out different or not come out at all, one step over the line and no direction home.

The last cut, 'Elegy', a tribute to Hendrix with Lanier on guitar, is over so fast that by the time you've gotten over 'Land' it's already gone.

Horses is an album in a thousand.

I'm not gonna jive you about how influential it's going to be (in terms of it stimulating dozens of toy Patti Smiths to come crawling out of the woodwork I hope it has no influence at all), but, God knows, it's an important album in terms of what rock can encompass without losing its identity as a musical form, in that it introduces an artist of greater vision than has been seen in rock for far too long.

It may not sell, it may never infiltrate the lives of more than a handful of people, but its existence means that there is some record of the most arrestingly bizarre set of perceptions of the American underlife to be set to music since the decline of Lou Reed and the death of Jim Morrison.

The fact that Patti Smith is a woman may well alienate listeners who are prepared to be receptive to a basically passive female intelligence (like Joni Mitchell), but may find an album of extrovert, ferocious female intelligence (like this one) somewhat unnerving.

Not to mention the fact that people always get weird in the presence of a powerful sexuality expressed by someone who they may not happen to find attractive.

And Patti Smith sure ain't Maria Muldaur (thank you, Lord). However, I'll say it again . . . first albums this good are pretty damn few and far between.

Listen.

Marquee Moon

NICK KENT

Television made their first furtive stab at a debut album in March 1975. Their first actual full-length vinyl exposition, released two years later, proved to be worth the wait. NME gave Nick Kent two pages to review the album and put Television on the front cover. And in many ways, Kent's review is as astonishing as the album it covered in laurels.

I concur thus.

Sometimes it takes but one record – one cocksure magical statement – to cold cock all the crapola and all-purpose wheatchaff mix'n'match, to set the whole schmear straight and get the current state of play down, down, down, to stand or fall in one dignified granite-hard focus.

Such statements are precious indeed. *Marquee Moon*, the first album from Tom Verlaine's Television, however, is one: a 24-carat inspired work of pure genius, a record finely in tune and sublimely arranged with a whole new slant on dynamics, centred around a totally invigorating passionate application to the vision of mastermind Tom Verlaine.

Forget all that New York minimalist punk stuff, Television's music is the total antithesis, and to call them punk rock is rather like describing Dostoevsky as a short story writer.

Television's music is remarkably sophisticated, unworthy of even being paralleled to that of the original Velvet Underground whose combined instrumental finesse was practically a joke compared to what Verlaine & Co. are cooking up here.

Each song is tirelessly conceived and arranged for maximum impact, the point where decent parallels really need to be made with the very, very best.

Dylan and early Love spring to mind, the Byrds' cataclysmic 'Eight Miles High' period, a soupçon even of the Doors and Captain Beefheart and their mondo predilichons, plus the very cream of those psychedelic-punk bands that only Lenny Kaye knows about.

Above all though, the sound belongs most undoubtedly to Television, and the appearance of *Marquee Moon* at a time when rock is so hopelessly lost within the labyrinth of its own inconsequentiality, where actual musical content has come to take a back seat to 'attitude', and all that word is supposed to signify, is to these ears little short of revolutionary.

My opening gambit about the album providing a real focus for the current state of rock bears a relevance simply because here at last is a band whose vision is centred quite rigidly within their music – not, say, in some half-baked notion of political manifesto mongery with that trusty, thoroughly reactionary three-chord backdrop to keep the whole scam buoyant.

Verlaine's appearance is simply as exciting as any other major innovators to the rock sphere – like Hendrix, Syd Barrett, Bob Dylan – and yes, Christ knows I'm tossing up some true-blue heavies here but goddammit I refuse to repent, because the talents of Verlaine's Television just damn excite me so much.

To the facts then – recorded in A & R studios, New York, produced by Verlaine himself and engineer Andy Johns, the album lasts roughly three-quarters of an hour and contains eight songs, several of which have been recorded in demo form at least twice before, and have been performed live innumerable times.

The wait has been worthwhile because the refining process, instigated by some hesitant non-recording contract months, has sculpted the songs into the masterpieces that are here, present for all to experience.

Side one makes no bones about making its presence felt, kicking off with the full-bodied thrust of 'See No Evil'. Guitars, bass and drums are strung together, fitting tight as a glove, clenched into a fist punching metal rivets of sound with the same manic abandon that typified the elegant ferocity of Love's early drive.

There is a real passion here, no half-baked metal cut and thrust – each beat reverberates to the base of the skull, with Verlaine's voice mixed perfectly into the grain of the rhythm. The chorus/climax is irresistible anyway – Verlaine crooning, 'I understand all destructive urges and it seems too perfect . . . I see . . . I see . . . no e-v-i-i-l-l.'

The next song is truly something else – 'Venus De Milo'. It's simply one of the most beautiful songs I've ever heard: the only other work to parallel it is Dylan's 'Mr Tambourine Man', a vignette of sorts, dealing with a dreamlike quasi-hallucinogenic state of epiphany.

'You know it's all like some new kind of drug/my senses are sharp and my hands are like gloves/Broadway looks so medieval, it seems to flap like little pages . . ./I fell sideways laughing, with a friend from many stages.'

'Friction' is probably the most readily accessible track from this album, simply because, with its cutting anarchic quasi-Velvets feel, plus (all important) Verlaine's most pungent methedrine guitar fretboard slaughter. Here it'll represent the kind of thing all those weaned on the type and legend, without hearing one note from Television, will be expecting.

The song has vicious instrumentation and a perfect climax which has Verlaine spelling out the title F-R-I-C-T-I-O-N, slashing his guitar for punctuation.

The album's title track closes the first side. Conceived at a time when rock tracks lasting over ten minutes are somewhat sunk deep below the subterranean depths of contempt, 'Marquee Moon' is as riveting a piece of music as I've heard since the halcyon days of . . . oh, God knows, too many years have elapsed.

Everything about this piece is startling, built around Verlaine's steely runs and meshed with Lloyd's intoxicating counterpoints.

Slowly a story unfurls – a typically surreal Verlaine ghost story involving Cadillacs pulling up in grave-yards and disembodied arms beckoning the singer to get in while 'lightning struck itself', and various twilight rejects from *King Lear* (that last bit's my own flight of fancy, by the way), babbling crazy retorts to equally crazy questions. The lyrics as a scenario for the music are utterly compelling. The song's structure is unlike anything I've ever heard before. It transforms from a strident two-chord construction, to a breath-takingly beautiful chord progression, which acts as a motif/climax for the narrative, as the song ends with a majestic chord pattern.

'Marquee Moon' is the perfect place to draw attention to the band's musical assets. Individually each player in Television is superb – Verlaine's guitar solos are sublime, they are, in short, a potential total redefinition of the electric guitar. As it is, Verlaine's solo constructions/Coltraneisms are always unconventional, forever delving into new areas, never satisfied with referring back to formulas. Simply, he can solo without ever losing the point.

Richard Lloyd is a good foil for Verlaine. Another fine musician, his more fluid conventional pitching and manic rhythm work is the perfect complementary force and his contribution demands to be recognized for the power it possesses.

Fred Smith on bass is an excellent solid player, he holds down and controls the undertow of the music with great skill. His understanding of what is required from him is a real pleasure to listen to.

Billy Ficca, a delicate but firm drummer, uses every portion of his kit to colour and embellish. I can only express a quiet awe at his inventiveness.

Individual accolades apart, the band's main clout lays in their ability to function as one and perhaps a good demonstration of this can be found in 'Elevation', side two's opening gambit. Layer upon layer of gentle boulevard guitar makes itself manifest, until Lloyd holds the finger-picked melody together and Verlaine sings in that truly incisive style of his.

The song again is beautiful, proudly contagious, with a chorus that lodges itself in your subconscious like a bullet in the skull – 'Elevation don't go to my head', repeated thrice until on the third line a latent ghost-like voice transmutes, 'Elevation into Television'. Guitars cascade in and out of the mix so perfectly.

'Guiding Light' is reflective, stridently poetic – a hymn for aesthetes – and shimmering with lovely piano lines played by Verlaine.

'Prove It', the following track, is a potential single; Verlaine spits and seats his command on the vocal – 'This case . . . this case I've been working on so long . . . too long.' And of course that chorus which I still can't hesitate quoting – 'Prove it . . . Just the facts . . . Confidential.'

Final song on the album is 'Torn Curtain'. A song of grievous circumstances (as with so many of Verlaine's lyrics), the facts – cause and effect – remain enigmatically sheltered from the listener. The structure is indeed strange, with Verlaine's vocals at their most yearning. The song is absolutely compelling and I can't think of a single number written in the rock idiom I could possibly compare it to.

So THAT'S IT. *Marquee Moon*, a work of real genius, suffice to say – oh listen, it's released on Elektra and reminds me of just how great that label used to be. I mean this is Elektra's finest record along with *Strange Days*. Tom Verlaine is probably the single most important rock singer/songwriter/guitarist of his kind since Syd Barrett.

If this review needs to state anything in big bold, black type it's simply this: *Marquee Moon* is an album for everyone, whatever their musical creeds and/or quirks. Don't let anyone put you off with jive turkey terms like 'avant-garde' or 'New York psychos'.

This music is passionate, full-blooded, dazzlingly well crafted, brilliantly conceived and totally accessible to anyone who (like myself) has been yearning for a band with the vision to break on through into new dimensions of sonic overdrive and the sheer ability to back it up.

Tom Verlaine and Television are out there hanging fire and cruising like meteors above all the three-chord wonder boys.

Prove it? They already have done, all you have to do is listen to the album, and levitate along with it.

They are one band in a million, the songs are some of the greatest ever.

The album is *Marquee Moon*.

The Sex Pistols (*are four months old*)

JONH INGHAM

Though Neil Spencer reviewed the Pistols in NME in February 1976, Ingham's and Sounds' unprecedented gesture, devoting a two-page spread to a band who, as the byline read, were barely four months old in April 1976, showed remarkable foresight. Much of what the Pistols had to say would soon provide a blueprint for an explosion of Pistolesque punk bands.

The small sleazoid El Paradise Club in Soho is not one of the more obvious places for English rock to finally get to grips with the seventies, but when you're trying to create the atmosphere of anarchy, rebellion and exclusiveness that's necessary as a breeding ground, what better place? Name a kid who will tell their parents they'll be home really late this Sunday because they're going to a strip club to see the Sex Pistols.

The front is the customary façade of garish, fluorescent-lit plastic and enticing tit pix, gold flocked wallpaper and a life-size gold-framed lovely beckoning you within.

Conditioning expects one to go down a hall or some stairs, but the minute you turn the corner you're there. A small room twenty to thirty feet long, bare concrete floor, a bar at one end, three and a half rows of broken-down cinema seats (the other half seems to have been bodily ripped out). It's an unexpectedly shocking sight at first, but after it gets comfortable the thought occurs that perhaps it's not sleazy enough. It needs more black paint peeling from the sweating walls, a stickier floor . . .

With luck, the second gathering occurred there last Sunday (the Maltese landlords can be a little difficult to unearth). The first such gathering accumulated entirely by word of mouth, and by midnight the joint was jumping.

Flared jeans were out. Leather helped. All black was better. Folks in their late twenties, chopped and channelled teenagers, people who frequent Sex, King's Road avant leather, rubber and bondage clothing shop. People sick of nostalgia. People wanting forward motion. People wanting rock & roll that is relevant to 1976.

At the moment that criteria is best embodied in the Sex Pistols. They fill the minuscule, mirror-backed stage, barely able to move in front of their amps. They are loud, they are fast, they are energetic. They are great.

Coming on like a Lockheed Starfighter is more important to them than virtuosity and sounding immaculate. This quartet has no time for a pretty song with a nice melody.

Guitarist Steve Jones doesn't bother much with solos, preferring to just pick another chord and power on through ('There's two reasons for that – I can't play solos, and I hate them anyway.' As he said that, 'I'm Mandy, Fly Me' came on the jukebox and we agreed the only good thing in it was the solo).

But imitating the roar of the Industrial Age doesn't mean they're sloppy. Although earlier reports reckoned their timekeeping somewhat off, to the point of cultivating an ethic of them being so bad they were good, Glen Matlock (bass) and Paul Cook (drums) seem to have the beast on the rails, and in this stripped-down form the beat is where it's at. One also has to remember that the Sex Pistols has only existed professionally since Christmas and that Steve has only played guitar for five months.

With inaudible lyrics the music is very similar from song to song, but a cranial trigger says that song is great (applaud), but that one is just OK (don't applaud). Everyone else seems to think similarly. Which annoys singer John Rotten endlessly – 'Clap, you fuckers. Because I'm wasting my time not hearing myself.' He begins a slow handclap; about three people join in.

John is a man who likes to confront his audience, not to mention the rest of the band. It's this Stooges-like aura of complete unpredictability and violence that gives the Sex Pistols that extra edge. Paul reckons the broken glass attitude will only disappear when they get as old as Pete Townshend and just do it for the money.

The Pistols' roots lie with Paul and Steve, who left school with a healthy desire to avoid work. The obvious alternative was rock, even though neither could play an instrument. Their musical models were the Stones and the Who and the early Small Faces, which doesn't say much for seventies rock, and was a reason for starting a band.

Out of the last six years Steve rates the Stooges. Paul admits to being fooled by Roxy Music for three albums. Later he added Todd Rundgren. 'Yeah, there's what acid does to you,' retorted Steve, adding proudly, 'There's no drugs in this group.'

Glen joined and they staggered on for a year, learning a Who/Small Faces repertoire ('but that didn't get us anywhere'), buying their threads from Sex and bugging Malcolm, the owner, to manage them. Having already spent seven months in New York handling the New York Dolls he wasn't too interested, but he helped them a bit and they kept bugging and, well, London could do with a seventies rock band.

Malcolm decided that Steve was hopeless as a singer, got him to learn guitar and the search was on. Into Sex walks John, who couldn't sing but looked the part. They tried to audition in the conventional manner, but finally settled on standing him in front of the shop's jukebox, telling him to pretend he was on stage.

John had never even considered joining a band.

We're sitting in a tacky pub in Charing Cross Road. Until now John has been sitting politely, looking a bit bored, while I talk to the others. He's wearing the ripped-up red sweater he wears on stage, a safety pin dangles from a thin gold ring in his right ear lobe. So how come you're doing it, John?

The intensity level immediately leaps about 300 per cent. He looks manic. 'I hate shit. I hate hippies and what they stand for. I hate long hair. I hate pub bands. I want to change it so there are rock bands like us.'

This is delivered at full tirade, with a sneer to match the voice. He clocks my tortoiseshell earring, the five weeks' laziness straggling across my cheeks and chin, and the sneer and the direct-eye blitz never stops. I'm inadvertently thinking, 'Gosh, I'm not a hippie now – that was a childhood error,' and I never was one in the first place. The kid's got style.

You know what end of a switchblade he would have been on in 1956. I'd love to be present when the middle-aged boogers who pass for rock critics on the nationals finally confront him.

But John's just winding up.

'I'm against people who just complain about *Top of the Pops* and don't do anything. I want people to go out and start something, to see us and start something, or else I'm just wasting my time.'

This last phrase is a favourite. He says it with just the right amount of studied boredom.

The Pistols found their first public by gatecrashing gigs, pulling up and posing as the support band. At the North East London Poly they succeeded in emptying the room, the same stylish feat being Shep Gordon's reason for signing up Alice Cooper. At St

Albans, where they supposedly played one of their worst gigs, they were asked back again. St Albans was also the first place to recognize the Doctors of Madness.

In London they rapidly depleted themselves of potential venues. For a start, they wouldn't play pubs.

Malcolm: 'The trouble with pubs is that they're bigger than the bands. They're all full of people playing what a crowd wants rather than what they want because they can make a reasonable living from it. If you want to change things you can't play pubs. You don't have the freedom.'

That left the Marquee, 100 Club and the Nashville; Eddie and the Hot Rods asked them to support at the Marquee. It was the first time they had ever used monitors, and hearing themselves caused slight o.d., John leaping into the audience and the others kicking the monitors about.

In the light of what the Pistols consider the Hot Rods' over-reaction to the incident, the group insist they did little damage to anything that wasn't theirs. They've also written a song on the matter.

I think the photos speak for the particular violence of the Nashville gig, but the band and the Nashville seemed to enjoy each other. Allan Jones of the *Melody Maker* described it: 'Their dreadfully inept attempts to zero in on the kind of viciously blank intensity previously epitomized by the Stooges was rather endearing at first ... The guitarist, another surrogate punk suffering from a surfeit of Sterling Morrison, played with a determined disregard for taste and intelligence.' Taste. Intelligence.

'Who's Sterling Morrison?' asked Steve.

When last heard of he was a university professor in Santa Fe.

'Oh, that's all right then. What's "surrogate" mean?'

They are going to play the Nashville again, but their problem, apart from finding it impossible to find a band they're compatible with musically, is that it's still not the right environment.

Malcolm decided early that France would understand much

better and envisioned a couple of weeks or more in Paris. The French promoter saw the Marquee gig and, fired with visions of Gene Vincent and Vince Taylor, has booked them across France and Switzerland for May. Meanwhile, El Paradise . . .

If things work out, Malcolm will obtain the old UFO premises. Apart from the difficulty of finding the landlords, the police arrived about 2.00 a.m. the first night, what with the noise of the steel rolling door going up and down all the time as people left, and it's not really the right thing to have Arrows spreadeagled against the wall being frisked as a nightcap to the evening's frivolities.

Basically, what Malcolm wants is a rumbling, anarchic, noisy, energetic rock scene, the likes of which haven't been seen in this country since the mid sixties. Any comparisons with the New York rock/club scene are briskly brushed aside.

'The trouble with the Dolls was that their hype was so much bigger than they were. They really had an opportunity to change it all around, but instead of ignoring all that bullshit about signing up with a company and a big advance they got sucked in.

'They get dazzled by the process. Every time the Ramones have a picture of them published it lessens their mystique. There's no mystery about the New York scene. Pretty soon Richard Hell is going to have to leave the Heartbreakers and Sire Records will dangle a contract in front of him and he knows it won't help and won't do any good, but he'll sign it because it's what's expected of him.

'The thing to do is just ignore all that. No one came to sign up the Stones, no one wanted to know. But when they saw a lot of bands sounding like that with a huge following they had to sign them. Create a scene and a lot of bands – because people want to hear it – and they'll have to sign them even though they don't understand it.

'The trouble with the pubs is that they're free, and people come for that reason. If you're at a Sex Pistols gig you wanted to go, because you spent money to get in. I opened the shop because I wanted people to make a certain statement if they wore my clothes. The Sex Pistols are another dimension of that.'

As for what the band think of comparisons . . .

'The New York scene has absolutely nothing to do with us,' sneers John. 'It's a total waste of time. All anyone talks about is the image. No one's ever mentioned the music.'

But there's a remote connection with the aesthetic and their seeming to try to get on with the future.

'I like that word, "remote",' he says real blankly.

(Is it always like this? 'No, he was rather polite tonight.')

Steve and Paul deliver the fatal blows.

'They're not like us. They all have long hair.'

'Yeah, Anglophiles with Brian Jones mopheads.'

So there they sit, waiting for a scene to build up around them, for the appearance of bands they can play with. They look rather glum at the prospect and when you consider it, we can at least go and see the Sex Pistols.

'Yeah,' sighs Steve, 'I wish I could see us.'

Another Sex Pistols Record (*turns out to be the future of rock & roll*)

ROY CARR

Roy Carr's NME *review of the Pistols' third single, 'Pretty Vacant', featured an immortal byline; with no less extravagant a claim than the one Landau had laid upon Springsteen. However, Carr was actually on the button, even if he refrains from mentioning the bamalam brilliance of the Pistols' six-minute cover of the Stooges' 'No Fun', insidiously planted on 'Pretty Vacant's derrière.*

In 1962, nobody really wanted a band looking like us and playing
what we wanted to play, because the people running the music
business couldn't understand anyone wanting to hear it!

(Mick Jagger)

In case anyone's forgotten, fifteen years have elapsed since then
and things really haven't changed that much, eh kidz!!

There are certain all-too-rare occasions when, without prior
warning, a record comes hurtling out of left field . . . stops you
dead in your tracks, floors your expectations, simply *shocks* you,
and promptly sets the adrenalin pumping around your system at
ten times the normal speed.

It happened to me (and I'm certain I'm speaking for countless
others), the very first time I heard Little Richard frantically scream
'Awobopaloobop – Alopbamboom', Chuck Berry motorvatin'
through 'Johnny B. Goode', the Kinks' brutalizing 'You Really Got
Me', Keith Richards's fuzz-guitar intro to '(I Can't Get No)
Satisfaction', and the psychotic delirium of Hendrix's 'Purple
Haze', the we-ain't-gonna-take-no-more-of-this-crap angst of the
Who's 'My Generation', the Velvets' cacophonic 'Sister Ray', the
contempt with which Dylan spat out 'Like A Rolling Stone',
hearing the Stooges' '1969' being played immediately after
CS&N's 'Marrakesh Express' one humid morning over a New
York radio station a couple of weeks after Woodstock, Tele-
vision's surreal 'Marquee Moon' . . .

I experienced the same feelings this Friday when I received an
acetate of the Sex Pistols' third single, 'Pretty Vacant'.

With few exceptions, up until now the seventies have been a
concept: take an idea and then build a band (like Kiss or
Aerosmith) around it and cold-bloodedly exploit it for every dollar
it's worth. That's, of course, if you have a taste for yesterday's
warmed-up leftovers!

The Sex Pistols are an exception – quite probably the only rock
band currently living and working in the present. Not last month,

not next year, but *now* – whilst all around them their immediate competitors, especially those embraced by new wave-ism, are lost in various half-cocked fantasies of what a 1977 rock & roll band should be like.

Contrary to expectations, the Sex Pistols turn out to be not merely somebody's idea of a band called the Sex Pistols, but the genuine article. What the Sex Pistols have in common with the likes of Jerry Lee Lewis, Little Richard, Chuck Berry, Keith Richard, Townshend, Dylan and Iggy – I'll even throw in Wayne Kramer – was that when they stood on the threshold of their respective careers – for a brief moment – not only were they devoid of illusion and pretension but they had their finger firmly on the pulse of a generation.

We have that situation recurring at this very minute.

Picture yourself trying to describe the sheer overwhelming impact of '(I Can't Get No) Satisfaction', 'My Generation', 'Raw Power' or even 'Dancing In The Street'. Truthfully, there aren't any appropriate words. And, unless you're terminally insensitive, you can't possibly fail to recognize the numbing shock of reality when, on such rare occasions as these, it presents itself with all the subtlety of an earthquake.

The Sex Pistols' 'Pretty Vacant' is one such instance.

With this disc, the Pistols positively cream their closest competitors with muscle to spare.

Forget about the acceptable face of outlaw chic. The Sex Pistols are a band virtually unable to perform before a public who helped to create them. It's a vacuum in which no other band has, until now, found itself thrust.

As a result of this dilemma, the only positive outlet for their frustrations is the comparative isolation of the recording studio and it's from there that 'Pretty Vacant' – the music, the noise, the intense atmosphere – boils over in sheer anger and desperation.

People have been trying to get back to this pitch of intensity throughout the seventies and the cumulative desperation seems finally to erupt on this seminal single.

Apart from anything else, 'Pretty Vacant' establishes that the Sex Pistols are not one-and-a-half hit wonders, and there's nothing about this record that should prevent any shop from stocking it, any radio station from keeping it off the playlist, except bloody-minded bigotry.

However, I'm sure that someone will find a 'suitable' excuse for, as we have all been made aware (during this Jubilee Year), both the Establishment and a good number of citizens of this Sceptred Isle are riddled with prejudice and hypocrisy to the extent that the Sex Pistols have been virtually branded the Niggers of Rock & Roll.

In the face of a media backlash, which has had quite the opposite effect to that intended, the Sex Pistols continue to gain momentum. In fact, if the heat were suddenly switched off, perhaps the desperation with which they approach their vocation might dissipate.

You see, the Sex Pistols are so much a part of the present social climate that next year they may be a spent force, maybe the Old Farts of the New Wave, maybe (if some people have their way) dead. However, let the future take care of itself. Whatever the outcome, we'll never ever forget 1977 in the same way we forgot 1973, 1974, 1975 and most of 1976!

Coming Up for Eire

DAVE McCULLOUGH

U2. Hmmmm. Difficult not to have an opinion about a man as supremely self-confident about his own importance as Bono. Credit goes to Sounds' Dave McCullough for hearing potential and possibilities when others just heard parody. It was 1979, after all.

The dichotomy that exists between Northern and Southern Ireland is a strange and jarring one. Travelling south from Belfast you can't but help noticing the hazy, subtle change of most aspects physical and spiritual which reveals itself in the transition from a louder, snarling land into an altogether more tranquil, withdrawn countryside.

The landscape changes into a sprawling, glorious affair, the pubs (ah, the pubs!) are dimmer and follow their own sets of rules, the people look different and are less given to thinking out loud, the bulk and body of Ireland resting on its limbs like some proud and majestic creature, motionlessly purring across its space of time and violence.

On the shiny wings of an Aer Lingus 737 tin can, I was last week reminded of the culture shock, floating with sidekick Slattery over the outskirts of Dublin town. Heathrow had taken its customary toll on us: loose-tongued security men had interrogated us, degraded us with a series of mind-games designed more to reassure the rest of the plane's passengers that they were conventional and safe compared to their hippy/punk long-haired/short-haired victims than to check that the aircraft was indeed secure.

The launching pad of English flights was indeed all noise and frenzy compared to the blank solemnity of Dublin airport, and the gulf of lifestyle and atmosphere was once again brought to mind. We were in another country, another rock & roll space altogether . . .

The Austin A40 that pulled out of Dublin airport some minutes later confirmed the notion. The car was a miracle of mechanical endurance, a sort of pathetic progression from pony and trap, Ireland's bid to keep up with the modern world, and more to the point, as we later discovered, a bid to make big-city top-cats McCullough and Slattery feel uncomfortable.

'We wanted to see how you'd react,' the machine's co-pilot, Bono, told me much later the following day. 'We've had people from record companies who've come over from England and they've taken one look at this car and gone "Whaat?" Don't worry though, you both passed the test.'

Bono is the lead singer of U2, the most important band to emerge from Ireland since the Boomtown Rats and the main objective of this trip to Dublin in the summer of '79. U2 are a very special band and part of a romance that flourished long distance between Dublin and myself ever since their first demo tape was brought to my attention earlier this year.

The tape, recorded in March, was a dazzling account of a band with quite amazing potential. Demos have an annoying habit of falling into narrow, obvious categories these days; for the most part they're fad-conscious or just plain incompetent.

The U2 tape, however, was different. Here was a band that defied trends, blends or bombast, a band that revealed direction, assurety and downright arrogance, letting you know from the Mickey Mouse confines of a C-60 cassette that they had something vital to contribute to the rock & roll of '79.

The sound was roomy and sharp, the songs, like the opening 'Another Time Another Place', reaching vast, breath-taking climaxes, the music dipping and soaring, taking its roots from everywhere you could imagine but defying direct bonds with past, present or, in the grandiose Bowiean sense, The Future. The Only Ones, Penetration, Banshees, Fall, all were there in the music somewhere but the essence was clearly a new (and when was the last time you heard a genuine new band?), significant name for the 'now space', as it were, of rock & roll present tense.

In the ensuing spring months and into early summer, U2 retained a low profile, leading me to re-establish my ideas of that dichotomy between the British Northern Irish and Southern Irish music scenes wherein Dublin and Southern Ireland remained quietly uninvolved, content only to throw forth the odd Rats, Horslips, Planxty freak.

Then word arrived from U2 to the effect that action was taking place between themselves and assorted mainland record companies, including CBS, and that other bands were now reaching stages of fruition (hard evidence including a remarkable tape from the Virgin Prunes) and could well require my attention.

In the midst of all this Paul McGuinness, manager of U2, had made a pointed remark over the phone: 'All that's missing over here, really, is somebody with the entrepreneurial skills of a Good Vibes to set things going. There's certainly enough talent about.'

As the A40 chugged its way into Dublin and U2 men Bono and Adam enthused over their own music and other bands from the city, what was happening became clear. In rock & roll terms, Dublin was a city that was growing up, like the U2 lyrics say 'from a boy to a man . . .'

Later that night we arrived and I finally had the pleasure of catching the fabled U2 live. The venue was the Bagott Inn, which lives up to its sleazy name with a vengeance. 'Tonight's something of a test night,' Bono explained. 'This is the first new wave type gig this place has put on and if it's a success then bands might be able to use it regularly.'

Gigs are a scarce commodity in Dublin. In fact, there are none, save the odd fortunate one-nighter at one of the many 'straighter' rock venues (ancient Skid Row and Horslips guitarists rool OK, y'understand), or the odd support slot at one of the city's two or three bigger, ballroom type venues (a band called DC Nien tonight having the unenviable task of warming up an AC/DC audience).

Bands, therefore, are hungry and they must search for gigs, as U2 have done. Their labour is not in vain, either, as the gig this night proves. The band give evidence to their burgeoning popularity in the city by cramming as many bodies into a scantily publicized Hope and Anchor-type gig as is physically (as opposed to legally) possible.

Their set is quite brilliant. It's an often disarming experience travelling out of London and seeing relatively unknown bands capable of taking on the prima donnas of the Hammersmith Odeon, Marquee and Nashville and wiping the proverbial floor with them (re: Tours and Undertones in the past) and this was yet another such occasion. U2 are total, solid music, naturally intended for the head and for the feet, inculcating meaning and innovation, expressing enough power in communication to knock the unsuspecting listener on his back.

Guitarist David Edge is the most flamboyant player I've seen since Stuart Adamson of the Skids (a major influence, as they say), creating a sizeable, unique niche of sound that spreads across U2's music with scintillating effect, joining together with Larry Mullen's drums and Adam Clayton's bass to form what the band constantly seek, namely a wide sound and a big impression.

Front man Bono is a new R & R performer. He takes the genre's tricks of the trade and tries them out on his audience, shifting their opinions and attitudes. In this sense U2 are unashamedly didactic; they attack their audience and hope maybe to leave them at the end of the night feeling shifted or moved in their attitudes.

Bono, like the rest of U2 and the Virgin Prunes, studies mime in order 'to use up every little ounce of space on stage'. The effect is totally absorbing. You follow Bono with your eyes as he counts on his fingers or runs across stage or spontaneously mimes something that is impenetrable but opposite to the moody, fat rolling sound. At the Bagott the mike broke in front of him. Instead of panicking he used the fluke, calling a kid from the audience down front, thrusting the mike into his upheld right arm, as it were, as a mike stand throughout the song.

And the songs are splendid, inspired impressions of that big sound the band seek, from the Skidsian raunch of 'Out Of Control', and analytical power of 'Twilight' and 'Stories For Boys' to the speedy pop of 'Boy Girl,' revealing an already established, remarkable songwriting force.

Like the Fall or the Zoo bands or Swell Maps, U2 have thrown the new wave over their collective shoulders and are now stepping out in the direction of more vital and contemporary expression while instinctively still retaining the clipped muscularity of the '76 revolution.

In this small space I can but present you with a whisper of the U2 vibe. Suffice to say that a single should be available soon in Ireland on CBS with an album to follow (tentatively titled *Boy*) and all hell will break lose over the coming months about this marvellous, mystical band. It's just a thought, but somebody suggested that if the Boomtown Rats were the John the Baptists of Irish R & R then U2 must be . . .

Tell Me When It's Over

BYRON COLEY

The Dream Syndicate never fulfilled the promise of their debut album, The Days of Wine and Roses, so enthused about by Coley in this return to the lost art-form of 'sleeve-note as signpost'. So you'll just have to take Coley's (and my) word that they were this rip-roaringly exuberant – or locate a copy of the 12-inch single on which he inscribed these words.

Like a pile of gladiators' bloodied kerchieves into which all local hepcats wished to plunge their snoots, the Dream Syndicate appeared on the ridge overlooking LA's musical netherworld in the early days of 1982. With one DIY EP and a brain-snapping series of shows (which showered heavy, metal stug-drops squarely on top of wondrously unguarded pates) their spectral presence soon assumed Herculean cool-to-the-x proportions both locally and nationally (their name was caressed by all the most in-groove lips); and this jumbo myth-profile was further heightened (and made populist) by the release of their unspeakably boss LP, *The Days Of Wine & Roses.* The vinyl casing you hold in your hands contains one cut from that most impossibly reet disc plus three selections that were recorded and broadcast a week prior at/from KPFK's Studio Zzzz.

Together, they offer evidence aplenty of the band's earnestly nondenominational greatness and the live cuts are especially remarkable in light of the fact that this gig was first to present the Syndicate to an audience not necessarily chained hand and foot to the temple of subterranean fashion (whose non-critically dogmatic first tenet, at this time, read 'Dream Syndicate Rules').

In short, the KPFK set was the band's premier opportunity to offer purely aural contours to a large-type crowd that, one presumes, was familiar with them primarily (if not solely) as a reported-in-the-press abstraction. In this setting they were not trapped fly-like in unctuous penned-webbage linking them with (ostensibly) fictional precursors (journalists of this period were notoriously lax in reporting that the Syndicate's sonics buggered description with the ease of a well-lubed and ogrish sodomite of Burroughsian design), but 'merely' were. Non humbly ear-directed proof of same is afore you.

This disc's one previously available buzz-portal is 'Tell Me When It's Over', and one would have a most devilish time finding a selection that more succinctly captures the Syndicate's apish essence.

Rather than opening with a note *per se*, 'Over' cascades forth with a fully matured RIFF, and its whole revolves around this riff's expansion and contraction. Now holding back for a trice, next stuttering wetly like a drunk's feigned apology, then surging forward once more, it describes the lyric's apparent intent as cagily as the solipsistic vocals and one must wonder whether the words were crafted to describe the playing or vice versa (so holistically intertwined yet functionally autonomous are they).

This song also affords us a characteristic peek at the artful humour simmering under the band's collective sombrero and the (easily graspable) evidence for this is threefold: (1) The song's witty placement (in this usage the word 'over' is generally associated with a terminus as opposed to a starting point) renders its title a jest; (2) One might extrapolate that Steve wrote the chorus's lyric as the imagined inner dialogue running through the head of a non-believer 'subjected' to one of the lengthy 'Suzie Q's with which the band delighted in teasing their audiences early on; (3) Karl's guitar, Kendra's bass and Dennis's drums seem a mite reluctant to accept Steve's vocal cues that the song is indeed 'Over', and, in fact, keep going until they're unceremoniously faded out. All right. It digs.

Of the three live cuts, 'Mr Soul' is perhaps the most fascinating on a simple selection-interest level since it serves as a curt slap on the kisser to those decrying the band as nth generation copycats passing off heisted notes as their own.

As every music history buff (worth even a tsp. of NaCl) is well aware, prior to mass acknowledgement of N. Young's pen voice as his own and the Buffalo Springfield's belated public reception as prime musical exponents (rather than shadow-Byrds), there were many who tabbed this song in its original form as nothing other than rank next-Dylanism. Hah! The vigour with which the Syndicate deal this thump is further amplified by the rhythm section's veering ever nearer and nearer to the coded beat they traditionally used for the short instrumental break contained between the second and third choruses of their keeningly sociopathic reading of (Dylan-proper's) 'Outlaw Blues'. The message of this teetering on the brink of double (triple?) glottal reverse is clearly, 'Don't Tread On Me!', but one can scarcely waste time wallowing in these specifics whilst the song's playfully monolithic raga structure ebbs and flows 'round his/her head. It's too too good to appreciate only on an academic level – by God, it moves.

Similarly persistent anti-taggability mixed with undeniably

righteous playing also coils through the core of the two originals here (both initially released on the aforementioned EP).

On that disc both 'Sure Thing' and 'Some Kinda Itch' were 'taken' (quite literally) with a roughneck's sense of time-with-end URGENCY – the guitars screaming like airport macadam under infinite p/s/i stress, the propulsive drum/bass-work rushing forward to presage and echo itself in the course of a single measure, and the vocals splitting the air in an insect fear torrent that physically gainsays their intellectually post-anxietal (as-seen-on-paper) message. Not so here.

For this date, the Syndicate spun the tables 360 degrees on those believing them to be a temple to loud/fast monotheism, and they permit these beauties to unveil their charms at a lilting (almost sexy) pace.

'Itch' is particularly notable, in that it began the evening's set on a completely unexpected note: bypassing its champing 'You're Gonna Miss Me'-styled intro in toto, and then turning what was usually one of the Syndicate's most ragingly GUITAR-stoked mind-burners into a highly civilized 'vocal with accompaniment'. The audience was thrown for a loop by this mangling of their expectations and one could taste the tension mounting as they waited (futilely) for the band to cut loose. At every new musical twist they girded their figurative loins for the ravaging noise onslaught they 'knew' would be forthcoming, but 'twas not to be. Karl's spatial-as-Cipollina fretwork led nowhere but back to the vocals, and ditto for the ferociously guttural (almost Faustian) pseudo bass loop that can be heard about four minutes in. Hurray!

This forceful dashing of accumulated mis-preconceptions forced the assembled neo-heps to rethink their acceptance-position pronto and, to their credit, they did.

'Sure Thing', as presented here, is another neat pop-quiz re: the audience's mettle.

It begins in the same light-hearted manner as 'Itch' (Steve's breath manipulation being especially coltish), thus giving yon crowd every reason to believe that it'll continue in a like manner. Midway through it even boils down to an elegantly circular melodic replay-statement via Kendra's bass (whose sent-sensate messages are sweet enough to bring visions of the Heidi/heather/goatherd trine to mind). At this point, the crowd is lulled into receptive approval of this ('obviously' heart-felt) modus when, out of the blue, Dennis's drums repeat their powerful opening run. This is a feint and the band again withdraws, but the drums reiterate their call to arms a split second later and the Syndicate explodes *en masse* into a clamorous din-hook that surprises the fudge out of the attendees (not leastly because it deeply scratches the itch that the song's lyrics – and heretofore its delivery – have implied is unscratchable).

Very neat formalist fisticuffs from a band with limitless destructive potential; and an excellent example of their protrusive mailed fist/kid glove dynamism. Never relax fully when you listen to this band. If they catch you napping they will crush your head like a vinegar-sotted egg.

Still, the musical bludgeoning/demolition of which they're capable is not without its own vast (albeit perverse) charms (and concomitant rewards), so if one night you startle to find that your face is drenched in blood – consider it not just a symbol of the Syndicate's victory, but of yours as well.

Dissolve/Reveal

PAUL WILLIAMS

Not many rock writers could display the necessary open-mindedness to witness and enthuse about two bands as diverse as cow-punkers Lone Justice and thrash exponents Black Flag within the same week.

Particularly when they're twenty years into critdom. Though, like Dream Syndicate, Lone Justice never repaid influential early media supporters like Robert Hilburn and Mikal Gilmore by delivering on vinyl, Williams's prose effortlessly conveys the joys of his first exposure to Maria McKee live.

Dissolve/reveal. It's Monday. I'm listening to the Stones' new single, 'Harlem Shuffle'. I've seen two more shows since catching the Beat Farmers and Mojo Nixon Thursday night: Lone Justice at the Stone in San Francisco Saturday, and Black Flag (same club, very different audience) Sunday. I have a new star in my universe. Her name is Maria McKee.

When I heard Lone Justice's album I was very impressed, especially with the lead singer, who has a great voice and a lot of presence. I liked the songs, and was knocked out by the energy of the hard rock numbers ('East Of Eden', 'Ways To Be Wicked,' Wait Till We Get Home'). Even the more overtly country numbers appealed to me. So I was excited to discover, practically the first day I was listening to the album, that Lone Justice would be performing locally the following weekend (me being lucky again).

The more I listened, the more excited I got. But I still wasn't prepared for the show I went to Saturday night. Maria McKee is a powerhouse performer, who at this stage in her career anyway is totally present in and totally committed to every word she sings and every movement she makes on stage. She sings with the kind of ease and speed Mick Jagger and Lou Reed had early in their careers, and she relates to her audience with the non-stop intensity and affection of Janis Joplin at her peak. Comparisons are dangerous, and I'm not necessarily saying she's as good as those people – in fact, I wouldn't even know how to measure such a thing. But, subjectively, my experience standing in the audience (on the dance floor, three or four heads back, maybe ten feet from the edge of the stage) was like my experience watching Jim Morrison in 1967 or Bruce Springsteen in 1973 or Janis Joplin New Year's Eve 1967 at the Ark in Sausalito. I was transfixed. I was filled with joy. And I was startled awake once again by the news that there is something bigger than me in this world, and I can be part of it. I got caught up in the performer's love of performing, her passion for reaching out through rock & roll.

Although there's a very strong country flavour to the album (balanced against an equally strong, almost contradictory rock flavour, creating an interesting tension), Lone Justice's show in San Francisco was rock all the way; the only overtly country aspects were a couple of ballads from the album included in the encores (great stuff), and Maria's stage persona, which is definitely country girl (cotton dress, she rolls her eyes a lot, comes on like a scrapper, calls her man 'honey' and affects just a touch of a drawl). The covers they sang that I recognized were the Rolling Stones' 'All Down The Line' (absolutely smokin', and a great choice), John Fogerty's 'Fortunate Son' (sung with an unexpected and heartfelt anger that transformed it from a rockin' oldie to a powerful, very timely political statement), Janis Joplin's 'Cry Baby' (she pulled if off; the woman has guts and style), and again, the Velvet Underground: climax of the first encore, a version of 'Sweet Jane' (incorporating the audience singing the background bit from 'Walk On The Wild Side', incredible) that stands easily with any 'Sweet Jane' I've ever heard. Then there were the originals, like her wonderful soliloquy with gospel quotations in the middle of 'Soap, Soup And Salvation,' and another audience response bit, in 'Wait Till We Get Home', unlike anything I've experienced before – she had us chanting over and over 'wait till we get home!' and then, us still chanting, she starts in on us, 'you're telling me to wait?!' Her presence is so strong she could get us singing not with her but against her, making us the son-of-a-bitch she's rebelling against, and keep us singing while she let us have it. Whew.

The Maria McKee I saw the other night was totally at home in the drama of her moment. When that happens to a performer, all the doors of creativity flow open. You get to a place (temporarily) where everything you try succeeds. All you have to do is throw your entire heart into it, give it everything you've got, spend all your love, trust, energy and talent right now. Believe that there's more where that came from, and if there isn't, at least you'll go out with a bang!

She's got this voice, and knows how to harness it with her band, on a rock & roll stage, and she has the ability to invent a role for herself and play it to the hilt, incorporating everything she's feeling and all the drama of the audience's hopes and expectations into each gesture, each phrase, each guitar chord. Part of how she does this is by being smart, and part is by being gifted, and part is by being lucky and in the right place at the right time, and part is by surrendering to the spirit. The greatest performances are channelled; the greatest performers are those who know how to stand in such a way that the lightning will strike and pass through them.

The only way I have of measuring a performance is subjective: after seeing Lone Justice perform, I feel like I'm living for the chance to see them again. And that's what I want from rock & roll. I want the shows and records to be so good that it's worth staying alive just to experience them.

Black Flag didn't move me to quite that degree, but I can see how they might have. They definitely got my attention. There were four guys – I expected more, somehow – and the singer, Henry Rollins, is a very powerful presence. He's tall, well-built, performed wearing nothing but black nylon boxer shorts (an elegant multicolour tattoo of the sun covers his back, with the words 'search and destroy' above it), when he wasn't singing he had his lips pursed angrily, always looking like he was about to spit on the audience (he did spit, frequently, but always back into the stage). While the music raged away behind him – drums, bass, electric guitar, and they were good; I suppose some of the heavy metal bands may play this well, but it's been impossible for me to tell at arena volumes with arena acoustics – he would stand at stage edge, microphone constantly gripped in his left hand, riding the music, moving his body hypnotically, not for the audience seemingly but rather as an acknowledgement of and response to the physicality of the music. He had the dignity and grace certain large simians in the zoo achieve, looking out at the gawking crowd with both hostility and a kind of distant compassion, as if aware that his suffering must be nothing compared to theirs. Between songs when people called out requests and other comments, he would lean forward, make eye contact, and move his lips, 'muh muh muh muh muh', mimicking them, communicating, but also in a strange way very giving; not holding himself back.

Black Flag is a hardcore band, which is what punk has evolved or devolved into, and as others have pointed out this music and heavy metal are definitely converging. But heavy metal is all pose and gesture; everything is formalized; and it seems to work best when the band is big enough to draw a large crowd, creating a sort of Nuremberg rally camaraderie (not that I regard heavy metal music as essentially fascist; it simply draws on the same human instincts, as do many rock shows, and, significantly, uses them for celebration – and profit-taking – rather than for political ends). (I have to add that I haven't seen a heavy metal show in a club or small theatre; possibly that would give me a whole other perspective.) Hardcore, on the other hand, is, at least in Black Flag's hands, a passionately sincere music. The loud guitar playing and the singer's screaming and sinuous movements are not formalized gestures intended to provoke ritualized responses, but rather an invocation of the dark muse, a spiritual and artistic and, often, political undertaking meant to call forward something wild and unknowable, something real and awakening and substantial in a dull and meaningless universe.

The audience at this show were not, for the most part, uniformed punks in mohawks and leather or skinhead regalia. It was a heterogeneous crowd, and if a lot of them were fans of the band, they were careful not to be obvious about it. There was plenty of slamdancing immediately in front of the stage, and people did dive off the stage into the crowd – I got hit pretty hard on the side of the head at one point, when I was watching the dancing from the side (actually, it attracted me, but I was unwilling to throw myself into the fray with my glasses on) and forgot to protect my flank. The slamdancing, in which people assault each other in a rough but impersonal, non-hostile, mostly fun-loving way, careening into their neighbours or sending others off with furious shoves, is exciting for the participants (like a bar-room brawl but safer; people are usually quick to help you up and protect you if you fall) and also creates an atmosphere of danger for the crowd as a whole, since people may come flying into you at any time wherever you stand on the sidelines. This reduces the distance between performers and audience – both are at risk in an unstable situation – even though on another level it can serve as a huge distraction. It's a fascinating phenomenon, far from harmless but also more fun than you might think, and worth experiencing if you get a chance and you dare.

But for Black Flag, I'm sure, the slamdancing is just another familiar piece of the environment, like urine-soaked alleys in back of urban clubs, not necessary to their act but not inappropriate either. What impressed me about the band, besides the power of the music and Rollin's striking visual and aural presence, was their evident commitment. I know they've been touring tirelessly, year in and year out, and while I trust that their hard work does earn them a little money (the show was not that well-attended, actually, maybe partly because the hardcore scene in San Francisco is being harassed and is starting to fall apart), it was clear to me watching them perform that what this is for them is a way of life and an artistic quest, they look like they live to play together on stage and that each night arrives as an opportunity to explore this thing a little further.

And their commitment is seductive. A lot of avant-garde artists beat the same old ideas to death endlessly and act like they're doing something important. Black Flag, on the other hand, strike me as real musicians and real risk-takers; I can see myself wanting to experience their show again before long, for the loud crashing angry fun of it and also to find out how much further and in what direction their hungers have taken them.

Drunk on the New Blood

DON WATSON

In his article on New York bands, the Swans and Sonic Youth, emerging in the early eighties from the embers of No Wave, Don Watson was among the first to recognize the beginning of a new avenue of exploration and a welcome diversion from the bastard children of thrash.

One o'clock Monday morning in New York . . .

Uptown, amidst the skyscrapers and the good old-fashioned futurism, M T V is transmitting as usual, broadcasting its neat little unruptured slices of corporate rock & roll.

The videodrone spirals on.

Downtown, on the edge of Alphabet City. The Pyramid Club downholds the tradition of the dream inverted. Here in authentic sleazerama, the performing transvestites are taking a break from dancing on the bar, snatching a quick gasp and gaping at the stage show. This is Foetus Flesh.

On-stage Roli Mosiman of the Swans plays keyboards, although it sounds like a cacophony of crashing juggernauts. Meanwhile from the floor – around ankle level of the first row to be precise – the vocals echo from deep in the chest of a writhing Jim Foetus.

His guttural cry is repetitious, infectious and insistent: 'LONG LIVE THE NEW FLESH/LONG LIVE THE NEW FLESH.'

From the mouths of germs and Foetuses . . .

New York, New York – so strange they named it twice.

The schizophrenia of the Big Apple Uptown/Downtown dichotomy has been well documented, but never has it seemed so firmly entrenched.

Uptown Manhattan is rapt in the Videodrone, convulsing in the clutches of a corporate rock boom, which explodes every three minutes across the ever-multiplying screens, the uptown thought bubble obscured by the horizontal grain of a video image.

The search for those who are trying to re-invent reality from the lifeless fabrications of the media blitz must take us out of the sealed and air-conditioned, antiseptic environs of Uptown's Toyland Futureworld and down to the haunt of all tourists of sleaze – the Lower East Side.

Where the Avenue numbers slide below zero and into the letters of Alphabet City is where obsessions can breed.

It's there, with the care and attention of the ever more hyperactive Foetus and Racontresse of Filth, Lydia Lunch, that the New Flesh is regenerating.

This time it takes the shape of Sonic Youth, dreams and desires channeled through a sound of adrenal fear, and the Swans, the sound of a heavy boot crushing a white hand.

Unlike their grandparents, Patti Smith and Television, this savage brood harbor no illusions of vaulting the ever-widening cultural gulf and invading the ivory towers of the uptown rock business.

The New Flesh will not be televised – they must be sought out in person.

The journey to the Lower East Side is safer now than it might have been a few years back.

Taxi drivers, once reluctant to venture into Alphabet City at all, now acknowledge that civilization stretches at least as far as Avenue B. But who cares anyway, on a night like this it's a scenic walk.

Outside my temporary abode, the Waterfront Loft, transvestite hookers stalk the beat on split-proportioned stilettoes. Adjusting high suspenders on torn fishnet stockings, they wait for often unsuspecting customers, looking far more real than the real thing.

Finally they retire to the late night bar La Bamba to gargle gin and bitch, while in the jukebox a cockroach scuttles between selection card and glass.

Further down, past heavy leather hang-out The Anvil, an all-male busking act on a late street corner stint look the picture of vulnerability, as they stand in the middle of a muscles-bulging and apparently predatory all-male crowd.

It looks like the countdown to a very nasty scene, until you check the street name. This is Christopher Street, New York's gay centre.

Past bookshops, still open and packed with pictures of strong-men that are cartoon strip representations of power, and bondage queens that are submission stylized and exaggerated to the point of art.

Then way east, along Third Street, past racks of motorcycles gleaming a muted yellow in the streetlamp light, and a building scarred with a huge SS in black aerosol. A Hell's Angel area, highly sought after in these parts, discourages breaks-ins, altogether safer than living near a cop station.

Just past midnight and we're down in the lowest numbers. It's late enough to pay an anti-social call on local vampyra turned brood mother Lydia Lunch, my favourite viper-tongued female.

Harpy doyenne of New York's No Wave, twisted torch singer of the Queen of Siam LP *Immaculate Consumptive*, Lydia sits at the window of her scrupulously tidy room. There is no bottle of Sunrise on the white table in front of her, but a bare light bulb bears a limited testament to the Americana Noir clichés of which we're both so fond.

The telephone rings, Lydia picks it up and flings it violently in the direction of Jim Foetus, who sprawls across the bed. Surrounding his outstretched figure are back issues of *Hustler*, the American porn magazine run by one-time presidential candidate and self-appointed horse-fly on the butt of the Moral Majority, Larry Flynt.

Far from the soft-focus liberalism of the sixties' *Playboy*, *Hustler* is real hardcore in every sense of the word, treating politics with all the delicacy it extends to its open-crotch photographic spreads.

'Definitely the best American magazine,' says Lydia. 'Politics and filth, what better combination could you have.'

Larry Flynt is Lydia's kind of guy; shot by a member of the Moral Majority during an obscenity case and paralysed for life from the waist downwards.

As well as working on her own stories, her little vignettes of degradation, and acting as brood mother to the Swans and Sonic Youth, she awaits the re-release of her back catalogue, on Cabaret Voltaire's Doublevision label.

This interest in the documentation of the past is new to Lydia. Previously, in the tradition of the No Wave from which she surfaced, she's been obsessively concise – records appear and are deleted as fast. If you missed out then you missed out and pay more attention in future.

All very well and good, but the result of such high principles is just that such renegades as the No Wavers are swallowed up by the historical process.

Now that the third wave is upon us, it's time for reactivation.

It began with Patti Smith, which is where rock & roll ended. Patti Smith was the last point of contact between two generations.

From that point on the American media, dominated as it still is by the previous generation of hoary old rockers, ceased to be able to understand, let alone interpret, what was going on. No Wave didn't care, it just continued to go its own sweet (and sour) way.

Deriving its name from the seminal Eno-produced LP *No New York*, No Wave's principal figures were Lydia's Teenage Jesus and the Jerks, the Contorions, Mars and DNA. They had in common a certain mode of sound which was like – Lydia?

'AAAAAAAAAAAARGH!'

What?

'It was like, roll your eyes back, stretch your hands out and scream.

'Its aim was to destroy rock, basically, eliminate the old dinosaurs that everything was based on. Emotional, artistic, musical, intellectual, everything, just to go AAAAAAAAAAAA-ARGH! I CAN'T TAKE IT ANY MORE! Just that – a cyclone burning itself up from the inside.

'What we were doing was influenced in an indirect way by the grandfathers, but it was a breakaway from that even then. It was almost rejecting the previous generation. The thoughts were on the same lines, but it sounded different because it was taking it to a different extreme.

'The No Wave thing took a lot of the more compassionate, humanist qualities that the forefathers had and eliminated them, reducing the whole thing to something much more cold and ugly and realistic, post-realistic. Not apocalyptic, but taking it to the ugliest extreme.'

It was always a rigorously apolitical revolution though, beginning with sex and taking it way beyond.

Trouble is, they were never there long enough for most people to even notice their existence.

'All the No Wave bands just self-destructed. They were all so concise in the music, the delivery, the point, and they just ended.

'It wasn't a premature death, it was an immediate and accurate one, they didn't extend the boundaries of their short lives. As I say, a cyclone that sucks into itself and disintegrates. Most people had no tolerance for it until it was over.'

Their legacy, though, is the third wave – the Swans and Sonic Youth, who have honed down the frenzy of the No Wave attack and are calmly taking it to the furthest extremes.

Sonic Youth, with their trashy cartoon slogan 'Kill Your Idols', bringing the malevolence of No Wave and the sound sensitivity of Glenn Branca to bear on the legend of the Stooges.

And the Swans, who further pursue the ends of ugliness in the belief that to perceive a thing as beautiful is necessarily to perceive it wrongly.

'To my ear,' says Lydia, 'the Swans are the ultimate end of this particular breed of music, which is not to say that nothing from the past is valid, it's just that this is the ultimate extreme of it. It is the end result of what has come before, for extremity and intensity.'

The mantle of the fatalist would fall all so easily on to Lydia's shoulders. Naturally, she would reject it.

'It's optimistic,' adds Lydia, 'when you realize that there is nothing, no hope left. The Swans and Sonic Youth are the end of this particular breed of music, and from that end will sprout something else. When you get to the end of the road, you don't fall off the edge. Yeah, I think I'm optimistic. I'm not jaded.'

No indeed. It's inevitably the darker side of the American split personality that I'm here to celebrate.

From Tennessee Williams and Henry Miller to Charles Bukowski, Hubert Selby Jr, and the Baron and Baroness of Filth, Larry Flynt and Lydia Lunch, *Horses* period Patti Smith through to New York's New Flesh, Sonic Youth and the Swans and their sickly fantasies of the super-real.

The renegades of Americana past and present, the Hard Corps of stubborn resistance, who with their blasphemous erections and iconoclastic ejaculations have released the anti-strain to the moral majority and their rampaging disease of conformist madness.

One o'clock, and as Tuesday morning's ushered in, it's time to penetrate deeper into the Lower East.

Hmmmmm ... you have to allow yourself a grimace at the irony. The last shopfront on the edge of Alphabet City is a funeral director's.

Down in the cramped surroundings of a two-room flat between A and B lives Swans vocalist Mike Gira.

You walk straight into the kitchen, past a squat little bath, and past the empty room of bassist Crosby. The door of the black-walled room is left ajar to highlight the noose that hangs in the frame.

Gira himself sits in his own room at the desk, framed against a gross cartoon of desperate sexuality that hangs on the wall – his own work.

We break open the first of the two six-packs I've brought along, and talk of Charles Bukowski. Gira tells me proudly of the time he had his stomach pumped in the ward his hard-drinking literary hero was known to frequent.

Poet, genius, novelist, and dirty old man, Bukowski's tales of bastards, whores and alcoholics make him one of the greatest of American writers. Ironic, because he denied its heritage entirely.

Equally though, for the sake of perversity, Gira would seek to dismiss the New York influences in which he's so obviously steeped. The Swans are perhaps the most New York of bands.

The nerve ends that the Swans scrape and stroke are sensitive ones. For those who expect music to concern itself with healthier matters they could easily be construed as somehow harmful.

'I don't think that's true,' Gira replies. 'Watching the Swans is a matter of losing yourself in the brutality of what you're watching. It's a musical performance, though it's not a permanent state. It's not a life-long lobotomy. No form of art can have an enduring effect on behaviour.'

So what in hell are the Swans?

'Honesty, directness, intensity of emotion. A sophisticated sound.'

269

Sophistication may not be the first word that springs to mind on hearing the raw power of the Swans, but such effective brutality essentially belies a great sensitivity to the use of sound.

Each element of the Swans, from Roli Mosiman's edgy psychotic drumming power through the euphoric combination of Crosby's bass, Wesberg's guitar and Gira's deadpan vocals, is direct and single-minded. Together they create a sound that is totally absorbed in itself, words and music in one pulsating mass.

The Swans simply wring everything possible out of the conventional line-up. But what, I wonder, sustains this fierce attack?

'Well, it's not just a musical venture, without the content and the desire to cut through things it wouldn't exist. It's not a matter of us getting together to make music. It's not like that at all.'

The Swans, claims Gira, have nothing to do with rock music. 'The Swans is just a dissatisfaction with basic ordinary experiences. It's a matter of trying to get more out of the human body.

'I suppose, as you say, it does have a lot to do with Theatre of Cruelty, although I wouldn't say Artaud is particularly a figure we invoke . . . I used to like him when I was a romantic.'

I leave Mike Gira in his small room to his profane tales, the extremes of his imagination and the remains of another six-pack.

As I close the door of his apartment, I hear the steady clacking of a typewriter begin. I walk down the dark green hall and outside again.

It's late and a quiet paranoia hangs over the streets as I head back up West, then way downtown to find Sonic Youth.

Sonic Youth are the most traditional of their axis, being the only ones who will profess an ideological alignment with rock & roll.

Guitarist Thurston Moore once intriguingly described them as a cross between Black Flag and Throbbing Gristle, and, like the former, they have the capacity for taking Raw Power's bastard offspring fiercely by the throat, strangling the life out of it, and all the time declaring their love for it.

Don Watson

Like the latter, their approach to sound is guided by an awareness of texture. They'll tear apart the standard formulations to dig innovation from their flesh.

Since their formulation in 1981, they've released two LPs. A debut produced by Glenn Branca – a work of deceptive fragility, ringing with frightened melodies and harmonies – and a fierce riposte in 1983's *Confusion Is Sex* which pulsed with the violence of the cornered.

It's only now, though, that they seem to have truly found their identity, with a forthcoming single 'Death Valley 69' recorded with Lydia Lunch and a third LP, both produced by Jim Foetus.

Theirs is the sound of the Velvet Underground and the Stooges, stretched, squeezed and distorted and finally brought to an electric currency.

Where in England, a country where traditions are a constant and stultifying force, we might see innovation as disregarding the past, for Sonic Youth, a self-confessedly very American band, it's a different story.

'The idea of America,' says bassist Kim Gordon, 'is that Progress is the God, so that what has happened is either totally steamrollered or it's rewritten.'

So true innovation is a matter of reactivating the past, not replicating it.

'To us it's more interesting to subvert the term rock & roll by applying it to what we do,' says Kim, 'than it is to claim to be something different, or to give ourselves a spurious "art" label.

'Because what is termed rock & roll in the land of MTV is actually a corporately induced replication, which in reality bears no resemblance to the original. It's like Philip K. Dick's electric sheep.'

But, no matter what they might say, what emerges, if it is rock & roll at all, is a mutant strain, but a fierce and virulent one all the same.

'That's because a lot of our idea was to radicalize what we love, like totally fuck it up.'

271

Whatever influences are churned through Sonic Youth's diverse imaginations, what comes out is a sound charged with fear and anxiety, that captures the human adrenalin rush. It certainly has nothing to do with the cosy fantasies of corporate rock & roll.

In their ability to penetrate to the roots of the rock clichés, Sonic Youth are closest to the Birthday Party, though in place of Cave's feverish imaginings they present a series of vivid abstractions, electric with violence and tension.

In contrast to the Swans, who are totally absorbed in their own darkness, Sonic Youth always seem scared of their own shadows.

There's also something uniquely personal about the interaction between Kim Gordon and Thurston Moore's guitars, Lee Renaldo's bass and Jim Sclavunos on drums.

Kim Gordon: 'One of the reasons that the last LP was called *Confusion Is Sex* is because a lot of what we do comes out of our own confusion, and how we come up with the structure is very intimate, almost sexual.'

Meanwhile, uptown, MTV continues, the electric sheep of America's new herd mentality.

'I think we rebel against hi-tech in the sense that it represents itself as a utopia,' says Thurston.

If this is heaven, we're bailing out. Sonic Youth pretended no mission, but by their very existence, in however limited a sphere, they rupture the glossover of America's history rewrite.

Outside Sonic Youth's downtown flat, a high crumbling structure held up by wrought-iron fire escapes straight out of *Once Upon a Time in America*, the garbage is spilling on to the streets. A grey dawn seeps over the skyline.

5. On the Road Again

"You don't have to wreck your hotel room this trip —
we're on holiday!"

'Going on the road', a perennial rock & roll experience, has changed dramatically since the Brits first managed to sell America's music back to it. Michael Braun's account of the Beatles' first trip to the US in 1964 seems remarkably tame twenty-eight years on.

If screaming girls, freeway hi-jinks and bad miming were soon to be superseded by sex, drugs and rock & roll seventies-style, the 'on the road' tales related by Nik Cohn and Stephen Davis, travelling across North America with the Who and Led Zeppelin, primarily detail orchestrated stunts by an extremely frazzled road crew, while the main concern of Mott the Hoople frontman Ian Hunter in his Diary of a Rock & Roll Star *is how he might get enough sleep.*

Lifestyle aside, Zeppelin's main claim to fame may well lie in the sizeable role they played in pushing rock bands down the unlit hallway to arenas with ping-pong acoustics. In a post-MTV world, bands seem increasingly reluctant to expose themselves to their fans close-up. Fewer gigs means, of course, bigger gigs, removing the essential intimacy of the experience.

Dylan's 1975 Rolling Thunder Revue was a necessary antidote to such cattle circuses, in particular the much-lauded Dylan/Band tour of the previous year, forty arenas in forty days. Dylan hated every moment. Nat Hentoff's major feature on the revue, 'Is It Rolling, Zeus?', proves that there is no success like failure.

The next concerted attempt to sweep arena rock into the ocean, the Sex Pistols' one and only US tour, ended with the band in disarray, berating 5,000 fans packed into Bill Graham's San Franciscan vision of a cross between an airplane hangar and a barn – Winterland. John

Helstrom provides a perceptive if dispiriting account of one of rock's most legendary tours.

Representing the post-Pistols world are two fictional accounts of life on the road, reflecting the extremes of arena-XS and club lo-life, one from the pen of jaundiced ex-journo Tony Parsons, the other from the twisted fingers of Sonic Youth's primo impresario, Thurston Moore. Some things never change. Or to quote John Entwistle, Who bassist and witness to most forms of road-mania:

> *I'm done screwing, spent my load*
> *Nothing doing, let's hit the road.*

America, America and Ed Sullivan

MICHAEL BRAUN

Michael Braun's paperback Love Me Do *was a pre-Rockspeak attempt (1964) to come to terms with Beatlemania. His detailed account of the reception awaiting the Beatles' arrival in America perfectly captures the goldfish-in-a-bowl existence they were required to adopt.*

After some trouble over visas with the American authorities, the Beatles received an H2 category, which was above H3 (trainees) but below H1, for 'persons of distinguished merit and ability'. Their work permits were valid 'as long as unemployed American citizens capable of performing this work cannot be found'.

A few days before the Beatles were to leave for the United

States it was announced that in addition to appearing on the Ed Sullivan television programme they would give two concerts at Carnegie Hall. Within hours after the announcement was made all the tickets were gone. They were being paid $10,500 for two shows at Carnegie Hall, and the New York impresario Sidney Bernstein offered them $25,000 plus $5,000 for the British Cancer Fund if they would give one performance in the mammoth Madison Square Garden. Epstein refused.

'Don't they realize,' said Bernstein, 'this isn't show business, it's history?'

Entering into the spirit of the occasion, the *Daily Express* revealed that according to high Washington sources the Beatles would be invited to the White House.

Two of the Beatles' records had been distributed in America a year earlier and had failed to make an impression. Then the steady publicity in the British national press had been picked up by the London offices of the American news media. *Time*, *Newsweek* and *The New York Times*, as well as NBC and CBS, all had stories on the Beatles, treating them as news phenomena rather than show business personalities.

In order to ensure that this gratuitous publicity was not dissipated, Epstein persuaded Capitol, the Beatles' American recording company, to spend fifty thousand dollars for what they called a 'crash publicity program'.

They plastered five million 'The Beatles Are Coming' stickers on telephone poles, washroom walls, and other appropriate places throughout the country. They distributed the record the Beatles had made in London to every disc jockey in the country. They issued a four-page newspaper on the Beatles and sent out a million copies. They photographed their top executives wearing Beatle wigs and distributed 'Be a Beatle Booster' badges to all their employees. They offered Beatle haircuts free to all their female employees and persuaded Janet Leigh to get one. They even tried, unsuccessfully, to bribe a University of Washington cheerleader into holding up a card reading 'The Beatles Are Coming' to the television cameras at the Rose Bowl.

'There was,' said Capitol Vice-President Doyle Gilmore, 'a lot of hype.'

On the morning of their departure from London, the *Daily Mirror*, in an article written by Donald Zec, said the Beatles were a passing phase as contrasted to Cliff Richard who had been studying his craft for years, but who nevertheless told Mr Zec he thought his colleagues from Liverpool were 'fab'. The national papers also carried reviews of Edward Albee's *Who's Afraid of Virginia Woolf?*, which had opened the night before. 'Why must we always look to America for excitement like this?' one of them asked.

Four thousand girls who had arrived at London Airport too early to read the papers gave the Beatles a screaming farewell as their plane left London.

Shortly afterwards, radio station WMCA in New York made the first of a series of announcements: 'It is now 6.30 a.m. Beatle time. They left London thirty minutes ago; they're out over the Atlantic Ocean headed for New York. The temperature is 32 Beatle degrees.'

Aboard the plane, the Beatles, accompanied by John's wife Cynthia, and Epstein, sat in the first-class compartment. Their fellow passengers included George Harrison (no relation), a columnist for the *Liverpool Echo* and *Liverpool Daily Post*; Harry Benson, a photographer for the *Daily Express*; and Maureen Cleave of the *Evening Standard*. Also aboard was Phil Spector, a constantly sun-glassed American who is responsible for earning millions of dollars by writing such songs as 'Da Doo Ron Ron'.

I was in the economy section of the plane with the Beatles' road manager, Neil Aspinall; his assistant Mal Evans; the photographer Bob Freeman, who was to record the trip for Epstein and the

Daily Mirror; the photographer Dezo Hoffman; as well as representatives of several other British publications and some British television stations. At one point during the trip Epstein came back and passed out a list of seventeen names who were 'press contacts' in every corporation with whom the Beatles would deal, from the Columbia Broadcasting System to the Hotel Deauville in Miami Beach.

In addition to the journalists there were several British manufacturers, who, tired of not being able to speak with Epstein in London, had decided that a plane 30,000 feet above the Atlantic was the best place to do business. Several of them sent products up to him with a note asking for an endorsement. They were all politely refused. Meanwhile the Beatles relaxed, laughed at the stewardess's life-saving instructions, and wondered about the reception awaiting them.

Paul was pessimistic. 'Since America has always had everything,' he asked Spector, 'why should we be over there making money? They've got their own groups. What are we going to give them that they don't already have?'

Maureen Cleave turned round and told Paul not to worry. 'You'll go like a bomb in America.'

'What?' asked Spector.

Someone came over to explain that what in England was a sign of confidence meant exactly the opposite in America, and the plane continued on its journey.

Harry Benson came back to tell several journalists that the Beatles liked him because 'I just play like I'm a daft soppy ha'porth.' He had tipped the stewardess to be allowed to take pictures exclusively during the trip and now he began lining the Beatles up for photos against the Manhattan skyline outside the window. When the plane began to descend, all they could see were the family houses of Queens that surround Kennedy International Airport.

'Hey!' said Benson, 'I think we've come to the wrong place.'

Any doubts that the Beatles (to say nothing of Benson) entertained were immediately settled when the plane came to a stop. Outside, what looked like the entire teenage population of the Greater New York area were waiting. From the window of the plane they seemed like a photo mural against the blue sky.

The mural quickly came to life when the plane's door was opened. The shouts of a hundred photographers crouched on a hydraulic crane blended antiphonically with the wailing wall of pubescence. As the Beatles reached the bottom of the stairway, a policeman who had been assigned to take them in hand came over and told them not to smile or wave 'or you'll excite them!' Then, turning to his companion, he remarked, 'Boy could they use a haircut!'

Everyone leaving the plane was handed a 'Beatle Kit' consisting of a wig, a button saying 'I like the Beatles' and an autographed photo. As the Beatles posed for pictures on the tarmac a Pan American Airways executive was trying to cover their BEAtle bags with the 'Beatles Kit'. During this lull an airport employee came over and asked for their autographs. When he received them he ran to show it to a few friends.

'Hey, look!' he said, 'Twenty bucks!'

It was 1.20 p.m. Beatle time.

The press room on the first floor of the arrivals building was jammed. From outside came the screams of the thousand teenagers who had chosen the customs section as their observation point. While the Beatles were declaring their baggage the press waited expectantly.

'Do you realize,' said one reporter, 'that if Beatle were in the dictionary it would come between "beatitude", meaning consummate bliss or blessedness, and "beat note", which is a note whose frequency equals the difference in the frequency of the two vibrators?'

Outside, several of the girls tried to hurl themselves over a retaining wall as the Beatles passed beneath.

Brian Sommerville, who had arrived in New York two days earlier to 'liaise' with the press, was now surrounded by them. A photographer from a New York paper that had bought a serial on the Beatles' lives from an English paper was complaining he couldn't get any pictures of them in the press room without New York credentials. A policeman tried to throw out a promotion executive from Capitol Records who didn't have an identification badge. From the back of the room came word that two girls had fainted outside.

'This', said Sommerville, 'has got entirely out of control.'

The Beatles are led into the press room where they stand on a platform talking and smiling quietly. Beneath them photographers cry: 'Down in front . . . gimme some room . . . whatsa matta . . . I can't see . . . please, down . . . more . . . no more . . . be a sport . . . hey, Beatles, look ovahere . . . whodda the left to rights . . . which one is George?'

Finally, Sommerville steps to the microphone. 'Would the photographers please be quiet now so the reporters can ask questions? Please.' This is met by cries of anguish from the photographers.

Sommerville grabs the microphone. 'Ladies and gentlemen, this is ridiculous! Hold up your hands, and I'll recognize you one at a time. If you won't be quiet we'll just stand here until you are. All right then!' he says. 'Shut up! Just shut up!'

The Beatles join in. 'Yeah, yeah, everybody shut up,' says John. Reporters applaud. Somebody asks, 'Aren't you embarrassed by all this lunacy?'

'No,' says John. 'It's crazy.'

'Will you sing something for us?' asks a reporter.

'We need money first,' says John.

'How do you account for your success?'

'We have a press agent.'

'What is your ambition?'

'To come to America.'

'Do you hope to get haircuts?'

'We had one yesterday.'

'Do you hope to take anything home with you?'

'The Rockefeller Centre.'

'Are you part of a social rebellion against the older generation?'

'It's a dirty lie.'

'What about the movement in Detroit to stamp out Beatles?'

'We have a campaign of our own to stamp out Detroit.'

'What do you think of Beethoven?'

'I love him,' says Ringo, 'especially his poems.'

At the back of the press room a woman reporter is talking on the phone. 'They are absolutely too cute for words and America is just going to love them.'

Epstein is being interviewed by a man with a tape recorder:

Man: 'I'm speaking with Brian Epstein, the Beatles' manager. Brian tell me: how was the reception?'

Epstein: 'Great, just great . . . the best reception ever.'

Man: 'Would you say it was the best reception ever?'

Outside four Cadillac limousines are waiting. Within ten seconds of the end of the press conference each contains a Beatle and is in motion. A policeman is shouting at the first chauffeur, 'Get out of here, buddy, if you want to get out alive!'

On the Long Island expressway leading into Manhattan, the caravan of Cadillacs is overtaken by a powder-blue Ford convertible that races alongside. A young man hangs out of the back window, waving a red blanket.

'So this is America!' says Ringo. 'They all seem out of their minds.'

A white convertible drives up with the word BEETLES written in the dust on either side. Brian Sommerville turns to George and says, 'Did you see that, George?'

George looks at the convertible with its emblem in the dust and says, 'They misspelled "Beatles".'

Halfway into Manhattan a crimson convertible drives up next

to Ringo's limousine. 'Ringo, Ringo,' shout the passengers, 'we go Ringo.' The girls squeal and the boy behind the wheel momentarily loses his grip, nearly smashing into the Cadillac's rear door.

Ringo rolls the window down. 'Hi, kids,' he calls.

'Yeah, yeah, yeah,' yell the kids.

'What's new?' asks Ringo.

'We love you, Ringo, we love you,' one girl screams. 'Oh – I'm about ready to die, DIE!'

'Don't do that,' says Ringo and rolls the window up.

At 63rd Street and Third Avenue, while waiting for a traffic-light, a young lady shouts into George's car: 'How does one go about meeting a Beatle?'

George leans out of his window.

'One says hello,' he says, but the light changes and the Cadillac lurches towards Fifth Avenue and the Hotel Plaza.

As Rome cherishes the Colosseum and Paris the Arc de Triomphe as symbols of a more glorious day, so New York feels about the Hotel Plaza. Generations of debutantes have danced in its *fin de siècle* ballrooms, and the most dissonant sound to be heard is the rare one of too much vermouth pouring into a martini.

Now the silver-haired ladies who cling to the Plaza like its reputation were looking askance. There were screaming hordes of adolescent girls surrounding the fountain where Scott and Zelda had bathed at midnight.

The Plaza management was petrified. Months ago they had accepted the Beatles' reservations, as businessmen, under their own names, checking only that they were 'financially responsible'. When the truth dawned, one of the Plaza executives went on the radio and offered the Beatles to any hotel in New York that wanted them.

During the first hour at the hotel the Beatles watched films of their arrival at the airport on television and posed for photographs. One of them asked John to lie on a bed and display his boots.

'Oh, no, please don't do that at the Plaza!' pleaded a distraught hotel official. 'That's not the image we want to project!'

'Don't worry,' said John. 'We'll buy the bed.'

To all Front Service:

During the stay of the Beatles at the Plaza Hotel I want extreme caution by all elevator operators as to the type of people you take upstairs to the 12th, 13th and 14th floors.

If in doubt please call the house officer, assistant manager or myself. Thank you for your co-operation.

Hilary Brown.

(from the staff bulletin board, Hotel Plaza)

Several girls climbed twelve flights of stairs to the wing where the Beatles' suite was located. In self-defence the Plaza hired guards to be on round-the-clock duty, and a desk was set up at the entrance to their wing.

'Why did you pick the Plaza?' a reporter asks George.

'I don't know,' he replies. 'I didn't pick it. Our manager did. All I can tell you is that the food is awful.'

In the hallway, Gail Cameron, a *Life* reporter, waited with a photographer. 'Listen,' she said to a press aide, 'I don't want to interview them, I just want their autograph for my managing editor – he told me not to come back without it.'

Several doors away is Brian Sommerville's suite. He is in the bedroom in tears. He has just had a fight with Epstein over the room arrangements and has been fired. 'I plan to return to London on the first available plane,' he says dramatically.

On the coffee-table in the sitting-room lies a box of candy with a telegram pasted to it, reading: 'I hope you like these better than jelly-babies. Good luck – Kitty Curowsky.'

Sitting on the sofa are Thomas Whiteside of the *New Yorker* and Alfred Aronowitz of the *Saturday Evening Post*.

'I don't feel very well,' says Whiteside, looking pale.

'Man,' says Aronowitz, a nervous, bearded type, 'don't you sense the excitement here?'

Sommerville has asked the hotel to put all of the Beatles' calls through to his room and the telephone keeps ringing. A radio station wants to tape thirty seconds of Ringo's conversation. A manufacturer wants to produce Beatle ashtrays. 'Uh, a group of us in the Village were wondering if the boys . . .' A promoter in Hawaii wants to book the Beatles for a tour there. 'Uh, this is Miss Grey of Capitol records. Could you have the Beatles call me at home tonight . . .?'

Sommerville re-enters the sitting-room. His argument with Epstein has been resolved. He is staying on.

The phone rings again. A charity organization wants to photograph a little girl in a wheelchair shaking hands with one of the Beatles. 'Oh dear, now that is a problem,' Sommerville says after hanging up. 'I always hate to have the boys photographed under those circumstances. You know what I mean – sort of gives the impression of a freak meeting a freak.'

They sit in silence for a minute. Then Aronowitz says: 'Listen, man, I don't want to talk to them. I just want to stand there and get images.'

'I'm definitely not well,' says Whiteside and leaves.

Lying opened on a table in the Beatles' suite is a note – one of hundreds, most of them still sealed.

Dear Beatles,

Here are some questions we hope you will answer for us:

1) John: Do you and your wife have any children?
2) Paul: Is it true that you have a special girl back in Liverpool?
3) To all four: What do you think of American girls?
4) To all four: Do you have an interest in your fans?

5) To all four: When are your birthdays?
6) Ringo: Where did you get your rings and how long have you played drums?
7) To all four: Do you see any difference in American fans and those of other countries?
8) George: Who picks out your clothes and haircuts?
9) To all four: What American do you admire?
10) To all four: Do you enjoy writing your music and what mood do you do it in?
11) To all four: What is your religion?

Sincerely yours,

Gayle

'We get 12,000 letters a day,' says Ringo. 'Yeah,' adds John, 'and we're going to answer every one.'

Neil Aspinall sits in a corner signing pictures of the Beatles. He has perfected their signatures, and these are being kept in anticipation of future requests. The door opens, and a New York disc jockey, called Murray the K, comes in with the Ronettes, an American recording group of three exotic-looking girls.

'We met the Beatles in London,' they say as if they are singing it.

In his room Sommerville is having dinner. One of the private guards walks in and introduces himself as 'Hughie'. As Sommerville eats, Hughie pours himself a drink and sits down. 'Say, Brian,' he says, 'last night I was at the Waldorf, where I had the honour of guarding the President. I was on the dais and everybody had to show me their pass to leave, even to go to the men's room. It was a great honour. I even had to wear a tuxedo. Of course, I still had my gun.'

Sommerville congratulates him and places a call to Lady Ormsby Gore, the wife of the British Ambassador in Washington. She has invited the Beatles to the Embassy after their performance in Washington on Tuesday.

He gets her on the telephone. 'We turned down Lady Dixon in Paris, you know,' he tells her. 'Bad marks in our copybook.' He says that 'Harold Macmillan can't wait to hear how we went over; he's breathless' and that 'Sir Winston sent the boys a cigar the other day to get an autograph for his niece.' After she has invited him to 'just a small dance' at the Embassy, Sommerville laughs politely and asks, 'Are you having trouble selling tickets? Why don't you auction off their autographs?'

A short time later George developed a sore throat and the hotel doctor ordered him to bed. A German measles epidemic had been declared in New York that day and the journalists descended on Sommerville's suite. After assuring them that George was not seriously ill, he ordered them out, but promised to meet the British press in the Oak Bar.

'Can we see the Beatles?' asked one of the journalists.

'Certainly not,' said Sommerville. 'My job is to keep you press boys away from them.'

Outside, on the street, behind police barricades, the girls are keeping their vigil. The sight of a shadow in the window – any window – any floor – incites hysteria. To keep warm they sing: 'London Bridge is falling down . . . 'cause we've got the Beatles.'

Everybody who walks out of the door is asked 'Did you see them?' 'Did you touch them?' A policeman comes out, and one of them yells: 'He touched a Beatle! I saw him!' Instantly he is covered with screaming, shrieking girls.

The waiters at the Plaza have been given orders to ask guests to remove Beatle wigs while in the lobby. In the Palm Court a violinist declines a request to play a medley of the Beatles' songs. He says the violin is not the proper instrument. The *Herald Tribune* asks Kay Thompson, author of *Eloise*, to write about what is happening.

In the Oak Bar, a reporter on the London *Daily Mirror* tells his colleagues of the British press, 'It's about time to start bursting these boys' balloons. Their heads are getting too big.'

At about one-thirty in the morning, after somewhat consoling the British journalists by giving them the news about the embassy ball, Sommerville went for a stroll around the block. As he re-entered the Plaza at the 58th Street door he was stopped by a guard who asked what floor he was going to.

'Twelve,' replied Sommerville.

'I'm sorry, sir,' said the guard, conscious of where he was, 'but they've got some sort of beetles staying up there. Could you show me some identification?'

The next morning is cold and rainy but this does not deter nearly one hundred of the faithful from maintaining their barricaded vigil on the Fifth Avenue side of the hotel.

On the twelfth floor George is still ill in bed. The *Express* wants to get a picture of him with a thermometer in his mouth. Chris Welles of *Life* is standing in the corridor explaining to Aspinall that 'We can only use a picture if it's exclusive. Couldn't we get them doing anything exclusively?' John Zimmerman, a photographer specializing in colour, is worried about the special equipment he has brought to shoot a cover for the *Saturday Evening Post*. 'It's worth $ 100,000,' he says. 'So the magazine is paying $50 a day for a suite to store it in and a Burns guard to watch that nobody steals it – while I wait for these guys.' Another photographer, Joe Covello, has turned Sommerville's sitting-room into a studio in order to shoot a cover for *Newsweek*. He had planned to pose the Beatles together but because of George's illness he settles for individual pictures.

While he is photographing Ringo, Sommerville walks in from the bedroom, where he has been on the phone. 'How can I make arrangements for Jackson, Mississippi,' he says, 'when I don't even know where it is?' Someone hands him a bouquet of flowers for Cynthia Lennon. A reporter called Mike Hennessy, of the British magazine *Today*, asked to interview Cynthia. Sommerville says he can't.

He then turns to the other photographers and reporters in the room and, waving the flowers, tells them he has made arrangements to photograph the Beatles at the boat-house in Central Park. 'Now remember, boys,' he admonishes them, 'you won't tell anybody where they are going, it's in your interest not to tell anyone.'

In the bedroom, Brown Megs, the public relations man for Capitol Records, is making arrangements with the police. 'Of course, officer,' he is saying, 'I can tell you where they're going but please don't let any of the fans know.'

At the other end of the twelfth floor, safely removed from the frenzy, was Epstein's suite. It was tastefully decorated in beige and white. His bedroom looked out on Central Park, and the sitting-room the fountain and Fifth Avenue. On the table were copies of *Show* and the *New Yorker*, as well as *Cashbox* and *Billboard*.

While he was in New York, Epstein used his suite as an office. He was sitting there now, dictating a memo to Wendy Hanson, an elegant blonde who was serving as his secretary during the period in New York. It was the proper ambience for dealing with important matters of high finance. The only disturbing notes were the constant screams of 'yeah, yeah, yeah' reaching the suite through the closed windows.

Shortly afterwards the Beatles (or rather, John, Paul and Ringo), having posed for photographs at the edge of the lake in Central Park; on a rock with the skyline in the background; with the daughter of one of the *Daily Express* correspondents with the skyline in the background; and driving a landau ditto; went into the boat-house to eat cheeseburgers, drink malted milks and speak with reporters.

As John sat down to his cheeseburger, a reporter for Associated Press, cigarette dangling from his mouth, took out his pad, looked up, and said: 'Listen, I'm not too familiar with all of this. What city are you from again?'

After they had finished talking to the reporters, the Beatles were put into two limousines and driven up the east side of Central Park to see Harlem and down the west side of the Park to the CBS studio at 53rd Street to rehearse for the *Ed Sullivan Show*.

Outside the theatre were a number of girls wearing yellow sweatshirts carrying the emblem 'WMCA Good Guys' printed on them (the Good Guys are disc jockeys on that station who had been pushing the Beatles). There was also a boy in a white sweatshirt which was labelled 'WQXR Bad Guys' (this is the local classical music station). A non-affiliated young man simply carried a sign reading 'Alonzo Tuske Hates the Beatles'.

Inside, the floor of the stage was painted blue, and there were half a dozen large white arrows pointing to the place where the Beatles would sing. Explaining the significance of this, the program's scenic designer, Bill Bohnert, said, 'I was attempting to symbolize the fact that the Beatles are here.'

The Beatles, with Aspinall standing in for George, rehearsed only for camera angles and whispered their songs. This was rather disappointing to Kathy and Nancy Cronkite – the daughters of the CBS newsman, Walter Cronkite – who had been admitted to the studio to watch the rehearsal. Three CBS vice-presidents had been turned down. 'I guess they know where they stand now,' said a press aide.

Towards the end of the afternoon George turned up for rehearsal. The press was assured that he would be able to take part in the show the next evening. 'He'd better be,' said Sullivan, 'or I'll put on a wig myself.'

After the rehearsal they went to a suite in the Savoy-Hilton, where George spent nine hundred dollars on a twelve-stringed guitar.

As they entered the Plaza they were enveloped in a squealing crowd of bridesmaids dressed in red velvet and white tulle. A man in a dinner-jacket came over and told them to 'stop congesting the lobby'.

Later that evening they were taken on a drive around Manhattan by Capitol executives. Passing the United Nations building George said the flagpoles would be good to hang sweatshirts on. Afterwards they were taken to dinner at 21 where they ate pork chops and Ringo asked the captain, 'Do you have any vintage Coca-Cola?'

When they returned from 21, John, George and Ringo stayed in their suite to watch television. Paul went across Fifth Avenue to the Playboy Club. After it had closed he returned to the Plaza with an off-duty Bunny and another couple. The other man suggested they should cross the street to the Chateau Madrid.

At the bar, the owner, Danny Lopex, introduced Paul to Angel Riera, the musical director of the Chavales de España, who were appearing at the club. Señor Riera is from Barcelona, and he and Paul talked about New York and music.

As Paul was turning to leave, Señor Riera looked up at him and said, 'Excuse me – I'm not much good at placing accents when English is being spoken. You're German, aren't you?'

Leaving the hotel the next morning the Beatles' limousine was surrounded by almost two hundred girls. The driver was forced to climb over the roof to get to the wheel. As the car started to pull away, someone asked John if he 'minded all this'. 'No,' he replied, 'it's not our car.'

An audience consisting mainly of teenage girls had been invited to watch the rehearsal for that evening's show as well as the taping of two additional songs for the programme in three weeks' time. They were reasonably quiet until Ringo's drums were rolled on stage. Then they began to scream. Before the Beatles appeared, Sullivan came on stage and asked the audience to give their attention to all the other fine performers besides the Beatles who were appearing, because if they didn't he would call in a barber. Then he said, 'Our city – indeed, the country – has never seen anything like these four young men from Liverpool. Ladies and gentlemen, the Beatles!'

What happened to the audience next led a writer in the *New York Herald Tribune* the following day to compare it with 'that terrible screech the BMT Astoria train makes as it turns east near 59th Street and Seventh Avenue.'

While the Beatles rehearsed, Cynthia Lennon stood in the back of the theatre talking to Maureen Cleave. Cynthia wanted to go shopping but was afraid to go out alone. 'The fans here seem a bit wackier than in England,' she said. A fan who happened to be standing near by overheard, and ten minutes later came back with a large parcel.

'There's no need for you to go shopping now,' she said as she presented her with a present for their six-month-old son – a 'Barracuda Atomic Sub'.

When the rehearsal and taping ended, Sullivan stood on the stage. 'It warms me to hear such enthusiasm,' he said.

'I'm going to be sick,' said a cameraman in the background. Someone asked Sullivan about the comment of his musical director Ray Bloch that had appeared in *The New York Times* that morning. Bloch had told *The Times*: 'The only thing that's different is the hair as far as I can see. I give them a year.'

Sullivan called Bloch over.

'Now, Ray,' he said, 'you can't say things like that.'

'They asked me how long I thought the Beatles would be making this kind of money,' replied Bloch, an elegant little man in a goatee, 'and I said about a year. Of course, I meant that they would then make a movie and make more money.'

On the other side of the stage a young man carrying a stenographic pad walked over to a CBS press aide. He worked for *Time* magazine and had been sent to New York from Washington. 'I don't know if this story is going in Music or Show Business,' he said.

'It should go in National Affairs,' said the CBS man.

Sullivan was talking about the Beatles. 'I remember the first time I saw them. I was at London Airport and there were mobs. There must have been 50,000 girls there and I later found out they had prevented Lord Home and Queen Elizabeth from taking off. I said to Mrs Sullivan, "Here is something." It was just like years ago when I was travelling in the South and I used to hear the name of Presley at fairs. Of course, he was all wriggling and sex. These boys are good musicians. When I finally saw them play in England, and the reaction, I said to Mrs Sullivan, "These boys have something."'

The *Time* man asked the press aide whether it was true that the Beatles had been invited to the White House.

'I understand the young girl is a big fan,' said the CBS man, 'but the Secret Service won't let her go to the Coliseum. I'm going to try and set up a performance at home.'

An hour before the Ed Sullivan programme was to begin, an instrumental trio wandered up and down the aisles serenading the largely teenage audience with soothing music. The fact that the only way backstage was through the men's room somewhat encouraged the girls to stay in their seats.

The troupe of boys from *Oliver* who were also to appear on the show arrived at the theatre. Someone asked them if they were Beatles.

'No,' replied a five-year-old with a Beatle cut and the broadest New York accent, 'we're roaches.'

Upstairs, the Beatles are having their pictures taken with Sullivan. A CBS press man is waving a pair of shears and a comb; 'C'mon, fellas,' he is saying, 'it's just a gimmick photo.'

Just before the programme is to begin, columnist Earl Wilson meets Sullivan backstage.

Wilson: 'It is true, Ed? Are you going to wear it?'

Sullivan: 'I've already worn it.'

Wilson: 'How did you look?'

Sullivan: 'It's a wig like any other. By the way, your hair looks great.'

The next day the photograph with Wilson's column shows him wearing a bald wig.

The Beatles' recording manager, George Martin, is in the audience. He plans to record their concert at Carnegie Hall. Someone asked him why, since all the songs have been recorded before.

'I don't know,' he says. 'It's just a bit of history, I guess.'

Be Happy! Don't Worry

NIK COHN

The antics of English bands like the Stones, Led Zeppelin and the Who – here documented by Nik Cohn – crisscrossing the North American subcontinent at the cleavage of the sixties and seventies became forever identified as a mandatory part of the rock & roll lifestyle. Sex, drugs and rock & roll became its nom de plume.

The first thing is the unreality. On the road you live in a capsule, a time machine, completely insulated against all normality or balance. You exist entirely in interiors – hotels and airports, limousines, dressing-rooms – and everything that you see has been filtered through glass. Night and day become meaningless, and cities are interchangeable. There are no restrictions or rules, and so you pass directly into fiction.

Each day presents a different gig, therefore a different landscape, therefore a different movie. There is no continuity, which means that you can do precisely as you choose, you can sink yourself and wallow in every possible and impossible outrage, excess, invention, since tomorrow you will be in a different script and everything will start afresh. You can't be reached and you can't be tied. Locked up safely inside your capsule, you skim above all retributions; can pretend to be infinite.

At first this feels quite marvellous – total release, speed, abandon. In the first week alone, I was P. J. Proby, Proust and Randolph Hearst in turn, before settling on Akim Tamiroff.

Why stop there? In New Orleans, I looked into the dressing-room and glimpsed the most beautiful girl, absolutely, that I had ever seen in my life. Ultimate teen angel – golden flesh, long blonde hair, big blue eyes and kisses, no doubt, much sweeter than wine.

At any other time, in real life, I would have dithered, fainted, let her slip away. But here, from within the capsule, it was the simplest thing in the world. Just walk up to her directly, look deep into her eyes and unleash the line of lines: 'Young lady,' I said, 'I believe I could make you a star.'

She did not scream, she did not strike me. On the road she merely flapped her eyelashes and, the very next morning flew with me to Hollywood, where I did not make her a star and she ripped me off in handfuls.

Or again. In Tuscaloosa, Keith Moon drank a bottle of brandy and began to feel quite frisky. So he destroyed his hotel bedroom. First he ripped down the curtains, smashed the mirrors, overturned the bed, slashed the mattress, fouled the sheets, put his fist through the bathroom wall. Then he kicked the TV until it expired, wrestled it through the door, heaved it over the balcony and watched it drop into the swimming-pool below. The splash was spiffing – groupies of every sex stood by the water and applauded. With the utmost dignity, Keith took a bow and went back into his room, where he lay down in the debris and straight away passed into deep and righteous slumber.

Next morning, when the management presented him with their bill for fifteen hundred dollars, he remembered nothing and felt no pain. No remorse, no trace of embarrassment, not even a hangover. And why should he? The limousines were waiting at the door, after all, and he was already in the next reel.

That's the benefit; the major drawback is psychosis. In a world without restrictions, there are also no guidelines, nothing left to cling to. You drift in weightlessness and, unless you have real resources of strength and imagination, this drives you into delirium.

No patterns are definite. Time and place evaporate, all norms are obsolete. You sleep in sunlight and soak in brandy for breakfast, Bloody Marys for elevenses, tequila for lunch; swallow uppers by the handful, downers by the tub, smoke and suck and sniff on whatever comes to hand, until you spin too fast to hold and fall down in a heap.

Minutes or hours or several days later, you come round and sit up. Immediately you start to whirl again, shuttling back and forth in time and space. You pass out in Dallas, which is 1964, and wake up in Los Angeles, 1980; expire in Phoenix, 1953, and are reincarnated in San Francisco, 1966. You go to bed with Lolita in Miami Beach and wake up next to her mother in Newark, New Jersey. Or you lay back on velvet cushions, you float in indoor swimming-pools, sleek and serene in Malibu, and the next thing you know you're destitute, besmirched and in jail, forty miles from Poplar Bluff.

If you can ride such games, you may fly faster, float freer than ever before; if you can't, you perish most horribly. Thus the tour is littered with numberless corpses. Roadies fall down elevator shafts, groupies suffocate in the shower. Promoters go bankrupt, security guards run amok with their nightsticks, the warm-up group blow themselves up. Journalists, almost always, are shipped home under sedation.

As for the Who themselves, their crises are now quite traditional, an integral part of the package. They have toured America fourteen or fifteen times and never once escaped without a major holocaust, so that they've learned to traipse through their traumas almost automatically, in a kind of formalized gavotte. So they break up, reform and break up again; threaten suicide, speak of murder; suffer, bleed, disintegrate and, in the epilogue, come home with a million dollars, more or less, for five weeks' work.

Even for such veterans, however, the tortures can sometimes be extreme. Early in the tour, Pete Townshend spent a couple of days at the ex-headquarters of Meher Baba, his avatar. The residents showed him the house where Baba had slept and left him alone in the avatar's bedroom. It was a stark little cell, like a third-rate hotel room, with only a bed and chair in it, and Pete could think of nothing to do but go on his knees, try to pray, meditate, whatever he could manage.

Straight away he could sense the Baba was present and waited to be blessed. But the avatar was not so benevolent – instead he took his disciple to pieces; poured, in Pete's own phrase, all the shit of the world on him; ravaged him, obliterated him, left him so smashed that, when the other followers opened the door again, they found him prostrate, unable to speak or move, scarcely able to breathe.

For the next few days, back on tour, he locked himself in his hotel room and talked to no one. On-stage he moved and played like a zombie; in dressing-rooms he crouched in corners, dead-eyed, drained, and twitched whenever anybody came close or touched him.

The rest of the group enjoyed this immensely. Baba has always made them sick and now was their chance of sweet revenge. So they took up the avatar's basic slogan – 'Be Happy Don't Worry' – and rubbed Pete's nose in it. A shattered shambling wreckage, he tried to back off but they pursued him, harried him relentlessly. 'Be Happy,' Keith kept chanting, exultant, flinging it out like a scarlet rag. 'Don't Worry, be happy, don't worry, be happy.' Pete made no response. Just sat there and continued to suffer.

One of the basic Who patterns is that their (very real) love for each other can only be released with extreme cruelty. They goad and downgrade each other continually, taking it in turns to play victim, until they reach breaking point and almost pass it. Halfway over the brink of total destruction, they suddenly relent and fall into each other's arms. For a moment they are satiated, and everyone embraces everyone. Soon enough, however, serenity begins to pall. Constant sweetness and light grow tiresome. Tempers fray, bickering begins again. A new victim presents himself and the cycle is launched once more.

At last, in Miami Beach, Pete broke surface. Somewhere out among the swamps, a fat rich freak laid on a house for us, complete with saunas and swimming-pools, unlimited alcohol and chemicals, and possibly thirty young ladies, of every colour, size and proclivity. Bad music played very loud and I lay down in a sand-pit, where I soon passed into a stupor. Minutes or days elapsed: 'You are floating on the astral plane,' someone kept telling me, not unkindly, and perhaps I was. But then I opened my eyes and there was Pete, half naked, extremely drunken, forcing his face into mine and demanding that I go swimming with him – skinny-dipping he called it.

I refused but he insisted; I refused again, and he grew abusive. 'Chicken,' he screeched. 'You're ashamed to show me your dick. All Jews are ashamed to show their dicks. You probably haven't even got one.'

When I still refused, he changed tacks and grew maudlin. 'Aren't you human at all?' he said, softly pleading (but of course I wasn't). 'When I wrote "Pinball Wizard" for you specially. My best song and I wrote it for you and now you won't even skinny-dip with me. One small favour and you turn me down.'

For a few moments he thought about weeping but decided not to and trailed off down the stairs instead, to frolic with large blonde nymphs beneath. Salvation through degradation, I suppose, and it must have worked, because next morning he fairly bounced, chipper as a chipmunk. From then on, right through the tour, he went from strength to strength – a still centre at the heart of chaos, while all around him capsized.

The next to crumble was me. On the seventeenth floor of the Playboy Plaza, looking out across the lake and its lurid technorama sunset, I was having my shoulders rubbed by a half-Mexican, half-Cherokee stripper named Shanda Lear, when there was a sudden flash of light and both of us felt an angel fly over our heads. Shanda Lear fell backwards on the bed, screaming and clutching her hands to her belly. Next morning her fingers, where they had been touching my flesh, were covered in festering blisters.

As for myself, I felt stunned but ecstatic. Since I had never had any mystic tremors before, and did not believe in such stuff anyhow, I made the very most of this and drifted through Memphis in a trance, borne up on waves of bliss. I was sanctified, my spirit had been saved. Then came the kickback. In New Orleans, I got staggering drunk and, hot to transmit my new condition, I jumped up in a nightclub, grabbed the microphone and broke into an impassioned, strangulated version of 'My Prayer'.

I must have made a truly horrendous figure: my voice was a croak, I couldn't stand straight and tears coursed down my cheeks in rivulets, plopping one by one on my shirt-front. I rambled and gurgled, dropped the mike and nobody reacted, nobody made a sound. All I could see were beady eyes in the dark, watching me. Without expression. I tried to run away but couldn't. My hands were shaking uncontrollably. Angels laughed in my face and I sank to my knees.

It was then that Keith rescued me from total and final decimation, jumping up on stage, commandeering the drums and playing along behind me, projecting such zest and conviction as he did so that fiasco was turned into high-camp vaudeville. People began to laugh and jeer, and I was released. Stumbling off into the night, I fell fast asleep and woke up next morning, purged and clean, ripe for a new beginning.

By nightfall I was already superseded. In my place one of the roadies, lost in acid, attempted self-crucifixion on a surfboard and all but succeeded. This game try made him the undisputed lion of the moment and, when he appeared backstage before the show, blushing but unbandaged, shyly triumphant, he received a massed ovation.

Glasses and silver spoons were hoisted in salute, the stigmata inspected with awe: 'Is this a Who tour?' cried Keith Moon, exulting, 'Or is this a fuckin' tour?'

At the Riot House

STEPHEN DAVIS

If Cohn's portrait of the Who on the road suggests a form of permanent mania in which participants outdo each previous excess, Stephen Davis's account of the Led Zeppelin '73 US tour seems to suggest a band going through the motions backstage as well as on-stage, bored by the now-humdrum ritual of excess.

At the Riot House there were the usual outrages. Led Zeppelin had the eleventh floor to themselves. At slack moments Richard Cole would roar down the corridor on a big Honda motor cycle that he had sneaked in via the freight elevator. On the plane to LA Jimmy had been shown a copy of *Star* magazine by Danny Goldberg. 'Jimmy went out of his mind,' Danny said. 'He said, "Look! There's a new generation of groupies in LA! Do you know them? Do you have phone numbers?"' Led Zeppelin's ground-zero in Los Angeles was the Rainbow Bar. There they were given their own cordoned-off section and were treated like royalty. Women knew where to find them. The whole entourage could go, so Led Zeppelin had safety in numbers and no chance of the rejection they had suffered during leaner years. They could get loaded, hold court all night, and go home with whomever they wanted. Their only worry was that the stray girls would get into the photographs and alarm their wives back home.

Jimmy was locked into his suite with Lori Maddox, who had now achieved the matronly age of fifteen. There had been several death threats against Jimmy, and private security guards were posted outside Jimmy's suite in shifts around the clock. At the same time Bonzo and the Zeppelin roadies observed their annual ritual of wanton hotel destruction. Entire suites of furniture went over the balconies. After the lads had been upbraided by the owner of a Lincoln convertible on to which they had been pouring their drinks and then their glasses from the eleventh floor, someone threw a table over the side and demolished the car. The televisions went next. Watching a big colour TV exploding on a pavement from a great height was a favourite Zeppelin pastime. The previous year at an old battleground, the Edgewater Inn in Seattle, Led Zeppelin had thrown all their televisions into the sea below. As Peter Grant was paying the bill, the hotel manager wistfully remarked that he had always wanted to chuck a TV out the window himself. 'Have one on us,' roared Grant, and peeled off another $500 bill. The manager went right upstairs and heaved a big Motorola off the balcony.

But it wasn't always like that, despite all the legends of non-stop mayhem. Danny Goldberg remembers a greater reality: 'My take on this period was that it was really boring. They were tired. One of the stories that doesn't get told was how many times there weren't wild parties, and how lonely and exhausted they would get, and how they would be so worried about what they looked like in a picture and would their wives be mad at them.'

On 2 June Led Zeppelin flew into San Francisco to headline an all-day show at Kezar Stadium promoted by Bill Graham. After Roy Harper had opened the show and the Tubes and Lee Michaels had played, it was 2.00 p.m. and Zeppelin was supposed to go on. But Led Zeppelin was in the air aboard the Starship, still *en route* from LA. After a wild limousine dash from the airport, Led Zeppelin went on at three-thirty. They played so loud that the leftover hippies along the famous Haight-Ashbury 'Panhandle' could hear them clearly a half-mile away. Three blocks away, patients at the University of California Medical Centre complained they couldn't sleep. Zeppelin played until six and then went backstage to confront Bill Graham, who was angry about the delayed show. Peter Grant and Bill Graham were like King Kong and Godzilla in terms of their personalities. They were two truly tough guys. And Graham couldn't believe he had to pay that kind of money to Led Zeppelin. So there were bad feelings and arguments about money all day, and Graham's people wouldn't let Zeppelin's photographer on-stage. In tricky situations Led Zeppelin would think of humiliating pranks and get Bonzo to perform them. So after the show Bonzo poured a bucket of cold water on Bill Graham, who was not amused. Bill Graham was treated like hip royalty from the sixties by every other manager, but not Peter Grant, who said, 'No one gets paid a premium for being hip by my band.' Graham disliked Led Zeppelin, but made a lot of money from them.

The first half of the tour ended the next day in Los Angeles, with Led Zeppelin reviving the Yardbirds' 'I'm A Man' and Freddie King's 'I'm Going Down' in the encore.

During the month-long break in June, Led Zeppelin scattered. Robert bought a sheep farm on the Welsh coast, and Jimmy bought the landmark Tower House in London's Kensington section from actor Richard Harris, paying £350,000 after outbidding David Bowie. Built as an eccentric home by an Edwardian architect, the house was a marvel of decoration and artisanry. Each room represented some natural theme – butterflies, the sea, astrology – and anyone walking its exquisite rooms and halls had the distinct feeling of being in the presence of some higher consciousness. Jimmy was still living at Plumpton Place, but the Tower House would soon become a refuge.

When Led Zeppelin met again in Chicago on 6 July for the second leg of the tour, conditions had changed. There had again been a serious death threat against Jimmy by a deranged man who had told a mutual friend to warn Jimmy that he would be killed while on tour. Jimmy claimed the man was later tracked down and put in a mental hospital. But the security guard remained outside his door twenty-four hours a day. 'Led Zeppelin was always the focus of death threats,' Danny Goldberg said, 'because of their occult association and their big success. The '73 tour was the first time that significant death threats had been directed towards Led Zeppelin, so it was taken very seriously. Later, the death threats became routine.'

Roy Harper was also back. 'Jimmy and Robert considered him a great thinker and visionary,' according to Danny. 'So Roy Harper was treated with tremendous deference, and catered to by everybody else. But he was also getting crazier and would stand off-stage holding this toy black rubber gorilla, which he would shake during Zeppelin's show as if the gorilla were some magical fetish that empowered the band.' This went on for several shows until one day Robert's roadie, Benji LeFevre, turned to Danny and said, 'I don't care what anyone says, this guy is six bricks shy of a full load.' Suddenly the bubble burst. The crew had been treating Harper like Dylan Thomas for weeks. Soon Richard Cole started grabbing the poet by the neck and throwing him into the last barge in Zeppelin's limo convoy, traditionally the conveyance of choice for Led Zeppelin's sleazy, unwanted entourage. The entourage was also later joined by B. P. Fallon and a film crew assembled on the spot by Joe Massot, whom Peter had called with three cities left in the tour after he had a revelation that film of the tour might be valuable after all.

By the time the film crew arrived, Led Zeppelin was headquartered at the Drake, a grand dowager of a hotel on New York's Madison Avenue. Every night the entourage would jump into a fleet of limos and drive to the Newark airport where the Starship waited, fueled and ready, at a private corner of the tarmac. On the first night of filming Led Zeppelin posed on the wings of the big jet, next to the huge letters of the group's name that had been painted on the fuselage, while the film crew clicked and whirred. In Baltimore the entire audience of 25,000 rose and fired their lighters as the group walked in, before Led Zeppelin had played a note, as a silent tribute to unadulterated charisma and unity. Jimmy was taken aback, stopped dead in his tracks by the honour. He later said that for him it was a moment of true magic.

A few nights later they flew to Pittsburgh. Danny Goldberg had convinced a writer from *Playboy* to come along. Also on the Starship were Ahmet Ertegun and half a dozen harlots in floppy silk playsuits (actually the roadies' girlfriends), who chatted with Jimmy and B. P. Fallon during the flight. Magnums of excellent champagne and very cold Thai beer flowed freely. Peter Grant, his gigantic bulk wrapped in a Hawaiian shirt, glowered menacingly at the team from *Playboy* and the man from the *Daily Express* that Danny had brought along as well. Bonzo berated the male member of the *Playboy* team because Led Zeppelin hadn't done well in *Playboy*'s music poll. Robert flirted with the female reporter the magazine had sent. 'See you later without your clothes on,' he said. The Zeppelin limo convoy got a sirens-wailing police escort from the airport to Pirates Stadium. The twenty-foot stage platform sat in the middle of the outfield in the big baseball park. Jimmy, in a white linen suit and a black shirt, had his red Gibson slung low along his crotch and his lips pulled into a tough pout; he did the gunfighter boogie all night, evoking noises from his theramin that sounded like Venusian police calls. Robert was in his usual skintight jeans and an open vest that revealed his bare chest. He strutted and preened, shook his hips and thrust out his breast, glistening with sweat. He bumped and ground, preened with exaggerated braggadocio and threw his hair back like some hippie Jesus. The thick July heat turned the concert into a delirious steam bath. At the show's climax, 'Whole Lotta Love', Led Zeppelin's Old Testament and standard edition of Freud condensed into one volume, two hundred white doves were released. Backstage, Richard Cole jostled the reporter from *Playboy* and then threw him off the stage. And by the time the show had finished and the first fans were reaching their cars in the parking-lot, Led Zeppelin was aboard its Starship, flying to New York.

The pace picked up even faster as the long, exhausting tour wore to its conclusion. In Boston the Zeppelin roadies went into action against a Teamsters Union goon squad that had appeared backstage at Boston Garden in an attempt to shake down Led Zeppelin. Peter Grant and his private army bloodied their faces and sent them away.

The tour ended with three shows at Madison Square Garden in New York. The Drake Hotel was plunged into the chaos. Richard Cole's suite was a madhouse of friends wanting tickets, publicists, hangers-on, groupies, people selling rare guitars and dope dealers. The telephones were ringing off the hooks with interview requests. The media were paying attention, at last! *Rolling Stone* had finally offered Led Zeppelin its cover if Page and Plant would do interviews, but was turned down flat. All the television offers were turned down as well. Led Zeppelin was proud of turning down those.

Robert would occasionally wander into Cole's suite, looking for Burmese beer and tickets for friends from Birmingham. Then Jimmy would materialize, pale, white and wraith-like in a black velvet suit. He was by then something of a basket case. His wounded hand was still bothering him, and it took a concerted effort of pure will to get it to play the guitar every night for three hours. Also, the past two weeks had been deadened by death-threat paranoia. Jimmy hadn't slept for a fortnight, sustaining himself on dope, booze and room-service hamburgers. On the night of the first New York concert, his limo had pulled up to the freight entrance of the hall when a long-haired kid threw himself on the car and shouted, 'Jimmy, Jesus is here!' The police dragged him off and beat him. It was unnerving. To a reporter, Jimmy whispered, 'We're all terribly worn out. I went past the point of no return physically quite a while back.'

Meanwhile, the film crew, which had been put together on three days' notice, had to keep shooting over and over again. They were, for some reason, unable to film a whole sequence of 'Whole Lotta Love', and couldn't persuade the truculent John Paul Jones to wear the same shirt for three nights for the sake of continuity.

Because the band had been hamming it up for the film crew, none of the New York performances was very effective. 'Dazed And Confused' ran more than a half-hour, as Jimmy used the violin bow to emit noon whistles and cybernetic death rattles before descending the purple haze into a jam on 'Route 66' as Robert yelled 'Oh, suck it!' and came in mock orgasm.

Led Zeppelin flew home to England the following day. When Jimmy's family saw the state he was in – exhausted, malnourished, sleepless, raving – they tried to get him into a sanitarium for a rest. Jimmy himself told a journalist that he thought he belonged either in a mental hospital or a monastery. 'I was thinking, "What the hell am I going to do?" because it was like the adrenaline tap wouldn't switch off. During those concerts to that many people, there was so much energy being stored up. I felt like a kettle with a cork in the top. I'd stay up for five nights at a trot. It didn't seem to affect my playing, but I'd come off-stage and I was not levelling off at all, not turning off the adrenaline. I couldn't. I felt I needed to go somewhere where there was a padded cell so I could switch off and go loony if I wanted. I was quite serious about it.'

Thursday, 23 November 1972

IAN HUNTER

Ian Hunter's ironically titled Diary of a Rock & Roll Star, *which catalogues the progress of Mott the Hoople's low budget '72 US tour, remains one of the few credible accounts of life on the road from the pen of a rock & roll musician. In this excerpt Hunter and the band have just arrived in Los Angeles, home of hedonists and health-nuts.*

Well folks, you won't believe this, but it's the 23 November and I'm sunbathing on the roof of the hotel. My lily-white body naked, but for Woolworth trunks. On Thanksgiving the town is quiet and peaceful, and Spanish-style villas slope down the one side of us. The flatness of this huge city lies on the other. It's been a long day. For some unknown reason we were all up at 8.00 a.m. and decided to check our bearings. We are, so the map says, situated in West Hollywood. So, taking the equipment lorry out of the car-park at the rear we turned right and headed up past the dreaded Whiskey to the famous Beverly Hills area. Here we parked at the perimeter, commercial vehicles aren't allowed today. We started to walk along Sierra Drive. This is the part of Hollywood where the majority of stars live and it has to be seen to be believed. Ritchie, Phil and me sat on the corner of Lorna Vista and Usher Drive just taking it all in. We saw lime trees, olive trees, poplars, palms – you name it. Automatic sprayers click on with the air-conditioning and start to spray over beautifully tended lawns, and the morning papers lie strewn, waiting for Rita Hayworth to pick them up.

Way up on a hill above the entrance to Greystone Park we can see cacti. We try to reach it but stop exhausted halfway. The houses could be Spanish, Italian or Mexican in design. They are all low and the hallmark of poverty is a three-car garage. Cars are everywhere, the usual combination being a Cadillac, Rolls or Bentley and a cheaper Ford of some type (junior's runabout) and a Volkswagen for the missus to wreck. Talking of shops, there are none. One pictures huge fridges and bars piled high with champagne and Rothmans. The architectural designs on some of these places are really something. Some are shaped in semi circles with gravel and rock roofs. Magic eyes stare at you from the trees and dogs growl and red pillar-box alarms duly alarm you. There are brilliantly coloured flowers: I don't know the names of them but I can dig 'em and all types of moss and fern. Huge gates compete for elaborateness. Was that Jane Russell I just saw in a Fleetwood? Rubber plants and other large-leaved climbing 'things' almost cover the windows giving those inside much needed privacy from the daily bus-loads of sightseers – and us. An amazing house at the top of a hill to our left looks just like a modern Parthenon. Cord, Wallace, Doheny, Sierra and Chris are just a few of the drives and alleyways we tramped looking for stars to come out and play, but the lazy bastards must still be in bed. They even paint the fire hydrants a bright silver here. And so, somewhere inside, the occupants sit. Probably with the bedside TV on and wanking, the mirrors arranged neatly around them. It's Beverly Hills on a quiet Thanksgiving morning, 78 degrees; it must be one of the most beautiful suburbs in the world. It makes Wembley look silly.

The sun is high now, really hot. Having been weaned on English winters it feels like cheating sitting here cheerfully burning. We truck back to the Hyatt.

Just one more thing about the hotel I forgot to mention; it rates as another example which ought to be copied by those idiot English hoteliers. As I walked through the foyer there's a picture of a guy with long hair. Underneath a caption says – 'Treat this man with respect, he may have just sold a million records.' Right on!

Out on to the patio and in the distance I can see mountains with snow on 'em and I keep wondering why, if it's so hot, why the fuck is the snow not thawing? Must be part of life's rich pattern in Film City.

Up on the roof I sit with Phally and Stan. Phally keeps on about how his underpants embarrass him, but he's too tight to buy swimming trunks, and Stan rambles on about some American bloke who just came up to the pool, flung all his clothes off and leaped straight in. He swam frantically to the other side, then jumped out and fainted on the spot. I put my foot in gingerly – it's bloody cold! There's a Hertz clock on the wall that says three minutes to 1.00 p.m.

Everybody's happy, but adjusting – where to now? Someone suggests we go to Disneyland, but apparently long hair is banned. A lot of Americans live *Peyton Place*. Certain segments of the society, particularly the middle-class families, annoy me. I find them nauseating and hypocritical. Over-reaction and the tendency to almost act their way through life – a television nation. Too much self-indulgence – unreal is a word that's been used many times before, but that about sums it up.

Back in the truck with Ritchie and left down Sunset Boulevard. It's an experience I'd love those poor out-of-work North-east English kids to see. It's just like the movies, and I'm Neil Cassidy, hitching a ride on Ritchie's International Harvester. What a buzz it would be to drive this heap up the M1. We keep going down Sunset until it gets a bit boring. On the right the vastness of LA and on the left the word HOLLYWOOD stands out of the hills behind and above.

Hundreds of hotels, motels, saloons, massage places, bars, clubs and dives. We stop at the corner of Hollywood and Vine – I once wrote a song about Hollywood and Vine with Kim Fowley, who's still hustling for us to record it. Will his persistence pay off? Listen to our next album and find out folks!

So here I am on poetic Hollywood and Vine. How the hell can you write about the corner of Wardour and Old Compton? The people who named British cities, towns and streets want a kick up the arse . . . 'I left my heart . . . in Watford,' etc . . .

So we turn right and it's just your average houses. They're wooden with shutters and toy cars, basketball nets and well-dressed little chicks, tiny Mexican boys and early sixties' cars (there's much more character in them than the shit they make today). Two dogs wait at a gate and a heavily lined spade parks the car after a hard day's work. It's good to see ordinary people in this extraordinary city. Back to Sunset Boulevard and more of those huge billboards. Mom's Apple Pie, the Bee Gees, Grand Funk and Chuck Berry – it's only a matter of time before Bolan's effigy adorns Piccadilly.

A shop called Sound City (no relation to the English one) sports a see-through drum kit and there's a club called Souled Out. Car-lots sell their wares at what seem to be extremely low prices. I think of the ridiculously high prices asked in England for ancient Mustangs. '69 and '70 models go for a song here. Huge supermarkets with vast car-parks making Safeway in Wembley look like a corner fag shop. Various sound studios and one film lot – all you can see is a hangar-like building – looks like a prison and probably is one.

We turn left on Sunset this time and intend heading for the hills but instead slow sharply as we find ourselves in a street full of adult movies and bookshops. I ain't got much of a memory for names but I do remember it was just off Hollywood Boulevard which runs parallel with Sunset. The pictures were closed so we went into the bookstore instead which was half porn and half straight. A door leads you to the porn section and a sign says fifty cents a look. Not feeling too randy, I don't bother. Instead I get *Rolling Stone*, *Changes* and *Rock*, the American equivalent of *Melody Maker*, *Sounds* and *Disc*. There's a review of our album

in *Rolling Stone* and it's great so decide to go back up to the hotel
and show the lads. On the way out I get *Close Up* and *International* . . . well, you never know – they're only cheap efforts.
We pay the middle-aged spiv in charge, whose nose is a mess, his
speech (if you could call it that) is slurred to the extreme, and I
realize coke isn't just the property of kids here.

We get back to the hotel and saunter into Pete and Buff's
room. Some chick called Rachel is ringing Pete once an hour and
Phal's having trouble getting rid of a bird he said hello to three
years ago. Excuses are made and the word's going round already
that we're not going to bother this time around. It's all fucking
boring anyway. They're lousy lays as a rule and you can never get
rid of them once you let them in. They don't even listen to the
music any more and as I've said, you run a big risk in the dose
stakes if you decide to dabble. The best thing to do, young and
inexperienced musicians (if there is such a thing), is to whip their
spotty little arses and lay back and enjoy a professional blow job;
then tell them you got crabs and they'll be gone before you know
it. Anyway, they don't make groupies like they used to.

Stan's red all over from spending too much time in the pool,
and he's hobbling around in Mick's boots. They're new ones and
Stan has smaller feet than Mick so he's wearing them in for him.
Peter and I engage in a game of chess and we draw one apiece.
Lucky old me, he usually does me every time; I can never
concentrate. Buff's eating a very large hamburger and Phal's
saying he's got to send some postcards. I go back to my room
(603) and ring my Mum and Dad. They've never gotten a phone
call from 6,000 miles away before so it will really knock them out.
I also try Trudy but they're all out for Thanksgiving dinner.

Red wine begins to tire me. Everyone else is tired too, even
though it's only 9.30, so we split up and I wander back to my
room, promising to meet the others later for the Whiskey.

I decide to sleep until midnight, but about 10.30 I'm woken by
the phone.

'Hi! I'm Lynn. I'm ringing to ask you if you'd like to see LA. Kim Fowley told me to look you up – oh, me and my friend Nancy too. No hassle really, I have a boyfriend already. We just want to talk.'

'Well, I don't know, I'm a newly married man. I mean . . . really no hassle?'

'Really, no hassle man.'

'OK.'

Five minutes later . . .

'Hello, we know Rodney at the E Club and Kim Fowley phoned Rodney and Rodney thought you might like to come round the club.'

'Well that's real nice of Rodney.'

'Oh, Rodney's a great guy – where's the rest of the band? Only we met Bowie, he's a beautiful cat . . . he taught us so much [I bet he fuckin' did]. And my boyfriend's group is going to back him in about a year from now, but I know how much we love each other [christ] so I don't care.'

'Well, thanks for dropping in. Give Rodders my humble thanks, but I heard all his ladies are ill this year.'

'Hey, I feel kind of weird. If you don't dig us just say so.'

'Hello, Nancy? How are you? No, I think you're both very nice, but I'm pretty tired at the moment.'

'See, some chicks are OK, but there's a thing about – it's not Vietnam clap, but guys are carrying it around and there's a few down in hospital . . .' (Oh my God.)

'Er, the roadies are in 606, why don't you nip round and see them. They're really nice people.'

'Do you think they'd mind? I mean, we don't really want to hassle them in any way you know.'

'No. It's great – go and knock them up. They'll like you and they're nice guys. I'm sorry to be unsociable but I really am tired.'

'OK then. But remember to come and see us at the E . . . really, no hassle. You look tired, try and get some sleep.'

'Great . . . thanks for coming. We'll be around. Don't forget the roadies are in 606. Tara.'

Ten minutes later . . . the phone rings . . .

'Cunt!'

Well now, that must have been 606.

Is It Rolling, Zeus?

NAT HENTOFF

The Rolling Thunder Revue which careered through bicentennial New England in the fall of '75 was not just a freewheelin' trek, at least not for Dylan, its main attraction and advocate. Rather it was an attempt to establish a permanent review, a perennial express that could be started up at will whenever he felt inclined to take his music to some hinterland of America. Though the Revue wound to an anticlimatic conclusion in May 1976, after a disastrous tour through the southern states in the spring, Hentoff's cover-story for Rolling Stone *captured some of its unique spirit during its halcyon days.*

Backstage at the Rolling Thunder Revue, Allen Ginsberg (who has just dedicated his book of *First Blues* to 'Minstrel Guruji Bob Dylan') asks the convener of these revels, these winds of the old days, 'Are you getting any pleasure out of this, Bob?'

The convener, who can use words as if they were fun-house mirrors when he is pressed, fingers his gray cowboy hat and looks at the poet. The first he had ever heard of Allen Ginsberg and the kind of people he hung out with was in *Time* around 1958 while he was still a kid in Minnesota. ('I'm Allen Ginsberg and I'm crazy.' 'My name is Peter Orlovsky and I'm crazy as a daisy.' 'My name is Gregory Corso and I'm not crazy at all.' That had broken up the kid in Minnesota.)

Now, here on the road with this hooting, rocking carnival of time present and time past, both perhaps present in time future, is Allen, who has survived, serene and curious, in a business suit.

'Pleasure?' Dylan finds the word without taste, without succulence. 'Pleasure? I never seek pleasure. There was a time years ago when I sought a lot of pleasure because I'd had a lot of pain. But I found there was a subtle relationship between pleasure and pain. I mean, they were on the same plane. So now I do what I have to do without looking for pleasure from it.'

'He is putting you on,' said a friend to whom Ginsberg, later in the tour, had described Dylan's exorcism of the pursuit of pleasure.

'No,' Ginsberg said firmly. 'Bob's attitude is very similar to the Buddhist view of non-attachment. The belief that seeking pleasure, clinging to pleasure, evokes pain. It stunned me when Bob said that. It meant that he's reached a philosophical level very few come close to. And it's a long-range, practical, workable, philosophical level. Bob has grown an awful lot. He's alchemized a lot of the hang-ups of his past. Like his insecurity, which has now become', Ginsberg laughs, 'an acceptance of and an ability to work with continuous change.'

On the other hand, a musician in Minstrel Guruji's band tells of an epiphany early in the tour: 'Joan and Bob are doing a duet. I forget the name of it, it's one of his old tunes. She's really moving. I mean dancing. She starts doing the Charleston and the audience is digging it and we're digging it. Dylan, though, he's plucking his guitar, moving his eyes around quick, like he does, looking at Joanie, looking at us, looking at the audience. Like, "What the hell is she doing that's going over so damn big?" It's over, and Joan walks off-stage, grinning, sees a friend in the wings, and says to him, "You won't be hearing that number again from this little old duo on this tour." And laughs because neither the friend nor the other standing there can figure out what she's talking about. But she's right. Bob's never called for that tune since. He couldn't stand the competition. Big as he is, in some ways he's still a kid scrabbling for his turf.'

'Not true,' says Joan Baez of the kid characterization. 'Or, not as true as it used to be.' She had once described Dylan as a 'huge ego bubble, frantic and lost, so wrapped up in ego, he couldn't have seen more than four feet in front of him'. But now, 'Bob has learned how to share,' Joan told me one night after a three and a half hour show in Waterbury, Connecticut, at an old rococo movie theatre that reminded me of Depression nights as a boy when we would go to just such a place to feel good anyhow and come home with some dishes besides. No dishes this time, but the most mellow feelings I've had from a concert since the Duke Ellington band on an exceptionally good night. The kicks were from the genuine mutual grooving of the music makers; but it was Dylan, as shaper of the thunder, who was responsible for lifting the audience and keeping it gliding.

A bounteous dispenser of thunder was Dylan this time around. At least three and a half hours every night, sometimes longer. (The concert in Toronto, one of the tour's more exalted evenings, ran close to five hours.) And yet always, or nearly always, the pacing, though relaxed, didn't go slack.

The right mix of back-up band, driving strong but sinuously so it never sounded like an assault. If you could keep T-Bone Burnett, Steve Soles, Howie Wyeth, Mick Ronson, Luther Rix and David Mansfield together – I was thinking as a once and former A & R man – you could have one hell of a house insurance band. Especially with Mansfield, nineteen and the kind of natural whom conservatory students prone to neurasthenia should never be

allowed to hear or see. Mandolin, pedal steel, dobro, violin –
Mansfield makes them all sing, for God's sake, as if he were the
sorcerer, not the apprentice he looks like.

Up front Rob Stoner, who doesn't get in the way, and the
authentically raffish Bob Neuwirth who may, he says, be in the
movies soon. Finally a Rhett Butler for our time. Put another way,
I think you have to see Neuwirth to remember his singing.

The substars. Ronee Blakley, who earnestly needs direction, as
her albums and her musical aimlessness on this tour rather painfully indicate. Roger McGuinn, who has become a large, jolly,
historic rocker, almost right for a Christmas mime show. And
surprisingly, most impressive of all in the second line some nights,
Jack Elliott. With his rambling white cowboy hat and folk collector's glasses, Jack is real serious, however idiosyncratic, and on
this tour quite moving in his seriousness. Watching and feeling
what 'Pretty Boy Floyd', let's say, still means to him, I started
thinking of Cisco Houston. Not that they sang alike, Cisco being
more of an original, but they trained a lot of memories. And Jack
is still spreading seeds.

All the way up front, Joan Baez and, as she calls him, the Kid.
Her voice has lowered and so the bodiless sound of medieval
caroling in a cathedral is also gone. But now there is more warmth
and flesh and survivor's humour ('Love is a pain in the ass'); and
still that surging vibrato which is so strong that when Joan sings a
cappella, the vibrato becomes her rolling rhythm section.

In her duets with Dylan, Joan, most of the time, is a secondary
strand. She could overpower him because her timbre penetrates
deeper and because she is more resourceful with her voice than he
is, but Joan is content to orchestrate Dylan. And Dylan – less
coiled, even dancing from time to time – cannot ever be called
relaxed but now is so in charge that even he believes he's in
charge. His singing, therefore, is more authoritative than ever
before. That is, the anxiety in his delivery has to do with the story
he's telling rather than the way he's telling it.

It feels good to him, this tour. The itch was there last summer. One liquid night, if you believe Bob Neuwirth: 'Me and Bob and Ramblin' Jack decided we were going to go out and tour in a station wagon, go out and play Poughkeepsie. That didn't turn out to be possible. So we did this instead. And this ain't no Elton John show, you know. This ain't no fucking one-fourth of the Beatles show or nothing like that. This show, we got it all, man. Between us we got it all. And it just gets better and better and better.'

'The feeling is good,' Joan handed me her glass of wine, 'because everybody has some room on-stage. Bob made sure of that. He didn't have to and I argued against it. I thought it would slow things up. But Bob insisted. He said the guys in the band have to work day and night and so each of them ought to get some attention for himself.'

He no longer seeks pleasure, he says. But what of the pleasure of attention? Why, that comes, it just comes.

Blood On The Tracks has been released and Allen Ginsberg, listening close, is moved to write the poet about a rhyme in 'Idiot Wind': 'Idiot wind blowing like a circle around my skull from the Grand Coulee dam to the Capitol.'

It's an amazing rhyme, Ginsberg writes, an amazing image, a national image, like in Hart Crane's unfinished epic of America, *The Bridge*.

The other poet is delighted to get the letter. No one else, Dylan writes Ginsberg, had noticed that rhyme, a rhyme which is very dear to Dylan.

Ginsberg's tribute to that rhyme is one of the reasons he is here with Bob and Joan and the rest of the merry motley. It was, says Allen, 'one of the little sparks of intelligence that passed between Bob and me and that led him to invite me on the tour.'

*

Joan, in faded jeans and multicoloured, boldly striped cotton shirt, is talking with amused affection about Dylan, about the tour, about herself. The Ghost of Johanna still marvels at the sparks that never cease coming from this 'savage gift on a wayward bus'. Throughout the tour, although Lord knows she knew his numbers well, Joan would slip into the audience to hear Dylan's sets or, if she were weary, she'd sit down backstage to listen.

'Bob has so powerful an effect on so many lives,' Joan says. She has been saying this for some thirteen years; and at the beginning, before his pop beatification, she pushed mightily to press that savage gift on those who had come to pay homage only to her. Dylan was the 'mystery guest' unveiled at her concerts, lurching on-stage to break the spell of high-born doom across the seas in someone else's history as he rasped about freak shows right outside.

'I'm still deeply affected by his songs,' Joan said. And by him? 'Well, of course, there's that presence of his. I've seen nothing like it except in Muhammad Ali, Marlon Brando and Stevie Wonder. Bob walks into a room and every eye in the place is on him. There are eyes on Bob even when he's hiding. All that has probably not been easy for him.' She says this entirely without her usual irony.

'Sometimes,' Dylan says to me on the phone in 1966, 'I have the feeling that other people want my soul. If I say to them, "I don't have a soul," they say "I know that. You don't have to tell me that. Not me. How dumb do you think I am? I'm your friend." What can I say except that I'm sorry and feel bad? I guess maybe feeling bad and paranoia are the same thing.'

On-stage, all during the Rolling Thunder Revue, Joan had put her arm around Dylan's shoulders, wiped the sweat off his forehead, kissed his cheek, and looked into his eyes, giving rise to a *frisson* voyeurism among those in the audience who yearn for 'Diamonds And Rust' to have a sequel, several sequels, for where else these days can you find that old-time mysterious rhapsody in the romances of the famous? 'It's on again,' a woman behind me whispers eagerly as Dylan and Baez intertwine in close harmony on-stage. 'It's on again.'

Later I ask the question and Joan laughs. 'This is a musical tour for me. Actually, I don't see much of Bob at all. He spends most of his time on that movie he's making. The movie needs a director. The sense I get of it so far is that that movie is a giant mess of a home movie.'

Joan, sitting back on the couch, as spontaneously straightforward as Dylan is cabalistically convoluted. And as he figures in who knows how many sexual fantasies of how many genders, so she is erotic, still freshly erotic, but probably stars in somewhat straighter fantasies. But who knows?

And she is funny, especially in self-defence. As on the day she showed up for her first rehearsal for the Rolling Thunder Revue.

'I'd like to hear that song off your new album,' Dylan asks the once and former girl on the half-shell. 'You know, "Diamonds And Rust".'

'You want me to do that on the show?' Joanie looks at him in solemn question.

'Yeah.' There is a distinct collector's gleam in Dylan's eyes. 'Yeah, I do.'

'You mean,' the ex-madonna grabs Dylan by the chin and looks him in the eyes, 'that song I wrote about my ex-husband?'

Dylan has been aced. 'I have to keep him spinning,' Joan says of the rout, 'in order to keep my balance.'

'Those duets', Joan says of what she's sometimes been thinking while also wiping Dylan's brow and looking into his eyes, 'are a hazard. It's hard singing with him because he's so devilish. There are times when I don't know what song he's plucking on that guitar until he starts singing. And he can be tricky. On one song, we'd been doing two choruses all along the tour but one night, just as I'm about to belt the second chorus, the song was all over. Done! Thanks a lot. Bob had worked out the new short ending with the band and hadn't told me. Oh, he's a lot of fun on-stage.'

Curtain! The second half of the nonpareil Rolling Thunder What-Might-Have-Been-and-What-Has-Been-Point-to-One-End-Which-is-Always-Present Revue is about to start!

Under the cowboy hat, the klezmer, the Jewish hobo musician with roots – roots by the centuries – turns to the sad-eyed lady from Chavez country. That lady who, he used to say, 'proved t'me that boys still grow'. Dylan looks up at Baez and says, 'Don't upstage me.'

She smiles her luminous smile and says, 'I'm going to use everything I have to do just that.'

The campaigner is still very fond of the klezmer. 'I used to be too hard on him. I used to be too hard on a lot of people.' Baez grins, sipping wine, 'Well, I'm not as stiff as I used to be. I've lightened up on people. I don't expect Bob to champion my causes any more. I've learned he's not an activist, which does not mean he doesn't care about people. If that were so, he wouldn't have written "Hurricane".'

Having shrived Dylan of her moral burden ('Singer or saviour it was his to choose/Which of us know what was his to lose'), what does she want for him now?

'I'd like to see him keep making music, keep creating. Why, I would like him to be happy.'

It all depends, of course. Or, as Jane Ace once said to Goodman Ace, 'If it makes him happy to be happy, then let him be happy.'

And what does she want for herself?

Joan Baez speaks to the wall. 'There must be something I can do with my life that will be worthwhile.'

You talk, I say, as if you've been a sybarite or a government official up to now.

'Oh, I've already done a fair amount of things; but in terms of what has to be done, how do you measure what you still ought to be doing? And maybe what I did wasn't done as efficiently as it could have been. Screaming at people may not be the most efficient way. I'm going to stay back a little from now on. I'm learning how to listen to people instead of preaching at them so much. And learning to listen to myself again. I'm thirty-thousand words into a book, an extension of *Daybreak*. And the songs. I'm going to write more personal songs. If they come. I go through some very long dry periods. But it's fun when it happens.'

She likes to laugh, always has, though in the past, as she knows, she has sometimes come on like Carry Nation wielding her axe with, as they used to say, an 'achingly pure soprano'.

'There are four of me, right?' Joan says. 'A mother, a woman, a musician and a politician. For a long time, I always put politics first. When Gabe was born, being a mother and being political took on co-equal importance. Music, like before, kept being shoved into the background. And the me that is a woman kept coming and going, depending on whether there was something going on in that part of my life.'

So, in the middle of the journey, the newsreel footage of the sixties having been locked up somewhere, which of the four Baezes is going to be in the forefront now?

'It's still getting sorted out,' says Joan. 'I'm always going to be involved in non-violence. I still feel very close to Chavez and the farmworkers, and I expect I'll be working again with Amnesty International. But on the other hand, I want to be with my kid. This is a very important year for him, a kind of transition year to when he starts moving away from as much need as he has now for his mother. I don't want to mess this year up. And then there's music. I can see myself getting more involved with the fun of the music, with allowing myself to be a musician for the sake of the music itself.'

And the woman part of Baez?

She grins. 'That comes and goes, depending on what happens. No way of knowing what's going to happen.'

One part of Baez, interlaced with all the others, remains stubbornly intact. 'I am', she says, 'your basic camp counsellor, I really am.'

All campers are to be treated equally, with justice and fairness for all. Or else.

By the twelfth stop of the Rolling Thunder Revue celebration of musical egalitarianism, the camp counsellor is furious. She is preparing a *pronunciamento* and a graphic drawing for the tour's internal newspaper. She is protesting rank injustice in the heart of all this here cultural freedom.

'They make the security people, the bus drivers and the crew', the burning bush speaks, 'eat at separate places and at separate hours from the rest of us. That is segregation.'

Who is 'they' – Lou Kemp?

'I don't know who it is. But this is going to stop. The drawing I'm putting in shows a pool of blood, and it's going to say that without these guys who are being segregated, one of us principals might be stranded, to say the least, in the wake of the Rolling Thunder Revue.'

What if your protest is ignored?

'Then a lot of us', says Joan, 'will go eat with the security people, the bus drivers and the crew. There are a lot of possible approaches to this kind of problem.'

Is Bob aware of this segregation?

Joan, customarily spontaneous, customarily candid, weighs her answer. 'I don't know,' she says.

*

Allen Ginsberg also speaks of protest, but as in a vision. Where once was a time to howl, now is the time to begin the harvest and to give thanks to the harbingers, then and now.

In Springfield, Massachusetts, Arlo Guthrie moves on-stage to play and sing with his father's other son, the hard-wishing, hard-travelling, earnestly self-adopted Jack Elliott. Backstage, the Midwestern klezmer (to whom Woody was his 'last idol') watches and listens.

'That's a strong lineage, Woody's,' says Allen Ginsberg, 'and Woody, of course, was part of an older lineage, that old good-time Wobbly idealism. That's all still going strong right in this show. Joan sings "Joe Hill". And "Hurricane" is part of that too, an old classic social protest song.'

Sound the news of injustice and the people will awake. How else can we begin?

'And look how we end,' says Walt Whitman's friend.

The end, a reasonably jubilant 'This Land Is Your Land', everybody on-stage, even Ginsberg-the-Keeper-of-the-Vision making silvery his finger cymbals, as Joan soars and swoops from the mountains to the prairies and Dylan, smiling, stands his ground, and all the rest move up to the hearty beat of the American Upanishad.

'There was a kind of vision of community in the sixties,' Ginsberg says after the show, 'and many people thought that once they'd had the vision, everything was solved. But as Jack Kerouac once said, "Walking on water wasn't built in a day". Another thing going on in the sixties was just people digging each other, digging each other's texture and character, hanging out. You can't do that fast either. You know, there was a lot of hanging out in the fifties too, in Kerouac.'

Dylan had been braced and shaped, in part, way back then, by Kerouac. *Doctor Sax*, *On the Road*, *Mexico City Blues*. The day after the Rolling Thunder Revue came to Lowell, Dylan, Ginsberg and Peter Orlovsky visited Kerouac's grave. Ginsberg had brought a copy of *Mexico City Blues* and Dylan read a poem from it. The three men sat on the grave, Dylan picking up Ginsberg's harmonium and making up a tune. When Dylan pulled out his guitar, Ginsberg began to improvise a long slow, 12-bar blues about Kerouac sitting up in the clouds looking down on these kindly wanderers putting the music to his grave. Dylan is much moved, much involved, a state of introspection closely captured by the camera crew that has also come along.

Before Lowell, before Boston, before Plymouth, the day the Dharma Carnival was to leave New York, Allen Ginsberg meets Muriel Rukeyser on the street. This soft-voiced, slow-speaking, hugely honest poet, who of late has been in South Korea trying to stop the terminal silencing of an anti-death poet there, is glad to see Ginsberg. She admires people with visions. She asks where he's going.

'I'm going on the bus,' Ginsberg says cheerily. 'It's a minstrel show!'

'But it's more than a minstrel show, isn't it?' she asks me the next day.

'It is a signal to the country,' Ginsberg tells me on the road. 'What happened in the San Francisco renaissance in the mid fifties was one of those signals that characterize the rise of a generation's poetic consciousness and its sense of social rebellion. And that happened in the very midst of McCarthyism. Then, in the mid sixties, the peace marches and the rise of rock – the Beatles and things like that – were among the signals for a further rising of consciousness, a wider sense of community. Now, the Rolling Thunder Revue will be one of the signal gestures characterizing the working cultural community that will make the seventies.'

I would like to truly believe, I tell the poet, but where, except in wish, is the basis for such joyous tidings in a time of torpor?

'Have you read Dave Dellinger's book, *More Power Than We*

Knew?' The poet must resort to prose. 'Dellinger shows that many of the demands that the youth generation or the left or the movement made in the sixties have actually been met. Congress did cut off funds for the Vietnam war and who would have thought that possible in the mid sixties? Then there were all the protests about the police state, and a police state paranoia to go with them. Now a great deal of that has been confirmed and exposed in public investigations. Not that everything has been all cleaned up but the work of the sixties did bear some fruit. It never was in vain.

'So now, it's time for America to get its shit together,' the poet says idiomatically. 'It's time to get back to work or keep on working, depending on who you are, because the work that went before has been good, even though people got discouraged. It's been as good as you can expect, considering what it takes to walk on water or reverse the machine age or deal with overpopulation or capitalism. Rolling Thunder, with its sense of community, is saying we should all get our act together. And do it properly and well.' The poet, bouncing his vision, laughs. 'Once you have a view of the right path, then you have to travel that path.'

That means Dylan's getting his act together too?

'Having gone through his changes in the sixties and seventies, just like everybody else,' Ginsberg says, 'Bob now has his powers together. On the show, he has all the different kinds of art he has practised – protest, improvisation, surrealist invention, electric rock and roll, solitary acoustic guitars, strumming, duet work with Joan and with other people. All these different practices have now ripened and are usable in one single show, just as there is also room for Mick Ronson and his very English kind of space-music rock, Joan and her sort of refined balladry and Roger McGuinn with his West Coast-style rock. All of these different styles turn out to be usable now.'

*

'Do you know what Dylan is talking about doing?' a principal of the tour says to me. 'Don't use my name, but he might start a newspaper! That blows my mind. It'll be a community newspaper, but for a community all over the country.'

I wonder who is going to be the music critic and, in particular, who is going to write about Dylan's records. Blind Boy Grunt?

'I am not able to tell you any details,' says Allen Ginsberg, 'but this tour may not end as all other tours have. There is some desire among us to have a kind of permanent community and Dylan is stepping very, very slowly to find out if that can work. Recordings would be one way and there may be other ways. One must proceed slowly and soberly – unlike the Beatles when they tried to expand their sense of community. Remember John Lennon trying to put together that whole Apple enterprise as a sort of umbrella organization for all kinds of collective work? But he didn't have the right personnel and so it wasn't done soberly and practically enough. This would be. Keep watching. The thing is to keep the Rolling Thunder spirit alive.'

Joan Baez's denunciation of class segregation aboard the Rolling Thunder Revue has appeared in the troupe's internal newspaper. Her sketch of some nameless star, lying on the ground with blood pouring out of his head, was not printed and has disappeared.

Did it work? I ask.

'Well,' says the ceaseless strategist of non-violent direct action, 'things kind of came together a bit after that. A lot of people, each in his or her own way, began committing small acts of civil disobedience – like taking the bus driver to their table. So the tone has changed and the segregation has lessened.' Some people, I am buoyed to see, are still overcoming.

The tour is old enough for retrospection.

'When you got that call from Bob,' an old acquaintance visiting Joan backstage says, 'I suppose you got on the plane without even knowing what you were going to get paid.'

Joan looks at the questioner as if the latter has just asked if the tooth fairy has gotten over its cold. 'When I got that call,' Joan says, 'I had already planned my fall tour. So I told the people dealing with the money that although it seemed like fun, they'd have to make it worth my while to change my plans. Well, after my lawyers got involved and we worked out a contract, a very detailed contract, they made it worth my while. Sure, I'm glad I came. This tour has integrity. And that's because of Bob.'

'Tell me,' the acquaintance asks, 'what are his children like?'

Joan hoots, 'I've never seen any of them. They're like mythology. It does gather around him, mythology. And he certainly helps it gather. Mythology and confusion. Like some of the songs. I know who "Sad-Eyed Lady Of The Lowlands" is, no matter who he says it is.'

'But at least we all know who "Sara" is,' the visitor observes.

'Dylan says', Ginsberg has overheard, 'that song is about Sara in the Bible.' And Ginsberg laughs.

Mythology has become palpable. Sara Lowndes Dylan has joined the Rolling Thunder Revue, and with her are several Dylan children and a nanny. Allen Ginsberg is impressed. 'Sara is very intelligent, very funny and I would say queenly. She's sort of aristocratic looking, like an old-time New York young Jewish lady who's been around a lot in the theatre, which she has been. Sara and Joan', Ginsberg chuckles, 'have had time to compare notes on Dylan.'

'No, I had never known her before,' Joan says of Sara, 'and yes, we have been comparing notes, and that is all I'm going to tell you about that. But I will say that for me, Sara is the most interesting female on this tour. Why? Because she's not a bore. That's the best thing I can say about anybody.'

Sara Lowndes Dylan has become part of the Rolling Thunder

Revue Acting Company, adding her skills and fantasies to what Allen Ginsberg estimates to be more than one hundred hours of film already in the can for the giant kaleidoscope being shot by Lombard Street Films, which is being financed – I am told for non-attribution by those close to Zeus – by Dylan himself. At least five or so complete concerts have been preserved and some special numbers, such as 'Isis', have been filmed more times than that. And there have been scores of scenes enacted by diversely mixed members of the troupe. Sara Dylan, for instance, has now portrayed a madam in a bordello in which one of the nubile employees is enacted by Joan Baez in a brazen French accent.

Joan, at first rather standoffish about what she had earlier regarded as a huge mess of a home movie, has now become more involved. In another scene, for instance, she and Dylan are in a bar and the bartender is Arlo Guthrie. 'My God, she has a lot of energy,' says Allen Ginsberg. 'And what a marvellous mime.'

Also intermittently involved are members of the band, virtuosic David Mansfield among them. As an educational insert in the Bordello sequence, Allen Ginsberg is seen in his business suit, taking Mansfield (playing a chaste 14-year-old) to lose his cherry, as Ginsberg puts it in the old-time vernacular. This being, in part, a musical, Mansfield of course has his violin along.

Like many of the scenes in this gargantuan movie – which will purportedly be cut and edited in the spring by Dylan and Howard Alk, who worked with Dylan on *Eat the Document* – the bordello section started as quite something else. Ginsberg had suggested a scene involving a number of women in the troupe, in part because he is much taken with the notion that the dominant theme in the Rolling Thunder Revue is respect for the 'mother goddess, eternal woman, earth woman principle'. He points to the songs in the show, such as 'Isis' and 'Sara', and notes as well that Sara Dylan had diligently researched this theme in such works as Robert Graves's *The White Goddess*.

The women having assembled, there was much discussion as to

the roles they would play – perhaps the graces or the goddesses or the nine muses. Somehow, however, Sara Lowndes Dylan said, 'After all that talk about goddesses, we wound up being whores.'

'None the less,' says Allen, 'Sara, as the madam, did talk about Flaubert.'

Dylan is consumed by this film. He conceives a good many of the situations, advises on the transmutation of others, does some of the directing, peers into the camera and works, picking up technique, with the film crew.

One day after much shooting, Ginsberg, wondering how Dylan keeps track of the direction of all this footage, asks him. Dylan wishes he hadn't.

'I've lost the thread,' Dylan, with some bewilderment, admits to Ginsberg.

A couple of days later, Ginsberg asks Dylan if the thread has been relocated. The singing film-maker nods affirmatively.

'So what is the thread of the film?' the poet asks.

'Truth and beauty,' says his ever-precise friend.

Along with the Dylan children and their nanny, Joan Baez's six-year-old son, Gabriel, is now on hand, together with Joan's mother and a nursemaid for Gabriel. What would Kerouac have made of this way of doing the road?

Also suddenly, triumphantly, materialized – a climactic re-affirmation of the eternal-woman principle – is Bob Dylan's mother, Beatty Zimmerman.

'A regular chicken soup Jewish mother,' Allen Ginsberg says approvingly. 'With a lot of spirit.'

Toronto. A cornucopian concert with Gordon Lightfoot and Joni Mitchell added to the Astartean cast. And also added in the fertile finale, 'This Land Is Your Land' – Bob Dylan's mother.

Seated at the back of the stage, Beatty Zimmerman is pulled up and on to stage centre and begins to dance and wave to the audience, none of whom, she is sure, knows who she is.

It is getting near the start of the second chorus and Joan Baez, chronically gracious, pulls Mrs Zimmerman toward the lead mike, the principals' mike. 'All of a sudden,' Joan says, 'Dylan kicks me in the ass. Gently. It was his way of saying, "I think I'd rather sing this chorus than have my mother do it." So I had to gracefully Charleston Mrs Zimmerman back a few steps and then leap to the mike and sing with Bob.'

And there, back a few steps, is Mrs Zimmerman, arms flailing, dancing to Woody's song and the music of Woody's children and the music of her own child, of all things. The first time she's ever been on-stage with that child.

'Sara, Joan, his children, his mother,' Allen Ginsberg meditates. 'He's getting all his mysteries unraveled.'

Not quite. Not yet. Earlier in the tour, listening to him as he chants what I took — wrongly, it turns out — to be kaddish for 'Sara', there is that mysterious, demonic force, in and beyond the words, that will last a long while beyond the tour. That cracking, shaking energy which reminds me of another klezmer on the roof, another Tateh in ragtime, Lenny Bruce. But Lenny, who certainly had his act together, never learned how to get his defenses together. Dylan, on the other hand, has developed a vocation for self-protection. If he has a mania, it is for survival. ('I'm still gonna be around when everybody gets their heads straight.') And part of the way of survival is keeping some of his mysteries damn well raveled.

One morning, as the caravan is about to break camp, a rock musician says, 'You know what makes him different. He sees the end of things. The rest of us, we're into something, it's as if it's going to last forever. Dylan, he's in just as deep, but he knows it's not going to last.'

I am mumbling about a stiff singer who phrases, however authoritatively, like a seal and plays nothing guitar on the side. Why, then, do I once again (unlike the '74 tour) find him powerful? 'It doesn't matter whether he's musical at all,' I am instructed by Margot Hentoff, a writer on these matters. 'He has in his voice that sense of the fragility of all things, that sense of mortality which everybody tries to avoid acknowledging but is drawn toward when they hear it. He's got it and nobody else has.'

It was my wife (quoted in a *New York Times* epitaph I had written of the '74 tour) who had greatly annoyed Dylan, a friend of his told me. 'He's not "The Kid" anymore,' she had said in print, 'so what can he be now?'

A year later, having come upon the Rolling Thunder Revue, she has an answer: 'A grown-up. Maybe a suspicious, secretive, irritating grown-up. But no longer a kid. He's lost that. And now, as he grows older, he'll get still more powerful because he'll reach the further knowledge that there is no way out of loss, and so he'll have a new truth to talk about.'

Late one night, at the Other End, before the trail boss was quite ready to get the wagon train going, Dylan and Bob Neuwirth and the rest of the gang are elevating their discourse.

'Hey, poet, sing me a poem!' one of them yells to Dylan.

'OK, poet,' says the Minstrel Guruji.

Delighted, Allen Ginsberg is saying, 'It's like in a Dostoevsky novel, the way they've taken to calling each other "poet". It's no more, "OK cowboy". It's "OK poet". They're using poet as an honorific, practical thing, and that means they've grown old enough to see that poetry is tough, that it's a lasting practice bearing fruit over decades.

'Dylan has become much more conscious of himself as a poet,' Ginsberg adds. 'I've watched him grow in that direction. Back in 1968, he was talking poetics with me, telling me how he was writing shorter lines, with every line meaning something. He wasn't just making up a line to go with a rhyme anymore; each line had to advance the story, bring the song forward. And from that time came some of the stuff he did with the Band – like "I Shall Be Released", and some of his strong laconic ballads like "The Ballad Of Frankie Lee And Judas Priest". There was to be no wasted language, no wasted breath. All the imagery was to be functional rather than ornamental. And he's kept growing from there.

'Like he's been reading Joseph Conrad recently. *Victory* in particular. I found out when we were talking about the narrative quality of some of the newer songs – "Hurricane" and "Joey" and "Isis". Bob related the way those songs developed to what he'd been learning about narrative and about characterization from Conrad. The way characterization and mood shape narrative. Now he's asking about H.P. Lovecraft. I wonder what that's going to lead to?'

It is near the end. In Toronto, Joan Baez is backstage. On-stage, Dylan is beginning his acoustic set. A member of Gordon Lightfoot's band begins to move some equipment. Baez glares at him and he stops.

'The jerk didn't know any better,' she says later, 'but I didn't want to miss a note. I didn't want to miss a word. Even after all these shows, the genius of the Kid was still holding it all together. I'd heard it all, every night, and here I'm sitting again as close to him as I can get. And not only me. You look around and you see every member of the band and the guys in the crew listening too.'

What is it? What is it he has? I ask.

'It's the power,' Joan says, 'it's the power.'

'Oh, I'm hurtin'.' It is the next morning. Bob Neuwirth groans and coughs in a most alarming manner. 'This is a rolling writers' show,' Neuwirth manages to say. 'Nobody's on this tour who isn't a writer. Oh, I'm really hurtin'. Even the equipment guys, the bus drivers, they're all jotting things down. It's a goddamn rolling writers' convention. Oh my God, I can't even cough. It's going to be such a drag when this tour is over.'

Joan Baez, mildly sympathetic when she's not laughing, says to the audibly aching Neuwirth, 'Do let me describe what happened to you last night.' 'Everybody has his own way of dealing with anxieties,' she explains to me, 'and his way was to get himself black and blue. He got very, very drunk and ornery and for an hour and a half four very large security guards were wrestling him in the hall because they didn't want him to leave the hotel and go wreck Gordon Lightfoot's house where we were having a party. Well, he got there anyhow and he did wreck the house just a little. But everybody had a grand time, and now Neuwirth feels fine too, except he can't walk very well.

'You see, it's going to be rough for all of us when this is over. And Neuwirth's way of handling that was to have an early blowout. God, it's depressing at the end.'

At the beginning, in Plymouth, Massachusetts, Elliott Adnopoz (long since transubstantiated into his vision, Ramblin' Jack Elliott) sees an old friend, the replica of the *Mayflower*, on whose rigging he, an expert sailor, had actually worked years before. Climbing to the top of the mizzen-mast, Elliott explodes with a long, joyous 'Ahoy!' and waves to the Minnesota poet in the cowboy hat below as Allen Ginsberg proclaims, 'We have, once again, embarked on a voyage to reclaim America.'

At least it is steady work, especially for a minstrel.

The Harder They Fall

JOHN HELSTROM

There have been few tours as brief and dramatic as the Sex Pistols' one and only American tour in January 1978. Lasting just ten days and seven shows, it ended with punk's premier iconoclasts in a state of dissolution, bassist Sid Vicious well on his way to an early appointment with his Maker and a disenchanted Johnny Rotten looking for a more suitable public image. Helstrom's account in New York's Punk *magazine remains the definitive account of this ten-day display of the Pistols' capacity for (self-)destruction.*

It's unbelievable that a rock group that played no more than one hundred live performances (less than fifty according to guitarist Steve Jones) and existed for only twenty-seven months could become as internationally disliked as the Sex Pistols were.

The Sex Pistols were designed by their manager, Malcolm McLaren, in the same way he designed clothes for his fashion shop. I always thought their image was lame – the anti-establishment stance belongs to hippies and their fashion strictly glitter – but they were a great rock & roll band. The fact that the English punk scene got so much publicity was as simple as being in an auto accident. English punk is a contradiction in terms – Marlon Brando could never come from England.

Armed with these prejudices, I set off to see the Sex Pistols tour. It was fun. For weeks the office buzzed with Sex Pistols rumours, like that Jimmy Carter was responsible for getting their visas. Everyone thought they were going to play CBGB when they stopped in New York to have their picture taken for the *NY Post*.

Malcolm was in England while the Sex Pistols played in Atlanta. Warner Brothers took over as soon as they landed. They called the shots now. McLaren didn't like this one bit.

Sid managed to get lost in Atlanta and gave himself a nice wound in his arm. It looked like he tried to shoot up with a Bowie knife, but the rumour said he was just having fun with a fish hook. Throughout the tour Sid tried to destroy himself every chance he got.

There was a riot outside the Taliesyn Ballroom in Memphis because two hundred ticket holders were refused entry – the fire marshall reduced the capacity that afternoon. When the bus was leaving for the ballroom, Sid couldn't be found. Everyone panicked. They finally found him outside by the pool, fresh from wandering around the Holiday Inn looking for you-know-what. He got severely disciplined by the tour security who kicked tour photographers Joe Stevens and Bob Gruen out of the bus before dragging Sid back. That night Sid looked strange – his eyes were red and his face was screwed up in a bizarre expression. John stood still. After the show that night they seemed depressed and miserable when they talked to a few fans and press.

I got a very close look at Memphis that night when I found I had no money for a cab and had to hitch-hike. A big luxury car pulled over. Inside, three black dudes tried to push dope on me. When I didn't buy any they pulled into a side road.

'How much money you got man?'

'About a dollar.'

'Give to me. NOW! Sheeeit! Dis ain't no dollar! Man, you said you had a dollar! What else you got?'

'Nothin'.'

'What you got in dat bag, man? What else you got? Lemme see what you got in dat bag?'

The car pulled over. As they swarmed over my suitcase, which contained a tape recorder, a sweater, a pair of socks and a toothbrush, I ran out the door. They came after me but were too fucked up on drugs to catch me.

The Memphis ghetto is a lot different from the ones in New York. The destruction is not as total, but the atmosphere is a lot more depressing. It's suburban waste and decay, if you can imagine that – dilapidated two-room houses, ramshackle cabins, guard dogs, abandoned Cadillacs, filthy front lawns, and a few blocks of undeveloped land. On the way down in the plane a resident was telling me how safe it was in Memphis and about the many clean city awards it wins all the time. Here I was hiding from every car that went by 'cause I'm white. I heard a fight going on in a house I passed. A car of noisy drunks careened by me. Finally I came to a part of town that looked like an Afro-American *Happy Days*.

Between Memphis and San Antonio the Pistols stopped in Austin. John and his bodyguard went to see *The Gauntlet*, while the rest of the group visited a massage parlour.

I met the group for the first time at the very plush Broadway Plaza hotel. I talked with Malcolm at length. He's a small intelligent man, whose manner is so subtle that he can become invisible. Although he's a bit spaced, he was the most eloquent person I spoke with on the tour. He gave me the impression that he knew what he wanted, how to get it, what to do with it when he got it, how to get rid of it, and how to blow up the world. He said he had to use the daily press in England to sell records because the Pistols couldn't get airplay and kids who go to concerts don't bother buying records. The front page scandals sell records to conservative workers with normal jobs who are curious about what the papers say.

Malcolm is dedicated to proving that you don't have to follow the established pattern of success in the music business, because once you can tell what's going to happen in a group, they become boring. Everyone is expected to play New York and Los Angeles for the press, and play big halls in between for maximum money and exposure. McLaren had a lot of trouble getting Warner Bros to go along with his ideas – the bus ('Planes are just so disorientating. You never have any idea of where you're playing', although Malcolm himself flies everywhere on the tour), skipping New York and Los Angeles, and playing in very strange clubs and ballrooms.

Our conversation was interrupted by Paul Cook, fresh from an interview with the prestigious *LA Times*. 'I said "fuck you" a few times and left.'

'Good,' said Malcolm. 'That's what they want to hear, all right.'

Steve Jones enters, and proudly announces that he's been farting in the reporter's face. He's hungry.

Randy's is a big Texas-style ballroom the size of two supermarkets with dozens of pinball machines in the back. There were more pretty girls at this place than I ever saw at a rock concert. Texas is great. The crowd is mostly rowdy drunken cowboys. Hundreds were packed in close to the very large stage, which was lit by giant spotlights – pure white light. The mob pelted the band with beer cans as they opened with 'No Future'. The sound took some time to get adjusted, but the Pistols proved themselves. They were pissed off and played with a vengeance.

John told the mob to stop throwing things. Sid yelled, 'You cowboys are all a bunch of fucking faggots! You cunts!'

The crowd growled back and threw showers of beer cans. Sid caught a full can in the teeth. He loved it, but when someone tried to fuck with his guitar he took it off and swung it at the guy's head. A couple of security guys tried to hold him back but he did it again. The spotlights turned off and there was a silence punctuated by the babbling crowd. It looked like the show was over. It looked like the mob was going to murder the Sex Pistols.

'Oh, what a pity. Sidney dropped his guitar,' John said. They played 'New York', John spitting the words 'You fucking little faggots' at the audience. He moved really strangely, hopping about like a cross between Groucho Marx and Quasimodo. 'We don't like your fucking free gifts!' he snarled, as beer cans continued to fly around.

'It's just like Iggy said – you're the fuckers who paid ten bucks to see us, so fuck you!' Sid proudly shouted.

'Shut up, Sidney, you're holding up the set!' John spat. John and Sid remind me of a comedy team, like Laurel and Hardy. Rotten finally said, 'Go ahead! Throw all the cans you want! It amuses us to watch fools throwing their money away!'

The next day the San Antonio front page headline screamed 'SEX PISTOLS WIN S.A. SHOOTOUT'.

Malcolm was excited after the show. 'Did you see that? We've been waiting three weeks for that one!' He asked Gruen if he got the Picture of Sid. Bob missed it.

'Too bad! Thousand pound shot, that one! The cover of the *Daily Mirror*!' (Stevens got it.) Malcolm is suddenly besieged by a group of English journalists who complain about the barbaric treatment they've received on the tour. Malcolm sympathizes with them. He's powerless. He smiled. These guys make up better stories than what actually happens. The media relies on exaggeration, lies, fabrications and bullshit and it was going to stay that way.

The Sex Pistols were at a sound-check when the *Variety* '77 television show presented them on national TV for the first time. Alan King and Telly Savalas made a point of announcing their appearance every five minutes – 'Coming up soon, the Sensational Sex Pistols!'

Sophie, Malcolm's assistant, arrived from London for the rest of the tour and was overheard saying 'I don't want to go on a tour with this poxy band.' She enjoyed the show that evening, as did everyone, although after Randy's, each show lost momentum. The other unforgettable incident occurred when someone threw a bunch of coins at Sid.

'Fuck this! Where's the hundred dollar bills?' he shouted. People handed and threw dollar bills to the group, who spent the second encore – 'Liar' – picking up dollar bills and stuffing them into their pockets and mouths.

After the show, Sid, Steve and Paul came out to the bar to talk to fans and pick up groupies. Sid made out the best. He got a blow-job in the men's room from a pretty good-looking shank.

Meanwhile, one of the English reporters complained to the tour manager, Noel Monk, about the treatment they'd received. Monk was standing behind one of his gorillas, leering down at this wimpy little reporter, shouting 'Oh yeah? We'll just say you took a swing at us. It'll be your word against ours, motherfucker!' The reporter stood up to Monk, trying to reason with him, but after persistent violent threats, he retreated to the bar.

I went backstage to find out how much money Rotten had collected. 'Fifteen dollars,' he said proudly. 'In England we're like starving Biafrans – Americans giving us money.'

Something about him reminded me of Tom Verlaine so I left the room. Paul Cook was getting a very high score on a pinball machine. I started stealing Sex Pistols posters off the wall. The owner of the club spotted me and took me into his office. He gave me a bunch of posters, instructing me to leave his Stevie Nicks poster on the wall. He also told me that the bottom fell out of progressive country a few years ago, and that he was booking a lot of punk acts – Ramones, Robert Gordon, Stranglers, Elvis Costello, etc.

I started for the bar. Suddenly a large gang of security apes grabbed a lone punk rocker. A friend of his objected. Another large gang appeared out of nowhere. The pair were dragged outside. This kind of thing was very typical on this tour so I didn't pay too much attention.

We were allowed to ride on the bus back to the hotel. Noel Monk menacingly ordered me not to write about anything that happened on the bus or at the hotel. No photos. He reminded me of Sgt Carter on *Gomer Pyle*.

As Roberta Bayley walked to the back of the bus, John spotted her (the only girl on a full bus of sex maniacs): 'This is highly inadvisable, young lady.'

The bus itself was very comfortable. It was crowded inside but there were bunk beds and cushioned chairs with built-in tables. While I sat in the back, the bodyguards eyed me suspiciously. Steve and Sid sat in the back with us. Sid looked for something to drink, then joked with Steve about how he learned everything about the guitar from him. Steve said he ripped everything off Johnny Thunders.

Johnny Rotten was off the bus fast and was walking down the hall carrying his bags as I got to the hotel. During the tour he spent most of his time locked up in his room or in the bus fighting with Sidney.

Sid was really drunk as usual, and started a friendly fight with Roberta after she declined to give him 'a portion'. Sid started slapping her, promising not to kick her with his work boots. Then Roberta began to win the fight, so he kicked her hand.

'O W W W H!'

Sid consoled her. 'Oh, I'm sorry, did I hurt you? . . . I'm sorry, I feel terrible about this . . . C'mon, hit me. Go ahead, I deserve it.'

Even though Sid really wanted to get beat up, Roberta declined. Next Sid came over to me and gave me an exhibition of his fighting skill, throwing punches at my face, faster and faster, missing by mere fractions of an inch. Then he punched my nose.

'I'm terribly sorry . . . Go ahead, hit me, I deserve it.'

The bodyguard was standing right back of him giving me more dirty looks so I turned down the offer. Sid whipped off his belt and left a really nice dent in the wall.

Steve fell asleep in one of the rooms, refusing to budge. He was tired of the bus. He and Paul talked Malcolm into letting them fly with him. I think this was part of the personality crisis they were having.

At the sound-check at the Longhorn Ballroom (once a topless

joint owned by Jack Ruby), I talked with Malc at length about his involvement with the New York Dolls. He stated that he never was officially their manager, that he merely helped them 'personally and financially'. People who knew him at the time say that he'd go to their apartments and drag them out of bed to get them to rehearsals. He compared the ego problems he had with David Johansen to the ones he has with Rotten now. It's a common problem – the lead singer gets so much praise and attention lavished upon him that he begins to believe it. They become very self-conscious and self-indulgent and imitate themselves. The group soon becomes fossilized, and the whole thing becomes self-congratulatory. As *Rolling Stone*'s Charles M. Young stands nearby stealing my interview, Malcolm admitted that he was sure about 1977, but he has serious doubts about 1978. 'There's got to be a group out there better than the Sex Pistols so they have something to compete against besides themselves.'

I asked him if the Sex Pistols hadn't been watered down by the media's stupid coverage. It didn't matter to him so long as the record was out – 'the document is there. The few good songs that don't become clichés in five years ['Anarchy', 'God Save The Queen', 'Holidays', and maybe 'Bodies', although 'the sentiment is a bit old fashioned'] will have proven the Sex Pistols. As long as they don't turn into entertainment.'

After the sound-check, where the Pistols rehearse 'Sod In Heaven', their latest tune, they went to the TV Bar, and mixed with the local clientele – mostly cops and hookers. In a corner of the bar Paul, Steve and Malcolm discussed the problems they were having with Rotten.

At the gig that night the Pistols seemed to have fun, at least Sid did. A punkette from LA gave him a bloody nose so he wiped the blood all over himself. He was so out of it he was playing with three busted strings on his bass.

Pistols fans climbed all over each other trying to tear down a curtain that framed the stage with portraits of C&W stars. During

'Anarchy' one fanatic tore Johnny's t-shirt off his body. John liked that bit so he shook the guy's hand.

There were even more security hassles than usual after the show. The LA punkettes complained to Malcolm that they were beaten by WB security for no reason. Two of them were holding up their friend whose face was badly bruised and could hardly stand up. Malcolm sympathized. 'Those wankers. Wankers. Warner Brothers is a bunch of wankers.'

It snowed in Tulsa, where they get snow only once or twice a year. Steve, John and Malcolm were all suffering from the flu.

At the sound check at Cain's Ballroom I picked up a copy of *Billboard*:

PUNK DISPLAYS

According to both Peter's International and Jem Records the *Never Mind The Bollocks* LP is already the biggest selling import item in memory. Jem Records is especially active in punk merchandizing, working with stores to put up a New Wave section.

The Pistols ran through a few songs, when suddenly I heard some off-the-cuff blues from Steve and Paul. Steve even played 'Amazing Grace', an old Rod Stewart favourite.

They played well that evening, but Sid Vicious is right – it's the attitude that made the Sex Pistols great.

After the concert Sid picked up a glamorous blonde with big tits. Everyone wondered if it was a man or a woman. When they got back to the hotel Sid tried to kill himself, as usual. First he smashed a gin bottle against a TV set. The bottle didn't break so he tried to jump out the window. That didn't work so he asked if anybody had any drugs. The blonde was pulling pot out of her socks when Noel Monk barged in. He went ape-shit when he saw drugs and started interrogating the blonde. 'Do you have anything else on you?' No, she didn't. Noel said he'd have to search her.

Soon Roman Polanski dressed in drag jumped out the window on television – *The Tenant*. Sid asked the blonde, ''Ere now, am I going to suck your cock or your cunt?'

'Cunt,' she whispered in such a deep voice that everyone in the room jumped ten feet.

Sid asked me which gig was the best. I told him Randy's. Sid asked, 'Was that in Dallas? Yeah, that was great!' Noel Monk took me aside to tell me that I should tell Sid that the band was best tonight. 'My job is to get these guys working as a band. The press wanted blood – they got their blood in Dallas. Now it's my job to turn them into a professional touring group.' Then Noel 'The Mad' Monk grabbed Sid's bottle of Jack Daniels. He pointed to an imaginary line. 'Don't drink past that line. See it there? Right there. No, there. That line.'

'All right, Noel. OK. Hey, Noel, I'm bein' good aren't I? I'm doin' OK, right?' Sid asked him sincerely. Noel, along with the bodyguards and road crew, had become close mates with Sid and Johnny. Even though they order them around like they were buck privates in the Marines, John was very impressed with the bodyguards' karate skill. When the Sex Pistols break up, though, the WB crew doesn't recognize Rotten's existence.

The next morning I was shaking a hangover in the coffee shop. Paul and John sat nearby. I showed *Punk* magazine to Paul, who was genuinely interested. Johnny snapped, 'That magazine is disgusting. It's hideous.'

'Shut up,' Paul said.

'It's disgusting! That magazine is hideous!'

'Will you shut up!' Paul complained.

About an hour later I walked to the elevator carrying a six-foot pair of steerhorns. John was waiting there with his bodyguard. He opened wide and he bent over funny.

'What the FUCK is THAT?'

'Steerhorns,' I mumbled. I handed them to John. 'Want them?'

Greed overcame his face in a strange smile. He nodded yes while his bodyguard nodded in approval.

'They're yours. A little gift from *Punk* magazine,' I said and started to leave.

'Yeah! Don't forget to slag us off in that magazine of yours.'

'Don't worry,' I answered. 'That'll be easy.'

The blonde, I found out, was a sex change. Sid described the bloody gash between her legs, and the stitches on her thighs. He got a decent blow-job out of it, anyway.

Until San Francisco, the tour was mildly successful. The Sex Pistols were a household name. The record was still moving up the charts. The tour was almost over and nobody was dead or in jail yet. Winterland, by far the biggest concert in the Pistols' short and stormy career, sold 5,000 seats in one day.

Rotten said in San Antonio that the group would not play shit-holes but here they were – poised to play the Biggest Shit-hole in the Decaying Hippie Capital of the World. To make things worse, Bill Graham, the biggest hippie promoter ever, the man responsible for the Fillmores, was promoting the concert.

On Friday 13th, the day before the Winterland gig, Malcolm had no idea where the bus carrying Sid and John was. He was busy making last minute arrangements – promotional ideas (giant squirt guns, billboards etc.), publicity photos of the group (a trip to Alcatraz was discussed) and creating the proper atmosphere of anarchy and chaos at Winterland.

Bill Graham wanted the doors to open at 5.00 p.m. and show the movies until 12.00, when the Pistols would be broadcast live on the radio. He booked the most professional and well-liked punk bands in the Bay Area to open. Malcolm wanted an open stage from 5.00 on, letting any kid who showed up with a guitar plug in and play. He tried to import a group of 12-year-old kids from LA called the Dickies and bought radio time to announce the open stage. 'Every kid should be allowed to play. Maybe a group will go on and blow the Sex Pistols off the stage. That would be fuckin' fantastic, wouldn't it?'

Meanwhile, the Sex Pistols were banned from Finland, the

Holiday Inn chain worldwide, and American Airlines. There was damage to the rooms in Tulsa (mostly the work of the road crew). On the flight from Tulsa, Steve and Paul were clowning around, fighting and rolling in the aisles. The stewardesses warned them that if they didn't stop at once they'd never fly on American Airlines again.

Suddenly there was a plan to fly the group to Brazil. Ronald Biggs, the Great Train Robber from England, invited the group to visit him and play at his nightclub in Rio de Janeiro. Biggs pulled off a multi-million dollar train robbery about twenty years before. He bought his way out of jail with the stolen money and absconded to Australia, then reappeared in Rio, where police couldn't extradite him because he was married and had a kid-citizenship. He's an infamous, legendary hero in England, and one of Malcolm McLaren's idols. There's even speculation that Biggs supported punk rock in England with some of his dough. Even though the Pistols would make the front pages in English newspapers, Warner Brothers didn't care. They didn't want to send them down there. Aside from the obvious expense, they were allegedly afraid that the military government would put them in jail.

'In view of the trouble they had with the US State Department, one wonders what the results of a future confrontation with the Brazilian military junta will be like. Stay tuned – our next communiqué might be the announcement of a bail fund' (from the '*Never Mind The Bollocks – Here's The Sex Pistols* 1st American Tour,' an extensive Warner Brothers publicity release sent out three weeks after the Pistols' break-up).

Malcolm had Warners by the balls this time, though. By contract they had to get the Pistols out of the country any way Malcolm said. McLaren's plans were to jet down to Brazil – get maximum publicity, forcing release of the LP in South America – fly to Europe for a short tour – film a big budget full-length theatrical film *A Star is Dead* starring the Pistols and based loosely on the Rolling Stones – record a second album – and play America again, perhaps doing as many as three tours before the end of the year. On the next tour, the Pistols would play New York City but in the same manner they played the rest of the country. Malcolm considered the Diplomat Ballroom in Manhattan (where Kiss was discovered), and high schools in the ghetto areas in all five boroughs. This way the media would have to cover the social conditions of the city when they came to do their stories.

Meanwhile the MiYako Hotel staff informed us that if one piece of furniture was nicked, if one lampshade was even slightly damaged, the Sex Pistols and everyone associated with them would be thrown out in ten minutes. The MiYako is where all visiting rock stars stay in San Francisco. While I was there I heard a lot of stories about the Tubes, the Babys, Kiss and record company staffs especially, and their penchant for destroying hotels. The best one was about stealing all the extension cords on the eighteenth floor, putting them all together, plugging in the set, turning it on, and throwing it out of the window to see what it looked like when it exploded in the street.

The next day Sid and John arrived and did an interview for KSAN-FM. They were so well behaved it was boring – they weren't allowed to say dirty words. Paul and Steve couldn't believe what pussies Sid and John were, because the night before they did a no-holds-barred dirtymouth interview on the same radio station. The speculation was that their bodyguards were keeping them in line.

Shortly afterwards, Noel Monk had photographer Roberta Bayley bodily removed from the sound-check. He had reason to believe that *Punk* magazine is connected with the CIA. He also made a concerted effort to have us blocked from attending the concert that night.

Right before the Pistols went on that night Rotten said in the dressing-room, 'Let's really fuck it up tonight. We'll fuck up these fucking hippies. We'll turn the tables, mates, and do something they haven't read about in the music press!'

Sid opened the concert with a few Ramones licks – 'Basement' and 'Blitzkrieg Bop'. It was all downhill from there. At one point the sound was so distorted all you could hear was John's vocals and Paul's drums – the mikes were completely off.

'If you can put up with this, you can put up with anything,' Rotten told the enthusiastic crowd. 'There's not enough presents. These ain't good enough. Cameras? Do we have any cameras?'

'Whoever hit me in the 'ead – it didn't hurt a bit, so tough shit!' Sid yelled as usual as he got pelted with a few cans. During the show several guys fainted and had to be dragged out over the stage.

'I think it's fun. Do you want your ears blown out some more?' Johnny yelled after an especially bad song. The house lights came on. 'Hey, the monitors are completely off. Wait – they just came back on. This song is about you. It's called "Problems".'

'One two three four!' shouted Sidney 'Ramone' Vicious.

The song ended as Rotten was at it again. 'Tell us what it's like to have bad taste.'

Malcolm was extremely depressed after the show. 'Fuckin' awful show, wasn't it? They were just like any other rock band.' Everyone connected with the band felt the same way.

The Winterland security tried to throw Rory Johnson, the Sex Pistols' American manager, out of the hall. 'I'm the fucking manager of the group!' he hollered. The security tried to throw him out anyhow.

'Flower-power fascists,' muttered Malcolm. 'Bloody fascists.' He refused to go to the backstage party, he hates those things. *Rolling Stone*'s Annie Leibowitz set up a bunch of lights and umbrellas at the party hoping to get a group shot for the cover. Rotten remarked to Joe Stevens – ''Ere now, what do you think I would do if you and Bobby [Gruen] did all that?'

Joe Stevens: 'You'd think we were over the top!'

Rotten: 'Fuckin' right mate, I'm not doin' it!'

That night, two hundred Sex Pistols fans tried to sneak into the

MiYako, where Steve Jones danced with Britt Ekland, Rod Stewart's old girlfriend. Did she spend the night with him? 'She told me not to say anything,' he said, 'but use that bit in your story!'

The road crew took great pleasure in relating to me how they ignored McLaren's attempts at getting unknown punk bands on-stage at the Winterland. They thought McLaren was a rank amateur who had no business being in rock & roll. They also considered him a security leak. 'Winterland was the best show, man. Graham sure knows how to put on a show!' Proof of this was that Bill Graham actually liked the music. The road crew didn't.

Rotten didn't want to go to Rio so he had Noel Monk book him into a hotel 25 miles away in San José. He was sick from the flu and had been throwing up blood. He was also tired of Malcolm's publicity stunts. He also hates flying.

Sid was staying with some punkettes in Haight-Ashbury, of all places. Noel figured that his job ended at Winterland, so if Sid killed himself at this point, it's not his fault.

At 6.00 a.m. on 16 January, Steve, Paul, Malcolm and the rest of the Pistols' staff piled into cabs and drove out to the airport to catch the flight to Rio. Malcolm drove out to John's hotel with Sid to talk him into going to Rio, but gave up on the whole mess. Everyone missed the flight, so they drove back to the MiYako. Paul and Steve hung around all day and were very depressed. Sid OD'ed that day, in addition to passing out on the plane on the way to New York.

If You're on the Road

TONY PARSONS

If The Boy Looked at Johnny *was damn close to fiction, co-author Tony Parsons went the whole hog in his first solo novel,* Platinum Logic. *The portrait he paints of 'The Biz' is only marginally diluted by the lack of a dose of Burchill-bile. This excerpt introduces Deuce Berner, Parsons's composite version of sixties rockstardom.*

If you're on the road and big enough, anything you want is available on room service. The slight, unnaturally gaunt-looking man dressed in black leather was Deuce Berner. He was big enough and it was taking its toll. He sprawled across three front-row seats in the first-class compartment of a Pan Am 747, bored, fatigued and ignoring *Coal Miner's Daughter* for the tenth time that year.

Berner had washed down a handful of Quaaludes with a bottle of duty-free cognac – those miniature booze bottles you get on airlines annoyed the hell out of him – but after a three-month tour of Europe he was beyond sleep.

He had been touring since he was seventeen. He was now thirty-one and had hated it for the last twelve years. Every city in the world looked exactly the same when all you saw of it was the venue, the hotel and whatever selection of the indigenous population were lucky enough to spend the night in your room. And then moving on the next morning, hours and hours of tedious travel, do the gig and get out, do the gig and get out, becoming more and more physically and mentally debilitated in too many identical, shiny, boring hotel rooms where there was no possible way to pass the time except watch television, take all the pills and powders on hand and come into yet another pathetically grateful orifice. He had run out of new ways to abuse groupies ten years ago, around the time when smashing up the hotel room became more effort than it was worth – though occasionally he would propel the TV through the window just for old time's sake.

The only thing that made it bearable was having the chance to go on-stage every night and feel like he was better than God. Sometimes it was so good he could even forget that he was bored shitless singing the same old songs night after endless night, and sometimes he could even remember why he originally became involved in rock, even before the early days when it was all for the cash, the chemicals and the cunt.

There was only one thing he loved more than performing. The five-hour flight from London to Kennedy was nearly over and he was looking forward to being back in New York City. He thought he would feel better once he was back in New York City.

Berner sat up and peered over the back of his seat. His manager was working on some papers.

'How long to go, Irving?' Berner asked.

Irving Landis took off his reading glasses and smiled at his boy tenderly. 'About fifteen minutes, Deuce. You need a drink there?'

Berner nodded indifferently and Landis ordered another bottle of cognac from the stewardess who had hovered nearby for the entire flight, from the minute she had seen the face from the papers. She was back within the moment. Landis paid her with some of the British sterling he had left and gave the bottle to Berner.

'What hotel we staying at?' Berner said, taking a long pull on the brandy and wiping his mouth with the back of his hand.

'The Americana,' Landis smiled. 'Last time you played New York fucken MOM booked us into a Holiday Inn. They're really giving us the treatment this time out.'

'Fuck 'em,' Berner sneered. 'We go where the money is . . .'

'The Big Six, Deuce, that's where the money is. We got our pick of 'em, Deuce!'

'They're all the same,' Berner said. 'Fucken record companies . . .'

'Once you've got a major pushing us, Deuce, it'll make all the difference, you'll see.'

Berner dropped back into his seat and Landis slipped his paperwork into the leather briefcase at his side so he could organize the Deuce Berner touring party for landing. He checked that the respectable-looking middle-aged man wearing a conservative blue serge suit was ready for their arrival.

'Everything's under control, man,' he said to Landis, giving him Berner's passport. 'Deuce left it in his stash bag.'

Landis put the passport in his inside pocket. Landis did everything for Deuce. Almost everything. What he didn't do for Deuce personally he arranged for minions to do. The minions complied without question. Some of them did so because they needed to be as close as possible to a rock star's reflected glamour. The rest of the minions, like the staid man who had found Deuce Berner's passport buried at the bottom of a bag full of drugs, did so because they were paid whatever it took for total obedience.

The man had once tried to bring down the walls of Babylon by writing poetry in a Greenwich Village loft in the fifties beat era. Now he was paid to carry all illicit chemicals in the possession of Deuce Berner through customs. This was his sole function. Qualifications for the job were a respectable appearance and not a nerve in your body.

'We always use a mule to carry Deuce's stuff through customs,' Landis often confided to associates he knew couldn't afford to make the information public knowledge. 'Mules come cheaper than F. Lee Bailey.'

Next Landis sat talking to the three foreign journalists who had accompanied the tour from Europe to interview Berner and cover his one-off appearance at the New York Palladium the following night. He laid out a line of cocaine for each of them while the stewardess turned a blind eye, after realizing she wasn't going to be offered a snort. Landis told the journalists how much he admired their musical knowledge, how abysmal the magazines and hacks they competed with were, how great a time they were going to have in New York. Landis worded the promise so that whatever particular fantasy the scribes were currently harbouring would appear to be nearing fruition.

He powdered their noses one more time – the pampered prickheads better come through with a fucking cover story, that's all – and left them, oozing such bonhomie that the pen-pushing revellers didn't notice that Landis had allowed himself exactly four minutes of small-talk to keep the press sweet.

'Give journalists whatever they want when they're writing good copy about you and broken legs when they ain't,' Landis was fond of saying.

Two teenage girls who had given Berner such superior blow-jobs in London that they were rewarded with return tickets to New York – Deuce had taken each of them into the toilet during the flight although it had been a few days since he had actually spoken to either of them – were told by Landis that there wouldn't be room for them in the limousines waiting at the airport. They didn't argue so Landis didn't tell them Deuce had grown weary of their skills and instructed his manager to throw them out of the plane.

'If a girl is on the road, she's there for one reason – fuck when, how and what she's told to until she's told to fuck off,' Landis was always saying. He briefed Berner's bodyguard on his duties for the airport – over-enthusiastic fans and jealous boyfriends were always a problem. Next Landis made sure that Berner's musicians, Berner's doctor and Berner's spectacular red-haired English model were all reasonably content, before taking his seat for the landing. The various VIPs and record company personnel who frequently attach themselves to a big name's tour were conspicuous by their absence – nobody who knew what a tour of the world's provinces entailed would be there until they had to be.

In New York, Landis thought happily, they'll cut their mother's throat to be there. He fastened his seat-belt for the Big Apple.

Berner automatically commandeered the first in the line of waiting limos for himself, his manager, his bodyguard and his model, while the rest of his touring party vied for positions in the remaining cars. If it wasn't for Deuce Berner there wouldn't even be a tour, and his entourage were never allowed to forget it.

In the haste to distance himself from the ramshackle reception committee waiting for him at Kennedy – the only admirers who waited for anybody who was somebody at an airport were invariably shrill, pawing fans with autograph books and cradle marks still on their fat asses, fans who had nothing that Deuce wanted – Berner and his select coterie failed to notice that there was anyone but the uniformed chauffeur in the limo until they were accelerating towards the towering, terrifying, exhilarating concrete and glass skyline.

Even when Berner noticed Ahmet Abbas sitting in the back seat of the limo, he ignored him. When the model had swiftly checked that Abbas didn't have a famous face she ignored him too, and hung on to the disinterested arm of her escort as though her life depended on it. Berner's bodyguard – a caricature of an Aryan supermensch who had been an ice hockey pro until his red Chevy Corvette hit a tollbooth at fifty miles an hour the day before a Stanley Cup lousy play-off and the cops found five grams of coke in the glove compartment and the National Hockey League told him to find a new career – glared at Abbas like the mother of a precious and threatened lion cub until Landis began to talk to the MOM executive with affable courtesy. The bodyguard felt at ease, staring at Berner hungrily.

'Ahmet, how are you?' Landis beamed. 'So good to see you! You're coming to the show tomorrow night, of course?'

'I'll be there, Irving,' Abbas said. He was amused by the manager's warm greeting – Landis's natural demeanour was old school Tin Pan Alley screaming steam-roller, the type of manager who talked to his boy's record company in either big league boasting or abused-artists angst. Being polite just didn't suit him. Obviously, Abbas thought to himself, he figures that Berner will be signed up with a major before the week is out and he can afford to indulge himself with some mild-mannered cordiality as though he was Brian Epstein or something, way above all the haggling, bickering and bullying of managerial responsibilities.

'How's Nathan?' Landis asked. 'And his lovely wife?'

'They're fine,' Abbas said, 'just fine.'

He suppressed the urge to laugh out loud. You bastard, Landis, you ain't going nowhere, he thought. Abbas wondered if Landis knew about the news story in *Rock International Press*. It was an English paper so he must have. Abbas concluded that Landis must be under the impression that the paper hadn't reached New York yet.

Berner was fiddling with the radio in the limo's dashboard. Snatches of rock, reggae, pop, soul and disco poured out intermittently – an aural melting-pot of New York's soundtrack, beyond barriers of age, social status, ethnic heritage, cultural legacy and tribal musical preferences – but he couldn't find what he was looking for, he kept getting this disco station which piped some piercing French eunuch backed up by the strings of a symphony orchestra so sweet that they could rot your teeth. The station he was looking for was nowhere to be found.

'I can't find WKTU-FM,' Berner complained. 'All I'm getting is this fucken disco shit!'

'That is WKTU,' Abbas said. 'They changed their format from rock to disco in July '78. They went from a point nine share of the city's radio audience to eleven point three just before Christmas, four points ahead of WABC...'

Berner stared at him incredulously. 'WKTU went disco?'

Abbas nodded. 'Nearly fifty stations have switched to disco already this year, Deuce.' Abbas talked to Berner respectfully because he was, after all, an artiste. Any act signed to a record company is an artiste and just how artistic they are has got nothing to do with it. 'There's a disco station in every big city in the country now, even the Midwest.'

'It's a fad man, it won't last,' Berner grumbled, feeling out of time. 'It all sounds the fucken same.'

Abbas thought of Stigwood and the Bee Gees, *Saturday Night Fever* and Studio 54, worldwide sales of the Village People single 'YMCA' topping the twelve million mark and the thirty per cent – over one billion dollars – of the record industry that the disco market had accounted for in the last year. But he said nothing, he just wondered how long before the rock-oriented label that he worked for had to start dancing to that disco beat.

'Oh, I don't know, Deuce,' the model girl made the mistake of saying. 'I think it'll last. Everyone knows it's impossible to dance to rock music!' She giggled. 'Maybe you'll have to change with the times, Deuce!'

Berner stared at her for a moment and then turned to the chauffeur. 'Stop the car,' he ordered, and the limo screeched to a halt. They were on the freeway into town where it was strictly no parking. Car horns blared all around them and drivers leaned out of their windows screaming abuse. Abbas leaned back in his seat and lit a cigarette.

'Get out,' Berner told the model girl.

'Wait a minute, Deuce, I was only joking! There's no need –'

'Get out! If there's one thing I don't need around me it's a fucken critic!'

Abbas thought of Stravinsky's dream of music critics, the musician's dream where his critics had appeared as small and rodent-like creatures with padlocked ears. He inhaled deeply, smiling.

'But, Deuce!'

'Get out, get out!'

The model girl stood by the side of the road staring after the limo's disappearing tail-lights. She bit her bottom lip and stuck out her thumb.

Berner found WABC and they rode the rest of the way to the Americana in silence except for the radio station's fifty thousand watts of power.

The caravan of limos began to arrive in front of the hotel and the Deuce Berner touring party swarmed into the luxurious, old-fashioned opulence of the Americana lobby.

Businessmen and well-heeled tourists gazed at them warily as they checked in. Berner collected his key and headed for the lift, followed by three uniformed bellboys struggling under the weight of his luggage.

'Did you book the road crew in here, too?' Landis asked Abbas. Normally the road crew – responsible for transporting, setting up and maintaining all of the equipment used in a live show – wouldn't be permitted in the tradesmen's entrance of a place like the Americana. Normally MOM's accommodation budget for Berner's roadies ran to putting them up in a two-star flop-house.

'They're booked in here too,' Abbas nodded, yearning for the moment when he would wipe the manager's triumphant smirk off his face. 'Where are they? Shouldn't they be here by now?'

'Yes,' Landis said. 'They were scheduled to catch the first flight to Kennedy out of Heathrow this morning. But they had a little trouble clearing customs. Some customs officer found a roach on the floor of one of the trucks and they dismantled every last speaker, amp and lamp.'

Abbas tried to hide his distaste. Every roadie is a dumb hippie, he thought. Long hair, joints and the groupies the musicians don't want. Unload the trucks, set up the PA system, rectify any faults that occur during the gig and take it all down and pack it all back in the trucks as soon as the show is over. They get up at dawn while the band are still bouncing off the walls of their hotel and drive to the next town. Maybe you'll get lucky and one of the musicians will let you hold his guitar, maybe even let you tune it for him. Hold on to that thought when an airport customs official takes a dislike to you and makes you show him the innards of every piece of equipment in the two giant trucks, just because the stoned chick – roadies still used expressions like that – who five of you had in there after the gig, when she couldn't gain entry to the dressing-room, didn't hide a roach. Abbas loathed roadies.

'Well, I hope they get here in time for the show tomorrow.'

'Don't worry,' Landis said. 'They'll be here long before then. We've got that NBC prime-time slot tonight, haven't we?'

'Right. And there's a couple of radio interviews for Deuce.' Abbas paused. 'Also I think we should discuss the question of Deuce's new contract as soon as possible.'

'OK, Ahmet, sure,' Landis said, grinning broadly. 'Let me get settled in my suite, take a shower and something to get rid of this jet-lag and I'll meet you in the bar in thirty minutes. OK, Ahmet?'

'Sure thing, Irving.'

Landis instructed a couple of bellhops to take his suitcases up to the suite, then started for the lift. 'I may be a little late,' he called to Abbas as he hit the button indicating his floor number. 'I've got a few calls to make.'

Abbas nodded as the doors closed. 'There's no rush, Irving,' he said, strolling to the bar, 'we've got all the time in the world.'

Stabb's Hand Touched Me and I Slept

THURSTON MOORE

In hard-rock fanzine, Forced Exposure, *Sonic Youth's Thurston Moore fabricates the sort of mid eighties travelling stint that might well be the logical culmination of thirty years refining rock's 'on the road' aesthetic.*

DAY 1 – 19 June – WASHINGTON DC
Punctuality is a suspicious speck in the rock roll cosmos. Time signatures, etc. are inherent necessities but getting to gigs on time, etc. is a whole nother pud. We split the NYC 5 hours after proposed take-off. DC was gig # 1. We had new not-even-out-of-the-box-yet amps and no sound-check looming ahead of us. Unprepared, frustrated and late. Two nights prior at CBGB it was vice-versa and we were set and confident and in check and everybody and their dog came and saw us and we bit the bag. DC gig was great. Sort of. Pussy Galore pre-Bob Bert kinda ruled but that's before they moved to NYC and I learned to hate them. That's a lie tho. I like Puss. Tar Babies ruled. And fuck this I got to meet the hero John 'Sky' Stabb of Govt Issue so eat me nazi pork.

DAY 2 – 20 June – WASHINGTON DC etc.
A day off and we did some shit. Ate BBQ in the land o' Go Go and that was heavy fat sticky kool. We crashed in a cheap-o-sleaze motel outside of Baltimore only to discover it was a quickie pull-in-pull-out sex-fuk joint with pussy-pole films on the TV. We nodded to the not-so-distant sounds of hump-n-pump.

DAY 3 – 21 June – PHILADELPHIA, PA
Unbelievable: a club worser than the New York Shitty Dunceteria – The Kennel Club in Philly. Three floors of drunken Fillyfolk shelling out 12 bux to get in and on disco dance floor #2w/ an immense PA and then checking out Sonic Puzz on Floor #3 pushing frogfart power through a not-quiet Radio Shack piece o' crank. Little Gentleman opened with a DOA shirt and a cover of 'Borstal Breakout' and I felt like I was at A7 two years ago stoned on shitweed, locked in the toilet w/ my head down and nothing coming out my butt while the Misguided played 'State Of War'. We made money.

DAY 4 – 22 June – RICHMOND, VA

Carpeted stages do not rule. They suqu les big deek. You need wood vibing/breathing into/thru yr bones. It's hard to move on a carpet – it's like wearing a Velcro suit. But fuggit, Richmond is bitchin' just for the fact that the girls are all a cross between the Shangri-Las and the Spahn Ranch babies. Southern foxed bellbottomed hip hugged mutant USA. Not for the fainthearted. The Happy Flowers are the Franken & Davis of punk. I guess that's it. ·

DAY 5 – 23 June – RALEIGH, NC

Raleigh rules with the Char-Grill where a hamburger says, 'I'm a mother-fucking hamburger – eat me' and the choclit shakes are like sucking a wrench out of the mud. Honour Role played and were hep. Subculture didn't show. The COC Crew were there hot and holy. We played Raleigh with Swans fucking years ago to nobody but 5 No Cores and recorded IG's 'Dog, I Wanna Be Yr' but this time things were a bit more pop-u-lar. It was Steve's birthday. We took the cake. Duh.

DAY 6 – 24 June – ATLANTA, GA

We pulled our van into 666 club late as fuck and bashed through the glass doors splintering glass and metal everywhere. There were hundreds and hundreds of kids waiting for us hanging heads outside, mostly chix. One guy got a shard of glass right through his fuckin head. It was sticking out his ear. Fuck him, he was in the way and we were drunk. I was sucking down Johnny Walker and Vodka and chasing it with Heinies for the last eight hours. I was pissed with puke globbing out my nose. I kicked the door open and immediately some teen lootch grabbed my crotch and whipped my boa out which was cool cuz I had a harding fucking on. I just looked at her and said, 'Bone meal'. Lee was carving SY in some kid's buttcheeks and sucking the blood out and then spitting it into Steve's laughing gomp. Kim was overly fucking dusted and frugging on top of the van banging dents into it and flipping the bird. It was cool. We missed sound-check but fuck it man who the fuck fucking needs it. We let everyone in free and sliced the heads off the wussy sticks who worked at this spermhole and played catch and frisbee with their brains. It was time go on so I tied up and shot shit heroin into my arm and banged mayonnaise into the other. I was boned and ready to motor. I stuck the microphone immediatefuckingly up my ass. Lee was actually fukking his guitar. Kim was just blindly bashing audience members with her bass, heads were popping like melons. Steve hung a noose over his drumkit and committed suicide.

DAY 7 – 25 June – ATHENS, GA
Proprietor: 'It was a good set, I thought more people would come.'
Me: 'Yeh, well, I don't know . . .'
Proprietor: 'The Replacements cancelled their show here this weekend so I thought people would come.'
Me: 'Yeh, I guess we're not too well known here or something . . .'
Proprietor: 'The Meat Puppets played here not too long ago and 400 people showed up and the Band walked out with $1000.'
Me: 'Yeh, jeez, don't these collegiate queers read the NME. We're famous.'
Proprietor: 'Yeh, well um, maybe it's kinda cuz you kinda suck.'

DAY 8 – THRU DAY 12 – 26 June THRU 30 June – NEW ORLEANS, LA – HOUSTON, AUSTIN, DALLAS, TX
Luck split the scene some time after the Athens 'Spinal Tap' gig. The details would be boring, not to mention petty. It has to do with business-cheese-fuckups. We demanded guarantees from promoters who were losing bundles. Not too many people showed up. Austin would've rocked as we were to gig with a reformed Meatjoy and Austin always rules and is a butthole blast but the promoter booked it on the same night as Dallas by accident and we had to move the show to the night before at a smaller scuzz

and couldn't play till 3.30 in the morning when the already scheduled evening events (Brave Combo) were over and out. The kids who got hep came and kicked tail grooving on what could be a new trend in late-late night shows. But not too many knew. And then Dallas was sick with identocops vs identiskins. Stupid and shitty. Our morale sucked. We look forward to Texas. The feeling is big. After all the letdown and bummage Texas still holds the most real promise of natural beauty in a dirt boy coon girl hot long ZZ magic emotion: the best pure bands are here. We escape, pull out, passion flower up the butt. Fuckingoddamn . . .

DAY 13 – 1 July – TUCSON, AZ

This begins the Sonic Saccharine Youth Trust jaunt. The club books the night as an all ages hardcore thrasharama slamboree and no one shows. The Tucson HC kids know better than to waste the green on us. The club owners are sub-moronic with very low IQ's, cheeze business suits, and pistols packed neath their vests. They ripped us and Saccharine off for big bux. It's called the Backdoor. If you play there you will suffer. Saccharine are amazing fucking christ. Jack Brewer now holds the secret of medallion power. He hypnotizes the audience and Baiza masters the universe. Our hope is restored.

DAY 14 – 2 July – PHOENIX, AZ

She's hot. We're up on the sun. We feel like real meat puppets. Broiling desert cacti muff. Saccharine are even more hippening. We're less. But people are fuckeen there so it's a killer time and we wake up and drive 6 hours thru the desert to California.

DAY 15 – 3 July – SAN DIEGO, CA

We don't have air-conditioning. We baked at 120 degrees in the desert. We picked up these hitch-hikers who had went swimming in Titty-Jello Pond and they cooled us off by taking off their bathing suits and wringing them over our bodies. They were funny young and stoned and liked to bounce and boop. San Diego was beat and outtatune. Lotsa Less-Than-Zero kids creeping into the scene. Strong desire to get foxy.

DAY 16 – 4 July – DAY OFF IN LA, CA
4th of July and we all dressed up like Lady Liberty and went and raped prostitutes behind the Hollywood sign. Then we ate burgers and 'mexican'. It was sick.

DAY 17 – 5 July – HUNTINGTON BEACH, CA
Met up with SST. We tell 'em our next LP is a triple called *Humpy Pumpy Cream Yr Butt* and they rolled their eyes and fell for it and we all had sexxx with Mugger, Greg, Pettibone, Henry, Rich, Ray, Watt, Spaceman, Davo, Dukowski. Twas ok. Safari Sam's is the club here. The owner's nice. The soundman's a stoner beach idiot. The security is failed-cop assholes usa. I was hanging outside drinking water when one of these oversized puds started pointing at me, 'Get rid of that bottle, get rid of that bottle. Now!' Me: 'It's only water, cool off dick.' It: 'I don't care, get rid of it now!' I bust it over his head, knock him down, pull his pants down, stick the cracked bottleneck up his bloodless ass and then I peed on his face. The gig was hot.

DAY 18 – 6 July – HOLLYWOOD, CA
Partied with the Lovedolls. Saccharine Trust kicked [word illegible] ass. We were Roxy rockstar on stage. Mike Watt jammed on 'Starpower'. Ate 2 humongous chili dogs at Pink's and said more than once, 'Yeh, I know Byron, why?'

DAY 19 – 7 July – SAN FRANCISCO, CA
Firehose: Watt, Hurley & Ed (fromohio): their van broke down and they didn't play. They're lucky. The PA was a piece of shit in a big disco called the I-Beam. It's where Rock Hudson used to 'come' and get buttfucked all night long. At least that's what Lee

told Steve. Cool place. It's on the Haight. Free love and dope. I think I killed somebody that night.

DAY 20 – 8 July – D A Y O F F
Tooling up the coast to Oregon. Took a walk through the Redwood forest at midnight. Shoulda been there.

DAY 21 – 9 July – P O R T L A N D, O R
At the end of the night this bleached blonde teen punkette got in our van and refused to leave so we drove on to the interstate, tied guitar strings around her neck and then threw her out the window and watched her bop and drag until nothing was left but nickel-wound bone dust.

DAY 22 – 10 July – S E A T T L E, W A
Local band Green River split the night with volumatic ig-pow glamkore. Twas hot. Sorta like very ultra. And like we kinda blew but the audience heaved, thank god.

DAY 23 – 11 July – D A Y O F F
Drove all day long. Jerked off. A lot.

DAY 24 – 12 July – D E N V E R, C O
Great sizzlin' all ages 13-year-old radbutt yeh i'll have a toke, thanks.

DAY 25 – 13 July – D A Y O F F
All day in the van the roof melting drops of corrugated scuzz on our 100 degree parched skin. Sweating and shitty and irritable. Living hell.

DAY 26 – 14 July – K A N S A S C I T Y, K S
Gift played their last gig with us. The singer Jimm being the guy who does *Blatch* fanzine from Oklahoma. They were tuff and

perverse. Maybe they'll get it back. Some kids drove 12 hours from Denver to dig the gig but were under 21. We snuck 'em in but they got tossed. I puked on stage and Lee stomped on it and it splat all over these lovely adults. We're getting burnt.

DAY 27 – 15 July – MINNEAPOLIS, MN
Home of Husker Du, Prince, the Replacements none of which came to say hi or even fuck you new york shit. Played the same club/stage *Purple Rain* was filmed on but you know everybody fucking has so fuck fuck. Soul Asylum was beered and hanging and nice gents at that and gave us the scoop on Bob Mould's office at Warner Bros. and his complete control contract and working relationship with the label and that was interesting. I got glad, then sorta sad.

DAY 28 – 16 July – MILWAUKEE, WI
Dinosaur played. One of the best coolest bands in the US. Albini showed up which was brave cuz this is the place where some promoter poured a glass of piss over Steve's face. This time the clubowners pulled him to the john and shoved his head into the men's stall and continually lashed him with their pee pees. We kinda saved him and said stop or we wouldn't play. Michael from Killdozer came and threw armadillo tails on stage. We reacted. Albini stage dived and in mid air some punk bashed in the head with a pitcher of beer. Sleep town.

DAY 29 – 17 July – CHICAGO, IL
We asked Sean Duffy if we could play with End Result, Pile of Cows, and Ono but he booked us with NOFX, Social Unrest and 86 Shred because he wanted a crossover audience. We said we didn't want to crossover, that we just wanted to fuck. He wouldn't have it. We asked him if we could put Steve Albini on the guest list and he said NO cuz Steve really hurt his girlfriend Patty Pezzatti by writing a lot of 'lies' about her being sexy and beauti-

ful. I fully understood and I popped a wicked boner. And I said I would bring Steve anyway. We met Steve at his fave Mex restaurant and watched him eat 3 pork burritos as big as new born babes laced with hot chihuahua sauce. Then he sucked down a pitcher of milk. He wiped his mouth on the waitress's shirt sleeve, pushed her away and pronounced, 'I own this fuckin' town, man.' We said nothing. 'If I knew Sean Duffy was to become the scene figurehead I wouldn'tve created Chi-town punk rock to begin with. I mean Vic Boni was bad enough, but kicking his ass outta town was easy. No sweat. Articles of Faith fucked things up for a while but I got it back in gear. Our next album cover has me in a red rubber diaper sucking a 13-yr-old girl's tit. It's cool. But this Duffy thing has to turn around and I think tonight is the fucking night. Let's go.' The waitress set the check in front of us and Steve instantly, though nonchalantly, heaved out his guts of puke-meat burying the once obtrusive bill of fare. We got to the Metroclub, walked to the desk and I said, 'This guy's on our list, jizz.' The guy had a ponytail and arms the size of whale dongs and said, 'No way.' I said, 'Fucking why?' and he held up a xeroxed copy of the Albini Wholesome fanzine interview where Steve lies about the Metro and Duffy as being, now get this, 'corrupt'. Steve grabbed the paper, crumpled it, dropped his drawers and stuck it half up his shit pit. He then got the ponytail stud in a headlock and shouted, 'EAT IT PANSY!' The dude was freaked as were we all but he ate it, he had to. Steve's power, his authority, was unreal. He then hammered the dude to the floor, kneeled upon his chest, took out his switchblade, flicked it, cut open his own left forearm and let blood drip and spill in the door-dude's gaping eyes. His screams were pure shrieking holy terror. The guy passed out. I just watched. Patty Pezzatti was in the ticket booth witnessing it all in stunned yet cat-like awe. She stepped from her post and in a nervous, courageous purr she muttered, 'Steve . . . I . . . I . . . I'.

He shut her up with a stare so fixed, so fucked, that the room quaked with a fevered finitude.

She took his knife.

He touched her tit.

The nipple was now poking the cotton.

Duffy was upstairs, Steve and Patty ascended, noiselessly.

The incredible wonderful hardcore bands playing before us had worked the audience into a bloodied, frothing menace. We got on stage and launched into 'Stepping Stone' without any vocal mikes, the whole slamming pit of punkdom howling along. Then we played 'My Girl Hates Heroin'. And then we split.

DAY 30 – 18 July – DETROIT, MI

We played this gig at Traxx promoted by Ken Waagner and Vice Bannon. They promised us in contract a lot of money and ripped us off 500 smackers. Maybe by now they've paid up but as my pen scrawls this scug we're ripped. All the kids who came said we shoulda played Corey Rusk's Graystone cuz they're honest and always hold true to the guarantee. We asked to play in Detroit for the best bux and best PA and got it. But something went wrong. Waagner and Bannon bailed. Corey and others didn't even come to the gig cuz they hate these fuckers so much. Detroit is the home of high energy and we thrive to come here. Talked to John Bannon for two hours about Alice Cooper. Dinosaur played and proved why they rule. Leaving Trains played with Jack Rabid on drums and they all hated each other and were quite sad. We were OK – the PA ruled. The club was cold and impersonal. I wish we dealt with Corey.

DAY 31 – 19 July – INDIANAPOLIS, IN

Tiny place. OK gig. The kids ruled. They gave us mushrooms. Got a tape by a group called Bramble Grit. Scratch Acid played in town a coupla weeks before at some Top 40 place and half the crowd were Dance Fever wannabees and David Yow (singer) was real drunk and he shit in his pants on stage in the middle of a song and proceeded to take out glumps of it and put it in his hair and fling it on the P A and wiped it on these big windows and terrorized the audience saying, 'Don't worry, it'll wash out.' And the management and P A people were furious cleaning and smelling the mikes and everything cuz there was a Top 40 cover band due on for the night nerds. I didn't see all this but I was told by all so you can probably believe it's true.

DAY 32 – 20 July – COLUMBUS, OH

We ate the mushrooms and I got trippy. I'm not into it. It gets too fucking in the way of how I really want to feel. Dinosaur fell down, destroyed their set and were holier than God. We sukked the big P.

DAY 33 – 21 July – CLEVELAND, OH

We forced Dinosaur on the bill and they whipped out their greatest set yet. Squirrelbait played that typical set of reggae-jazz-nugent with an enticing bit of gamelan music teasing thru the din. That they took showers before and after they went on was a bit bothersome but they're young and they seem to like school. I like Redd Kross. We played with razor blades instead of picks. I met Fraser Suicyde of Starvation Army, a childhood hero of mine and Dinosaur's, I'm afraid it was awesome.

DAY 34 – 22 July – BUFFALO, NY

The people who put on the gig were great. They lost money but they figured they might cuz Buffalo is kinda snoring. I like a good sleepy atmosphere and wish we stayed longer. We again forced Dinosaur on the bill and they played 'Cortez The Killer' by Neil Young with Lee singing. You missed it man.

DAY 35 – 23 July – ROCHESTER, NY

Kim was born here and hadn't been back since she was a wee lass and some lighting guy tripped over a wire and smashed her bass amp into nonworking mode and it skrewed up the gig but we rocked on through. Lydia Lunch was brought up here and we checked out the streets she used to 'hang' on and went to House of Guitars where she used to want to work and Armand Schaubroeck wasn't there. Boring.

DAY 36 – 24 July – PROVIDENCE, RI

Tour is almost over and I'm tired of having to write in this stoopid journal. This gig was a white cross. Happiness, ok you satisfied. Byron, Jizzy and Philerrup came and missed the gig. The only people we knew. Lotsa peops. Some were nice. Some were retarded.

DAY 37 – 25 July – WASHINGTON DC

Back to where we started. It's my birthday. Gone and G.I. are playing. I'm introduced to Sab Grey and if you know who I'm talking about you're probably thrilled. It is extremely fucking hot now and humid and the middle of summer. Sab left right as we were plugging in cuz his girlfriend was tired. Big black dj was playing Bang Zoom by Roxanne/UTFO and didn't care that I thought it was great. We drove all fucking day broiling and shitty to here from RI. Am I bumming you out? I'm just making all this up.

DAY 100000000 – THE END – BOSTON, MA

Schizophrenic landscapes are a dime a dozen at their most extravagant, I declare bothered n snidely.

I-give-up.

6. Voices from the Other Side

" How does this sound? — 'I dreamed the band was playing to
a capacity audience of stoned thousands at a top Los Angeles
venue, and when I woke up, we were!'"

The writer–rocker dialogue has not been entirely one-way. Plenty of rock singers have felt the need to comment first hand on their predicament. In several notable instances the would-be rock star has started out writing about the form, Chrissie Hynde, Bob Geldof, Bono Vox and Patti Smith (here represented by her 'final' essay for Creem, *'Jukebox Cruci-fix') all making the transition.*

Would-be wordSmith Steven Morrissey even aspired to writing about rock & roll, though the sum of his efforts was little more than editing one cut'n'paste scrapbook and writing assorted letters to the English music press, all dealing with the same theme – the absolute primacy of the New York Dolls in the history of rock & roll. In two letters he wrote to New Musical Express *and* Melody Maker *in 1976 he managed to first praise and then damn the discordantly audacious Sex Pistols. In June 1976, the Pistols warranted praise because:*

> . . . despite their discordant music and barely audible audacious lyrics . . . the Sex Pistols are very New York and it's nice to see that the British have produced a band capable of producing atmosphere created by the NY Dolls and their many imitators, even though it may be too late. I'd love to see the Pistols make it.

By December of the same year, the Pistols had apparently forsaken the mantle of natural heirs to the Dolls:

> If the music they deliver live is anything to go by, I think that their audacious lyrics and discordant music will not hold their

heads above water when their followers tire of torn jumpers and safety pins. British Punk Rock is second to the New York equivalent in that it does not possess the musical innovation . . . [of bands like] the Shirts and Jobriath.

Cough! Figures like Frank Zappa and Thurston Moore are represented elsewhere in the Penguin Book of Rock & Roll Writing. *In this section, the rock & rollers are primarily concerned with detailing their own situation. Even Lou Reed's feature, 'Fallen Knights and Fallen Ladies', though ostensibly about the casualties of rock & roll – notably Brian Epstein, Brian Jones, Jimi Hendrix and Janis Joplin – allows autobiography to impinge. Indeed, it is tempting to view this piece as part of the decision-making process Reed underwent between abandoning the Velvet Underground in 1970 and re-entering the rock & roll arena in 1972.*

Like Reed, most of Richard Hell's prose writing reflects back upon himself. In my chosen article, Hell, in the guise of Theresa Stern, reviews an early show at CBGB by his then-band, the Heartbreakers. Hell remains fascinated by the process of being his own critic.

Dylan was for a time equally intrigued by the possibility of manipulating his own press, constructing his own interviews for Playboy *and* Village Voice *and arranging his own stage-circuses-cum-press conferences. 'A Night With Bob Dylan' was published in December 1965. Al Aronowitz later owned up to the piece, then admitted that Dylan had 'rewritten' it. Whatever the truth, it is an insider's account of Dylan's surreal socializing as his wheel began to catch fire.*

Pete Townshend's Rolling Stone *review of the compilation of Who singles,* Meaty, Beaty, Big & Bouncy, *reads as an historic piece of bravado, asserting the Who's pre-eminence in rock through fourteen slabs of three-minute madness while Steve Albini, producer extraordinaire, chooses to utilize the medium of the record review to unload pent-up producer's blues.*

A Night With Bob Dylan

AL ARONOWITZ AND BOB DYLAN

When the New York Herald Tribune *ran a photographic portfolio of Dylan by Daniel Kramer in December 1965, at the height of Dylan's hipness, they also ran an uncredited piece purporting to detail a typical night in the company of the master bard.*

Bob Dylan picked himself up from the revolving turntable; staggered into an armchair, waved his hands above his head and sat down to watch the tube. On it, Soupy Sales was grinning from behind a mask of cream pie.

'Mmmmmm,' said Dylan, 'what a horrible, terrible, obnoxious way to make a living!'

Behind him a double exposure of Elvis Presley fired two six-guns into the room from a well-silvered Andy Warhol canvas covered with Cellophane.

'I hate it . . .' Dylan said. 'I'm going to cut a hole in its abdomen and put a water hose through it.' He got up, walked with cowboy bow-legs into the kitchen and asked someone to make him some tea. The reflection of Soupy Sales still grinned from his grey-coloured shades.

It wasn't Dylan's pad; he had borrowed it from somebody or other. On the floor, a mink rug played tablecloth for several cups and saucers, ashes and the ashtrays that the ashes had been intended for. Several other people wandered about the room, some of them while still sitting in their chairs.

The doorbell rang. It was Brian Jones of the Rolling Stones

with a limousine waiting outside. Dylan wiped Soupy Sales's face off the TV tube, Robbie Robertson wiped the autoharp off his lap and everybody split. Dylan was the last to leave. He took the Temptations record off the turntable, hid it under his double-breasted corduroy jacket and winked at a light bulb. His tea, unsipped, was left to cool in its cup.

In the limousine, Dylan asked to be left off at the next block.

'You must be joking,' said Brian Jones.

Inside the limousine, Charlie, the chauffeur, asked if the group was going downtown. 'I'm getting off at the next block,' said Dylan. 'These other people're going downtown . . .' 'Thank you, sir,' said Charlie. 'No, we're not going to any downtown,' said Milly, a friend of Brian's. 'Shut up!' said Dylan, 'shut up and quit making that racket or else you'll be thrown to the fire inspectors. . . . and they are very hungry.' 'What?' yelled Milly. The car stopped at the corner and Milly, one way or another, was thrown out . . . 'Watch the fire inspectors!' yelled Brian. 'Nonsense,' said Dylan, 'I'm just fooling. We really don't have them over in America.' The limousine eventually stopped at a bar in the Eighth Avenue district. After everyone in the party had entered, a very muscular woman ran up and very surprisingly hugged Dylan. 'You're not supposed to do that without an eyepatch!' he jolted. 'Hug my friend there, Brian, he looks more like me!' . . . 'You can write on the walls here,' said Dylan later at the table. 'This is the only bar I know of where you can write on the walls and nobody calls you a poet.' . . . Sailors began wandering over towards the table and eventually everyone decided to leave. 'Where's Harold the Driver?' asked Bob Neuwirth, a third cousin of Bob Dylan's. 'That's not Harold,' said Dylan. 'That's Mr Egg, and there but for fortune go you or I.' 'Ahhhhhh,' said Bob Neuwirth. 'You must give me two pints!' said Dylan. 'And anyway, how do you know his name ain't Egg?' 'Where are we going?' said everyone called Hare-up. 'We're going to the zoo.'

'You Americans must all be soft,' said Brian Jones. 'Do you have any coyotes?' A sailor leaped on the table, grinning at Brian, who snarled back. 'I like your hair,' the sailor said. 'What about hair?' Dylan said. 'I thought we were going to the zoo,' said Bob Neuwirth. 'That's what we need,' said Brian Jones, 'some coyotes.' 'Are you sure you mean coyotes?' said Dylan. 'Are you sure we're going to the zoo?' said Brian Jones. 'Be yourself,' said Dylan. Everybody walked towards the door with the sailor leaping off the table and following them.

'We're not going anyplace,' said Bob Neuwirth. Dylan leaped on Brian Jones and asked, 'Tell me, Brian, why is it that your lead singer does not have a little, pencil thin moustache?'

Back in the limousine, someone directed the driver to an underground movie house on Lafayette Street. Later on, when questioned about it, Dylan said they were all blindfolded and taken there at gunpoint. On the stage inside, there was no movie, but instead a group of green painted musicians were presenting a spontaneous ritual which had taken them three months to prepare. Timothy Cain, a friend of Dylan's, whom they had run into under the marquee, grabbed the seat next to Dylan. 'Can you smoke here?' he asked Dylan. 'Of course you can smoke here,' replied Dylan. 'Put that cigarette out!' said a long-haired flowery girl who turned out to be an usherette. Timothy ignored her. The usherette left in a huff, returning moments later with a chubby man who wore a handlebar moustache and slippers. 'Put that cigarette out,' the chubby man said. 'Oh, my God,' said Dylan, 'it's Porky Oil.' Immediately, Timothy rose, grabbed the usherette's flashlight, unscrewed it, took the batteries out and threw the batteries at the Exit signs and proceeded to punch the chubby man in his ample stomach. At the same time, everyone in the party got up to leave as Dylan mumbled. 'What good are exits anyway?' 'I'm not an art fanatic,' said Timothy, 'I'm a cigarette-smoker.' 'I like you,' said Dylan. 'I wish we were both alive during Napoleon's time.'

After several more stops, which included a pinball arcade on 42nd Street, the back room of a fortune-teller in the Chelsea district, the Phonebooth, a discotheque, and St Paul's Cathedral, the limousine wound up in front of a bar in Greenwich Village. Four people remained in the group, the others having been left behind by accident. 'Plenty more people inside,' said the chauffeur. 'Watch your tongue,' said Dylan.

The group got out to go inside the bar, but it was already closed. 'Back to the pad,' said Dylan. There was a small number of people gathered around the mink rug when they returned. Dylan took the Temptations record out from beneath his double-breasted corduroy jacket and put it on the record-player. Then he went to another room and closed the door.

There was a W. C. Fields movie on the TV set. Dylan walked into the kitchen to get a bandage. 'I think Marlon Brando should play the life of W. C. Fields,' he mumbled. He fiddled around in the kitchen. 'I also think that Warren Beatty should play the life of Johnny Weismuller,' wrapping the bandage around his finger. Dylan returned to his room, stopping to say, 'As for me, I plan to do the life story of Victor Mature.' 'Is he serious?' said the mild-mannered, petite coloured girl, who was sitting cross-legged on the floor. She was immediately thrown out.

Fallen Knights and Fallen Ladies

LOU REED

'Fallen Knights and Fallen Ladies' was originally part of an anthology of essays about rock fatalities, No One Waved Goodbye. *Reed chose not to single out one victim, but rather to concentrate on cause – fame and its vicarious requirements. It was written in 1970. As Peter Doggett has written,* 'over the next four years, Reed was made to live out the implications of his valediction(s).'

At the age when identity is a problem some people join rock & roll bands and perform for other people who share the same difficulties. The age difference between performer and beholder in rock is not large. But, unfortunately, those in the fourth tier assume those on stage know something they don't. Which is not true. It simply requires a very secure ego to allow yourself to be loved for what you do rather than what you are, and an even larger one to realize you are what you do. The singer has a soul but feels he isn't loved off-stage. Or, perhaps worse, feels he shines only on stage and off is wilted, a shell as common as the garden gardenia. But we are all common as snowflakes, aren't we?

Brian Epstein built an empire but lived long enough to have a lot of time on his hands. Those who hate the nine-to-five regime do not know the blessing that it holds. It masters the mind and protects it from itself. It soothes the ego. This is what I do. I have a family and I provide. When one has free time one tries to enjoy it, if only for its rarity. We are a race that needs to work. Brian Jones died for the lack of it and Janis Joplin and Jimi Hendrix from too much of the wrong kind.

I remember the early days of the Beatles well. I had recently been asked by the Tactical Police Force of the city which housed my large eastern university to leave town well before graduation because of various clandestine operations I was alleged to have been involved in. In those days few people had long hair and those who did recognized each other as, at the very least, a good guy and one who smoked marijuana. And so I was lining up medical proof in order to evade the draft when along came the moptops, with their pictures in every window and their records on the jukebox where the local poets furrowed their brows and read to each other, where sophisticated elderly townies came to prey on callow youth and where I often went to drink along to that week's lost everything. It was the world of Kant and Kierkegaard and metaphysical polemics that lasted well into the night and it was into this world that the Beatles' music came, first as novelty and later as the style, the Spanish heeled boots, the banged haircuts, the accents (so delightful, cooed the girls to their Wellington-footed American counterparts), a style which was to proliferate and finally dominate the sixties.

I had recently been introduced to drugs at this time by a mashed-in Negro whose features were in two sections (like a split-level house), named Jaw. Jaw gave me hepatitis immediately, which is pathetic and laughable at once, considering I wrote a famous amplified version of the experience in a song. Anyway, his bad blood certainly put an end to my abortive excursions and consequently tempered whatever enthusiasm I might have had for pop music at this time. The Beatles were innocent of the world, and its wicked ways, I felt, while I no longer possessed this pristine view. I, after all, had had jaundice.

This other-worldly approach vanished however, and after my mind and my liver kept me from the army, I, too, danced to Beatles music. Had Epstein realized what he had unleashed on the world? Did he tie his kite to their comet or was it vice versa? Had it been a sure thing any fool could have bumbled through or was the whole enterprise a masterful scheme of plotting (ten records in the Top 10 at once!)? We will never know and if John or Paul do, it does not seem they are talking.

If Brian Epstein had nothing to do, really, with the Beatles' success, one can understand his death more easily. We see him worthless, feeling perhaps, the pawn of circumstance, to which he had not added his true bit of fuel. Feeling that he had nothing to give. After all he did, in his autobiography, describe himself as bland, as having only come to life through them. Had he not failed at becoming an actor? I remember him on the old *Hullaballoo* TV show looking so pale and wan and out of place. So quiet! Was this the mastermind tycoon, the successor to Col. Parker, the new Barnum?

But perhaps he was the genius some say, filling up his day with devious and splendid machinations, plotting and coursing the trail of our idols so that they did eventually blaze above each and every one of our heads. If he was a great businessman, expressing his will through four musicians, bringing honesty and integrity to an otherwise murky business, how he then must have suffered when the Beatles decided to tour no longer. What is left after two movies and no tours? No more organizational meetings, plots, plans and devices. Does one pore endlessly over monstrous manuscripts praying to find the sacred words, to resurrect once again the excitement, the glory and the power?

Or do you spend your time flitting from one party to another, continent to continent, experimenting with this or that, savouring the fruits of one's endeavours but endeavouring no more? Do you find new groups, Gerry and the Pacemakers, the Cyrkle, Cilla Black? There is only one group. And they do not want to perform.

I remember him best for a story that may or may not have been true. In his mansion Brian Epstein kept Spanish servants, none of whom could speak English. Let that be a lesson to us all in discretion.

After the Beatles came the Stones and of the Stones one could never have ignored Brian Jones with his puffed-up Pisces, all-knowing, suffering fish eyes, his incredible clothes, those magnificent scarves, Brian always ahead of style, perfect Brian. How could Brian have asthma, a psychological disease (we're told) and certainly something strange for a member of a rock & roll group? We read in interviews that Brian saw himself as the original lead Stone, a position he held until their American tour singled out Mick for the honour in the hearts of the American female.

Can you remember 1964 when the Stones were called homosexual for having long hair? (Were you?) Brian, with two 14-year-old girls draped on each arm, must have laughed. And yet, the centre of attention was drifting. In a group the attention may be evenly distributed (we all knew and loved John, Paul,

George and Ringo) but in the Stones it was to be Mick. Now normally in a group an instrumentalist can never overshadow a lead singer (exception: the Yardbirds where Eric Clapton, Jeff Beck and Jimmy Page did just that to poor Keith Relf). In the Stones there was Mick, the pivotal centre. Charlie and Bill were for gourmets. That left Keith and Brian. Lead guitar always, always beats rhythm guitar for popularity, so that left Brian, who one assumes therefore turned to more and more exotic instruments to establish his presence both to himself and others. This is what I'm worth. Let me see you play the damn thing.

It would be a mistake I think for someone to compete with Jagger on his own terms. Jagger has literally rewritten the book on strut scowl and scruffy and the role of street urchin versus society he played perfectly and mercilessly. Had Brian thought of competing it would have been a mistake. No one can overtake the lead vocalist.

New drugs, new countries, new sounds, back to the blues, my own music (everyman's conceit and dream), I must redefine myself because the self I wanted to become is occupied by another body. And still he was identified as a Stone which was contrarily identified as Mick's group, a back-up band, a sideman. Now connoisseurs of course know that the band is a Band, but the great mass looked to Mick not Brian to be their leader through this Fall from Grace. And how can you take that? 'But I started the thing,' you might say. 'It was my records in the first place, I turned them on, must I be a damn singer to turn on the world?' Yes. Or the champion of guitar.

Then, of course, there are more problems, the drug arrests, the constant mental turmoil. What if they tour without me? Financial. Could I starve? (He died well in debt.) If they play without me I shall be disgraced and have nothing whereas if I leave and strike out on my own I'm out before they get me (how sad! how inevitable!), and I create my own myth, style, voice, the eyes will be on me, I have a future, there's so much I know, music, music, music, who would know it from *that*, I can do it, I have to do it, I will do it, I must do it.

And of course the disorientation, am I backwards, forwards, the asthma attack (I am going to choke), the fall (where is the pool?!), and everything settles like a quiet bubble coming in spurts and then thin streams until finally the last one has popped itself right out of earthly existence.

Do people realize that at the age some of our entertainers are, most people have settled into a lifestyle from which they will reap rewards the rest of their lives? That is security of job and family. Most have found their soul-mate and are busy with one child, if not two, and life seems ordered and with purpose. No strange meanderings for them. That is for lesser or greater or at the very least different mortals from you or I. And yet there is no son more delinquent, no family more in chaos than the audience which comes to sit at the table of rock. Who else withdraws emotions so arbitrarily? And yet if the audience is just one big person, it should not be thought any more or less dependable than anyone else. Therefore performer beware. If you come looking for love, come prepared with a thick skin or a thick heart. Or, as my analyst put it, don't depend on anyone, not your lover, your friend, or your doctor.

Hendrix, that most supple of guitarists, the true electronic extension, depended on his audience to take him anywhere but where he was. But, as he insisted on taking their trip rather than taking them on his, he was ultimately forced to face a vision of himself which screamed clown. One cannot get to the top and switch masks. The lover demands consistency, and unless you've established variance as your norm *a priori* you will be called an adulterer. You can accept illogic as logic if it's presented all the time but not when sprung as a ripe pomegranate in a grove of erstwhile peaches.

Hendrix was at the mercy of so many people, one wonders how he stood it as long as he did. He was the other side of Joplin's coin. If she traded off the black, he was trading off the white. When his management brought him here from England with two white sidemen, the die was cast. For Jimi Hendrix could never have been accepted in white America as a first-rate phenomenon had he an all-black band.

When Jimi Hendrix came over, the most striking thing besides his truly incredible guitar virtuosity was his savage, if playful, rape of his instrument. It would squeal and whine, going off into a crescendo of leaps and yells that only change could program (see, we are extensions of Mr Cage, it's all so modern and primitive at the same time, how simultaneous). Anyone who does that night after night must go mad. It was the frenzy of self, for frustration can only so long be acted out in violent ways, never mime. If any part of it becomes sham, then vital energies are used to mimic the worst aspects of self and both mind and body are soon exhausted.

Jimi Hendrix's shows became sex shows, the idol erotically gliding, so ... diffident, through a performance with two playmates clearly not in his league. Bitterness developed over attention to the star. But he was the star, wasn't he (lead guitarist and vocalist)? So the group dissolves. Comes the amorphous dawn and he realizes, I am not a strip-teaser, an Ann Corio con artist of the pelvis, I am a guitar player, now that I have, uh, arrived, why don't they take me seriously? The zenith of burlesque wants to play rock Macbeth and so, they say, do all comedians, ha, ha, want to be tragedians. But I! Am! An! Artist! I! Can! Play! And he could (running counter to the Cassandra-like predictions of management) have played a sinewy Lear or a sweet and loving Hamlet, for Jimi played music beautiful music every waking minute moment, noon and sun-music permeated his every thought and action and it had to be, I repeat, had to be, that he would have to say I must play real music or shrivel up and die one wind-swept morning.

And so, as Joplin is to do also, he forms a new band, to play what he attempts. And yet, there is no money for that, it is not so successful (where are the fans?) and so the old band is sporadically reformed for jobs in Oregon and the need to perform for an audience goes on, only this time to be forced to, this time knowingly violate the self and soul (the body is a temple that houses the soul activated by the spirit which is energy), it was all right before, when we didn't understand what we were doing (the Shadow of Men witnesses all we do), when we had to get there . . . but to break the principles (so newly discovered) now! the spirit breaking, now! And so one runs back to the room to clarify the goals, get one's head straight, get it together, sort it all out, and dimly, dimly, may or may not perceive that management was lying.

Who can you talk to on the road? Long-haired dirty drug people wherever you look. The boy passes over a bag of green powder (for Christ's sakes as Holden would put it, Samwise come protect the master) and passes out. Don't take that, it has horse tranquilizer in it. Oh, I shot up to your song. I got busted to your song. Oh please bless me and touch me and make it all go away. I loved to you.

Who did Janis Joplin talk to on the road? She brought excesses of feeling into moribund white music. On the road when one sees only nights, never the pretty days of a flat midwestern sun. And all your companions are drugged and hip and so sophisticated (we talk on such a high level only dogs can hear us) about the scene and who did what to whom and three puns on why, far out . . . She's so . . . twisted. Who can you talk to when you're famous and alone and all the people idolize you and want . . . to . . . get high with you and show you that they too are *hip*, that they *know* what is happening and watch let's get her drunk she's so funny when she's drunk you'll love her do you remember . . .

I remember people who do encore after encore and after being pressed into a role they may have wanted, either consciously or unconsciously emulate a pattern, gradually become the persona and, then alone, have to live up to it because the wretched *they* want it and what if they are right? Perhaps I should die. After all, they all (the great blues singers) did die, didn't they? But life is getting better now, I don't want to die. Do I?

And if it's true all so true that you can't live up to everyone's expectations, and if it's true you cannot be all things to all people, and if it's true you cannot be other than what you are (passage of time to the contrary), then you must be strong of heart if you wish to work the problem out in public, on stage, through work before 'them' who fully expect and predict in print their idol's fall. And if it was true it was inevitable and oh yes we know sad, and oh nothing could be done about it after all that's how she started out she just realized too late the habits of years are not undone in days, then if it's true that princesses are besmirched, then all of us are fallen knights.

Meaty, Beaty, Big & Bouncy

PETE TOWNSHEND

Pete Townshend has always been the sixties figure to most self-consciously ruminate upon rock's heritage and so when in 1972 MCA put together a collection of Who singles, he used Rolling Stone *magazine as a medium for these alternative sleeve-notes, in which he reveals much about not only the quirks of fate that gave us so many classic 'Oo singles, but also his abiding faith in the 7-inch 45.*

On listening to this album, it's very easy to imagine that the whole Who world has been made up of singles. Where Tommy and his lengthy and finally expatriated self come in, it's hard to say. Probably nearer the time of the second album, *A Quick One*, or *Happy Jack*, as it was called in the States. Before we even approached the idea of making an album that was an expression of our own feelings, or in the case of *Happy Jack*, an album expression of our own insanity, we believed only in singles. In the Top 10 records and pirate radio. We, I repeat, believed only in singles.

In England albums were what you got for Christmas, singles were what you bought for prestige. It was the whole re-creation of the local dancehall-cum-discotheque in your own sweet front room. You had to have the regulation tin speaker record-player, tin, not twin, housed artistically in a vinyl-covered box under a lid with a two-watt amplifier worthy only of use as a baby alarm, and a record deck on which the current Top 20 singles could be stacked twelve or fifteen high for continuous dancing of the latest dance – which differed only from last week's in the tiniest possible hip-waggling details. A long sentence, but a single sentence. One sentence and you have the truth about singles. We made them tinny to sound tinny. If you made them hi-fi to sound tinny you were wasting your time, after all.

Shel Talmy, who produced our first three singles, was a great believer in 'making groups who are nothing, stars'. He was also a great believer in pretending the group didn't exist when they were in a recording studio. Despite the fact that I go on to say that our first few records are among our best, they were the least fun to make. We only found out recording was fun when we made 'Happy Jack' and the ensuing album with our latter-day producer Kit Lambert. However, dear Shel got us our first single hits. So he was as close to being God for a week as any other unworthy soul has been. Of course it was a short week; I quickly realized that it was really the brilliant untapped writing talent of our lead guitarist, needless to say myself, that held the key to our success. Talmy and all following claimers to Who history are imposters.

As you can see, I feel pretty good about my own contributions to this, the greatest of Who albums. John Entwistle's contribution should have been a single too, that's why it's here. Without a hint of guilt I shout aloud that singles just could be what life is all about. What rock is all about. What the Spiritual Path is all about! Ask Kit Lambert about shortening a song two hours long with 24 verses, 6 choruses and 12 over-dubbed guitar solos down to two minutes fifty or preferably shorter. Ask him how he did it without offending the composer. Deceit. Lies. Cheating! That's what rock is all about.

It really is the most incredible thing that after two years of brainwashing himself into being a producer of singles for Top 10 radio play, Kit Lambert actually turned his brain inside out and came up with Rock Opera. Enigmatic paradox. But good thinking for a group who stopped getting hits. Listen to 'Magic Bus' and 'I Can See For Miles' and tell me why those cuts weren't hits. Tell me why *Tommy* was. Kit Lambert knows some of the answers, and perhaps because this album covers not only a huge chunk of our English success record-wise, but also our evolving relationship with Kit as our producer, it is, in my opinion (doubly prejudiced, and tainted by possible unearned royalties helping to pay for the tactical nuclear missile I am saving up for) the best collection of singles by the Who there is.

It's all our singles, and it includes all our earliest stuff, excluding 'I'm The Face' which might be released soon on the Stones label. 'I'm The Face' was our very first record on an English label called Phillips. It was 'written' by our then-manager Pete Meadon, fashioner of our mod image. He pinched the tune of 'Got Love If You Want It' by Slim Harpo and changed the words to fit the groovy group. That is another, even earlier story, which if ever told, would banish the Who mystique forever.

'Can't Explain', more than any other track here, turns me on. We still play this on stage, at the moment we open with it. It can't be beat for straightforward Kinks copying. There is little to say about how I wrote this. It came out of the top of my head when I was eighteen and a half. It seems to be about the frustrations of a young person who is so incoherent and uneducated that he can't state his case to the bourgeois intellectual blah blah blah. Or, of course, it might be about drugs.

'Anyway, Anyhow, Anywhere', our second record, was written mainly by myself, but those were political days in late '64. Or was it '65? Roger helped a lot with the final arrangement and got half the credit. Something he does today for nothing, bless him. I was lying on my mattress on the floor listening to a Charlie Parker record when I thought up the title (it's usually title first with me). I just felt the guy was so free when he was playing. He was a soul without a body, riding, flying, on music. Listening to the compulsory Dizzy Gillespie solo after one by Bird was always a come-down, however clever Gillespie was. No one could follow Bird. Hendrix must have been his reincarnation especially for guitar players. The freedom suggested by the title became restricted by the aggression of our tightly defined image when I came to write the words. In fact, Roger was really a hard nut then, and he changed quite a few words himself to toughen the song up to suit his temperament. It is the most excitingly pig-headed of our songs. It's blatant, proud and – dare I say it – sassy.

Musically it was a step forward. On 'Can't Explain' we had been fully manipulated in the studio, the like of which hasn't been seen since (aside from my dastardly treatment of Thunderclap Newman). Jimmy Page played rhythm on the A side and lead on the B, 'Bald Headed Woman'. He nearly played lead on the A, but it was so simple even I could play it. The Beverly Sisters were brought in to sing backing voices and Keith has done poor imitations on stage ever since. 'Can't Explaaaain,' he screams, hurling drumsticks at the sound man who turns the mike off because he thinks it's feeding back.

'Anyway' was the first time we encountered the piano playing of Nicky Hopkins, who is a total genius, and likes the Who. He likes John Lennon too and a lot of other people who give him work. A lot of bands breathed a sigh of relief when he and his missus showed their weary cheery faces in England again this summer. We did, and so on. He's still working.

Kit Lambert described 'Anyway, Anyhow, Anywhere' to reporters as, 'A pop art record, containing pop art music. The sounds of war and chaos and frustration expressed musically without the use of sound effects.' A bored and then cynical Nik Cohn – Christ, he was even more cynical than me – said calmly, 'That's impressionism, not pop art.' I repeated what Kit had briefed me to say, mumbling something about Peter Blake and Lichtenstein and went red. Completely out of order while your record is screaming in the background: 'I can go anyway, way I choose, I can live anyhow, win or lose, I can go anywhere, for something new, Anyway anyhow anywhere.'

Then we released 'My Generation'. The hymn. The patriotic song they sing at Who football matches. I could say a lot about this, I suppose I should say what hasn't been said, but a lot of what has been said is so hilarious. I wrote it as a throwaway, naturally. It was a talking blues thing of the 'Talking New York' ilk. This one had come from a crop of songs which I was, by then, writing using a tape recorder. Kit Lambert had bought me two good-quality tape decks and suggested I do this; it appealed to me as I had always attempted it using lesser machines and been encouraged by results. But when you sit down and think what to play, it's a little hard. The whole point is that blues patterns, the ones groups use to jam with one another, are somehow the only thing forthcoming when you are gazing at a dial and thinking mainly of how good it's going to be to play this to Beryl and proudly say, 'I played all the instruments on this myself.' All the instruments being guitar, guitar, bass guitar and maracas.

Anyway, ensconced in my Belgravia two-room tape recorder and hi-fi showroom, I proceeded to enjoy myself writing ditties with which I could later amuse myself, over-dubbing, multi-tracking and adding extra parts. It was the way I practised. I learnt to play with myself. Masturbation comes to mind and as a concept making demos is not far off. 'Generation' was then praised by Chris Stamp, our 'other' manager, who was worshipped only as a source of money from his ever-active roles as assistant director in various film epics. He was convinced it could be the biggest Who record yet. Bearing in mind the state of the demo it shows an astuteness beyond the call. It sounded like (I still, of course, have it) Jimmy Reed at ten years old suffering from nervous indigestion.

Kit made suggestion after suggestion to improve the song. He later said that it was because he was unsure of it. I went on to make two more demos in my den of magnetic iniquity, the first introduced the stutter. The second several key changes, pinched, again, from the Kinks. From then on we knew we had it. I even caught a real stutter which I only lost recently.

Over the period of rewriting I realized that spontaneous words that come out of the top of your head are always the best. I had written the lines of 'Generation' without thinking, hurrying them, scribbling on a piece of paper in the back of a car. For years I've had to live by them, waiting for the day someone says, 'I thought you said you hope you'd die when you got old in that song. Well, you are old. What now?' Of course, most people are too polite to say that sort of thing to a dying pop star. I say it often to myself. The hypocrisy of accusing hypocrites of being hypocritical is highly hypocritical. See the new Lennon album. See 'My Generation'.

It's understandable to me, perhaps not to you, that I can only think of inconsequentially detrimental things to say about the emergence of lyrics from my various bodily orifices. 'Substitute', for example, was written as a spoof on 'Nineteenth Nervous Breakdown'. On the demo I sang with an affected Jagger-like accent which Kit obviously liked, as he suggested the song as a follow-up to 'My Generation'. The lyric has come to be the most quoted Who lyric ever. It somehow goes to show that the 'trust the art, not the artist' tag that people put on Dylan's silence about his work could be a good idea. To me, 'Mighty Quinn' is about the five Perfect Masters of the age, the best of all being Meher Baba of course, to Dylan it's probably about gardening, or the joys of placing dog shit in the garbage to foul up Alan J. Weberman. 'Substitute' makes me recall writing a song to fit a clever and rhythmic-sounding title. A play on words. Again it could mean a lot more to me now than it did when I wrote it. If I told you what it meant to me now, you'd think I take myself too seriously.

The stock, down-beat riff used in the verses, I pinched from a record played to me in 'Blind Date', a feature in *Melody Maker*. It was by a group who later wrote to thank me for saying nice things about their record in the feature. The article is set up so that pop stars hear other people's records without knowing who they are by. They say terrible things about their best mates' latest and it all makes the pop scene even snottier and more competitive. Great. The record I said nice things about wasn't a hit, despite an electrifying riff. I pinched it, we did it, you bought it.

'The Kids Are Alright' wasn't a single in England; it was in the States. Funnily enough, this broke really well in Detroit, an area where both Decca Records and the local community were a little more hip to the Who than they were elsewhere. Detroit, or at least Ann Arbor, was the first place in the States we played after New York.

There are a few cuts on this album that are good because they are as simple as nursery rhymes. 'Legal Matter', for example, is about a guy on the run from a chick about to pin him down for breach of promise. What this song was screaming from behind lines like, 'It's a legal matter baby, marrying's no fun, it's a legal matter baby, you got me on the run', was 'I'm lonely, I'm hungry, and the bed needs making.' I wanted a maid I suppose. It's terrible feeling like an eligible bachelor but with no woman seeming to agree with you. 'Pinball Wizard' is, quite simply, quite pimply,

from *Tommy*. It's my favourite song on the album and was actually written as a ploy to get Nik Cohn, who is an avid pinball
player, to be a little more receptive to my plans for a Rock Opera.
Nik writes on and off for *The New York Times*. I know which
side my Aronowitz is buttered, mate!

From the superb production of 'Pinball' it is hard to imagine
that anything produced by Kit Lambert with the Who before
'Pinball' could stand up. There are two songs that do. 'Pictures of
Lily' just jells perfectly somehow. Merely a ditty about masturbation and the importance of it to a young man, I was really digging
at my folks who, when catching me at it, would talk in loud
voices in the corridor outside my room, 'Why can't he go with
girls like other boys.' The real production masterpiece in the
Who/Lambert coalition was, of course, 'I Can See For Miles'. The
version here is not the mono, which is a pity because the mono
makes the stereo sound like the Carpenters. We cut the tracks in
London at CBS studios and brought the tapes to Gold Star studios
in Hollywood to mix and master them. Gold Star have the nicest
sounding echo in the world. And there is just a *little* of that on the
mono. Plus, a touch of home-made compression in Gold Star's
cutting-room. I swoon when I hear the sound. The words, which
ageing senators have called 'Drug Orientated', are about a jealous
man with exceptionally good eyesight. Honest.

Two of the tracks here are produced by the Who, not Kit
Lambert. One is 'Substitute'. We made this straight after 'Generation' and Kit wasn't really in a position to steam in and produce,
that honour being set aside as a future bunce for Robert Stigwood,
God forbid. A blond chap called Chris at Olympic studios got the
sound, set up a kinky echo, did the mix etc. I looked on and have
taken the credit whenever the opportunity has presented itself
ever since. Keith can't even remember doing the session,
incidentally, a clue to his condition around that period. The other
Who-produced cut was 'The Seeker'. 'The Seeker' is just one of
those odd Who records. I suppose I like this least of all the stuff.

It suffered from being the first thing we did after *Tommy*, and also from being recorded a few too many times. We did it once at my home studio, then at IBC where we normally worked, then with Kit Lambert producing. Then Kit had a tooth pulled, breaking his jaw, and we did it ourselves. The results are impressive. It sounded great in the mosquito-ridden swamp I made it up in – Florida at three in the morning drunk out of my brain with Tom Wright and John Wolf. But that's always where the trouble starts, in the swamp. The alligator turned into an elephant and finally stampeded itself to death on stages around England. I don't think we even got to play it in the States.

The only non-Townshend track on the album is also a non-single. Politics or my own shaky vanity might be the reason, but 'Boris The Spider' was never released as a single and could have been a hit. It was the most requested song we ever played on stage, and if this really means anything to you guitar players, it was Hendrix's favourite Who song. Which rubbed me up well the wrong way, I can tell you. John introduced us to 'Boris' in much the same way as I introduced us to our 'Generation': through a tape recorder. We assembled in John's three feet by ten feet bedroom and listened incredulously as the strange and haunting chords emerged. Laced with words about the slightly gruesome death of a spider, the song had enough charm to send me back to my pad writing hits furiously. It was a winner, as Harry would say. It still is, for the life of me I don't know why we still don't play it, and the other Entwistle masterpiece 'Heaven And Hell', on stage any more. There is no peace for the wicked, John's writing is wicked, his piece here is 'Boris'.

Of interest to collectors is 'I'm A Boy'. This is a longer and more relaxed version of the single which was edited and had fancy voices added. The song, of course, is about a boy whose mother dresses him up as a girl and won't let him enjoy all the normal boyish pranks like slitting lizards' tummies and throwing rocks at passing cars. Real Alice Cooper syndrome. Of course,

Zappa said it all when he wrote his original Rock Opera. Nobody noticed, so he had to write a satire on the one Rock Opera people did notice. 'I'm A Boy' was my first attempt at Rock Opera. Of course the subject matter was a little thin, then what of *Tommy*?

We get right down to the Who nitty-gritty with 'Magic Bus'. Decca Records really smarmed all over this one. Buses painted like Mickey Mouse's first trip. Album covers featuring an unsuspecting Who endorsing it like it was our idea. 'Magic Bus' was a bummer. For one thing, we really like it. It was a gas to record and had a mystical quality to the sound. The first time ever I think that you could hear the room we were recording in when we made it. The words, however, are garbage, again loaded with heavy drug inference. For example, 'thruppence and sixpence every way, trying to get to my baby'. Obviously a hint at the ever-rising prices of LSD.

When I wrote 'Magic Bus', LSD wasn't even invented as far as I knew. Drug songs and veiled references to drugs were not part of the Who image. If you were in the Who and took drugs, you said 'I take drugs', and waited for the fuzz to come. We said it but they never came. We very soon got bored with the drugs. No publicity value. Buses, however! Just take another look at Decca's answer to an overdue *Tommy*: *The Who, Magic Bus, On Tour*. Great title, swinging presentation. Also a swindle as far as insinuating that the record was live. Bastards. They have lived to regret it, but not delete it. This record is what that record should have been. It's the Who at their early best. Merely nippers with big noses and small genitals trying to make the front page of the *Daily News*. Now Peter Max – there's a guy who knows how to use a bus! They pay him to ride on them.

To wind up, this album is a piece of history that we want you to know about. It's really a cross-section of our English successes, and when in the States, and we get compared to come-and-go heavies who, like everyone else, influence us a little, we get paranoid that a lot of American rock fans haven't heard this stuff.

They might have heard us churn out a bit on the stage, but not the actual cuts. As groups, Cream, Hendrix and Zeppelin etc., have gotten bigger than the Who ever did and a lot quicker. But they don't have the solid foundation that we have in this album. This album is as much for us as for you, it reminds us who we really are. The Who.

Heartbreakers

THERESA STERN

Theresa was the original neon girl, a fully fledged heartbreaker from day one, authoress of a thin sliver of poetic works – Wanna Go Out? – constantly lurking in the shadows, a Second Woman to Richard Hell's Third Man. Here s/he not-so-detachedly assesses the original Heartbreakers before Hell left them behind and they reverted to the simple sound of Thunder.

I hate white 'rock & roll'. The only person who can break my heart is myself. Whose idea is the 'heart' anyway? The man who can break my stomach can have my heart on the popsicle stick. Undoubtedly the Heartbreakers have made a lot of girls sad, but I testify here that they have helped to make me bad.

As I was saying . . . you do not 'gotta have heart', the delusion that you do has produced more unhappy homosexuals than even Richard Hell can hope to mentally torture. The plea 'you gotta have heart' is merely words anyway and as modern minds automatically realize, a picture's worth a billion of 'em. These particular words are probably the only important ones left. I'm imaginary. The Heartbreakers exist in the images they create out of desperation. For love and money. A couple of them want to die as well. In other words the Heartbreakers are imaginary. The desperation is real, they are aware of these two things, and the result is a large number of people (myself included) willing to pay to have their hearts broken. 'I will break your heart or die trying.' This inspires my gratitude. An irreversibly 'broken heart' is the door to permanent illumination. The Doors had the wrong organ (break hearts, not balls). Paradise is dead.

What remains is blank. Love, in fact, comes in spurts. Albert Cossery wrote *A Life Full of Holes*. The only available human pleasures are 1, the facts of life (love), and 2, dreams (the facts of death). Every parent is a liar and a murderer, they stick you with life to relieve their boredom and pretty soon you die. If you are lucky you may become aware of this, thereby breaking your heart, from which flows beautiful nothing like a fire you can gaze at and have a good dream. It is very moving and exciting to watch people who are aware of these things attempt to be entertaining. It's also funny and scary like if you answered the door one night to find Daffy Duck quacking with rage.

Rock & roll has become more than its own history. The best rock & rollers, like the Heartbreakers, are human beings of rock & roll. Like mutations. Having been born roughly simultaneously with the sound, they've absorbed it, it's modified them and they have the unprecedented and mysterious ability to turn a teardrop into a driving question mark. Time after time.

Johnny Thunders is quintessential rock & roll. Baseball was out because even though he was the only freshman on his High School varsity, he wouldn't cut his hair for the coach. He dropped out, moved to the Lower East Side and pretty soon was the 18-year-old guitarist of the most famous group in America. Rock & roll is life and death. No exit. To my knowledge he has never met anyone outside of R&R over the age of twenty-five who didn't leave mad and/or disgusted. Teenage girls adore him.

Jerry Nolan was also a New York Doll. When their original drummer died, hundreds lined up to audition for the most highly publicized unrecorded group since Cybill Shepherd, consequently Jerry was the best musician in the group. He's been playing professionally since he was fourteen, and his instincts are infallible. What's more, he's sexy, a gentleman, and can lose four quarts of blood just because his mind's on something more important.

Richard Hell, unlike the rest of the group, who were born in New York, was born and raised in Lexington, Kentucky, where he was a teenage car thief. He met Tom Verlaine at the age of fifteen, they ran away from home together, arrived in New York soon after and a few years later co-founded the group Television. When it became obvious that they were incompatible as group members, Richard left and within a week received a call from Jerry and Johnny, who by complete coincidence had split from the Dolls the same week, thus the Heartbreakers were born. Hell is a master rock conceptualist and student of facial expressions. On stage he generally appears completely blank, very tired, extremely angry or profoundly agonized. That's because he feels that way. He's responsible for the lyrics and vocals (and much of the music) for such songs as 'I Belong To The Blank Generation', 'Love Comes In Spurts', 'New Pleasure' (it's about hypnosis), and 'You Gotta Lose' (from which comes 'My mother was a pinhead and my father was a fly/That's why I love you darlin with a love that's so unique/Your glistenin wings they complement your head's impressive peak'). It's sort of a rhythm and blues and doesn't stay funny for long.

To pick up our tale . . . the trio were now in need of another guitar player. They searched for weeks, even appearing once in a disastrous debut at the now defunct Coventry in Queens as a trio. Finally on a dead night at CBGB, they heard the tall dark thin chords of a player named Walter in a local band called the Demons. He was invited to a rehearsal and the following week the band was complete. He's the most lovable member of the band, with his hip twitches and secret smile, and he also wrote and sings one of its most popular songs, 'Flight'.

Though writing is the only thing I do that gives me any semblance of satisfaction, I write very little because I'm hard as a rock and can only write when I've been hit pretty bad. The Heartbreakers have only existed for seven months and they hit harder every week.

Jukebox Cruci-fix

PATTI SMITH

Patti Smith's seminal 'Jukebox Cruci-fix', a prose-poem version of 'Break It Up', relates a vist to Jim Morrison's grave and a vision that she saw there. Smith finally decides she would rather be a live dog than a dead lion and walks away from the grave.

I was at this party but nothing was happening at all. a lot of chicks were leaning over a pale neon wurlitzer jukebox. the way dead voice boxes rolled up it came on like a coffin. It was the kind of party to leave behind. 8 millimetre footage of Jimi Hendrix jacking his strat. girls sobbing and measuring the spaces between his fingers. I went out in the hallway and stood there drinking a glass of tea. 'riders on the storm' was rolling from a local transistor, the boy slipped on some soap and the radio fell in the bathtub. I gulped my tea too fast and some of it went up my nose it made me choke and stammer and my lungs started pumping like erratic water wings . . .

I woke up and the room was gone the radio was playing 'riders on the storm' and the D J cut in and said that Jim Morrison was dead. I reached over for my air rifle and took shaky aim, ducks with musical notes etched in their little wax skulls were revolving on the ceiling. Camus said that it's death which gives gambling and heroism their true meaning. but me I prefer another french saying – better a live scoundrel than a dead miracle. I kicked the shit outa the radio and went looking for a heavy handed game of chance. local bingo – fascination – or when the chips are down handle some poker . . .

Johnny Ace was cool he came east from Texas to knock 'just a Dream' off the charts with 'pledging my Love'. 'dream' was tender but who could imagine humping it up to Jimmy Clanton? all the girls would oil their nylons when Johnny came to town. white girls. there were no black girls in the fifties. flashes of pony tail hair, girls with chiffon triangles tied tight around their hot soft throats. girls with flesh like wonderbread, and Johnny Ace sang for them, a hero with no R&B no spanish blood, no sweat. ballads tender as Boston lettuce, more soft spots than a baby's head, until he pushed his own finger in. one Christmas Eve the black velvet Sinatra was a little long backstage. Ace was playing solitaire. he took a .45 calibre outa his tux. rolled the barrel like his own hit record and blew his brains out.

some say Vladimir Mayakovski was the first rock 'n' roll star. russian poet adolescent anarchist, handsome 22 years old rushing the streets howling blue face. a guy with huge piano teeth and a marshall amp installed in his chest. he was always crashing church meets bars parties pool halls. were there pool halls in russia? who knows. but if there were he hit them all. he was the seven feet tall poet bully with the amazing megaphone mouth. did God know about revolution rhythm of the painful promise of a poem? well Mayakovski knew and thousands of kids rocked in russian behind him.

until one morning while the crowds were waiting. our hero was penning his last booming aria; 'me and life are quits' he writ. and like our own Johnny Ace he held the wild card. he put on a clean shirt. swaggered to the window. maybe glanced in the mirror russia's Marlon Brando cocked the lever pulled the trigger and blew his heart out. russian lit was in the red. the funeral was like after the pop festival. you know – those last shots of monterey – no sound – minds blown. all the women wore black cloaks. russia was a rainy nunnery, cause Mayakovski – a God unto himself to say nothing of his fans – had pulled the rug from his own life.

you take a chance when you put your stakes on somebody else. like a horse race it often pays but sooner or later you're gonna be left standing in the rain. genius is meant to peak and pull out or be wiped out permanently. we is a fickle lot. the champ ain't champ unless he keeps on winning. the minute some flash knocks him outa the ring or outa the charts he's thru. like Pabst Beer says 'ya don't get the blue ribbon for being second.'

see it's like this. first let me move outa metaphor. there was no poker game. I'm lousy at cards. there was the dream though and I got splattered. we been creamed up the ass since Buddy Holly Kennedy. platinum porches miniature airplanes switchblades poisons saturday night specials motorcycles hypodermics pills thrills old fords. ever see Jackson Pollock in motion. that bull ballet and dripping blue poles. premeditation was his action he didn't believe in accidents. his blood spattered like his own pain cause like most heroes he was a crazy driver. it's okay though. it was the rules of an old game, and me I got to admit I like the photographs. the twisted steel the outstretched hand the broken neck of a fender. the instant replay of Lee Harvey Oswald getting dead live on television. they were the assassinating rhythms of our generation.

but rhythms like rules shift. something new is coming down and we got to be alert to feel it happening. something new and totally ecstatic. the politics of ecstasy move all around me. I refuse to believe Hendrix had the last possessed hand that Joplin had the last drunken throat that Morrison had the last enlightened mind.

they didn't slip their skins and split forever for us to hibernate in posthumous jukeboxes.

they are gone and we're still moving. I went to Jim Morrison's grave and there was nothing. a dirt site in Section 6. I sat there like some jack ass sobbing in the mud all alone in Paris when there is so much work to do so much flesh to consume. there is nothing there – no headstone no vibration no flowers no feeling. just a little plastic plaque with the word A M I friend the only thing Jim Morrison ever wanted.

I went to Paris to exorcise some demons. some kind of dread I harbored of moving forward. I went with this poetic conceit that we would meet in some melody hovering over his grave. but there was nothing. it was pouring rain and I sat there trying to conjure up some kind of grief or madness. I remembered this dream I had. I came in a clearing and saw a man on a marble slab. it was Morrison and he was human. but his wings were merging with the marble. he was struggling to get free but like Prometheus freedom was beyond him.

I sat there for a couple of hours. I was covered with mud and afraid to move. then it was all over. it just didn't matter anymore. racing thru my skull were new plans, new dreams voyages symphonies colours. I just wanted to get the hell outa there and go home and do my own work. to focus my floodlight on the rhythm within. I straightened my skirt and said goodbye to him. an old woman in black spoke to me in broken English. look at this grave how sad! why do you americans not honour your poets?

my mind moved before my mouth. I finished the dream. the stone dissolved and he flew away. I brushed the feathers off my raincoat and answered:

because we don't look back.

Our Town

MIKE MILLS

In 1985 REM bassist Mills imbued this insider account of Athens, Georgia as The Happening Place To Be with enough small-town sense to convey something of how it might have happened while no one was quite sure what was happening.

When you mention 'the Athens scene' to anyone who's been here for four or five years, they get weird. When we started – when the Side Effects were starting and Pylon and the Method Actors were playing – it was just people playing for the fun of it at parties or makeshift clubs. It was not a scene at all, and now it kind of is. We were originally here as University of Georgia students – come and go. There's always this big turnover of horse-flesh.

Athens is a great town, a college town. There's about 24,000 students. The entire population is about 60,000. It's a small place. When summer school is over in August, and everyone's on vacation, you can lie down in the middle of Broad Street. They might as well turn the traffic-lights off because it is dead with a capital D.

Largely, it's just the chemistry of a lot of kids together in one place. But that's true for almost any college town; some more than others. We've got a big, powerful radio station – WUOG – one of the most powerful college stations I've ever heard anywhere – 10,000 watts. And they support local bands really well. They supported us when we needed it. College radio is the saviour of rock & roll in America right now. If it were not for college radio, all the good bands that are doing well would have nowhere to go. There's nowhere they could tour if there were no college radio stations to play their records and insure that they would have some kind of crowd when they came there.

There are some great bands here. Number one: The Kilkenny Cats. They used to be non-melodic, drone, gloom-and-doom stuff. But they've grown as a band and as musicians and added a lot more melody to what they've been doing. Now they are kind of a dark band, but pop.

The second-best is the Squalls. The Squalls deserve to be famous. They've got an EP. I don't mean to use 'hippies' in a derogatory sense, but it's a bunch of people that are a little older than me. They're not students; they live here, have been here for a long time. They're not trying to be trendy, famous or successful. They're just playing because they're having a good time and they're a lot of fun to see. That's the way it oughta be. In a perfect world, they'd get rich.

Dreams So Real – good band, name's far too hard to say. Also worth mentioning are Banned 37, the Barbecue Killers – great name, even if the band was really sloppy – and Fashion Battery. Normally, I don't care that much for fusion, but the Land Sharks do fusion with a really good kick. They add a lot of energy to it, instead of just technical proficiency.

There are only two clubs worth mentioning for live music: the 40 Watt and the Uptown Lounge. There are other clubs with different kinds of music, but nothing I'm really interested in.

The 40 Watt Club has had three different locations before its present one. The one that it's in now used to be a fern bar. The Uptown Lounge is right across from the police station. It used to be a porno theatre and they've been working on it steadily since then, trying to rearrange it. I guess they've got all the stains off the floor. None of these places has been around more than a year.

Tyrone's was the best club Athens has ever seen. Unfortunately, it burned down a year and a half ago. It was a sad, sad day.

Everybody was upset. The suspended heater broke off its moorings, fell on to the stage, and BANG – there everything went. It happened about four in the morning. It would have been better if people had been there because they would have been able to stop it. It was a total loss.

It was great because the people that ran it would let anybody play there, and get the door. You charge two dollars and you get all the money. I made $30 and I thought I was rich. They made their money off the bar – and they made a ton. The only thing that didn't burn in the fire was my tab. They went sifting through the rubble and found it – $40.

Most kids here drink. They drink a lot of beer – pitchers of beer. As it gets warmer they hang out at the pool, or go downtown. Downtown is the main drag. There's downtown, then there's north campus, and the dorms, so it's really accessible. You don't need a car. Up on College Street: Ruthless Records. Good store. But the one that's been here the longest, right up across the corner from Ruthless, is Wuxtry. It's really small and all it has is used records.

Fraternities are very much a part of what goes on here. They have huge parties. They're maybe 15 or 20 per cent of the total student population. It's usually the ones with money. There are not too many art students in the fraternities and sororities. They're a real conservative, right-wing group of people. But fine, so what? That's the way it is. They don't completely ignore music, such as what's playing at the 40 Watt. They come out and lots of times they enjoy it. That was what we did, when we first started. We were the first band among several that drew a cross-section of people. Pylon and the Method Actors would draw the creative left-wing people that cared. Then, when we started, we got everything from dormies and fraternity people to the arty types. We were accessible – without trying to be.

Every college in the country, University of Georgia included, is getting more and more conservative. It's changed since I started going to school here – the way it has everywhere else. Most kids in college, all they care about is getting a degree and getting a good job. Who's to say that they're wrong? A lot of kids here are for Reagan. Not most of them, but as many here as in Topeka, or Houston, or Albuquerque, or New Brunswick, New Jersey.

If you compare youth culture now to the sixties, it's certainly not the same. Bob Dylan changed people's lives. People listened to Bob Dylan and wanted to go out and change the world. If you want to think about youth culture as one spearhead that's gonna make a difference in the world, it's not gonna happen. The sixties were a time of political activism. It went from innocence to cynicism really quickly. And now the situation is not so much apathy as realization and there's not a lot you or anyone else personally can do.

Any rock star who thinks he's gonna make a big difference is deluded. Look at the biggest: Prince, Michael Jackson, Bruce Springsteen. Are they gonna inspire anyone to do anything? No! They're gonna inspire them to go out and buy a record – that's it. Millions have, and millions will. Great. That's what music is about; it's entertainment. What do kids in Athens or anywhere want? They don't want anything. Nobody's that dissatisfied that they need an icon to lead them into the new age. It just isn't that way any more. Nobody's gonna change the world, and everybody might as well realize that.

I guess my attitude is more of what a small-town mentality is about. If you grew up in New York or in LA, it would change your viewpoint on just about everything. There's no time to sit back and think about things. Our music is closer to everyday life – things that happen to you during the week, things that are real. It's great just to bring out an emotion, rather than a jingoism – better just to make someone feel nostalgic or wistful or excited or sad. You are the world and everybody is the world, but who needs to be told that? I don't. I don't want to hear about it. I know my place in the world, and most people do, and they don't want to hear it from a bunch of over-inflated musicians.

It's not isolated here – you can't act like this is Antarctica. But that's the way people think – that you're down here in the pine forests 'hangin' niggers from trees'. The South is a weird place. If you go out in the woods you're gonna end up with a lot of inbreeding and the kind of people that are behaving really strangely. But would you want to live in the suburbs of Boston, or Long Island, or the south side of Chicago? Take your pick. People are deadly anywhere you go. Human nature is a sorry thing. All you can do is try to improve it.

Some guy down the street and his 12-year-old son beat an 11-month-old dog to death yesterday. He said the dog was getting in his yard and chasing birds, and enticing his dog to chase birds. They beat the dog to death with a board with a nail through it. They pounded the fuckin' dog in the head. The guy's a nut, a psycho. He doesn't belong in human society. But that could happen in Iowa, or in Wyoming.

Look at those two mountain men in Montana. The man and his son kidnapped that jogger for a wife. The father was afraid that his son, who was like seventeen, was getting tired of living all alone in the mountains. So the father said. 'Wehull, we gawna getchoo a waafe, boy.' And they went down to the National Park and kidnapped this woman jogger. It's the truth! You get out in the woods anywhere – not just Georgia, not just the South – and there're gonna be some weird people doing weird things.

Reverend Howard Finster lives in Summerville, Georgia, up near Rome, about three hours from here. We go up and see him all the time. He very seldom leaves Summerville, but lots of art students from here and the University of North Carolina, South Carolina and North Carolina State all come down and help him with whatever projects he's doing.

He's a tremendous guy. His idea is that he is a traveller in space and was put here to bring the word of God to people through folk art. That's all he does. He sleeps about three hours a night and every waking hour he churns out his great folk art.

For years he was a travelling evangelist and finally he had a vision. He is 'Howard Finster, Man of Visions', that is his title. His vision said: 'Don't travel any more. Sit here in Summerville and make your church and have people come to you.' He built a church by himself, three stories high with a big steeple, on his property. He buried all his tools in a cement walkway and said, 'I give up my tools. I don't need them any more because I'm dedicating my life to God.' He's selling in New York for unbelievable amounts of money. He was on *The Tonight Show* and blew Johnny Carson away. It's part of his religion – reaching people through art. He is making art to spread the word of God.

He helped Michael [Stipe] with the album cover for *Reckoning*. Michael drew the outline for this two-headed snake, and gave it to Howard to fill in. And Howard did – in incredible detail. It was screwed up in the way it was printed. What Howard did was so much more detailed than finally came out.

Dave Pierce is the publisher of *Tastyworld*. He's put out five issues in about nine months – it's an iffy thing. If and when, usually when. Right now it's 95 per cent local, but I think he has ambitions of eventually expanding it into a national thing. But it's great – because there are a lot of bands here. And a lot of bands come through from out of town, playing at the 40 Watt, or the Uptown, or at Legion Field, which is the university-sponsored concert that they have outdoors. There's something to talk about – especially if you come out every two months. There's plenty to fill up the pages. If you come out every month, there might not be so much.

Athens is not the incredible, bizarre happening that people would peg it as. It's just not as unique as people think, but it's a great place. The fact that the B-52s left Athens and became famous, that a lot of media attention is focused here, makes it easier for people to get into bands and do things – because they know there are going to be people paying attention. When we started touring, we'd say, 'We're from Athens.' People would go: 'Oh, Athens –

the B-52s, Pylon – great. We'll book you.' But after we played there once or twice, Athens became totally irrelevant.

You're out-of-the-way here. You can do things as a band without all the pressure. When we started out, we were terrible, just like every band that starts out. But we had a whole year just to play around the South and get better – and to learn to deal with adversity, playing at pizza parlors and biker bars and gay discos. We can play down here, we can go to Tennessee, North Carolina, Florida, South Carolina, Alabama, and improve the band – our songwriting, stage presence, everything – without ever hearing about it. But in New York or London, the minute you start playing – ZANG! There's the local rock magazine reviewing your show and making all these judgments about you.

People come here thinking, 'It's a scene and I'm going to nurture my musical talent.' That's a mistake. By this point, the other bands that were our contemporaries have broken up, and most of the bands in Athens now are of a different attitude. A lot of them are thinking, 'We can be a band, and we can attract attention, and get out of Athens.' That never occurred to Pylon or the Side Effects or us. It was totally unselfconscious. The only important thing was playing around town, playing at parties, having fun.

The innocence is gone. I don't want to be sentimental and maudlin about it – it's not as though that was the golden age of Athens. But at the same time, there was just a different sort of attitude. That sort of thing, just by the nature of what it is, can't last.

The booking policies of the clubs now are no more exclusive. Anybody can play at the 40 Watt, anybody can play at the Uptown. There's competition for the weekends. The trouble is, during the week it's gotten really slack and people don't go out; everybody's studying. Most of these kids here know they're in school. People think it's a scene, and there's gonna be five hundred people in a club of a Wednesday night. It ain't gonna happen.

Athens is a great place – I love it. You get a band together –

great. You've got your chance. But that happens lots of places. If the Embarrassment from Lawrence, Kansas, had become a huge national hit, people would have gone, 'God, there's Get Smart and the Mortal Micronauts – LOOK AT ALL THOSE BANDS! What is it about Lawrence, Kansas, that produces these bands?' Look at Austin, Texas – Stevie Ray Vaughan, Willie Nelson. It could be anywhere.

People, especially if they're far away, like to see this grouping coming out of an area: You've got the North Carolina group – Mitch Easter, the dBs, Chris Stamey, whatever else. You've got Athens – Oh OK, Lets Active, the Method Actors, R E M, Love Tractor, the Side Effects, the B-52s. It's enticing, it's romantic, it's easy and it's a lot of fun to think of a town: 'Wow! What's going on in this town that keeps churning out these great groups?' Three or four years ago, no one would have thought of this being a 'scene.' It was just people having a good time, and people playing at parties and enjoying themselves.

People actually moved here thinking, 'I'm going to get in on the Athens scene.' And they end up hating us and people that've been here five years because we're not out every night supporting local bands. I'll go ahead and say it: I think a lot of the local bands resent us. It's a backlash because it's like our fault that we made Athens a 'scene'. And a lot of people here go: 'Oh, there go those hot-shot rock stars.' Sorry! I just live here because I like it. I didn't ask to be in this band, it just happened that way.

I go to New York all the time. I know exactly what the difference is. I want to keep living in Athens. I spend half my time somewhere else, which is what makes Athens so great. To me it's a relief to come here. I have lots of friends, there's a lot to do. I get out on the road for three months at a time and I'm wired to the max. I'm just nuts and I go home to Athens and go, 'Aaahh'. You wind down – what a great place to come home to.

Eyewitness Record Reviews

STEVE ALBINI

Another wonderful idea comes to fruition in Forced Exposure: *a record producer gets to review the finished product of sessions he has recently worked on! The producer has always held a decidedly ambivalent role in the creative process. Though expected to turn both shit and shit-hot into shellac, he has only minimal editing powers. So Steve Albini, of Big Black and assorted hipper than hip screen-credits, conjures up* The Revenge of the Producers.

Record reviewers have been at an enormous disadvantage since the advent of multi-track recording in the late 1950s. No longer can any assumptions be made about the conditions under which a record was recorded. I am now able to write the first truly informed series of record reviews since the dawn of that accursed technology. I can comment on records I saw being made.

When I am hired to record a band, I make it plain to my clients that I do not wish to be associated with their charming little records. I will do a good job for them, but that does not include shouldering any responsibility for their lousy tastes and mistakes.

When I was employed as a photo re-toucher, I was often involved in the alteration of reality for the noble purpose of increasing cigarette sales. Not once did I expect or desire to see 'produced by Steve Albini' on a Marlboro ad, simply because it was this, and not some poor other sap, who toned down the excessive lipgloss on Darryl's pout or removed the unfortunate sarcoma from his forehead. I apply the same logic to my current occupation.

Often these clients disregard my wishes and publicize the fact that I worked on their records. Oh, man. Today, they get their just desserts.

I will make little comment about the actual music on any of these records (figuring everybody has formed an opinion already or couldn't care less), and will say nothing except 'Bless you' about those who have respected my anonymity.

A word about my fees: I charge whatever the hell I feel like at the moment, based on the client's ability to pay, how nice the band members are, the size and directly proportional gullibility of the record label, and whether or not they got the rock. For example, Slint or Mudhead I would lend money to, the Didjits or Fugazi I would do for free. Shadowy Men on a Shadowy Planet and Jesus Lizard would pay beans. Most everybody else pays $150 – $450 a day, except that anybody on a major label gets fucked wholedong outright, figuring that they're never going to get paid anyway, unless it's somebody like Ministry or Depeche Mode or Guns N' Roses or Bullet LA Volta who suck so wildly that I wouldn't endure them for a fortune.

The straight skinny from an eyewitness:

The Pixies *Surfer Rosa* LP: A patchwork pinch loaf from a band who at their top-dollar best are blandly entertaining college rock. Their willingness to be 'guided' by their manager, their record company and their producers is unparalleled. Never have I seen four cows more anxious to be led around by their nose rings. Except that I got to rewrite their songs with a razor-blade, thought the drums sounded nice, and managed to get Nate the Impaler on the LP as a cameo, I remember nothing about this album, although I thought it was pretty good at the time. During the recording, a sibling of the sexual partner of a Pixie was lounging around making little fuck me noises, so I took her home and got stiffed.

Had to retreat to Byron's 'den of satisfaction' and run a batch off by hand. I seem to remember that their Filipino guitar player was pro-Marcos, but I could be wrong. The album took about a week; maybe two all tolled. Fee: $1,500.

I later recorded a single track with them for a label-stroke compilation album. The band had been getting the Big High Building 'pampered performer' treatment for a couple of years by then and were consequently bored and dour. It took a couple of hours after dinner one night. Fee: $4,000. About a year later, Bob Krasnow, the geeb at Elektra's Big High Building who fathered this dumb idea sent me a truly revolting nickel-and-gold Omega wristwatch (the kind Record Producers wear), with tacky Biz inscription and tacky presentation case. As soon as somebody at the pool room offers me what it's worth, I'm gonna have a hell of a nice dinner.

The Wedding Present 'Brassneck' single: I was told they wanted to record three songs, we ended up recording six, the most embarrassing of which is an as-yet-unreleased adenoidal rendition of Penetration's 'Don't Dictate'. I should say right out that the band are truly swell guys. Nice enough to go out with your sister and everything, but Jesus, are they vulnerable. They started out like any independent band, and now are in the unenviable position of trying to operate like one while unquestionably in the jaws of a High Building-type record company. These poor guys are under the delusion that the staff of RCA actually gives a shit about whether they draw breath or not. They sweat their tours out in a tiny rented van, pinching every penny, lost in the assumption that the label dorks back in the Big High Building 'feel' for them in some way. Meanwhile, I'm chatski on the cellular phone in the limo, keeping my appointment with the club car of a Britrail, where I'll be treated to a fucking filet on my way to my private room in the four-star Hotel Piccadilly in Manchester (where the three telephones and electric towel warmer are an ergonomic distance away from the toilet, but the closed-circuit porn movies have the penetrations and cum shots excised). 'Not to worry,' the grand dork says, snapping the Amex down on whatever Formica is handy, 'it's recoupable.' It took about four days. Fee: $9,500 plus 'niceties'.

The band recorded three songs in Chicago during a break in their US tour, and while the music was otherwise a big improvement over the songs recorded for 'Brassneck', I have to report that they also did a version of a Steve Harley song called 'Make Me Smile'. Supposedly this was a smash hit in the Bad Music Era across the pond, but back in Montana I only knew one guy who ever listened to Steve Harley. He was a Sparks fan and he later died of a brain tumour. I'm not going to risk it myself. Fee: $ 4,260.

The Breeders *Pod* LP: For reasons too subtle to describe accurately (boing! – Hat Ed.), I really enjoyed going to Scotland and working on this. The actual record is nothing special, of course, but I have a much deeper understanding of the twin phenomena of synchronous menses and breast swelling than I previously would have dreamed. The only chafingly unpleasant thing about the experience was an unbearable shit-head label gopher who loitered around the studio during those hours when he wasn't actually engaged in plugging the guitar player (the only function he truly served). Josephine, the bass player, looks quite a bit like an emu, except that her hair is thinner. The studio owner had a pathological fear of raw eggs, and entertained us with stories about the ex-Bay City Roller he buys reef from. His wife, a voluptuous, once-attractive singer, would occasionally strip down to her frillies at the bountiful dinner table. I ate haggis and enjoyed it. I pounded everybody through the album in about a week, but the label insisted that we stay at the studio and dreamed up another three weeks of work for me to do. The drummer accepted any excuse to go across the road to the pub and get stupid drunk, and finished one evening dancing in the arms of a Freemason transvestite named 'Dora' (John). On the last night in Scotland, the drummer went to a meeting of the Anglers' Club, and didn't return until well after closing time. Presented to the front door by two Anglers, each holding an elbow (the little drummer's legs had failed hours earlier), Shannon was completely blackened with soot from the fire, except for bright blue rings drawn with pool table chalk around nose and chin. Anglers, I swear! The well-plugged guitar player (noted above) tipped me to a bit of Boston gossip. It seems that Suzy Rust has been getting some social mileage out of a rumour that she and I are well acquainted with the contours of each other's nakedness, and once traded orgasms in the growler at Chet's. Let me make one thing perfectly clear: I have never been in the toilet at Chet's. Fee: $4,000.

Tad *Salt Lick* EP: There has been debate in some quarters about the validity of the whole Tad thing. Such talk comes from mouths unassociated with either ears or brains. That Tad now introduces himself as 'Tiny' whenever he gets a chance is only further evidence of apparent genius. His first words after stepping off the plane and enveloping my forequarter with a handshake however, were, 'Say, do you know where we can get any pot?' Fortunately, a terrible band of my acquaintance was recording in the studio upstairs from us, with a singer known to travel with commercial quantities, so I made the introductions. 'I'm not carrying much pot nowadays,' said the singer, his expression inverting. 'I'm tired of getting arrested all the time.' Tad was not a happy Tad that weekend. Fee: $600.

Poster Children *Flower Power* LP: They had a really fruity drummer for a while, but I think he died of the syph. This one took two days. Fee: $300.

Daisy Chain *Reaction* LP: Their current drummer, Crazy Bob, does occasionally scream 'Hey, fuck me in the ass, Steve, right here, right now!' from across a crowded room at me, but somehow that isn't as irritating as wearing a beret and scarf simultaneously. While recording their second record Crazy Bob got to meet Aerosmith, whose drummer shared this joke with him: How do you get a nun pregnant? – Fuck her. I laughed. Fee: $2,400.

Bitch Magnet *Star Booty* EP: Listen, all I did was help three college bozos remix some sorry class-project recordings, and all of a sudden, Ding! I'm their 'producer'. Listening to this poor wittle wecord is about the dumbest thing you can do with it, especially if you're short on dinnerware. I did work on an actual record of theirs later, and it wasn't unpleasant, but Orestes 'Toast' Delatorre, their drummer and interesting member, has left the band to pursue dog grooming in Alaska or some place, so who really cares. That B'gnet routinely fires Jon Fine (token hebe) immediately after each recording session is testament to his personality. Fee: $100 I think.

Jesus Lizard *Pure* EP: Recorded before the band existed, and therefore neither representative nor any good. They recorded with a drum machine, against all advice, instead of waiting for their excellent actual drummer (a sort of tragic genius) to materialize. A shame, considering how tremendous a band they've become. This record is a blight on a soon-to-be-enormously-significant career. Bands have overcome more shabby beginnings. But not many. The only one of their three records that is not absolutely stellar, but boy is it lunar. Fee: about a buck, I think.

Bastro *Rode Hard And Put Up Wet* LP: See previous review. In my opinion, a Zoviet France tattoo is stupid even when compared to genital piercing.

Whitehouse 'Thank Your Lucky Stars' 45 and LP: William Bennett can effortlessly play almost any Yes song you could be pained to mention on Spanish guitar. I shit you not. Each of the songs Whitehouse recorded was structurally mapped by a famous heavy metal song. So much so, in fact, that all Bennett used as a head-phone cue was a cassette recording of whichever Black Sabbath, Iron Maiden or Deep Purple song the track was based on. Tidbit – three guesses which later-famous synthesizer guy that is on the back of that Prag Vec record you haven't listened to since 1980. Ding! Give that man a banana. Fee: $600.

Membranes *Kiss Ass Godhead* LP: I did not produce this record, despite what it says on the jacket. I worked on a couple of songs in Chicago, and helped them mix a few more songs in Leeds, but I no more 'produced' it than did I reach into my butt crack and discover it. (Speaking of which, I have a good friend and billiard associate named Jon Spiegel whose magic act involves the disap-pearance of a volunteer's hankie and the subsequent appearance from between his own magnificent butt cheeks. It's a real P T A pleaser.) Neither Homestead nor Glass, the Membranes' two labels, ever paid me. John Robb is a stand-up fellow, but he has lousy business associates, and talks like a Ferriner. Fee: still nothing in the mailbox, Seymour, you lying fuck.

Gore Wrede LP: The title is a Dutch pun combining the words 'cruelty' and 'peace'. Oh you guys, you crack me up. This is a double album, made up of four monolithic instrumentals, the longest of which clocks in at near half an hour. I arrived after the band had spent three weeks recording, so there was basically nothing for me to do except oversee over-dubs and mix one song. And take sauna baths. And eat like a pig. My favourite victual in Dykenland is a peppered raw beef called 'filet American'. Must be another Dutch pun. I also learned to love Vlokken, a chocolate shred that is eaten on toast. I met a writer for the Dutch music magazine *Oor* (Ear), who always wore a glove on his right hand, which was always balled-up in a fist. I found out why when the conversation turned to fireworks, and he demonstrated (by sticking a thumbtack in it) that his hand was wooden. He had blown it off with fireworks as a boy. He asked me why Americans have such a low opinion of the Dutch. I told him that Americans seldom even thought of the Dutch, except for their elm disease, which we thought highly of. He gave as evidence the expressions 'being in Dutch', 'Dutch courage', and worst of all 'Dutch treat – why that's no treat at all!' I told him they were all puns. The other engineer on the record was Theo Van Eeenbergen, a swell guy who now handles live sound for Henry Rollins, a fate I wouldn't wish on a dog I didn't like. Theo told me about the pot farm he used to live on. Sometimes he and his friends would run naked through the plants and collect the resins from their skin to smoke like hashish. Neat. Things I now know how to say in Dutch: *'Zet je koptelefoon op, mietje, voor ik je tegens jehersens knal'* ('Put your headphones on, you little faggot, or I'll come out and crush your brains'); *'Vall kapot! Late we eten'* ('Fuck it, this is a disaster! Let's eat'). I also learned why you should never ask a Dutch guitar player to hand you his 'pick'. Fee: $1,200.

Head of David *Dustbowl* LP: The original artwork for this album said 'Dustbowel', which I quite liked, even when I found out it was a mistake. My involvement here was limited to remixing a record that was fine before I touched it and got no better for the effort. I also had to endure the presence of Justin Pile, HOD's measly drummer, who spent long hours bemoaning the state of his haemorrhoids, playing with his dreadlocks and eating greasy vegetarian food (the better to fart you with, grandma) – the turd. Fee: about $500, I think.

7. Satires and Short Stories

" This is going to knock the rest of pop literature into a cocked hat. It's called War and Peace and Sex and Drugs and Rock and Roll."

Given the potency of its internal myth-making machinery, it is surprising that there has been so little fiction written from within the rock milieu. Perhaps it's because there is more than enough of the fiction-in-the-guise-of-fact variety. Who needs fiction when there is Bob Spitz's Dylan biography or Mark Elliott's Rockonomics? Rock fiction seems to be primarily satirical, whether it be the ascerbic cartoons originating from the pens of Ray Lowry, Tony Benyon, John Crawford and Savage Pencil, or that last resort of reviewers and the spoof review.

The three spoof reviews within are entirely fictitious. The albums do not exist (the Masked Marauders album came after the review and does not correspond to its contents) though in each case the respective magazines received mail asking when the album was due for release.

The three short stories which make up the bulk of this section all deal with a different kind of invention – the fantasies of rock & roll fans. Jonh Ingham's fan-figure, Len Zeppelin, is at the centre of a simple parable about hipness and the collector mentality. Tama Janowitz, on the other hand, takes on the real-life mythology surrounding the Boss of the boardwalk, His Royal Bruceness.

The third and final short story is a much sharper, more intense slice of real life. Allen Ravenstine's 'Music Lessons' is based on his early days in Cleveland combo Pere Ubu, the days when 'Billy' (i.e. Peter Laughner) was in the band. Lester Bangs's obituary of Peter Laughner, who died at the age of twenty-four, is well-known from the Bangs anthology, Psychotic Reactions and Carburettor Dung. Ravenstine paints an equally harrowing but considerably more sympathetic

419

portrait of a man whose faith in rock & roll's redemptive qualities failed to save him from his own heart of darkness.

One Step Forward, Two Steps Back

DUNCAN CAMPBELL

The Dylan enigma has provided ample opportunity for serious spoofing, from N M E's missing 1965 Christmas album, Snow Over Interstate 80, *to Michael March's fabricated 'I Wanna Be With You' interview.* International Times's *spoof review of Dylan's 'first' post-New Morning vinyl statement, the fabled* Holy Land, *came at a time (1973) when there seemed little prospect of a genuine sequel to 1970's* New Morning.

There we stood, twenty-odd members of the music press on the sweat-dappled corner of East 55th and Madison, waiting for the promised limousines to pick us up.

'What's goin' on?' asked the wrinkled pretzel-seller eyeing the collection of satin hats, striped blazers and glitter sandals. 'This a faggots' convention or something?'

But no. We were Men – and Women, for there too on that June morning were Annie Leibowitz and Susanne Schneider – with a Mission. We had been summoned to New York a week before by an embossed invitation card coyly inviting us to 'An Historic Musical Event', a ticket and instructions had been enclosed. There were veteran reporters of rip-offs who had been flown over for Brinsley Schwartz's abortive launching; there were hood-eyed commentators who could recite you the words of 'Johnny B. Goode' backwards; and there were unimpressed slicksters who had given away their complimentary tickets to the Bowie tour. Yet they were all there, carried away by the sheer ballsiness of such a transparently exploitive come-on.

'No, man,' said Paul Gambachi of *Cream* to the little pretzel guy, in a voice loud enough to bring a shudder to the snow-capped sinuses of the rest of the musical establishment, 'we're waiting to go off and hear a preview of the new Bob Dylan album.'

Gambachi had spoken the unspeakable. For although there had been rumours – 'Dig-this-man, we're-gonna-be-hearin'-Bob's-new-one' – filtering their way through the elegant corridors of the Chelsea Hotel where we were staying, few of us had had the cool, or lack of it, to utter the words.

Now it was out. And so were we. Waiting another ten minutes for caramel-coloured limos, marked cryptically 'Zimmerman Tours Inc' to take us to the airport and off on a private plane to Hibbing, Minnesota, birthplace of Bob Dylan.

The black stewardess served Tequila Ponderosa (two shots of tequila, one of guava juice and a drop of pimento with crushed ice) as the stereo sound system blared out the soundtrack from *High Society*. We were off.

Off to a slightly over-warm welcome from Dylan's manager, Albert Grossman, chin shrouded in a new beard, stomach tucked in below an Apache-bead belt.

As we landed, the shiny limousines were absent. In their place – pick-up trucks with foam-rubber sheets at the back, under a Bombay silk canopy.

For the doubters who had been mumbling, 'Jeez, man, this is just another Columbia rip-off, man – they'll introduce us to some pimply patsy with his first album still hot from the presses,' Grossman's appearance was something of a downer.

Perhaps indeed Dylan was waiting for us. Perhaps indeed we were about to hear his latest since 'George Jackson'. Perhaps indeed we were moments away from witnessing 'An Historical Musical Event'.

Hibbing itself is no great shakes: a Holiday Inn, a bowling alley, Al's Ices and a new concrete fire station with no windows on the ground floor were all that cried for notice on the drive to the Birthplace. Jake Eriksen of *Reggae USA* was sick over the side of the second truck.

We drew up outside an unpretentious two-storey whitewood house with a small, anxiously green garden in front of it. This, said the driver of the first truck, was the birthplace of 'the finest musician and composer of the twentieth century'. Suffering as we were from jet-lag, general weariness and the effects of those mean tequilas, we were in no position to disagree.

Nor would we have done. For just at that moment, as if scripted by some over-zealous Hollywood writer, appeared one Bob Dylan.

Now I never have seen Him in the flesh before. Movies, yes. Record sleeves by the gross. Posters, a million times. But there's something awe-laden about encountering a myth in his birthplace, a legend in his womb.

Tanned from a Woodstock summer and filled out somewhat by a wife's cream-cheese-and-almond burgers, he still had that same vulnerable quality that drove a kazoo-shaped stake thru the hearts of the East Villagers in the early sixties, clad as he was in baggy white corduroy Levis, blue collarless shirt and turquoise Star of David.

'Howdy,' he said, 'we got some food and stuff inside.'

It was, I think, the only complete sentence he uttered throughout our entire four-hour visit.

Half an hour later, we were in the barn that belonged to his neighbour, Mr Andrews, gazing in wonderment at the quadrophonic sound system, the split-new speakers and Japanese Hora amps that had been mounted the better for us to hear The Album.

The Album: right, let's start at the beginning, with the song most closely related to the album's title.

'Wailing Wall' said the handout, printed in black on violet paper, featuring Al Kooper on Jew's harp, Andy Mulhone on Moog and Ken Buttrey on Drums. And away it went. It was, as became obvious after two lines, an account of Dylan's trip to Israel, poignant, slightly over-romantic, simplistic:

> We got no bouquet of roses
> For such a heavy dude as Moses
> Don't wanna die, just wanna give
> Bethlehem and Tel-Aviv

Jean-Claude Bisonnier, the only French music correspondent in the bunch, giggled slightly and we all looked the other way.

Better was to follow.

'Answer To Joanie' came booming out through the barn. We consulted our sheets to find out that Roger McGuinn was playing Mountain Dulcimer on it, along with a series of unknown (to me anyway) musicians. This was Dylan's reply to Joan Baez's plaintive song, 'Song For Bobby', in which she asked him why he was no longer politically involved. The message came through strong:

> Don't judge Quasimodo by his backbone,
> There's a heart buried deep inside
> I'm seakin'
> I'm freakin'
> But not for a place to hide

The *LA Free Press* critic applauded mildly, found no one else was doing so and tried to pretend he'd been wiping the sweat from his hands.

Track number three came on, eleven minutes of it. Ah, here was the old Dylan, here was the echo of a million articulate childhoods:

Who needs a Weberman when the body-snatcher whispers
Amen?
Who wants an eagle when a child cries out for a wren?

and, shifting into an attack on all those people who'd accused him
of being a junkie, Dylan sang,

Why should I cook my goose when someone does it for me?
Why should I saddle me up when I see skeletons before me?

The second side, as it will become when the album is finally
released in August, starts with 'Did He Fall Or Was He Pushed'.
It's a subtly political song, never pushy, never obvious, but straight
out of the 'Hattie Carrol', 'Blowin' In The Wind' genre.

Then, 'The Man In The White Suit', possibly the least musically
imaginative despite the Robbie Robertson mid-stanza riffs, which
catalogues Dylan's feelings about the Isle of Wight concert.

They wanted to see stigmata, they wanted a child grown old
They prayed for a bright slice of lightning, they craved a
stone that had rolled.

Considering that 'Sam Sam Sam' featured, according to our
notes, the Mormon Tabernacle Choir, I would have expected a
longer, more complex piece than this rerun of 'All The Tired
Horses'. This is, of course, a song about director Sam Peckinpah
in whose latest movie, shot in Mexico, Dylan stars. But I doubt if
Sam will be ecstatic about the lyrics:

Shoot a chicken through the neck
Ask your way to the nearest Aztec.

Nice bit of banjo from John Prine though.
Almost as if we had been expecting it came the next song, a

laid-back love-tribute to his wife and kids called 'Truly – In The Lap Of The Gods', which, incidentally, McGuiness Flint are bringing out as a single in a few weeks. It's simple, balladic, reminiscent of the *Nashville Skyline* album with its basic chords and hummable rhythm.

And what would be the last track, we wondered? An electric slide back to 'Leopard Skin Pill Box Hat'? A tip-of-the-hat to Woody or Johnny or Eric? The cribsheet said it had been recorded in Dynamic Studios, Kingston, Jamaica, with J. J. Cale, Al Kooper and Kendel Kardt, but we still had little idea of what to expect.

Being from this side of the Atlantic, I was able to recognize the tune before urbane *Rolling Stone* Jann Wenner, fetchingly attired, as he was, in a tartan jump suit – not that he'd been concentrating too hard; he spent a great deal of our time in Hibbing trying to get the Great Man's autograph, 'for his kid' he said.

'It's an old Irish song,' I told him.

And it was. None other than the 'Wild Colonial Boy' with a fine piece of double tracking and the most righteous of slide-guitar playing from Kooper.

And that was it. Thirty-nine minutes of the new-old Dylan: some political, some sad, some nostalgic, some plain electric. As we eased ourselves out of the waterbed-armchair comfort of Mr Andrews's barn, we could just hear the final chuckles on the album. Couldn't make out the word quite but the last one seemed to rhyme with 'suckers'.

We stepped out into the late evening to shake hands with Mr D. who had changed from his baggy cords into a pair of green dungarees and a Muscle Shoals t-shirt.

'Good t' see you, man,' he said to everyone, including the ladies, 'hope you dug it.' And off he went into the Minnesota sunset, waving wanly as we hit the trucks and headed off for our steamy flight back to New York.

There was a special *Holy Land*-by-Bob Dylan t-shirt on every seat in the plane. I sold mine for $15 to a youth in the Orange Julius on 39th Street.

Release This Album, Virgin!

APRIL FULE

The spoof review enters the punk era. NME produces a rather authenti-
cally implausible account of the 'lost' Sex Pistols live album, Anarchy
in the USA. The page-long review even fooled some people into
thinking such an artifact existed, despite the article's author – April
Fule – and its publication date, 1 April 1978.

NME has gained exclusive access to a master tape copy of what
should have been the Sex Pistols' 'memorial album' – *Anarchy in*
the USA.

It is now clear that Johnny Rotten's stop-over in New York
after the Pistols broke up in San Francisco was actually designed
to enable him to have top-level consultations with executives and
A & R men at Warner Bros., the Pistols' American label.

During this period, without the knowledge of the other band
members, was born the *Anarchy in the USA* concept, involving
live tapes from the band's shows in the States at the beginning of
January – Atlanta, Memphis, San Antonio and San Francisco.

Rotten flew back to London with the tapes. There he played
them to Virgin Records boss Richard Branson, who expressed
dissatisfaction with the sound quality. Nick Lowe, Phil Spector
and Mickie Most were apparently just three of the candidates for
remix duties, but eventually, at Rotten's request, the two of them
– Branson and Rotten – flew out to Jamaica, where they hoped to
enlist the services of a top reggae producer to knock the album
into shape.

However, Rotten's sojourn in JA was less than successful, and he arrived home in London with a set of very rough mixes.

By this time Messrs Cook and Jones had also returned home from their jaunt to Brazil, where they had laid down a couple of cuts with Rio de Janeiro's most celebrated resident, Great Train Robber Ronald Biggs. These they left with Virgin, simply as demos, but Virgin considered one track – 'Birds And Bees' – so good that they immediately added it to the *Anarchy in the USA* album.

At this point, with the album still in rough mix form – and with only Rotten, Branson and a couple of other WB and Virgin execs aware even of its existence – plans for its release went ahead. Covers were printed up (which is how *NME* landed this exclusive preview, after Warners approached photographer Joe Stevens to ask permission to use one of his shots on the sleeve), a tentative catalogue number was assigned, and a release date was set.

That date was 1 April.

But then problems set in.

First, Malcolm McLaren learned of the proposed release, and promptly slapped injunctions on it to prevent the record companies upstaging the launch he had planned for the Jones, Cook & Biggs trio. (Malcolm's plan was for the 'New Pistols' to perform their debut gig during the half-time break at the World Cup in Argentina.)

Then Virgin, so they claim, got cold feet due to the dubious quality of the mixing – which remains unresolved. Also, they decided to delay in order to avoid hurting sales on the newly released Tangerine Dream album, *Cyclone* – 'Most Pistols fans groove on the Tangs,' said a company spokesman.

Anyway, this is the 'unofficial' track listing of the Sex Pistols' *Anarchy in the USA* album:

Side 1: 'Belsen Was A Gas' (the controversial 'next' single which never saw the light of day), 'Substitute' (the Who song which was a stand-out of their earliest gigs), 'Anarchy In The USA, ('Anarchy' as we know and love it with just a title change), and 'Pretty Vacant'.

Side 2: 'Holidays In The Sun', 'Birds And Bees' (the studio track with Ronnie Biggs on vocals), 'God Save The Queen', and 'Bodies' (which disintegrates into a hail of cans and feedback halfway through).

Judging by the extremely rough mixes we've heard, it's one of the most anarchic 'official' releases ever put out by any major record company. How they ever hoped to salvage anything listenable from the sea of sirens, explosions, bleeps, crowd noises, feedback and general chaos, Rotten only knows. The whole thing sounds like they parked the Virgin Mobile outside the hall and recorded it from there – which is, in fact, what they did.

The most interesting track, of course, is 'Birds And Bees', where Ronald Biggs performs a superbly basic lyric in a toneless Cockney accent any punk singer would be proud of over an energetic, if somewhat low-fidelity backing track. The chorus – which comprises most of the song – is brilliantly incisive: 'I hate the flowers/I hate the trees/I hate the birds/And the fuckin' bees.'

So what happens now?

The famous Al Clark, Virgin's stalwart press person, had this to say: 'As Virgin Records have always maintained, we have no ongoing plans to release any further Sex Pistols artefacts in the foreseeable future. It may be true that an album by the title of *Anarchy In The USA* exists. I have also heard *Live Bollocks, Bollocks In The West, Bollocks Goes To Randy's Rodeo, Radio WB-OLLOX* and *Bollocks – What Kinda Damn Limey Talk Is That* mooted as possible nomenclatures for as-yet unheard works by Messrs Rotten, Vicious, Cook, Jones, Biggs, McLaren, Matlock, Wally and no doubt positive galaxies of session stars of the Chris Spedding ilk.

'That notwithstanding, any moves to issue any Sex Pistols record at this moment in time must inevitably be confounded by the veritable maze of legal transactions which are attendant upon the disintegration of any major rock band – and the Sex Pistols are no exception.'

Meanwhile, Virgin boss Richard Branson commented: 'Anyone trying to get a copy of this album is wasting their time. However, we do have some very nice Steve Hillage and Henry Cow albums, available for £1 off in all Virgin stores if you buy six copies of Mike Oldfield's boxed collection at the same time . . .'

In London, Warner Brothers refused to comment on behalf of their American arm – though the Yanks are supposedly most keen to get something on the market to recoup some of their enormous financial investment in the band. Their next project, apparently, is to set up a duet between Linda Ronstadt and Johnny Rotten on a well-known Jackson Browne song whose title escapes me.

When approached by *NME*, Glitterbest, the Pistols' own organization, merely commented: 'Bugger off, you stupid bunch of hacks.' Asked whether Malcolm McLaren was personally available for comment, a Glitterperson simply yelled: 'We deny that Malcolm is on the planet, OK? Let alone in bloody London!'

The Masked Marauders

T. M. CHRISTIAN

The Masked Marauders was a piss-take that became a product. Originally a fabrication of Rolling Stone's staff, the Masked Marauders album was a super session to end all thoughts of inbreeding, featuring the combined talents of that sixties 'Holy Trinity', Dylan, the Beatles and the Stones. When some wise-ass went as far as to construct a hard-copy version, the results suggested that a Masked Marauders album was far better left to the imagination of Rolling Stone's readers.

They began months ago, the rumours of an event that at first seemed hardly believable but which in the end was accepted as all but inevitable. After all, with *Grape Jam*, *Super Session*, *The Live Adventures of . . .*, *Blind Faith*, Joe Cocker's LP, Crosby Stills Nash & Young, *Jammed Together* and *Fathers & Sons*, it had to happen. Set for release later this month, the 'Masked Marauders' two-record set may evoke an agonizing tip-of-the-tongue, lobe-of-the-ear recognition in some, or cries of 'No, no, it can't be true' in others. But yes, yes it is – a treasured, xeroxed sheet of credits (which, for obvious contractual reasons, will not be reproduced on the album) and the unmistakable vocals make it clear that this is indeed what it appears to be: John Lennon, Mick Jagger, Paul McCartney and Bob Dylan, backed by George Harrison and a drummer as yet unnamed – the 'Masked Marauders'.

Produced by Al Kooper, the album was recorded with impeccable secrecy in a small town near the site of the original Hudson Bay Colony in Canada. Cut in late April, only three days were required to complete the sessions, though mixing and editing involved months of serious consultations on both sides of the Atlantic. Word has it that the cover art was intended as a 'send-up' of *Blind Faith*, but none of the principals were willing to comment on the situation.

The LP opens with an eighteen-minute version of 'Season Of The Witch' (lead vocal by Dylan, on which he does a superb imitation of early Donovan). The cut is highlighted by an amazing jam between bass and piano, both played by Paul McCartney. Then, the tone of the album is set by the next track, 'With A Little Help From My Friends' (all), followed by a very brief 'In

The Midnight Hour', which collapses in giggles and is the 'joke' of the set.

Side Two begins with an extremely moving a cappella version of 'Masters Of War', sung by Mick and Paul. You'll truly wish, after hearing this cut, that you 'could stand over their graves until you're sure that they're dead'. This is followed by an indescribable twelve-minute John Lennon extravaganza, James Brown's 'Prisoner Of Love', complete with a full ten-minute false ending. 'Don't let me be a prisoner . . . ak, ow, arrrggghhh, ooo.'

The oldies craze is not slighted; Dylan shines on Side Three, displaying his new deep bass voice with 'Duke Of Earl', Jagger with 'The Book Of Love', and John, of course, with 'I'm The Japanese Sandman'. Paul showcases his favourite song, 'Mammy', and while his performance is virtually indistinguishable from Eddie Fisher's version, it is still very powerful, evocative, and indeed, stunning. And they say a white boy can't sing the blues!

After the listener has recovered from this string of masterpieces, Side Four opens with a special treat, two songs written especially for this session: Dylan's 'Cow Pie', which is very reminiscent of Billy Ed Wheeler's 'The Interstate Is Coming Through My Outhouse' and Mick Jagger's 'I Can't Get No Nookie'.

In line with the present trend toward 'simplicity', the album nears an end with a very simple duet on acoustic guitars – George and Bob – a marvelously sensitive, yearning, melancholy exploration of 'Kick Out The Jams'. The final cut, a group vocal is, what else, 'Oh Happy Day'. This track will probably be released as a single.

All the hassles of creating a special label, of rearranging schedules, chartering planes and minimizing the inevitable 'ego-conflicts', were worth it. It can truly be said that this album is more than a way of life; it is life.

Tripping Down Blackberry Way

JONH INGHAM

Though Jonh Ingham would later make a name for himself at Sounds *as an early champion of the Pistols and punk, it was with this whimsical short story, published in a 1973 issue of* Let It Rock, *that he first hinted at an understanding of the rock & roll disease. In this cautionary tale, Ingham relates the story of Len Zeppelin and his love for English beat-combo the Move, a band who, by Len's own admission, he has never heard.*

On the first day of each month, Len Zeppelin, rushing home from high school to listen to *Disraeli Gears*, would religiously pull his battered '62 Ranchero into the Thriftmart parking-lot, rush in, grab the latest glossy copy of his favourite rock mag *Eye*, throw fifty cents in the direction of the check stand, and race to his buggy. With 'Strange Brew' familiarly filling the atmosphere as it had every afternoon for the six months he had owned the album, Len would turn to the centre of the mag for the real meat: a feature called 'The Electric Last Minute'. In neat columns with appropriate pictures was the latest rock news of the world, from Digby Diehl in Los Angeles to Nik Cohn in London. Although he read every word with reverence, he believed Nik Cohn almost to obsession. Next to San Francisco, London was the most mystical city Len could think of, and Nik managed to convey its essential swingingness with such fervour that Len almost wished he lived there, even though San Francisco was a mere three-hour drive to the north.

On one such occasion in the spring of 1968 Nik unleashed the Move into 17-year-old Len's consciousness. Some bands he would just have to read about to be a life-long fan. Thus it was with the Move. Nik so glorified them that young Len became one of their most fervid fans. Only God and the English knew what they sounded like, but with a blond singing skull and general destruction of televisions and autos on stage, who cared? And that smutty Harold Wilson postcard . . . It took Len three years' patient waiting before he found out the contents of that card, but he knew the perpetrators of a publicity stunt like that had to be a major force in the music world.

Circumstances took Len to Australia during the summer of 1968, and his mom, always taking an interest in her son's affairs, knew of his secret passion and one day brought home a record. The Record. A dark purple cover with a sloppily painted pinwheel over which was painted in atrocious psychedelia: MOVE. He didn't have a phonograph, so Len contented himself with looking at the cover for hours, imagining what the grooves must say. Did they really sing 'Zing Went The Strings Of My Heart'? It wasn't until he was home in the oven heat of Fresno, back among his blacklight posters and stacked copies of *Eye*, that he discovered his mother had forgot to pack the record. He almost threw his copy of *The Grateful Dead* at the window in rage.

Beset with these temporary set-backs he still knew that the Move was Where It Was At. Even Ralph J. Gleason said so, and he certainly knew. Len tried to explain all this one night to Marcia, his girlfriend. She didn't understand how someone could love without reservation a band they had never heard.

Hell, she thought, I bet even at his school nobody knows about them. Not even the seniors. It occurred to her that their relationship might soon have to end, but on the other hand, he always had good dope. She decided to be helpful.

'What do they look like?' Maybe one of them looked like Mick Jagger, or even Brian Jones, though she doubted anyone would ever look that beautiful.

'Ummm . . . Well, one guy's called Ace Kefford – great name, huh? – and Nik Cohn says he looks like a blond singing skull. But he freaked out and left the group.' Marcia didn't think it was a great name, and was repulsed by the concept of a singing skull. He sounded more repellent than Bill Wyman, but she kept her thoughts to herself.

'And Roy Wood – he's the leader – he looks like . . . Ummm . . . You know David Mankoff?' Marcia nodded. He was the star high school quarterback and cooked french fries at McDonald's, and was always trying to take her out. She did not like David Mankoff.

'Well, Roy Wood looks a little like him . . . very little.' Marcia rolled over in disgust. Len shrugged and turned out the lights.

He moved to Los Angeles, where the Move actually played the Whiskey, but Len was penniless, so he stood outside four nights in a row staring at the sign advertising their presence while 17-year-olds from San Fernando Valley tried to sell him reds and THC. One night in a record store he asked the proprietor whether the Move had ever released a second album and the owner replied that they had just received the first copies of it from England. A mere $5 and Len could have this freshly released bonanza *Shazam!* for his very own, but Len's old paranoia that maybe it wouldn't sound good reasserted itself (a paranoia he had never been able to rationalize – how can the Move not sound good when he's a Move fanatic?) and he opted for *Déjà Vu*. After all, CSN&Y were a known commodity. One listen, and Len wished that he had taken the Move. A year later he found a secondhand copy of *Shazam!* for 95 cents. He was surprised when he didn't like it.

By various means he acquired *Looking On* and *Message From The Country* and *Shazam!* Three years of faith justified. Later, he found 'Blackberry Way', 'Here We Go Round The Lemon Tree' and 'Fire Brigade' in a Thrifty drug store for ten cents each. It was his first experience that Nik Cohn could be wrong. Len did not like 'Fire Brigade'. He loved the other two. In fact, he played them with a regularity unpractised since *Disraeli Gears*. He picked up another copy of *Shazam!* and grew to like it, confusing though it was. He read every work he could find on the newly formed Electric Light Orchestra. Rummaging through seedy second-hand record stores, as was his wont, he came across the Move's Birmingham Brothers, the Idle Race. Len's rock & roll collector friend said the Idle Race made the best produced psychedelic album of all, and he was right. Len even spent an hour looking at the cover trying to figure out which one was Jeff Lynne.

Finally, in 1972, he moved to England. And he did see the Move, but not quite in the way expected. The English were sensible; they liked the Move so much they'd been Top 10 faves since 1967. But in the odd dichotomy of the English mind and music scene, a group that in the US were considered heavy and underground and all out rocking was here thought of as a commercial pop group trapped within the endless success of three-minute spectacles of production and technique. They were still releasing smash singles, but they hadn't performed live for ages, unless you count prime-time fandango *Top of the Pops*.

The particular Thursday we are concerned with differs from any other Thursday only in that 'California Man' is lurking somewhere in the Top 10. Len tuned in not knowing what to expect. Tonight's compère was Tony Blackburn, possibly the worst deejay in Britain, if not the world, but Len's favourite. He actually awoke just to hear Tony's 7–9 a.m. show on the radio, complete with requests, Going Steady spots, and Tony's almost encyclopediac non-knowledge of music. A morning without Tony was like an acid trip without hallucinations.

Thus it was that Tony introduced one of Len's major hallucinations. The Move. The camera opened on Jeff Lynne at the piano, decked out in his Teddy Boy best, slowly panned across the rest of the group, and the plot became clear. Tonight the Move were back in the 1950s and Roy Wood led the onslaught with the neatest DA anyone with two-foot long hair has ever managed to pin up, wailing on his glittering sax as if the spit-curled spectre of Haley was on his back. It was all clean fun of course, and maybe the studio audience understood it, even the end when Woody rolled around on his back with his horn pointed to heaven, divinely inspired 12-bar blasts coursing from the mouth, and another guy did the same with his stand-up bass, spinning it around with his winkle-pickered feet. To a surprised Len it was divine. Four years' patient waiting lacked vindication only because of the kinescope tube and the fact that all the music had been dubbed. But you can't expect everything.

Two weeks later the Move/ELO/Wizzard plans were announced, and Len foundered for a moment in the inadequacies of his own myths. He wanted to see the Move, and now they weren't ever going to play live any more. Not only that, Roy Wood was leaving the ELO to form Wizzard, which sounded suspiciously like another ELO. Len was crestfallen, but even more determined to see one of these incarnations.

He fervently scoured the *Melody Maker* each week for an ad announcing a performance from ELO/Wizzard. When notice of an ELO concert finally occurred he celebrated by dropping their record on to the phonograph, twisted the volume knob on 10, and sank back in ecstacy, oblivious to the irate pounding coming from the ceiling and walls on either side of him.

The actual event at first seemed anti-climactic. Having travelled to a somewhat obscure part of London via all available forms of public transport, he had to sit through an obscure pop group, whiling away the time by trying to discern the extent of the marvellous Art Deco architecture the proprietors of this particular pleasure palace had cunningly obliterated beneath gallons of purple paint. When the Electric Light Orchestra finally walked out Len felt a strange ecstacy coupled with a supreme sense of fulfilment and destiny. His only disappointment was that Woody wasn't present.

They sure looked weird, almost everyone bedecked in hats, one cellist in a tux with tennis shoes and a Batman-type skull cap, the other cellist surrounded by a brilliant yellow cape, Jeff Lynne condescending to the current glamour craze with a regal purple sequined codpiece surmounting his gaily striped pants. The audience, a mere few hundred, split themselves generationally, the young fanatics clustering around the stage, the older Move fans lying down in the back.

The opening few minutes practically nailed Len to the floor. More than a mere wall, the music clawed and sawed through his cerebrum and body, a steam-roller on the rampage. The cellists wandered the stage at random, handling their instruments like vertical guitars, dropping to their knees, bowing each other's cellos. The violinist stepped into the spotlight for his solos, the wandering gypsy entertaining the rich of the Ritz. Bev Bevan beat out those rhythms in the grand traditions nurtured by Ringo Starr and Charlie Watts, and the keyboardsman and bassist admirably fulfilled their duties in anonymity. Jeff Lynne stood front and centre, a kindly father watching his brood at play.

All critical and emotional response bypassed Len; he merely absorbed. Only '10538 Overture' and 'Roll Over Beethoven' produced conscious reactions; intense enjoyment on the former, amusement and appreciation of the use of Ludwig Van's glorious Ninth as an introduction to the latter. For all his fantasizing and pretense, he couldn't shake the notion that although half the Move was better than none, the fact is he was very audibly and visually reminded that this wasn't the Move, but Jeff Lynne and supporting musicians.

With heavy heart he finally acknowledged that he was once again victim of the rock & roll time, that he had missed out on the coincidence of circumstances that enables someone to see Eric Clapton with the Yardbirds or Dylan in 1965 or Elvis way back when. It seemed to Len that periodically, for short times, a certain musician or combination created an aura in his or their music and a stance that was an embodiment of the ultimate magic of rock & roll.

He had always believed that the innate quest of the music was to hit the ultimate peak and then move on. But he had no doubt that it would end popular music as we know it and everything associated with it, and probably destroy irreplaceably a lot of things in the process. That was part of the mystique. People had come so close so often and then either been destroyed by mundane interests (possibly protecting themselves) *à la* the Beatles, or else pulled away just before they shot over the cliff. There's more to motorcycle accidents than broken bones.

Len had never thought of the Move in quite these terms, but he knew it was implicitly understood by them and their musical peers, and as such affected their music. Even the audience was in on the secret, going so far as to invert excitement until James Taylor convinced them that high-decibel noises teetering on the brink of collapse wasn't really what they wanted at all. But you can only pull wool over the people's eyes for so long, and Led Zep and Black Sabbath and Slade were right there to help the kids move the fleece from their orbs to their ears.

The trouble with these pantywaist nowhere bands of recent birth, thought Len, is that they're too damn smug and happy with their feeble lot, and have no desire to see what's Over There. What they need is a good dose of acid.

A sadder Len travelled silently home, where he roamed yet again through Nik Cohn's book, cataloguing rock & roll's teenage lusts and hopes, from Johnnie Ray to the Beatles, with even a few pages devoted to the Move. Sadder, but no wiser. Now if only the Stones would come to town. He'd been waiting to see them since 1964.

You and the Boss

TAMA JANOWITZ

Tama Janowitz conceives the ultimate fan fantasy – taking the place of a rock icon's wife – and turns it into a wry little parable.

First, you must dispose of his wife. You disguise yourself as a chambermaid and get a job at a hotel where Bruce is staying with his wife on the tour. You know you are doing the right thing. Bruce will be happier with you. You are educated, you have studied anthropology. You can help Bruce with his music, give him ideas about American culture. You are a real woman.

You go into Bruce's room. His wife is lying on the bed wearing a t-shirt that says 'Number 1 Groupie' and staring straight up at the ceiling. You tell Bruce's wife that Bruce has arranged for you to give her a facial and a massage: it's a surprise. 'Isn't he sweet?' she says with a giggle.

You whip out an ice-pick hidden under your clothes and quickly give her a lobotomy: you've watched this technique in the *Frances Farmer Story* on TV. Bruce's wife doesn't even flinch.

After the operation, you present her with a bottle of Valium and an airplane ticket to Hollywood; the taxi's waiting outside. To your amazement, she does exactly what you tell her to do.

You're a bit worried about how Bruce will adjust to her absence and your presence, but when he returns to the room at three in the morning he doesn't even seem to notice the difference. You're dressed in her nightie, lying in bed, looking up at the ceiling. Bruce strips down to his jockey shorts and gets into bed with you.

'Good-night, honeybunch,' he says. In the morning he still doesn't seem to realize there's been a change in personnel.

In real life, Bruce is larger than life. Though he appears small on television and on record covers, when you stand next to him for the first time you understand that Bruce is the size of a monster. His hands are as large as your head; his body might take up an entire billboard. This is why, you now know, he must have guitars made specially for him.

At breakfast Bruce puts away a dozen eggs, meatballs, spaghetti and pizza. He sings while he eats, American songs about food. He has plans, projects. He discusses it all with his business manager: the Bruce Springsteen Amusement Park, the Bruce Springsteen Las Vegas Casino, a chain of Bruce Springsteen bowling alleys.

Bruce decides that today you will buy a new home.

You are very excited about this prospect. You imagine something along the lines of Graceland or an elegant Victorian mansion. 'I'm surprised at you,' Bruce says. 'We agreed not to let my success go to your head.'

He selects a small ranch-style house on a suburban street of an industrial New Jersey town. 'You go rehearse, darling,' you say. 'I'll pick out the furnishings.'

But Bruce wants to help with the decoration. He insists on ordering everything from Sears: a brown-and-white plaid couch trimmed with wood; a vinyl Laz-Y-Boy recliner; orange wall-to-wall carpeting. The bedroom, Bruce decides, will have mirrors on the ceiling, a waterbed with purple satin sheets, white shag carpeting, and two pinball machines. Everything he has chosen, he tells you, was made in the USA.

In the afternoon, Bruce has a barbecue in the backyard. 'Everybody's got to have a hobby, babe,' he tells you. He wears a chef's hat and has his own special barbecue sauce – bottled Kraft's, which he doctors with ketchup and mustard. Though he only knows how to make one thing – dried-out chicken – everyone tells him it is the best they've ever had. You think it's a little strange that no one seems to notice that his wife is gone and you are there instead; but perhaps it's just that everyone is so busy telling Bruce how talented he is that they don't have time.

Soon you have made the adjustment to life with Bruce.

The only time Bruce ever feels like making love is when the four of you – you, Bruce and his two bodyguards – are driving in his Mustang. He likes to park at various garbage dumps outside of Newark and, while the bodyguards wait outside, pull you into the back seat. He finds the atmosphere – rats, broken refrigerators, old mattresses, soup cans – stimulating. He prefers that you don't remove your clothes; he likes you to pretend to fight him off. The sun, descending through the heavy pollution, sinks slowly, a brilliant red ball changing slowly into violet and then night.

When Bruce isn't on tour, rehearsing with his band, recording an album, or writing new songs, his favourite pastime is visiting old-age homes and hospitals, where he sings to senior citizens until they beg him to stop. He explains that he finds it refreshing to be with real Americans, those who do not worship him, those who do not try to touch the edges of his clothing. But after a short time, even the sick old people discover that when Bruce plays to them they are cured.

The terminally ill recover after licking up just one drop of Bruce's sweat. Soon Bruce is in such demand at the nursing homes that he is forced to give it up. There is nothing Bruce can do that doesn't turn to gold. One day Bruce has a surprise for you. 'I'm going to take you on a vacation, babe,' he said. 'You know, we were born to run.' You are thrilled. At last you will get that trip to Europe; you will be pampered, you will visit the couture houses and select a fabulous wardrobe; you will go to Bulgari and grab a handful of jewels. You will be deferred to; everyone will want to be your friend in the hope of somehow getting close to Bruce.

'Oh Bruce, this is wonderful,' you say, 'where will we go?'

'I bought a camper,' Bruce says. 'I thought we'd drive around, maybe even leave New Jersey.'

You have always hated camping, but Bruce has yet another surprise – he's stocked the camper with food. Dehydrated scrambled eggs, pancake mix, beef jerky. 'No more fast food for us,' he says.

You travel all day; Bruce has decided he wants to visit the Baseball Hall of Fame. While Bruce drives he plays tapes of his music and sings along. You tell him you're impressed that he's memorized all the words. 'So what do you think?' he says. 'You like the music?'

Though your feet hurt – Bruce has bought you a pair of hiking boots a size too small – you tell him you think the music is wonderful. Never has a greater genius walked the face of the earth.

Unfortunately, Bruce is irritated by this. The two of you have your first fight. 'You're just saying that,' Bruce says. 'You're just the same as all the rest. I thought you were different, but you're just trying to get on my good side by telling me I'm brilliant.'

'What do you want from me?' you ask.

Bruce starts to cry. 'I'm not really any good,' he says.

'That's not true, Bruce,' you say. 'You mustn't feel discouraged. Your fans love you. A small boy was cured of cancer when he saw you on TV. You're up there with the greats: the Beatles, Christ, Gandhi, Lee Laccocca. You've totally restored New Jersey to its former glory. Once again, it's a proud state.'

'It's not enough,' Bruce says, 'I was happier in the old days, when I was just Bruce, playing in my garage.'

You're beginning to feel unhappy in your life with Bruce. Since Bruce spends so much time rehearsing, there is little for you to do but shop. Armed with credit cards and six bodyguards (to protect you from Bruce's angry women fans), you search the stores for some gift for Bruce that might please him. You buy foam coolers to hold beer, Smurf dolls, candy-flavoured underwear, a television set he can wear on his wrist, a pure-bred Arabian colt. You hire three women to wrestle on his bed covered in mud.

Bruce thanks you politely but tells you, 'I'm only interested in one thing.'

'Me?' you say.

Bruce looks startled. 'My music,' he says.

To your surprise you learn you are pregnant, though you can't figure out how this could have happened. You think about what to name the baby. 'How about Benjamin Springsteen?' you say.

'Too Jewish immigrant,' says Bruce. 'This kid is going to be an American, not some leftist from Paterson.'

'How abut Sunny Von?' you say.

'Sunny Von Springsteen?' Bruce says. 'I don't get it. No, there's only one name for a kid of mine.'

'What?' you say, trying to consider the possibilities. Bruce is sitting on the couch, stroking his guitar. The phones are ringing non-stop, the press is banging on the door. You haven't been out of the house in three days. The floor is littered with boxes from Roy Rogers, cartons of White Castle burgers, empty cans of Coke. You wonder how you're going to fill up the rest of the day. You've already filed you nails, studied the Sears catalogue, made a long-distance call to your mother.

At last Bruce speaks. 'I'm going to call the kid Elvis,' he says.

'What if it's a girl?' you say.

'Elvis,' Bruce says, 'Elvis either way.'

You fly to Hollywood to try and find his real wife. You finally track her down: she's working as a tour guide at a wax museum. 'Admission to the museum is $5,' she says at the door. 'The museum will close in fifteen minutes.'

'Don't you remember me?' you say. 'I'm the person who gave you a lobotomy and shipped you off to Hollywood.'

'If you say so,' says Bruce's wife. 'Thank you.'

'I made a mistake,' you say. 'I did wrong. I have your ticket here. You go back to Bruce.'

His wife is willing, though she claims not to know what you're talking about. 'But what about my job here?' she says. 'I can't just leave.'

You tell her you'll take over for her. Quickly, you rush her to the airport, push her on to the plane. You tell her to look after Bruce. 'He can't live without you, you know,' you say.

You wait to make sure her plane takes off on time. A sense of relief comes over you.

You have nowhere to go, nothing to do; you decide to return to the wax museum and make sure it's locked up for the night.

You have the keys to the door. The place is empty, the lights are off. Now you wander through the main hall. Here are Michael Jackson, Jack the Ripper, President Reagan, Sylvester Stallone, Muhammad Ali, Adolf Hitler. You are alone with all these men, waxy-faced, unmoving, each one a superstar.

Something violent starts to kick, then turns, in your stomach.

Music Lessons

ALLEN RAVENSTINE

Allen Ravenstine provided the strange synthesizer soundtracks to all but one 45 during Cleveland underground combo Pere Ubu's first fifteen years of travails. In 'Music Lessons' he relates a thinly veiled slice of autobiography about a high-school prom these avant-garde rockers were booked to play in their early days, 'when Billy was in the band'.

In those days we'd play wherever they'd let us. We were in our early twenties, still alert keyboards for the devilish fingers of adolescent heart-warp, and we thought it was not true that we were untested. We had piloted ourselves through the mazes of failed love and the temptations of the material world. We knew the realm of the spirit. We had chosen our poisons. We had learned to speak, and we were certain that our voices were endowed with something to say. We lacked only opportunity, but its arrival was foretold. There was a certain current that ran through the air around us, something that seemed to be in the light that fell everywhere we went, a vibration that ran through all of our conversations; our antennae were up and singing. It was like putting your ear to the rail, and we could hear the rumble of that train any time we bothered to listen; our time would come. It was as tangible as the modern noise we made. When it arrived, we would board with a giddiness that seemed unmanly to express, so we rode smugly in those windows with an understated arrogance that fueled all of our bad decisions. There would be a trail of goodbyes mottled with the kind of smiles that accompany the departure of a train headed for trouble, one in which the passengers are ignorant of their destination and certain of it at the same time. Those who remained on the platform were glad to be left behind. We were the lover you have to say goodbye to, the one you can't live with. And while they no doubt felt a hole opening up at the parting, one that in some cases would be a long time filling, they were glad the fighting was over. I, too, would stand waving one day, having found that the empty places in me would have to be filled elsewhere. But all of that was still a few years away, these were still the days before the record contracts and the European tours, the days when Billy was alive.

We were preparing to play at a high school, a spring celebration dance-prom of sorts. A cousin of our bass player, and student at the school, had volunteered himself to the prom committee. And in an instance where blood ties won out over common sense, he told them he knew of a good band. They believed him. We were not the kind of band that plays at a prom. But we had been told we had the job, and we did not say no to work (that would come later when we had learned to think of it as a business tactic). We pushed our equipment along the gleaming hallways whose lines and corners hummed the idiot tune of sterility. The castors left tracks in the wax and the clatter we raised echoed sharply back and forth across the polished hallways until all of the individuality was washed out of the sound and we were just a nasty noise proceeding. The lockers frowned at us from their louvers, the classroom doors turned a blank face. We were missionaries, but we had not come to appeal to the ethereal, we were not there to make promises about a better tomorrow, we were not the bearers of good news. We bore a darkness whose weight we foolishly felt was ours to wield, and we had come to share it. We were not pretty. And as those dreamy Christians had no doubt felt on their way down the rivers into the shady interior of Africa, the very ground seemed hostile, the unnaturally bright environs seemed to recede from our every step.

Billy arrived late, as he always did. For him it was a question of station, he was the guitar player and everyone knew he was a great guitar player, and it was his privilege, if not in fact his duty, to show up late. To question him on this point was to fly in the face of Rock & Roll itself. I hated Billy a good part of the time, hated him for being free of guilt, hated him for finding a life swum against the stream so easily assimilated. But when he got on stage and pulled from the guitar what was his alone to take, I forgave him everything and felt something go through me that must surely have been love of some kind. I envied him the depth of his heart, and I could not forgive him for knowing the value of that depth, nor for the way he usurped the space he felt was his. He seemed born with a sense of his true limitations and aware that within those invisible walls there were no limits.

Billy stopped the shoe with his forehead and the argument was over. He let go a burst of laughter that started and stopped as if it were wired to a switch, then he sat down on the couch with the blood running from the gash that the six-inch heel had left in his head. He took a long pull from the bottle of Jack Daniels and ripped the tab off the top of a Rolling Rock. The warm beer foamed over on to the coffee table and formed a small ringed pool when he lifted the can.

Jane got up from the living-room floor. The coat tree had missed her but in dodging it she had caught her hip on the corner of a speaker and both she and it had sprawled across the shining oak boards. She limped to the couch and sat next to Billy. Neither of them said anything. Billy slid the whiskey bottle toward her with the back of his hand.

It was three o'clock in the afternoon and life went on in its usual way. Outside the apartment delivery trucks went about their business, drivers hitting the pavement on the trot, pencils stuck in their caps, clipboards in hand with sheets to be signed. Car horns, air-brakes, and the cat-calls of hookers flagging down the cash laden lonely – no credit cards please.

In number 35 the windows were closed, the blinds were drawn. Billy and Jane kept it that way. With the windows open, the phone rang with complaints about the music, and eventually Black Dave would climb the stairs and pound on the door. Then Billy would have to look at all those gold teeth while Dave blew spit in his face and yelled about the way he had to climb all those stairs just to tell him something that he already knew. Why the hell couldn't he just take the hint when the phone rang and knock it off?

Billy opened the guitar case and lifted out the white Stratocaster. He left the loaded revolver in the well he had cut in the case. He held the guitar in both hands and pulled the lid closed with the heel of his boot. It was time for work.

The halls were suddenly bellowing with the sound of reggae music, it ricocheted from the shiny walls like hammers on tin pans, and I spun around to see Billy coming toward me with a boom-box on his shoulder, black Ray-Bans, white shirt, torn jeans, motorcycle boots, and that twisted smile. It was all in the smile, the story of a belief in a dream, a go for broke faith in illusion. A little boy who had once bought a record and found in it something that seemed more true than the trees outside his window, than the words spoken by his father, than the figures scratched on the blackboards at school. Something that would hold him for life. And out of that sound grew a need and a reason, something to do, and something to live for. The smile of a boy who never lost the joy that came from stealing the coil wire off the school principal's Buick. A smile fuelled by the lust of a dream fulfilled.

We made our way to the cafeteria and moved our gear around on the folding stage. We found our place and ran our cords. The little red lights came up on the amps and we made some noise. Everything worked, and that was all we could hope for, there were no acoustics to consider. It was not a room made for sound.

Standing at my synthesizer I looked around at the decorations. Crêpe paper hung draped from the lights like bunting. Daffodils and tulips cut from coloured paper dangled from the fixtures and bright yellow letters spelling 'Welcome Spring' clung to the wall behind me. I could see the girls from the decorating committee as if they were projected on thin air, flickering like old film, all smiles and giggles, on ladders, stretching streamers and hanging flowers. Their lips formed the shapes of letters belonging to colours and fabrics, their hands moved to show the cut of dresses, their ankles described small circles in space as they talked of shoes. I could hear them speaking of boys, rolling their eyes, and talking about what love felt like. We were in the wrong place.

I stepped down to the speckled tile floor and looked at the

stage. Sometimes, with the instruments in their stands seeming puffed-up with the breath of anticipation, the power lights winking from the amp faces like mischievous eyes, and the chrome threads in the speaker grilles gleaming in harmony with the microphone stands in the coloured lights, a stage can seem like an engine idling confidently on high octane possibility. And in those moments, while the stage purrs quietly and the crowd filters in, scooting chairs and clinking glasses, there is some comfort to be drawn against a life that sometimes seems like stealing. A kind of acknowledgement that all things are equal, that this world really is illusion, and that passion is the only logical choice. Find something that you love and let convention smother the hindmost. But standing in the accusing wash of white from the fluorescent cafeteria, it was hard to feel anything like confidence or worth. The power of those lights overwhelmed like doubt.

We went out into the parking-lot. We smoked Camels from Virginia, and marijuana from Thailand, while the energy swirled around us. We became a wire waiting to be plugged in. Billy had his own ritual, he waved off the joint as we knew he would, and leaned on the oxidizing fender of the drummer's navy blue Impala, drinking from a bottle of Jack Daniel's. He chased the whiskey with green cans of beer and dexedrine. Life never went fast enough. It was never bright enough. It was never loud enough. The tone was never quite right. The angle from which life was seen required adjustment, the mind had to be tuned just like a guitar.

Billy listened to the voices at the party and tried to think of them as just sound. He could almost hear the people in the room as if they were birds in a stand of trees and it made him smile. It was all nonsense anyway. He had filled his arm with methamphetamine before he came. It was the Cadillac of speed; the rush was like having skin for the very first time. Running his hand through his hair sent a wave of ecstasy through him that was nearly unbearable. All thoughts were brightly lit avenues that led to better places. All problems were merely puzzles sent to amuse. The seconds slowed as his heart jumped forward, leaping from each beat as if from a burning ship. The past was a useless wreck and the future, a sucker's paradise; at best it was useful as collateral against the indulgences of the present. Life ran lovingly toward death. If you felt good, then everything was all right. What other gauge was there? Billy felt fine. He took a long drink of whiskey and felt sure that everything was all right. He took the revolver from his guitar case and started firing at the wall. It was funny the way everybody got so excited. Didn't they understand that everything was all right?

We hung around in the failing light, waiting for the mercury lamps to come on and the time to arrive. We laughed too loudly and too easily. We watched the cars pull in and rollicked in sarcasm as the girls in long dresses were helped out of sombre-coloured sedans by pimple-faced boys in ruffled shirts and rented suits.

In that voice that always made me think of Drano on raw muscle, a painful rasp he was too young to possess, Billy said, 'They can't help it. That's all they know. They've just managed to believe what they've been told. That's all.' And then, like it was meant for ears closer to him than ours, he said, 'Sometimes I think it wouldn't have been so bad.' We were quiet for a second and I think he realized that we had heard him. He shook it off and smiled and said, 'But then sometimes I'm a real asshole.' We all laughed, but not with certainty.

A man in a suit that was hideously red in the mercury light crunched toward us across the gravel lot like a man walking through a bowl of cornflakes. I could feel the tension that swarmed around him as he came. His face bore a pinched expression. Here was a man who had drawn the short straw on the prom detail. Somewhere there was a TV that had his name on it, and he wanted to be there drinking down whatever it had to offer. Watching over brats and rock & roll bands on a Saturday night wasn't part of his job description.

He made an effort against the heat that was in him, and in a voice that imitated patience he said, 'Uh, are you boys ready? They're all waiting inside, I thought you'd realize that.'

'Relax, man, we saw them go in. We were just getting ready. You know, waiting for the drugs to kick in,' Billy said, and just to put the cap on it, he threw in a little machine-gun, air-guitar solo. Now it was really starting, I could feel myself go rigid.

In another light, the man's suit might have been a pedestrian brown, and in another place, his face might have been the one a child looked into for understanding. But mercury vapour, and that parking-lot, was all we had. He turned away from Billy and looked at me showing a face pumped hot with blood. 'He'd better be kidding!' he roared.

'He is,' I said and my voice was small and I wondered why he was asking me. But I knew why, like a man with a birthmarked face knows why no one's eyes ever really meet his. People are attracted to a handicap. My doubt surrounds me like a layer of strange clothing. They come to me with their rage because I will accept it. I will drink it down and let it unsettle me. I am unsure and waiting to be told. I am waiting for the lights to come up and that sure arm to come under mine and pull me away with a steady voice saying softly, 'It's all over now, son. You're coming with us.' I'm guilty, and it shows.

'Well then, let's go!' said the raging chaperone. 'And you had better not give me any trouble or I'll have all of your butts in a sling!' He turned and crunched off without waiting to see if we were following. His hands curled in and out of fists at his side like they were part of the engine that drove him.

'Chicken shit!'

I turned to see Billy looking at me, 'Oh right, like I was supposed to tell him you were serious and get us all thrown out!'

'Chicken shit.'

'You know, you were right before. You really are an asshole sometimes.'

'Chicken shit.'

We mounted the stage and the singer bowed. The crowd looked into each other's eyes, they were expecting people who looked like them. There was a low murmuring as they searched for a way to place us. We didn't wait for them, we played.

Billy turned his hands loose and lit up his guitar, he released from its strings the things stored deep in the metal and wood. The things that were his alone to find. There were sounds that moved beyond the stroke and placement of his fingers, things that happened when he didn't seem to be moving. The guitar gave itself willingly, it bent itself to what he wanted. There was power and there was release.

We told the truth as we knew it, but we didn't sing about love.

The crowd didn't let themselves move, they were waiting for the real music to start. They waited and wondered if this might be some practical joke. Maybe there was a camera somewhere, perhaps there would be a picture of those incredulous looks in the yearbook. Sure, that was it, little black and white photos with captions: 'James Oliver looks into the future and sees the tapes of his fumble at the Super Bowl', 'Mary Campbell learns of her Pulitzer Prize nomination.'

The music spilled from the stage and struggled on the floor. It danced alone there self-consciously like a gatecrasher at a country club. And then a few did hear it, they moved past the stunned and frozen and walked out to the floor. They danced and smiled and their bodies moved inside their clothes in a way that made you see how they didn't fit. These were the people we had come to play for, the ones whose parts didn't fit together in the prescribed way. The ones who look out a window and wonder if what they see is

452

what their neighbour sees. The ones who aren't sure that Maybelline and General Motors have what they want.

The others were now certain that this was no joke, that the real music was not going to start and they'd be damned if they were going to be made fools of by these misfits. They booed and hooted, and some of the boys, feeling like they had to be men and defend the sensibilities of their womenfolk, approached the stage and swore at us.

'Turn that shit off!'

'Play something we can dance to!'

With that the singer pulled the mic from its stand and screamed, 'Dance? You people don't know how to dance! I'll teach you how to dance!' He threw himself from the stage and with the true abandon of the insane he spun and tottered and writhed on the floor. He danced a reckless ballet befitting a man talking in tongues.

And then the man with the pinched face pulled the plug. Only the drums carried on, and loud as they were, they sounded small and abandoned. The singer pulled himself up and bowed. A few of the very brave applauded and were given looks by the others that foreshadowed trouble in the hallways on Monday. One of the dancers came over to my end of the stage and said, 'I loved it! Why did you stop?'

'Somebody pulled the plug on our equipment,' I said and I looked up to see the man in the brown suit. His face was purple, the chemicals of rage were shaking him in overdose.

'The police have been called! And I suggest that if you want to avoid going to jail, you get your equipment out of here just as quickly as you can! And if you think I'm kidding, just hang around and find out! I'd love to see you morons go to jail!'

'Relax, Pop,' I said. 'We're going.' My voice was not small, and I felt a sort of peace. I was like a radio tuned to some other frequency. This small man's purple anger was firing right past me, off to waste itself in some other space. I stood looking at him, but not really seeing him. I was inside myself noting the absence of his rage in my stomach. He walked stiff-legged toward the hallway like a man in search of reinforcements.

Billy looked up from packing away his guitar, smiled at me and said, 'Chicken shit.'

We left that room as brothers, bonded loosely by the trappings of renewed exile. It was not to last. There was no life-line in Billy's hand. Soon he would be consumed by paranoia, fear would become a second skin. He would find himself sleeping in hotels because the apartment was too well known. He would change hotels two and three times a night because the law was almost on him. He would break into a parked car that he knew to be full of listening devices even though at the same time he knew it was all in his head. He was telling himself it was all in his head as he broke out the window and unlocked the door. He was telling himself it was all in his head as he pulled the seats apart.

He started bringing the gun to rehearsals. He'd lay it on top of his amp as part of setting up, like it was another piece of his equipment. He took up a spot in the corner away from the windows and facing the door. He drank constantly and vacillated between sullen silence and animated chatter. Sometimes he was funny, something resembling his old self, and we embraced these moments like drowning men, laughing quickly and trying to keep the conversation rolling on a parallel course. But his attention was fickle, and he drifted away from us with lightning speed, launching into near mystical tirades about the FBI agents who were following him and had the ability to disappear when they turned sideways.

It took a long time to work up the courage to ask him to leave, but when the time finally came, there wasn't much of a response. He looked around the room at us for a moment, then he packed his guitar case and walked out. He never said anything.

He disappeared for a while after that. When he surfaced, he was worse. The enemy was everywhere. He was arrested for setting a tree on fire. He was convinced that the pine cones were cleverly disguised microphones. I don't think there was anything we could have done.

He was twenty-four when he died. Heart failure. There are just so many beats and Billy had used them up. He had been living at home, no one else would have him. His mother found him in the morning when she went to wake him for breakfast. He was lying where he had fallen from the bed, face down in the deep pile carpet. She rocked him in her arms while she waited for the ambulance. Looking into his purple face, she saw only a small boy.

Two days after the funeral, a record label called from London, they had heard the tapes we made, they wanted to know if we had someone to represent us. They wanted to make a deal, and by the way, who was this guitar player?

'He's dead,' I said. There was a long pause, I thought we had been disconnected, and I was about to hang up when the voice said, 'I'm sorry, did you say he was dead?'

'Yes, his name was Billy and he's dead.'

'I'm very sorry to hear that. Did this just happen? Should I call back another time?'

'No need to, it's been going on for a long time. We have another guitar player, and we're writing material.'

A few months later I was watching my breath turn to steam as I read the names and messages left by Londoners hiding from Hitler's blitz in the chalk caves of Chislehurst. I was waiting for the fans to arrive on the buses that were bringing them to the 'Mystery Gig'. Waiting for showtime.

It had been magical and incomprehensible to watch the English countryside appear through the clouds from the windows of a jet.

Seven hours of noise and darkness and then we slid beneath the clouds and England came up to meet us. There were limousines at the gate and interviews at the BBC. It never seemed real and it moved quickly.

We spent two or three months in England and Europe every year for ten years after that. There were rainy nights in Berlin, spent stumbling through the shiny darkness looking for a perfect Martini. There were soccer games with Hungarians in the pre-dawn streets of Paris. There was a drunken boat in the Baltic Sea; the deep bell tones of ice breaking under the hull, the automated arc-lights sweeping the darkness from the bridge, while below on the restaurant deck reeling drunks watched *Laverne and Shirley* with something like true reverence. There had been the colliding rhythms of weaving street bands in the snow-lit alleyways of Zurich at carnival time. The steel-toothed Russians in Budapest who told us, 'We know your music in Russia, you must come to play, but not in Moscow, nobody plays in Moscow. You must come with us to Siber, the snows and the trees of Siber, this is where you must play.' Their dentures were made by them with hammers, their eyes were focused on places that only vodka can take you. But most of those years I don't remember, most of them are deep in an alcoholic haze.

I wore myself close to the surface, and played the sounds that seemed to echo what I felt. Maybe it was the subconscious knowledge of a world clinging to a precipice, a faint memory of the Sword of Damocles, a vision of the Iron Curtain. I don't mean the political animal, but the nightmares of a child born into a world described in those terms. I was a young man contending with mustang emotions in a landscape moulded by a vision of men with their fingers poised over the button; the red phone in the White House; the backyard bomb shelter. The sun came and went and with it went the days of school and the concepts of career and family. The spectre of the bomb stayed on and on. Life around the water cooler; how was I supposed to take that seriously? Who could have looked at what had been done and said, 'Yeah, cash me in for some of that too!' No, the only sensible path was one of resistance, but it, like life itself, went against the laws of physics, and it stood to reason that a price must be levied. Loneliness and alienation? Those were just the parking fees, the real price was pain, a subtle, invading, mercurial pain, a thing that infected your brain, a thing that became the surface on which your heart stood, and it needed to be ministered to.

I poured alcohol on the pain, dusted it with cocaine, inflated it with marijuana and opium, and in the end I decided I liked it. I decided it was the box from which creativity flowed. I decided it was the fate of the artist. I took it into my arms like a lover and I pulled it to me, I forgave it everything. As I have done with no other thing, I accepted it unconditionally. And like a man with a game leg, I moved on.

8. The Biz

"Perhaps a little unwisely, Colonel Parker has decided to try and carry on Elvis' work."

A record company is there to market records – not dictate terms.
(Johnny Rotten after A&M had just sacked the Sex Pistols)

There is no pretence of objectivity in this chapter, which is an unasham-edly jaundiced look at the music biz and, more pertinently, its relation-ship with the rock & roll punters. Not surprisingly, the biz has always maintained an ambivalent attitude to rock music and particularly the rock consumer, fickle and fiercely suspicious of the industry as he has generally proved to be.

And while the industry repackages its past in spruced-up 3- or 4-CD anthologized sets, pock-marked with the occasional rarity to prise loose the presidents from collectors, mittens, coffee-table rock dominates the airwaves with interminable Classic Rock radio stations all spewing out the message that rock died when peace, love and understanding went out the window. Meanwhile, the weight of the industry is exerted against the few thousand who seek alternatives like home taping and the purchase of bootlegs, rather than consider what aspects of consumer demand they are failing to satiate. Welcome to the machine.

While the industry has pressed for legal powers so that it may operate its own form of censorship – not just the exclusive right to release product by artist X but the ability to tax anyone who uses blank tape just in case it might be used to record copyrighted material – it has shown a distinct lack of will when required to stand tall against the most recent manifestation of America's deep-rooted puritan-ism, the PMRC (Parents' Music Resource Center), a rather innocuous euphemism for Small-minded Bigots Inc., something Frank Zappa, in his statement to Congress, holds up to some truly righteous ridicule.

461

The Rock & Roll Liberation Front?

JOHN MORTHLAND AND JERRY HOPKINS

With the benefit of hindsight it seems astonishing that rock fans took until 1969 to follow the lead of their blues brethren and begin bootlegging their more cultish artists. This detailed article, from the days of Rolling Stone *in-depth investigations, provides an enormous amount of information about the beginning of what has become a veritable hive of hot wax.*

Even as Columbia Records was going to court to prevent further bootlegging of Bob Dylan's *Great White Wonder* album, two more bootleg Dylan LPs and an amazing live Rolling Stones album were being made available on the black market. And, according to bootleggers, you can expect to find Dylan's Isle of Wight concert with the Band in your local record store any day now.

If the fact that the bootleggers have a release schedule now seems to indicate that their 'business' is stabilizing, it's only illusory. For everybody's getting into the act, and people are going out and buying an 'underground' album, then pressing a few thousand copies for themselves. All five albums on the market today are being distributed by at least three different producers, and competition is driving the price down.

In fact, bootlegging was just getting to be a damned lucrative business when KSAN-FM in San Francisco put the word out over the air that the underground albums are shucks, with a life span of, maybe, twenty playings. The top layer of vinyl is very cheap, KSAN claims, and the needle scrapes it off pretty quickly. The result is nothing but a grating scratchy noise through the speaker, and probably a damaged needle. The cheap vinyl is also full of bubbles.

Some people are finding this true of the bootlegged albums they bought; others claim to have played the records many times more than that with no ill effects. With so many new 'distributors' playing the bootleg game, it could well be that some of them are, indeed, inferior products.

It all started late last summer, when two LA freaks put out the *GWW* set, a double album consisting of unreleased Dylan tapes originally recorded in a Minneapolis hotel room in 1961 and a Woodstock basement (with the Band) in 1967, plus one song copped directly from the TV set, when Dylan sang on the Johnny Cash show. Quality of the tapes was poor, but the album still sold well, especially on the West Coast. There soon followed the *Troubled Troubador*, which duplicated some of the material already being bootlegged, but added some new songs as well.

Columbia believes it has caught up with the producers of the *GWW* set. Attorneys for CBS, Dylan and Dwarf Music teamed up to get a restraining order in the US District Court here which prohibits further manufacture and sale of all Dylan material. Four persons and a suburban Gardena pressing plant were named in the court order, each charged with violating the Federal Copyright Act, 'unfair competition and unjust enrichment'. The underground Stones album – aptly titled *LIVE r Than You'll Ever Be* – is actually a major coup for the bootleggers. Recorded live at the Forum in LA and the Oakland Coliseum, it is one of the finest albums of 1969. For a bootleg, the sound quality is excellent. It is so far superior to the Stones' legitimate live LP that comparisons are unfair.

Although the Chuck Berry composition 'Little Queenie' is the only song not available on a London-released album, the undergrounder is selling well enough and is available in large enough quantity that the price has dropped almost a dollar since it first came out during the Christmas season. The album is put out on 'Lurch Records' and the Stones are identified only as 'The Greatest Group on Earth'.

The Dylan album put on the black market just in time for Christmas shopping is called *Stealin'*, and by January there were at least three versions being sold – some with labels (Har-Kub Records), some without; some with a rubber-stamped title, some without even that much identification. Much of it is of excellent sound quality, seeming to consist of alternate takes of songs appearing on either *Bringing It All Back Home* or *Highway 61 Revisited*. Columbia spokesmen are especially incensed over this album, since they believe these tracks were stolen right out of their vaults.

And the week after Christmas, still another Dylan album was made available, this one called *GWW John Birch Society Blues*. This one also duplicated some songs on other underground Dylan, but presented new material as well.

For a while, a recording of the Plastic Ono Band's concert at Toronto was being bootlegged. However, Apple scotched that by releasing *Live Peace In Toronto*, featuring John and Yoko with friends including Eric Clapton.

Thus, the underground record scene, at the turn of the decade, has become a noticeable industry. Not so big Columbia or London Records or anyone else has any real fear of being knocked off, but large enough to warrant a flurry of angry retaliatory activity in the offices of Dylan's manager and the Stones' manager and lawyers for their record and music publishing companies.

Columbia has been the only one to get results, though, and those only of the bootleggers on the first Dylan album. And it wasn't easy tracking them down. The original producers of that album had reportedly split to Canada, taking with them the proceeds from an estimated 8,000 albums, one step ahead of the draft. Supposedly, they purchased a gas station there.

Apparently one of them gave the bootleg business some second thought, though, and he returned to Los Angeles – only to find others had jumped aboard, duplicating the original *GWW* and selling at least 40,000 copies. For the moment, he remained out of sight.

By then, of course, Columbia and Dylan and Dwarf Music were involved, assigning the case to attorneys on both coasts and employing private detectives to conduct a full investigation. The story they pieced together is fascinating, and the major characters are two of those subsequently named in the court order, Norton Beckman, owner of Norty's Discount Records, and Ben Goldman, owner of Do-Re-Mi Records, both of them small shopkeepers in the Fairfax district of Los Angeles. Apparently they were the ones who'd copied the original *GWW*, evidently making a tape from a bootlegged album one of them had purchased from the people who started all this. This was in early September.

According to affidavits filed with the US District Court, Beckman then took the tape to Austin McCoy, who runs AMC Audio Engineering out of his rather nondescript home in downtown LA. He was to make the acetates – which would be used to manufacture the metal disks called 'mothers' or 'masters' which in turn were to be used to produce the 'stampers', which were finally used to press the records sold in retail stores. McCoy said Beckman told him he was the rightful owner of the tapes; the acetates were made, and Beckman was charged $161.76.

The acetates then went to the James Lee Record Processing Company in nearby Gardena, where the 'mothers' and 'stampers' were made. Gardena is one of several dozen anonymous communities in Los Angeles, memorable mostly for its countless all-night poker parlours, and James Lee is one of the many record processors in the city who asks no questions. 'We've had lots of stuff come through here that's later turned up stolen or dirty, but we don't know that,' an employee said. 'We don't play the records when we get them, because if we do that we have to be responsible.' The masters cost $12.50 each, the stampers $9.

From Lee the masters and stampers went to S&R Record Manufacturers, also in Gardena. S&R is a pressing plant, and it was here the finished copies of *GWW* were made and then stuffed into plain white album sleeves, ready for delivery to retail stores all over the country. In a show of generosity, apparently Beckman and Goldman even authorized the slight additional cost of shrink-wrapping the albums – wrapping the unmarked package in Cellophane.

Meanwhile, a private detective named Richard Dunn was surveying Los Angeles area record shops. The company he worked for, Raymond Boyd and Associates, had been employed by John Faughnan, chief of security for Columbia Records. They'd been told to find out everything they could. Dunn said in an affidavit that he visited 45 stores and had seen copies of *GWW* in 23 of them; he suspected they were being sold 'under the counter' in several others.

But in so far as Columbia determining who the bootleggers were, none of this was especially useful. If the shopkeepers weren't worried about displaying the records openly, they still weren't talking to strangers. Most didn't know the names of the bootleggers anyway.

The break in the case finally came when someone in the Columbia A&R department in Los Angeles got an anonymous phone call from a woman who said she knew who the bootleggers were. She told Mrs Sandi Spidell that the guys on Columbia's most wanted list were Beckman and Goldman, and, as a matter of fact, if Columbia really wanted to see something, they could go down to S&R in Gardena and watch the albums coming off the press. Thousands of them.

Mrs Spidell was so astonished and excited that she hung up on the woman. The woman called back to explain why she had called in the first place. Beckman and Goldman had been bad-mouthing some friends of hers, she said, saying they were the guys who were bootlegging the Dylan LP. Not true, she said, and she hung up.

Columbia sent another of its private eyes, Pete Brito, to Norty's Discount Records to take a picture of Norton Beckman. He then started with S&R and worked his way back through the production companies involved, using the picture to identify Beckman as the man who had *GWW* produced. (It was determined that at each step, Beckman had used an alias, Gerald Feldman – the third name listed in the court order.) The private eye also saw all those albums coming off the press, and told S&R that Columbia thought they were breaking the law and they'd better stop. S&R, owned by Anastacio and Ofelia Sapian, told Brito they'd stop when a court told them to, and no sooner.

It was getting very legal now. The plea for a restraining order said Beckman and Goldman and all the others have 'wrongfully appropriated and exploited for their own benefit, the artistry, labour, expenditure and skill of Dylan . . .' It was, the brief said, 'a simple case of piracy of Dylan's private musical performances for defendants' profit, and a brazen disregard of the Copyright Act provisions respecting recording licenses, copyright royalties and elementary fair play . . .' Not only that, but 'defendants have caused and are causing great injury to plaintiff Dylan . . .'

They also asked for $20,000, saying this was the smallest amount that could be figured against loss of income and goodwill, and said this figure would be amended.

Judge Harry Pregerson waded through the pleas and affidavits (the file was fully two inches thick) and signed the restraining order. Norty Beckman, his neighbourhood pal Ben Goldman and S&R Records were told to stop fooling around. So was Michael 'Dub' Taylor, a third individual named in the court order. Trouble was, Columbia's private eyes couldn't find Taylor.

'The truth of the matter is we aren't even sure who he is,' said Columbia's lawyer in Los Angeles, Thomas J. Ready. 'We think he was one of the youngsters to start this thing, to make the first *Great White Wonder*. But that's speculation on my part. We haven't been able to serve him with papers. We understand he's left the country.'

But three out of four isn't bad. And apparently the action taken was paying off. Norty Beckman and Ben Goldman refused to talk to the press in early January – two weeks after the court order – but a woman who identified herself as manager of Norty's Record Store told a customer, 'They told us to stop selling. We stopped, just as simple as that. Maybe I scare easy, but the way I see it, I'm David and they're Goliath. Who needs it?'

She apparently had forgotten how that Biblical story ended, but there were no bootleg records on display in her shop that day. Nor were there any in Goldman's a mile or so away. And a similar action by Columbia, this one instituted in Canada against International Record Corp Ltd., the Canadian distributor of *GWW*, was also successful, with the defendant agreeing to 'cease and desist'.

By now, the underground Stones album had been released. At first, it was available only in small numbers. Shortly after Christmas, most stores on the West Coast had sold out. Suddenly, it became available again in larger quantities than ever before, and a price war ensued.

In the Bay Area, Leopold's, the non-profit record store owned and operated by Berkeley students, got it first. In fact, they were told that they'd have it exclusively by the LA distributors who supplied them. But one other store in Berkeley got it immediately (200 copies), another a week later, and pretty soon a Palo Alto store and one in San Francisco were handling it as well.

Over a two-week period, Leopold's had received about 1,600 copies of the Stones album. They had planned to hold on to them all until they had saturated their market, and then start shipping them out wholesale to other stores in Northern California.

Leopold's had also been the prime Berkeley outlet for *Great White Wonder*. They had sold about 3,000 copies at prices ranging from $6.67 down to $5.24 after paying $5 to $3.50.

They got the Stones album from the same distributor who supplied them with *Great White Wonder*. Shortly after receiving the Stones LP, Gervich and a couple others took a few copies over to KSAN in San Francisco, which hadn't yet received a copy. And who should be there but Sam Cutler, road manager for the Stones on their recent US tour. 'Cutler listened to it and really dug it, the sound, the music and everything. He bought a copy from us, then bought five more for each of the Stones. So we ended up selling the Stones their own album,' Gervich laughed.

Other stores in Berkeley weren't taking the matter quite as lightly. One manager, who had stocked everything he could get his hands on, had been told by his Columbia sales representative that he should be expecting a letter in the mail pretty soon. The sales rep didn't give any hints about what the letter would say, but the store owner assumed it would be a cease and desist order.

And at Discount Records in Berkeley, manager Don Ellis was saying, 'Our policy is not to sell the bootlegs. We sold *Great White Wonder* for a while, because I really hadn't thought about it. Like, all I could think about was, wow, it's Dylan, and I really didn't think about the moral question. Then some Columbia attorneys came in the store and asked me if I realized what I was doing. The artist should have some say about what's released, and he should get paid.'

Discount Records is owned by CBS. Ellis said there was no coercion on the part of Columbia attorneys, but that they just convinced him selling bootlegs was a bad idea. 'When I see it now, I know it's bad,' Ellis added. 'This will make the artist afraid to appear in public. It's bad for him to play around.'

On 20 December, the Stones album turned up in Chicago. Noel Gimble, owner and manager of seven record stores there, was doing good business with them. He'd sold about 1,000 copies of *Great White Wonder* at $9.95, and cleared his shelves of 2,000 Stones albums at $5.50 each.

'I do a service to my customers, if you want to look at it that way,' Gimble said, 'because I can make more money off a normal record. These are a headache in a way. I can't exchange them, I don't know who I'm dealing with, it's getting out of hand. It's a bit of a touchy subject here. My distributors are concerned, but really pretty easy-going. They know it won't re-occur to a great proportion. It's not the kind of item I can keep restocking.'

By early January, the prime movers of *LIVE r Than You'll Ever Be* were willing to speak openly, but anonymously, about their business. A young man with long hair and a full beard, one of the partners, said the whole operation started in New York about two weeks before Christmas. He and a friend bought 5,000 copies back East at $2.50 each, plus shipping charges, with the understanding that they'd have an exclusive on the record in the LA area.

'There's really nothing exciting about this,' one of them remarked. 'It's just an ordinary operation, cut-and-dried.

'Do you really think the Stones miss the money we're making? Whatever we take out of their pockets, we're doing as much for them in terms of publicity and interest in their music. The word moral doesn't apply. It's a matter of get what you can, and when someone else pops up copying our stuff, we do what we can to get more product at less cost. Maybe that's what the big record companies should do – compete with us. They weren't going to release this material anyway, were they?'

At Sam Goody's largest record store in the East, executive buyer Sam Stolen said, 'We wouldn't buy them. We're a public company which isn't allowed to buy such an album. We wouldn't sell them at a nickel apiece. The dealer is as responsible as the manufacturer.'

Village Oldies, however, moved about 200 copies of *Great White Wonder* at $4 or $5 each. *Stealin'* went for $6 even though a single album, because the quality was much better. They sold 50 copies. At the House of Oldies, *GWW* went for $15, about the highest price in the country; they sold a three-record set (including *Troubled Troubador*) for $25. These two store managers have been told by their distributors that they have access to unlimited numbers of the Stones album if they want it, but both refused to sell it.

One customer in a New York store said he'd bought a cassette recording of the Beatles' as-yet-unreleased album, *Let It Be*, when he was in Miami for the pop festival.

One of the producers of the *Stealin'* album was interviewed by John Carpenter of the *Los Angeles Free Press*, and afterwards refused all further press contact. 'Some of these songs are better than the shit that Columbia has released,' the bootlegger said. 'They just keep sitting on them, so you might say, in a sense, we're just liberating the records and bringing them to all the people, not just the chosen few.'

Among the songs 'liberated' are new versions of 'It Takes A Lot To Laugh, It Takes A Train To Cry', 'She Belongs To Me', 'It's All Over Now, Baby Blue', and 'Love Minus Zero No Limit' (misidentified on the label as 'My Love Waits Like Silence').

Considering what these albums cost to produce, the new capitalists are doing pretty good for themselves.

Talking with salesmen at record pressing plants in Los Angeles – where there are more than fifty, probably more than anywhere else – a clear picture is formed. In a run of anything over, say, 3,500 records, cost per record shouldn't top thirty-five cents, and that could include blank labels and record sleeves, if the 'capitalist' is charming and persuasive enough. The price they get for their albums also depends on how charming and persuasive they are.

'It's a bargaining thing,' said Emanuel Aron of Aron Records in LA. 'I'm dealing with five or six different people now, and they ask whatever they think they can get. It's always a cash and carry thing anyway. They don't leave a phone number. If I ask them what if I run out, they say they'll be stopping by occasionally, they'll keep me supplied, not to worry. The hell of it is, some of them are juggling tapes; they're taking the same tapes and mixing them up, including some songs on one album, some of the same but some different on others, and selling them as different LPs.

471

They are different, of course, but only slightly. The odd thing is, it doesn't seem to matter. They all sell. I've sold hundreds of everything I can get.'

Making bootlegging even more attractive is the anonymity that seems to accompany it. (So long as you don't make any enemies, as Beckman and Goldman apparently did.) It is, for example, extremely difficult to trace a product back to a pressing plant. Many believe the catalogue or matrix numbers etched into the wax near the centre of the record tell an educated observer which pressing plant was involved, but this isn't true. The numbers normally are used only for internal record-keeping and besides that, on most of the bootleg records issued thus far, there are no identification numbers present at all.

Nor is it difficult for a bootlegger to find someone who will press his records for him. Competition is stiff in most cities, and it often seems merely to be a matter of working one's way through the yellow pages under Phonograph Records – Whlse & Mfrs – to find a promising pressing plant.

Besides that, the laws which supposedly protect an artist from this fate are archaic. According to Brian Rohan, a San Francisco attorney who handles several rock groups, the worst that can happen is that the bootleggers and record stores will be enjoined by the courts from continuing their trade. If they refuse to cease and desist, they can be held for contempt of court. The plaintiff can also sue, as Columbia has done, for the amount of money they think they lost. This figure, Rohan said, is usually 'just picked out of the air', since the companies can't really set a precise figure. And to sue each record store for their sales would only amount to a couple hundred dollars per store, which probably wouldn't cover court costs. To prevent any store from bootlegging at all, each store has to be enjoined separately.

'It's like trying to stamp out a bunch of ants,' Rohan stated. 'It's worth more to the companies and artists in publicity and glamour than they could get back in money. Anyhow, it's not widespread enough to made a dent.'

Hence, Columbia's and now London's problems in stopping the bootleggers. Columbia spokesmen take the position that bootlegging doesn't hurt the company at all in terms of sales (which seems to be true, at least at Leopold's), but does hurt the performers and composers because they lose out on royalties. Also because they have a right to determine which material is fit for release. It's all a matter of the audience's respect for the artist, they say. London, the Stones' label, won't even say that much, referring all inquiries to Allen Klein and Abkco, who likewise refuse comment.

Several record store managers, however, say that they've been told by Columbia sales representatives that sales are hurt by the bootleg album. And in light of Rohan's statement, it becomes more than just a question of the audience's respect for the artist, but also a question of to what lengths the record companies are willing to go to protect their artists. It seems fairly obvious that outside of Dylan, the Stones and the Beatles, this type of bootlegging would be unprofitable, due to lower demand for the product.

In Los Angeles at the moment, things are 'hot', and most pressing plants are asking callers to come in for a chat and then checking tapes and credentials if it seems there is anything dodgy about one's motivation and 'company'. Many bootleggers are, as a result, turning to the East Coast, where they are finding companies perhaps less profitable, but certainly less inquisitive. Some say this is the beginning of the end – that New York and New Jersey have always been headquarters for the counterfeit-Mafia-bootleg business, and that the kids are being sucked into it. Others say this is bullshit.

The fact that the records themselves may be defective may take the record companies off the hook, for if it costs too much to get a durable product, bootlegging of even the big three groups may be unprofitable. No one would be in on it then except the burn artists, and record-buyers would get hip to them pretty quick. That would solve everything. Meanwhile, record stores on the West Coast have been promised Dylan's Isle of Wight performance around mid January, some unreleased Beatles material shortly thereafter . . . and that, bootleggers say, is just the beginning.

Money: Rock for Sale

MICHAEL LYDON

'Money doesn't talk, it swears.' Discuss in 5,000 words or less. Cometh the counter-culture, cometh the conundrum: how to take the cash and retain integrity. Lydon confronts the issue head-on, unimpressed by gestures of sixties solidarity.

In 1956, when rock & roll was just about a year old, Frankie Lymon, lead singer of Frankie Lymon and the Teenagers, wrote and recorded a song called 'Why Do Fools Fall In Love?' It was an immediate million-selling hit and has since become a rock classic, a true golden oldie of the sweet-voiced harmonizing genre. The group followed it up with other hits, starred in a movie, appeared on the *Ed Sullivan Show*, toured the country with Bill Haley and the Comets, and did a tour of Europe. Frankie, a black kid from Harlem, was then thirteen years old. Last year, at twenty-six, he died of an overdose of heroin.

Despite the massive publicity accorded to rock in the past several years, Frankie's death received little attention. It got a bit more publicity than the death in a federal prison of Little Willie John, the author of 'Fever', another classic, but nothing compared to that lavished on the break-up of the Cream or on Janis Joplin's split with Big Brother and the Holding Company. Nor did many connect it with the complete musical stagnation of the Doors, a group which in 1967 seemed brilliantly promising, or to the dissolution of dozens of other groups who a few years ago were not only making beautiful music but seemed to be the vanguard of a promising 'youth culture revolution'.

In fact these events are all connected, and their common denominator is hard cash. Since that wildly exciting spring of 1967, the spring of *Sgt Pepper's Lonely Hearts Club Band*, of be-ins and love-ins and flower power, of the discovery of psychedelia, hippies and 'doing your thing' – to all of which 'New Rock', as it then began to be called, was inextricably bound – one basic fact has been consistently ignored: rock is a product created, distributed and controlled for the profit of American (and international) business. 'The record companies sell rock & roll records like they sell refrigerators,' says Paul Kantner of the Jefferson Airplane. 'They don't care about the people who make rock or what they're all about as human beings any more than they care about the people who make refrigerators.'

Recently, the promoters of a sleazy Southern Californian enterprise known as 'Teen Fair' changed its name to 'Teen Expo'. The purpose of the operation remains the same: to sell trash to adolescents while impressing them with the joys of consumerism. But nine years into the sixties, the backers decided that the fifties image of nice-kid teenagerism had to go. In its place, they have installed New Rock (with its constant companion, schlock psychedelia) as the working image of the 'all new!' Teen Expo.

By the time the word gets down to the avaricious cretins who run teen fairs, everybody has the message: rock & roll sells. It doesn't make money just for the entertainment industry – the record companies, radio stations, TV networks, stereo and musical instrument manufacturers, etc. – but for law firms, clothing manufacturers, the mass media, soft drink companies and car dealers (the new Opel will 'light your fire!'). Rock is the surest way to the hearts and wallets of millions of Americans between eight and thirty-five – the richest, most extravagant children in the history of the world.

From the start, rock has been commercial in its very essence. An American creation on the level of the hamburger or the billboard, it was never an art form that just happened to make money, nor a commercial undertaking that sometimes became art. Its art was synonymous with its business. The movies are perhaps closest to rock in their aesthetic involvement with the demands of profitability, but even they once had an arty tradition which scorned the pleasing of the masses.

Yet paradoxically it was the unabashed commerciality of rock which gave rise to the hope that it would be a 'revolutionary' cultural form of expression. For one thing, the companies that produce it and reap its profits have never understood it. Ford executives drive their company's cars but Sir Joseph Lockwood, Chairman of EMI, the record company which, until Apple released the Beatles' records, has always admitted that he doesn't like their music. The small companies like Sun and Chess Records which first discovered the early stars like Elvis Presley and Chuck Berry were run by middle-class whites who knew that kids and blacks liked this weird music, but they didn't know or really care why. As long as the music didn't offend the businessmen's sensibilities too much – they never allowed outright obscenity – and as long as it sold, they didn't care what it said. So within the commercial framework, rock has always had a certain freedom.

Moreover, rock's slavish devotion to commerciality gave it powerful aesthetic advantages. People had to like it for it to sell, so rock had to get to the things that the audience really cared about. Not only did it create a ritualized world of dances, slang, 'the charts', fan magazines and 'your favourite DJ coming your way' on the car radio, but it defined, reflected and glorified the listener's ordinary world. Rock fans can date their entire lives by rock; hearing a 'golden oldie' can instantaneously evoke the whole flavour and detail of a summer or a romance.

When in 1963–4 the Pop Art movement said there was beauty in what had been thought to be a crass excretia of the Eisenhower

Age, when the Beatles proved that shameless reveling in money could be a stone groove, and when the wistful puritanism of the protest-folk music movement came to a dead end, rock & roll, with all its unabashed carnality and worldliness, seemed a beautiful trip. Rock, the background music of growing up, was discovered as the common language of a generation. New Rock musicians could not only make the music, they could even make an aesthetic and social point by the very choice of rock as their medium.

That rock was commercial seemed only a benefit. It ensured wide distribution, the hope of a good and possibly grandiose living style, and the honesty of admitting that, yes, we are the children of affluence: don't deny it, man, dig it. As music, rock had an undeniably liberating effect; driving and sensual, it implicitly and explicitly presented an alternative to bourgeois insipidity. The freedom granted to rock by society seemed sufficient to allow its adherents to express their energies without inhibition. Rock pleasure had no pain attached; the outrageousness of Elvis's gold lamé suits and John Lennon's wildly painted Rolls Royce was a gas, a big joke on adult society. Rock was a way to beat the system, to gull grown-ups into paying you while you made faces behind their backs.

Sad but true, however, the grown-ups are having the last laugh. Rock & roll is a lovely playground, and within it kids have more power than they have anywhere else in society, but the playground's walls are carefully maintained and guarded by the corporate élite that set it up in the first place. While the White Panthers talk of 'total assault upon the culture by any means necessary, including rock & roll, dope and fucking in the streets', *Billboard*, the music trade paper, announced with pride that in 1968 the record industry became a billion-dollar business.

Bob Dylan has described with a fiendish accuracy the pain of growing up in America, and millions have responded passionately to his vision. His song 'Maggie's Farm' contains the lines, 'He gives me a nickel, he gives me a dime, he asks me with a grin if I'm having a good time, and he fines me every time I slam the door, oh, I ain't gonna work on Maggie's farm no more.' But along with Walter Cronkite of the New York Yankees, Dylan works for one of Maggie's biggest farms, the Columbia Broadcasting System.

Mick Jagger, another adept and vitriolic social critic, used rock to sneer at the 'under assistant west coast promotion man' in his seersucker suit; but London Records used this 'necessary talent for every rock & roll band' to sell that particular Rolling Stones record and all their other products. For all its liberating potential, rock is doomed to a bitter impotence by its ultimate subservience to those whom it attacks.

In fact, rock, rather than being an example of how freedom can be achieved within the capitalist structure, is an example of how capitalism can, almost without a conscious effort, deceive those whom it oppresses. Rather than being liberated heroes, rock & roll stars are captives on a leash, and their plight is but a metaphor for that of all young people and black people in America. All the talk of 'rock revolution', talk that is assiduously cultivated by the rock industry, is an attempt to disguise that plight.

Despite the aura of wealth that has always surrounded the rock & roll star, and which for fans justified the high prices of records and concerts, very few stars really make much money – and for all but the stars and their back-up musicians, rock is just another low-paying, insecure and very hard job. Legend says that wild spending sprees, drugs and women account for the missing loot; what legend does not say is that most artists are paid very little for their work. The artist may receive a record royalty of two and a half per cent, but the company often levies charges for studio time, promotion and advertising. It is not uncommon for the maker of a hit record to end up in debt to the company.

Not surprisingly, it is the black artists who suffer most. In his brilliant book, *Urban Blues*, Charles Keil describes in detail how the blues artist is at the mercy of the recording company. It is virtually impossible, he states, for an unknown artist to get an honest contract, but even an 'honest' contract is only an inexpensive way for a company to own an artist body and soul.

A star's wealth may be not only non-existent, but actually a fraud carefully perpetuated by the record company. Blues singer Bobby Bland's 'clothes, limousine, valet and plentiful pocket money', says Keil, 'are image bolsterers from Duke Records (or perhaps a continual "advance on royalties" that keeps him tied to the company) rather than real earnings.' And even cash exploitation is not enough; Chess Records last year forced Muddy Waters to play his classical blues with a 'psychedelic' band and called the humiliating record *Electric Mud*.

Until recently, only a very few stars made any real money from rock; their secret was managers shrewd to the point of unscrupulousness, who kept them under tight control. Colonel Parker molded the sexual country boy Elvis into a smooth ballad singer; Brian Epstein took four scruffy Liverpool rockers and transformed them into neatly tousled boys-next-door. 'We were worried that friends might think we had sold out,' John Lennon said recently, 'which in a way we had.'

The musicians of New Rock – most of them white, educated and middle class – are spared much of what their black and lower-class counterparts have suffered. One of the much touted 'revolutions' that New Rock has brought, in fact, has been a drastic increase in the power of the artists *vis-à-vis* the record company. Contracts for New Rock bands regularly include almost complete artistic control, royalties as high as ten per cent, huge cash advances, free studio time, guaranteed amounts of company-bought promotion, and in some instances control over advertising design and placement in the media.

But such bargaining is at best a futile reformism which never challenges the essential power relationship that has contaminated rock since its inception. Sales expansion still gives the companies ample profits, and they maintain all the control they really need (even the 'revolutionary' group, the MC5, agreed to remove the word 'motherfucker' from an album and to record 'brothers and sisters' in its place). New Rock musicians lost the battle for real freedom at the very moment they signed their contracts (whatever the clauses) and entered the big-time commercial sphere.

The Doors are a prime example. Like hundreds of New Rock musicians, the four Doors are intelligent people who in the early and mid sixties dropped out into the emerging drug and hip underground. In endless rehearsals and on stage in Sunset Strip rock clubs, they developed a distinctively eerie and stringent sound. The band laid down a dynamo drive behind dramatically handsome lead singer Jim Morrison, who dressed in black leather and, writhing with anguish, screamed demonic invitations to sensual madness. 'Break on through,' was the message, 'yeah, break on, break on through to the other side!'

It was great rock & roll, and by June 1967, when their 'Light My Fire' was a number one hit, it had become very successful rock. More hits followed and the Doors became the first New Rock group to garner a huge following among the young teens and pre-teens who were traditionally the mass rock audience. Jim Morrison became rock's number one sex idol and the teenyboppers' delight. The group played bigger and bigger halls – the Hollywood Bowl, the garish Forum in Los Angeles, and finally Madison Square Garden last winter in a concert that netted the group $52,000 for one night's work.

But the hit 'Light My Fire' was a chopped-up version of the original album track, and after that castration of their art for immediate mass appeal (a castration encouraged by their 'hip' company, Elektra Records), the Doors died musically. Later albums were pale imitations of the first; trying desperately to recapture the impact of their early days, they played louder and Morrison lost all subtlety: at a recent Miami concert he had to display his penis to make his point.

Exhausted by touring and recording demands, the Doors now seldom play or even spend much casual time together. Their latest single hit the depths; *Cashbox* magazine, in its profit-trained wisdom said, 'The team's impact is newly channeled for even more than average young teen impact.' 'Maybe pretty soon we'll split, just go away to an island somewhere,' Morrison said recently, fatigue and frustration in his voice, 'get away by ourselves and start creating again.'

But the Doors have made money, enough to be up-tight about it. 'When I told them about this interview,' said their manager, Bill Siddons, sitting in the office of the full-time accountant who manages the group's investments (mostly land and oil), 'they said, "Don't tell him how much we make".' But Siddons, a personable young man, did his best to defend them. The Doors, he said, could make a lot of money if they toured more often and took less care in preparing each hall they play in for the best possible lighting and sound; none of the Doors lives lavishly, and the group has plans for a foundation to give money to artists and students ('It'll help our tax picture too'). But, he said, 'You get started in rock and you get locked into the cycle of success. It's funny, the group are out there on stage preaching a revolutionary message, but to get the message to people, you gotta do it the establishment way. And you know everybody acquires a taste for comfortable living.'

Variations of the Doors' story are everywhere. The Cream started out in 1966 as a brilliant and influential blues-rock trio and ended, after two solid years of touring, with lead guitarist Eric Clapton on the edge of a nervous breakdown. After months of bitter fighting, Big Brother and the Holding Company split up, as did Country Joe and the Fish (who have since reorganized with several replacements from Big Brother). The Steve Miller Band and the Quicksilver Message Service were given a total of $100,000 by Capitol Records; within a year neither one existed in its original form and the money had somehow disappeared.

Groups that manage to stay together are caught in endless conflicts about how to make enough money to support their art and have it heard without getting entangled in the 'success cycle'. The Grateful Dead, who were house and bus minstrels for Ken Kesey's acid-magical crew and who have always been deeply involved in trying to create a real hip community, have been so uncommercial as to frustrate their attempts to spread the word of their joyful vision.

'The trouble is that the Grateful Dead is a more "heard of" band than a "heard" band,' says manager Rock Scully, 'and we want people to hear us. But we won't do what the system says – make single hits, take big gigs, do the success number. The summer of '67, when all the other groups were making it, we were playing free in the park, man, trying to cool the Haight-Ashbury. So we've never had enough bread to get beyond week-to-week survival, and now we're about $50,000 in debt. We won't play bad music for the bread because we decided a long time ago that money wasn't a high enough value to sacrifice anything for. But that means that not nearly enough people have heard our music.'

The Jefferson Airplane have managed to take a middle route. A few early hits, a year of heavy touring (150 dates in 1967), a series of commercials for White Levis and the hard-nosed management of entrepreneur Bill Graham, gave them a solid money-making popular base. A year ago they left Graham's management, stopped touring almost entirely, bought a huge mansion in San Francisco and devoted their time to making records (all of them excellent), giving parties and buying expensive toys like cars and colour TVs. They've gone through enormous amounts of money and are now $30,000 in debt. But they're perfectly willing to go out and play a few jobs if the creditors start to press them. They resolve the commercial question by attempting not to care about it. 'What I care about,' says Paul Kantner, 'is what I'm doing at the time – rolling a joint, balling a chick, writing a song. Start worrying about the ultimate effect of all your actions, and in the end you just have to say fuck it. Everybody in the world is getting fucked one way or another. All you can do is see that you aren't fucking them directly.'

But the Airplane also profess political radicalism, and, says Kantner, 'The revolution is already happening, man. All those kids dropping out, turning on – they add up.' Singer Grace Slick appeared in blackface on the Smothers Brothers show and gave the Black Panther salute; in a front window of their mansion is a sign that reads 'Eldridge Cleaver Welcome Here'. But Kantner said he hadn't really thought about what that meant: would he really take Cleaver in and protect him against police attack, a very likely necessity should Cleaver accept the welcome? 'I don't know, man, I'd have to wait until that happened.'

Cleaver would be well advised not to choose the Airplane's mansion for his refuge. For Kantner's mushy politics – sort of a turned-on liberalism that thinks the Panthers are 'groovy' but doesn't like to come to terms with the nasty American reality – are the politics of the much touted 'rock revolution'. They add up to a hazy belief in the power of art to change the world, presuming that the place for the revolution to begin and end is inside individual heads. The Beatles said it nicely in 'Revolution': 'You say that it's institution, well, you know, you better free your mind instead.'

Jac Holzman, president of Elektra Records, said it in business-man's prose: 'I want to make it clear,' he said, 'that Elektra is not the tool of anyone's revolution. We feel that the "revolution" will be won by poetics, and not by politics – that poetics will change the structure of the world. It's reached the kids and is getting to them at the best possible level.'

There is no secret boardroom conspiracy to divert antisocial youthful energy into rock and thus render it harmless while making a profit for the society it is rebelling against, but the corporate system has acted in that direction with a uniformity which a conspiracy probably could not have provided. And the aware capitalists are worried about their ability to control where kids are going: 'There is something a bit spooky, from a business point of view,' a *Fortune* issue on youth said recently '. . . in youth's widespread rejection of middle-class lifestyles ("Cheap is in") . . . If it . . . becomes a dominant orientation, will these children of affluence grow up to be consumers on quite the economy-moving scale as their parents?'

So the kids are talking revolution and smoking dope? Well, so are the companies, in massive advertising campaigns that co-opt the language of revolution so thoroughly that you'd think they were on the streets themselves. 'The Man can't bust our music', read one Columbia ad; another urged (with a picture of a diverse group of kids apparently turning on): 'Know who your friends are. And look and see and touch and be together. Then listen.' We do.

More insidious than the ads themselves is the fact that ad money from the record companies is one of the main supports of the underground press. And the companies don't mind supporting these 'revolutionary' sheets; the failure of Hearst's *Eye* magazine after a year showed that the establishment itself could not create new media to reach the kids, so squeamish is it about advocating revolution, drugs and sexual liberation. But it is glad to support the media the kids create themselves, and thereby, just as it did with rock, ultimately de-fang it.

The ramifications of control finally came full circle when *Rolling Stone*, the leading national rock newspaper, which began eighteen months ago on a shoestring, had enough money in the bank to afford a $7000 ad on the back page of *The New York Times*. Not only was this 'hip rock' publication self-consciously taking its place among the communication giants ('NBC was the day before us and *Look* the day after,' said the 22-year-old editor), but the ad's copy made clear the paper's exploitive aim: 'If you are a corporate executive trying to understand what is happening to youth today, you cannot afford to be without *Rolling Stone*. If you are a student, a professor, a parent, this is your life because you already know that rock & roll is more than just music; it is the energy centre of the new culture and youth revolution.' Such a neat reversal of the corporate-to-kids lie into a kids-to-corporate lie is only possible when the kids so believe the lie they have been fed that they want to pass it on.

But rock & roll musicians are in the end artists and entertainers, and were it not for all the talk of the 'rock revolution', one would not be led to expect a clear political vision from them. The bitterest irony is that the 'rock revolution' hype has come close to fatally limiting the revolutionary potential that rock does contain. So effective has the rock industry been in encouraging the spirit of optimistic youth take-over that rock's truly hard political edge, its constant exploration of the varieties of youthful frustration, have been ignored and softened. Rock musicians, like their followers, have always been torn between the obvious pleasures that America held out and the price paid for them. Rock & roll is not revolution-ary music because it has never gotten beyond articulation in this paradox. At best it has offered the defiance of withdrawal; its violence never amounting to more than a cry of 'Don't bother me.'

'Leave me alone; anyway, I'm almost grown'; 'Don't step on my blue suede shoes'; 'There ain't no cure for the summertime blues'; 'I can't get no satisfaction': the rock refrains that express despair could be strung out forever. But at least rock has offered an honest appraisal of where its makers and listeners are at, and that radical, if bitterly defeatist, honesty is a touchstone, a starting point. If the companies, as representatives of the corporate structure, can convince the rock world that their revolution is won or almost won, that the walls of the playground are crumbling, not only will the constituents of rock seal their fate by that fatal self-deception, but their music, one of the few things they actually do have going for them, will have been successfully corrupted and truly emasculated.

1973: A Year in Singles

SIMON FRITH

Simon Frith has been one of the few successful rock critics to maintain a resolute balance between sociology and genuine enthusiasm for the Music. His analysis of 1973's single releases in the UK provides a damning indictment of the wastefulness of the industry, while also reminding the reader that the product not the process counts!

Now that nostalgia's a way of life, I've begun to remember how much I disliked all those old records. The reason I never bought the Searchers' 'Sugar And Spice' was that it was so tedious and, eight weeks running on the new Jimmy Savile oldie show, it still is. But I did get a buzz from it the first week and I remembered it note perfect. And that's the thing about singles – there's no escape. Even if you only buy albums and carefully avoid Radio One, you've still got to negotiate pubs and shops and football matches. And never go public dancing. And only go to certain select parties. I don't think it's possible. There's no way to avoid the current Top 20 except in a nunnery. I've never had to listen to ELP or Yes or any of the other progressive prophets but I've suffered 'Eye Level' at least thirty times already and, like it or not, it's now part of the experience of 1973. Hit singles, whatever the sales trends and the profit figures, are still the essence of pop culture.

Singles can become important for us whether we like them or not; the problem of a 45 is not just whether (and why) it's good, but whether (and why) it's a hit. 'Eye Level' was released in November 1972 – few people knew, no one bought it. A year later it was number one – the same music but different significance. And what interests me is not whether it's a good record (it isn't) but why and how it became popular. Because a hit record emerges from a long process of selection – by record companies of what they will release and promote, by D Js of what they will play and plug, by customers of what they will buy. It's not a simple matter of aesthetics or commerce or taste or fashion but a complicated mixture of all these things. The process is usually obscured – by nostalgia which takes hits as given, by critics searching for histori-cal significance, both uninterested in how hit selection works. Which is the point of this piece.

The year I've taken is 1 September 1972 to 31 August 1973. For most singles buyers this is how the year works – around education. It's September which means a new year, new class, school, college. The music business reflects this rhythm; tailing off during the summer, launching records and groups and tours in the autumn. Any isolation of a year is artificial but this seems less arbitrary than taking the usual January to December.

The most extraordinary thing about the singles market is how many there are. In 1972–3, 2,941 singles were released; 57 or so new records were available every week. And the supply was constant, faltering only over Christmas and (to a lesser extent) during July and August. It's a lot of shit and very little sticks: 6 per cent, 180 records, three new hits a week. Why do they bother?

It varies from company to company; not all records are aimed at the charts. There are specialist markets: kids (Disneyland released 14 singles), country-lovers and brass band enthusiasts (labels like Nashville and Waverley), train-spotters and soul freaks. With relatively few promotion costs these markets can be big enough for profits – even if the records don't get hit status. Trojan and its associate labels issued at least 200 singles and only four were hits; presumably the reggae market is big enough to make Judge Dread-style success a nice perk but not a necessity. The same is true for the various hard-soul labels – Contempo (23 releases), Stax (19 releases), Mojo (2 hits from 28 releases); soul success is measured not by immediate sales but by the long-term habits of discos and disco dancers. All in all about a sixth of the year's singles weren't released or promoted with chart success in mind; these records weren't expected to and didn't become pop music.

Another group of singles is released to be popularly heard but not necessarily sold; the records are album trailers, advertisements. EMI, for example, are the English distributors of several US rock labels – Neighborhood, Fantasy, Asylum, Signpost, Dot/ Paramount – and released 55 of their singles. None of them were hits but few of them were promoted to be hits. The point was to get them heard, to get people interested in the artists concerned, to sell albums. This attitude lies behind the singles policy of all the self-consciously rock labels, whether big American – like WEA (15 hits from 184 releases) and CBS (15 hits from 266 releases) – or small British – like Island (4 hits from 26 releases) and Charisma (one hit from 14 releases). A high proportion of the 45s they release were made and conceived as album tracks; the best thing about the occasional single success, about a Carly or a Paul Simon, is the effect it has on album sales. I calculate that another sixth of a year's singles are album tracks, album trails. Sometimes chart success will be pushed for as part of the overall sales strategy; mostly, though, these releases are routine, token, like a couple of weeks' full page ads in *NME*.

Remove specialist and promo records, and we're left with two-thirds of a year's supply of singles aimed at pop chart success – about 2,000 records in 1972–3. There were 180 hits and some of these strayed in from other markets; in short taking pop singles alone, the success rate is about one in eleven. What this means for profits I don't know, but success certainly isn't distributed evenly.

The most successful labels were Bell (16 hits from 69 releases), MGM (8 hits from 33 releases), Rak (7 hits from 21 releases) and Tamla Motown (12 hits from 46 releases). It's clear that in the singles business a company getting a hit from every five releases or less is doing extraordinarily well; one in ten is just fine (Jonathan King's UK label, for example, had 4 hits from 37 releases); the big companies get by on considerably less. Take EMI. The Columbia/Parlophone/EMI labels managed 6 hits between them, from 166 releases; Capitol added one hit from 33 releases, Regal Zonophone one from 23. EMI's single profits seemed dependent on its distribution deals – with Tamla, Rak, Apple (5 hits out of 7) – and (thanks to Roy Wood) its progressive label, Harvest (3 hits from 21 releases). It was the same pattern at Decca – good old Decca got only 5 hits from 98 releases, MAM and UK got as many hits from half the number of records; and progressive Deram label got 4 hits from 36 releases, while 69 MCA/UNI singles were issued without any success whatsoever. At Phonogram the Philips/Fontana labels had 2 hits from 117 releases and the company's singles success was based on its distribution of American labels – Avco, Westbound etc. – 5 hits from 27 releases; Pye had one hit from 99 releases (plus one from 13 on Dawn); Polydor had 9 hits from 127 releases, UA 2 hits from 100. Of the big companies, only RCA (14 hits from 153 releases) and A&M/Ode (7 from 65) did respectably.

Various things emerge from these figures. First, the single sales of most record companies are based on the continuing appeal of very few artists – MGM's eight hits were all by the Osmonds. And if a success rate of one in eleven is normal and acceptable, then a company doesn't need many stars. RCA did OK simply because they had the Sweet and David Bowie; Polydor did less well because although they had Slade, the New Seekers didn't repeat the sales of the previous year; DJM released 52 singles, but their three hits were all from Elton John. The implications of this are obvious: for most record companies what's important is to produce and sell an act, an image, and not just a record – in the long run it's easier to run a star with assured sales than to have to work on a series of one-offs.

The second revelation of the statistics is that the companies that did worst in 1972–3 were the English pop giants – EMI and Decca, Philips and Pye. The traditional record biz was definitely out of touch; this was reflected by the equally poor results of all the old-fashioned independents: Chapter 1, no hits from 16 releases: Dart, no hits from 23 releases; York, no hits from 35 releases; President, no hits from 27 releases; Penny Farthing, no hits from 18 releases. These companies were out of touch with the pop market, misjudging taste, unable to sell.

Compare the year's successes, Bell and Rak in England, Tamla and the Phonogram group of US labels. All these companies work on a policy of releasing a limited number of carefully chosen records and giving all of them a solid push. The exact market is decided in advance and determines the sales approach. To quote Dick Lehy of Bell: 'The first essential factor, of course, is selection of product. I hope we know what records to reject. We don't go picking up product just for the sake of it – we always first ask "who is going to buy it?" If we can't answer that question we don't release the record.'

Having decided who is going to buy, the only problem is to make sure they do, and techniques vary from market to market. Cassidy and the Osmonds were sold through magazines, Glitter and the Detroit Emeralds through discotheques. Listen to Radio Luxembourg, and Pye and Decca and EMI are pushing a different record every week, in time-honoured fashion. By contrast, UK with Shag and 10CC, Bell with Barry Blue, Phonogram with Limmie and Family Cookin', got hits by plugging away for months.

The object of record companies is to defy the uncertainties of mass taste; to produce certain hits. The most certain hit is the new release of a big star – RCA have been able to rely on Elvis for years – and the major concern of all companies is to produce stars first, records second. Beyond that the record business has traditionally tried to ensure success by working to formula (imitating other hits, other stars) and by releasing a sufficient range of material that something must sell. The 1972–3 success of newer record companies reflected a more sophisticated attempt at certainty, a more calculated attempt at giving the public what it wants. Bell's policy, for example, was based not on an indirect measure of taste (previous hits and sales) but on a direct investigation of who buys records, what for, where from. What did they find?

Everybody knows that only kids buy singles. I don't know how they know 'cos I've never seen the market research figures published, but the charts reveal some other things. Old-fashioned, grown-ups' pop survives – Shirley Bassey and Perry Como got their usual hit, the Eurovision Song Contest (Anna-Marie David) and *Opportunity Knocks* (Peters and Lee and Stuart Gillies) had their usual success. If kids were buying these records it was as Mum's birthday present and throw in Elvis and Cliff while they're at it. And there's always room for a good tune and a tidy act on television – Gilbert O'Sullivan and Blue Mink and the New Seekers, the Carpenters, Dawn and Olivia Newton-John. Or a novelty. Lieutenant Pigeon, the Royal Scots Guards. These sorts of record are a permanent fixture in the British pop mind. A Place Must Be Found For Them. In 1972–3, 27 places and the year's football song, 'Nice One Cyril'.

Elsewhere were weeny boppers; eight hits for the Osmond Family, four for the David Cassidy/Partridge Family, five for the Jackson Family – though I'm not sure how much of the Jacksons' appeal was weeny. The pictures and posters were there but they're also good to dance to.

And danceability is still the determinant of most hits. In 1972–3 there were two movements on disco floors – to smooth American soul and to rough British stomp. The soul revival was sharp and sweet – 31 hits – but mostly of a particular kind of soul: smooth, the blues edges blunted, carefully produced emotion, quiet voiced – Harold Melvin and Billy Paul, New York City and the Detroit Emeralds, the O'Jays and the Stylistics. Gamble/Huff, Thom Bell,

Stevie Wonder and his electric piano, are the masters now. Intricate and subtle music for intricate and subtle dancing.

The English stomp (47 hits) is different; crude and brash music for crude and brash dancing. It's built on strong foundations. Slade (four hits) football rock – stamping feet and chanted lyrics, crowd music, scarf swaying with Noddy and Geordie and Gary Glitter, who pared the style down to its elements; the T. Rex (four hits) boogie – bass plus guitar and bongo beat, sexy, monotorock; and the David Bowie (four hits) glamour – wisps of green hair, an arrogant ponciness leaning against the door with baggy pants, a cocked finger and the Rolling Stones beat. Mix Slade, T. Rex and Bowie and get Chinn and Chapman, who ruled 1972 OK. Mud from nowhere; Suzi Quatro, the first female number one for five years; Sweet above all, 'cos they're in on the joke and you can prance and preen and stomp and sway to them *all at once*.

This was the market that the *knowing* labels tapped – Tamla and Phonogram provided the soul, Rak and Bell and UK the stomp. Discos were gayer and brighter than the year before. Few reggae records and predictable taste and most things sound good if they're loud enough. It isn't difficult to give the public what it wants, decide what it wants, even. How else do you explain Shag and Kenny and Barry Blue? The most interesting disco hits were Wizzard and 10 CC because they weren't so easy, so calculated, but came from private obsessions; both groups carry their own weight. The other British stompers know the fun, the excitement, the violence, even the green hair, belong to the kids. It's their exhilaration, and the records sound in the background as gestures, walls the dancers put up around themselves. New years, new steps. Glitter rock and glam rock and all the trends won't last because the same dance gets boring. But it was the sound of 1972–3, there's no denying. Are you ready for your good memories of Gary Glitter, c. 1984?

For dance hits, easy-listening hits, it's the context that counts.

The customer may set the scene, but if you can place your record right – Phonogram in discos, MAM on TV shows, Philips on *Opportunity Knocks* – then you're in with a chance. Product and promotion, available and appropriate. Phonogram push their soul records to a network of key DJs, reward chart success with free albums; the English entry into the Eurovision Song Contest is a guaranteed hit as the BBC's plug of the year. The records that for a casual Radio One listener seem to come from nowhere actually come from very specific situations – Peters and Lee schmaltz, Limmie and Family Cookin's magic. But there's another group of hit singles – forty odd in 1972–3 which don't come from the dance floor or the TV screen. Which people buy because they've heard them on the radio – the radio doesn't play them because they've been bought. Which people dance to because they're there – they weren't made for people to dance to. Mainstream pop. A hotchpotch and a rag-bag of a year's singles with no obvious market or place or use except as nice records to play on the radio.

It's this group of hits that is the most difficult to explain. Record companies release them with great uncertainty. They depend for success on Radio One plays. They reveal the vagaries of public taste. Some I can understand – the latest records of established stars, the various Beatles, the Who and Roger Daltrey, Elton John, the Faces and Rod Stewart and Python Lee Jackson (which certainly wasn't a hit when it was first released, pre-Rod-fame, in 1970). Some hits are a spill-over from (or a spill-into) the album market – Paul Simon, Cat Stevens, Focus, Roxy Music. But there remain the incomprehensible hits – incomprehensible not because they aren't good records ('You're So Vain' and 'God Gave Rock'n'Roll To You'), but because equally good records, equally played, weren't hits. Why, for example, was Lou Reed's 'Walk On The Wild Side' a flop first time out and a smash hit six months later?

One way into this question is to survey the records that weren't hits despite (radio) availability. Some things then become clearer; there's a limited market for weeny wonders – no joy for Rick Springfield or Marty Kristian, let alone Jonathan King's unplayed stable; the BBC prefers to stick with old artists, long after they've lost a mass appeal, and only the biggest acts keep a mass appeal through thick and thin – the Kinks, Tremeloes and Dusty Springfield haven't; similarly, the BBC will always push a follow-up even though the public is resistant to being sold the same sound twice – Jimmy Helms, Peter Skellern; American easy-listening is difficult to break without the necessary TV backing – Helen Reddy's 'I Am Woman', for example; there's presently no large market for continental grand gloom – Joe Brown's 'Hey Mama' – for reggae (tough on Jimmy Cliff), for instrumentals or Californian sunshine.

And then some records (I can't keep up this detachment for ever) were just plain bad – CCS, Raw Holly's 'Raining In My Heart', 'Don McLean's 'Dreidle' offered no incentive to anyone to buy them. Something else I hadn't realized is how often an artist/style/sound needs to be heard on two or three records before it breaks as a hit – Stealers Wheel, Geordie, Clifford T. Ward. The last two are especially sad cases. Both recorded unsuccessfully on John Peel's Dandelion label, both are doing nicely now – for Polydor and Charisma.

All this manic categorization still leaves me unable to account for the failure of the following fine records:

'Anything' by Al Green
'Night' by Frankie Valli
'I Saw The Light' by Todd Rundgren
'Living Next Door To Alice' by New World (even M. Most's touch falters)
'Free Ride' by Edgar Winter
'Drift Away' by Dobie Gray (which got the Radio One push twice)

(and I'm surprised, though less sorry, at the failure, despite weeks of exposure, of the Sutherland Brothers' 'You've Got Me Anyway', Steely Dan's 'Do It Again' and Blue's 'Little Jody').

All I know is that these records moved me, enough to buy them. Which was my contribution to the hit selection process, and brings me to two final points. First, one of the joys of singles, of the Radio One/Jukebox/Disco razzmatazz, is the tension between what you like and what everyone else likes, the public struggle between your taste and everyone else's. There are hundreds of singles that no one ever hears – on radio, TV or dance floor. They might be brilliant and they might as well not exist; pop music is what you do hear, not what you could or should hear. Secondly, I have treated singles throughout this article as the industry treats them – as products, profits, figures on balance sheets. But somewhere in this process are musicians and their music. The reason I bought 'Drift Away' and 'Free Ride' and 'Night' and my other single favourites of the year was because I liked the music. And even though it's important to know how records reach you, how they are released and promoted, marketed and distributed, once they've gone through this it's down to you. And the music. And that raises a whole lot of other questions.

The Man Can't Scotch Our Taping

PETER TITUS

The record industries on both sides of the Atlantic spent much of the eighties attempting to institute a blank tape levy. Titus, in this 1982 article from New York Rocker, *picks his targets well and provides a considered defence of the consumer's rights and the need to ensure that 'home tapers' do not become a generic scapegoat for the industry's own wastefulness, ineptitude and greed. It remains a live issue, as recent attempts to impose a levy on digital (DAT) tape serve to illustrate.*

To guard music creators from the 'serious threat' posed by audio home taping, the US record industry has hit the war-path with a red-white-and-blue crusade called 'Save America's Music'. Their goal: an across the board surcharge on blank tape and recording equipment. Because this tax may cost music consumers hundreds of millions more dollars a year, it's worth taking a hard look at the SAM battle plan, who it really serves, and how.

Home taping, it is charged, threatens the diversity and abundance of American music; the copyright system which promotes this cultural wealth; and the 'well being of a major industry contributing to the economy of the United States'. Not surprisingly, the last point takes top priority in SAM literature.

As put by Stanley Gortikov, silver-haired president of the Recording Industry Association of America: 'Last year our industry sold the equivalent of 475 million albums. But at the same time, about 455 million albums were home-taped. So for about every album we sold, one was taped. One for one! In our hen-house, the poachers now almost out-number the chickens.'

Coming as it does from those making money off music, the charge of 'poaching' may puzzle some readers. They are referring to a 1980 home-taping survey taken by Warner Communications, one of the poachees.

According to this study, 52.5 million Americans currently buy blank tapes and use about 75 per cent of these tapes to record music at home. Since consumers shell out about $609 million for these tapes, record executives draw an angry conclusion: 'We believe that, at the very least, consumers would have spent this $609 million on pre-recorded product had they been unable to home tape.'

This hand-wringing has a broader social context. Like the rest of the US economy, the record business has been hit with a wicked slump. Sales leveled off last year at about $3.6 billion, while some 55 million fewer units were shipped than the year before. The Savers, however, never mention recession politics. All their fire is directed at renegade tapers, and it's backed up by Congressional action in Washington.

Legislation is now pending that would require the Copyright Royalty Tribunal to determine 'fair compensation to copyright owners'. The fee in question would be payable by importers and manufacturers of blank tape and recording equipment, to be held by the government for distribution. Those entitled to a share of these funds could file a claim with the Tribunal.

Exactly who gets what is still undetermined. Considering the murky world of copyright ownership, it may never be very clear. Presumably, major music publishers like Warner Communications, a principal SAM backer, would benefit handsomely. In any case, the likeliest distribution formulas will reflect ongoing chart action and airplay, with the lions' share going to established hit-makers. The legislation also bans record rentals unless sanctioned by the copyright owner.

For pop fans, the overriding issue is restricted access to musical variety, since the immediate effect of the surcharge will be an increase, probably substantial, in the cost of tape decks and blank cassettes. All but the rich will face new budget-related constraints.

Of course, as industry strategists know, it's hard to argue with the idea of a fair return to copyright owners for use of their work. What they fail to address, however, is the reason for the rise of home taping in the first place. Understanding this issue leads to a whole nest of unsavoury problems for the Save America drum-beaters.

The price of pre-recorded music has exploded. Pre-recorded cassettes jumped 52 per cent over eight years, and in '79 averaged $7.70 list. LPs rose 74 per cent over the same period, according to

RIAA figures, and today cost about the same as tapes. The price tag on singles has doubled.

These increases occurred as the industry developed big savings through new manufacturing technologies and wholesale roster and staff cutbacks.

The results of the larger consumer survey from which Warner's home-taping study is compiled found that virtually none of the 2,700 people questioned thought pre-recorded music cost 'too little' and most, 58 per cent, thought it was too high.

The incredible thing is that it is considerably cheaper to tape at home, on equipment bought at retail prices, than to buy comparable music pre-recorded. With vastly more efficient manufacturing abilities, the industry should in all reason be able to provide a much cheaper product and still have plenty left over to pay healthy royalties to performers, composers and producers. Virtually no other commodity in America has been so overpriced as to drive people into home production on this scale.

It is only surprising that larger numbers have not done so. According to figures provided by SAM itself, 75 per cent of all music tapers do so 'most often' for reasons other than to avoid a purchase. These reasons range from making copies for use in automobile tape decks, to preserving the quality of recordings, to the sheer fun of creating one's own program. It is probably the weight of these numbers, in fact, that keeps the industry from demanding an outright ban on blank-tape technology.

Furthermore, the figures ballyhooed by the industry ignore the substantial amount of taping – documented in the Warner survey – that people do from records they already own. Accounting for these uses of blank tape would lower the number of so-called 'poached' albums from Gortikov's 455 million by a factor of some 80 million units per year.

For concerned observers, this type of statistical gerrymandering should sound an alarm. This is important because clouds of florid rhetoric surround SAM's economic points. Once alerted, it's easy to see gaping holes in their born-again logic. Following are a few glaring examples from Save America literature:

> 'The huge losses to the record industry have already reduced the diversity of music available to consumers. In the past three years, new releases have declined by one third.'

Actually, far from contributing to the decline of diversity, home taping has opened the doors for many to expand their access to music. On the other hand, the trend toward fewer new titles stretches back twenty years, not just the past 'home taping' period. Between 1963 and 1978, new releases declined by almost 50 per cent, while the record industry grew sixfold in terms of units shipped. The logic of this process is simple: because of the economics of mass production and distribution, fewer numbers of larger-selling titles are many times more profitable than large numbers of smaller selling releases.

This sobering fact may not sit well with the Savers because it flies in the face of the notion that what is good for Big Music is automatically good for America, a central tenet of their crusade.

> 'Classics, jazz and new music forms are especially likely to suffer, since they are largely subsidized by hit recordings.'

The idea that less commercial music somehow depends on hits for subsidization has never held water. Record companies don't release losers on purpose. In fact, their executives work night and day trying to eliminate losers altogether. This practice won't be reversed by transferring revenue from foreign tape manufacturers to American record firms.

> 'Home taping reduces sales and forces prices upward, an unfair result for those who buy recordings.'

On the contrary, high record prices have stimulated much home taping. Blaming consumers for inflation is an old trick, usually pulled at clobbering time.

'It hurts artists, composers and musicians, depriving them of deserved revenue for the use of their music and songs.'

Book authors coexist nicely with the public library system that circulates their work widely at no expense to readers. Most see it as an ideal way to get people involved with their work. Indeed, authors would likely join composers and performers in citing a long list of bitter grievances that, in their eyes, rank well ahead of copyright abuse, unless by that we mean unpaid record company royalties. Losses to home taping must pale, for example, compared to those inflicted by a sick economy or the huge sums extracted by the owners of America's record corporations.

Putting these insights together leads to a dim view of the crusade to 'Save America's Music'. High record prices combined with depressed markets spell big trouble for the industry and the artists who depend on it for survival. The Savers dodge the issues, however, blaming all their woes on home taping. Given the protectionist urge in business circles, it's easy to see how this largely imported merchandise got singled out. In any case, people who've made music a part of their lives face another round of killing price rises plus a nasty blow to their freedom to enjoy the widest possible access to musical variety. That doesn't add up to saving anything at all.

Statement to Congress, 19 September 1985

FRANK ZAPPA

If one needed proof of the clout that puritan elements retain in American society, the censorship debate of recent years would provide it. In 1985, Tipper Gore, now wife to a potential vice-president, outraged by a reference to masturbation on a Prince track ('Sugar Walls') she had bought for her 8-year-old daughter, enlisted assorted Senators' wives into a cabal whose express intention was to censor the record industry. The Parents' Music Resource Centre – their chosen moniker –convinced their Senate spouses to set up a hearing in front of the Commerce, Technology and Transportation Committee to consider their proposal to introduce a rating system for rock albums. Inevitably it was artists, not the industry, who attempted to resist the Mothers of Prevention, as Frank Zappa would later dub them. Zappa's statement to Congress is a typically incisive assault upon the motives underlying the Washington wives' moral crusade.

The PMRC proposal is an ill-conceived piece of nonsense which fails to deliver any real benefits to children, infringes the civil liberties of people who are not children and promises to keep the courts busy for years, dealing with the interpretational and enforcemental problems inherent in the proposal's design.

It is my understanding that, in law, First Amendment issues are decided with a preference for the least restrictive alternative. In this context, the PMRC's demands are the equivalent of treating dandruff by decapitation.

No one has forced Mrs Baker or Mrs Gore to bring Prince or

Sheena Easton into their homes. Thanks to the Constitution, they are free to buy other forms of music for their children. Apparently they insist on purchasing the works of contemporary recording artists in order to support a personal illusion of aerobic sophistication. Ladies, please be advised: the $8.98 purchase price does not entitle you to a kiss on the foot from the composer or performer in exchange for a spin on the family Victrola. Taken as a whole, the complete list of PMRC demands reads like an instruction manual for some sinister kind of 'toilet training programme' to housebreak *all* composers and performers because of the lyrics of a few. Ladies, how dare you?

The ladies' shame must be shared by the bosses at the major labels who, through the RIAA, choose to bargain away the rights of the composers, performers and retailers in order to pass H.R. 2911, the blank tape tax: *a private tax, levied by an industry on consumers, for the benefit of a select group within that industry.*

Is this a consumer issue? You bet it is. PMRC spokesperson Kandy Stroud announced to millions of fascinated viewers on last Friday's ABC *Nightline* debate that Senator Gore, a man she described as 'a friend of the music industry', is co-sponsor of something referred to as 'anti-piracy legislation'. Is this the same tax bill with a nicer name?

The major record labels need to have H.R. 2911 whiz through a few committees before anybody smells a rat. One of them is chaired by Senator Thurmond. Is it a coincidence that Mrs Thurmond is affiliated with the PMRC? I can't say she's a member, because the PMRC *has no members*. Their secretary told me on the phone last Friday that the PMRC has *no members . . .* only *founders*. I asked how many other DC wives are *non-members* of an organization that raises money by mail, has a tax-exempt status, and seems intent on running the Constitution of the United States through the family paper-shredder. I asked her if it was a cult. Finally, she said she couldn't give me an answer and that she had to call their lawyer.

While the wife of the Secretary of the Treasury recites 'Gonna

drive my love inside you . . .' and Senator Gore's wife talks about
'*Bondage!*' and 'Oral sex at gunpoint' on the CBS evening news,
people in high places work on a tax bill that is so ridiculous, the
only way to sneak it through is to keep the public's mind on
something else: *porn rock*.

The PMRC practises a curious double standard with these
fervent recitations. Thanks to them, helpless young children all
over America get to hear about oral sex at gunpoint on network
TV several nights a week. Is there a secret FCC dispensation
here? What sort of end justifies *these* means? PTA parents should
keep an eye on these ladies if that's their idea of 'good taste'.

Is the basic issue morality? Is it mental health? Is it an issue at
all? The PMRC has created a lot of confusion with improper
comparisons between song lyrics, videos, record packaging, radio
broadcasting and live performances. These are all different
mediums, and the people who work in them have a right to
conduct their business without trade-restraining legislation,
whipped up like an instant pudding by the Wives of Big Brother.

Is it proper that the husband of a PMRC *non-member/
founder/person* sits on any committee considering business pertaining to the blank tape tax or his wife's lobbying organization? Can
any committee thus constituted 'find facts' in a fair and unbiased
manner? This committee has three. A minor conflict of interest?

The PMRC promotes their programme as a harmless type of
consumer information service, providing 'guide-lines' which will
assist baffled parents in the determination of the 'suitability' of
records listened to by 'very young children'. The methods they
propose have several unfortunate side-effects, not the least of
which is the reduction of all American music, recorded and live,
to the intellectual level of a Sunday morning cartoon show.

Teenagers with $8.98 in their pocket might go into a record
store alone, but 'very young children' do not. Usually there is a
parent in attendance. The $8.98 is in the parent's pocket. The
parent can always suggest that the $8.98 be spent on a book.

If the parent is afraid to let the child read a book, perhaps the $8.98 can be spent on recordings of instrumental music. Why not bring jazz or classical music into your home instead of Blackie Lawless or Madonna? Great music with *no words at all* is available to anyone with sense enough to look beyond this week's platinum-selling fashion plate.

Children in the 'vulnerable' age bracket have a natural love for music. If, as a parent, you believe they should be exposed to something more uplifting than 'Sugar Walls', support Music Appreciation programmes in schools. Why haven't you considered *your child's needs for consumer information*? Music appreciation costs very little compared to sports expenditures. Your children have a right to know that something besides pop music exists.

It is unfortunate that the PMRC would rather dispense governmentally sanitized heavy metal music than something more 'uplifting'. Is this an indication of PMRC's personal taste, or just another manifestation of the low priority this administration has placed on education for the arts in America? The answer, of course, is *neither*. You can't distract people from thinking about an unfair tax by talking about Music Appreciation. For that you need *sex* . . . and *lots of it*.

Because of the subjective nature of the PMRC ratings, it is impossible to guarantee that some sort of 'despised concept' won't sneak through, tucked away in new slang or the overstressed pronunciation of an otherwise innocent word. If the goal here is *total verbal/moral safety*, there is only one way to achieve it: watch no TV, read no books, see no movies, listen to only instrumental music or buy no music at all.

The establishment of a rating system, voluntary or otherwise, opens the door to an endless parade of Moral Quality Control Programmes based on 'Things Certain Christians Don't Like'. What if the next bunch of Washington Wives demand a large yellow 'J' on all material written or performed by Jews, in order to save helpless children from exposure to 'concealed Zionist doctrine'?

Record ratings are frequently compared to film ratings. Apart from the quantitative difference, there is another that is more important: people who act in films are hired to 'pretend'. No matter how the film is rated, it won't hurt them personally. Since many musicians write and perform their own material and stand by it as their art (whether you like it or not), an imposed rating will stigmatize them as *individuals*. How long before composers and performers are told to wear a festive little P M R C *armband* with their Scarlet Letter on it?

The P M R C rating system restrains trade in one specific musical field: rock. No ratings have been requested for comedy records or country music. Is there anyone in the P M R C who can differentiate *infallibly* between rock and country music? Artists in both fields cross stylistic lines. Some artists include comedy material. If an album is part rock, part country, part comedy, what sort of label would it get? Shouldn't the ladies be warning everyone that inside those country albums with the American flags, the big trucks and the atomic pompadours, there lurks a fascinating variety of songs about sex, violence, alcohol and *the devil*, recorded in a way that lets you hear *every word*, sung for you by people who have been to prison and are *proud of it*?

If enacted, the P M R C program would have the effect of protectionist legislation for the country music industry, providing more security for cowboys than it does for children. One major retail outlet has already informed Capitol Records sales staff that it would not purchase or display an album with *any kind of sticker on it*.

Another chain of outlets in shopping malls has been told by the landlord that if it racked 'hard-rated albums' they would lose their lease. That opens up an awful lot of shelf space for somebody. Could it be that a certain Senatorial husband-and-wife team from Tennessee sees this as an 'affirmative action programme' to benefit the suffering multitudes in Nashville?

Is the P M R C attempting to save future generations from *sex itself*? The type, the amount and the timing of sexual information given to a child should be determined by parents, not by people who are involved in a tax scheme cover-up.

The PMRC has concocted a Mythical Beast, and compounds the chicanery by demanding 'consumer guidelines' to keep it from inviting your children inside its *sugar walls*. Is the next step the adoption of a 'PMRC National Legal Age for *comprehension* of Vaginal Arousal'? Many people in this room would gladly support such legislation, but, before they start drafting their bill, I urge them to consider these facts:

(1) There is no conclusive scientific evidence to support the claim that exposure to any form of music will cause the listener to commit a crime or damn his soul to hell.

(2) Masturbation is not illegal. If it is not illegal to do it, why should it be illegal to sing about it?

(3) No medical evidence of hairy palms, warts, or blindness has been linked to masturbation or vaginal arousal, nor has it been proven that hearing references to either topic automatically turns the listener into a social liability.

(4) Enforcement of anti-masturbatory legislation could prove costly and time-consuming.

(5) There is not enough prison space to hold all the children who do it.

The PMRC's proposal is most offensive in its 'moral tone'. It seeks to enforce a set of implied religious values on its victims. Iran has a religious government. Good for them. I like having the capitol of the United States in Washington, DC, in spite of recent efforts to move it to Lynchburg, Virginia.

Fundamentalism is not a state religion. The PMRC's request for labels regarding sexually explicit lyrics, violence, drugs, alcohol, and especially *occult content* reads like a catalogue of phenomena abhorrent to practitioners of that faith. How a person worships is a private matter, and should not be *inflicted upon* or *exploited by* others. Understanding the fundamentalist leanings of this organization, I think it is fair to wonder if their rating system will eventually be extended to inform parents as to whether a musical group has homosexuals in it. Will the PMRC permit musical groups to exist, but only if gay members don't sing, and are not depicted on the album cover?

The PMRC has demanded that record companies 're-evaluate' the contracts of those groups who do things on stage that *they* find offensive. I remind the PMRC that *groups* are comprised of *individuals*. If one guy wiggles too much, does the whole band get an 'X'? If the group gets dropped from the label as a result of this 're-evaluation' process, do the other guys in the group who weren't wiggling get to sue the guy who wiggled because he ruined their careers? Do the *founders* of this *tax-exempt organization with no members* plan to indemnify record companies for any losses incurred from unfavourably decided breach-of-contract suits, or is there a PMRC secret agent in the Justice Department?

Should individual musicians be rated? If so, who is qualified to determine if the *guitar player* is an 'X', the *vocalist* is a DA, or the *drummer* is a 'V'? If the *bass player* (or his senator) belongs to a religious group that dances around with poisonous snakes, does he get an 'O'? What if he has an earring in one ear, wears an Italian horn around his neck, sings about his astrological sign, practises yoga, reads the Kabbala or owns a rosary? Will his 'occult content' rating go into an old CoIntelPro computer, emerging later as a *'fact'*, to determine if he qualifies for a home-owner loan? Will they tell you this is necessary to protect the folks next door from the possibility of 'devil-worship' lyrics creeping through the wall?

What hazards await the unfortunate retailer who accidentally sells an 'O'-rated record to somebody's little Johnny? Nobody in

Washington seemed to care when Christian terrorists bombed abortion clinics in the name of Jesus. Will you care when the *'Friends of the Wives of Big Brother'* blow up the shopping mall?

The PMRC wants ratings to start as of the date of their enactment. That leaves the current crop of 'objectionable material' untouched. What will be the status of recordings from the Golden Era prior to censorship? Do they become collector's items . . . or will another 'fair and unbiased committee' order them destroyed in a public ceremony?

Bad facts make bad laws, and people who write bad laws are, in my opinion, more dangerous than songwriters who celebrate sexuality. Freedom of speech, freedom of religious thought, and the right to due process for composers, performers and retailers are imperiled if the PMRC and the major labels consummate this nasty bargain. Are we expected to give up Article One so the big guys can collect an extra dollar on every blank tape and ten to twenty-five per cent on tape recorders? What's going on here? Do *we* get to vote on this tax? There's an awful lot of smoke pouring out of the legislative machinery used by the PMRC to inflate this issue. Try not to inhale it.

Industry's Bane, Fans' Bonanza

JON PARELES

The same basic issues raised in the previous article – the failure of the companies to release what fans want; the hypocrisy and greed of the Biz; and their attempts to divert attention from their own profiteering by the use of their favourite scarlet fish, bootlegging – all rear their heads in this 1991 article from the August pages of The New York Times.

Record collectors, watch out for the Feds. People who order bootleg CDs by mail have lately been finding Federal agents at their doors, as *Rolling Stone* recently reported. It's part of a new crackdown on bootleg recordings, abetted by the anti-piracy program of the Recording Industry Association of America.

To music fans, piracy is one thing and bootlegging is another. I'm all for efforts to eliminate pirated recordings, those cheap counterfeited cassettes that offer fuzzy copies of both the music and the packaging. Performers who have slaved to perfect an album deserve to have it heard clearly; recording companies have a right to recoup their investments in recording and promotion. And the person who buys a pirated tape probably won't buy the real thing. (Of course, a price cut for legitimate CDs and cassettes would undermine the pirates.)

Bootlegs are different. Bootlegs aren't part of a musician's official recorded output; they preserve concerts, television appearances, radio broadcasts, studio out-takes, discarded songs, stray noise. How such material ends up on CDs is a shady business that may involve surreptitious concert-goers with tape recorders or illicit purchase of material. People who buy bootlegs know they're taking a chance, they expect middling sound and hit-or-miss quality. But what bootlegs provide is the chance to hear music that hasn't been worked over, edited, sanitized; they are the unauthorized audio biography of a performer – genius and warts and all.

Many musicians don't like bootlegs. They want to be immortalized in perfected form, with royalties, on their own timetable (or that of their label). On *As An Am Zappa*, a Frank Zappa bootleg that has just been issued in a facsimile version by Rhino Records, Mr Zappa is heard complaining that bootleggers who attended his concerts were able to release his newest songs before he could.

Yet unlike pirated albums, bootlegs don't seriously hinder sales of copyrighted recordings. Fans who lay out two or three times the price of a regular release to buy a bootleg CD of Prince's

Black Album, or a Bruce Springsteen radio broadcast, or a Smiths concert tape, are likely to be collectors, people who own the complete catalogue and crave more. They'll be first in line when a new legitimate album comes out.

While a musician doesn't receive royalties for bootlegs, the superstars bootleggers are interested in aren't starving, and royalties from a few hundred, even a few thousand, bootlegs wouldn't make them significantly richer. The Grateful Dead, an endlessly bootlegged band, simply shrug and smile; they set aside a place at concerts for people who want to make tapes.

At this point, someone generally says, 'Suppose your newspaper could be copied and sold more cheaply on the street? Then you would be up in arms about copyright protection.'

Well, Xeroxing the front page would be piracy. Bootleggers, on the other hand, would be distributing (at premium prices) alternate versions of articles, stray public statements and rough drafts full of typos, clearly designated as such. I wouldn't object.

The recording business has whined for more than a decade about sales lost to unauthorized recordings, trying hard to conflate pirates, bootlegs and even home-made party tapes. This month, after years at odds, the electronics industry and the recording business have reached an agreement in which they would jointly support a royalty of two per cent on home digital recording machines and three per cent on blank digital tapes and discs.

If Congress approves their proposal, the royalty would be paid by equipment manufacturers (and, sooner or later, consumers) and distributed to copyright holders: recording companies (a whopping 38 per cent), performers (25 per cent), songwriters and publishers (about 17 per cent each). For the moment, analog cassettes are safe, but the foot is in the door.

It probably doesn't hurt that major electronics manufacturers (Philips, Matsushita, Thorn-EMI and Sony) now own four of the six major recording companies (Polygram, MCA, Capitol and what used to be CBS), so they would be paying royalties to themselves. (Is that tax deductible?) With the agreement, pre-recorded digital audio tapes (DAT) have a chance to reach the market just before recordable CDs make them obsolete.

The royalty agreement and the bootleg furore are part of a new assault on a favourite recording business bugaboo: the outside entrepreneur. When sales are sluggish, recording nochos don't blame themselves, their products or their prices; they proclaim that sales are diverted by technology or unfair competition. In the early 1980s, as the Walkman changed listening habits, the big threat was that people were supposedly copying vast numbers of albums on to cassettes. So the recording business lobbied Congress for a royalty; noting that recording companies continued to make profits, Congress demurred. The companies eventually did what they should have done in the first place: they geared up to release pre-recorded cassettes.

Another alleged menace was imported albums, and there, American recording companies prevailed. Some imports were exactly the same as American releases (yet different from pirate recordings, since performers received foreign royalties); others contained music unavailable here. With too many choices, consumers might not have bought what American labels were pushing. Recording companies sued importers. Now, no recording owned by an American company, whether or not available here, can be imported without the company's consent.

Fans who want an Elvis Costello song that appears only on a British album, or collectors who want various album covers from different countries, are out of luck. If a German or Japanese company reissues a favourite old Jerry Lee Lewis album, and the American company is keeping it in the vault, the American company can block import sales; die-hard fans might travel overseas, attempt a mail-order or pray for a reissue.

And now, not content to prevail over the music they paid to produce, recording companies are on the war-path about the music they didn't finance, give or take some studio out-takes.

The issue is control. Recording companies don't want anyone else to sell recordings; they don't get a piece of the action. They also don't want to admit that there are options; if listeners and musicians decided they didn't need 64-track studios and state-of-the-art computerized sound mixes, bands might not need recording-company capital. The companies also want passive consumers who'll buy what's being marketed, not smart alecks who search out alternatives.

Musicians have got used to the current system, too, lingering in studios and nit-picking every millisecond of digitally recorded data. Even purportedly live albums routinely have post-production credits, likely to mean that wrong notes were tuned up electronically or re-recorded. Over a career of any duration, musicians become hypersensitive; they hear infinitesimal glitches and convince themselves that everyone else can hear them, too. After all their work they can't bear to think that a version of the song they belted out years ago in some nondescript arena might eventually show more passion, even if they missed a high note. Lately, some have been admitting it, as reissue and out-take and fake bootleg CDs made their way into the market.

What bootlegs offer, and performers and companies are reluctant to let out, is testimony that the musicians are fallible – that they make mistakes, have false starts and, sometimes, put out glossy productions that are stillborn. They also challenge the notion that music belongs to big companies and can be doled out at their convenience.

One of my favourite unauthorized recordings is a cassette of a Keith Richards concert at the Beacon Theater. Taped, I happen to know, on a pocket recorder with a one-point stereo microphone, hidden under the seat, the cassette is sonic sludge, particularly after a few generations of cassette to cassette copies. The singing is way out of tune, the bass and drums are muddy and the audience whoops and hollers continually. Any recording company would dread putting it out; most of the songs had just appeared on Mr Richards's *Talk Is Cheap*. But it sounds real – wild, sloppy, riotous. It has the secret of a prime bootleg: it sounds like an occasion, not a product.

9. The Promise is Broken

When the promise is broken
You go on living
But it steals something
From deep down in your soul.
                    (Bruce Springsteen – 1977)

'The Promise Is Broken' was a song that Bruce Springsteen recorded for Darkness On The Edge Of Town. *It may well be his most perfect song. It tells the tale of a man who follows a dream until, having 'lived a secret I should have kept to myself', he gets drunk one night and blurts it out. The song ends with the singer 'farway from home, sleeping in the back seat of a borrowed car', a scary* déjà vu *image of Hank Williams slumped, dead, in the back seat of his Cadillac on New Year's Day 1953.*

In this section the promise is broken repeatedly, at least in the eyes of the writers. Sometimes it's a temporary lapse, more often it is evidence of a more permanent disconnection.

Dylan and Lou Reed in particular have been written off repeatedly. Yet they have survived, they have endured. Unlike Peter Laughner, whose review of Lou Reed's Coney Island Baby *Lester Bangs considered his finest prose piece. It is certainly a highly personalized response from someone who put his stakes on someone else, then was surprised when they inevitably failed to live up to the perfected image.*

Marcus's legendary response to Dylan's career-assassination album

517

Self Portrait – 'What is this Shit?' – just summed up a generation's confusion at Dylan's maddening perversity.

More permanent forms of amnesia are also represented here – Marcus again, this time on Elvis's increasing refusal to take chances; Jules Siegel's eye-witness account of the gradual disintegration of Brian Wilson's Smile project; Nick Kent's compassionate 1974 profile of the Rimbaud of rock, Syd Barrett.

There are also some typically hostile, if brilliant, deconstructions: of the Bruce Springsteen phenomenon by Richard Meltzer, at a time (1985) when it seemed that the Boss could do no wrong; and of that sacred cow of rocklore, Sgt Pepper's Lonely Hearts Club Band, by Richard Goldstein, a solitary dissenting voice back in June 1967. Finally, Joe Carducci and Charles Shaar Murray do battle over whether one should admit to drinking one's coffee black. Both attack the question of whether rock & roll has a future, from separate poles.

Presliad: Fanfare

GREIL MARCUS

The public spectacle of inexorable artistic decline is the primary theme of this section from Greil Marcus's much lauded volume on Americana in rock, Mystery Train. Written two years before Presley's death, it hangs an arc of inevitability over the eventual nemesis.

Elvis Presley is a supreme figure in American life, one whose presence, no matter how banal or predictable, brooks no real comparisons. He is honoured equally by long-haired rock critics, middle-aged women, the City of Memphis (they finally found something to name after him: a highway), and even a president. Beside Elvis, the other heroes of this book seem a little small-time. If they define different versions of America, Presley's career almost has the scope to take America in. The cultural range of his music has expanded to the point where it includes not only the hits of the day, but also patriotic recitals, pure country gospel and really dirty blues; reviews of his concerts, by usually credible writers, sometimes resemble biblical accounts of heavenly miracles. Elvis has emerged as a great artist, a great rocker, a great purveyor of schlock, a great heart-throb, a great bore, a great symbol of potency, a great ham, a great nice person, and, yes, a great American.

Twenty years ago Elvis made his first record with Sam Phillips, on the little Sun label in Memphis, Tennessee; then a pact was signed with Col. Tom Parker, shrewd country hustler. Elvis took off for RCA Victor, New York and Hollywood. America has not been the same since. Elvis disappeared into an oblivion of respect-ability and security in the sixties, lost in interchangeable movies and dull music; he staged a remarkable comeback as that decade ended, and now performs as the transcendental Sun King that Ralph Waldo Emerson only dreamed about – and as a giant contradiction. His audience expands every year, but Elvis transcends his talent to the point of dispensing with it altogether. Performing a kind of enormous victory rather than winning it, Elvis strides the boards with such glamour, such magnetism, that he allows his audience to transcend their desire for his talent. Action is irrelevant when one can simply delight in the presence of a man who has made history, and who has triumphed over it.

Mark now, the supreme Elvis gesture. He takes the stage with a retinue of bodyguards, servants, singers, a band, an orchestra; he applies himself vaguely to the hits of his past, prostrates himself before songs of awesome ickiness; he acknowledges the applause and the gasps that greet his every movement (applause that comes thundering with such force you might think the audience merely suffers the music as an excuse for its ovations); he closes with an act of showbiz love that still warms the heart; but above all, he throws away the entire performance.

How could he take it seriously? How could anyone create when all one has to do is appear? 'He looks like Elvis Presley!' cried a friend, when the Big E stormed forth in an explosion of flashbulbs and cheers; 'What a burden to live up to!' It is as if there is nothing Elvis could do to overshadow a performance of his myth. And so he performs from a distance, laughing at his myth, throwing it away only to see it roar back and trap him once again.

He will sing, as if suffering to his very soul, a song called 'This Time, You [God, that is] Gave Me A Mountain', which sums up his divorce and his separation from his little girl. Having confessed his sins, he will stand aside, head bowed, as the Special Elvis Presley Gospel Group sings 'Sweet Sweet Feeling (In This Place)'. Apparently cleansed of his sins, he will rock straight into the rhythm and blues of 'Lawdy Miss Clawdy' and celebrate his new-found freedom with a lazy grin. But this little melodrama of casual triumph will itself be a throwaway. As with the well-planned sets, the first-class musicians, the brilliant costumes, there will be little life behind the orchestration; the whole performance will be flaccid, the timing careless, all emotions finally shallow, the distance from his myth necessitating an even greater distance from the musical power on which that myth is based.

Elvis gives us a massive road-show musical of opulent American mastery; his version of the winner-takes-all fantasies that have kept the world lined up outside the theatres that show American movies ever since the movies began. And of course we respond: a self-made man is rather boring, but a self-made king is something else. Dressed in blue, red, white, ultimately gold, with a superman cape and covered with jewels no one can be sure are fake, Elvis might epitomize the worst of our culture – he is bragging, selfish, narcissistic, condescending, materialistic to the point of insanity. But there is no need to take that seriously, no need to take anything seriously. 'Aw, shucks,' says the country boy; it is all a joke to him; his distance is in his humour, and he can exit from this America unmarked, unimpressed and uninteresting.

'From the moment he comes out of the wings,' writes Nik Cohn, 'all the pop that has followed him is made to seem as nothing, to be blown away like chaff.' That is exactly what that first moment feels like, but from that point on, Elvis will go with the rest of it, singing as if there are no dangers or delights in the world grand enough to challenge him. There is great satisfaction in his performance, and great emptiness.

It is an ending. It is a sure sign that a culture has reached a dead end when it is no longer intrigued by its myths (when they lose their power to excite, amuse and renew all who are a part of those myths – when those myths just bore the hell out of everyone); but Elvis has dissolved into a presentation of his myth, and so has his music. The emotion of the best music is open, liberating in its commitment and intangibility; Elvis's presentation is fixed. The glorious oppression of that presentation parallels the all-but-complete assimilation of a revolutionary musical style into the mainstream of American culture, where no one is challenged and no one is threatened.

History without myth is surely a wasteland; but myths are compelling only when they are at odds with history. When they replace the need to make history, they too are a dead end, and merely smug. Elvis's performance of his myth is so satisfying to his audience that he is left with no musical identity whatsoever, and thus he has no way to define himself, or his audience – except to expand himself, and his audience. Elvis is a man whose task it is to dramatize the fact of his existence; he does not have to create something new (or try, and fail), and thus test the worth of his existence, or the worth of his audience.

Complete assimilation really means complete acceptance. The immigrant who is completely assimilated into America has lost the faculty of adding whatever is special about himself to his country; for any artist, complete assimilation means the adoption of an aesthetic where no lines are drawn and no choices are made.

That quality of selection, which is what is at stake when an artist comes across with his version of anything, is missing. When an artist gives an all-encompassing Yes to his audience (and Elvis's Yes implicitly includes everyone, not just those who say Yes to him), there is nothing more he can tell his audience, nothing he can really do for them, except maybe throw them a kiss.

'Only the man who says No is free,' Melville once wrote. We don't expect such a stance in popular culture, and anyone who does might best be advised to take his trade somewhere else. But the refusal that lurks on the margins of the affirmation of American popular culture – the margins where Sly Stone and Randy Newman have done their best work – is what gives the Yes of our culture its vitality and its kick. Elvis's Yes is the grandest of all, his presentation of mastery the grandest fantasy of freedom, but it is finally a counterfeit of freedom: it takes place in a world that for all its openness (Everybody Welcome!) is aesthetically closed, where nothing is left to be mastered, where there is only more to accept. For all its irresistible excitement and enthusiasm, this freedom is complacent, and so the music that it produces is empty of real emotion – there is nothing this freedom could be for, nothing to be won or lost.

At best, when the fans gather around – old men and women who might see their own struggles and failures ennobled in the splendour of one who came from the bottom; middle-aged couples attending to the most glamorous nightclub act there is; those in their twenties and thirties who have grown with Elvis ever since he and they created each other years ago (and who might have a feeling he and they will make their trip through history together, reading their history in each other) – at best, Elvis will confirm all who are there as an audience. Such an event, repeated over and over all across the land, implies an America that is as nearly complete as any can be. But what is it worth?

When Elvis sings 'American Trilogy' (a combination of 'Dixie', 'The Battle Hymn Of The Republic', and 'All My Trials', a slave song), he signifies that his persona, and the culture he had made out of blues, Las Vegas, gospel music, Hollywood, schmaltz,

Mississippi and rock & roll, can contain any America you might want to conjure up. It is rather Lincolnesque; Elvis recognizes that the Civil War has never ended, and so he will perform The Union.

Well, for a moment, staring at that man on the stage, you can almost believe it. For if Elvis were to bring it off – and it is easy to think that only he could – one would leave the hall with a new feeling for the country; whatever that feeling might be, one's sense of place would be broadened and enriched.

But it is an illusion. A man or woman equal to the song's pretension would have to present each part of the song as if it were the whole story, setting one against the other, proving that one American really could make the South live, the Union hold and slavery real. But on the surface and beneath it, Elvis transcends any real America by evading it. There is no John Brown in his 'Battle Hymn', no romance in his 'Dixie', no blood in his slave song. He sings with such a complete absence of musical personality that none of the old songs matter at all, because he has not committed himself to them; it could be anyone singing, or no one. It is in this sense, finally, that an audience is confirmed, that an America comes into being; lacking any real fear or joy, it is a throwaway America where nothing is at stake. The divisions America shares are simply smoothed away.

But there is no chance anyone who wants to join will be excluded. Elvis's fantasy of freedom, the audience's fantasy, takes on such reality that there is nothing left in the real world that can inspire the fantasy, or threaten it. What is left is for the fantasy to replace the world; and that, night after night, is what Elvis and his audience make happen. The version of the American dream that is Elvis's performance is blown up again and again, to contain more history, more people, more music, more hopes; the air gets thin but the bubble does not burst, nor will it ever. This is America when it has outstripped itself, in all of its extravagance, and its emptiness is Elvis's ultimate throwaway.

There is a sense in which virtually his whole career has been a throwaway, straight from the time when he knew he had it made and that the future was his. You can hear that distance, that refusal to really commit himself, in his best music and his worst; if the throwaway is the source of most of what is pointless about Elvis, it is also at the heart of much of what is exciting and charismatic. It may be that he never took any of it seriously, just did his job and did it well, trying to enjoy himself and stay sane – save for those first Tennessee records, and that night, late in 1968, when his comeback was uncertain and he put a searing, desperate kind of life into a few songs that cannot be found in any of his other music.

I suppose it is the finality this 'comeback TV special' performance carries with it that draws me back to Elvis's first records, made when there was nothing to take for granted, let alone throw away. Those sides, like 'One Night', catch a world of risk, will, passion and natural nobility; something worth searching out within the America of mastery and easy splendor that may well be Elvis's last word. The first thing Elvis had to learn to transcend, after all, was the failure and obscurity he was born to; he had to find some way to set himself apart, to escape the limits that could well have given his story a very different ending. The ambition and genius that took him out and brought him back is in that first music – that, and much more.

Goodbye Surfing! Hello God!

JULES SIEGEL

Jules Siegel's immensely detailed 'Goodbye Surfing! Hello God!' provides both the best and the most contemporary account of the making, and ultimately the aborting, of Brian Wilson's grand project, the pop album that would transcend pop, Smile. Siegel's text places the gradual easing of Wilson's previously sure touch and the fragment-

ing of his fragile vision in a sympathetic light, all the while leaving just the barest hint of what might have been.

It was just another day of greatness at Gold Star Recording Studios on Santa Monica Boulevard in Hollywood. In the morning four long-haired kids had knocked out two hours of sound for a record plugger who was trying to curry favour with a disc jockey friend of theirs in San José. Nobody knew it at that moment, but out of that two hours there were about three minutes that would hit the top of the charts in a few weeks, and the record plugger, the disc jockey and the kids would all be hailed as geniuses, but geniuses with a very small g.

Now, however, in the very same studio, a Genius with a very large capital G was going to produce a hit. There was no doubt it would be a hit because this Genius was Brian Wilson. In four years of recording for Capitol Records, he and his group the Beach Boys, had made surfing music a national craze, sold 16 million singles and earned gold records for ten of their twelve albums.

Not only was Brian going to produce a hit, but also, one gathered, he was going to show everybody in the music business exactly where it was at; and where it was at, it seemed, was that Brian Wilson was not merely a Genius – which is to say a steady commercial success – but rather, like Bob Dylan and John Lennon, a GENIUS – which is to say a steady commercial success and hip besides.

Until now, though, there were not too many hip people who would have considered Brian Wilson and the Beach Boys hip, even though he had produced one very hip record, 'Good Vibrations', which had sold more than a million copies, and a super-hip album, *Pet Sounds*, which didn't do very well at all – by previous Beach Boy sales standards. Among the hip people he was still on trial, and the question discussed earnestly among the recognized authorities on what is and what is not hip was whether or not Brian Wilson was hip, semi-hip or square.

But walking into the control room with the answers to all questions such as this was Brian Wilson himself, wearing a competition-stripe surfer's t-shirt, tight white duck pants, pale green bowling shoes and a red plastic toy fireman's helmet.

Everybody was wearing identical red plastic toy fireman's helmets. Brian's cousin and production assistant, Steve Korthoff, was wearing one; his wife, Marilyn, and her sister, Diane Rovelle – Brian's secretary – were also wearing them, and so was a once dignified writer from the *Saturday Evening Post* who had been following Brian around for two months trying to figure out whether or not this 24-year-old oversized tribute to Southern California who carried some 250 pounds of baby fat on a 6 foot 4 inch frame, was a genius, Genius or GENIUS, hip, semi-hip or square – concepts the writer himself was just learning to handle.

Out in the studio, the musicians for the session were unpacking their instruments. In sport shirts and slacks, they looked like insurance salesmen and used-car dealers, except for one blonde female percussionist who might have been stamped out by a special machine that supplied plastic mannequin housewives for detergent commercials.

Controlled, a little bored after twenty years or so of nicely paid anonymity, these were the professionals of the popular music business, hired guns who did their job expertly and efficiently and then went home to the suburbs. If you wanted swing, they gave you swing. A little movie-track lushness? Fine, here comes movie-track lushness. Now it's rock & roll? Perfect rock & roll, down the chute.

'Steve,' Brian called out, 'where are the rest of those fire hats? I want everybody to wear fire hats. We've really got to get into this thing.' Out to the Rolls-Royce went Steve and within a few minutes all of the musicians were wearing fire hats, silly grins beginning to crack their professional dignity.

'All right, let's go,' said Brian. Then, using a variety of techniques ranging from local demonstration to actually playing the instruments, he taught each musician his part. A gigantic fire howled out of the massive studio speakers in a pounding crush of pictorial music that summoned up visions of roaring, windstorm flames, falling timbers, mournful sirens and sweating firemen, building into a peak and crackling off into fading embers as a single drum turned into a collapsing wall and the fire engine cellos dissolved and disappeared.

'When did he write this?' asked an astonished pop music producer who had wandered into the studio. 'This is really fantastic! Man, this is unbelievable! How long has he been working on it?'

'About an hour,' answered one of Brian's friends.

'I don't believe it. I just can't believe what I'm hearing,' said the producer and fell into a stone silence as the fire music began again.

For the next three hours Brian Wilson recorded and re-recorded, take after take, changing the sound balance, adding echo, experimenting with a sound-effects track of a real fire.

'Let me hear that again.' 'Drums, I think you're a little slow in that last part. Let's get on it.' 'That was really good. Now, one more time, the whole thing.' 'All right, let me hear the cellos alone.' 'Great. Really great. Now let's do it!'

With twenty-three takes on tape and the entire operation responding to his touch like the black knobs on the control board, sweat glistening down his long, reddish hair on to his freckled face, the control room a litter of dead cigarette butts, Chicken Delight boxes, crumpled napkins, Coke bottles and all the accumulated trash of the physical end of the creative process, Brian stood at the board as the four speakers blasted the music into the room.

For the twenty-fourth time, the drums crashed and the sound-effects crackle faded and stopped.

'Thank you,' said Brian, into the control-room mike. 'Let me hear that back.' Feet shifting, his body still, eyes closed, head moving seal-like to his music, he stood under the speakers and listened. 'Let me hear that one more time.' Again the fire roared. 'Everybody come out and listen to this,' Brian said to the musicians. They came into the control room and listened to what they had made.

'What do you think?' Brian asked.

'It's incredible. Incredible,' whispered one of the musicians, a man in his fifties, wearing a Hawaiian shirt and iridescent trousers and pointed black Italian shoes. 'Absolutely incredible.'

'Yeah,' said Brian on the way home, an acetate trial copy or 'dub' of the tape in his hands, the red plastic fire helmet still on his head. 'Yeah, I'm going to call this "Mrs O'Leary's Fire" and I think it might just scare a whole lot of people.'

As it turns out, however, Brian Wilson's magic fire music is not going to scare anybody – because nobody other than the few people who heard it in the studio will ever get to listen to it. A few days after the record was finished, a building across the street from the studio burned down and, according to Brian, there was also an unusually large number of fires in Los Angeles. Afraid that his music might in fact turn out to be magic fire music, Wilson destroyed the master.

'I don't have to do a big scary fire like that,' he later said, 'I can do a candle and it's still fire. That would have been a really bad vibration to let out on the world, that Chicago fire. The next one is going to be a candle.'

A person who thinks of himself as understanding would probably interpret this episode as an example of perhaps too-excessive artistic perfectionism. One with psychiatric inclinations would hear all this stuff about someone who actually believed music would cause fires and start using words such as neurosis and maybe even psychosis. A true student of spoken hip, however, would say hang-up, which covers all of the above.

As far as Brian's pretensions toward hipness are concerned, no label could do him worse harm. In the hip world, there is a widespread idea that really hip people don't have hang-ups, which gives rise to the unspoken rule (unspoken because there is also the widespread idea that really hip people don't make any rules) that no one who wants to be thought of as hip ever reveals his hang-ups, except maybe to his guru, and in the strictest of privacy.

In any case, whatever his talent, Brian Wilson's attempt to win a hip following and reputation foundered for many months in an obsessive cycle of creation and destruction that threatened not only his career and his future but also his marriage, his friendships, his relationship with the Beach Boys and, some of his closest friends worried, his mind.

For a boy who used to be known in adolescence as a lover of sweets, the whole thing must have begun to taste very sour; yet, this particular phase of Brian's drive toward whatever his goal of supreme success might be began on a rising tide that at first looked as if it would carry him and the Beach Boys beyond the Beatles, who had started just about the same time they did, into the number-one position in the international pop music fame-and-power competition.

'About a year ago I had what I considered a very religious experience,' Wilson told Los Angeles writer Tom Nolan in 1966. 'I took LSD, a full dose of LSD, and later, another time, I took a smaller dose. And I learned a lot of things, like patience, understanding. I can't teach you or tell you what I learned from taking it, but I consider it a very religious experience.'

A short time after his LSD experience, Wilson began work on the record that was to establish him right along with the Beatles as one of the most important innovators in modern popular music. It was called 'Good Vibrations', and it took more than six months, ninety hours of tape and eleven complete versions before a 3-minute 35-second final master tape satisfied him. Among the instruments on 'Good Vibrations' was an electronic device called a theramin, which had its debut in the soundtrack of the movie

Spellbound, back in the forties. To some people 'Good Vibrations' was considerably crazier than Gregory Peck had been in the movie, but to others, Brian Wilson's new record, along with his somewhat earlier release, *Pet Sounds*, marked the beginning of a new era in pop music.

'THEY'VE FOUND THE NEW SOUND AT LAST!' shrieked the headline over a London *Sunday Express* review as 'Good Vibrations' hit the English charts at number six and leaped to number one the following week. Within a few weeks, the Beach Boys had pushed the Beatles out of first place in England's *New Musical Express*'s annual poll. In America, 'Good Vibrations' sold nearly 400,000 copies in four days before reaching number one several weeks later and earning a gold record within another month when it hit the one-million sale mark.

It was an arrival, certainly, but in America, where there is none of the Beach Boys' California-mystique that adds a special touch of romance to their records and appearances in Europe and England, the news had not yet really reached all of the people whose opinion can turn popularity into fashionability. With the exception of a professor of show business (right, professor of show business; in California such a thing is not considered unusual) who turned up one night to interview Brian, and a few young writers (such as the *Village Voice*'s Richard Goldstein, Paul Williams of *Crawdaddy*, and Lawrence Dietz of *New York Magazine*), not too many opinion-makers were prepared to accept the Beach Boys into the mainstream of the culture industry.

What all this meant, of course, was that everybody agreed that Brian Wilson and the Beach Boys were still too square. It would take more than 'Good Vibrations' and *Pet Sounds* to erase three and a half years of 'Little Deuce Coupe' – a lot more if you counted in those J. C. Penney-style custom-tailored, kandy-striped short shirts they insisted on wearing on stage.

Brian, however, had not yet heard the news, it appeared, and was steadily going about the business of trying to become hip. The Beach Boys, who have toured without him ever since he broke down during one particularly wearing trip, were now in England and Europe, phoning back daily reports of enthusiastic fan hysteria – screaming little girls tearing at their flesh, wild press conferences, private chats with the Rolling Stones. Washed in the heat of a kind of attention they had never received in the United States even at the height of their commercial success, three Beach Boys – Brian's brothers, Dennis and Carl, and his cousin, Mike Love – walked into a London Rolls-Royce showroom and bought four Phantom VII limousines, one for each of them and a fourth for Brian. Al Jardine and Bruce Johnston, the Beach Boys who are not corporate members of the Beach Boys enterprises, sent their best regards and bought themselves some new clothing.

In the closing months of 1966, with the Beach Boys home in Los Angeles, Brian rode the 'Good Vibrations' high, driving forward in bursts of enormous energy that seemed destined before long to earn him the throne of the international empire of pop music still ruled by John Lennon and the Beatles.

At the time, it looked as if the Beatles were ready to step down. Their summer concerts in America had been only moderately successful at best, compared to earlier years. There were ten thousand empty seats at Shea Stadium in New York and eleven lonely fans at the airport in Seattle. Mass media, underground press, music industry trade papers and the fan magazines were filled with fears that the Beatles were finished, that the group was breaking up. Lennon was off acting in a movie; McCartney was walking around London alone, said to be carrying a giant torch for his sometime girlfriend Jane Asher; George Harrison was getting deeper and deeper into a mystical Indian thing under the instruction of sitar-master Ravi Shankar; and Ringo was collecting material for a Beatles museum.

In Los Angeles, Brian Wilson was riding around in the Rolls-Royce that had once belonged to John Lennon, pouring a deluge of new sounds on to miles of stereo tape in three different recording studios booked day and night for him in month-solid blocks, holding court nightly at his $240,000 Beverly Hills Babylonian-modern home, and, after guests left, sitting at his grand piano until dawn, writing new material.

The work in progress was an album called *Smile*. 'I'm writing a teenage symphony to God,' Brian told dinner guests on an October evening. He then played for them the collection of black acetate trial records which lay piled on the floor of his red imitation-velvet wallpapered bedroom with its leopard-print bedspread. In the bathroom, above the wash basin, there was a plastic colour picture of Jesus Christ with trick effect eyes that appeared to open and close when you moved your head. Sophisticate newcomers pointed it out to each other and laughed slyly, almost hoping to find a Keane painting among decorations ranging from Lava Lamps to a department-store rack of dozens of dolls, each still in its plastic bubble container, the whole display trembling like a space-age Christmas tree to the music flowing out into the living-room.

Brian shuffled through the acetates, most of which were unlabelled, identifying each by subtle differences in the patterns of the grooves. He had played them so often he knew the special look of each record the way you know the key to your front door by the shape of its teeth. Most were instrumental tracks, cut while the Beach Boys were in Europe, and for these Brian supplied the vocal in a high sound that seemed to come out of his head rather than his throat as he somehow managed to create complicated four and five part harmonies with only his own voice.

'Rock, rock, Plymouth rock roll over,' Brian sang. 'Bicycle rider, see what you done done to the church of the native American Indian ... Over and over the crow cries uncover the cornfields ... Who ran the Iron Horse ... Out in the farmyard the cook is

chopping lumber; out in the barnyard the chickens do their number
. . . Bicycle rider see what you done done . . .' A panorama of
American history filled the room as the music shifted from theme
to theme; the tinkling harpsichord sounds of the bicycle rider
pushed sad Indian sounds across the continent; the Iron Horse
pounded across the plains in a wide open rolling rhythm that
summoned up visions of the old West; civilized chickens bobbed
up and down in a tiny ballet of comic barnyard melody; the
inexorable bicycle music, cold and charming as an infinitely
talented music box, reappeared and faded away.

Like medieval choirboys, the voices of the Beach Boys pealed
out in wordless prayer from the last acetate, thirty seconds of
chorale that reached upward to the vaulted stone ceilings of an
empty cathedral lit by thousands of tiny votive candles melting at
last into one small, pure pool that whispered a universal amen in
a sigh without words.

Brian's private radio show was finished. In the dining-room a
candle-lit table with a dark blue cloth was set for ten persons. In
the kitchen, Marilyn Wilson was trying to get the meal organized
and served, aided and hindered by the chattering suggestions of
the guests' wives and girlfriends. When everyone was seated and
waiting for the food, Brian tapped his knife idly on a white china
plate.

'Listen to that,' he said. 'That's really great!' Everybody listened
as Brian played the plate. 'Come on, let's get something going
here,' he ordered. 'Michael – do this. David – you do this.' A
plate-and-spoon musicale began to develop as each guest played a
distinctly different technique, rhythm and melody under Brian's
enthusiastic direction.

'That's absolutely unbelievable!' said Brian. 'Isn't that unbelievable? That's so unbelievable I'm going to put it on the album.
Michael, I want you to get a sound system up here tomorrow and
I want everyone to be here tomorrow night. We're going to get
this on tape.'

Brian Wilson's plate-and-spoon musicale never did reach the public, but only because he forgot about it. Other sounds equally strange have found their way on to his records. On *Pet Sounds*, for example, on some tracks there is an odd, soft, hollow percussion effect that most musicians assume is some kind of electronically transmuted drum sound – a conga drum played with a stick perhaps, or an Indian tom-tom. Actually, it's drummer Hal Blaine playing the bottom of a plastic jug that once contained Sparklettes spring water. And, of course, at the end of the record there is the strangely affecting track of a train roaring through a lonely railroad crossing as a bell clangs and Brian's dogs, Banana, a beagle, and Louie, a dark brown Weimaraner, bark after it.

More significant, perhaps, to those who that night heard the original instrumental tracks for both *Smile* and the Beach Boys' new single, 'Heroes And Villains', is that entire sequences of extraordinary power and beauty are missing in the finished version of the single, and will undoubtedly be missing as well from *Smile* – victims of Brian's obsessive tinkering and, more importantly, sacrifices to the same strange combination of superstitious fear and God-like conviction of his own power he displayed when he destroyed the fire music.

The night of the dining-table concerto, it was the God-like confidence Brian must have been feeling as he put his guests on his trip, but the fear was soon to take over. At his house that night, he had assembled a new set of players to introduce into his life game, each of whom was to perform a specific role in the grander game he was playing with the world.

Earlier in the summer, Brian had hired Van Dyke Parks, a super-sophisticated young songwriter and composer, to collaborate with him on the lyrics for *Smile*. With Van Dyke working for him, he had a fighting chance against John Lennon, whose literary skill and Liverpudlian wit had been one of the most important factors in making the Beatles the darlings of the hip intelligentsia.

With that flank covered, Brian was ready to deal with some of the other problems of trying to become hip, the most important of which was how was he going to get in touch with some really hip people. In effect, the dinner party at the house was his first hip social event, and the star of the evening, so far as Brian was concerned, was Van Dyke Parks's manager, David Anderle, who showed up with a whole group of very hip people.

Elegant, cool and impossibly cunning, Anderle was an artist who had somehow found himself in the record business as an executive for MGM Records, where he had earned himself a reputation as a genius by purportedly thinking up the million-dollar movie-TV-record offer that briefly lured Bob Dylan to MGM from Columbia until everybody had a change of heart and Dylan decided to go back home to Columbia.

Anderle had skipped back and forth between painting and the record business, with mixed results in both. Right now he was doing a little personal management and thinking about painting a lot. His appeal to Brian was simple: everybody recognized David Anderle as one of the hippest people in Los Angeles. In fact, he was something like the mayor of hipness as far as some people were concerned. And not only that, he was a genius.

Within six weeks, he was working for the Beach Boys; everything that Brian wanted seemed at last to be in reach. Like a magic genie, David Anderle produced miracles for him. A new Beach Boys record company was set up, Brother Records, with David Anderle at its head and, simultaneously, the Beach Boys sued Capitol Records in a move designed to force a renegotiation of their contract with the company.

The house was full of underground press writers; Anderle's friend Michael Vosse was on the Brother Records payroll out scouting TV contracts and performing other odd jobs. Another of Anderle's friends was writing the story on Brian for the *Saturday Evening Post* and a film crew from CBS-TV was up at the house filming for a documentary to be narrated by Leonard Bernstein.

The Beach Boys were having meetings once or twice a week with teams of experts, briefing them on corporate policy, drawing complicated chalk patterns as they described the millions of dollars everyone was going to earn out of all this.

As 1967 opened it seemed as though Brian and the Beach Boys were assured of a new world of success; yet something was going wrong. As the corporate activity reached a peak of intensity, Brian was becoming less and less productive and more and more erratic. *Smile*, which was to have been released for the Christmas season, remained unfinished. 'Heroes And Villains', which was virtually complete, remained in the can, as Brian kept working out new little pieces and then scrapping them.

Van Dyke Parks had left and come back and would leave again, tired of being constantly dominated by Brian. Marilyn Wilson was having headaches and Dennis Wilson was leaving his wife. Session after session was cancelled. One night a studio full of violinists waited while Brian tried to decide whether or not the vibrations were friendly or hostile. The answer was hostile and the session was cancelled, at a cost of some $3,000. Everything seemed to be going wrong. Even the *Post* story fell through.

Brian seemed to be filled with secret fear. One night at the house, it began to surface. Marilyn sat nervously painting her fingernails as Brian stalked up and down, his face tight and his eyes small and red.

'What's the matter, Brian? You're really strung out,' a friend asked.

'Yeah, I'm really strung out. Look, I mean I really feel strange. A really strange thing happened to me tonight. Did you see this picture, *Seconds*?'

'No, but I know what it's about; I read the book.'

'Look, come into the kitchen; I really have to talk about this.' In the kitchen they sat down in the black and white hound's-tooth check wallpapered dinette area. A striped window shade clashed with the checks and the whole room vibrated like some kind of pop art painting. Ordinarily, Brian wouldn't sit for more than a minute in it, but now he seemed to be unaware of anything except what he wanted to say.

'I walked into that movie,' he said in a tense, high-pitched voice, 'and the first thing that happened was a voice from the screen said "Hello, Mr Wilson." It completely blew my mind. You've got to admit that's pretty spooky, right?'

'Maybe.'

'That's not all. Then the whole thing was there. I mean my whole life. Birth and death and rebirth. The whole thing. Even the beach was in it, a whole thing about the beach. It was my whole life right there on the screen.'

'It's just a coincidence, man. What are you getting all excited about?'

'Well, what if it isn't a coincidence? What if it's real? You know there's mind gangsters these days. There could be mind gangsters, couldn't there? I mean, look at Spector, he could be involved in it, couldn't he? He's going into films. How hard would it be for him to set up something like that?'

'Brian, Phil Spector is not about to make a million-dollar movie just to scare you. Come on, stop trying to be so dramatic.'

'All right, all right. I was just a little bit nervous about it,' Brian said, after some more back and forth about the possibility that Phil Spector, the record producer, had somehow influenced the making of *Seconds* to disturb Brian Wilson's tranquillity. 'I just had to get it out of my system. You can see where something like that could scare someone, can't you?'

They went into Brian's den, a small room papered in psychedelic orange, blue, yellow and red wall fabric with rounded corners. At the end of the room there was a jukebox filled with Beach Boys singles and Phil Spector hits. Brian punched a button and Spector's 'Be My Baby' began to pour out at top volume.

'Spector has always been a big thing with me, you know. I mean I heard that song three and a half years ago and I knew that it was between him and me. I knew exactly where he was at and now I've gone beyond him. You can understand how that movie might get someone upset under those circumstances, can't you?'

Brian sat down at his desk and began to draw a little diagram on a piece of printed stationery with his name at the top in the kind of large fat script printers of charitable dinner journals use when the customer asks for a hand-lettered look. With a felt-tipped pen, Brian drew a close approximation of a growth curve. 'Spector started the whole thing,' he said, dividing the curve into periods. 'He was the first one to use the studio. But I've gone beyond him now. I'm doing the spiritual sound, a white spiritual sound. Religious music. Did you hear the Beatles album? Religious, right? That's the whole movement. That's where I'm going. It's going to scare a lot of people.

'Yeah,' Brian said, hitting his fist on the desk with a large slap that sent the parakeets in a large cage facing him squalling and whistling. 'Yeah,' he said and smiled for the first time all evening. 'That's where I'm going and it's going to scare a lot of people when I get there.'

As the year drew deeper into winter, Brian's rate of activity grew more and more frantic, but nothing seemed to be accomplished. He tore the house apart and half redecorated it. One section of the living-room was filled with a full-sized Arabian tent and the dining-room, where the grand piano stood, was filled with sand to a depth of a foot or so and draped with nursery curtains. He had had his windows stained gray and put a sauna bath in the bedroom. He battled with his father and complained that his brothers weren't trying hard enough. He accused Mike Love of making too much money.

One by one, he cancelled out the friends he had collected, sometimes for the strangest of reasons. An acquaintance of several months who had become extremely close with Brian showed up at a record session and found a guard barring the door. Michael Vosse came out to explain.

'Hey man, this is really terrible,' said Vosse, smiling under a broad-brimmed straw hat. 'It's not you, it's your chick. Brian says she's a witch and she's messing with his brain so bad by E S P that he can't work. It's like the Spector thing. You know how he is. Say, I'm really sorry.' A couple of months later, Vosse was gone. Then, in the late spring, Anderle left. The game was over.

Several months later, the last move in Brian's attempt to win the hip community was played out. On 15 July, the Beach Boys were scheduled to appear at the Monterey International Pop Music Festival, a kind of summit of rock music with the emphasis on love, flowers and youth. Although Brian was a member of the Board of this non-profit event, the Beach Boys cancelled their commitment to perform. The official reason was that their negotiations with Capitol Records were at a crucial stage and they had to get 'Heroes And Villains' out right away. The second official reason was that Carl, who had been arrested for refusing to report for induction into the army (he was later cleared in court), was so upset that he wouldn't be able to sing.

Whatever the merit in these reasons, the real one may have been closer to something another Monterey board member suggested: 'Brian was afraid that the hippies from San Francisco would think the Beach Boys were square and boo them.'

Whatever the case, at the end of the summer, 'Heroes And Villains' was released in sharply edited form and *Smile* was reported to be on its way. In the meantime, however, the Beatles had released *Sgt Pepper's Lonely Hearts Club Band* and John Lennon was riding about London in a bright yellow Phantom VII Rolls-Royce painted with flowers on the sides and his zodiac symbol on the top. In *Life* magazine, Paul McCartney came out openly for LSD and in the Haight-Ashbury district of San Francisco George Harrison walked through the streets blessing the hippies. Ringo was still collecting material for a Beatles museum. However good *Smile* might turn out to be, it seemed somehow that once more the Beatles had outdistanced the Beach Boys.

Back during that wonderful period in the fall of 1966 when everybody seemed to be his friend and plans were being laid for Brother Records and all kinds of fine things, Brian had gone on a brief visit to Michigan to hear a Beach Boys concert. The evening of his return, each of his friends and important acquaintances received a call asking everyone to please come to the airport to meet Brian, it was very important. When they gathered at the airport, Brian had a photographer on hand to take a series of group pictures. For a long time, a huge mounted blow-up of the best of the photographs hung on the living-room wall, with some thirty people staring out – everyone from Van Dyke Parks and David Anderle to Michael Vosse and Terry Sachen. In the foreground was the *Saturday Evening Post* writer looking sourly out at the world.

The picture is no longer on Brian's wall and most of the people in it are no longer his friends. One by one each of them had either stepped out of the picture or been forced out of it. The whole cycle has returned to its beginning. Brian, who started out in Hawthorne, California, with his two brothers and a cousin, once more has surrounded himself with relatives. The house in Beverly Hills is empty. Brian and Marilyn are living in their new Spanish Mission estate in Bel-Air, cheek by jowl with the Mamas and the Papas' Cass Elliott.

What remains is 'Heroes And Villains', a record some people think is better than anything the Beatles ever wrote.

Richard Goldstein

I *Blew My Cool in* The New York Times

RICHARD GOLDSTEIN

As every rock fan knows, one of the seminal works of modern music was recorded at Abbey Road studios in the early months of 1967. But enough about Pink Floyd's Piper At The Gates Of Dawn. *What of the album being recorded across the way* – Sgt Pepper's Lonely Hearts Club Band? *Eric Idle called it 'a millstone in pop music history' in his satirical documentary* All You Need Is Cash. *Richard Goldstein had the nerve and insight to make the same judgement on the day of the album's release.*

The Beatles spent an unprecedented four months and $100,000 on their new album, *Sgt Pepper's Lonely Hearts Club Band*. Like fathers-to-be, they kept a close watch on each state of its gestation. For they are no longer merely superstars. Hailed as progenitors of a pop avant-garde, they have been idolized as the most creative members of their generation. The pressure to create an album that is complex, profound and innovative must have been staggering. So they retired to the electric sanctity of their recording studio, dispensing with their adoring audience and the shrieking inspiration it can provide.

The finished product reached the record racks last week; the Beatles have supervised even the album cover – a mind-blowing collage of famous and obscure people, plants and artifacts. The twelve new compositions in the album are as elaborately conceived as the cover. The sound is a pastiche of dissonance and lushness. The mood is mellow, even nostalgic. But, like the cover, the overall effect is busy, hip and cluttered.

If being a critic were the same as being a listener, I could enjoy *Sgt Pepper's Lonely Hearts Club Band*. Other than one song which I detest ('Good Morning, Good Morning'), I find the album better than 80 per cent of the music around today. But it is the other 20 per cent – including the best of the Beatles' past performances – which worries me, as a critic.

When the Beatles' work as a whole is viewed in retrospect, *Rubber Soul* and *Revolver* will stand as their major contributions. When the slicks and tricks of production on this album no longer seem unusual, and the compositions are stripped to their musical and lyrical essentials, *Sgt Pepper* will be Beatles baroque – an elaboration without improvement.

Like an over-attended child, this album is spoiled. It reeks of horns and harps, harmonica quartets, assorted animal noises, and a 41-piece orchestra. Sometimes, this elaborate musical propwork succeeds in projecting mood. The 'Sgt Pepper' theme is brassy and vaudevillian. 'Lucy In The Sky With Diamonds' is scored with stinging dissonance, and 'She's Leaving Home' is drenched in maraschino strings. In what is becoming a Beatles tradition, George Harrison unveils his latest excursion into curry and karma, to the saucy accompaniment of three tamburas, a dilruba, a tabla, a sitar, a table harp, three cellos and eight violins.

Harrison's song, 'Within You Without You', is a good place to begin dissecting *Sgt Pepper*. Though it is among the album's stronger cuts, its flaws are distressingly typical of the work as a whole. Harrison's voice – hovering midway between song and prayer chant – oozes the melody like melted cheese. Because his raga motifs are not mere embellishments but are imbedded into the very structure of the song, 'Within You Without You' appears seamless. It stretches, but fits. What a pity, then, that Harrison's lyrics are dismal and dull. 'Love You Too', his contribution to *Revolver*, exploded with a passionate sutra quality, but 'Within You Without You' resurrects the very clichés the Beatles helped bury: 'With our love/We could save the world/If they only knew.'

All the minor scales in the Orient wouldn't make that profound.

An obsession with production, coupled with a surprising shoddiness in composition, permeates the entire album. John Lennon's raunchiness has become mere caprice in 'Being For The Benefit Of Mr Kite'. Paul McCartney's soaring pop magnificats have become politely profound. I find it easier to support those allegations by comparing 'She's Leaving Home' with 'Eleanor Rigby', because while the musical motifs are similar, a profound sense of tragedy is conveyed in the earlier song through a series of poignantly ironic vignettes. The expression of agony through triviality has exercised a profound influence on the poetry of rock; you can feel it in Donovan's 'Young Girl Blues' and in the Bee Gees' stark 'New York Mining Disaster'.

'She's Leaving Home' is unlikely to influence anyone except the Monkees. Its lyrical technique is uninspired narrative, with a thin icing of irony. All its despair is surface, and so, while 'Eleanor Rigby' seethed with implications, 'She's Leaving Home' glistens with the flourish of tragedy. Even the instrumentation is explicit in its portrayal of theme. One of the most characteristic things about Beatle music is its intrinsic irony. Orchestration flows from mood; you dig 'Norwegian Wood' without even knowing it uses a sitar, because its melancholy moansound fits the mood. 'Yesterday' feels baroque on its own melodic terms; it doesn't depend on its arrangement. In both these classic Beatle songs, production follows, never determines, function. But in 'She's Leaving Home', harps and strings dominate what are essentially a weak melody and shallow lyrics.

I feel the same about most of the songs on this album. For the first time, the Beatles have given us a package of special effects, dazzling but ultimately fraudulent. In *Revolver*, I found a simplicity and empathy that was staggering. But in *Sgt Pepper* I sense an obsession with the surrogate magic of production, and a new sarcasm masquerading as cool.

Most distressing, I sense a dangerously dominant sense of what is chic. Much of the radicalism on this album has appeared elsewhere in a less sophisticated form. It was possible months ago to predict the emergence of the extended pop song, because it had already appeared in its infancy (the Fugs: 'Virgin Forest'; Love: 'Revelation'; the Stones: 'Goin' Home'; Doors: 'The End'). The Beach Boys introduced the multi-melody with 'Good Vibrations' and the Mothers of Invention – not the Beatles – are the pioneers of pop oratorio.

Still, the Beatles will probably receive credit for most of the 'innovations' on this album, including, of course, the removal of 'banding', or space between the cuts. Unfortunately, there is no thematic development to justify this wholeness; at best, the songs are only vaguely related. In unadorned fact, the Beatles had composed a healthy chunk of this material before they thought of centralizing it. Only in mid-production, did the idea of producing an album which would resemble a concert take hold, and the finished product shows this hesitant commitment to the idea of unity. George Harrison's piece has no place in a band concert, and neither do 'A Day In The Life' or 'Lucy In The Sky'.

The cohesive structure of *Sgt Pepper* cries out for interpretation. I am told that this album is all about the despair of loneliness, but is anxiety really the message we get in 'Lovely Rita', 'Fixing A Hole', or 'With A Little Help From My Friends'? Some say the Beatles are head composers. To turn on, goes the reasoning, will admit the enlightened to a whole range of associations and subtleties unfathomable to the straight mind. My experience till now has been that what I like straight, I like all the time. The idea that certain progressions, tonal nuances and lyrical flights are comprehensible only to the turned-on smacks of critical fascism. I think of the psychedelic experience as an elaboration of a given reality – not a substitute.

The only conceivable way to treat *Sgt Pepper* would seem to be as caprice. 'Sit back and let the evening go.' But you and I know the best Beatle music is only deceptively casual. Part of the trouble with this album is its determination to be a game, and the shallow-est cop-out is to excuse this work by reporting jubilantly that it has no meaning. It does. In fact, some of the songs are soggy with content. The difficulty comes in defining the work as a whole. It is much more sensible to talk of mood than actual meaning in *Sgt Pepper*. The Beatles have always avoided producing 'theme' albums, and despite its quasi-continuity, this one represents no significant break with that tradition. There are no recurrent themes, and only hints of what should have been repeating musical motifs. Nevertheless, this album has a definite mood, even if it is only expressed in its aims. *Rubber Soul* strove for tonal beauty and it is lushly melodic. *Revolver* attempted to be eclectic; its compositions stand as utterly distinct and self-contained. *Sgt Pepper* is a circus of sour.

With one important exception, it is precious but devoid of gems. 'A Day In The Life' is such a radical departure from the spirit of the album that it deserves its peninsular position (follow-ing the reprise of the 'Sgt Pepper' theme, it comes almost as an afterthought). It has nothing to do with posturing or put-on. It is a deadly earnest excursion into emotive music with a chilling lyric. Its orchestration is dissonant but sparse, and its mood is not whimsical nostalgia but irony.

With it, the Beatles have produced a glimpse of modern city life that is terrifying. It stands as one of the most important Lennon–McCartney compositions, and it is an historic pop event. 'A Day In The Life' starts with a description of suicide. With the same conciseness displayed in 'Eleanor Rigby', the protagonist begins: 'I read the news today, oh boy.' This mild interjection is the first hint of his disillusionment; compared with what is to follow, it is supremely ironic. 'I saw the photograph,' he continues, in the voice of a melancholy choir boy:

> He blew his mind out in a car,
> He didn't notice that the lights had changed.

'A Day In The Life' could never make the Top 40, although it may influence a great many songs which do. The aimless, T. S. Eliot-like crowd, forever confronting pain and turning away, will become a common symbol. And its narrator, subdued by the totality of his despair, may reappear in countless compositions as the silent, withdrawn hero.

Musically, there are already indications that 'A Day In The Life' is a key to the new music. Electronic rock, with its aim of staggering an audience, has arrived in half a dozen important new releases. None of these songs has the controlled intensity of 'A Day In The Life', but the willingness of many restrained musicians to 'let go' means that serious aleatory-pop may be on the way.

Ultimately, however, it is the uproar over the alleged influence of drugs on the Beatles which may prevent 'A Day In The Life' from reaching the mass audience. The song's refrain, 'I'd love to turn you on', has rankled disc jockeys supersensitive to 'hidden subversion' in rock & roll. In fact, a case can be made within the very structure of 'A Day In The Life' for the belief that the Beatles – like so many pop composers – are aware of the highs and lows of consciousness.

The song is built on a series of tense, melancholic passages, followed by soaring releases. In the opening stanza, for instance, John's voice comes near to cracking with despair. But after the invitation, 'I'd like to turn you on', the Beatles have inserted an extraordinary atonal thrust which is shocking, even painful, to the ears. But it brilliantly encases the song and, if the refrain preceding it suggests turning on, the crescendo parallels a drug-induced 'rush'.

The bridge begins in a staccato crossfire. We feel the narrator rising, dressing and commuting by rote. The music is nervous with the dissonance of cabaret jazz. A percussive drum melts into a panting railroad chug. The words fade into a chant of free, spacious chords, like the initial marijuana 'buzz'. But the tone becomes mysterious and then ominous. Deep strings take us on a

Wagnerian descent and we are back to the original blues theme, and the original declaration, 'I read the news today, oh boy.'

Actually, it is difficult to see why the BBC banned 'A Day In The Life', because its message is, quite clearly, the flight from banality. It describes a profound reality, but it certainly does not glorify it. And its conclusion, though magnificent, seems to represent a negation of self. The song ends on one low, resonant note that is sustained for forty seconds. Having achieved the absolute peace of nullification, the narrator is beyond melancholy. But there is something brooding and irrevocable about his calm. It sounds like destruction.

What a shame that 'A Day In The Life' is only the coda to an otherwise undistinguished collection of work. In substituting the studio conservatory for an audience, the Beatles have lost crucial rapport, and that emptiness at the roots is what makes their new album a monologue. Nothing is real therein, and nothing to get hung about. Too bad: I have a sweet tooth for reality. I like my art drenched in it, and even from fantasy, I expect authenticity. What I worship about the Beatles is their forging of rock into what is real. It made them artists; it made us fans; and it made me think like a critic when I turned on my radio.

We still need the Beatles, not as cloistered composers, but as companions. And they still need us, to teach them how to be real again.

Altamont, California

GEORGE PAUL CSICSERY

The spirit of the sixties died prematurely on 6 December 1969 at a speedway track on the outskirts of San Francisco. Csicsery's account of the events that day at Altamont suggests that the devil no longer confined his interest to the blues, and if Jagger's incantation of 'Sympathy For The Devil' had summoned them up, the hellhounds now wielded sawn-off pool cues.

6 December, 1969

In the beginning there was rock & roll. The Beatles came and made it good with love and the Bluebird of Paradise. But even while the children lifted their faces to the sun, Mick Jagger coiled himself around the tree of flesh, offering a sweet bite of chaos. Saturday, the children swallowed that bite, after chewing and tasting their alliance with evil for nearly a decade.

Until Saturday, evil was value-free, something to dig for its own sake. A lot of people who thought they were children of chaos dropped out of their sugar-coated camp trips Saturday to see the core of their religion at work.

Altamont, like the massacre of Song Mi, exploded the myth of innocence for a section of America. As the country grows more sophisticated, it learns to confront its own guilt.

The media projected WOODSTOCK. A great people event put on by the younger generation to celebrate its freedom. Traffic jams creating technological time-space motion transcending normal blurb time events. Birth, death, dope, violent, groovy teenyboppers dancing – an instant consumer package of life. Look at all the hippies, America. They're grooving while the rest of you schmucks have to watch it on TV, because you're too uptight. The media needs hippies now more than ever, to show there is still someone in America who can dig on a scene.

But this time it didn't work. The helicopters could not feel that something more than a happening with three hundred thousand people was going on below. Altamont was America. Years of spreading dope, hair, music and politics came together and reflected nothing less than the whole trip.

Those who expected the illusion of their own inherent goodness to last forever are still freaked. Others, who pay less attention to the rhetoric of a cultural revolution, say they had a good time. Putting it all together reads like America's pulse *now*. After all, we not only make beautiful music, love and beadwork; we pay our pigs to exterminate Black Panthers, we fry Vietnamese in their own homes and we elect Spiro Agnew to govern our lives.

Altamont was a lesson in micro-society with no holds barred. Bringing a lot of people together used to be cool. Human be-ins, Woodstock, even a Hell's Angel funeral, were creative communal events because their centre was everywhere. People would play together, performing, participating, sharing, and going home with a feeling that somehow the communal idea would replace the grim isolation wrought on us by a jealous competitive mother culture.

But at Altamont we were the mother culture. The locust generation come to consume crumbs from the hands of an entertainment industry we helped create. Our one-day micro-society was bound to the death-throes of capitalist greed. The freeway culture delivered the crowd, separate, self-contained in Methedrine isolation, to an event where they could not function as private individuals. The crowd came from a country where everything is done for you. Welfare state – relax, work and pay your taxes. We'll take care of the war in Vietnam and the war at home.

Yeah, but nobody made sure the machine would function at Altamont. Three hundred thousand people sucked on a dry nipple because it was free. Everyone tried to get to the same place all by himself, and since everyone made it there was no pie. The pie was watching yourself at the spectacle, watching the spectacle watching you at the spectacle doing your own thing watching.

America at Altamont could only muster one common response. Everybody grooved on fear. One communal terror of fascist repression. The rest was all separate, people helping, people walking, people eating, people standing in line to shit. The revolutionaries were there too. Everybody related to people freaking out as well as the mother culture relates to Yippies. Here they were running through the crowd naked, stoned, trampling on our thinning privacy.

They expressed our own lack of control, our desire for space, for the freedom to live out our own body lives. But the crowd reacted with blind hatred, paranoia pressing them forward to get a better look at their own private crush on his satanic majesty.

But it wasn't all a freak-out. Back up the slopes of Altamont Speedway, as in the secluded suburbs and woods of America, people kept to the illusions of better dope and more space. The loners, couples and communes saw nothing, heard nothing, and cared less about the crowded valley of fear. Most of them say they had a good time, but few escaped the heavy vibes from below.

Around the stage, at the epi-centre, the Angels lost control. Their violence united the crowd in fear. Even people who had no fear of the Angels grew tense from a repressed feeling of panic that swirled around the stage. Mostly it was a fear of being trampled that was intensified by fights and people who did freak out. Since the Angels were the only group there who were together enough to organize their violence, they became a clear focus of crowd hatred. Thousands of times we've blamed pigs for less while holding the myth of right-wing Anarchist sacred. Marlon Brando, freewheelin' agent of chaos, another of Saturday's toppled camp heroes.

The Angels protected Mick, their diabolic prince, well. He escaped without serious injury. Later on KSAN they, too, defended their actions on the grounds that their private property was violated '. . . ain't nobody going to kick an Angel's bike and get away with it . . .' The official cover-up came Ronald Reagan style from the Stones' manager Sam Cutler. When asked about the Angels' violence he answered '. . . regrettable, but if you're asking for a condemnation of the Angels . . .'

It was over. No explanation was needed, only a feeble plea for someone in America to clean it up. The stirrings of a young but growing movement to salvage our environment. The job of cleaning up Altamont, or America, is still up for grabs. America wallows in the hope that someone, somewhere, can set it straight. Clearly nobody is in control. Not the Angels, not the people. Not Richard Nixon or his pigs. Nobody. America is up for grabs, as she sinks slowly into Methedrine suffocation with an occasional fascist kick to make her groan with satisfaction.

What Is This Shit?

GREIL MARCUS

Marcus's famous Rolling Stone *review of Dylan's 1970 two fingers to his audience,* Self Portrait, *carried no byline, but its opening statement will forever define the general response to Dylan's sprawling exercise in commercial suicide. I mean to say . . .*

(1)

What is this shit?

(2)

'I don't know if I should keep playing this,' said the disc jockey, as the album made its debut on the radio. 'Nobody's calling in and saying they want to hear it or anything . . . usually when something like this happens people say "Hey, the new Dylan album"', but not tonight.'

Later someone called and asked for a reprise of 'Blue Moon'. In the end it all came down to a telephone poll to determine whether radioland really cared. The D J keeps apologizing. 'If there is anyone who needs . . . or deserves to have his whole album played through it's Bob Dylan.'

(3)

'What was it?' said a friend, after we'd heard thirty minutes of *Self Portrait* for the first time. 'Were we really that impressionable back in '65, '66? Was it that the stuff really wasn't that good, that this is just as good? Was it some sort of accident in time that made those other records so powerful, or what?

'My life was really turned around, it affected me – I don't know if it was the records or the words or the sound or the noise – maybe the interview: "What is there to believe in?" I doubt if he'd say that now, though.'

We put on 'Like A Rolling Stone' from *Highway 61 Revisited* and sat through it. 'I was listening to that song, ten times a day for the last few months, hustling my ass, getting my act together to get into school . . . but it's such a drag to hear what he's done with it . . .'

(4)

G M: 'It's such an unambitious album.'
J W: 'Maybe what we need most of all right now is an unambitious album from Dylan.'
G M: 'What we need most of all is for Dylan to get ambitious.'
J W: 'It's such a . . .'
G M & J W: '. . . *friendly* album . . .'

(5)

'It's hard,' he said. 'It's hard for Dylan to do anything real, shut off the way he is, not interested in the world, maybe no reason why he should be. Maybe the weight of the days is too strong, maybe withdrawal is a choice we'd make if we could . . .' One's reminded that art doesn't come – perhaps that it can't be heard – in times of crisis and destruction; art comes in the period of decadence that precedes a revolution, or after the deluge. It's a prelude to revolution; it's not contemporary with it save in terms of memory.

But in the midst of it all artists sometimes move in to re-create history. That takes ambition.

(6)

The four questions: The four sons gazed at the painting on the museum wall. 'It's a painting,' said the first son. 'It's art,' said the second son. 'It's a frame,' said the third son, and he said it rather coyly. The fourth son was usually considered somewhat stupid, but he at least figured out why they'd come all the way from home to look at the thing in the first place. 'It's a signature,' he said.

(7)

Imagine a kid in his teens responding to *Self Portrait*. His older brothers and sisters have been living by Dylan for years. They come home with the album and he simply cannot figure out what it's all about. To him, *Self Portrait* sounds more like the stuff his parents listen to than what he wants to hear; in fact, his parents have just gone out and bought *Self Portrait* and given it to him for his birthday. He considers giving it back for Father's Day.

To this kid, Dylan is a figure of myth; nothing less, but nothing more. Dylan is not real and the album carries no reality. He's never seen Bob Dylan; he doesn't expect to; he can't figure out why he would want to.

(8)

'Bob should go whole-hog and revive the Bing Crosby Look, with its emphasis on five-button, soft shoulder, wide-collar, plain country-club lounge jackets (Pendleton probably still makes them). And, like Der Bingle, it might do well for Dylan to work a long-stemmed briar pipe into his act, stopping every so often to light up, puff at it, raise some smoke and gaze, momentarily, toward the horizon, before launching into [this is John Burks in *Rags*, June 1970] the next phrase of "Peggy Day". Then, for his finale – the big "Blue Moon" production number with the girls and the spotlights on the fountains – he does a quick costume change into

554

one of those high-collar 1920s formal shirts with the diamond-shaped bow tie, plus, of course, full-length tails and the trousers with the satin stripe down the side, carnation in the buttonhole, like Dick Powell in *Gold Diggers of 1933*. Here comes Dylan in his tails, his briar in one hand, his megaphone in the other, strolling down the runway, smiling that toothpaste smile. "Like a roll-ing stone . . ."'

(9)

'It's a high school yearbook. Colour pictures this year, because there was a surplus left over from last year, more pages than usual too, a sentimental journey, "what we did", it's not all that interesting, it's a memento of something, there's a place for autographs, lots of white space, nobody's name was left out . . . It is June, after all.'

(10)

Self Portrait most closely resembles the Dylan album that preceded it: *Great White Wonder*. The album is a two-record set masterfully assembled from an odd collection of mostly indifferent recordings made over the course of the last year, complete with alternate takes, chopped endings, loose beginnings, side comments and all sorts of mistakes. Straight from the can to you, as it were. A bit from Nashville, a taste of the Isle of Wight since you missed it, some sessions from New York that mostly don't make it, but dig, it's Dylan, and if you wanted *Great White Wonder* and *Stealin'* and *John Birch* and *Isle Of Wight* and *A Thousand Miles Behind*, *Self Portrait* will surely fill the need.

I don't think it will. It's true that all of the bootlegs (and the Masked Marauders, which was a fantasy bootleg) came out in the absence of new music from Dylan, but I think their release was related not to the absence of his recordings but to the absence of the man himself. We are dealing with myth, after all, and the more Dylan stays away the greater the weight attached to anything he's done. When King Midas reached out his hand everything he touched not only turned to gold, it became valuable to everyone else, and Dylan still has the Midas touch even though he'd rather not reach out. It is only in the last two years that the collecting of old tapes by Dylan has really become a general phenomena, and there are many times more tapes in circulation than are represented on the bootlegs. There is a session with the Band from December of 1965, live albums, ancient recordings, tapes of Dylan at the Guthrie Memorial, with the Band last summer in Missouri, radio shows from the early sixties, and a live 'Like A Rolling Stone'. It sometimes seems as if every public act Dylan ever made was recorded, and it is all coming together. Eventually, the bootleggers will get their hands on it. Legally, there is virtually nothing he can do to stop it.

He can head off the theft and sale of his first drafts, his secrets, and his memories only with his music. And it is the vitality of the music that is being bootlegged that is the basis of its appeal. The noise of it. *Self Portrait*, though it's a good imitation bootleg, isn't nearly the music that *Great White Wonder* is. 'Copper Kettle' is a masterpiece but 'Killing Me Alive' will blow it down. *Nashville Skyline* and *John Wesley Harding* are classic albums; but no matter how good they are they lack the power of the music Dylan made in the middle sixties. Unless he returns to the market-place, with a sense of vocation and the ambition to keep up with his own gifts, the music of those years will continue to dominate his records, whether he releases them or not. If the music Dylan makes doesn't have the power to enter into the lives of his audience – and *Self Portrait* does not have that power – his audience will take over his past.

(11)

In the record industry music is referred to as 'product'. 'We got Beatle product.' When the whirlwind courtship of Johnny Winter and Columbia was finally consummated everyone wanted to know when they would get product. They got product fast but it took them a while longer to get music. Such is showbiz, viz. *Self Portrait*, which is already a triple gold record, the way 'O Captain! My Captain!' is more famous than 'When Lilacs Last In The Dooryard Bloom'd', is the closest thing to pure product in Dylan's career, even more so than *Greatest Hits*, because that had no pretensions. The purpose of *Self Portrait* is mainly product and the need it fills is for product – for 'a Dylan album' – and make no mistake about it, the need for product is felt as deeply by those who buy it, myself included, of course, as by those who sell it, and perhaps more so.

As a throw-together album it resembles *Flowers*; but it's totally unlike *Flowers* in that the album promises to be more than it is, rather than less. But its title alone, *Self Portrait*, makes claims for itself as the definitive Dylan album – which it may be, in a sad way – but it is still something like an attempt to delude the public into thinking they are getting more than they are, or that *Self Portrait* is more than it is.

(12)

'. . . various times he thought of completing his baccalaureate so that he could teach in the college and oddly enough [this is from *A Rimbaud Chronology*, New Directions Press] of learning to play the piano. At last he went to Holland, where, in order to reach the Orient, he enlisted in the Dutch Army and sailed for Java in June of 1876. Three weeks after his arrival in Batavia

[Charles Perry: "We know Dylan was the Rimbaud of his generation; it seems he's found his Abyssinia"] he deserted, wandered among the natives of the jungle and soon signed on a British ship for Liverpool. After a winter at home he went to Hamburg, joined in a circus as interpreter-manager to tour the northern countries, but the cold was too much for him and he was repatriated from Sweden, only to leave home again, this time for Alexandria. Again, illness interrupted his travels and he was put off the ship in Italy and spent a year recovering on the farm at Roche. In 1878 he was in Hamburg again, trying to reach Genoa to take a ship for the East. Once more he tried to cross the Alps on foot [Charles Perry: "We know that Dylan was the Rimbaud of his generation; it seems he's found his Abyssinia"] but in a snow-storm he almost perished. Saved by monks in a Hospice, he managed to reach Genoa and sail to Alexandria where he worked as a farm labourer for a while. In Suez, where he was stopped on his way to Cyprus, he was employed as a ship-breaker to plunder a ship wrecked on the dangerous coast at Guardafui. Most of the first half of 1879 he worked as foreman in a desert quarry on Cyprus, and went home in June to recuperate from typhoid fever.'

(13)

I once said I'd buy an album of Dylan breathing heavily. I still would, but not an album of Dylan breathing softly.

(14, 15, 16)

'. . . very highly successful in terms of money. Dylan's concerts in the past have been booked by his own firm, Ashes and Sand, rather than by [this is from *Rolling Stone*, 7 December 1968] private promoters. Promoters are now talking about a ten-city tour with the possibility of adding more dates, according to *Variety*.

'Greta Garbo may also come out of retirement to do a series of personal appearances. The Swedish film star who wanted only "to be alone" after continued press invasions of her life is rumoured to be considering a series of lavish stage shows, possibly with Dylan . . .'

And we'd just sit there and stare.

(17)

Before going into the studio to set up the Weathermen, he wrote the Yippies' first position paper, although it took Abbie Hoffman a few years to find it and Jerry Rubin had trouble reading it. A quote:

> I'm gonna grow my hair down to my feet so strange till I look like a walking mountain range then I'm gonna ride into Omaha on a horse out to the country club and the golf courses carrying a *New York Times* shoot a few holes blow their minds.

'Dylan's coming,' said Lang.

'Ah, you're full of shit,' [said Abbie Hoffman in *Woodstock Nation*] 'he's gonna be in England tonight, don't pull that shit on me.'

'Nah, I ain't kiddin, Abbey-baby, he called up and said he might come . . .'

'You think he'd dig running for president?'

'Nah, that ain't his trip, he's into something else.'

'You met him, Mike? What's he into?'

'I don't know for sure but it ain't exactly politics. You ever met him?'

'Yeah, once about seven years ago in Gertie's Folk City down in the West Village. I was trying to get him to do a benefit for civil rights or something . . . hey, Mike, will you introduce us? I sure would like to meet Dylan . . . I only know about meetin' him through Happy Traum . . .'

'There's an easier way . . . Abbs . . . I'll introduce you. In fact he wants to meet you . . .' Would *Self Portrait* make you want to meet Dylan? No? Perhaps it's there to keep you away?

(18)

It's certainly a rather odd 'self portrait': other people's songs and the songs of a few years ago. If the title is serious, Dylan no longer cares much about making music and would just as soon define himself on someone else's terms. There is a curious move toward self-effacement; Dylan removing himself from a position from which he is asked to exercise power in the arena. It's rather like the Duke of Windsor abdicating the throne. After it's over he merely goes away, and occasionally there'll be a picture of him getting on a plane somewhere.

(19)

Because of what happened in the middle sixties, our fate is bound up with Dylan's whether he or we like it or not. Because *Highway 61 Revisited* changed the world, the albums that follow it must — but not in the same way, of course.

(20)

Ralph Gleason: 'There was this cat Max Kaminsky talks about in his autobiography who stole records. He stole one from Max. He had to have them, you know? Just had to have them. Once he got busted because he heard this record on a jukebox and shoved his fist through the glass of the box to get the record out.

'We all have records we'd steal for, that we need that bad. But would you steal this record? You wouldn't steal this record.' You wouldn't steal *Self Portrait*? It wouldn't steal you either. Perhaps that's the real tragedy, because Dylan's last two albums were art breaking and entering into the house of the mind.

(21, 22)

That splendid frenzy, the strength of new values in the midst of some sort of musical behemoth of destruction, the noise, the power – the *totality* of it! So you said well, all right, there it is . . .

The mythical immediacy of everything Dylan does and the relevance of that force to the way we live our lives is rooted in the three albums and the two incredible singles he released in 1965 and 1966: *Bringing It All Back Home*, *Highway 61 Revisited*, *Blonde On Blonde*, 'Like A Rolling Stone' and 'Subterranean Homesick Blues'. Those records defined and structured a crucial year – no one has ever caught up with them and most likely no one ever will. What happened then is what we always look for. The power of those recordings and of the music Dylan was making on stage, together with his retreat at the height of his career, made Dylan into a legend and virtually changed his name into a noun. Out of that Dylan gained the freedom to step back and get away with anything he chose to do, commercially and artistically. The fact that more than a year now separates one album from another heightens their impact, regardless of how much less they have to offer than the albums which established this matrix of power in the first place. In a real way, Dylan is trading on the treasure of myth, fame and awe he gathered in '65 and '66. In mythical terms, he doesn't have to do good, because he has done good. One wonders, in mythical terms of course, how long he can get away with it.

(23)

Vacation as a vocation: Dylan is, if he wants to be, an American with a vocation. It might almost be a calling – the old Puritan idea of a gift one should live up to – but it's not, and vocation is strong enough.

There is no theme richer for the American artist than the spirit and the themes of the country and the country's history. We have never figured out what this place is about or what it is for, and the only way to even begin to answer those questions is to watch our movies, read our poets, our novelists, and listen to our music. Robert Johnson and Melville, Hank Williams and Hawthorne, Bob Dylan and Mark Twain, Jimmie Rodgers and John Wayne. America is the life's work of the American artist because he is doomed to be an American. Dylan has a feel for it; his impulses seem to take him back into the forgotten parts of our history, and even on *Self Portrait*, there is a sense of this vocation; Bob is almost on the verge of writing a western. But it's an ambitious vocation and there is not enough of that, only an impulse without the determination to follow it up.

Dylan has a vocation if he wants it; his audience may refuse to accept his refusal unless he simply goes away. In the midst of that vocation there might be something like a *Hamlet* asking questions, old questions, with a bit of magic to them; but hardly a prophet, merely a man with good vision.

(24)

Self portrait, the auteur, and home movies: 'Auteur' means, literally, 'author', and in America the word has come to signify a formula about films: movies (like books) are made by 'authors', i.e. directors. This has led to a dictum which tends to affirm the following: movies are about the personality of the director. We should judge a movie in terms of how well the '*auteur*' has 'developed his personality' in relation to previous films. His best film is that which most fully presents the flowering of his personality. Needless to say such an approach requires a devotion to mannerism, quirk and self-indulgence. It also turns out that the greatest *auteurs* are those with the most consistent, obvious, and recognizable mannerisms, quirks and self-indulgences. By this approach *Stolen Kisses* is a better film than *Jules and Jim* because in *Stolen Kisses* we have nothing to look for but Truffaut while in *Jules and Jim* there is this story and those actors who keep getting in the way. The spirit of the *auteur* approach can be transferred to other arts; and by its dictum, *Self Portrait* is a better album than *Highway 61 Revisited*, because *Self Portrait* is about the *auteur*, that is Dylan, and *Highway 61 Revisited* takes on the world, which tends to get in the way (*Highway 61 Revisited* might well be about Dylan too, but it's more obvious on *Self Portrait*, and therefore more relevant to Art, and . . . please don't ask about the music, really . . .).

Now Dylan has been approached this way for years, whether or not the word was used, and while in the end it may be the least interesting way to listen to his music it's occasionally a lot of fun and a game that many of us have played (for example, on 'Days Of '49' Dylan sings the line 'just like a roving sign' and I just can't help almost hearing him say 'just like a rolling stone' and wondering if he avoided that on purpose). One writer, named Alan Weberman, has devoted his life to unraveling Dylan's songs in order to examine the man himself; just as every artist once had his patron now every *auteur* has his critic, it seems.

Self portrait, the auteur, and home movies cont.: We all play the *auteur* game. We went out and bought *Self Portrait* not because we knew it was great music – it might have been but that's not the first question we'd ask – but because it was a Dylan Album. What we *want*, though, is a different matter – and that's what separates most people from auteurists – we want great music, and because of those three albums back in '65 and '66, we expect it, or hope for it.

I wouldn't be dwelling on this but for my suspicion that it is exactly a perception of this approach that is the justification for the release of *Self Portrait*, to the degree that it is justified artistically (the commercial justification is something else – self-justification). The *auteur* approach allows the great artist to limit his ambition, perhaps even to abandon it, and turn inward. To be crude, it begins to seem as if it is his habits that matter, rather than his vision. If we approach art in this fashion, we degrade it. Take that second song on *John Wesley Harding*, 'As I Went Out One Morning', and two ways of hearing it.

Weberman has determined a fixed meaning for the song: it relates to a dinner given years ago by the Emergency Civil Liberties Committee at which they awarded Bob Dylan their Thomas Paine Prize. Dylan showed up, said a few words about how it was possible to understand how Lee Harvey Oswald felt, and got booed. 'As I Went Out One Morning', according to Weberman, is Dylan's way of say he didn't dig getting booed.

I sometimes hear the song as a brief journey into American history; the singer out for a walk in the park, finding himself next to a statue of Tom Paine, and stumbling across an allegory: Tom Paine, symbol of freedom and revolt, co-opted into the role of Patriot by text-books and statue committees, and now playing, as befits his role as Patriot, enforcer to a girl who runs for freedom – in chains, to the South, the source of vitality in America, in America's music – away from Tom Paine. We have turned our history on its head; we have perverted our own myths.

Now it would be astonishing if what I've just described was on Dylan's mind when he wrote the song. That's not the point. The point is that Dylan's songs can serve as metaphors, enriching our lives, giving us random insight into the myths we carry and the present we live, intensifying what we've known and leading us toward what we never looked for, while at the same time enforcing an emotional strength upon those perceptions by the power of the music that moves with his words. Weberman's way of hearing, or rather seeing, is more logical, more linear, and perhaps even 'correct', but it's sterile. Mine is not an answer but a possibility, and I think Dylan's music is about possibilities, rather than facts, like a statue that is not an expenditure of city funds but a gateway to a vision.

If we are to be satisfied with *Self Portrait*, we may have to see it in the sterile terms of the *auteur*, which in our language would be translated as 'Hey, far out, Dylan singing Simon and Garfunkel, Rodgers and Hart, and Gordon Lightfoot . . .' Well, it is far out, in a sad sort of way, but it is also vapid, and if our own untaught perception of the *auteur* allows us to be satisfied with it, we degrade our own sensibilities and Dylan's capabilities as an American artist as well. Dylan did not become a figure whose every movement carries the force of myth by presenting desultory images of his own career as if that was the only story that mattered – he did it by taking on the world, by assault, and by seduction.

In an attack on the *auteur* approach, as it relates to film, Kevin Brownlow quotes an old dictionary, and the words he cites reveal the problem: 'The novel (the film) (the song) is a subjective epic composition in which the author begs leave to treat the world according to his own point of view. It is only a question, therefore, whether he has a point of view. The rest will take care of itself.'

Crazy Diamond

NICK KENT

'Remember when you were young/You shone like the sun', sang the Floyd in 1974, just as NME were running Nick Kent's sorry tale of ex-Floyd mainstay Syd Barrett's slide into a nether-world of hobgoblins. Written at a time when, despite three years of terminal silence, people were still wondering whether Barrett might come out of his hermetic state, Kent's portrait suggested that Barrett was unlikely to falter in his role as a modern-day Rimbaud.

There is a story that exists pertaining to an incident which occurred during one of Syd Barrett's last gigs with the Pink Floyd. After a lengthy interval, the band decided to take to the stage (there is a certain amount of dispute as to which venue this all took place at) – all except for Syd Barrett, who was left in the dressing-room, manically trying to organize his anarchically inclined hairstyle of the time.

As his comrades were tuning up, Barrett – more out of desperation than anything – emptied the contents of a jar of Mandrax, broke the pills into tiny pieces and mixed the crumbs in with a full jar of Brylcreem. He then poured the whole coagulated mass on to his head, picked up his Telecaster, and walked on stage.

As he was playing his customary incoherent, sporadic, almost catatonic guitar phrases, the Mandrax–Brylcreem combination started to run amok under the intense heat of the stage lighting and dribbled down from his scalp so that it looked like his face was melting into a distorted wax effigy of flesh.

*

This story is probably more or less true. It exists amidst an infinity of strange tales – many of them fact, just as many wistful fiction – that surround and largely comprise the whole legend-in-his-own-time schtick of which Syd Barrett is very much the dubiously honoured possessor.

Barrett is still alive and basically functioning, by the way.

Every so often he appears at Lupus Music, his publishing company situated on Berkeley Square which handles his royalties situation and has kept him in modest financial stead these last few dormant years. On one of his last visits (which constitute possibly Barrett's only real contact with the outside world), Brian Morrison, Lupus's manager, started getting insistent that Barrett write some songs. After all, demand for more Syd Barrett material is remarkably high at the moment and EMI are all ready to swoop the lad into the studio, producer in tow, at any given moment.

Barrett claimed that no, he hadn't written anything, but dutifully agreed to get down and produce some sort of something.

His next appearance at the office occurred last week. Asked if he'd written any new tunes, he replied in his usual hazy condition, hair grown out somewhat from its former scalp-shaved condition, 'No.' He then promptly disappeared again.

This routine has been going on for years now. Otherwise Barrett tends to appear at Lupus only when the rent is due or when he wants to buy a guitar (a luxury that at one point became an obsession and consequently had to be curtailed).

The rest of Barrett's time is spent either sprawled out in front of the large colour TV in his two-room apartment situated in the hinterland of Chelsea, or else just walking at random around London. A recent port-of-call was a clothes store down the King's Road where Syd tried on three vastly different sizes of the same style of trousers, claimed that all of them fitted him perfectly and then disappeared again, without buying any.

And that's basically what the whole Syd Barrett story is all about – a huge tragedy shot through with so many ludicrously comic aspects that you could easily be tempted to fill out a whole article by simply relating all the crazy anecdotes and half-chewed tales of twilight dementia, and leave it at that. The conclusion, however, is always inescapable and goes far beyond the utterly bogus image compounded of the artist as some fated victim spread out on an altar of acid and sacrificed to the glorious spirit of '67.

Syd Barrett was simply a brilliant, innovative young songwriter whose genius was somehow amputated, leaving him hamstrung in a lonely limbo accompanied only by a stunted creativity and a kind of helpless, illogical schizophrenia.

The whole saga starts, I suppose, at least for convenience's sake, with a band called the Abdabs. They were also called the 'T'-Set and no one I spoke to quite knew which had come first. It doesn't really matter though.

The band was a five-piece, as it happens, consisting of three young aspiring architects, Richard Wright, Nick Mason and Roger Waters, a jazz guitarist called Bob Close and – the youngest member – an art student called Roger Keith Barrett (Barrett, like most other kids, had been landed with a nickname – 'Syd' – which somehow remained long after his schooldays had been completed).

The band, it was generally considered, were pretty dire – but, as they all emanated from the hip élitist circles of their home-town Cambridge they were respected after a fashion at least in their own area. This hip élite was, according to fellow-townsman Storm of Hipgnosis (the well-respected record-sleeve design company who of course have kept a close and solid relationship all along with the Floyd), built on several levels of acquaintances, mostly tied by age.

'It was the usual thing really, 1962 we were all into Jimmy Smith. Then 1963 brought dope and rock. Syd was one of the first to get into the Beatles and Stones.'

Storm remembers Barrett as a 'bright, extrovert kid. Smoked dope, pulled chicks – the usual thing. He had no problems on the surface. He was no introvert as far as I could see then.'

Before the advent of the Pink Floyd, Barrett had three brooding interests – music, painting and religion. A number of Barrett's seniors in Cambridge were starting to get involved in an obscure form of Eastern mysticism known as 'Saint Saji' which involved heavy bouts of meditation and much contemplation on purity and the inner light.

Syd attempted to involve himself in the faith, but he was turned down for being 'too young' (he was nineteen at the time). This, according to a number of those who knew him, was supposed to have affected him quite deeply.

At any rate, Barrett lost all interest in spiritualism after that and soon enough he would also give up his painting. Already he'd won a scholarship to Camberwell Art School in Peckham which was big potatoes for just another hopeful from out in the sticks.

Both Dave Gilmour and Storm claim that Barrett's painting showed exceptional potential: 'Syd was a great artist. I loved his work, but he just stopped. First it was the religion, then the painting. He was starting to shut himself off slowly then.'

Music, of course, remained. The Abdabs . . . well let's forget about them and examine the 'Pink Floyd Sound', which was really just the old band but minus Bob Close who 'never quite fitted in'. The Pink Floyd Sound name came from Syd after a blues record he owned which featured two bluesmen from Georgia – Pink Anderson and Floyd Council. The two names meshed nicely, so . . .

Anyway, the band was still none too inspiring – no original material, but versions of 'Louie Louie' and 'Road Runner' into which would be interspersed liberal dosages of staccato freak-out. Kinda like the Blues Magoos, I guess.

'Freak-out' was happening in the States at the time – the time being 1966, the year of the Yardbirds, the Mothers of Invention and the first primal croaks from the West Coast. Not to mention *Revolver* and 'Eight Miles High'.

The fat was obviously in the pan for the big 1967 Summer of Love psychedelic bust-out. However, the Pink Floyd Sound weren't exactly looking to the future at this juncture.

Peter Jenner, a lecturer at the LSE and John 'Hoppy' Hopkins were in the audience for one of their gigs and were impressed enough to offer them some sort of management deal.

Admits Jenner: 'It was one of the first rock events I'd seen – I didn't know anything about rock really.' (Jenner and Hopkins had in fact made one offer prior to the Floyd – to a band they'd heard on advance tape from New York called the Velvet Underground.)

'Actually the Floyd then were barely semi pro standard, now I think about it, but I was so impressed by the electric guitar sound. The band was just at the point of breaking up then, y'know. It was weird – they just thought, "Oh, well, might as well pack it all in." But we came along and so they changed their minds.'

The first trick was the light show and the UFO concerts. The next was activating a policy of playing only original compositions.

This is where Syd Barrett came into his own. Barrett hadn't really composed tunes before this – the odd one here and there – a nonsense song called 'Effervescing Elephant' when he was maybe sixteen – and he'd put music to a poem to be found in James Joyce's *Ulysses* called 'Golden Hair', but nothing beyond that.

The first manifestation of Barrett's songwriting talents was a bizarre little classic called 'Arnold Layne'. A sinister piece of vaguely commercial fare, it dealt with the twilight wanderings of a transvestite/pervert figure and is both whimsical and singularly creepy.

The single was banned by Radio London who found its general connotations a little too bizarre for even pirate radio standards.

The Floyd were by now big stuff in Swinging London. Looking back on it all, the band came on just like naïve art students in Byrds-styled granny glasses (the first publicity shots are particularly laughable), but the music somehow had an edge. Certainly enough for prestigious folk like Brian Epstein to mouth off rhapsodies of praise on French radio, and all the 'chic' mags to throw in the token mention.

There were even TV shows – good late night avant-garde programmes for Hampstead trendies like *Look of the Week* on which the Floyd played 'Pow R. Toc H'.

The Floyd Cult was growing as Barrett's creativity was beginning to hit its stride. This creativity set the stage in Barrett's songwriting for what can only be described as the quintessential marriage of the two ideal forms of English psychedelia – musical rococo freak-outs underpinning Barrett's sudden ascendancy into the artistic realms of ye olde English whimsical loone, wherein dwelt the likes of Edward Lear and Kenneth Grahame. Pervy old Lewis Carroll, of course, presided at the very head of the tea-party.

And so Arnold Layne and washing-lines gave way to the whole Games-for-May ceremony and 'See Emily Play'.

'I was sleeping in the woods one night after a gig we'd played somewhere, when I saw this girl appear before me. That girl is Emily.'

Thus quoth the mighty Syd himself back in '67, obviously caught up in it all like some kite lost in spring.

And it was glorious for a time. *Piper At The Gates Of Dawn* was being recorded at the same time as *Sgt Pepper* and the two bands would occasionally meet up to check out each other's product. McCartney stepped out to bestow his papal blessing on *Piper*, an album which still stands as my fondest musical memory of 1967 – even more so than *Pepper* or *Younger Than Yesterday*. (All except for 'Bike' which reeks of crazy basements and Barrett eccentricities beginning to lose control – psychedelic whimsy taken a little too close to the edge.)

You see, strange things were starting to happen with the Floyd and particularly with Barrett.

'See Emily Play' was Top 5 which enabled Barrett to more than adequately live out his pop star infatuation number to the hilt – the Hendrix curls, kaftans from 'Granny's', snakeskin boots and Fender Telecasters were all his for the asking – but there were the, uh, unstabilizing influences.

First came the ego problems and slight prima donna fits, but gradually the Floyd, Jenner et al. realized that something deeper was going on. Take the Floyd's three *Top of the Pops* appearances for Emily.

Jenner: 'The first time Syd dressed up like a pop star. The second time he came on in his straightforward, fairly scruffy clothes, looking rather unshaven. The third time he came to the studio in his pop star clothes and then changed into complete rags for the actual TV spot.'

It was all something to do with the fact that John Lennon had stated publicly he wouldn't appear on *Top of the Pops*. Syd seemed to envisage Lennon as some sort of yardstick by which to measure his own situation as a pop star.

But there were far darker manifestations of a definite impending imbalance in the Barrett psyche.

He was at that point involved in a relationship with a girl named Lynsey – an affair which took an uncomfortably bizarre turn when the lady involved appeared on Peter Jenner's doorstep fairly savagely beaten up.

'I couldn't believe it at the time. I had this firm picture of Syd as this really gentle guy, which is what he was, basically.'

Something was definitely awry. In fact there are numerous fairly unpleasant tales about this particular affair (including one that claims Barrett to have locked the girl in a room for a solid week, pushing water biscuits under the door so she wouldn't starve) which are best not dwelt on.

But to make matters worse, Syd's eyes were often seen to cement themselves into a foreboding, nay quite terrifying stare which really started to put the frighteners on present company. The head would tilt back slightly, the eyes would get misty and bloated. Then they would stare right at you and right through you at the same time.

One thing was painfully obvious: the boy genius was fast becoming mentally totally unhinged.

Perhaps it was the drugs. Barrett's intake at the time was suitably fearsome, while many considered his metabolism for such chemicals to be a trifle fragile. Certainly they only tended towards a further tipping of the psyche scales, but it would be far too easy to write Barrett off as some hapless acid amputee – even though certain folks now claim that a two-month sojourn in Richmond with a couple suitably named 'Mad Sue' and 'Mad Jock' had him drinking a cup of tea each morning which was, unknown to Syd, spiked with a heavy dosage of acid.

Such activity can, of course, lead to a certain degree of brain damage, but I fear one has to stride manfully blindfolded into a rather more Freudian landscape, leading us to the opinion of many of the people I talked to who claimed that Syd's dilemma stretched back to certain childhood traumas.

The youngest of a family of eight, heavily affected by the sudden death of his father when Syd was twelve years old, spoilt by a strong-willed mother who may or may not have imposed a strange distinction between the dictates of fantasy and reality – each contention forms a patchwork quilt-like set up of insinuations and potential cause-and-effect mechanisms.

'Everyone is supposed to have fun when they're young – I don't know why, but I never did' (Barrett talking in an interview to *Rolling Stone*, autumn 1971).

Jenner: 'I think we tended to underrate the extent of his

problem. . . . One thing I regret now was that I made demands on Syd. He'd written "See Emily Play" and suddenly everything had to be seen in commercial terms. I think we may have pressurized him into a state of paranoia about having to come up with another "hit single". Also we may have been the darlings of London, but out in the suburbs it was fairly terrible. Before "Emily" we'd have things thrown at us on-stage. After "Emily" it was screaming girls wanting to hear our hit song. So the Floyd hit the ballroom circuit and Syd was starting to play up.'

An American tour was then set up in November – three dates at the Fillmore West in San Francisco and an engagement at LA's Cheetah Club.

Barrett's dishevelled psyche started truly manifesting itself though when the Floyd were forced on to some TV shows. *Dick Clark's Bandstand* was disastrous because it needed a miming job on the band's part and 'Syd wasn't into moving his lips that day.'

The *Pat Boone Show* was quite surreal: Boone actually tried to interview Barrett on the screen, asking him particularly inane questions and getting a truly classic catatonic piercing mute stare for an answer.

So there was the return to England and the rest of the Floyd had made the decision. On the one hand, Barrett was the songwriter and central figure – on the other his madness was much too much to handle. He just couldn't be communicated with.

Patience had not been rewarded and the break-away was on the cards.

But not before a final studio session at De Lane Lea took place – a mad, anarchic affair which spawned three of Barrett's truly vital twilight rantings. Unfortunately only one has been released.

'Jugband Blues', the only Barrett track off *Saucerful Of Secrets* is as good an explanation as any for Syd not appearing on the rest of the album.

'Y'see, even at that point, Syd actually knew what was happening to him,' claims Jenner. 'I mean, "Jugband Blues" is the ultimate self-diagnosis on a state of schizophrenia . . .'

> It's awfully considerate of you to think of me here.
> And I'm most obliged to you for making it clear that I'm
>   not here.
> And I'm wondering who could be writing this song.

Barrett even had a Salvation Army Band troop in during the middle of the number. The two unreleased numbers are both unfinished creations – one a masterful splurge of blood-curdling pro-Beefheartian lunacy – 'Scream Your Last Scream' . . .

> Scream your Last Scream
> Old Woman with a basket
> Wave your arms madly, madly
> Flat tops of houses
> Houses. Mouses. She'll be scrubbing apples on all fours
> Middle-dee-riddle with Dumpy Mrs Dee
> We'll be watching telly for all hours.

The other, 'Vegetable Man', is a crazy sing-along.

'Syd,' recalls Jenner, 'was around at my house just before he had to go to record and, because a song was needed, he just wrote a description of what he was wearing at the time and threw in a chorus that went "Vegetable man – where are you?"'

A nationwide tour of Great Britain followed – Jimi Hendrix, the Move, the Nice and the Floyd on one package – which distanced things out even further. Syd often wouldn't turn up on time, sometimes didn't play at all, and sat by himself on the tour coach.

The rest of the Floyd socialized with the Nice (guitarist David O'List played with the band when Barrett was incapable). But surely the two uncrowned kings of acid-rock – Hendrix and Barrett – must have socialized in some capacity?

'Not really,' states Jenner. 'Hendrix had his own limousine. Syd didn't really talk to anyone. I mean, by now he was going on-stage and playing one chord throughout the set. He was into this thing of total anarchistic experiment and never really considered the other members of the band.'

There was also this thing with Syd that the Floyd were 'my band'. Enter Dave Gilmour, not long back from working with various groups in France – an old mate and fair guitar. The implications were obvious.

Jenner: 'At the time Dave was doing very effective take-offs of Hendrix-style guitar playing. So the band said "play like Syd Barrett".'

Yeah, but surely Dave Gilmour had his own style – y'know, the slide and echo sound?

'That's Syd. On-stage Syd used to play with slide and a bunch of echo-boxes.'

Hmmm.

The Floyd played maybe four gigs with the five-piece and then Barrett was ousted. It was a courageous move – he reacted and everyone seems to agree that it was all perfectly warranted. Except, maybe, Syd.

From here on in, the whole Barrett saga goes a trifle haywire.

Barrett himself loped off into the back country of Earl's Court to greet the usual freak show, but not before he'd stayed over at South Kensington awhile with Storm.

'Syd was well into his "orbiting" phase by then. He was travelling very fast in his own private sphere and I thought I could be a mediator of some sort. Y'see, I think you're going to have to make the point that Syd's madness was not caused by any linear progression of events, but more a circular haze of situations that meshed together on top of themselves and Syd. Me, I couldn't handle those stares though!'

By that time, the Floyd and Blackhill Enterprises had parted company, Jenner choosing Barrett as a brighter hope. What happened to the Floyd is history – they survived and flourished off their own more electronic tangent, while Syd didn't.

The Madcap Laughs, Barrett's first solo album, took a sporadic but none the less laborious year to complete. Production credits constantly changed hands – Peter Jenner to Malcolm Jones (who gave up half the way through), ultimately to Dave Gilmour and Roger Waters.

By this time Barrett's creative processes refused to mesh properly and so the results were often jagged and unapproachable. Basically they were essays in distance – the Madcap waving whimsically out from the haze. Or maybe he was drowning?

On 'Dark Globe' the anguish is all too real.

Many of the tracks though, like 'Terrapin', almost just lay there, just scratching themselves in front of you. They exist completely inside their own zone, like weird insects and exotic fish, the listener looking inside the tank at the activity.

In many ways, *Madcap* is a work of genius – in just as many other ways, it's a cranked-up post-acid curio. It's still a vital, thoroughly unique album for both those reasons.

Jenner: 'I think Syd was in good shape when he made *Madcap*. He was still writing good songs, probably in the same state as he was during "Jugband Blues".'

Storm: 'The thing was that all those guys had to cope with Syd out of his head on Mandrax half the time. He got so "mandied" up on those sessions, his hand would slip through the strings and he'd fall off the stool.'

Barrett, the second album, was recorded in a much shorter space of time. Dave Gilmour was called in to produce, and brought in Rick Wright and Jerry Shirley, Humble Pie's drummer, to help.

Gilmour: 'We had basically three alternatives at that point, working with Syd. One, we could actually work with him in the studio, playing along as he put down his tracks – which was almost impossible, though we succeeded on "Gigolo Aunt". The second was laying down some kind of track before and then having him play over it. The third was him putting his basic ideas down with just guitar and vocals and then we'd try and make something out of it all. It was mostly a case of me saying "Well what have you got then Syd?" and he'd search around and eventually work something out.'

The Barrett disintegration process continued through this album giving it a feel more akin to that of a one-off demo. The songs, though totally off the wall and often vague creations, are shot through with the occasional sustained glimpse of Barrett's brainbelled lyricism at its most vivid.

Like 'Wolfpack', or 'Rats', which hurtles along like classic *Trout Mask Replica* Beefheart shambling thunder, with crazed double-edged nonsense lyrics to boot.

> Rats, rats
> Lay down flat we don't need you
> We act like cats
> If you think you're unloved
> Well we know about that.

'Dominoes' is probably the album's most arresting track, as well as being the only real pointer to what the Floyd might have sounded like had Barrett been more in control of himself. The song is exquisite – a classic kind of Lewis Carroll scenario which spirals up and almost defies time and space – 'You and I/And dominoes/A day goes by' – before drifting into an archetypal Floyd minor-chord refrain straight out of *More*.

Gilmour by this time had become perhaps the only person around who could communicate with Barrett.

'Oh, I don't think anyone can communicate with Syd. I did

those albums because I liked the songs, not, as I suppose some might think, because I felt guilty taking his place in the Floyd. I was concerned that he wouldn't fall completely apart. The final remix on *Madcap* was all mine as well.'

In between the two solo albums, E M I, Harvest or Morrison had decided to set up a bunch of press interviews for Barrett, whose style of conversation was scarcely suited to the tailor-made ends of the media.

Most couldn't make any sense whatsoever out of his verbal ramblings, others tumbled to a conclusion and warily pin-pointed the Barrett malady in their pieces. Peter Barnes did one of the interviews.

'It was fairly ludicrous on the surface. I mean, you just had to go along with it all – y'know Syd would say something completely incongruous one minute like "It's getting heavy, innit" and you just have to say "Yeah, Syd, it's getting heavy", and the conversation would dwell on that for five minutes. Actually, listening to the tape afterwards you could work out that there was some kind of logic there – except that Syd would suddenly be answering a question you'd asked him ten minutes ago while you were off on a different topic completely!'

Hmmm, maybe a tree fell on him. Anyway, another Syd quirk had always been his obsessive tampering with the fine head of black hair that rested firmly on the Barrett cranium. Somewhere along the line, our hero had decided to shave all his lithesome skull appendages down to a sparse grizzle, known appropriately as the 'Borstal crop'.

Jenner: 'I can't really comment too accurately, but I'm rather tempted to view it as a symbolic gesture. Y'know – goodbye to being a pop star, or something.'

Barrett, by this time, was well slumped into his real twilight period, living in the cellar of his mother's house in Cambridge. And this is where the story gets singularly depressing.

An interview with *Rolling Stone* in the Christmas of '71 showed

Barrett to be living out his life with a certain whimsical self-reliance. At one point in the rap, he stated, 'I'm really totally together. I even think I should be.'

Almost exactly a year later, from the sheer frustration of his own inertia, Barrett went temporarily completely haywire and smashed his head through a basement ceiling.

In between these two dates, Syd went into the studio to record.

'It was an abortion,' claims Barnes. 'He just kept over-dubbing guitar part on guitar part until it was just a chaotic mess. He also wouldn't show anyone his lyrics – I fear actually because he hadn't written any.'

Jenner was also present: 'It was horribly frustrating because there were sporadic glimpses of the old Syd coming through, and then it would all get horribly distorted again. Nothing remains from the sessions.'

And then there was Stars, a band formed by Twink, ex-drummer of Tomorrow, Pretty Things and Pink Fairies.

Twink was another native of Cambridge, had previously known Barrett marginally well, and somehow dragged the Madcap into forming a band including himself and a bass player called Jack Monck. It is fairly strongly considered that Barrett was used – his legendary reputation present only to enhance what was in effect a shambling, mediocre rock band.

The main Stars gig occurred at the Corn Exchange in Cambridge where they were second-billed to the M C 5. It was an exercise in total untogetherness and, after an hour or so, Barrett unplugged his guitar and sauntered off the stage to return once again to his basement.

Since that time, Syd Barrett may or may not have worked in a factory for a week or so/worked as a gardener/tried to enroll as an architectural student/grown mushrooms in his basement/been a tramp/spent two weeks in New York busking/tried to become a Pink Floyd roadie.

All the above are stories told to me by various semi-authentic sources.

More than likely, most of them are total fabrications. One thing, though, appears to be clear: Syd Barrett is unable to write songs ('Either that or he writes songs and won't show them to anyone' – Jenner).

In the meantime, Barrett has been elevated into the position of becoming perhaps the leading mysterioso figure in the whole of rock. Arthur Lee and Brian Wilson are the only other figures who loom large in that echelon of twilight zone notoriety and myth-weaving.

Zowie Bowie

SIMON FRITH

The impact of David Bowie on the course of modern music seems to far outweigh his actual contribution. In this brief piece from the heights of Bowiemania, 1973, Frith deals with the Bowie conceit: making himself rock's ultimate star.

Arguing about pop stars is mostly a loony thing to do. So many of the judgements involved are subjective that the inarticulacy of a *Juke Box Jury* is entirely right – I love the backing and so what? David Bowie is pretty and witty but he'll have to convince you, not me. The only words worth flinging about have a much more general concern – not with Bowie's aesthetic appeal but with his purpose and effect. So, Bowie bashing (roll up! roll up!) isn't much different from Bolan bashing and other past delights. It's the back page of *Melody Maker* and the selling-out argument.

Bowie has sold his talent for fame, fortune and a white fur rug; a once creative artist is now slipping on Woolworth's glitter; shameless, Bowie has become a showbiz star.

I know who Bowie's sold out to; I don't understand what he's sold out from. Where is this authentic rock tradition, pose-less and glamour-free? Elvis? The Beatles? No way. Dylan wasn't a bootlace maker, pulling himself up. They're all pop stars, big business, livery-chauffeured. Rock is not some pure order, under constant threat of worldly corruption; it operates from the heart of the beast itself and its achievement is the result of its context. Rock is entertainment that suggests – by its energy, self-consciousness, cultural references – something more. The Bowie question is not whether he's sold out, but whether the music he makes from his pop star stance is more than good fun, whether it illuminates its situation.

Bowie constructs his music around an image rather than a sound or a style and it's this that disturbs rock purists. I mean, what a cheek, deciding to be a star before he'd even got a fan. But it isn't a con trick. Ziggy Stardust is the loving creation of a genuine rock addict and the purpose of the Bowie show isn't to give pop a falsely glamorous glow but to point up the reality of the continuing star/audience relationship. Since 1967 and peace and love, rock has been faking a community, as if Jimmy Page, by being scruffy, became a man of the people. But smoking dope together in a field doesn't turn an audience into a society and it's this pretence that Bowie rips apart.

I'd welcome Bowie to rock if only because his live act (down to the flaunted bisexuality) makes explicit aspects of pop usually ignored. But it's equally fascinating to follow his attempts to create a musical style to support the theatrics. His aim is to combine a tone of voice (world-weary narcissistic), an instrumental urgency (Mick Ronson's aggressive and melodic riffs) and a lyrical mythology (science fiction plus New York depravity). It doesn't always work but when it does the result is a gripping rock statement. Cold and calculated, maybe, but a scarily complete vision of life in the rock culture – sensual, selfish, endless. Heartbreak Hotel has become a Drive-in Saturday (Seattle–Phoenix).

If You Choose, Choose to Go

PETER LAUGHNER

When Laughner died in June 1977, Lester Bangs wrote, in his famous obituary, 'Peter was a great writer as well as being a gifted musician. You can get some idea of his style from what was probably the best thing he ever had published, his review of Lou Reed's Coney Island Baby *in the March 1976 issue of* Creem.' *Here it is.*

Coney Island Baby made me so morose and depressed when I got the advance copy that I stayed drunk for three days. I didn't go to work. I had a horrible physical fight with my wife over a stupid bottle of 10 mg Valiums (she threw an ashtray, a brick and a five-foot candelabra at me, but I got her down and sat on her chest and beat her head on the wooden floor). I called up the editor of this magazine (on my bill) and did virtually nothing but cough up phlegm in an alcoholic stupor for three hours, wishing somewhere in the back of my deadened brain that he could give me a clue as to why I should like this record. I came on to my sister-in-law, 'C'mon over and gimme head while I'm passed out.' I cadged drinks off anyone who would come near me or let me into their apartments. I ended up the whole débâcle passing out stone cold after puking and pissing myself at a band rehearsal, had to be kicked awake by my lead singer, was driven home by my long-suffering best friend and force fed by his old lady who could still find it in the boundless reaches of her good heart to smile on my absolutely incorrigible state of dissolution . . . I willed her all my worldly goods before dropping six Valiums (and three vitamin B complex's, so I must've figured to wake up, or at least at the autopsy they would say my liver was OK). Well, wake up I did, after sleeping sixteen hours, and guess what was running through my head, along with the visual images of flaming metropolises and sinking ocean liners foaming and exploding in vast whirling vortexes of salt water . . .

> Watch out for Charlie's girl . . .
> She'll turn ya in . . . doncha know . . .
> Ya gotta watch out for Charlie's girl . . .

Which is supposed to be the single off *Coney Island Baby* and therefore may be a big hit if promoted right, 'cause it's at least as catchy as 'Saturday Night' . . . if they can just get four cute teens to impersonate Lou Reed.

Now, when I was younger, the Velvet Underground meant to me what the Stones, Dylan etc. meant to thousands of other Midwestern teen mutants. I was declared exempt from the literary curriculum of my upper-class suburban high school simply because I showed the English department a list of books I'd glanced through while obsessively blasting *White Light/White Heat* on the headphones of my parents' stereo. All my papers were manic droolings about the parallels between Lou Reed's lyrics and whatever academia we were supposed to be analysing in preparation for our passage into the halls of higher learning. 'Sweet Jane' I compared with Alexander Pope, 'Some Kinda Love' lined right up with T. S. Eliot's 'Hollow Men' . . . plus I had a rock band and we played all these songs, fueled pharmaceutically by our bassist who worked as a delivery boy for a drugstore and ripped off an entire gallon jar full of Xmas trees and brown and clears. In this way I cleverly avoided all intellectual and creative responsibilities at the cleavage of the decades (I did read all the Delmore Schwartz I could steal from local libraries, because of that oblique reference on the first Velvets LP). After all, a person with an electric guitar and access to obscurities like 'I saw my head laughing, rolling on the ground' had no need of creative credentials . . . there was the rail-thin, asthmatic editoress of our school poetry mag, there was the unhappily married English teacher who drove me home and elsewhere in her Corvette . . . there were others (the girl who began to get menstrual cramps in perfect time to the drums in 'Sister Ray'). Who needed the promise of college and career? Lou Reed was my Woody Guthrie, and with enough amphetamine I would be the new Lou Reed!

I left home. I wandered to the wrong coast (can you imagine what it was like trying to get people in Berkeley, California, to listen to *Loaded* in 1971? Although maybe they all grew up and joined Earth Quake . . .). When Lou's first solo album came out, I drove hundreds of miles to play it for ex-friends sequestered at small exclusive Midwest colleges listening to the Dead and Miles Davis. Everyone from my high school band had gone on to sterling careers as psych majors, botanical or law students, or selling and drinking for IBM (Oh yeah except the drummer became a junkie and had a stroke and now he listens to Santana). All the girls I used to wow into bed with drugs and song married boys who were just like their brothers and moved to Florida or Chicago; leaving their copies of *Blonde On Blonde* and *White Light* in some closet along with the reams of amphetamine-driven poetry I'd forced on them over the years. By the time *Metal Machine Music* came out, I'd lost all contact. The only thing that saved me from total dissolution over the summer of '75 was hearing Television three nights in a row and seeing *The Passenger*.

So all those people will probably never pay any attention to *Coney Island Baby*, and even if they did it wouldn't do much for what's left of their synapses. The damn thing starts out exactly like an Eagles record! And with the exception of 'Charlie's Girl' which is mercifully short and to the point, it's a downhill slide. 'My Best Friend' is a six-year-old Velvets out-take which used to sound fun when it was fast and Doug Yule sang lead. Here it dirges along at the same pace as 'Lisa Says' but without the sexiness. You could sit and puzzle over the voice-overs on 'Kicks' but you won't find much (isn't it cute, the sound of cocaine snorting, and is that an amyl popping in the left speaker?). Your headphones would be better utilized experiencing Patti Smith's brilliant triple-dubbed phantasmagoria on *Horses*.

Side Two starts off with the *worst* thing Reed has ever done, this limp drone self-scam where he goes on about being 'a gift to the women of this world' (in fact this whole LP reminds me of the junk you hear on the jukeboxes at those two-dollar-a-beer stewardess pick-up bars on First Ave. above 70th). There's one pick-up point, 'Oo-ee Baby', with the only good line on the record, 'your old man was the best B&E man down on the street', then this Ric Von Schmidt rip-off which doesn't do anything at all.

Finally there's 'Coney Island Baby', just maudlin, dumb, self-pity: 'Can you believe I wann'd t'play football for th' coach' . . . Sure, Lou, when I was all uptight about being a fag in high school, I did too. Then it builds slightly, Danny Weiss tossing in a bunch of George Benson licks, into *still more* self-pity about how it's tough in the city and the glory of Love will see you through. Maybe. Dragged out for six minutes.

Here I sit, sober and perhaps even lucid, on the sort of winter's day that makes you realize a New Year is just around the corner and you've got very little to show for it, but if you are going to get anything done on this planet, you better pick it up with both hands and *do it yourself*. But I got the nerve to say to my old hero, hey Lou, if you really mean that last line of 'Coney Island Baby' – 'You know I'd give the whole thing up for you' – then maybe you ought to do just that.

Situation Vacant

PATRICK ZERBIB

Public Image Limited, Johnny Rotten's post-Pistols statement of contempt for the constraints of rock & roll, was launched in 1978 as an audacious part-band, part multi-media organization who would have their fingers in all the 3.14s of modern technology, rejecting the mundane album-tour-album circuit. In 1983, when Zerbib's scathing analysis of the great pretender was published in The Face, *John Lydon aka Rotten was PiL's sole survivor as the band embarked on its first ever UK tour, to promote the* Live in Tokyo *album.*

Stuffed into a crumpled grey suit, John Lydon bursts into the room. He scans the scene quickly, like a wary animal . . .

Since his return from New York, Lydon has been widely fêted. He has given a press conference to launch *Order of Death*, in which he makes his acting debut; he has been to Newcastle to appear on the *Tube*, and today he has just come back from Germany where he appeared on another TV show. Tomorrow he will give his first concert in the UK for almost five years.

He sits down in front of the tape recorder and fixes me with his renowned manic stare. He seems to be on his guard.

'How did you get the part in the movie?' I ask, trying to avoid his obvious agitation.

'The casting agent rang me up and said: there's a part. I went there and I thought it would be a good laugh. Then I read the part and thought, ah ha! I'd better take this one seriously!'

Lydon sinks back into the sofa and puffs on his Silk Cut,

evidently pleased to be talking about *Order of Death*. The film recounts the war between Leo Smith, a schizophrenic young aristocrat, and Fred O'Connor, the corrupt chief of the New York Bureau of Narcotics. Leo Smith is the cop-killer, an angel of death who assassinates one by one the corrupt cops of the Narcotics Bureau. Next on his list is Fred O'Connor. But here Smith achieves the height of refinement; he transforms O'Connor into a murderer, and obliges him to cut his own throat. O'Connor is played by Harvey Keitel, veteran of countless thrillers. But in this duel John Lydon is the winner; far more fascinating on screen than Keitel.

'When the Italian director chose you,' I tell Lydon, 'people warned him he would have trouble.'

'Yeah, they were convinced I would destroy the whole thing. But they had faith enough, they let me do it. The fact is, I was much more professional than all of them put together!'

'How come?'

'Well, you know what the Italians are like: fucking chaos! They just loved arguing, and I kept saying: Work! Just work!'

Lydon suddenly stands up. 'They would argue like this all the time . . .' He gesticulates wildly. 'What do you mean, put the camera here? You crazy?' Adopting an Italian accent: 'Eh! Who is the director here? You, or me?'

Physically, Lydon has changed over the last few years. There is still the same carrot-top hair, but the tufts are thinner, and he has put on some weight. At twenty-six, his stomach is starting to bulge, his cheeks are chubby and there is the beginning of a double chin. He sits down again and continues . . .

Lydon describes an altogether different person on set from the Lydon we thought we knew. Here is a new Lydon, diligent, punctual, always ready with his lines, prepared to shoot and re-shoot the same scenes without quibbling. The same Lydon that went to the Metropolitan Opera in New York with Hugh Fleetwood, author of the novel on which the film is based.

Before the light fades in the studio, John must have his picture taken. He sits on a tall, narrow chair, folds his arms tightly, and leans towards the camera, eyes open wide as though the lens were a zombie about to steal his soul. Again that fixed manic stare . . .

Anyone old enough to remember punk will remember that look. Pupils burning, eyes glaring, the look of Johnny Rotten, a glint of mischievous lightning. Lydon deploys it on cue, but it has grown pale and frozen. And when the photographer asks, he won't take it off.

Nor will he talk about his group, Public Image Ltd.

'No way,' he moans, 'I'm tired. Make it up, I'm sure you can.'

Since his return from New York, Lydon has evaded any direct questions about Public Image Ltd, whilst being loquacious enough on other subjects. It's now three years since the group emigrated to New York, and in three years all they've produced is one single. 'This Is Not A Love Song' is honourable enough but hardly adds to the body of work before they left. And the album, *Live In Tokyo*? Lamentable. These two records have found a ready place in the charts but that doesn't alter the question: Have Public Image got anything left to say?

When they were formed nearly five years ago the group threatened to become a remarkable force in music. At least, that was the fervent desire of music critics in Britain and the US suffering from post-punk triste and anxious to find a new stimulus. Who better to provide it than the former Johnny Rotten?

The son of working-class Irish Catholic parents, John Lydon grew up in Finsbury Park, North London, where one of his best friends was Keith Levene. He left school and worked in a number of dull jobs before he found himself in a clothes shop called Sex in the King's Road, owned by a certain Malcolm McLaren. You all know the rest. To complete his group the Sex Pistols, Malcolm needed a singer. Why not John? With a face both angelic and demonic, and his voice utterly hopeless, as though he had swallowed a cat, John would make the ideal anti-idol of rock. For two years Johnny Rotten wore his famous manic glare on the pages of every tabloid. But the farce grew too much for him. In California at the end of the Pistols' first US tour, he walked out of a motel room and never came back.

'At the end of the Pistols, it was like he was finished,' recalls Keith Levene now. 'Then we got together and talked about changing a few things. But he would lie around and sleep. He wanted to be treated like a star. Nice bloke, but such a lazy bastard.'

John was being pulled apart. On the one hand, he knew he had to rid himself of the past, of Rotten, of No Future. He decided to call himself by his real name: John Lydon. On the other hand, he had a real fear of sinking back into anonymity, of losing the place that he had snatched for himself. He kept on at Keith, who had no shortage of ideas for their proposed new group.

Together they drew up the principles of Public Image. (1) PiL is not a group, but a wide-ranging corporation, which deals with other corporations (Virgin, for example; PiL produces music, but it also produces images and graphics). (2) PiL refuses to deal with middle-men, notably managers. (3) PiL is composed of individuals who make music separately and the music of PiL is a collage of their individual work. (4) PiL does not tour. There is no question of becoming a production line. Each concert is an event. (5) PiL doesn't put out records, but objects. Their first single, 'Public Image', was packaged in a parody of a tabloid newspaper. The *Metal Box*, their second album, comprised of three 12-inch singles packaged in a metal container like those used for storing reels of films, stamped with the label PiL.

The third key member of PiL was Jah Wobble, one of the few people who could hold his own with Lydon, sometimes physically. John and Keith chose him because of his taste in reggae; since he had never played an instrument, they hoped he would be able to invent new bass lines.

At the end of 1978, at the Rainbow in London and in Paris, PiL's first performances galvanized their audiences. Jim Walker concentrated all his force on the snare drum, drowning the other instruments. Wobble played his bass sitting on a chair, because he didn't know how to hold it otherwise. Keith Levene, hardly visible on stage, plucked noises from his guitar at random.

As for Lydon, he spent the greater part of the concert with his back turned to the audience, screaming anguished words at the wall. Sometimes he would erupt into his own peculiar version of the skank. And as he and Levene wanted, the group sounded pretty much like a collage of four autonomous musics. In sum, a kind of anti-rock. Performed at an anti-concert.

Compare this with PiL of 1983. Lydon is about to consummate the most banal tour of his career, with a group of session musicians who have learnt every agonized inflection of his songs by heart. His last album, *Live In Tokyo*, is a disgrace. And as for managers, Lydon nowadays has all the management he needs from Larry White, the new guiding force of the group. Meanwhile, the group itself has lost both Jah Wobble and Keith Levene.

What's going on in John Lydon's head? Has he come unstuck? Has he caught the superstar sickness? Has he no longer any rapport with his public? Perhaps he no longer has a public.

In 1978, he bought a house in Gunter Grove, Chelsea, where he played host to an endless stream of friends and visitors. Five years later he has decided to leave New York because 'three years is enough'. But he isn't going back to Gunter Grove because 'England is finished'. Instead he is staying in a suite at the Royal Garden Hotel in Kensington – home from home for visiting rock stars – before moving to Los Angeles where his manager Larry White has an office with six employees.

In 1979, Lydon lived like a prince surrounded by his court jesters. 'I love visitors,' he once said. 'They are here for my amusement.' Nearly every night, a dozen or so would arrive at Gunter Grove to demolish the inevitable cans of lager. There was Ari Up, the singer with the Slits, whose mother, Nora, now lives with John. The daughter of a rich German right-wing publisher, Nora recently left Chris Spedding for Lydon. Don Letts was a frequent visitor, with his waist-length dreadlocks and super-8 camera, now swapped for a professional U-matic. There was also a journalist from *Melody Maker*, a well-known photographer, and a retinue of friends who seemed to be forever on the look-out for an angle to make some money.

During this time in London, much amphetamine was inevitably being taken and heroin too was catching on. John abhors heroin, but his door was open to its *habitués*. In fact, he liked to be surrounded by them; their weakness consoled his own insecurity. But he was no help to them. If they started to turn white, he would panic and scream at Nora to call an ambulance. Then he would disappear for the next hour.

In other respects, Lydon was an excellent host. He had a store of anecdotes, an appetite for conversation and an ear for gossip. He enjoyed the power he wielded with his court, playing his acolytes off against one another, betraying eager confidences.

When he tried to play a musical instrument, though, his friends would do their best to stop him. Nevertheless, he began to develop a musical sensibility of sorts. His Arabic melodies on 'Albatross' and 'Poptones' surprised both Levene and Wobble. And for the first year the group felt they were making creative headway. But, bit by bit, the enthusiasm dwindled.

In the middle of 1980 Jah Wobble was sacked from PiL, supposedly because, without telling the others, he had used some tracks they had recorded together. And Keith Levene?

The statement was terse. John and Keith argued over the mix of 'This Is Not A Love Song', and as a result of this disagreement Keith Levene has quit the group. John refuses to elaborate:

'What happened to Keith?' asked a journalist at the press conference.

'He quit.'

'How come you've had so many quitters?'

'Dunno. There's an awful lot of weak people in this world.'

Keith Levene is still living in New York. When I called him, at 11 o'clock in the morning, he was just waking up.

'Listen, it became impossible to work with John. I wasn't getting any feedback from the band. Only ideas to make money.'

Such as?

'You know, in the beginning, PiL had a few basic ideas. Play interesting music, offer interesting gigs. And what? In the US John started wearing tuxedos and singing "Anarchy In The UK". Dreadful.'

How come?

'It all started when he got back from Italy. After the shooting of *Order of Death* everything went sour. And I lacked courage, I should have quit a year ago.'

From talking to Keith Levene and others close to the group, it's possible to garner an accurate enough impression of the three years that John Lydon and Public Image spent in New York.

No need to make it up, as Lydon suggested.

PiL left London early in 1981, exasperated by incessant police raids. 'We lived very near to the Chelsea nick,' said Lydon. 'That's apparently where they train the drug squads. So, you know, they needed places to practise. I suited their purpose. They even sent me the bomb squad once: "Uh, we have reason to believe there are bombs on these premises." Why? I said. "Because an Irish flag was raised through your window!"'

For the first few months in New York, PiL lived very well thanks to an advance from Virgin Records on their next album. After all, *Metal Box* hadn't done so badly; nearly 50,000 copies worldwide. The group installed themselves in a luxury hotel. A star in America must act like one. But the dollars soon disappeared and PiL fled to the Chelsea Hotel, infamous refuge of bankrupt stars. As well as John, there was Martin Atkins, the drummer, Keith Levene and Jeanette Lee, in charge of the group's videos, posters, sleeves.

With no more money left, Keith called Richard Branson, head of Virgin Records, to ask for another advance.

'I want to hear some tapes first,' said Branson.

'But I'm telling you, we can't afford the studio!'

'And I'm saying: make a tape and send it to me.'

'You know that won't make any difference. You'll have to release the tapes anyway.'

'That's the idea.'

Meanwhile, all New York wanted to meet John. They would take him to dinner in the best restaurants, delighted to be seen beside the former Johnny Rotten. It was not so long ago that America too had been scandalized by the first and last US tour of the Sex Pistols.

But they were still broke. To alleviate this misery, PiL gave concerts in faraway suburbs in New Jersey and upstate New York. 'We charged as much as possible,' recalls Levene, 'but because we were so disorganized we spent just as much hiring the equipment and getting there.'

It was about this time that Keith came across South Park Studios, owned by two lawyers who wanted to help the group. 'Pay us what you can now,' they proposed. 'And we'll get the rest back from Virgin later.' Public Image Ltd could finally go into a studio . . .

If John wanted to, that is. He preferred to pass the time in bed watching quiz shows on the TV while working his way through fifteen cans of beer a day. Tired of this inactivity, Jeanette Lee abruptly left the group and returned to London.

Soon after this, Bonnie Zimmerman called Lydon at the Chelsea. Bonnie, a casting agent, was looking for an actor for Italian director Roberto Faenza. He wanted a young Englishman, preferably a rock singer, for the role of Leo Smith in *Order of Death*. She had contacted Sting and Elvis Costello. Both too busy. After their first meeting, Bonnie decided to help Lydon prepare for the interview, painstakingly reading the script through with him.

'He worked hard,' she recalls. 'He really wanted to do it right.'

On the day of the casting, Roberto Faenza arrived with Harvey Keitel. Keitel already knew his role by heart. By the time they started shooting, he would be the person he was playing. He carried a loaded revolver strapped to his ankle and even spent time in a real Narcotics Bureau beforehand. Lydon, of course, already had plenty of experience playing the schizoid brat.

Ten other candidates were tested with Lydon, young actors, rock musicians from New York ... almost instantly, the director chose John.

'I didn't know what he had done before, although of course I'd heard about the Sex Pistols,' says Faenza. 'But I liked his personality very much. And his face ... John has a great face.'

The producer apologized for only being able to offer him 10,000 dollars. Given his circumstances, Lydon could hardly refuse.

With the first cheque, he paid his bill at the Chelsea and rented a huge loft on West 19th Avenue. 'Just a warehouse area,' he says, 'a commercial zone. The loft was enormous. Enormously filthy. Don't worry, we managed to fill it very well. There were twenty of us there at one point.'

John was happy. He was going to make his acting debut and Nora had decided to join him in New York. Keith was able to pay the studio and would continue working on the tapes, while Lydon plunged into a new world, whose denizens knew nothing of rock, neither its codes nor its poses. There was no point in employing a front with Faenza, Keitel and Fleetwood, who was on hand for the shooting; they hardly ever listened to rock music. Nor any question of playing the prima donna, which he had tended increasingly to do with his friends in PiL. In the cinema, Lydon had everything to prove ...

But after his return from Rome, John had changed. 'That's when it started to go wrong,' affirms Levene. Just when they had landed an unexpected contract with a Japanese promoter, for a ten-date concert in Japan for a fee of 9,000 dollars, plus expenses – enough to pull PiL out of the rut for some time to come.

It was at this point in time that John decided to go to Los Angeles. He had been invited there by Larry White, a sound engineer, road manager and all-round American music-business-man. John, for some reason, hit it off with him.

Lydon, by his own admission, is fascinated by Americans. They, at least, don't have any unnecessary complexes about money. True, they never think about anything else, but . . .

'That's the thing about this place,' he once said. 'If you're earning money, they love ya, they want ya, they'll insist.'

'You'll never make it,' Larry White told John. 'With your sound; what a bunch of wankers! The people want to see Johnny Rotten, man. Do you realize what you've got in your hands? Besides, you need a real band. Get your act together!'

Larry introduced him to his protégés: three session men from New Jersey. They knew the Sex Pistols repertoire off by heart. As for the music of Public Image, they could pick that up in a couple of days. To see for himself, John tried out the show in a club in Los Angeles. He ended with 'Anarchy In The UK', and the LA neo-punks pogoed with joy. There, right in front of their eyes, an essential metamorphosis had taken place; John Lydon had once again become Johnny Rotten.

A joke at first maybe, but Johnny soon found himself seduced by his new persona; a cynical, immoral Lydon, divested of all the principles that had inspired PiL at the start. 'Sure,' shrugged Johnny, 'a long time ago I said that if I ever find myself singing "Anarchy In The UK" again, it'll be the end.'

But so what? Since when has an artist not had the right to contradict himself?

Meanwhile, in South Park Studios, Keith Levene and drummer Martin Atkins were listening to the mix of 'This Is Not A Love Song' that John had done before he left for LA. Levene liked the result, but wanted to try another mix.

'I don't think John will like it,' Atkins kept repeating, 'I don't think John will like it . . .'

Atkins called John in Los Angeles to warn him about what was happening in the studio.

'Let me talk to Keith,' John snapped.

'What's wrong with you?' asked Keith. 'I'm just trying another mix. It sounds much better.'

'No you don't, Keith. You just send the bloody tape to Virgin!'

'But –'

'YOU JUST GET OUT OF THE FUCKING STUDIO OR YOU WON'T BE PART OF PIL ANY MORE!'

'I don't like what I've been hearing about you in LA,' retorted Levene. 'It's a joke! Singing "Anarchy In The UK" ... We're doing all the things we said we'd never do. Is that what you want? A sell-out?'

'Who tells me what I want to do?'

And John hung up.

Johnny Lydon returned to New York soon afterwards with Larry White, to prepare for the tour of Japan. The meeting between Larry and Keith was a disaster. 'I wanted to kill him,' says an exasperated Levene.

That day, Lydon lost a friend. And not for the first time. One by one, over the years, they have given him up. Because he's a fatalist. Because he believes in nothing, except himself. But he swallows each new loss and feels stronger.

And so, I went to see Johnny Lydon at the Top Rank Suite, Brighton – his first performance in Britain for almost five years. Johnny walks on stage, to be greeted by a hail of gob and plastic beer glasses.

'That's it,' he declares. 'Good-night. I'm going.'

But he keeps the microphone in his hand.

'Spit one more time, I say ONE MORE TIME, and I'm gone!'

At the same moment, his group launch into 'Public Image', the song that marked the birth of John Lydon from the ashes of Johnny Rotten.

Apart from Martin Atkins, the three other musicians are all new. With their blow-dried hair, their freshly cleaned jackets, their archetypal poses, they seem hopelessly out of place. The sound they make is perfunctory.

The audience is a mess of 'wacky hairdos', as Lydon himself sarcastically tells them; old punks nostalgic for the pogo, new punks with heads full of glue. All the same, as he unleashes the four-year-old fragments of Public Image, it's clear that Johnny still has his magnetism.

'Give up, John. You're finished!'

'Fuck off,' replies Johnny. 'You get what you give!'

A slap in the face for the crowd, just like old times. But this time around there is no response – save perhaps for the can of tear-gas that clears the hall for ten minutes.

Watching the scene from the edge of the crowd are a young couple, both nineteen years old, still at college, and readers of *The Face*.

Are they enjoying the concert?

'No, not at all.'

Did they expect something better?

'No.'

So they spend their money for nothing?

'Well, you see, there's not much to do in Brighton tonight. And we missed punk. I heard some of the records though because my brother was a punk. So we thought: Let's go and see Johnny Rotten!'

A pogo-er leaps in front of me. In his hand is a can of beer that splashes over his jeans. He is wearing a PiL t-shirt. A fan?

'Nah,' he pants. 'I just bought the t-shirt. But Johnny's great. He's singing "Anarchy In The UK", just like before.'

He is indeed singing 'Anarchy In The UK'. But it's not just like before. He follows this with 'This Is Not A Love Song', and hurriedly disappears.

Will Lydon really succeed in donning once again the mask of Rotten, simply to haul himself up to the rank of superstar? There is a contradiction here, an awful irony, but rock can safely mock such ironies. Rock has a short memory. But at least Johnny has reminded us of the level of banality to which rock has sunk.

The whole of the rock business has its eyes glued to the charts. It produces nothing but pin-ups for adolescent bedrooms, while the Rolling Stones are making more money than ever.

Does that bring anything to mind?

1974, perhaps? Now almost ten years past.

Music was then monopolized by superstars giving super-concerts in super-stadiums. The new superstars – you name them – are equally remote from their equally disenfranchized audiences, who prefer to fall together with each other now and go to nightclubs than to fall together behind Madness, Boy George, Siouxsie, Gary Numan etc. etc. . . .

But in 1974, the new rebels were hatching their whirlwind. Soon, the whirlwind came, the whirlwind named punk. Johnny Rotten screamed 'No Future' and fixed us with his manic stare.

Bring on the new whirlwind.

The Meaning of Bruce

RICHARD MELTZER

In recent years Meltzer has clearly revelled in his role as the cantanker-ous ol' man of Rockspeak. His musings in a 1985 issue of Spin *upon the Bruce phenomenon fired a number of scabrous volleys in the direction of the squeaky clean Boss.*

Bruce, uh, Springsteen? The youth-demographic Wayne Newton/ Bette Midler? Is he even an issue anymore? (Don't tell me he's on the cover – I'll find out soon enough.)

I have never liked the youth-demographic Newton/Midler. I have nearly always loathed him. I've rarely been able to even look at the boring little prick without muttering expressions like 'master of ersatz', 'the absolute voice of the status quo', or 'the emperor's new news and workshirt'. Pompous as knee-jerk responses go, maybe, but here's this guy, see, the absolute non-irony of whose most prevalent guise ('earnestness') has always struck me, on sheer scale alone, as more than a trifle pompous incarnate. But fuck me (right) – whuddo I know?

Basically, I've just never gotten the point. Well, I have gotten the point of his appeal to consumers of the rampantly consumable. That much is obvious. 'Boogie on down, not only without guilt but with social conscience' – all bases, or let's just say both bases, covered – three hours for the price of one.

It makes total sense, for inst, what my lady-friend Irene sees in this shit. She's a show fan, see, Broadway and whatnot, a somewhat late (but eager) arrival to the rock–roll shores. She finally takes to rock and what she takes to is Bruce – and I ain't listening. Eventually she gets her way, sits me down perchance to educate me (lout that I am), plays me some Bruce and, lout that I am, I jump up (she forgot to tie me down), wave my arms (to the beat so she knows, at least, I am no crackpot), conduct the room to a round of 'O! . . . klahoma! Where the wind comes sweepin' down the plain!' and dang me if she does not chuckle (as opposed, y'know, to sending me home) (lout I forever will be) because a) she is no fool and b) I have got the *sturm und drang* of it not far from purt near correct. And I know – and she knows that I know – that Bruce is naught but her long-awaited Conrad Birdie, or whatever their names are from *West Side Story*, made flesh. Or at least made ongoing product.

Which is fucksure cool but, um, note the connection. Just note it.

Or, for further inst, take my pal Scott Kempner. Scott's basic rhythm-of-life shtick has always been The Rock & Roll Fan Club Meets Here. Before Bruce was his boss boy it was Peter Townshend. But ever since that week in '75 when its Face made the cover of *Time*, *Newsweek* and all three trades, the Bruce Gestalt has, for Scott, role-played one consistently grand advertisement for the Power and Glory of Rock Rock Rock & Roll, as if by the mere fortuity of its scale 'n' bombast (not to mention its benignity) we are assured that – this time around – they cannot and will not dare bust 'our music'. Somehow, in this picture a seminal (and terminal) wedding of creative life-blood to market-place/culture death is overlooked (or ignored). But, heck, that's cool too – there's people, I'm told, who actually regard rock videos as gifts (as primary objects of experience!). And, hey, couldn't the, y'know, fact of Reagan be regarded as glorious evidence of the persistence of electional demo- ... what's the word? ... demogracy??? i.e. you want a ring implanted in your cultural nose, well someone (by golly) will implant it.

But, *mea culpa*, I digress. The specific side of the Kempner plug-in to Bruce – sorry, Scott, but use you I must for nefarious purpose – is ... well I'm not sure about now, but in '75 I asked him flat-out 'Whuh?' and he says, 'If the Fonz had a band it would be Springsteen.' Yes! The Fonz!! This, of course, was before we knew, or could know, that the incredible lovable li'l leather schmuck, the most palatably inaccurate (yet life-affirming) peer group arche-TV-type since Maynard G. Krebs, was but an accident on the road to grown-actor oblivion for one Henry Winkler. Can't knock actors as pump-primers for purported real thingers in principle, no sir, but when you've got your Ersatz Quotient up there in a supreme falsification-of-reality range ... hey (weepy-eyed stick-in-the-mud humanist that I am), I'm knock-ing. But not mocking. It is sad what folks sometimes fall for. And remain fallen for ten fucking years down the chute ... fuggit.

Or for final inst, 'cause I'm itching to get to what genuinely pisses me off – back at the dawn of the eighties I had this punk show on a Pacifica station that the Revolutionary Communist Party was bugging me to play their band Prairie Fire on. Finally, I go see 'em and they're, well, they're not Public Image (or the Fall) (or even the Clash). They're just your basic formally reactionary get-down boogie band with largely implicit rad/topical 'message' superadded. Structurally sound reiteraters of an already mega-told tale (American Music Revisits American Myth); one more entry in – and I don't really mean to insult them – the Springsteen Sweepstakes. Far from being insulted, their spokesperson hears the Bruce reference and . . . like wow. Gee, she tells me, if only they could harness that familiar sound, Bruce's or its ilk, which People and y'know Workers already relate to, and wow, like songs're so liberating and freeing and . . . and god am I one godless stick in the mud.

I hit her with (and she rejects) my whole entire rant re: the need to reject Prevailing Form (the 'No Excuse for Bruce After Punk' routine). She winces at but stands up to my drivel re: Bruce as a) Hubert Humphrey (if even that much) in contempo-softshoe drag; b) nose-ring yanker of the palace guard; c) learning-disabled child of the sixties to whom that decade never even registered. We're bouncing all this one-dimensional quasi-political claptrap and then we start talking lyrics, poetics. Bruce's, that is. We're no longer talking Prairie Fire. We bounce 'bourgeois' about. I ask (pray tell) what the non-bourgeois – shall we even maybe say revolutionary? – import might be of such Springsteenisms as wind blows through my hair (and yours) in my '56 Chevy and my wonderful new sneakers embrace bright lights of etc. And she says, 'Bourgeois romantic or not, such lyrics give hope to so many.' And so be it.

And so be it all. I mean, yeah, I certainly can dig how among the teeming zillions various lames and non-lames alike have plugged into Bruce. It seems like the sum of the some-of-the-people you can fool all of the time has gotten a little unwieldy, but at heart I'm a pluralist. Not all mass delusions make me puke. I just cannot see, really I can't, a single sight, sound or accident within the delusion that is anything but monochromatic blah.

Is there anything grimmer and grayer than the Myth of America? I am sick of the Myth of America. Granted, Bruce's America is at least fractionally different from Rambo's – a good bad sitcom compared to a bad bad one – but since we're talking belief systems and the goddam market-place, how many billion consumers do you think have bought both? Bruce and Rambo. Without missing a beat.

None of which would mean shit to a shitbook – and, really, let's not be so *ad* mass *hominem* – if it weren't for what Bruce, or his shrill Dave Marsh, did last October to avoid endangering any possible cross-constituency of consumers of the left and/or right. A couple weeks left till the election – remember? – and Reagan starts quoting Bruce. But instead of saddling his *sturm und drang*, riding out and yelling, 'Vote for Walter! Our President wants us dead!' (and winning Walt Delaware and possibly Hawaii in the process), the little cocksucker passes it on to his publicist Barbara Carr, who passes it to her wonderful husband David. I don't remember the exact words, I've looked and I just can't find it, but 'rock critic Dave Marsh' did an outstanding hem-haw on page one of the respected news-sheet I happened to catch. Something to the effect that if the President would only look at such and such a Springsteen album cut, he would clearly see that *au contraire* blah blah bluh. Don't say anything, don't stir anything, don't lose a single customer! Fuck these people!!

And fuck me for getting so steamed. I'm an old grouch all right, but after punk, after Reagan – after everything and anything – why does this transparent dogshit remain an issue, for crying out loud? Next, we'll be asked to write about Garfield the Cat.

What Have They Done to my Blues, Ma?

CHARLES SHAAR MURRAY

If the recent transformation of certain long-standing exponents of Rockspeak from level-headed rock critics to 'If It's Black It's Good' zealots has been at times dispiriting, Murray's 1984 feature regarding heavy metal's wholesale appropriation of the blues makes some typically incisive points.

The Blues had a grandson, too, a malformed idiot thing that stays chained up in the cellar most of the time.

When visitors call or when it is taken out for an airing, it gibbers and hoots, flexing its muscles and masturbating frantically.

It brags incessantly of its strength and its masculinity, its great and noble heritage and its direct line of descent from both black and white geniuses, but it takes good care to avoid all but the most superficial trappings of its ancestry.

It fuels itself on fantasies of adventure and power and sexual conquest; it sees itself as Conan or Mad Max.

It says it will never die.

This thing's name is heavy metal. It is the result of obsessive inbreeding reinforced by cultivated ignorance. The village idiot of popular music, to be sure, but of all the descendants of Mama Blues, it is possibly the only one currently acknowledging its heritage as well as the one that betrays its heritage most profoundly.

Nowhere else outside the comparative commercial backwater

of white R&B would a band record as obscure a blues item as John Brim's 'Ice Cream Man' – as Van Halen did on their first album – and nowhere else would anyone turn it into such a grotesque, bloated monstrosity.

Nowhere else then does the blues receive as much lip service as it does in heavy metal (let alone as much guitar service), but nowhere else in popular music today contains as much explicit rejection of black music, black culture and black people, unless you count the real Nazi-pinhead faction of Oi.

Metal leans on the blues for most of its guitar language and a few of its themes, and metal musicians often cite the blues as justification for arrant sexist misogyny and for endless boring road songs, but this is the purest sophistry. Metal is the culmination of a long line of events and causes and effects: it's what happened when someone subtracted the number that they first thought of. It is the result of the transplanting of a number of complex cultural codes from their original milieu to another – very different – setting.

Heavy metal is an outgrowth of the white blues-rock of the sixties, though it is ultimately a very different animal, and the result of Britain's re-exporting of blues themes and devices. Unlike their British contemporaries, American white blues-rockers like Paul Butterfield, Michael Bloomfield and Johnny Winter learned their trade through intimate association with black bluesmen on their home turf. In Chicago, Bloomfield, Butterfield and others like Charlie Musselwhite and Elvin Bishop, hung out in Chicago taverns and gained the respect of the men who taught them – Muddy Waters, Magic Sam, Otis Rush, Buddy Guy, Big Joe Williams, Sonny Boy Williamson – by their devotion to the music and their willingness to absorb and to participate in its culture.

In Texas, Johnny Winter was doing the same thing, playing with all the local bluesmen and with everybody who came through town, making blues sides for local labels that sold to black record buyers whether they realized he was (incredibly) white or not.

In the UK, musicians like Eric Clapton, Mick Jagger and all the musicians who eventually formed groups like the Rolling Stones, the Yardbirds, the Who, the Animals and legions more, were studying the same music from records without any grounding in the music's culture other than what they could deduce from the records themselves and whatever skimpy literature on the blues they could find, most of which disdained contemporary urban blues as a perversion and concentrated almost exclusively on the rural blues of the twenties and thirties.

The result was that British blues was an exclusively white phenomenon. British blacks brought with them the cultures of Africa and the West Indies, which by no means failed completely to interest and involve young whites, but it wasn't the blues rockers who checked out the black clubs of Britain's major cities. Freddie King and Little Walter were thousands of miles away.

In Texas and Chicago, Winter, Bloomfield and the others played in integrated bands – the Paul Butterfield Blues Band was never, in all of its history, an all-white band. Winter hung out in the black clubs until soul came in and whites were no longer welcome whatever their credentials.

British blues-rock began to mutate within months of reaching the stage. Unlike American blues audiences, British blues crowds were predominantly young, which made R&B a youth music: fast, tough, danceable, adult and sophisticated in its themes and language, simple in structure and with limitless scope for improvisation. It was often sloppy and pretentious, but it was also in its way quite perfect.

It also completely changed the texture and meaning of the music: the volume and the tempo were revved up as far as they could go, and as the music reached a wider audience and was played in bigger rooms, a new technology had to be developed accordingly (this is why the Marshall amplifier had to be invented).

But an equally significant change occurred almost subliminally: the significance of the lyrics and themes shifted as the songs were transferred from the black taverns of Chicago's South Side to the clubs and dancehalls of the UK.

No matter who had the licks down pattest, Winter and Bloomfield knew what Muddy Waters or Bo Diddley meant when they sang 'I'm A Man', whereas Clapton and Jagger didn't. In Muddy's 'Manish Boy' or Bo's 'I'm A Man', the unspoken punch line to the title is 'I'm a man (don't ever call me "boy")'. It's expressed through sexual braggadocio, but the sentiment was clear to any black radio or club audience of the time. Transplanted to the Marquee Club and sung by, say, Keith Relf of the Yardbirds, the song becomes 'I'm a Man (you're a woman – get 'em off)'. British R&B in its most extrovert form became two things: a testing ground for musical and technological explorations which completely changed the vocabulary of pop, and the most convincing and saleable focus for laddishness and sexual experimentation since rockabilly.

(The similarity is not coincidental. Though rockabilly was developed in the American south, where black and white lived together like a couple who hate each other, side by side but rarely touching, the billies were distanced from the blackness of the music they borrowed in similar manner to the UK blues-rockers, though not to the same extent.)

Anyway – to cut a long and often-told story short – the British blues-rockers went to the States and cleaned up, mainly because they were about seventeen trillion times more exciting than anything that the white American music biz could put up against them. Wide-eyed, they went to see Ray Charles and to meet Howlin' Wolf and record at Chess in Chicago, but the form was set: blues-rock was a lot of bum-shaking, fast tricky guitar solos, walls and walls of speakers and simultaneous pursuit and put-downs of gurls. White America went ape-shit and bought British blues-rock lock, stock and barrel.

Enough of this interest in the music spilled over on the origina-
tors to provide a sizeable boost to the careers of some two or
three dozen leading bluesmen, but basically this wrought the final
transformation of blues via blues-rock into heavy metal, and of
the blues into a music consumed and supplied principally by
young whites.

However, the musical transformations weren't strictly on the
white side of the fence. Jimi Hendrix, a black American guitarist
who moved to the UK in late '66 and re-exported himself to the
States as an English blues-rock superstar nine months later,
bridged the two traditions more perfectly than anyone before or
since, and since he was easily the hardest and most unanswerable
guitarist around, carved considerable tracks into the black
American music of the late sixties and early seventies and a
Hendrix-derived abstraction of the new 'blues' guitar began to
creep into the soul hits (black record producers not only have a
sharp ear for new licks and noises but a great willingness to sell
records to white audiences by including an easy reference point
for them – you didn't think this started when Quincy Jones
blagged Eddie Van Halen into a Michael Jackson session, did
you?).

Isaac Hayes's 'Shaft' would've been completely impossible if
Hendrix hadn't recorded 'Voodoo Chile (Slight Return)', and if
Hendrix and Sly Stone had both fallen under buses when they
were small children there's no telling what Norman Whitfield and
Miles Davis would've had to come up with in that era.

The grand culmination of this tradition in soul music came
with the Isley Brothers' 'Who's That Lady', a wonderful, yearning
song spiced by Ernie Isley's exquisitely sinuous guitar solo. Over
on the white side of the fence there was Grand Funk Railroad.
Black and white American pop were beginning the lengthy separation which has only just started to thaw.

Old clips of US pop shows from the fifties and early sixties –
like the lengthy compilation excerpts from *Dick Clark's American*

Bandstand that showed up on TV a year or two back, or the TAMI Show – depict a sizeable amount of musical integration, with the likes of James Brown, the Beach Boys, the Rolling Stones and Martha and the Vandellas following each other in quick succession amidst no visible trauma. In the sixties, soul and blues artists played primarily white concerts and festivals and were received with standing ovations: B. B. King appeared at the Fillmore West and was greeted with a solid minute of applause. Otis Redding tore up Monterey and two integrated bands – the Jimi Hendrix Experience and Sly and the Family Stone – were the pre-eminent groups of their time. The Rolling Stones risked their reputations by hiring the likes of B. B. King, Stevie Wonder, Ike and Tina Turner and Muddy Waters to open for them (would you like to follow talent like that?).

These days, even the Clash can't guarantee their black guest artists freedom from racist abuse. Can you imagine the response to a black opening act on a bill with Ted Nugent or Van Halen? The end result of the whitewashing of the blues has been that heavy metal is now (in America anyway) the music of the urban white racist – and with the eclipse of the kind of pop R&B that scored a few UK hits for the likes of Dr Feelgood and the Inmates a few years ago, virtually nobody but heavy metal bands ever plays a blues to a mass audience now.

And as whites took over the neighbourhood, the blacks moved out. Blues audiences had been slipping for a while as soul came along with its sharper rhythms and more urgent articulation, but the music of men like John Lee Hooker was now damned by association. There are no major bluesmen in the States who could support themselves solely on their black audience.

Heavy metal musicians often cite the blues as influence, but comparatively few of them mention Muddy Waters or B. B. King. Their 'blues' is more likely to be Cream, or Jeff Beck, or Led Zeppelin – the first group to clean up by completely trashing the blues and inflating its corpse with an air pump.

Influential sixties rock bands like the Who or the Rolling Stones abandoned much of the conceptual machinery of the blues as they went their various ways, but even at their worst they have been informed by its ethos and its spirit. A modern metal band will give little evidence of knowing that the stuff existed in the first place.

So what's left, in 1984, of the received heritage of the bluesmen of America, some of the greatest artists ever to walk this earth?

Where once there was an easy openness about human sexuality and a rueful acknowledgement of the difficulties of holding a family or a relationship together in the extremes of urban poverty, there is now a total contempt for women that expresses itself in songs that are nothing more or less than rape fantasies (an aptly named group called Great White have a song called 'On Your Knees' which goes in part: 'Knockin' down the door, pull you to the floor/'cause you need it so bad/takin' what I choose, never lose . . . gonna drive my love inside you/nail your ass to the floor/down on your knees'). Yeah, but all them old blues geezers 'ad songs about birds an' that didn't they?

Where guitarists like T-Bone Walker and B. B. King and Muddy Waters used string-bending or a slide to vocalize their instruments, to communicate what was important to them by the most precise gradations of pitch and rhythmic accent as a talking-drummer might, Michael Schenker or K. K. Downing simply jabber high-speed babble, regurgitated licks where nothing counts except velocity. Bill Nelson describes the transition perfectly in an article in the current *One Two Testing*: 'Not only did every other guitarist learn to speak the new language, but they all began to repeat the same sentence – an unforgivable grim cavalcade of mindless and hysterical riffs, perpetrated by the kind of people who saw nothing more challenging in the instrument than a socially acceptable means of pointing their willies at an audience.'

Heavy metal bears superficial resemblances to rock & roll. There's tight pants, loud guitars, a certain amount of celebration,

610

a shared dissatisfaction, a lot of lights, movement . . . but where heavy metal sets itself apart from the kind of rock & roll that sustains and engages something other than blind reflex is in its total lack of concern for what happens in people's lives when they're flat-back to the wall and the thing you didn't want – loss of a lover, lack of money, lack of friends, nuclear war, whatever – is right in front of you, and you need to make some kind of arrangement with the human condition.

Whether you give in or stand and fight is immaterial: first you have to know it's there. Heavy metal is the most dishonest form of rock music extant: it lives in a world of fraudulent masculine power, of violence as a metaphor for everything at all. It's rock & roll with all that ever made any kind of rock & roll worthwhile squeezed out.

Its spiritual sterility is part of its appeal. It has only produced one interesting musician in the past dozen or more years (Eddie Van Halen), and its imagery is now so confused that Judas Priest's absurd vocalist Rob Halford could pass his stage gear on to Prince Charles or Frankie Goes to Hollywood and no one would know the difference. Nothing is ever communicated apart from the fact that The Willie Rules and if you don't have one you'd better button your lip when around people who have. It's Conan without the pretty pictures or the clever dialogue.

Since the days when guitar music was regarded as so uncool and rockist that A Certain Ratio were forced to play Hammersmith Palais with their backs to the audience in case a passing structuralist were to accuse them of indecent full-frontal exposure of a guitar, the guitar has become halfway respectable again, thanks to Stuart Adamson, the Edge, Adrian Belew, Nile Rodgers and the brilliant African guitarists like Pablo, King Sunny and the geniuses who play with Orchestras Makassy and Super Mazembe. The rock guitar tradition is being enriched by a whole world of new influences, and the stranglehold of the post-Jimmy Page school of guitar players is being broken.

But the ideological stranglehold of heavy metal will never be broken until Britain and America advance to the point where white people can accept black music without first having to detach it from black people. The way Michael Bloomfield did, the way Johnny Winter and many, many other musicians of honour and courage and soul did. It was, after all, a British white guitarist who taught himself the complete works of Freddie King and Hubert Sumlin from records who made the unforgivable remarks which sparked the formation of Rock Against Racism.

Heavy metal: the transformation of precious jewels and gold into lead.

Narcorockcritocracy!

JOE CARDUCCI

Antithesis. Joe 'C for controversial' Carducci decides that he wishes to nail the notion of modern black rock music to the wall, preferably upside down in a vat of rotting gourds.

Mailer and other intellectuals . . . turned this fascination (with black America) into a strange, often unintentional rape of black ideas and styles . . . In perpetuating the romance of blackness, supporting the notion that black jazzmen, for example, were in touch with some primal sexual energy, Mailer was as guilty of stereotyping blacks as the rednecks and social mainstreamers his white Negro opposed.

(Nelson George, *The Death of Rhythm & Blues*, 1988)

Nelson George in his book is less melodramatic than its title might lead you to suspect. In his study it is crossover (to white audience) that helped a few artists commercially, but destroyed a music and its cultural tradition. This is parallel to certain analyses of black business troubles since the end of segregation (and the captive market that went with it). He neglects, however, to focus on the changes wrought by recording technology, which, if they allow pop fabrications such as Poison the appearance of rock music, certainly also have all but destroyed the aesthetically crucial band format in black music. This format was the necessary foundation for all the musical innovations of Louis Jordan, Muddy Waters, James Brown, Jimi Hendrix, Sly and the Family Stone. What is currently missing across the board in black music (exceptions include the blues, zydeco, go go and serious jazz) is a real rhythm section that plays, gets sweaty, gets funky, gets down on to tape and heard. This jamlessness is so basic a bad trip that it is bound to haunt the next stages of black music. We can hope for an aesthetic backlash, but rap and hip hop and house ain't it. Those are essentially parasitic in relation to their antecedent forms – a holding pattern. Technology, imagination and street culture may have spiced it up considerably, but the essence – the thing of it – is either missing, or borrowed and frozen solid. Rap groups like Public Enemy and Stetsasonic generally talk a good game when it comes to respecting the black American tradition of music, but they don't even believe in the band format. They believe in redeeming the pop scam. And in order to do that they end up exploiting their antecedents in a way that doesn't even allow for the possibility of combustion.

It was the just-off-the-plantation black pop audience's desire for 'sophistication' that led it to reject the blues, Chuck Berry, the Jimi Hendrix Experience, in fact the guitar itself as an artifact of the share-cropping cotton-picking bluesman – a too recent, too painful past or perhaps just socially embarrassing in the new environment (interestingly, you can hear an echo of this same guitar shame in most countrypolitan, or country and western crossover product). Soon enough James Brown's audience was as white as Berry's and Hendrix's. The hardest working man in show business was unable to project the fantasy of leisure that the grandchildren of slaves and sharecroppers demanded.

As James's father Joe Brown told Gerri Hirshey for her book, *Nowhere to Run*: 'White folks, some young white folks, run away from America. They ashamed. Black folks, they run all over, up North, everywhere, tryin' to get into America.'

The drive of the black masses to get into America – even when it is camouflaged as it must be when black (or white) ideologues' charges of 'Uncle Tom-ing' and 'trying to be white' are so quickly thrown around – plays too easily into the hands of the purveyors of slick chic: Motown, Gamble and Huff, Prince. (Although Prince had tried to assume a persona of a Bob Dylan or a Miles Davis – that of a deep, rule-breaking genius recluse – his music is at best on the cutting edge of recording production and arrangement technology. He appears to be translating the archness of George Martin and Kraftwerk to a pop R&B framework – a surprisingly late development. The 'Brownian' jams in his live set are for his rock critic constituency. They were and are important to him as must all mirrors be. These contrived jams also help cover his ass regarding the new rap scene and its implicit finger pointing at the crossover culture, even as rap itself crosses over; yielding what, crap? Just asking.)

The black, new wave inspired rock band, the Bus Boys, must have been 'thinking white' when they named their band because its lowly labour connotation all but precludes it firing the imagination of the black pop audience. Other interesting examples of contemporary cultural deracination can be heard in the vocalizing by Cory Glover of Living Colour and Doug Pinnick of King's X. Both bands are fitfully good hard rock bands and as you might then guess of their black vocalists they display a certain distance from the gospel/R&B root. Their vocals generally favour an overly broad and mechanically emotive style. Neither has quite musically interfaced with white rock and contemporary rock while remaining rooted in black essence, as the Bad Brains' H. R. Paul Hudson has done.

As Leroi Jones foretold (on the verge of the Motown sound): 'I am proposing that the weight of the blues for the slave, the completely disenfranchised individual, differs radically from the weight of the same music in the psyches of most contemporary American Negroes' (*Blues People*, 1963).

And in this new high tech producer-dominated pop game you let in the white imitators like flies on shit because that rhythm section edge black pop music has had on white pop music is surrendered. Any producer/engineer can now program or cop the rhythm he wants out of the placebo syn-drum.

Nelson George, in concluding his book, remarks about his list of contemporary 'white Negroes' (Peter Gabriel, Robbie Neville, Steve Winwood, Paul Young, George Michael, Phil Collins): 'You realize that whites no longer have to imitate R&B, but have, to a degree unprecedented in the post-war era, matched their black contemporaries. How? Through a deeper understanding and (dare I say) love for the currents in black music history' (*The Death of Rhythm & Blues*).

Certainly these limeys (all but one) he mentions 'love' R&B singers of the past and present. But they too underestimate the value of the rhythm section as the heart of any music and ambition to be more than pop ($), even as they profit from advancements in microchip technology. Perhaps in the live situation a real drummer plays and even wails on the skins (or pads or syn-drums), but in real terms music is heard and handed down – immortalized even – on disc and tape. And in today's record stores all you see are rows and rows of CDs that are digital products cradle to the grave. We are in a new ice age. If the cradle is to keep rocking then that first stage in the recording process – the playing – is going to have to in fact be played by a band of musicians.

And for all the blather we've heard over the years from black ideologues and music writers about the superior inherited African sensitivity to timbre, tone and rhythm, you would think we would now hear a little commotion from them when the whole of their popular music is paved over with synthetic percussion leaving any drummer just a performance adjunct – a human triggering device for pre-programmed digitally rendered sound bites. That's show biz I guess.

Rap, hip hop, and house are not musics *per se*, but are rather the points where performance art and a strong but displaced black disc jockey culture meet dance music. Good disc jockeys who are about music and radio style have been banished from radio for nearly two decades. They went instead to clubs to experiment with mixing records. Clever bastards that they are, they even found a way to condense their mixes to the point where they could release them on records – radio on records! The performance art influence comes in by way of its general modern connotation of art attempting to move beyond artifact. That is, such artists are following a market-place evolutionary tendency toward more efficient culture production. Musical craft, like any artistic craft, has a discipline and is measurable. Where possible this is anxiously traded away by the unmusical artist who has focused instead on the marketing of style, mystique and persona by previously successful artists. Students of Warhol and Bowie have learned that if you feed the media a personal mystique you can more efficiently generate an audience for your art than if you concentrate on actually working out an honest attempt at art (which requires a full commitment of time and energy). And if your art is conceptual rather than interpretive or expressive you can escape criticism and your achievement will not be measurable. Just read any writing on rap, hip hop or house. I can prove that critics have missed an aesthetic point *vis-à-vis* rock music, but in the case of the coverage of these contemporary black 'musics' there is simply nothing to prove.

What *Billboard* writer Nelson George has missed is this correlative: the new technology – particularly synthetic percussion – allows any singer who can hire a competent producer to compete in the pop market-places of rhythm-oriented musics. Love has nothing to do with it. This technology has not only led new wave incompetents like the Cure, New Order and Billy Idol, disco queens like George Michael and the Communards, and unheavy metalheads like Motley Crue and Anthrax, right past the real music on the *Billboard* charts, it has also buffaloed real musicians into sinking to their level: pop. No one, after all, wants to lose their contract.

If you pull out pre-1981 releases by European new wavers, you may hear interesting melodic or textural ideas, but you won't hear shit in the rhythm section. There are very few exceptions. This has changed with the new technology and now Euro pop – soulless as it may be, rockless as it may be – sounds rhythmically convincing and alluringly glossy. Disco's Tin Pan Alley promise has delivered via second generation Brit new wave and hip hop (soul on ice).

Such concerned professional observers as Nelson George might miss the implications of such a fundamental development because the pop language is to date the only one with any currency in the real world of rock, pop, funk, rap, metal, blues and country. Abstract concepts such as 'jam', 'hot', 'cook' (all likely generated in the early gospel and jazz worlds), should be applied to all considerations of rhythmic musical languages, but are presently at a distinct disadvantage in mediated discussions and promotions of music. Any observer conversant with pre-disco funk and R&B surely has felt the temperature of black music drop from hot to damn near chilly over the past fifteen years. But it is all so well produced, ain't it. People – even apparently the professionals – do not consciously listen to the rhythm instruments during a musical performance (unless they solo). As Nelson George likely assumes, while focusing on the vocals and arrangements, that he is hearing processed rhythm. Should he hear something with some life in it, it had better be jazz (in its élitist non-body guise) or my guess is he would reject it from consideration as serious contemporary music.

There simply is no more soul music, *per se*. Black music, with isolated exceptions, is either body music, processed and designed for dancing, stirring up hormone levels and introducing the background of sexual intent for the awkward young so gathered, or head music, processed and designed to demonstrate the author/rapper's superior rank in a tough world. What soul vocalizing remains is inevitably encased in the ice of contemporary pop production technology and is therefore an ersatz soul, without musical root or resonance. The only regularly broadcast black music that is hot and full measure is that by the school marching bands at half time on BET's black college football coverage.

Black aesthetiticians are also frequently led down the wrong rhetorical road because so much of their spiel is conceived in response to mainstream pop music and its unequal rewards. However, since 1970 most rock music has been a largely underground phenomenon, and by 1974 that underground economy had shrunk to the point where the rewards were strictly functional at best. That is, they allowed a band to keep recording and keep touring with little prospect to someday buy castles in Spain or fly to Denver for cheeseburgers. Any serious black artist ought to focus on his true aesthetic counterparts in the rock underground (the independent labels and small clubs) when measuring his relative rewards and society's level of racism, because if he pegs his commercial expectations at the level of Van Halen and U2 then he will of necessity by such logic surrender that which alone might make his music worth discussing. That is, real musicians who are African-American should stop defusing themselves in attempts to con their way to pop success, just as real musicians of any race ought. Because cash reward or no cash reward, that con always backfires aesthetically. The pop market is no longer racist; it is rather prejudiced against music – especially that made from the small band format. Therefore, congratulate Michael Jackson. Welcome Living Colour to the club. Thank MTV for mixing in black pop. Thank CBS's Yetnikoff for threatening to pull all his videos from MTV if they didn't add Michael's 'Beat It' video. But if you're serious about music, then stay serious about it!

Wimps 'R' Us

DEBORAH FROST

The release of Use Your Illusion I *and* II, *two sprawlingly diluted 'double-album' length CDs by Guns N' Roses, may not represent a landmark in the history of rock & roll, but it certainly marks a turning point in the history of hype. Deborah Frost's* Village Voice *piece suggests Marshall McLuhan might have been right all along, and that the medium may indeed be the message.*

Smart boys don't talk about anarchy; stupid boys don't know about it. It's hard to imagine, say, Emma Goldman (who, true, was not really a boy, only a garden-variety anarchist) starting a riot, then complaining she lost her contact lens, like Axl Rose did after his recent débâcle at St Louis's Riverport amphitheater. For Guns N' Roses, 'anarchy' is as good as any other limp excuse they've unzipped and waved in public lately. Then again, Guns N' Roses, capitalist tools that they really are, know they can wave anything they want and the marketing geniuses at their record company will figure out how to package it.

The English (whose youth culture is only a few aeons younger than the monarchy, but almost as institutionalized) have learned to cope with the inevitable pop flavour of the month as gracefully as the next equally inevitable round of cucumber sandwiches. But in America, by dint of national size, shape and bloodsport, we have been forced to develop something bigger, better and uglier, mofos of the minute. And duck, duck, duck, Guns N' Roses are IT. This is no accident – of nature, or anything else. Even as I type, someone in the house turns on the tube, and whaddyaknow, it's Guns N' Roses night on MTV. Not that every night hasn't been Guns N' Roses night since the channel began hyping the band's tour last June, when *Use Your Illusion I* and *II* (Geffen) were originally expected. The hourly promo ops included lots of Kurt Loder on the spot with heads of Slash and Axl (all the effect of which was not unlike sending Ted Koppel in search of Saddam Hussein) and the contest giveaway of Rose's former Sunset Strip apartment (which Rose toured as graciously for the camera as anyone on a soft real estate market might have expected). But as MTV rolls a GN'R block of the hit clips from the band's brief but lucrative career – which until last week consisted of one full-length big money album, a stop-gap EP, and a few spare change singles – their success is no great mystery. Yes, the music mostly recharges ideas Aerosmith got from the Rolling Stones and Led Zeppelin and the Yardbirds, who in turn took 'em off the hands of a lot of Black folks who never got to toss color TVs out of hotel windows. Still from 'Welcome To The Jungle' to the *Terminator 2* tie-in, 'You Could Be Mine,' GN'R's greatest riffs are packed with enough grit, sweat and plain ornery 400-mule kick to guarantee significant recognition in any rock or radio climate. It just might have taken them a few more years at the bottom of AC/DC bills.

But it isn't only the music, distinguished by the voice that loads it like a lethal injection, a voice dosed with some of the familiar discomforts of Morrison, Jagger and, most eerily, Janis Joplin, and shot through with a whinny, rage and pathos all its own.

Guns N' Roses are the biggest, scariest monsters that ever escaped MTV's lab. Axl Rose absolutely dominates the video screen – territory that has been previously creatively and profitably used by a whole host of videogenic species from Madonna to Mellencamp. But like Garbo or Dietrich, who managed to register a similarly indelible and incomparable presence in a different realm, right now Rose transcends his medium better than anyone else on the box. Not that Rose accomplishes the same feat anywhere else – least of all on record or the concert stage. In fact, what is really scary about the 'You Could Be Mine' clip isn't cyber-Arnold's humongous artillery; it's how the inspired camera angles and spectacular editing completely alter what was, in reality, at the Ritz last May, an often embarrassingly minor-league rehearsal from a supposedly world-class band. Then again, as *Rolling Stone's* me-decade drone unwittingly prophesied: perception is reality. And even without packing the Gunners and the Terminator into one teeter-towering monument to modern iconography, a veritable semiotic gorge-fest gabba hey, what you see and hear of the band is so electrifying on the box that anything before, after, or remotely near it seems very, very small. Just now, when we returned from our GN'R block to regular programming, with a Dutch Ken doll V J posing outside some race-car track where the action zipped by at a mere hundred-odd m.p.h., it felt like the air had just been sucked out of every tire in the world.

When reduced to a sound bite, Guns N' Roses – in particular, Axl and his Glimmer Twin *manqué*, Slash (whose guitar playing often does glimmer with something approaching greatness) – loom as large as any mythical creation. Perhaps because bread is getting scarcer, our circuses need to be enormous, and Guns N' Lemmings have been only too willing to throw themselves and their dirtiest laundry in all three rings, even if it means impaling themselves on a few tent spikes in the process. Guns N' Roses have ingested not only all of arena rock's attitudinal riffs, but punk's as well, and eagerly regurgitate it all. If fore-gunners the Sex Pistols and New

York Dolls never racked up the same sales figs, it had a lot to do with their inability to adequately confront arena rock's musical riffs. Of course, the antics with which GN'R have sought to establish a rep as rock's most authentic outlaw dudes are not even unique to rock; it's the behavior of any pack of men on the road, whether they be jocks, travelling salesmen, or presidential candidates. GN'R's 'private' lives (which they and their appointed messengers have gleefully detailed since day one) may be even less original than their aesthetic stance. Like the plots of a few late seventies rock novels, GN'R have almost been programmed for destruction. (No doubt, when it happens, MTV will remind us to tune in.) So, maybe it's all for the best that they've swept up all the cutting-room floor odds and sods – the rough sketches, in-jokes, dirty jokes, off-stage lines and studio parties – and slapped them together into the two double balls of confusion, *Use Your Illusion I* and *II*. Better they clean out the vaults than, say, Alan Douglas.

10. And in the End

"Well, you didn't expect me to wear the corny old cowl and the shabby threads did you?"

Hope I die before I get old.
(*Pete Townshend – 1965*)

Brian Jones, Jimi Hendrix, Janis Joplin, Jim Morrison, Gram Parsons, Marc Bolan, Elvis Presley, Ian Curtis, John Lennon and Johnny Thunders. A list of casualties which could as easily include Lowell George, Sid Vicious, Peter Laughner, Lester Bangs, Phil Lynott and Nico. Rock & roll has certainly tended to chew up its surrogate progeny and spit 'em out at a terrifying rate.

If Jonathan Richman used to sing about looking forward to a time when he could be dignified and old, he was definitely the exception. If sex and rock & roll had only a marginal bearing on this roster of handfuls of dust, Drugs N. Drink should certainly take due credit for terminating a few mortal coils.

I've included a cross-section of the sermonizing obituary – Landau's piece on Joplin, Murray's on Presley, Hell's on his friend Johnny Thunders, one of rock's more expected casualties. I've tried to balance these with more personalized recollections: Al Aronowitz on Brian Jones and Jim Morrison, Adrian Thrills and Paul Morley on Ian Curtis, Greg Mitchell on Gram Parsons.

In the midst of these valedictions and tributes comes a healthy dose of irreverence from Lester Bangs, whose posthumous interview with Jimi Hendrix says a lot more about what ailed Hendrix than all the belated exposés of the financial shenanigans that surrounded him could.

Over Their Dead Bodies – Memories of Brian and Jim

AL ARONOWITZ

Brian Jones was not the first post-Rockspeak casualty. Brian Epstein and Otis Redding beat him to the punch. Nor was Jim Morrison the last. But their 'drug-induced' deaths – book-ending the years which claimed Jimi Hendrix and Janis Joplin – signified the end of a naïve faith in the drug-culture's beneficence.

I am standing with Brian Jones at the window of his hotel suite when we look down into this open sore in the bedrock fifteen flights below and see the steel mesh blanket jump like a dog being shot and then hear the deadly thump of the dynamite charge beneath it.

They are sending up another New York City skyscraper and I turn to Brian and say, 'It's an omen, man. Wherever I see you, they're building something.' I stand there remembering all the times Brian and I have looked through a hotel window to find a construction pit across the street, and yet I realize I am actually saying this to be kind to Brian. Already he drawls with the decay of his oncoming martyrdom to drugs and you have to put an ear against his mouth to hear what he is saying.

It is the fall of 1967 and, although Brian has always hated New York, he keeps telling me he'll be back in a month, after he takes care of his dope busts. Of course, he never returns. How many evenings can you keep waking up to find your cigarette burned through the bedclothes and into the mattress, not knowing how many days ago you fell asleep or how many Desbutols you took before you did?

This is the last time I see him, and he is wearing a collar of Day-Glo sequins and a bracelet of watermelon seeds and he shows me his lavender suede boots. If he gave nothing else to this world, Brian Jones was the first heterosexual male to start wearing costume jewelry from Saks Fifth Avenue. Shall I tell you about the 7. 00 a.m. he wanted me to take him to the top of the Empire State Building with his orange blond hair still oozing blood from where a girlfriend had cracked his skull with a Coke bottle? 'Well,' he used to say, 'what do you expect from a pop star?'

Oh, yes, Brian was always a dandy. In the end, he was like a princeling who had run out of toys to play with. Once he kept a box score of his women and it added up to sixty-four in one month, a pace which didn't even allow for the luxury of a one-night stand. That was all right with Brian. He used to find them waiting in his bathroom and in his closets and in his bed, and he'd take them on two at a time.

When it came to lifestyles, Brian wrote the definition of an English pop star. Was he the real hero of the Rolling Stones? Certainly he was the most photogenic. John Lennon once told Brian Epstein that the Rolling Stones would break up over Brian Jones's dead body. Epstein said he didn't understand what John meant. Of course he never lived to find out. Only Lennon could have known how necessary Brian Jones was to the chemistry that kept the Rolling Stones together. Doesn't John still carry the same sack of cement for the Beatles?

I met Brian in 1964 when the Stones first arrived in America faced with the emotional mathematics of trying to fill the footsteps of the Beatles. To walk into Carnegie Hall to hear them for the first time was to have a bucket of sound splashed into your face. The Stones didn't play concerts in those days. What they played were riots. It soon became apparent that they were the only group in a position to challenge the Beatles for leadership in that first storming of the ramparts of England's palsied caste system.

Shall I tell you about the time two cops stopped us for doing eighty around London's Marble Arch? It may as well have been Fifth Avenue and Washington Square, but we were drunk out of our skulls on Scotch. Behind the wheel, all Brian did was laugh that asthmatic laugh of his and the cops grinned and let us go. It was Brian who founded the Stones and discovered all those obscure black blues records by Bo Diddley and Chuck Berry and Willie Dixon that he somehow imported from America and put into the Stones' own language. 'I was the undisputed leader of the group,' he used to say. 'The undisputed leader.'

His undisputed leadership lasted only until the Stones started making enough money for it to be worthwhile for someone to dispute. Lead singer Mick Jagger and lead guitarist Keith Richard joined co-manager Andrew Loog Oldham in a *coup d'état* and the next thing Brian knew was that the Rolling Stones were cutting two sides in LA without him. From then on, it was only a matter of time before John Lennon could say I told you so.

Brian suffered through an Ed Sullivan show and most of an American tour before taking an overdose of pills in Chicago. They kept him in the hospital for more than a week. In the beginning, he had sung harmony and played the harmonica but he was quickly reduced to an ornament with the Rolling Stones, the kind of bright spot that they couldn't get out no matter how hard they rubbed.

Shall I tell you about the time the Stones threw a party in the $ 500-a-day penthouse of the New York Hilton and Brian brought Bob Dylan along with Bob's guitarist, Robbie Robertson? Bob sat down at the piano, Robbie played the guitar and Brian blew harp. He blew and blew until his lips were red. When he wiped his mouth, he found it was blood. It always made Brian nervous to play with Bob. 'Don't be paranoid, Brian,' Bob would smile. On the night of New York's great harvest moon blackout, Bob led a party of visitors up the five flights of stairs to Brian's room at the Lincoln Square Motor Inn. They played guitars and sang by candle-light.

One of the first things Brian ever told me was about a vision that he once had coming out of a nightclub in London's 3. 00 a.m. dawn. It was as if the heavens had called upon him to look up and see the face of a goddess angel telling him to work for human good. It was a vision that guided him for as long as I knew him and yet he always kept cursing himself as one who used his power for evil. Shall I tell you about the dog chain he used to carry to beat his girlfriend? He refused to be satisfied by whatever he did. 'I don't just play rhythm guitar,' he would say. Once he stayed up all night writing a treatise on his paranoia. One of his greatest fears was that he had made it on his good looks and really had no talent.

He died at twenty-six, a man whose vision had somehow carried him into decadence. He died as one of the leaders of a generation that was determined to build the biggest monument to itself in the history of mankind even if the monument turned out to be a whirlwind. He died taking the rap for all the drug-users of Britain. Even when he tried to beat the rap by committing himself to a rest home, he merely walked into the rest home carrying his dope with him.

After he was kicked out of the Rolling Stones' leadership, a friend suggested that Brian get the best musicians available on both sides of the Atlantic and start the first Anglo-American supergroup. 'No,' he said, 'if I left the group, I'd just be an ex-Rolling Stone.' In the end, there were reports that Mick Jagger had become impatient. On the one hand the Stones needed Brian for the group's image. On the other, the group wanted to tour again but Brian couldn't get an American visa because of his trouble with the police. It was only several weeks ago that Brian announced he was leaving the Stones and Mick Jagger announced that a guitarist named Mick Taylor would replace Brian. Replace Brian?

Over his dead body.

We all make our deals with the devil.

I suppose Jim Morrison must have realized that he made his. Listen to Jac Holzman, the president of Elektra Records, the company that helped create the great fireworks display that Jim became.

'Superstardom is a speed trip,' Jac said, paraphrasing something he once read by Michael Lydon. 'The flash is incredible, but it kills you in the end.'

Jac was remembering how quiet Jim really used to be, storing up his anger only to let it out in quick and unexpected public detonations. He remembered the first time he saw Jim singing with the Doors in the Whiskey A Go Go, Los Angeles.

It was only a short time after the Doors had got their release from Columbia and Jac could understand why.

'They were not very good,' he said, 'but there was something there that made me keep coming back.' He signed them up and put them in a studio with producer Paul Rothschild. It was the summer of 1966. They completed their album in ten days but Jac didn't release it until the following January. By the summer of 1967, the album was selling a quarter of a million copies a month.

It was a success that came long past the point of anticlimax for Jim. I remember Nico, the tall, blonde beauty, telling me how Jim used to bite his hands until they bled in the dressing-room after a show. She and Jim ran together for a while.

The first time I saw Jim perform was in Steve Paul's Scene, the old cellar club on 46th Street. It was back in 1966 and I was with Brian Jones. Jim went through his gimmick of opening his mouth to the microphone as if he was about to sing and then closing it again and both Brian and I got up and walked out. Before long, 'Light My Fire' hit number one on the charts.

It was soon afterwards that Jim and the Doors were telling

reporters to 'think of us as erotic politicians'. I couldn't quite figure out what they were running for but it was easy to spot their constituency. The teenyboppers kept telling me that while the Beatles had been optimists, the Doors were pessimists. Meanwhile, Jim was quickly getting burnt out.

I didn't meet him until after he had outgrown all that baloney. It was at Mike McClure's house in San Francisco, where Jim used to go to take lessons in what he really wanted to be, a poet. I remember playing *Nashville Skyline* for him. He said it was Dylan's most 'sensual' album, but then Jim was always hung up on sensuality. When Mike talked about writing a science-fiction screenplay, Jim said, 'Yeah, let's make it pornographic science-fiction.' We got drunk that night, sitting at Mike's round wooden kitchen table with Jim chomping on a cigar and doing imitations like he was somebody's Uncle Charlie. It was the first time I had seen him with a beard and somehow he reminded me of Charlton Heston. I could visualize him acting heroic roles in great cinemascopic epics.

All the friends I've talked to now say they knew intuitively that Jim was dead as soon as they got the final phone call. But the sadness for me is that I really expected him to go on to greater things.

We went to Chinatown the next afternoon, to one of those restaurants with formica-top tables, and we had a rip-roaring meal, with Jim playing Uncle Charlie again. Jim and Mike talked about Artaud. Jim was one of the most voracious readers I've ever met, but that's the way it is with people who are as serious about their writing as Jim was.

Actually, Jim and Mike did get to finish a film script they were working on together, an adaptation of Mike's novel, *The Adept*. They also were kicking around an idea for an original movie musical.

In addition to his book of poetry, *The Lords*, and his collection of short prose fragments, *The New Creatures*, Jim also printed a private edition of poetry, *American Prayer*, for distribution among his friends. He was working on a partially completed manuscript when he died.

'I didn't expect Jim to live very long,' Mike now says, 'not at the intensity at which he lived. He was on a very self-destructive level. But I don't think of it now as Jimi Hendrix, Janis Joplin and Jim Morrison. I think of it as Jack Kerouac, Charles Olson and Jim Morrison.'

Jim had already spoken with the Doors when he went to Paris to chase after Pamela, the one woman he always went back to out of the countless he knew. He hadn't been getting along with the rest of the group for a couple of years and they had been looking for a new lead singer for some time.

In the old days, at the height of the Doors' success, Jim had constantly kept telling the others that he wanted to quit and they'd take it out on him on-stage, sometimes dropping notes and imitating his phrasing.

To most of his friends, he was always a tragic figure. His audience refused to let him mature. When he tried to read his poetry on-stage, the crowd would ask for 'Light My Fire'. They wouldn't let him stop being the Lizard King. He wanted to be considered a poet and a writer.

He is buried now in the Perelachaise cemetery in Paris, near the grave, I am told, of Molière. Superstardom is a speed trip. The flash is incredible, but that's the deal you make.

He had quit his heavy drinking the last couple of months. According to his friends, the death certificate said he died of a heart attack brought on by respiratory complications.

He died peacefully. When Pamela found him in the bath-tub, there was a smile on his face.

A Posthumous Interview

LESTER BANGS

Bangs's deliciously irreverent posthumous interview with Hendrix, which one imagines to be delivered in a laid-back, hippy patois, conveys the sense of a man careening out of control who woke up one day to find himself dead, an open verdict hanging over his head.

LB: Jimi, you used to sing a lot about astral planes, the cosmos and such when you were on earth. Now that you're out there, how does it stack up against what you originally envisioned?

JH: Well, I'll tell ya. It's not like the advertisements [laughs]. But then, neither was I. Because see, a lot of people got the wrong idea about me.

LB: Like who?

JH: Me, for starters. I didn't know what I was doing, except I dug R&B and Dylan, and found out howta get all these weird sounds outa my axe. That's where things got confused, just a little bit. Like I'm jammin' my ass off one night on-stage at the Fillmore, playin' some kinda dirt bike ride round the rings of Saturn, and I look out at the crowd and they're like one big pinball machine I'm lighting up, making 'em go buzz and tilt by playing 'See See Rider' backwards or something, I didn't know because my fingers were turning into celery stalks and I'm afraid to look at that, so I shut my eyes a second but there was some kinda Marvel Comic

633

S & M Thor's Mistress flashing this whip and snorting at me in there so I open 'em up again fast as I can and now everybody in the audience is Bob Denver.

LB: What? What do you mean?

JH: I mean that every face out there looked identical, like Bob Denver on *Gilligan's Island*, with the little hat and the ratty shirt and everything, and they were all staring up at me with that goofy Gilligan's look like 'What're we supposed to do now?' so I screamed out right in the middle of a chorus of another song I'd forgot anyway, 'I'm the Skipper and I want you to go get Marianne and bring her here to me! I want that bitch on her KNEES!' It seemed to make sense in the context of the lyrics at the time.

LB: Well, it was a time of great experiment and innovation, after all.

JH: I know I changed some things, not nearly as much as some people seem to give me credit for, but I coulda really *changed* things, I think, if I knew then what I know now. But at the time the alternative was so irresistibly tempting, and I was tellin' ya about screamin' my lungs out at Gilligan. I had no idea in hell what Noel and Mitch were doing, they coulda been on a Greyhound to Tuscon, Arizona, for all I knew or cared. So I just tore up into a long high note, held it, tore it off and decided to get the hell out of there.

Now, no sooner do I get off the stage than who do I practically smash foreheads with but Bill Graham. Asshole's been standin' there on the side of the stage watchin' me this whole time. Now he just blocks my way, grabs my arm, stares deep into my eyes and says: 'Jimi, why do you go out and play shit like that, when we both know you're capable of some of the best blues I've ever heard in my life, man?'

Well, I hate to say it, but I just niggered out, played even more spaced than I was, because I didn't wanna hassle with the cat, I just wanted outa there. But if I'd been physically and psychologically capable of staying, man, I woulda said: 'Because there are times when I strongly suspect, deep down inside, that I hate the fuckin' blues. Every broke-down nigger behind a mule he don't own can sing the blues. I only do blues because it's fun and easy to get into once in a while, and because I know all them fans don't think a music show by a black person is their money's worth unless they get to hear some.'

LB: Yeah, but what about cuts like 'Red House' and 'Voodoo Chile'? They were incredible songs, fantastically played!

JH: They weren't exactly what you would call original compositions. They were good takes, especially the second 'Voodoo Chile'. The long version had a nice feel, but it was there to fill out a double album, and Winwood played the same damn solo he played in 'Pearly Queen' and every other damn session he did for about three years. I played good blues on 'Red House', but it got way more attention than it deserved, probably because it was so hard to get in America for a long time. I mean, 'I Don't Live Today' is real blues, modern blues – it's what happens when you drop a hydrogen bomb on the blues, which is what it deserves.

Listen. The blues is white music, and so was most 'free jazz'. All the musicians know it, everybody in the ghetto knows it because they'd be boppin' to James Brown and Stanley Turrentine, don't own Muddy Waters albums much less Robert Johnson, and 98 per cent of 'em never heard of Albert Ayler. My music was at least 70 per cent white. If I'd played what black people wanted to hear at that time I'da been spectacularly unsuccessful in the hip rock superstar world, and if I'd gone down to the Apollo Theatre and played what I played at the Fillmore I probably woulda been laughed off the stage. And knowing that has dogged my ass all the way to this moment. That and the fact that to a certain extent and in the interests of image, I had to shuck and jive because you know niggers is just s'posed to be bad and screw good wid big dicks an' be finger poppin' all de time. I just added a little acid and feedback. And hell, for all of that I didn't even get laid that much either, or at least not as much as I should. I mean, you would think with me bein' JIMI HENDRIX and all the big deal was made out of it, *I'd be gettin' more pussy* than Haile Selassie's whole harem and better quality than, I dunno, who's the hottest screw you can think of?

LB: Uhmmmmm . . . Wilma Flintstone.

JH: Thanks a lot. Like, I coulda dug gettin' into som'a that Julie Christie. You know, or maybe som'a that Ursula Andress, you know movie stars, continental flash class pussy. Instead I get all these dopey bitches wanna read my Tarot and always gotta i ching in the Bantam edition in their back jeans pocket ready to spring on you at any second and tell you just the exact state of the gobbledegook. Well, I got more gobbledegook than I know what to do with already, as even a passing listen at my songs will tell you. You think I wrote all them fuckin' cosmic lyrics because I had the Universal Mind on tap? Hunh. I liked *Star Trek* but I ain't Paul Kantner. I got more out of it than Paul Kantner, who shoulda profited by my bad example. I just dropped this and snorted that, and pretty soon a lotta shit was swirling around my head. Same shit as hit everybody else, really, especially Dylan, who was as inspiring and as bad an influence on me as anybody. I started out sincere, but half the time I couldn't fuckin' think straight, so stuff I knew was sloppy-ass jive time mumbo-jumbo come tumblin' out, and people jump up like whores for a blow of coke: 'Oh wow, Jimi, far out . . .' And maybe that's where things started to really go wrong. When I saw that folks'd buy that jive as profound, well I just spaced it all a-way.

LB: Are you saying you were a suicide?

JH: I ain't saying nothing, man. Except maybe that no dead niggers are suicides. But it's got nothing to do with me now. 'Cause there ain't no race bullshit Out Here. Ain't no races – 'Just us angels up heah, boss!' Maybe I'll come back – just once – and do a three-night stint of God's Trombones as a rock opera, with Gil Scott-Heron and Stevie too. 'Cause I wanna lay some shit on Stevie – that cat is off and I don't care if he's blind. I don't care if his mama sent him to seven churches for each day of the week, he is flat wrong, period, I mean, nobody should know this 'Heaven' shit better'n me. I allow myself as something of an expert on the subject. It's been nothin' but blow-jobs 'n' soma since I bailed out back in '70. Don't ever go ta heaven man. It's the shits. Only reason not to split is Hell is worse, we went down there one weekend on a binge and it's the dregs. Heaven is like total stardom with a constant-touring clause, nothin' but arenas and hotels, but Hell is like Baltimore. The whole Afterlife trip is rigged to the rim jobs, and like New York cabaret cards it's one system you can't beat.

LB: Your rap is ... well ... I honestly can't think of another question right now.

JH: That's OK, I'm on speed, I'll fill in [Lights a cigarette, with compulsive urgency but steady hands].

LB: I get a feeling you're pretty critical of your fellow musicians, dead and living.

JH: Yeah, but it's cool, see, because there's nobody I'm more ruthlessly critical of than myself. I was a good guitar player, no Django, but I did manage to come up with a few new riffs and a few new ideas about how to finger or get some weird noises outa the thing. But there ain't much percentage in ego-tripping when you're dead, so I gotta cop that that was about it. The songs I wrote that had actual melodies, that you could hum or have a real zinger cover, can be counted on the fingers of one hand. 'Angel' I'm still proud of as a composition, and a couple others. But the rest is mostly just metal riffs, with mostly jive lyrics and I talked instead of sang. I got a lotta credit for introducing 'advanced technology', or whatever they're callin' it these days, to rock. But the thing that almost everybody missed was that once the distortion and technology became a 'required' part of the whole style and, like, institutionalized, then it was all over. Because technology is cold – so's technique, for that matter – and humans are hot. Or at least they should be. Because the emotion behind the distortion is the whole thing. And what we didn't realize was that all of us cultivating distortion so much was just digging our graves, emotionally speaking. And literally too, I guess, in some cases.

Because as time went on I began to realize that what people craved was just noise. Now, I took a lotta care with my own albums, the first three anyway – they were very carefully produced, all that shit. They were tight. But I was beginning to really, really wonder. Because when I listen to *Are You Experienced?*, at least half of what I hear and remember is just this really crazed unhappy desperation and pissed-offness that can't make no sense out of nothing. It's there in the lyrics and in the music too. Because that was where I was at the time. When I said 'Ain't no life nowhere', I meant it! Meanwhile I'm thinking do they expect me to bring the can of lighter fluid in my pocket on-stage every night? Obviously something is wrong somewhere.

LB: Well, what was it about distortion that started bothering you so much?

JH: Well, like Graham wants blues, so do the fans, but Graham don't want distortion and they do. He thinks that's shit and blues is 'real'. Well, I don't know what the fuck is real. I never exactly did. Like, do I play two chords or three or just fuck around with tremelo and feedback and make funny noises and burn my guitar and swallow the strings and cannibalize my sidemen and then stand there alone on the stage with the buttons poppin' off my shirt like Brock Peters singing 'John Henry' and 'Cotton Fields' back home and a selection of word songs personally recorded on Parchman by Alan Lomax? See, it seems to me when I look back that there was something larger that I always really, really wanted to do, but I could never quite get a firm grip on it.

On one level I'm really glad I got out when I did. Because it's like Kennedy see, a legend – everybody can sit around saying, 'Well, gee, nothin' happening, but if Jimi was around now, he'd show us where it was all goin' next!' But they're wrong. I wouldn't have a fuckin' clue what to do now, if I was so unfortunate as to be 'around'. I'd probably be just like the rest of 'em, repeating my same shit over and over until everybody is as bored as I am and we mutually agree to call it quits and I'll go sit in the islands and listen to reggae or something. Or maybe, what would be even worse, I'd be one of the ones that keeps grinding out the same old shit and doesn't know it: 'Yeah, Jimi, your new album *Toe Jam Asteroid* is the absolute best thing you've done!' 'Yeah, like dig, I'm hip, pops . . . just be cool.' Yeah, that's how I'd cop out, come on as a real jive throwback spade wearing shades all the time, a little hat and cigarette smoke, the old Lonely Unapproachable Jazz Musician routine, sitting around in smoky clubs, sidewalk cafés, talk nothin' but bebop jive shit. 'Yeah, cook, ah, that was a wiggy scene. Later.' [He breaks up laughing.] The Thelonious Monk of the wah wah. Either that or just go hide and do session work. Become like Louie Shelton. Because I know I couldn't do what I started out to do and make it really cook.

And it ain't that I don't still got my chops. I do. Everybody's too fucking hung up on chops, though. I think the only studio album where I really burned all the way was my first one. And that's after practising night and day, year after year, trying to learn it all and do it better, coming up hard and fast and paying dues and busting your chops and out to whip ass on everybody, when suddenly one day I discovered somehow that I could be fuckin' Segovia; that if some other weird component is missing, then I might as well be Louie Shelton.

LB: What is that component?

JH: I wish I knew. I know I lost it somewhere. I take consolation from the fact that just about everybody else came up same time I did too. Maybe we all just got too high.

LB: How do you feel about people like Eric Burdon and Buddy Miles, whom some observers have accused of cashing in on your name or their association with you after your death?

JH: Listen, once you kick out you tend to let a lotta bad shit just go under the bridge. Fuck it, I hope they copped a few extra bucks. Besides, nobody lives forever, and I'm gonna have to sit down and have a serious talk with poor old Eric whenever he gets up here, in lieu of busting his face open. It's actually amusing, and besides, he really didn't know any better. Buddy Miles is a different case – I'd be afraid of getting my ass kicked, but anybody racks up as many bad records as that cat's probably gonna end up on the first coal cart to Hell anyway, so hopefully I'll never chance to see his fat face again.

LB: Ever see any of the others who kicked off close to the time you did, hanging around up here?

JH: Nah. I hear about them once in a while, but I don't hang out with 'em. You wouldn't either. Morrison – I heard all about him, although I didn't see it. He put up such a big stink how he wanted

640

into Hell and was gonna make 'em all wish he'd never died, and on and on . . .

I identify with him on a certain level. We both came along at the right wrong time, right to become figureheads, wrong in terms on longevity. We were like the test models for crap like Alice Cooper and David Bowie. We both got suckered, but I like to think he got suckered far worse than I did. He, like, had more complicity in his own destruction. I like to think I just got more confused musically as much as in life, until it was all too much of a mess and there was no way out. I let too damn many people intimidate me, for one thing, because I knew I was off but I never had the simple street-smarts to figure just maybe they were off too, maybe ten thousand times worse than me, so I just kind of ended up laying myself in everybody's hands. I mean, I was really an innocent, and it wasn't comfortable then.

LB: What about Janis?

JH: I was hoping you weren't going to ask me that. Jeez, you fuckin' journalists, always after the next lurid headline. Well . . . she was pathetic there and she's pathetic here. It's not her fault, but she doesn't do anything, particularly, to try to improve it, either. That's all I got to say about that.

LB: How do you feel about being a hot chart artist still, and record companies over-dubbing other accompanists on your old tapes?

JH: My records still selling is just like Jefferson Starship being more popular then Jefferson Airplane – quality has nothing to do with it, it's just people hanging on to things they know were good and represented something once, instead of taking a chance on a dubious unknown artist.

As far as the over-dubbing goes, I feel almost as much

indifference there. It sounds weird and egotistical for a dead guy to crow about how he was actually a one-man show, especially since his old sidemen really have no means of retorting, so obviously the smart position for me to have is no position. Why don't you go ask John Coltrane the same question, and see if connubial fidelity extends beyond the grave?

LB: You seem pretty negative about the people who've followed you musically on earth, though.

JH: Yeah. I am. Because they're cold. I may have played real dogshit some gigs, and cut some tracks that were too smooth for my taste. But I was loose. There was something bigger than me sweeping me along and it killed me in the end, but some pretty incredible music came out of it at times, too. My only regret is that I wonder how much of it, under those circumstances, was really my music, when you get right down to it. If a lightning bolt strikes you, and out of it you get a masterpiece, well, is it you or the lightning bolt? And in the final analysis it's just no contest. You know you lost control, you let the music and the life play you, and that's why you went under. But it really happened, it was real fire and real dues, and nothing can erase that. It should be pretty obvious by now that I consider my life and my art a failure, but it was an honest failure.

What bugs me is these cats now – no bolt. And no them either! I don't mind people copping my riffs, but they're like a buncha college students! Most of my riffs I copped off somebody else, but then I went on and played and forgot about it. I didn't sit around with seven candles burning in a shrine to Chuck Berry. So who even cares if cats like this Trower or that guy in Canada succeed or fail, what's the fucking difference? There is more happening in any bar on Friday night when the dance floor's full, than in all those cats' albums and concerts put together.

What's even worse is that they missed the biggest lick of all, the thing that was so discouraging to me – that I saw the end of it coming. I don't mean rock & roll or popular music or even heavy metal – just the kind of particular experimental, technological branch we riffed out on and sawed through. There's got to be something else. Because one thing I learned while killing myself was that a hell of a lot of that shit was just sound and fury kicked up to disguise the fact that we were losing our emotions, or at least the ability to convey them. Most of *Electric Ladyland* and the second album sound real cold to me now. I don't know what it sounded like to me then, because I was too spaced out to make any accurate judgement except that it had all the ingredients. I got some rocks off especially in things like 'Voodoo Child (Slight Return)', the albums were relatively slick and I knew they would sell.

I guess that's what I was trying to get at before when I talked about the missing component. I just forgot how to feel unless I was getting electric shocks or something – and after a while even electric shocks began to feel all the same. And even saying it like that doesn't really explain it. It's really THE great mystery, for everybody Out Here. And nobody's come up with any solid answers yet. So when you get back, when you publish this, if anybody comes up after that and tells you they got some kind of a line on it, I don't care how thin it is, well, you'd be doing me the biggest favour of my death if you'd pass it on back. I'd like that more than anything in the . . . Cosmos.

[He laughed again, briefly, then stared through us into some sort of distance. It was obviously time to go.]

643

The Death of Janis Joplin

JON LANDAU

In his contemporary obituary of Joplin, Jon Landau – rather than perceiving drugs as the be-all and end-all of her decline – makes them just one particularly lethal manifestation in the process of 'pop' fame.

We tell ourselves we are a counter-culture. And yet are we really so different from the culture against which we rebel? The truest expression of middle-class culture lies within the star system. The star system entails the glorification of a single personality beyond reason. It involves the selection of one person who is made to stand for all of our fantasies and all of our misplaced frustrations. It is the crudest and most primitive form of escape, in which we express dissatisfaction with ourselves by endowing another with superhuman qualities. And it is a cornerstone of what is pretentiously called the counter-culture.

Hollywood has always been viewed cynically by educated members of society because it supposedly glorifies our mass fantasies and myths. Its only demand on the intellect is that we accept what is blatantly untrue: the good guy versus the bad, the impossible romances between high and low, the inevitable triumphs of diligence, hard work and perseverance over dishonesty, laziness or whatever. Of course these propositions are nothing less than the myths and lies of the culture. And the star system, the system of vicariously living these lies through some superhuman image, is the biggest lie of all. For within it we are taught to identify with the superhumans who act out these fantasies and make them believable, attractive, stimulating and erotic. We are taught to believe that the unreal existence they present is not only possible, but that we ourselves are inadequate because we return to our mundane and unexceptional existence once we leave the movie theatre or the concert hall.

And what of the individuals who are stars? How does their participation affect them? Stars are often people who believe the myths of the star system more intensely than anyone else and therefore become participating members of the myth. It is not something that is forced upon them; it is something they crave. Stars are narcissistic. And they seldom anticipate the problems that achieving their limited goals must inevitably create for them.

For stars are invariably denied their own humanity. Forced to fulfill the fantasies of an audience, forced to pursue the fantasy that made them stars in the first place, they have no room left for a private existence within which they can be free to face the problems and situations common to us all. They are expected to be above that. The star is supposed to be what we think s/he is.

Janis Joplin was admired and loved for her capacity to drink. It is not surprising that people find it hard to believe she died of a heroin overdose just because she wasn't supposed to do that. It wasn't part of the Janis we saw on the stage. It wasn't part of *Rolling Stone*'s Janis. It wasn't part of our Janis.

Marilyn Monroe was supposed to be the all-American beauty, the dumb blonde. The fact that she was a sensitive, intelligent, complicated human being who could never adjust to the superhuman status she achieved in our society destroyed her capacity to face her real problems. She never had enough time to sort out what was hers and what was theirs. Dylan saw the problem impending, and left the arena before the demands of an adoring public got so great he could no longer cope with them.

It is not uncommon for successful stars to have no real private lives. They learn to act out their public identity so well they seem capable of repressing their basic needs and qualities as human beings forever. In a recent, brilliant article by J. Anthony Lukas called 'This is Bob (Politician-Patriot-Publicist) Hope', Hope emerges as a man with no inner self at all. Everything he does or says is done in the character of a public person. There is no hint of any inner reflection or an inner existence. He is what the public and press have made him, and he has done his damnedest to extinguish anything that doesn't fit the role.

More often than that, the star is a human being, like Marilyn, who is much more fragile and is unable to cope with the impossible demands of his/her position at all. The end result can often be some dramatic act in which the star reveals to the public that s/he is a human being, that s/he feels pain, and that s/he suffers the same problems as the rest of humanity and that no amount of adoration can make the suffering any less real than that of any other member of society. Suicide is not the least common of such acts.

The star system is empty because it offers us nothing real. It offers us only fantasies and lies. And yet our budding counter-culture thrives on stars as much as Hollywood did in the forties. And the unreality of our system, the exaggerations and contortions we force on our stars, may well be greater than that of any previous star system.

Janis was our star. She wanted to be a star, and in a sense she got what she wanted. But being a star didn't satisfy her. Towards the end her energy was going more and more into becoming something else: a professional and a craftsman. She had, with the formation of her fine new group, the Full Tilt Boogie Band, re-dedicated herself to the music. The local concert at Harvard Stadium last August showed her about to blossom into the fine musician she always had the potential to become. She seemed to have absorbed all the musical mistakes of her past, and she looked forward to the future with justified excitement.

But she was, of course, still ready to act out our fantasies for us. A member of the audience that night screamed out to her, 'I wanna ball you, Janis. We all wanna ball you.' And she answered, exactly according to script, 'Whew now, fellas, that's gonna take me a year and a half.' She also told us that 'My music ain't supposed to make you wanna riot. It's supposed to make you wanna fuck.'

Janis's creed – one that excited her audience with its simplicity – was to get high and get laid, and to take it all today because there may be no tomorrow. That creed wasn't enough, any more than the idiot creeds of twenty years ago weren't enough. And anyone who believes it is enough is living in precisely the kind of fantasy world that Janis died in.

Janis's death is frightening because so many people believed they loved her, even if it was from a distance, and because so many identified so intensely. But who among us wants to identify with her death? Who wants to follow her that far? Those who do must be getting scared about their own potential for self-destruction.

Janis Joplin was known to us as a star. Our picture of her was based on a pact between Janis and ourselves, satisfying some mutual need to make the world a little easier to bear by making it a little less real. And of course we could never be satisfied with her and Janis finally exhausted herself trying to keep her end of the bargain.

Janis Joplin was a human being and was never any of the things we wanted to believe about her. She was beset by the same fears and problems as anyone who sat in the audience watching her. The difference lay only in her ability to express herself for ourselves, through her music and her ability to perform. The rest we made up.

Elmore James sang a song I'm sure Janis knew, maybe too well. He used to say, 'When things go wrong, so wrong with you, it hurts me too.'

The only thing to add to that: as much as we may be hurt, no one will ever be able to tell how much more we hurt her.

Crazy Eyes' Goodbye

GREG MITCHELL

What made the Eagles famous, made a loser out of Gram Parsons. Parsons rewrote the book of rock & roll excess, so it is perhaps not too surprising that his posthumous renown has been more related to his outrageous lifestyle than for being one of, if not the, founding father of 'country rock'.

> Lived the life you sang about
> Carried me through when I had my doubts
> Now there's an emptiness inside of me
> All I've got left is your memory
>
> (Chris Hillman, 'Heavenly Fire')

One lazy day in the summer of '68 I'm listening to the album with the weird cowgirl cover (Dylan had dropped a hint with *John Wesley Harding* but who'd a thunk it would have come to 'this') and trying to identify all these upstart Byrds listed on the back.

After being rescued from confusion by the all-too-familiar voices of Roger McGuinn and Chris Hillman on the first four cuts, suddenly something interesting is happening on the fifth. 'You're Still On My Mind'. A snappy tune? No, more than that. 'An empty bottle, a broken heart, and yer still on . . . my . . . mind!' The voice, 'Fresh and slick', like cornbread and molasses. A 'new' voice, but whose?

No clue on the *Sweetheart Of The Rodeo* album jacket. Turn the record over. First song 'In South Carolina . . .' Damn voice again! 'There's many tall pines . . .' Purtiest song ah ever heard. 'Hickory Wind'. Sounds like an old song from a long time back, but the label says it's written by a G. Parsons. One of the new Byrds is Gram Parsons who plays 'guitar'. Aha . . .

'. . . thank you very much!' Emmylou Harris is back for her second encore. Beacon Theatre, New York City, Spring '76. She plunks into the first notes of an unfamiliar melody. As if on cue, three strangers call out from different corners of the hall: 'HICKORY WIND!' Emmylou pauses, stops, signals her band, closes her eyes, sings. 'Now when I'm lonesome . . . I always pretend . . . that I'm getting the feel . . . of hickory wind.' It's 60 degrees out, but deep inside, I'm freezing.

Emmylou wasn't the only pretender in the crowd that night and I wonder if any of us knew what ghost we were conjuring. Gram Parsons never recorded a hit single, appeared on only six albums – all commercial flops – and wasn't even a prolific writer, leaving behind no more than thirty-five songs when he OD'ed at twenty-six on pills and booze, 19 September 1973.

> You sing songs about brass buttons
> And shiny silver shoes
> Crazy eyes, what had you to lose?
> (Richie Furay, 'Crazy Eyes')

I never could explain Gram's cult attraction. There were enough contradictions about Parsons to make him mysterious – this was a Waycross, Georgia country boy who went to Harvard, wore Nudie suits with reefer lapels and took amphetamines to get 'mellow' – but it had to cut deeper than that. When the news of his death and desert immolation arrived, I took off my shoe and threw it across the room, where it cracked the plastic on my telephone. When Jimi and Janis croaked, I'd barely shrugged.

Strangely enough, I can listen to Gram's music today with the most compelling of mixed emotions. The best of it still makes me want to cry or 'try' harder than anything else around. Without straining, I can compare this effect to that of Hank Williams, another smart martyr-cowboy, whose voice lived even after his lyrics and the melodies died young. Something about hitting the fundamental note, stretching the human chord 'cross country – experience not so much shared as relinquished in a moment of oppressive sadness.

> His song came from deep down inside
> You could hear it in his voice
> And see it in his eyes.
> (Bernie Leadon, 'My Man')

Parsons's songs were, if not inevitably brilliant, at least bizarre even when they weren't. Often in a religiously symbolic way. 'The New Soft Shoe', 'Hot Burrito #2' ('You better love me – "Jesus Christ!"') and 'Return Of The Grievous Angel', among others, illustrate the difference between writing country-rock jingles and composing personal anthems that intersect the universal. Parsons considered Eagles et al. bubblegum; he is to Dan Fogelberg what Bob Dylan was to Tom Paxton – a mad 'scientist', not a facile technician. Like Ray Davies, Parsons reaches me in a lot of inexplicable ways, even though the three of us have nothing in common but a certain resigned humanity and a vulnerable – even morbid – fatalistic spirit.

In his last interview, with *Crawdaddy* in the summer of '73, Parsons said he spent a lot of time in the desert 'up at Joshua Tree [where he was to die only weeks later] just looking at the San Andreas fault, and saying to myself: "I wish I was a bird drifting up above it."' Now he's with all 'the truckers, and the kickers and the cowboy angels' in honky-tonk heaven, leaving me to sit here remembering something that he once told me. Eight years later, I'll be damned if it did not come true. 'An empty bottle, a broken heart, and yer still on . . . my . . . mind.'

A Marc in Time

PAUL MORLEY

*After spending the first three years of the seventies producing the most
contagiously nonsensical singles ever to scale the heights of the British
charts, Bolan's star faded. He seemed on the verge of a commercial
comeback when he met his untimely death in September 1977. Paul
Morley took the opportunity of 1980 repeats of Bolan's final TV
shows to re-evaluate the T. Rex legacy.*

Independent Television are currently repeating five shows from
the three-year-old *Marc* series. Marc Bolan was star in and
presenter of a pop show that was very much in the low budget,
early afternoon Granada tradition – the *Marc* season followed
similar series featuring the Bay City Rollers and the Arrows. ITV
are repeating the five shows following considerable pressure from
members of the still substantial Marc Bolan fan club. Marc magic
has lingered three years after his tragic death.

It is magic. There was magic around much of what Bolan
achieved or attempted, a magic in the relationships he established
with his followers. Bolan's whole art was formed around a singular
integration of his belief in 'magic' (myth, mystery, exotica) and an
obsession with the magic of the most fundamental rock & roll
essentials. He considered the pop single to be 'a spell', and
although it took him some time to articulate that potently, and it
was only achieved for three or four years, when he did he
determined the commitment and direction of what turned out to

be the third generation of rock fans. Bolan was a considerable catalyst: most of his effect was outside magic.

Seeing the show again induces some sadness. Sadness because the shows were Bolan's last public appearances, because what seemed special then isn't special now: time has not been kind.

Despite what at the time seemed to be both a resurgence of Bolan's creativity and interest in it, the *Marc* shows depict a lively but limited trouper tenaciously remembering fabulous times, self-consciously parodying the original parodies and almost willingly exposing the transience of his music.

Bolan's pop music was impermanent (although some songs transcend that): he made it so because he recognized that the pop song was a moment, a mark in time, at most a period. He knew that the Pop Star, through the very nature of the phenomenon, faded away. He always said he would have three or four years at the very top – as far back as 1965 he was claiming that he would be an idol for four years and that the idea appealed to him, and in 1972 he was aware the Rex impact would burn away quickly – and through *Marc* it's as if he was masochistically rubbing in that as a pop person he was essentially passé, half-heartedly indulging in being a pop personality.

But even a shaky, echoey remembrance of one of pop's heroes is better than nothing. Bolan looks happy but haggard – he'd just emerged from a shocking pop star period – not thin but gaunt. He wears stark make-up, a horror hangover from his glam days. There's no T. Rex backing him but ugly session musicians. The shows are neither the surrealistic extravaganzas he wanted, nor a recapturing of the unrehearsed, spontaneous tackiness of the sixties' pop shows he grew up loving. The show was not his: it was hung around him and his past. The choice of guests is mostly awful.

But, for moments, Bolan's elemental and elusive uniqueness can be spotted. His sense of camp could never desert him. His imperfectly perfect miming is classic. There's the way he holds and caresses his meticulously positioned guitar – never a great guitarist, he was a great *user* of the guitar, often using it to emphasize the absurdity of it all. Most of all there's the wide grin that lets everyone into the secret: look what I'm getting away with! It was simple but outrageous gestures such as these, supported by a fierce belief in his own destiny, that profound love for the rock & roll spirit, androgynous sensuality and enormous self-confidence, that helped him win his fame.

He was no artist, but artisan. He was actor, sometimes forgetting his lines, having to bluff his way through. He was cartoonist. He caricatured the rock & roll dream. He lived the dream and suffered through it. And there through *Marc* we see him vainly reliving his own caricature.

But that Bolan caricature, the years when Bolan was on top, in control and loving every minute, should never be underestimated. Whether by design or accident – a mixture of both ultimately – Bolan rediscovered pop's potency and value. He was an exaggeratedly bright light in the early seventies' darkness. He invented what was termed glam rock – it was cosmic pop, teenage music, at a time when rock was drifting into a late-twenties slumber.

Marc Bolan introduced more people to the wonders of pop than almost anyone. He didn't let anyone down. He was offering nothing more than excitement. Bolan personified vitality in life. He was a believer in the magic of life as well as the magic in life. Live it to the full, laugh at and with it, live it to the end.

On 16 September 1977 he died in a car crash in London, just four weeks to the day after the death of Presley, two weeks before his thirtieth birthday.

There was nothing tidy about Bolan's death. It was no romantic conclusion, it created no instant glamour. It brutally cut him off when he was at last beginning to compromise, seek out attention in new ways. It left behind a jagged legend. A legend wrapped around three mad years.

Rhapsody in Blue

CHARLES SHAAR MURRAY

For many ambulance chasers, Presley's death was proof positive that every day spent inside the cauldron of mass fame chipped another piece off the real person. Murray successfully conveys the shocking price Presley paid.

The death of Elvis Presley was truly the stuff of which nightmares are made.

The first great symbol of rock music as youth-culture jailbreak, dying alone of a heart attack brought on by an over-strenuous game of squash, dying as a sick, obese, tortured hulk, dying lonely, miserable, dope-riddled, dying empty, dying exhausted, dying – finally – as a man who had everything he ever wanted but found it all wanting.

Elvis Presley was a symbol, yeah. He was an icon, he was rock & roll incarnate, he was an idol, he was a hero. He gave the kids a look and a sound and an attitude: he gave us his identity and once he gave it to us he was left with nothing of his own except the useless trash accumulated by millionaires who have nothing but money which can buy nothing but objects.

That was all he had because it was all we could give him: an adulation and an idolatry that dehumanized him, left him as flat and two-dimensional as the Elvis poster on my wall. Just as – to a certain extent – everybody who plays or consumes rock & roll has become something of what Elvis made them, Elvis became what we made him.

And once we turned him into a poster, transformed him into an effigy, became something new by sucking on his soul, he became a monster: first a young, beautiful and awesome monster, then a bland, castrated monster and finally a hideous, pitiful monster who inspired a mixture of pity and derision and – maybe – a shudder of mortality, a *frisson* of decay.

Dorian Gray for Our Generation. The human poster was gruesome by the end, and much of his pain must have come from the fact that he knew it. If we make a man into a god, he must suffer as a man does, but his suffering must be on a godlike scale.

And how can a man survive the torments of a god and still remain unscathed?

The bloated bulk that was Elvis Presley's body was the outward sign of the death by attrition of Elvis Presley's spirit.

He stuffed himself with food, napalmed his brain with smack and cocaine – even though true to the dictates of his beloved deceased mum, he kept off smoke and booze, an All-American boy! – surrounded himself with more and more toys; any damn thing to make it stop hurting.

By the time I discovered the superhero of the fifties, he was already the bland-out of the sixties. Everybody knew who Elvis was – he was a likely contender for the Most Famous Person in the World title even though the Beatles and Stones and Dylans and Hendrixs were making their waves – and, for some, this memory of the golden creature who redefined 'youth' created an indulgence for what Presley was becoming. For others it created contempt.

It seemed that the only one who didn't know who Elvis was any more was Elvis. Obviously you can't be a teenage mutant from outer space/inner Memphis for all your life, but it seemed like a betrayal that Elvis was conforming to the dictates of fifties adult orthodoxy just as a new sixties generation – fuelled on Chess blues, Motown soul and the finest moments of fifties rock – was starting to tear down a new set of barricades.

Elvis the man and Elvis the living tabernacle were slowly beginning to move apart, and when the irresistible force and the immovable object are one and the same, then it is inevitable that something has to give. In the seventies, Elvis made his heroic attempt to rejoin his severed selves, to come to terms with the legend, to roll away the stone and become unified once more.

He did a TV special, got back in front of people once more and for a while it was an almost supernatural visitation, the resurrection shuffle.

And then the two images separated once more, the man and the god, the flesh and the spirit. Body and soul began to destroy each other.

The man grew ugly, the legend grew tarnished, the god became a joke.

Elvis Presley, ultimately, became the nightmare B side of the Great Rock Dream. So you wanna be a rock & roll star? So you wanna be Elvis Presley? So you want to be someone who millions of women want to ball and millions of men want to be? So you want fame, talent, beauty, riches, admiration, love, power?

Have it, baby. Have it with my compliments. Have it and enjoy it and see if it's what you really want once you've got it. The only catch is that once you've got it you can't give it back.

Imagine, then, what Elvis Presley, 19-year-old truckdriver of Memphis, Tennessee, would have thought if somehow he could've had some prescient flash of Elvis Presley, 42-year-old superstar of Memphis, Tennessee, killing his pain with an obscene blend of cheeseburgers and scag.

Don't Walk Away in Silence

ADRIAN THRILLS AND PAUL MORLEY

Ian Curtis's membership of Joy Division, and therefore the rock pantheon, had minimal bearing on his suicide. Despite his attempts to externalize his inner anguish in song, Curtis never seemed comfortable with life itself. For Curtis did not take the familiar route of drugs or drink but a deep-rooted melancholy he felt that Joy Division's music sought, but failed, to expiate.

Rock's such an infuriating thing it's a marvel we get so consumed. Mostly rock is an unstable slab of crudity and stupidity; an endless roll of superficiality and lies. Some people, though, achieve within it even more than the usual palatable, topical noise, and create something beautiful enough to sustain our faith. The rock music that is above and past the status quo and narcissism of the enduring rock tradition, that reaches us through business channels, that doesn't set up as its restraining barrier the cynical elements of Good Time and consolation, can be broadly split in two.

Good rock music – the palatable, topical stuff – is an amusement and an entertainment; the perfect pastime for this current season of hell. The very best rock music is created by individuals and musicians obsessive and eloquent enough to inspect and judge destinies and systems with artistic totality and sometimes tragic necessity; music with laws of its own, a drama of its own. The face of rock music is changed by those who introduce to the language new tones, new tunes and new visions.

The very best rock music will frighten us as much as it will entertain us.

657

It will always be the rock music that reflects the enormity of our struggle and our unease, that achieves a language you feel in your heart, your spine, your eyes, rather than that which submits to fame, fortune and fashion, that supports our faith in rock music. It's a faith worth having. It's certainly not a problem.

Joy Division throw us out of balance. Their music is undoubtedly filled with the horror of the times – no cheap shocks, no rocky horror, no tricks with mirrors and clumsy guilt, but catastrophic images of compulsion, contradiction, wonder, fear. The threatening nature of society hangs heavy; bleak death is never far away; each song is a mystery, a pursuit. The music is brutally sensual and melancholically tender. The songs never avoid loneliness, cruelty, suffering; they defy these things.

All this isn't only a love for deep oppressive seriousness, we're not celebrating gloom. More it's a loathing for mediocrity and hypocrisy and complacency, the deceptions rock often seems proud to mould. There can be nothing so silly as believing that rock is a saviour, and nothing as outrageous as accepting it as an artificial attractive network of trash and flash. People tend to take rock music for granted – and never think what it could be.

Joy Division never took it for granted and pushed its possibilities to the limits.

The very best rock music is art, and that is nothing to be ashamed of. Good rock music is entertaining and amusing, legitimate and intelligent, and from week to week, single to single, upset to upset, it keeps us going. The very best rock music – that is because of the roots, the hedonism, the delinquency and the screaming of rock tradition – is dramatic, neurotic, private, intimate and draws out of us more than just admiration and enthusiasm.

Whether it's Jimi Hendrix or Joy Division, it suggests infinity and confronts squalor. In direct opposition to the impersonal exploitation of the rock structure it miraculously comes from, it cares for the inner person.

It is rarely straightforward intelligence and wit that produces the very best rock music, it is dreams, naïvety, aspirations, intuition, exuberance . . . there are dreams that shout for a better world and a deeper understanding. These are the dreams of the very best rock music.

Joy Division make art. The prejudice that hangs around the word 'art' puts people off, makes them think of the untouchable, the unreachable and the unrealistic. Joy Division put reality into rock. Yet for all the intensity and violence of their images, the music never relinquishes a classic accessibility; rhythm, melody, atmosphere, are awesomely sophisticated.

Joy Division make art. Joy Division make the very best rock music.

This is heavy stuff, and why not? Joy Division achieve something unique. Joy Division are not merely a hip new wave group on a fashionable independent label. Oh no!

The month before what were to have been their first American gigs, Joy Division completed an impromptu set of British dates. In keeping with their corporate aversion to regulation and routine, the gigs hardly qualified as a tour proper.

Spread through April, they followed hot on the heels of the fortnight spent in Islington's Britannia Row studios on the new *Closer* album. The dates took in London venues as diverse as the Rainbow, where they supported the Stranglers, to three nights at the Moonlight Club. Out of town, they were largely unannounced or were advertised only locally. Though a few of the dates were cancelled as Ian Curtis fell ill, it was a period of hectic and intense activity for the group.

The last of the gigs was in the University of Birmingham's High Hall on Friday 2 May. It was also, fatefully, the last public appearance Ian Curtis made as vocalist in Joy Division.

Four days before the Birmingham gig, a video was filmed in

Manchester for the forthcoming 'Love Will Tear Us Apart' single. The location – a disused, windswept Dickensian warehouse converted into a rehearsal studio – seemed the ideal place for a Joy Division video. But the band's attitude to proceedings was withdrawn and disinterested. Even on camera, they seemed to have little time for such promotional niceties.

Such lethargy could hardly have been further removed from the mood in the university dressing-room later that week as the band prepared for the Birmingham gig: Joy Division, despite their reputation as sober individuals, despite the myth of romanticized gloom that seemed to extend way beyond the vivid musical imagery, despite the cryptic humour of manager Rob Gretton, were earthy and easygoing people.

As Tony Wilson says, 'To people they seemed a very gloomy band, but as human beings they were the absolute opposite.'

The absolute opposite. Indulging in the customary dressing-room horseplay and practical joking, beer swilling and football talk – Ian Curtis was a Manchester United supporter. Just because they painted graphic musical landscapes of unprecedented power in their work, didn't mean that Joy Division never joked or smiled in their quieter moments.

Or even split their sides laughing, as when 'Twinny', their red-headed roadie-in-chief, managed to shatter the dressing-room window as he tried to sneak a couple of fans into the gig and then lied brazenly to the gig promoters when they came to investigate the rumpus.

But the earthy off-stage demeanours – the blunt, wary Peter Hook, the mischievous Bernie Albrecht, the quiet, easygoing Stephen Morris and the shy, fragile, polite Ian Curtis – were transformed the minute the group stepped out into the misty blue and green glare of the stage spotlights.

Though a reticent student audience were sluggish in warming to them, Joy Division's power and purity of purpose was immediately apparent in the undiluted vigour of their music.

Their ultimate live set, characteristically, made few concessions to rockbiz tradition, the opening number being an unfamiliar, untitled instrumental built around a revolving drum motif, one of two new songs already written and rehearsed in the few weeks since the completion of the LP.

A ripple of cheers greets a feedback-ridden, faster than usual 'Shadowplay'. But Joy Division never stooped to easy games, and follow the familiar song with two choppy, strident ones from the new album, 'Means To An End' and 'Passover'. Indeed, it is only with the end of the slow, mournful 'New Dawn Fades' that Ian Curtis acknowledged the audience for the first time with a curt 'hello'.

But the crowd, surprisingly, stand transfixed, their feet taking all of five numbers to warm to the dark dance music as the swirling, shifting guitar and drum patterns of the hypnotic '24 Hours' give way to the pulse-beat of the throbbing bass introduction to 'Transmission'. The band's third single suddenly seems to take on the aura of the hit it should have been as the audience finally begin to respond with any real vigour for the first time during the entire gig, their reticence melting in the face of the frightening intensity of Joy Division's performance.

The euphoria rises through 'Disorder', Curtis's flailing robotic juggle dance taking on almost violent proportions as Morris and Hook hold down the back-beat with precision and power and Albrecht studiously picks out the purest improvised guitar solo.

The guitarist takes over on synthesizers for the two closers, both again from the new LP, the translucent 'Isolation' and the serene 'Decades', a track, like the awesome 'Atmosphere' or 'Love Will Tear Us Apart', that accentuates the delicate side of the group and provides a sharp counterpoint to the more physical hard rock that comprises most of their set.

Curtis, however, stumbles from the stage before the end of the song, totally exhausted and obviously showing signs of strain. The band, despite demands for more, return for only a sharp one-song encore, a revamped version of the 1978 Factory sampler track 'Digital' . . .

It doesn't really need saying, but Ian Curtis was highly emotional, deeply romantic and acutely sensitive. It was these qualities, plus an irrational willingness to take the blame for things, combined with a set of problems it's not relevant to reveal, that made him decide to leave us. A change of scenery. For him, perhaps, freedom.

On Saturday 17 May, four days before Joy Division were to fly to America, he had visited his old house in Macclesfield to watch the televised film *Stroszek* by his favourite director, Herzog. Hours later, in the early hours on the Sunday morning, he hung himself. He was twenty-three.

That a myth will develop is inevitable, if only because of the 'type' of group Joy Division seem to be, the passions they arouse. Ian Curtis's words are vivid and dramatic. They omit links and open up perspectives; they are set deep in untamed, unfenced darkness. He confronted himself with ultimate realities.

However it's written, this piece contributes to the myth. Things need to be said, things that would have been said anyway, without perhaps so much unconstrained emotion. Ian's leaving gives his words and his images a final desperate, sad edge of clarity. It's a perverse way for Joy Division to get their deserved attention.

When we listen to past and future Joy Division records the myth takes on new shape and stature. Our memories add to the myth. Ian Curtis's own myths, the myths he dragged up from the deep and turned into our reality, inspire it.

The myth gets stronger . . . we might as well get on with it. Ian would love this myth. Ian Curtis was young, but he had already seen the depths. His death is a waste, but he had already given us more than we dare hope from anyone.

We were looking towards him. And he was no longer there.

My Brilliant Career

SIMON FRITH

Despite ten years of execrable solo albums and marriage to the impossibly unpopular Yoko Ono, a tidal wave of valedictions poured out of the world media on the death of John Lennon, all seemingly implying that he had been murdered a decade earlier but no one had seen fit to report it. Thankfully Simon Frith's belated article in the March 1981 New York Rocker *sought to assess Lennon's significance in the here and now.*

'DEATH OF A HERO!' it said in big black letters across the front of the *Daily Mirror*, and if I hadn't known already I'd have expected a story about a policeman or a soldier in Northern Ireland. The British media response to John Lennon's death was overwhelming, and what began as a series of private griefs was orchestrated by disc jockeys and sub-editors into a national event, but it was difficult to decide what all this mourning meant. The media themselves seemed less slick than usual, more ragged in their attempts to respond to a genuinely popular shock. What came through was not just Beatle-nostalgia but a specific sadness at the loss of John Lennon's Beatle qualities – qualities that never did fit easily into British populist ideology. 'The idea,' as Lennon once told *Red Mole*, 'is not to comfort people, not to make them feel better, but to make them feel worse.'

John Lennon was a 1950s, not a 1960s, teenager and he didn't have a great youth, but he did grow up in Liverpool where there was an aggressive way of leisure that survived television and the fifties rise of family consumption. By the time I was a teenager, with the mods in the sixties, the young were the only people left out at night and no one was very tough. The Liverpool sound was the sound of gangs and territory being claimed, and the Beatles always had to stand for something. They played their gigs in Liverpool and Hamburg clubs in which there was no space for subtlety or self-pity, no room for preening. The Beatles' noise was hoarse and harsh, an effect of the unrelieved nightly sets, and even the best of the sixties' live bands, the Stones and the Who, were indulged youth groups by comparison, with a flabbiness that the original Beatles couldn't afford. The Beatles sang American music in a Liverpool accent – nasal rather than throaty, detached, passion expressed with a conversational cynicism.

John Lennon was the only hero I've ever had. His genius is usually described with reference to the songs he wrote, but it was his voice that always cut through me. He sang with a controlled, forthright intimacy that demanded a hearing even on uninteresting material (like *Double Fantasy*). He was the only rock singer who ever sang 'we' convincingly.

The day John Lennon was shot in New York I got the Clash's *Sandinista!* I've played it incessantly since, as an exorcism of those old Beatle records that I don't want to hear again. *Sandinista!* is infuriating, indulgent, exciting and touching. It is packed with slogans and simplicities, guns and liberation, images of struggle and doubt, and it is a wonderful tribute to Lennon's influence – a record that would have been impossible to imagine without him. Jones and Strummer always were closer to Lennon and McCartney than their Jagger/Richards pose lets on.

John Lennon believed, more intensely than any other rock performer, that rock & roll was a form of expression in which anything could be said, and he believed, too, that rock & roll was the only form of expression in which many things – to do with growing up working class, mostly – could be said. His music (and the Clash's) involves an urgent need to be heard (a need which often obscures what is actually being said). In 1956 John Lennon found in rock & roll an anti-authoritarian voice that everywhere else was silenced, and most of his life afterwards was committed to keeping faith with this voice, preserving its edge, cutting through the ideological trapping of pop.

John Lennon refused to be trivialized and Yoko Ono was truly his partner in this, facing him with many of the issues that were later addressed by punk. She questioned the taken-for-granted masculinity of the rock & roll voice, rock conventions of spontaneity and realism, rock assumptions about the 'truth' of the singing voice and the relationship between the public and the private.

Since Lennon's death I haven't done anything much, but before it I was watching old films: *Top Gear* from 1964, a flat studio showcase of the year's British stars with two good incidents – the Beatles cheerful on stage, and the spine-chilling moment when the young Steve Winwood opened his mouth and that extraordinary white soul voice came pouring effortlessly out: and *Rude Boy*, a shoddy piece of flimflam designed to trivialize not only the Clash but the entire punk moment of 1976–9 – working-class 'experience' is mimicked through the medium of bourgeois realism and I walked out. The Clash concert footage is good enough though, and does raise questions about the shifting rules of rock meaning. These days, for example, the annual berk of a British Christmas is Rod Stewart, who releases an album and goes on tour. Once upon a time his singing style (a refinement of the white soul vocal) was the epitome of emotional sincerity. Now he just sounds silly, and it is Joe Strummer's narrow range and tight-throated projection or John Lydon's wailing inarticulacy which are the sounds that mean it.

'Imagine no possessions', John Lennon sang, but I never thought he could (John Lydon maybe). There was a sloppiness to John and Yoko's concept of peace and love and changing things by thinking them so, that concealed what mattered more – an astute sense of the mass market and how it worked. The central contradiction of John Lennon's artistic life lay in the uneasy enthusiasm with which he packaged and sold his dreams (which were, to begin with, real enough). The problem for the working class, he told *Red Mole* in 1971, is that 'they're dreaming someone else's dream, it's not even their own'. The problem for a working-class hero is that he too is defined in other people's dreams.

John Lennon was murdered by a fan, by someone who pushed the fantasies that pop stardom is designed to invoke into an appalling, stupid madness. But the grief that the rest of us Beatle fans then felt drew on similar fantasies, and the bitter fact is that John Lennon, whose heroism lay in his struggle against being a commodity, whose achievement was to express the human origins of pop utopianism, should be trapped, finally, by a desperate, inhuman, nightmarish version of the fan's need to be a star.

The Party's Over

RICHARD HELL

It is difficult to conceive of the death of Johnny Thunders surprising anyone ('My God, Mr Death! You look like Johnny Thunders warmed up'). The week after Thunders's funeral, Richard Hell, performing at a tribute to Tim Buckley, dedicated his final number, '(I'm Living On) Chinese Rocks', to Buckley and Thunders. Hell's obituary of his old friend, published in Melody Maker *the following week, displays that same refreshing lack of sentimentality about the death of his junkie friend.*

Johnny's Party is over. Thinking about him this morning (9 May) in New York, it's another drizzly colourless day, as it was for his funeral last week.

I hope when I die people don't go soft about me. It's stupid. Apart from his family and four or five livelong friends, probably the people who'll miss Johnny most are those he exploited. The ones who were made to feel important because he spent time with them in order to get them to do things for him. Of course, he never really had to try to get this kind of treatment: people fell over each other to get next to him. They liked to be near him just to look at him, like a jungle carnivore. And a girl could not be wrong to have him at her side. That's how he made his living, like many (of us) in rock & roll. I don't think Johnny would want people to go soft about him.

Then again, he lit into journalists a lot for not treating him with enough respect. He even wrote a song ('I Tell The Truth Even When I'm Lying') replying to what he considered their insulting, unjust treatment of him. It included this 'open letter to the music press: Revoke your poetic licence you probably got on 42nd Street, the same place you got your lover, the same place your mother got your father . . .' When he told me how much he liked Japan, it was mostly because the people were 'real polite and kind. I tell you I did forty or fifty interviews and not one person asked me about drugs.' That's what he attacked them for. While, of course, he himself consistently exploited heroin's significance in the maintenance of his bad boy image. He included conspicuous syringes in publicity photos, and frequently mimed jamming needles into his forearm during his stage act.

I've found the effort to write this (which includes viewing videos of recent shows, reading old interviews, listening to tapes and records, talking to some of his closest old and new friends and, especially, being forced to recall in detail a lot of time I spent with Johnny myself) spooky and scary as well as sad (where's the good part?). Mainly because I find myself identifying with him, so that it becomes almost as if something I say about him I'm saying about myself. And that to feel something or evoke a feeling about him is to feel the same thing about myself.

The main qualities, the virtues, that set Johnny apart were that he didn't give a fuck and he dressed great.

Johnny, of course, was the rock & roll Dean Martin of heroin, at least in his last decade. I'd known him since 1974, which I think was the last year before he had a narcotics habit. I admired the Dolls; they inspired me. They were the first pure rock & roll group. Pure in that they knew and operated on the assumption that rock & roll is at least 50 per cent (maybe 100 per cent, maybe 200 per cent) attitude.

They were the first group that regarded themselves as stars rather than thinking of themselves as musicians, or writers, or vocalists. The Dolls were for New York groups what the Sex Pistols were for British groups. They excited everybody by being flawless: in it for fun, never pretentious or pretending to be anything they weren't; they were ballsy, noisy, tough, funny, sharp, young and real. Stupid and ill. They mocked the media, threw up on grown-ups, and kidded with the kids in a language of drugs and sex.

And I don't think there's really much of an argument to be made against the observation that Johnny peaked with the Dolls, when he was twenty. Even his most recent sets undeniably picked up considerably whenever he played a Dolls tune (he didn't do many of them, but you'd hear a 'Lonely Planet Boy' or 'Personality Crisis'). The next seventeen or eighteen years were just spent getting to know him a little better.

There was something perfect about Johnny. Though because he was a legendary archetype, you tended to think of him as predictable, as a type. You tended to condescend to him because you thought you had him nailed (and otherwise he might be a threat). But he always surprised me when I talked to him. The surprising thing was how smart he was. He was smart in the same way he dressed so perfectly. Smart the same way Elvis Presley was rather than in the way, say, Ludwig Wittgenstein was. The thing was, you could imagine you could be smart like Wittgenstein by just thinking hard enough but Elvis just had it. It was almost spiritual, a kind of grace, a kind of innate ruling of the world. That's what you wanted and Johnny had it. And he knew it; to him, the highest compliment was to be 'as good as Frank Sinatra and Elvis'.

He was perfect because he made no apologies. He was just graceful. He instinctively knew how to make do with what he had (though he made a lot of bad records).

Rock & roll, of course, is about not growing up and settling down, defying those who have, and living for sex and other types of fun. That's who Johnny was. The New York version. Johnny made his choice, or lived out his destiny, and he had a right to it. He always went to drugs to be able to face the day, and he always went to his guitar to be himself (though he spent most of his time watching TV). There's no judging to be done. It's like Marlene Dietrich in *Touch of Evil* when she says, 'He was just a man . . .'

I've got to admit it annoys me to see cynical, exploitive, self-centred, death-drive get glamorized. I hated the Chet Baker documentary for that reason and Chet and Johnny had a lot in common. They were both junkies who always put themselves first and treated their talent as just another little windfall they could squeeze for all the narcotics and fancy clothes they might be able to drain from it.

(Johnny: 'I would never become righteous. Everybody's entitled to do what they want if they don't hurt me.' It took Johnny to say 'me'.)

He could definitely be a scumbag. I remember when we started the Heartbreakers and first gigged at CBGB how I found him stealing cases of beer from outside the dressing-room. That was not cool; the club owner had always been good to the bands. Then there was how after I left the group he tacked the entire band's names as songwriters on the number which had become their anthem, 'Chinese Rocks', even though the song had been entirely and exclusively written by Dee Dee Ramone and me.

Johnny, though, was the kind of guy you always forgave. He did everything with such impenetrable confidence, everything about him was so up-front, with his soulful murmur in your ear making you feel like a human insider, you could only say, 'Well, that's JT . . .' and write it off.

It was impossible to insult him to his face; he could hold his own with anyone. You wouldn't want to anyway; he was so sweet and soft-spoken (still conveying that you'd better not touch his hair).

(I also remember this: his most frequent companion of the last year telling me with real fondness how he'd always bring her something – some knick-knack from his bedroom wrapped in a scarf – before he asked to borrow money.)

One of the most widely felt reactions to Johnny's death was that the conclusion had been foregone for so long that there wasn't any drama left. In other words, we'd considered him dead since 1980. That's a nasty thing to say, and, though I admit it occurred to me, it isn't really true or fair. In fact, one of Johnny's distinctions was that he was always worth seeing (for all the above reasons: he had that kernel of talent, he didn't give a fuck and he dressed great).

29 April. Johnny's funeral today. At the cemetery, as words are spoken over his coffin, and flowers dropped on it, out in the dreary day, finally tapping into the sadness. Like the sadness is a dimension that is always there but we have developed over the years such a way of avoiding.

Sort of like the way in his last concerts, in the light, he looked scary, like an accusation or a reminder you'd rather not get.

Some Notes on the Contributors

ALBINI, Steve – 'Eyewitness Record Reviews' was first published in Issue 17 of *Forced Exposure*. Albini remains one of America's leading contemporary independent record producers and co-founder of Big Black.

ANON. – There are four anonymous contributors to the *Penguin Book of Rock & Roll Writing*: the author of the sleeve-notes to the 1956 *Elvis* album; and the staff writers responsible for 'One Step Forward, Two Steps Back' in *International Times* No. 157, 'Release This Album, Virgin!' in *New Musical Express* 1 April 1978 and 'The Masked Marauders' album review in *Rolling Stone* 18 October 1969.

ARONOWITZ, Al – 'Memories of Jim and Brian' was originally published separately as 'Over His Dead Body' and 'Memories of Jim', both in the *New York Post*. Aronowitz was also an uncredited co-author of 'A Night With Bob Dylan' in the *New York Herald Tribune* 12 December 1965. He is currently putting the finishing touches to his autobiography, *If I Knew I Was Going to Live This Long, I Would've Taken Better Care of Myself*.

BANGS, Lester – 'In Which Another Pompous Blowhard . . .' is an edited version of a chapter from Bangs's *Blondie*, while 'Jimi Hendrix:

A Posthumous Interview' was first published in *Creem* magazine in 1971. Bangs died in 1982. An anthology of some of his best writings was published in 1989, *Psychotic Reaction and Carburettor Dung*, edited by Greil Marcus.

BRAUN, Michael – 'America, America and Ed Sullivan' is an edited version of the chapter of the same name in Braun's 1964 account of the Beatles' rise to fame, *Love Me Do*.

BURCHILL, Julie – 'Germs' is the opening chapter in Julie Burchill's and Tony Parsons's *The Boy Looked at Johnny*, subtitled *An Obituary of Rock & Roll*. It remains Burchill's only book-length exposition on rock & roll.

CARDUCCI, Joe – 'The Thing of It and the King of Thing' and 'Narcorockcritocracy!' are both excerpts from *Rock and the Pop Narcotic*. Privately published, this invigorating study is available direct from Redoubt Press, P.O. Box 476750, Chicago, IL 60647.

CARR, Roy – 'Another Sex Pistols Record (turns out to be the future of rock & roll)' was first published in *New Musical Express* 2 July 1977. Roy Carr is co-author of *The Beatles: An Illustrated Record* and *David Bowie: An Illustrated Record*, and sole author of *The Rolling Stones: An Illustrated Record*.

COHN, Nik – 'Classic Rock' and 'America After the Beatles' were both originally parts of *Awopbopaloobop*. The re-edited version of 'Classic Rock' included in this anthology and 'Be Happy! Don't Worry' are both derived from the 1990 anthology of Cohn's rock writings, *Ball the Wall*.

COLEY, Byron – Coley's writings are represented by his sleeve-notes to the 12-inch single of Dream Syndicate's 'Tell Me When It's Over', released in 1983 on Rough Trade Records.

COON, Caroline – 'Rebels Against the System' was first published in *Melody Maker* 7 August 1976. Coon subsequently published a fuller account of the punk explosion, *1988*, which remains in print.

CSICSERY, George Paul – 'Altamont, California' was originally published in the *New York Daily News* 8 December 1969. It was first anthologized in *The Age of Rock 2*.

DAVIS, Stephen – 'At the Riot House' is an excerpt from Davis's history of Led Zeppelin, *Hammer of the Gods*.

DYLAN, Bob – is credited with rewriting 'A Night With Bob Dylan', first published without a by-line in the *New York Herald Tribune* 12 December 1965. At this time he was also responsible for 'constructing' fake interviews in the *Village Voice* and *Playboy*. His most recent album is *Under The Red Sky*.

FOWLER, Pete – 'Skins Rule' was first published in *Rock File 1*.

FRITH, Simon – '1973: A Year In Singles' was originally published in *Rock File 2*. 'Zowie Bowie' was first included in the April 1975 issue of *Let It Rock*. 'My Brilliant Career' originates from Issue 37 of *New York Rocker*. Frith is also the author of *Sound Effects* and co-edited the 'Rock File' series.

FROST, Deborah – 'Wimps 'R' Us' is an edited version of an article in *Village Voice* 1 October 1991.

GILLETT, Charlie – 'Five Styles of Rock & Roll' is drawn from Gillett's hefty account of the origins of rock & roll, *The Sound of the City*. Gillett also co-edited the five 'Rock File' volumes.

GOLDSTEIN, Richard – 'San Francisco Bray' first appeared in the *Village Voice*, 'A Quiet Night at Balloon Farm' in *New York* magazine, and 'I Blew My Cool in *The New York Times*' in *The New York Times*. All three were subsequently included in the 1970 anthology *Goldstein's Greatest Hits*.

HELL, Richard – 'Heartbreakers' was originally published in the first issue of *New York Rocker* under the pseudonym Theresa Stern. A book of poetry, co-written with Tom Verlaine, was also published under the Stern alias, *Wanna Go Out?*. 'The Party's Over' first appeared in *Melody Maker* 18 May 1991. Hell's most recent album is a collaboration with Thurston Moore of Sonic Youth, *Dimstars*. Hell also recently published excerpts from his seventies diaries, *Artifact*, published by Hanuman.

HELSTROM, John – 'The Harder They Fall' was first published in *Punk* No. 14. Helstrom remained editor of *Punk* throughout its three-year existence.

HENTOFF, Nat – 'Is It Rolling, Zeus?' was first published in *Rolling Stone* 15 January 1976.

HOPKINS, Jerry – co-authored 'The Rock & Roll Liberation Front?', first published in *Rolling Stone* 7 February 1970 and subsequently included in the *Rolling Stone Rock & Roll Reader*. He is best known as the co-author of the highly successful Jim Morrison biography, *No One Gets Out Of Here Alive*.

HOSKYNS, Barney – 'The Meaning of Bile' first appeared in *New Musical Express* 18 February 1984. Hoskyns is currently working on a history of The Band, provisionally entitled *Tears of Rage*.

HUNTER, Ian – 'Thursday, 23 November 1972' is an excerpt from *Diary of a Rock & Roll Star*. Ian Hunter was founder of Mott the Hoople and has enjoyed a sporadically successful solo career since their dissolution in 1974.

Some Notes on the Contributors

INGHAM, Jonh – 'Tripping Down Blackberry Way' originally appeared in the January 1973 edition of *Let It Rock*. 'The Sex Pistols (are four months old)' was first published in *Sounds* 24 April 1976.

JANOWITZ, Tama – 'You and the Boss' was originally published in the November 1985 issue of *Spin* as part of a seven-writer symposium on Springsteen called 'The Meaning of Bruce'. Janowitz remains best known for her first novel, *Slaves of New York*.

KAYE, Lenny – 'The Best of Acappella' was first published in *Jazz and Pop* magazine. It was anthologized in *The Age of Rock 2*. Kaye subsequently co-founded the Patti Smith Group and now works primarily as a producer.

KENT, Nick – Kent's review of *Marquee Moon* was first published in *New Musical Express* 5 February 1977. 'Crazy Diamond' was first published in *New Musical Express* 14 April 1974. Kent is currently compiling a collection of the best of his rock writings.

LANDAU, Jon – 'It's Too Late to Stop Now' and 'The Death of Janis Joplin' have both been derived from Landau's own 1972 collection of his writings *It's Too Late to Stop Now*. 'I Saw Rock & Roll Future . . .' is an edited version of a review in Boston's *The Real Paper* 23 May 1974.

LAUGHNER, Peter – was co-founder of Cleveland art-rockers Pere Ubu. He died of acute pancreatitis at the age of 24 in June 1977. 'If You Choose, Choose to Go' was first published in the March 1976 issue of *Creem* magazine.

LYDON, Michael – 'Money: Rock For Sale' was first published in *Ramparts* magazine before being anthologized in *The Age of Rock 2*. A collection of Lydon's late sixties rock & roll musings, *Rock Folk*, has recently been republished in the US by Citadel Press.

MARCUS, Greil – 'Fanfare' is an excerpt from the 'Presliad' section of *Mystery Train*. 'What Is This Shit?' is an edited version of Marcus's untitled review of Bob Dylan's *Self Portrait* album in the 23 July 1970 issue of *Rolling Stone*. Marcus's most recent book, *Dead Elvis*, collects together many of his previous articles on the Presley phenomenon.

McCULLOUGH, Dave – 'Coming Up for Eire' was first published in *Sounds* 15 September 1979.

MELTZER, Richard – A version of 'The Aesthetics of Rock' was first published in *Crawdaddy* magazine in 1967. It was then collected in *The Age of Rock*. A book of the same title was published by Something Else Press in 1970 and recently republished by Da Capo Press in the US. 'The Meaning of Bruce' was part of a symposium on the Springsteen phenomenon in the November 1985 issue of *Spin* magazine. Meltzer's most recent collection of his writings is *Gulcher*.

MILLS, Mike – has been bassist in Athens combo REM since their inception. 'Our Town' was originally published in the July 1985 edition of *Spin* magazine.

MITCHELL, Greg – 'Crazy Eyes' Goodbye' was originally published in *Crawdaddy* magazine.

MOORE, Thurston – has been a leading light in New York noise merchants Sonic Youth, who recently signed to Geffen Records. 'Stabb's Hand Touched Me and I Slept' was originally published in Issue 14 of *Forced Exposure*.

MORLEY, Paul – 'New Pop UK' originally appeared in Issue 20 of *New York Rocker*. 'A Marc in Time' and 'Don't Walk Away in Silence', the latter co-written with Adrian Thrills, were both first featured in *New Musical Express* in the 20 September 1980 and 16 June 1980 issues respectively.

Some Notes on the Contributors

MORTHLAND, John – 'The Rock & Roll Liberation Front?', co-written with Jerry Hopkins, first appeared in *Rolling Stone* 7 February 1970.

MURRAY, Charles Shaar – 'What Have They Done to my Blues, Ma?', 'Rhapsody in Blue' and 'Weird Scenes Inside Gasoline Alley' all originally appeared in *New Musical Express*, in issues dated 3 March 1984, 27 August 1977 and 22 November 1975 respectively. A collection of some of CSM's articles, including 'Rhapsody in Blue', was recently published in the UK by Penguin under the title *Shots From The Hip*. His most recent book was *Crosstown Traffic*, assessing the impact of Jimi Hendrix.

PARELES, Jon – 'Industry's Bane, Fans' Bonanza' was originally published in *The New York Times* 21 July 1991.

PARSONS, Tony – 'If You're on the Road' is an excerpt from Parsons's first novel *Platinum Logic*. 'Germs', co-written with Julie Burchill, has been taken from *The Boy Looked at Johnny*. Parsons's most recent book was his co-authored autobiography of George Michael, *Bare*.

RAVENSTINE, Allen – 'Music Lessons' originally appeared in the *Cleveland Edition*. It is an excerpt from a much larger work, a fictionalized account of Ravenstine's time as the landlord of The Plaza and synthesizer player in Pere Ubu.

REED, Lou – 'Fallen Knights and Fallen Ladies' originally appeared in Issue 34 of *Zigzag* and the *No One Waved Goodbye* collection. Lou Reed co-founded the Velvet Underground in 1965 and has pursued a solo career since 1970. His most recent album was *Magic And Loss*. A collection of some of his most notable lyrics was recently published under the title *Beyond Thought and Expression*.

SIEGEL, Jules – 'Goodbye Surfing! Hello God!' was originally published in the October 1967 edition of *Cheetah* magazine.

SMITH, Patti – 'Jukebox Cruci-Fix' and 'The Rise of the Sacred Monsters' were both published in *Creem* magazine in 1973 and 1975, shortly before Smith gave up rock journalism to concentrate on the Patti Smith Group, which disbanded in 1980. Smith has recently published a new book, *Wool Gathering*, as part of the Hanuman pocket book series.

STERN, Theresa – see Richard Hell.

SUGARMAN, Danny – 'It's My Life and I'll Do What I Want' is an excerpt from Sugarman's autobiography, *Wonderland Avenue*. Sugarman's most recent book is an account of the rise of Guns N' Roses, *Appetite for Destruction*.

THRILLS, Adrian – 'Don't Walk Away in Silence', co-written with Paul Morley, was first published in *New Musical Express* 16 June 1980.

TITUS, Peter – 'The Man Can't Scotch Our Taping' was first published in Issue 53 of *New York Rocker*.

TOWNSHEND, Pete – Townshend's review of the Who's *Meaty, Beaty, Big & Bouncy* was first published in the 7 December 1971 edition of *Rolling Stone*. Since the disbandment of the Who in 1982, Townshend has been both an editor at Faber & Faber and a solo recording artist. His most recent album was *Deep End Live*.

WATSON, Don – 'Drunk on the New Blood' was first published in *New Musical Express* 24 November 1984.

WILLIAMS, Paul – 'What the Sixties Had . . .' and 'Dissolve/Reveal' are both excerpts from *The Map*. 'How Rock Communicates' was originally published in *Evergreen Review* and was first collected in *Outlaw Blues*. The second volume of *Performing Artist*, Williams's account of Bob Dylan's most notable performances and recordings, is due to be published this autumn.

WOLCOTT, James – 'A Conservative Impulse in the New Rock Underground' was first published in *Village Voice* 18 August 1975.

WOLFE, Tom – 'The First Tycoon of Teen' was first published in the *New York Herald Tribune*. It has been part of two previous collections, Wolfe's own *The Kandy-Kolored Tangerine-Flake Streamline Baby* and *The Age of Rock*.

ZAPPA, Frank – Zappa's Statement to Congress (19 September 1985) has been entered into the Congressional Record. It has also been published as part of Zappa's 'Porn Wars' section in *The Real Frank Zappa Book*. Zappa continues to issue prodigious amounts of retrospective material from his thirty-year career as a musician. A second *Beat the Boots* boxed-set is his most recent release.

ZERBIB, Patrick – 'Situation Vacant' first appeared in Issue 44 of *The Face*.

Acknowledgements

We would like to thank the following authors, publishers and literary representatives who have given permission to reprint copyright material in this collection. (For full bibliographical information, readers should consult 'Some Notes on the Contributors'.)

Duncan Campbell for 'One Step Forward, Two Steps Back'.

Joe Carducci for 'Narcorockcritocracy!' and 'The Thing of It and the King of Thing'.

Jonathan Clowes Ltd, London, on behalf of Michael Braun, for 'America, America and Ed Sullivan', copyright © 1964 by Michael Braun.

Byron Coley for 'Tell Me When it's Over'.

Dutton, an imprint of New American Library, a division of Penguin Books USA, Inc., and David Higham Associates, Ltd for 'Presliad: Fanfare', copyright © 1975 by Greil Marcus.

Farrar, Straus & Giroux, Inc. for 'The First Tycoon of Teen', copyright © 1965 by Thomas K. Wolfe, Jr.

Forced Exposure for 'Eyewitness Record Reviews' by Steve Albini; 'Stabb's Hand Touched Me and I Slept' by Thurston Moore.

Simon Frith for 'My Brilliant Career', '1973: A Year in Singles' and 'Zowie Bowie'.

Deborah Frost for 'Wimps 'R' Us'.

Richard Hell for 'The Party's Over' and 'Heartbreakers', copyright © Richard Meyers.

John Holmstrom for 'The Harder They Fall'.

Jonh Ingham for 'The Sex Pistols (are four months old)' and 'Tripping Down Blackberry Way'.

Acknowledgements

International Press Syndicate for 'The Meaning of Bruce' by Tama Janowitz (subsequently published under the title 'You and the Boss' in *Slaves of New York*); and 'Our Town' by Mike Mills.

Lenny Kaye for 'The Best of Acappella'.

Nick Kent for 'Crazy Diamond' and *'Marquee Moon'*.

Michael Lydon for 'Money: Rock for Sale'.

Macmillan London, Ltd for 'It's My Life and I'll Do What I Want' by Danny Sugarman.

Richard Meltzer for 'The Aesthetics of Rock, and 'The Meaning of Bruce'.

Paul Morley for 'A Marc in Time' and 'New Pop UK'.

New Musical Express for 'Another Sex Pistols Record . . .' by Roy Carr; 'Don't Walk Away in Silence' by Adrian Thrills and Paul Morley; 'Drunk on the New Blood' by Don Watson; 'The Meaning of Bile' by Barney Hoskyns; 'Release This Album, Virgin!'; 'Rhapsody in Blue' and 'Weird Scenes Inside Gasoline Alley' by Charles Shaar Murray.

New York Herald Tribune for 'A Night With Bob Dylan' by Bob Dylan and Al Aronowitz.

New York Post for 'Over His Dead Body' and 'Memories of Jim' by Al Aronowitz.

The New York Times for 'Industry's Bane, Fans' Bonanza' by Jon Pareles, copyright © 1991 by The New York Times Company.

Omnibus Press for 'In Which Yet Another Pompous Blowhard Purports to Possess the True Meaning of Punk Rock' by Lester Bangs.

Pluto Press for 'Germs' by Julie Burchill and Tony Parsons.

Allen Ravenstine for 'Music Lessons'.

Rogers, Coleridge & White, Ltd for 'America After the Beatles', 'Be Happy! Don't Worry' and 'Classic Rock' by Nik Cohn.

Savoy Books for 'A Posthumous Interview' by Lester Bangs.

Charles Shaar Murray for 'What Have They Done to my Blues, Ma?'

Sister Ray Enterprises, Inc. for 'Fallen Knights and Fallen Ladies' by Lou Reed.

Acknowledgements

Patti Smith for 'Jukebox Cruci-Fix' and 'The Rise of the Sacred Monsters'.

Souvenir Press, Ltd for 'Five Styles of Rock & Roll' by Charlie Gillett.

Straight Arrow Publishers, Inc. for 'Is It Rolling, Zeus?' by Nat Hentoff; 'The Masked Marauders' by T. M. Christian; 'Meaty, Beaty, Big & Bouncy' by Pete Townshend; 'The Rock & Roll Liberation Front?' by John Morthland and Jerry Hopkins; 'What Is This Shit?' by Greil Marcus.

Peter Titus for 'The Man Can't Scotch Our Taping'.

Village Voice for 'A Quiet Night at Balloon Farm' and 'San Francisco Bray' by Richard Goldstein.

A. P. Watt, Ltd on behalf of Tony Parsons for 'If You're on the Road'.

Paul Williams for extracts from *The Map*, copyright © 1988 by Paul Williams and 'How Rock Communicates', copyright © 1969 by Paul Williams.

Patrick Zerbib for 'Situation Vacant'.

Every effort has been made to contact or trace all copyright holders. The publishers will be glad to make good any errors or omissions brought to our attention in future editions.

682